Handbook of Sexual Orientation *and* Gender Diversity *in* Counseling *and* Psychotherapy

Handbook of Sexual Orientation and Gender Diversity in Counseling and Psychotherapy

EDITED BY

Kurt A. DeBord

Ann R. Fischer

Kathleen J. Bieschke

Ruperto M. Perez

American Psychological Association • Washington, DC

Chapter 7 was coauthored by an employee of the United States government as part of official duty and is considered to be in the public domain.

Published by
American Psychological Association
750 First Street, NE
Washington, DC 20002
www.apa.org

To order
APA Order Department
P.O. Box 92984
Washington, DC 20090-2984
Tel: (800) 374-2721; Direct: (202) 336-5510
Fax: (202) 336-5502; TDD/TTY: (202) 336-6123
Online: www.apa.org/pubs/books
E-mail: order@apa.org

In the U.K., Europe, Africa, and the Middle East, copies may be ordered from
American Psychological Association
3 Henrietta Street
Covent Garden, London
WC2E 8LU England

Typeset in Goudy by Circle Graphics, Inc., Columbia, MD

Printer: United Book Press, Baltimore, MD
Cover Designer: Mercury Publishing Services, Inc., Rockville, MD

The opinions and statements published are the responsibility of the authors, and such opinions and statements do not necessarily represent the policies of the American Psychological Association. Any views expressed in Chapter 7 do not necessarily represent the views of the United States government, and the author's participation in the work is not meant to serve as an official endorsement.

Library of Congress Cataloging-in-Publication Data

Names: DeBord, Kurt A., editor.
Title: Handbook of sexual orientation and gender diversity in counseling and
  psychotherapy / edited by Kurt A. DeBord, Ann R. Fischer, Kathleen J. Bieschke, and
  Ruperto M. Perez.
Description: Washington, DC : American Psychological Association, 2017. |
  Includes bibliographical references and index.
Identifiers: LCCN 2016009029 | ISBN 9781433823060 | ISBN 1433823063
Subjects: LCSH: Transgender people—Mental health. | Transgender people—Counseling
  of. | Sexual minorities—Mental health. | Sexual minorities—Counseling of. | Sexual
  orientation—Psychological aspects. | Sex role—Psychological aspects. | Psychotherapy. |
  Cultural psychiatry.
Classification: LCC RC451.4.G39 H365 2017 | DDC 616.89/140867—dc23 LC record
  available at https://lccn.loc.gov/2016009029

British Library Cataloguing-in-Publication Data
A CIP record is available from the British Library.

Printed in the United States of America
First Edition

http://dx.doi.org/10.1037/15959-000

CONTENTS

CONTRIBUTORS

Kathleen J. Bieschke, PhD, Head, Department of Educational Psychology, Counseling, and Special Education, Pennsylvania State University, University Park

Kurt A. DeBord, PhD, Professor, Social & Behavioral Sciences, Lincoln University, Jefferson City, MO

Cori Deitz, PhD, Psychological Counselor, Coordinator of Online Services, Counseling and Psychological Services, Eastern Washington University, Cheney

lore m. dickey, PhD, Assistant Professor, Department of Psychology & Behavioral Sciences and Director, Psychological Services Clinic, Louisiana Tech University, Ruston

Weston V. Donaldson, PhD, Clinical Geropsychologist, Aurora Mental Health Center, Aurora, CO

Ruth E. Fassinger, PhD, Professor Emerita, Department of Counseling, Higher Education, and Special Education, University of Maryland, College Park

Ann R. Fischer, PhD, Adjunct Associate Professor, Department of Psychology, Southern Illinois University, Carbondale

Brian R. Fitts, MA, doctoral student, Urban Education Doctoral Program—Counseling Psychology Specialization, College of Education and Human Services, Cleveland State University, Cleveland, OH

John C. Gonsiorek, PhD, ABPP, retired

Douglas C. Haldeman, PhD, Clinical Psychology Program, College of Graduate and Professional Studies, John F. Kennedy University, Pleasant Hill, CA

Kristin A. Hancock, PhD, Clinical Psychology Program, College of Graduate and Professional Studies, John F. Kennedy University, Pleasant Hill, CA

Christopher G. Hawkey, MA, graduate student, Department of Psychology and Neuroscience, University of Colorado, Boulder

Susan Kashubeck-West, PhD, Professor, Department of Counseling & Family Therapy, University of Missouri–St. Louis

Brett M. Millar, MA, doctoral student, Health Psychology and Clinical Science, City University of New York and The Center for HIV Educational Studies and Training, Hunter College of the City University of New York, New York

Bonnie Moradi, PhD, Professor of Psychology and Director, Center for Women's Studies and Gender Research, University of Florida, Gainesville

Tyson Pankey, MPH, doctoral student, School of Education, University of Wisconsin, Madison

David W. Pantalone, PhD, Associate Professor and Director, Clinical Psychology Doctoral Program, Department of Psychology, University of Massachusetts Boston and Behavioral Scientist, The Fenway Institute, Fenway Health, Boston, MA

Charlotte J. Patterson, PhD, Professor, Department of Psychology and Director, Women, Gender & Sexuality Program, University of Virginia, Charlottesville

Parrish L. Paul, PhD, Licensed Psychologist, independent practice, Nashville, TN

Ruperto M. Perez, PhD, Director, Counseling Center, Georgia Institute of Technology, Atlanta

Julia C. Phillips, PhD, Associate Professor, Department of Counseling, Administration, Supervision and Adult Learning, and Codirector of Training, Counseling Psychology Doctoral Program, Cleveland State University, Cleveland, OH

Carol Robinson, MEd, National Certified Counselor, doctoral student, Department of Counseling and Family Therapy, University of Missouri–St. Louis

Glenda M. Russell, PhD, Research Associate, Ethnographic & Evaluation Research, University of Colorado, Boulder

Francisco J. Sánchez, PhD, Assistant Professor, College of Education, University of Missouri, Columbia

Ariel Shidlo, PhD, Codirector, Research Institute Without Walls and Clinical Assistant Professor of Psychology in Psychiatry, Weill Cornell Center for Human Rights, Weill Cornell Medical College, New York, NY

Jillian C. Shipherd, PhD, Clinical Psychologist, Women's Health Sciences Division, National Center for PTSD, VA Boston Healthcare System; Director, LGBT Program, Patient Care Services, Department of Veterans Affairs, Boston, MA; and Associate Professor, Department of Psychiatry, Boston University School of Medicine, Boston, MA

Anneliese A. Singh, PhD, Licensed Professional Counselor, Associate Professor, Department of Counseling & Human Development Services, The University of Georgia, Athens

Tyrel J. Starks, PhD, Assistant Professor of Psychology and Faculty Affiliate of the Center for HIV Educational Studies and Training, Hunter College of the City University of New York and the Health Psychology and Clinical Science Program at The Graduate Center of the City University of New York, New York

Jennah N. Strathausen, MEd, Graduate Assistant, Counseling Center, University of Missouri, Columbia

Tammi Vacha-Haase, PhD, Associate Dean, Graduate School, Colorado State University, Fort Collins

Sarah E. Valentine, PhD, Clinical and Research Fellow in Psychology, Department of Psychiatry, Massachusetts General Hospital/Harvard Medical School, Boston, MA

Tara Vossenkemper, MA, Licensed Professional Counselor, doctoral student, Department of Counseling and Family Therapy, University of Missouri–St. Louis

Amber M. Whiteley, BS, doctoral student, Counseling Psychology, University of Utah, Salt Lake City

Roger L. Worthington, PhD, Professor and Chair, Department of Counseling, Higher Education, and Special Education, University of Maryland, College Park

ACKNOWLEDGMENTS

When we began to discuss the possibility of developing this book, we felt privileged to have the guidance afforded to us by our prior work in producing two other handbooks in this area. We felt grounded in our knowledge of the subject and confident in our abilities to engage in every step of the editorial process. However, we worried about being able to keep up with the pace of social and political changes in relation to the lives of sexual minority and transgender and gender nonconforming people during the 3 years that this book was in development (see the Introduction). Fortunately, we found a great way to respond to that apprehension. We invited an incredibly talented set of authors to challenge, inspire, and educate us as we moved through the production process. The authors in this book are, quite simply, remarkable. They are exceptionally knowledgeable about their topics and delightfully skilled in applying their knowledge and insight to counseling and therapy. In addition, they demonstrated tremendous patience, flexibility, and professionalism in responding to the many rounds of editorial feedback we provided during this time. We are grateful to them for their service and the outstanding chapters they contributed. They are a dedicated group that we admire greatly.

We would also like to express our thanks to the Books Department of the American Psychological Association. Susan Reynolds, Andrew Gifford,

Liz Brace, and Neelima Charya were enormously helpful to us with their guidance and input. This book could not have been completed without their hard work. Andrew recruited two anonymous reviewers to provide feedback on the first draft of the manuscript. His synthesis of their comments with his own led to a much stronger final manuscript.

Each of us would like to thank specific individuals and groups for their feedback, insights, and support during the development of this book. Kurt DeBord would like to thank Caitlin Bartley for her consistent and valuable comments on the chapters in this book. He would also like to thank Yemna Khan and Monica Hees for their comments. He is exceptionally grateful to Wayne Mayfield and Mara Aruguete for their support and encouragement. Ann Fischer would like to thank Eric Morris, Marc Fischer, Linda Gannon, Yu-Wei Wang, and the many students and colleagues who have taught her about gender and sexuality over the years. She appreciated the helpful chapter feedback provided by Elom Amuzu, Donna LaBarge, and Max Schmitz at Southern Illinois University. She sends special thanks to the Association for Women in Psychology, which has always been about more than "just" women. Kathy Bieschke would like to thank members of her research team, James Geckler and Carly Scarton from Pennsylvania State University, for their invaluable assistance. Toti Perez would specifically like to thank his colleagues at the Georgia Tech Counseling Center and the Division of Student Life for their generous support and encouragement and also Stephen Cook, Jill Lee-Barber, and his family for their continued care and support.

Finally, Kurt, Kathy, and Toti have felt very fortunate as editors of the first two editions of the handbook to have enjoyed the company, counsel, and camaraderie of one another. And yet, in searching for another voice to join in the production of this new handbook, we could not have been more excited and more appreciative to have Ann Fischer join us as a coeditor. She brought a fresh perspective and a deep understanding of the issues. Most important, she was able to seamlessly integrate herself into our editorial team. This is no small task given that we have worked together for 10 years and have established a level of honesty that the three of us have rarely experienced among collaborators. Her presence greatly enriched the quality of the group. Ann would like to add her thanks to us, as well. She states, "You welcomed me, challenged me, and listened to me as both a scholar and friend. As we shared visions, critiques, frustrations, and joys, the give-and-take of our Monday afternoon conference calls has been a highlight of my career." We all look forward to working with one another again on the next edition of this handbook.

Handbook of
Sexual Orientation
and Gender Diversity
in Counseling *and*
Psychotherapy

INTRODUCTION: THE PACE OF CHANGE AND THE CHALLENGE TO KEEP UP

KURT A. DeBORD, ANN R. FISCHER, KATHLEEN J. BIESCHKE, AND RUPERTO M. PEREZ

The social and political landscape for sexual minority (SM) and transgender and gender nonconforming (TGNC) people has improved in the United States during the past several years. The Supreme Court's ruling that made same-sex marriage legal in all 50 states was a visible, dramatic, and (for some) surprising change that affected the quality of life for many SM individuals. Shifts in attitudes and policies on other key issues (e.g., domestic partnership benefits, adoption, parenting) affecting both SM and TGNC communities have gained positive ground (American Civil Liberties Union, 2015) since the last publication of this handbook. However, in comparison with people in the general population, SM and TGNC people still face high rates of discrimination, interpersonal harassment and violence (Federal Bureau of Investigation, 2014), and mental health challenges (e.g., Burgess, Lee, Tran, & van Ryn, 2008; Mustanski, Garofalo, & Emerson, 2010). In this latest edition of the handbook, we examine the ongoing challenges faced by

http://dx.doi.org/10.1037/15959-001
Handbook of Sexual Orientation and Gender Diversity in Counseling and Psychotherapy, K. A. DeBord, A. R. Fischer, K. J. Bieschke, and R. M. Perez (Editors)
Copyright © 2017 by the American Psychological Association. All rights reserved.

SM and TGNC people and offer a contemporary guide to affirmative therapy for this population. This, too, was the primary goal we had for our last two handbooks (Perez, DeBord, & Bieschke, 2000; Bieschke, Perez, & DeBord, 2007), but we came to realize that an update was needed: Sociocultural factors change over time, and so too does the shape of affirmative therapy. Affirmative therapy still incorporates therapeutic ways of being, questioning, and exploring, but the focus and sophistication of these processes continue to evolve. This handbook attempts to define, characterize, and guide the current state of affirmative therapy, while situating it within the social values and forces that have molded it. In this Introduction, we identify a number of the factors that motivated our decision to pursue this goal at this time. We start by addressing some of the sociocultural changes that have occurred in the United States and some of the changes that have occurred in the mental health profession. Next, we describe themes identified by our authors and themes we asked our authors to address. We then consider the critical significance of language use. We conclude by providing brief descriptions of the chapters that follow.

CULTURAL SHIFTS

"Why would you even need a book on that?" was a question recently posed to one of the editors of this handbook. The discussion that followed made clear the questioner's opinion that by now, the social climate for SM and TGNC people had improved so dramatically that there was no need to articulate a distinct therapeutic approach. Furthermore, he seemed to assume that most mental health care providers would already be affirming of SM and TGNC people, making a book on affirmative therapy redundant. Those sentiments represent some of the challenges to capturing and refining the description of affirmative therapy with SM and TGNC clients. Unfortunately, those sentiments are not uncommon, yet they ignore the experiences of trauma, hardship, and stress so frequently endured by SM and TGNC people that are well documented in this handbook (see, e.g., Chapters 7 and 13). It is true that social changes have led to improvements in the lives of SM and TGNC individuals at a pace that has been unparalleled. A few years ago a pollster commented about same-sex marriage: "Attitudes on this issue are changing faster than on any other issue in the history of public-opinion polling" (quoted in Clift, 2012; see also Chapter 3 this handbook). The attitude changes have been accompanied by swift changes in the law. During the development of this handbook, we asked some authors to repeatedly revise their commentary on the number of states with legalized same-sex marriage because the numbers were changing so fast. We had no idea that by the completion of this text, same-sex marriage would be the law of the land in the United States.

However, it is important to keep in mind that many progressive political and social changes are often met with backlash in the interpersonal experiences of SM and TGNC people. The National Coalition of Anti-Violence Programs announced that the network's calls in 2013 from lesbian, gay, bisexual, transgender, and queer (LGBTQ) individuals or HIV-positive survivors requesting support after physical hate crimes increased by 21% in comparison with the previous year. A substantial majority (59%) of these survivors were people of color, and about one third (32%) had disabilities. Transgender women in the sample suffered physical violence in interactions with police at a rate about six times higher than other survivors. Because of such realities, this handbook is necessary.

The pace of social change on SM and TGNC issues has been complemented by responses from researchers and policymakers in the arena of mental health that have informed and nurtured the growth of affirmative therapy in recent years (see Chapter 13, this volume). Statements about therapeutic guidelines, best practices, and standards of care for SM and TGNC clients have been recently developed and revised by several organizations (e.g., American Psychological Association, 2012, 2015; Association for Lesbian, Gay, Bisexual, and Transgender Issues in Counseling, 2009; World Professional Association on Transgender Health, 2012). Being cognizant of this progress, we asked our authors to incorporate into their chapters the most recent and relevant empirical work on SM and TGNC mental health. They responded by creating a text that can serve not only as a guide for providing affirmative therapy but also as a launch pad for those interested in expanding the research base in this area. Furthermore, some authors (see Chapters 5 and 15) used the guidelines and recommendations of the professional bodies in this field to stimulate consideration of how complex SM and TGNC affirmative therapy can be. This handbook is intended to summarize and synthesize the factors that have shaped the face of affirmative therapy to this point in time.

THEMES IN THE HANDBOOK

A number of topics are addressed consistently by the authors in this handbook. The authors' unique and creative approaches to these topics provide refreshing and enhanced appreciation for their complexity, addressing as they do such themes as minority stress, stigma management, resilience, and intersectionality.

We invited authors to entertain and explore the sometimes conflicting schools of thought that collectively inform the state of affirmative therapy today—and we were not disappointed. Complexity may be the defining feature of how SM and TGNC lives are currently depicted in the scholarly literature. This complexity presents both challenges and promises to those who seek to offer affirmative therapy to their clients. One example of how this kind of complexity can present challenges is illustrated by Fassinger (Chapter 1), who probes the complexity and depth of the academic work in this field by reviewing perspectives that question the very validity of the identities that the SM and TGNC abbreviations stand for. Also addressing the complexity of therapy, Russell and Hawkey (Chapter 3) address the multiple, shifting contexts of clients' lives, in which external stigma experiences (e.g., prejudice, discrimination) may come to be internalized. By adopting a cognitive perspective that encourages clients to see how specific events in time are related to broad, long-term social and political movements, these authors identify ways to help clients connect their suffering to societal forces without succumbing to the helplessness that sometimes comes from awareness of oppressive systems. As a third example of complexity, dickey and Singh (Chapter 16) discuss the basic contradiction of mental health providers being both gatekeepers and evaluators, on the one hand, and supporters or advocates, on the other hand, for gender nonconforming individuals who wish to make a medical transition. Another example of the challenges posed by the complexity of this field is the paradox identified by Phillips and Fitts (Chapter 14). They question how it is possible to endorse a form of therapy that, by its existence, reifies and strengthens the idea that normalcy is represented by heterosexual and cisgender lives.

As we encountered the questions that naturally emerged from our authors' exploration of the complexities inherent in SM and TGNC lives and in affirmative therapy, we realized that there were no clear-cut answers to them. Nevertheless, deliberation of possible responses to those questions consistently leads to rich understandings of effective therapeutic services. At times, our authors offer inspired and imaginative suggestions for how to tackle the dilemmas posed by providing affirmative therapy. We believe that readers benefit from contemplation of this complexity.

We were not overly surprised when chapter authors spontaneously converged on the themes of minority stress (Meyer, 1995, 2003), stigma management, and resilience factors in the practice of affirmative therapy today. In the first edition of the handbook (Perez et al., 2000), lesbian and gay identity development models were popular and assumed to be important to providing sound affirmative therapy. In the second edition (Bieschke et al., 2007), Fassinger and Arseneau described the identity development process as having a critical social component, with connection to a lesbian, gay, bisexual, and transgender community being a unique and important facet of the mental health outcomes of our populations of interest. Today, a sociological perspective has successfully inverted the focus of affirmative therapy from one that emphasized individual problems to one that challenges providers to adopt a strengths-based approach for clients and to actively consider the pathologizing influences of a culture plagued with prejudice. This approach opens the potential of affirmative therapy to actively nurture the multiple pathways of individual expression encompassed by the endless intersectional identities of SM and TGNC people. As editors of a handbook that endeavors to depict the current nature of affirmative therapy, we support and appreciate the marked shift that this signifies.

As editors, we were excited to see the themes that spontaneously emerged from the minds of our authors, but we also invited them to consistently concentrate on some topics. Intersectionality was one of them. Moradi (Chapter 4) calls on readers to resist dismissing this crucial topic as "buzzworthy" and faddish; she illustrates that a thoughtful consideration of intersectionality compels one to analyze how social and political power are wielded by certain groups in a society. She asks us all to examine how some SM and TGNC experiences become prototypes while others become invisible. With this idea in mind, we asked all of our authors in the second section of this handbook to develop a case study for each of their chapters that featured the application of affirmative therapy to a client whose identity represented the intersection of multiple, often stigmatized, backgrounds. In doing so, we sought to use our positions as editors to inspire readers to always think about the unique challenges and resilience factors that SM and TGNC people bring to the consulting room. Also, we hoped engaging in such reflection would bring to the forefront the issues of power and privilege and how they play out in clients' lives and counselors' lives and in the interaction between the two. We also invited authors to describe the impact of their own social positions and biases on their topics; our purpose was to encourage contributor transparency. (We note that not all contributors decided to reveal this information about themselves.) This type of analysis and reflection calls into question the language and words we use in discussing and doing affirmative therapy, a topic we turn to next.

USE OF TERMS IN THE HANDBOOK

The titles of our three handbooks—*Handbook of Counseling and Psychotherapy With Lesbian, Gay, and Bisexual Clients* (first edition; Perez et al., 2000); *Handbook of Counseling and Psychotherapy With Lesbian, Gay, Bisexual, and Transgender Clients* (second edition; Bieschke et al., 2007); and the present *Handbook of Sexual Orientation and Gender Diversity in Counseling and Psychotherapy* (third edition)—reflect shifts in social power about who was included in the discussion of SM and TGNC lives in the scholarship and research literature relevant to affirmative therapy. The first handbook did not include discussion of TGNC people. The second handbook did, but the discussion was limited to two chapters. In this handbook, we asked all but three sets of authors to include consideration of empirical or theoretical work on TGNC people and to offer suggestions about the implications of their chapter for TGNC people. (The chapters on affirmative therapy and physical health for SM and TGNC clients are separate. In addition, the chapter on sexual orientation change interventions focused only on SM people.) This inclusivity demanded careful deliberation about what terms to use to refer to people not only in the TGNC community but in all of our populations of interest.

The use of appropriate terms in lesbian, gay, bisexual, transgender, queer, questioning, intersex, asexual, and ally (LGBTQQIAA) communities is a complex issue loaded with political implications and emotional valence. Many people in these communities shun the use of labels, sometimes arguing that labels cannot, and should not, try to reflect lived experience. Some people feel that many of the commonly used terms do not adequately represent the diverse backgrounds and subcultures that exist within the community (see Scholz, 2013). No term is perfect; many are cumbersome. Not one is all-inclusive. The dynamic nature of language itself translates into an ever-evolving use of terms that will be different tomorrow than it is today.

As editors of this handbook, we had to decide which terms to consistently use throughout the text in referring to the client populations of interest. We concluded that the best way to proceed was to consult the literature, the popular websites for political activism in these communities (e.g., GLAAD, Williams Institute, the National Center for Transgender Equality), authors with a history of professional writing in the area, leaders in Division 44 (Society for the Psychological Study of Lesbian, Gay, Bisexual, and Transgender Issues) of the American Psychological Association, and members of the communities we knew personally. We were confronted with more complexity and controversy than we had bargained for. Repeatedly we were told that no matter what terms we decided upon, we could expect to anger and alienate some while satisfying others.

After careful consultations and consideration of the implications, we selected the terms *sexual minority* and *transgender and gender nonconforming* because of their perceived inclusiveness and simplicity. We recognize that there will likely not be consensus on which terms are best for anybody given the varieties of backgrounds, situations, and temporal fluidity that can affect self-selected identities. In fact, Scholz (2013) challenged researchers to avoid invoking categories of identity unless we explicitly acknowledge their conditionality as "local, situational, and temporary" (p. 271). We also acknowledge that some people consciously choose not to self-identify at all, refusing to participate in a system of naming that may limit, silence, or render unacceptable experiences that do not easily fit within identity boundaries. One set of boundaries of particular relevance is the *gender binary*, an overarching cultural construction that shapes what we see and experience in terms of sex and gender. The gender binary in the United States, for example, structures institutions and individual experience to "allow" for two and only two sexes and genders (male and female, masculine and feminine).

We had the privilege of inviting authors to write about the factors that optimize affirmative therapy with SM and TGNC clients. In our review of chapters, it became clear that a wide variety of terms was being defined and used. For the sake of clarity and efficiency, we asked authors to consider using the terms described below and to write about how and why their use of terms might differ from ours. Although many authors agreed with our recommended terms, others preferred variations on the LGBTQ abbreviation. Russell and Hawkey (Chapter 3) used the term *sexual minority and gender expansive individuals*, for reasons they explain in their chapter. As editors, we found the definitions used by dickey and Singh in Chapters 6 and 16 to be enlightening and helpful in distinguishing concepts that often get confused in common usage or simply are used differently by different individuals or groups. Therefore, much of what we have included below represents their good work.

Sexual orientation is used in this volume to describe one's typical patterns of sexual and affectional attractions. If one assumes a gender binary (that people fall neatly into categories of male and female), a *gay* or *lesbian* sexual orientation refers to a person's same-sex sexual/affectional orientation. *Bisexuality* is descriptive of those who have attractions to people of both sexes. *Men who have sex with men, questioning, queer, sisters,* and *same gender loving* are words and phrases often used by people to describe themselves as involved in some way in same-sex attraction or behavior. Individuals and groups often self-identify with these terms in order to distinguish themselves from gay and lesbian cultures perceived to reflect the norms, values, and standards of privileged, White, gay, or lesbian people. We use the term *sexual minority* as an umbrella term that includes all of the groups described here.

Gender identity refers to how one defines, understands, and experiences his or her gender (e.g., woman, man, transgender individual). As editors, we agreed that *gender nonconforming* was a term that provided the most inclusivity for people who were opposed to living in and seeing the world in a way that forced gender into a binary status. Consultation with our authors led us to understand the importance of including *transgender* as a unique identity because some people who identify as transgender embrace and adopt the gender binary. Thus, throughout the text we have encouraged authors to use the abbreviation TGNC to refer to transgender and gender nonconforming people.

There are many words that TGNC clients may use to describe themselves. Some clients may shorten *transgender* to *trans* or *trans** (see Chapter 13), or they may use *trans man* or *trans woman* to designate a TGNC status and their current gender identity. Other TGNC clients may feel strongly about using words such as *woman* or *man* or *male* or *female* to describe their gender identity. *Genderqueer* is another term some people who do not associate with a gender binary may use. It is typically claimed either by someone who consciously refuses to participate in hegemonic, binary social constructions of gender or someone who identifies with components of stereotypically masculine, feminine, and/or gender-neutral expressions (or something else altogether; Lambda Legal, 2015). *Gender expression*, unlike gender identity, refers to one's outward behaviors (e.g., clothing) in experiencing and communicating gender. Words such as *masculine, feminine*, and *gender neutral* are common ways to describe one's gender expression.

Other terms that are often used in TGNC-affirmative counseling include *cisgender* and *cisgender privilege*. *Cisgender* refers to people whose gender identity is aligned with the sex they were assigned at birth (Lambda Legal, 2015). *Cisgender privilege* includes all of the (unearned) societal advantages that are provided to individuals whose originally assigned sex is consistent with their preferred gender expression and presentation. These privileges can range from being able to easily access safe public bathrooms and not being pushed to defend one's gender presentation to having responsive health care.

Because language is continuously evolving in TGNC communities, TGNC-affirmative therapy requires that practitioners are not only knowledgeable about the various words and expressions that TGNC clients use to describe themselves but also are prepared to use these words and understand their meanings. In cases where a TGNC client uses a term that the practitioner does not understand, asking for clarification respectfully is often the best strategy. Affirmative counseling also involves using pronouns or words that TGNC clients express as important to them. There are helpful glossaries of TGNC terms that can be found in a number of the websites listed in the Appendix (e.g., Lambda Legal's *Bending the Mold*). It is important to remember, however, that variation and fluidity in usage of terminology are constants in the continuing journey toward affirmative practice.

STRUCTURE AND ORGANIZATION OF THE HANDBOOK

The vast majority of material in this book is new and unique to the third edition. In Chapter 12, Charlotte J. Patterson offers an update to her previous version of this chapter (Patterson, 2007) about family issues in the second edition. This handbook contains three parts, each relating uniquely to affirmative therapy.

Part I: Foundational Information for Practitioners

The chapters in Part I challenge readers to consider how their therapeutic work with SM and TGNC people is supported by assumptions that have powerful implications for the nature and outcomes of their work. Fassinger (Chapter 1) tackles social constructionism, the way in which all meanings are created through social discourse; the implications for the construction and enactment of identity are provocative. Her critique of essentialist notions requires readers to contemplate how their assumptions about the essence of sexual orientation and gender identity might allow for a focus and validation of certain ways of being while negating others. She offers a model of therapy that is "transgression-affirmative," encouraging clients to create their own stories while acknowledging the influences of broader social systems. Sánchez and Pankey (Chapter 2) elaborate upon the essentialist assumptions that underlie research on the physiological bases of sexual orientation and gender identity. They also offer an extensive review of the often conflicting findings published in the biomedical research on the influence of genes, hormones, and brain structures on SM and TGNC identities.

The politics of stigma, oppression, and privilege are explored in the remaining two chapters of Part I. Russell and Hawkey (Chapter 3) describe the impact of shifting social attitudes and policies on SM and TGNC lives. They offer an approach to therapy that focuses on responding to stigma, both internalized and external, in ways that draw on clients' strengths and that encourage active reframing and coping with stigma-related stressors. Stigma and resilience are also themes in Moradi's chapter on intersecting identities (Chapter 4); she critically analyzes how social power influences the questions we ask that shape our research and practice with SM and TGNC people. In addition, she offers a series of questions that all practitioners should consider while engaging in affirmative therapy (e.g., With which clients do I attend to group differences and culture as explanatory factors for presenting concerns?). Taken together, the four chapters in this section provide the groundwork for the self-reflection and self-awareness that are necessary for effective affirmative therapy with SM and TGNC clients.

Part II: Affirmative Counseling With Sexual Minority, Transgender, and Gender Nonconforming Clients

In this section, readers are invited to explore what affirmative therapy can look like with specific subpopulations of SM and TGNC people. Authors in this section identified and applied research findings to counseling and therapeutic practice and considered intersectional identities. TGNC people were included in all but one of the six chapters in this section. The exception was made because we wanted one chapter on affirmative therapy for SM clients and a separate chapter for affirmative therapy with TGNC clients. A case study was included in each of the chapters within this section.

In Chapter 5, Paul describes the relevance of minority stress, resilience, and microaggressions and the positive aspects of being a SM to affirmative therapy while simultaneously inviting clinicians to scrutinize their potential biases that could interfere with providing care. He maps the application of several crucial guidelines and recommended competencies identified by two professional bodies, the American Psychological Association (2012) and the Association for Lesbian, Gay, Bisexual, and Transgender Issues in Counseling (ALGBTIC; Harper et al., 2013), to his case work. In Chapter 6, Singh and dickey describe affirmative therapy with TGNC clients, providing excellent direction for counselors needing to learn how to work with TGNC clients who are facing social transitions as opposed to medical transition. They, too, discuss the minority stress model (Meyer, 2003) and the role of resilience factors that permit effective coping among TGNC individuals.

The next two chapters deal with SM and TGNC clients who experience trauma and conflict. In Chapter 7, Pantalone, Valentine, and Shipherd delve into the prevalence of trauma, provide guidance on how to assess it, and apply empirically based interventions to two cases using prolonged exposure therapy (Foa, Hembree, & Rothbaum, 2007) and cognitive processing therapy (Resick & Schnicke, 1992). Chapter 8 examines how stigma, rooted in a variety of religious traditions, can affect the mental health of SM and TGNC clients. Kashubeck-West, Whiteley, Vossenkemper, Robinson, and Deitz explore the statements authorities from a few religious perspectives have made publicly regarding their views on sexual orientation and gender identity. They consider approaches to resolution for those who experience conflict between their religious identities and their SM and TGNC identities.

The final two chapters in Part II review crucial aspects of affirmative therapy with younger and older portions of the SM and TGNC populations. In Chapter 9, Starks and Millar adopt a decidedly data-based approach to considering how best to work with SM and TGNC youth. After exploring the health and mental health disparities between SM and TGNC youth and their counterparts, they apply research to developing interventions in areas key for adolescents and young adults, including substance abuse, mental health, sexual health, and relationship skills. Chapter 10 calls for providers to consider how to provide affirmative therapy for aging adults. Vacha-Haase and Donaldson examine numerous generational and cohort effects that could influence how and with what issues older clients present for therapy. Issues of health, finances, social support, sexual health, caregiving, residence, and end-of-life planning are investigated.

Part III: Essential Areas for Practice, Research, Training, and Health

As its title suggests, Part III addresses topics that readers should find useful for providing affirmative therapy, understanding the research base for practice with SM and TGNC people, developing training programs for students, and recognizing the physical health needs of SM clients and TGNC clients who are interested in physical transition. These chapters prepare readers to enhance the field of affirmative therapy by establishing the empirical groundwork in the areas of sexual orientation change interventions (SOCIs), SM and TGNC family and other relationship dynamics and influences, practice delivery, and physical health.

Chapter 11 explains the context for and nature of SOCIs. Shidlo and Gonsiorek thoroughly consider why people might seek SOCIs and what the ethical problems are with attempting to provide these interventions. The authors provide alternatives to SOCIs and potential follow-up strategies for clients who have participated in them. Patterson (Chapter 12) depicts how SM and TGNC people and their family relationships (including couples) are continuing to be affected by the evolving legal and policy landscapes across the United States that pertain to such issues as job discrimination, parental rights, adoption, and marriage. In a revision of her similar chapter (Patterson, 2007) in the second edition of this book, Patterson uses updated research findings to characterize patterns of relating and sharing power in same-sex relationships.

Chapters 13 and 14 will be especially valuable to those involved in establishing and advancing research agendas and graduate training programs that address the needs of SM and TGNC people. Worthington and Strathausen explore the relevance of intersectionality to the empirical research base and then provide a comprehensive review of research findings related to many aspects of SM and TGNC mental health and to the delivery of counseling services since the publication of the second edition of this handbook (Bieschke et al., 2007). In Chapter 14, Phillips and Fitts explore the methods and outcomes of studies that have been conducted on the effectiveness of training programs in producing practitioners competent in aspects of SM and TGNC affirmative therapy. Their identification of factors that facilitate best practices in the training of competent counselors and psychologists will be especially informative to academicians and trainees.

The final two chapters in this part address physical health issues. Haldeman and Hancock adopt a minority stress model to frame the many obstacles and risks faced by SM people in achieving optimal physical health. They shed light on health care access barriers, negative coping strategies, and specific health related problems that disproportionately affect SM lives. They respond to the health challenges faced by SM people by additionally describing SM resilience characteristics and positive changes in health care practices, and they list recommendations for providers to help them promote the physical well-being of their SM clients. The final chapter (Chapter 16) enlightens readers about the health care issues faced by TGNC people who are considering physical transition processes. dickey and Singh explore the controversy associated with a diagnosis of gender dysphoria as defined in the fifth edition of the *Diagnostic and Statistical Manual of Mental Disorders* (American Psychiatric Association, 2013), the recent standards of care produced by World Professional Association for Transgender Health (Coleman et al., 2012), the assessment of readiness for medical transition, and the specifics of hormone therapies and gender-affirmation surgeries, including their costs. The authors also advise mental health care providers on the follow-up care that is essential for TGNC clients who have participated in medical interventions. These chapters should be included on the reading lists of those interested in providing quality mental health care to SM and TGNC clients.

CONCLUSION

With topics as rich, dynamic, and politically charged as sexual orientation and gender identity, our talented authors strove to provide a comprehensive guide to the complex issues that underlie and characterize the provision of affirmative counseling and therapy. In the chapters that follow, the authors' expert reviews of previous research and their creative applications of the body of evidence will substantively enhance the quality of services provided to clients who identify as SM or TGNC. In addition, the handbook will serve as a resource for furthering dialogue and generating new ideas among researchers, practitioners, advocates, and students.

REFERENCES

American Civil Liberties Union. (2015). *LGBT & AIDS project case profiles.* Retrieved from https://www.aclu.org/hiv-aids-lgbt-rights/lgbt-aids-project-case-profiles

American Psychiatric Association. (2013). *Diagnostic and statistical manual of mental disorders* (5th ed.). Arlington, VA: Author.

American Psychological Association. (2012). Guidelines for psychological practice with lesbian, gay, and bisexual clients. *American Psychologist, 67,* 10–42.

American Psychological Association. (2015). *Guidelines for psychological practice with transgender and gender nonconforming people.* Retrieved from http://www.apa.org/practice/guidelines/transgender.pdf

Association for Lesbian, Gay, Bisexual, and Transgender Issues in Counseling. (2009). *Competencies for counseling with transgender clients*. Alexandria, VA: Author.

Bieschke, K. J., Perez, R. M., & DeBord, K. A. (Eds.). (2007). *Handbook of counseling and psychotherapy with lesbian, gay, bisexual, and transgender clients* (2nd ed.). Washington, DC: American Psychological Association. http://dx.doi.org/10.1037/11482-000

Burgess, D., Lee, R., Tran, A., & van Ryn, M. (2008). Effects of perceived discrimination on mental health and mental health services utilization among gay, lesbian, bisexual and transgender persons. *Journal of LGBT Health Research, 3*(4), 1–14. http://dx.doi.org/10.1080/15574090802226626

Clift, E. (2012, July 31). Why the Democrats backed a gay marriage plank for the party convention. *The Daily Beast*. Retrieved from http://www.thedailybeast.com/articles/2012/07/31/why-the-democrats-backed-a-gay-marriage-plank-for-the-party-convention.html

Coleman, E., Bockting, W., Botzer, M., Cohen-Kettenis, P., DeCuypere, G., Feldman, J., . . . Zucker, K. (2012). Standards of care for the health of transsexual, transgender, and gender nonconforming people, Version 7. *International Journal of Transgenderism, 13*, 165–232.

Federal Bureau of Investigation. (2014, December 8). *Latest hate crime statistics report released*. Retrieved from http://www.fbi.gov/news/stories/2014/december/latest-hate-crime-statistics-report-released/latest-hate-crime-statistics-report-released

Foa, E. B., Hembree, E. A., & Rothbaum, B. O. (2007). *Prolonged exposure therapy for PTSD: Emotional processing of traumatic experiences therapist guide (treatments that work)*. New York, NY: Oxford University Press. http://dx.doi.org/10.1093/med:psych/9780195308501.001.0001

Harper, A., Finnerty, P., Martinez, M., Brace, A., Crethar, H. C., Loos, B., . . . ALGBTIC LGBQQIA Competencies Taskforce. (2013). Association for Lesbian, Gay, Bisexual, and Transgender Issues in Counseling competencies for counseling with lesbian, gay, bisexual, queer, questioning, intersex, and ally individuals. *Journal of LGBT Issues in Counseling, 7*(1), 2–43. http://dx.doi.org/10.1080/15538605.2013.755444

Lambda Legal. (2015). *Changing birth certificate sex designations: State-by-state guidelines*. Retrieved from http://www.lambdalegal.org/know-your-rights/transgender/changing-birth-certificate-sex-designations/

Meyer, I. H. (1995). Minority stress and mental health in gay men. *Journal of Health and Social Behavior, 36*, 38–56. http://dx.doi.org/10.2307/2137286

Meyer, I. H. (2003). Prejudice, social stress, and mental health in lesbian, gay, and bisexual populations: Conceptual issues and research evidence. *Psychological Bulletin, 129*, 674–697.

Mustanski, B. S., Garofalo, R., & Emerson, E. M. (2010). Mental health disorders, psychological distress, and suicidality in a diverse sample of lesbian, gay, bisexual, and transgender youths. *American Journal of Public Health, 100*, 2426–2432. http://dx.doi.org/10.2105/AJPH.2009.178319

National Coalition of Anti-Violence Programs. (2013). *Lesbian, gay, bisexual, transgender, queer, and HIV-affected hate violence in 2013 (2014 release edition)*. Retrieved from http://avp.org/storage/documents/2013_ncavp_hvreport_final.pdf

Patterson, C. J. (2007). Lesbian and gay family issues in the context of changing legal and social policy environments. In K. J. Bieschke, R. M. Perez, & K. A. DeBord, *Handbook of counseling and psychotherapy with lesbian, gay, bisexual, and transgender clients* (2nd ed., pp. 359–377). Washington, DC: American Psychological Association. http://dx.doi.org/10.1037/11482-015

Perez, R. M., DeBord, K. A., & Bieschke, K. J. (Eds.). (2000). *Handbook of counseling and psychotherapy with lesbian, gay, and bisexual clients*. Washington, DC: American Psychological Association. http://dx.doi.org/10.1037/10339-000

Resick, P. A., & Schnicke, M. K. (1992). Cognitive processing therapy for sexual assault victims. *Journal of Consulting and Clinical Psychology, 60*, 748–756. http://dx.doi.org/10.1037/0022-006X.60.5.748

Scholz, J. (2013, June). Queer psychology: Let's focus on the theoretical approach instead of preserving identities. In *Coming-out for LGBT psychology in the current international scenario: Proceedings of the 1st International Conference on LGBT Psychology and Related Fields* (pp. 272–274). Lisbon, Portugal.

World Professional Association on Transgender Health. (2012). *Standards of care for the health of transsexual, transgender, and gender nonconforming people*. Retrieved from http://www.wpath.org/uploaded_files/140/files/Standards%20of%20Care,%20V7%20Full%20Book.pdf

I

FOUNDATIONAL
INFORMATION
FOR PRACTITIONERS

1

CONSIDERING CONSTRUCTIONS: A NEW MODEL OF AFFIRMATIVE THERAPY

RUTH E. FASSINGER

CASE STUDY

In my therapy practice a decade ago, Shawna,[1] a 34-year-old, single, professionally successful African American woman, presented with sleep deprivation, anxiety, and depression related to severe job-related stress. She gradually revealed that she might be attracted to women and acknowledged this as an important source of her stress. Over time, she explored what this meant for her in her family, at work, and in her African American and Christian communities; her fear of damnation caused her to take brief breaks from therapy several times. Throughout her therapy, I used a feminist, affirmative approach in which I provided openness, collaboration, support, education, and validation of whoever and wherever she was

---

[1]Client identifiers have been changed to protect confidentiality.

http://dx.doi.org/10.1037/15959-002
Handbook of Sexual Orientation and Gender Diversity in Counseling and Psychotherapy, K. A. DeBord, A. R. Fischer, K. J. Bieschke, and R. M. Perez (Editors)

in her identity journey—which eventually led her to romantic relationships with women. Preoccupied with a need to self-label, Shawna agonized over whether she was "really gay," and she asked me often (with my ever-unfolding understanding of her) to pronounce my judgment on her "true" self, that is, her "real" sexual orientation. She regarded the fact that I could/would not do so as an excuse to refuse her growing feelings of attraction to me, but we successfully worked through this and mutually agreed to end therapy about 3 years later. At that point, Shawna identified herself somewhat hesitantly as "bi" and was in a satisfying three-way relationship with an African American lesbian couple. She kept in touch with me over the next several years. At last contact, she was happily in a relationship with a multiethnic woman, identified herself as "sort of a bi-lesbian" (although she "no longer care[d] about labels and such"), and eagerly awaited the legalization of same-sex marriage in Maryland so that she and her "wife" could "tie the knot."

This case illustrates a core dilemma for any therapist attempting to enact affirmative therapy with a client claiming or considering a sexual minority identity, in that it foregrounds and implicitly presumes the existence of an identity that both the client and the therapist are trying to explore freely and about which neither is certain. In the case cited here, I consistently validated whatever identity my client claimed at any given time, so certainly I was being affirmative, but I would argue that most therapy probably is aimed at being affirmative if conceptualized in this broad way. What makes LGBTQQIA-affirmative therapy unique, however, is all of those prefatory letters (which stand for lesbian, gay, bisexual, transgender, queer, questioning, intersex, asexual, ally)—that is, the therapy very specifically focuses on affirming identities that are organized around sexual orientation or gender diversity (i.e., expression, identity). Thus, gay- (or the more inclusive LGBTQQIAA) affirmative therapy, by label and definition, requires understanding and validation of the very identities that therapists and their clients are trying to be flexible about in honoring the individual unfolding of clients' stories.

There is an assumption that both the client and the therapist can comprehend and name an essence of the client's experience of the world that is grounded in self-identification within a specific range of sexual orientation and gender diversity labels (e.g., gay, lesbian, bisexual, transgender, queer, gender nonconforming). Even if neither the client nor the therapist is certain of the self-identification of the client for various clinically relevant reasons, there still is an implicit imperative that the therapist portray openness to, positive attitudes toward, and willingness to explore aspects of identity connected to sexual orientation and gender diversity. The expectation that therapeutic time and attention be given to these particular realms of human experience implies that they are considered to be a critically important part of what makes up this individual human being who is presenting for intervention and that the intervention is judged to be "affirmative" when it is organized around these specific dimensions of sexual orientation and gender diversity.

However, a sizeable number of scholars have adopted a stance that identity is socially constructed—that it is a complex amalgam of sociocultural expectations, beliefs, messages, stereotypes, and assumptions that are inculcated into and internalized by individuals in a society and then come to be seen as essential aspects of self, tied to and embodied in perceived biological, physical, genetic, or evolutionary phenomena (e.g., genitalia, chromosomes). From a constructionist standpoint, there is nothing that really is an essential aspect of the self, and identity is simply an artifact of a social organizational process, a collective set of societal constructs created to categorize people along dimensions that society deems important to categorize (primarily to enact systems of power and privilege around those categories). It follows that any system (including a system of therapeutic intervention) that relies on interactions pertaining to an identity that is socially constructed is potentially problematic. It is based on constructs that are temporally, historically, and culturally bound. At best, such identity anchors are unstable: Affirmative therapy is affirmative of what, exactly, in terms of identities that are continually evolving? At worst, these identity anchors can be seen as rigidly constraining the free expression of selfhood—that is, affirmative therapy affirms arbitrary, limiting, perhaps ill-fitting categorizations of the self.

This chapter explores what it means to enact LGBTQQIA-affirmative therapy within a paradigm that questions the very existence of those LGBTQQIA identities. I begin with a description of the social constructionist stance, including more radical queer theory, and the relation of this approach to identity, particularly pertaining to sexual orientation and gender diversity; this account includes historical background to trace the emergence of the social constructionist approach in relation to the historical unfolding of conceptions of gender and sexuality. Then I outline a recently articulated social constructionist approach to counseling focused on work and relationships (M. S. Richardson, 2012), which I believe can be applied effectively to affirmative therapy related to sexual orientation and gender diversity. I draw a distinction between constructionist and constructivist points of view, and I again use vocational theory (Savickas, 2013) to detail how these approaches might inform therapeutic practice. Finally, I propose a transgression-affirmative nested-narrative identity construction and enactment (NICE) model of therapy. I conclude with a return to my opening case example and consider the ways in which my proposed model might enhance therapeutic effectiveness with sexual minority clients.

OVERVIEW OF THE SOCIAL CONSTRUCTIONIST STANCE

The main tenet of a social constructionist stance rests on the observation that societies create meanings around particular dimensions of human bodies and behaviors, which are transmitted throughout the society by direct teachings, stereotypes, institutionalized beliefs, and assumptions—that is, through social discourse or discursively. These socially transmitted meanings and the dimensions to which they are attached become internalized and eventually come to be viewed as essential aspects of human experience, complete with explanatory fictions based in factors presumed to be observable (e.g., bodies, drives, behaviors, emotions, historical interpretations). The assumption that there are fundamental essential aspects of the self has been termed *essentialism,* and an essentialist stance posits many human dimensions (e.g., gender, race, sexual orientation) as inborn, culturally independent factors that constitute an important axis of reality for the individual. (See Chapter 2 for further discussion of essentialist perspectives.)

Much has been written about the motivation to create categories and fit people into them, with explanations ranging from internal–individual and cognitively oriented (a need to classify and simplify complex phenomena so that the mind can process them readily) to external–contextual and sociopolitically motivated (a need to create hierarchical systems of power, privilege, and advantage so that society can accord approval and mete out resources). Prentice and Miller (2007) noted that the tendency to essentialize varies greatly across types of human categories; those based on gender, race, and ethnicity seem to demonstrate robustness across cultures and subcultures, whereas other kinds of categories (e.g., personality, politics) do not. According to these authors, psychological essentialism is a heuristic that provides a "good enough" explanation of deeper structure (usually not fully understood), and the extent to which a category is essentialized is independent of entitativity (the extent to which it is perceived as unified into a coherent meaning). Moreover, psychological essentialism has crucial social consequences: the accentuation of similarities within and differences between categories of people (based on belief in an underlying essence); lack of motivation to change oneself or members of essentialized groups (based on a belief in stability and immutability); and greater prejudice toward stigmatized groups (based on "belief that an immutable essence causes many of a category's observable features"; Prentice & Miller, 2007, p. 204).

An essentialist stance applied to sexual orientation is a belief that sexuality itself (and particularly the sex of one's partner[s]) is a core, definitive determinant of one's being. According to essentialists, categories of sexual expression and orientation, as well as gender expression and identity, can be appropriately applied to people because they capture intrinsic aspects of humans that occur across culture and history. Essentialism can take several forms related to gender and sexuality, and these evoke the mechanisms described by Prentice and Miller (2007): an assumption that human sexual behavior is natural; that it is predetermined by biological, physiological, or genetic factors and is thus immutable; a belief that human behaviors demonstrating some similarity in form are the same and thus constitute a manifestation of an underlying essence (e.g., a tendency or drive); and an assumption that behaviors sharing an observable similarity also share an underlying, coherent meaning (Vance, 1992).

Social constructionists, by contrast, assert that there are no innate or intrinsic characteristics of people related to sexuality and gender, but rather that an individual identifies with or is identified by sexual orientation or gender diversity because those are the labels and words, the categories, and the means of self-knowing offered to people in that culture at that time. Bohan (1996) noted,

> By defining individuals in terms of their erotic and affectional attachments and by enumerating categories to describe such attachments, we actually create precisely the situation we think we are describing. Individuals do, in fact, understand their identity to be grounded in the nature of their affections . . . Thus, experiences come to define individual identity; the adjective "homosexual" . . . becomes a noun (the homosexual) . . . The concept of sexual orientation transforms something one experiences into something one *is*. (pp. 6–8)

Social constructionists are concerned about the context in which essentializing of categories takes place and the discourses that drive the hierarchical conceptualizations of the categories that are formed. For example, social constructionist scholar Celia Kitzinger has pointed out that the concept of race was constructed and justified within the socioeconomic reality of black slavery. Similarly, the concept of gender is regarded by Kitzinger and other feminists as a political category—that "to describe women as a natural category is to biologize the historical situation of domination" (Kitzinger, 1995, p. 143). In a now-classic discussion of "doing" gender, West and Zimmerman (1987) noted how the daily reenactment of gender (based on deeply internalized, unquestioned categories) continually reinforces those categories, such that

> we simultaneously sustain, reproduce, and render legitimate the institutional arrangements that are based on sex category. If we fail to do gender appropriately, we as individuals—not the institutional arrangements—may be called to account (for our character, motives, and predispositions). (p. 146)

Similarly, Gagnon (1990) highlighted the politics of social control implicit in discourse related to sexual orientation:

> "homosexual" and "homosexuality" are names that have been imposed on some persons and their conduct by other persons—and this imposition has carried the right of the latter to tell the former the origins, meaning, and virtue of their conduct. . . . the authorized explainers . . . are in the process of inventing social and psychological facts as often as they are discovering them, and such authorized facts are often "disproved" or at least "disbelieved" when a revisionist group of authorized speakers seize the means of communication. (p. 183)

Gagnon's (1990) observation raises the question of who the authorized speakers have been and are currently, and how present-day discourses and conceptualizations of sexual orientation and gender diversity have come about. A brief historical account of two threads of this discussion are presented in the following sections: the social construction of (homo)sexuality during the past century and the evolution of social constructionism and queer theory in the past several decades.

Construction of (Homo)sexuality

There are several excellent, detailed histories of (homo)sexuality (e.g., D'Emilio & Freedman, 1988; Greenberg, 1988; Katz, 1995), including more focused historical accounts of women (Faderman, 1981, 1991; Tavris, 1992), homosexuality and religion (Boswell, 1980), and transgender people (Feinberg, 1996). The study of homosexuality has been summarized as one of resistance, because the authorized speakers evolved from being experts outside of homosexual communities to becoming the increasingly assertive voices of those in sexual minority communities themselves (Minton, 1997). Historians generally agree that the first use of the term *homosexual* was in 1869 in a pamphlet by Karl-Maria Kertbeny, a Hungarian journalist decrying Germany's antisodomy laws. The term was popularized, however, in Richard von Krafft-Ebing's 1893 *Psychopathia Sexualis*, intended for the medical and sexological communities, and by the 1890s, this terminology was in common usage.

Foucault (1978) traced the 19th-century shift from a legal and moral discourse focused on sexual practices (e.g., sodomy) to a medical–psychiatric and sexological discourse emphasizing a condition exhibited by individuals. At the time, this condition was seen as "inversion" (the belief that male homosexuals were essentially female, and female homosexuals essentially male), a congenital defect that was distinguished from the "perversion" of willfully immoral (same-sex) sexual acts. Krafft-Ebing's work led to the gradual displacement of the concept of inversion by the broader term *homosexuality*, and his own thinking also evolved over time; he came to view homosexuality not as a nervous disorder but as an object choice, with homosexual love equivalent to heterosexual love (Bullough, 2001). Nonetheless, the medicalized, sexological view of homosexuality progressed in the late 19th and early 20th centuries, with increasing case reports in medical journals in Europe and America from asylums as well as neurologists (Minton, 1997). Preeminent clinicians such as Sigmund Freud were important shapers of the dominant discourse, with biological sex and its aberrations at the heart of explanations of sexual desire and preferences. Moreover, the successful medicalization of homosexuality meant that most information on same-sex inclinations was based on medical and mental health cases.

Gagnon (1990) described the radical shift in the United States during the first four decades of the 20th century as a movement from a country composed of small, localized (regionally, linguistically, religiously) cultures to a large national economy, polity, and culture, with a growing urban middle class detached from regional cultures and with new forms of communication (e.g., radio, cinema) to unite the populace into common knowledge and ideas. It was in this context that a new science of sexuality, focused on the behavior of the emergent middle class (versus clinical populations), began to take root. By the 1930s, new sources of information on sexuality appeared in the form of research participants, and studies of homosexuality became widespread, with sex researchers such as Havelock Ellis and Magnus Hirschfeld making important contributions. Perhaps best-known in the United States was the sex variants study, led by sex researcher Robert Dickinson and psychiatrist George Henry, and relying on extensive community liaison work by lesbian Jan Gay and gay Thomas Painter. Published in 1941, this research used a case study method to provide detailed interviews with 80 men and women in New York City. Minton (1997) identified this study as especially important because it was the first time that participants were able to collaborate with researchers and thus expose the realities of their own lives. Sadly, however, "their objectives of empowerment and social acceptance were not to be realized" (Minton, 1997, p. 342), because the researchers maintained adherence to medical explanations throughout the study and pathologized the experiences of interviewees. However, Henry and Dickinson introduced Painter to Alfred Kinsey, and he assisted Kinsey in his research.

Kinsey's groundbreaking work, published in the 1940s and 1950s (Kinsey, Pomeroy & Martin, 1948; Kinsey, Pomeroy, Martin, & Gebhard, 1953) radically changed the way in which same-sex behavior was perceived. Kinsey's research subjects were largely young, middle class, educated, and liberal, and Kinsey's published accounts of their sexual behavior reflected a deep shift from the sexual ignorance of the past to a more liberated sexuality at mid-century; indeed, "what Kinsey supplied, under the banner of science, was a legitimation of the sexual lives that many middle-class persons were already living" (Gagnon, 1990, p. 187). Kinsey's now-famous 6-point scale revealed considerable variation in sexual behavior among normative males and females, with a substantial portion of them reporting both same-gender and other-gender activity (including fantasies). Thus, homosexuality and heterosexuality could be viewed as continuous rather than discrete dimensions of behavior; they did not represent unitary, separate identity categories; and homosexuality could be judged a natural form of sexual desire in humans (Broido, 2000). Kinsey's findings upended what was considered normative in psychosexual development and paved the way in the 1950s and 1960s for studies focusing on cultural context and societal oppression as definitive in the lives of same-sex-oriented people (Gagnon, 1990).

Tiefer (2000) noted the enormous impact of Kinsey and other 20th-century sex researchers (e.g., William Masters and Virginia Johnson), asserting that they had created a "modern sexuality: positive, physical, healthy, and ambivalent about romanticism, in reaction to the sexual repressions of Anglo-American Victorianism" (p. 90). Researchers finally were free to study same-sex sexuality without the lens of pathology, as did Evelyn Hooker in her landmark studies. Urged by a student in one of her classes to study gay men, she obtained a National Institute of Mental Health grant and compared matched samples of noninstitutionalized gay and heterosexual men using several projective psychological measures interpreted by three leading experts in projective assessment. Her results (Hooker, 1957) indicated that experts could not distinguish between the profiles of gay and nongay men, thus debunking the long-assumed association between homosexuality and pathology.

By the 1960s, the homosexual rights movement was moving beyond seeking acceptance to demanding civil rights, and the work of Kinsey, Hooker, and other sex researchers was central to its arguments. Indeed, Gagnon (1990) asserted that the convergence of politics and science became the foundation for the lesbian and gay communities and subcultures that were formed in the 1970s. In 1970, the gay community began a campaign to remove homosexuality from the American Psychiatric Association's diagnostic manual (the *Diagnostic and Statistical Manual of Mental Disorders* [DSM], the second edition of which was published in 1968); this was accomplished in 1973, and in 1975 the American Psychological Association followed suit, adding their powerful call for advocacy in erasing the stigma around sexual orientation (Conger, 1975). The "medical erasure" of homosexuality (completed in 1986 with removal of ego-dystonic homosexuality from the third revised edition of the DSM, published in 1987), combined with the liberatory politics of 1970s, allowed lesbians and gay men to speak in their own voices and finally wrest control from scientific and medical experts who previously had spoken for them, thus gaining "freedom from the official restraints of heterosexist hegemony, such as psychiatric diagnosis" (Minton, 1997, pp. 345–346). One outcome of this new focus was the advent of homosexual identity development or "coming out" theories, which made sense at a time when owning one's same-sex sexuality demanded an internal recognition and an often-public declaration process. These early theories (e.g., Cass, 1979; Coleman, 1982; Minton & McDonald, 1983–1984) posited a process of recognition of feeling different from prevailing heterosexual expectations, confusion, and gradual identification with a lesbian or gay identity, to acceptance and, ultimately, integration of identity into an overall sense of self.

At the same time that the liberation movements of the 1960s and 1970s were culminating in questioning the status quo and shrugging off the chains of oppression, intellectual movements were engaging in revisionist views of knowledge and questioning the voices of the authorized speakers regarding many social identities, such as those related to race, gender, class, and sexual orientation. Attention became focused on the mechanisms by which society inculcates beliefs into its members, and feminists began to question the very roots of empiricist science, arguing that the way science is done cannot be separated from the doers of that science. Moreover, the radical claim was made that there is no such thing as objective reality, but only what we think we "know" collectively through shared assumptions, biases, and beliefs, and the agreed-upon methods we use to articulate and support those beliefs. Thus, the social constructionist paradigm was born.

Social Constructionism and Queer Theory

Precursors to social constructionism in the sexuality arena include anthropologists doing cross-cultural work on sexuality in 1960s, who believed that culture shaped customs and local expressions of sexuality but did not question the existence of basic essentialist constructs such as sex drives, desires, and tendencies (Vance, 1992). It was sociologist Mary McIntosh's (1968) groundbreaking paper on the homosexual role that obviated the historical construction of sexuality. McIntosh drew upon labeling theory to characterize the homosexual as playing a social role as opposed to having some sort of condition (as per medical models). McIntosh demonstrated the constructed nature of the homosexual role by arguing that the role did not exist in many societies, that it emerged in England only in the late 19th century as a distinguishing characteristic of a person, and (based on Kinsey's estimates) was adopted by a relatively small minority of people. Moreover, McIntosh asserted that viewing homosexuality as an essential condition had led to inappropriate questions about etiology and obscured the centrality of social discourse in constructing roles.

Other researchers frequently cited as pioneers in the social constructionist point of view are sociologists John Gagnon and William Simon, who drew upon the symbolic interactionist tradition to develop what they termed *script theory* (e.g., Gagnon & Simon, 1973). They asserted that sex is not an instinctive force or biological drive controlled by one's inner psyche, hormones, or physiological drives, but rather is socially constructed and regulated by sexual scripts, which are fluid, flexible, changeable, and subject to constant revision and editing. A person is not a being with a sexual orientation that is an expression of her or his essential self, but is an actor fulfilling a role, complying with a socially created script that dictates what is forbidden, expected, and viewed as healthy. Similarly, Kitzinger (1987, 1995) observed that the social control of sexuality represses lesbians and gay men, producing and shaping them according to societal proscriptions of acceptability. I offer a concrete example: Sex with multiple partners tends to be frowned upon in the United States, and contemporary acceptance of same-sex marriage is consistent with a dominant sexual script that supports monogamous, long-term relationships; indeed, some of the rhetoric supporting the 2015 U.S. Supreme Court decision on same-sex marriage emphasized the importance of legal support in helping gay people lead "normal" lives (subtext: out of the bars and bathhouses and into their own bedrooms, just like their presumably-monogamous heterosexual peers). A legal right thus encourages adherence to a social script.

Also influential in the development of social constructionist ideas were feminists and gay liberationists writing in the mid-1970s, locating stories that had been lost, silenced, or made invisible by an oppressive society—searching for the historical roots of women's and sexual minority communities and documenting "herstory" and "gay ancestors" through time and place. This activist history countered the prevailing sexist and heterosexist discourses, but the emerging gay history (like the coming-out models) still was rooted in essentialist categories of sexual orientation. Nonetheless, these focused efforts gave rise to the new field of gay and lesbian studies, which put sexual orientation at the heart of an entire area of multidisciplinary scholarship. Although much of the new discipline was rooted in essentialist assumptions, some writers began to question meanings of sexual acts and behaviors within culture and time, acknowledging that what existed in the past may not have constituted "gayness" as it is understood in present-day Western societies. Writers began to question whether the categories of gay and lesbian had always existed or whether sexual acts had always had the same meanings. If not, how was meaning constructed, and what were the implications for present-day beliefs and assumptions about (homo)sexuality?

Kitzinger (1995) traced social constructionist origins in the field of psychology to Kenneth Gergen's (1973) groundbreaking *Social Psychology as*

History, which undermined psychology's claims to an objective, fact-based science. Gergen observed that what we study are social rather than natural products, that our notions about what it is to do science, what count as scientific facts, and what constitutes good scientific practice are the products of the particular place, time, and culture in which they are embedded. It follows that if science is merely a localized, habituated observance, it really cannot be proven empirically, nor can it provide objective truths. This critique of science has been embraced by feminists (e.g., Gavey, 1989; Gergen, M. M., 1988; Harding, 1986; Hare-Mustin & Marecek, 1988; Unger, 1983, 2011) and applied to the deconstruction of many entities often considered "natural" in psychology: gender (Bohan, 1996; Fausto-Sterling, 2000; Shields & Dicicco, 2011; Tavris, 1992), race and ethnicity (Guthrie, 1998), intelligence (Selden, 1999), and mental illness (Szasz, 1970). However, despite the radical revisioning of psychology, science, and social identities ushered in by social constructionists, it is a paradigm of many challenges, three of which are enumerated briefly below.

Challenges of Social Constructionism

Degree of Strength of the Social Constructionist Stance

The social constructionist theoretical stance is not a unitary, coherent position, and there is disagreement about how far to take the critique of essentialism. "Weak" social constructionists (Kitzinger, 1995) incorporate varying degrees of essentialism into their thinking; for example, one might believe that the direction of sexual desire or lust (toward same-sex or other-sex partners) is demarcated by socially created categories within which people unknowingly direct their desire, but that the desire itself is an innate, undifferentiated impulse that resides in the body, based on physiological sensation, brain waves, genetics, or the like. A "strong" social constructionist, however, would assert that there is no such thing as sexual desire unshaped by culture or history and that what we perceive as a sexual desire or sexual impulse is itself a product of a culture organized around sexual desire as a necessary part of that culture's relational patterns, reinforced continually in discursive practice.

The emphasis on discourse in the social constructionist stance gives rise to judicious attention to language, and one need only consider the evolution of language in many categories that have been psychologically essentialized to observe how temporally and contextually bound such labels are: ladies versus women; Miss or Mrs. versus Ms.; colored versus Negro versus Afro-American versus Black versus African American; homosexual versus lesbian/gay/bisexual versus queer; transgender versus gender nonconforming; or homophobia versus heterosexism versus sexual prejudice. One of the main contributions of the social constructionist focus on discourse is the recognition that naming is important and carries immense power to define and shape experience.

Political and Advocacy Goals

The preeminence of essentialist perspectives cannot be denied in the development of sexual minority group history and solidarity, as well as in arguments necessary to framing civil rights demands, which are based on demonstrating enduring, inborn, unchangeable aspects of the self as a member of a "natural" group deserving "protected class" status to ensure treatment equal to other groups. By contrast, the social constructionist stance—that categories of sexuality are simply socially agreed upon labels particular to time and place—leaves questions about what a sense of community with like others means and how an advocacy agenda can be advanced. How do we protect individuals from discrimination based on sexuality-related categories and yet dismantle the very existence of those categories at the same time? Vance (1992) noted that this tension is also present in feminism, which holds two simultaneous, somewhat contradictory goals: to attack the primacy of the gender system as a social organizer and to defend women as a group. The latter involves emphasizing their status as a group with a unique collective interest, different from men, and therefore "replays and perhaps reinforces the very gender binary crucial to the system of gender oppression" (Vance, 1992, p. 143). Similarly, the gay movement both "attacks a naturalized system of sexual hierarchy which categorizes and stabilizes desires and privileges some over others, and . . . defends the interest of 'gay and lesbian' people, which tends to reify identity and essential nature in a political process" (Vance, 1992, p. 143).

Feminist social constructionists also have pointed out that there are political dangers in essentialist arguments for civil rights. They have noted that arguments can be defensive and apologetic: Sexual minorities must be tolerated because they can't help who they are—it is beyond their control—a slippery slope that risks reinforcing notions of gay people as sexual predators. Moreover, the tacit acceptance of sexual minorities as living "alternative lifestyles" keeps them on the margins and obscures the recognition of sexual orientation as a product of and capitulation to a coercive patriarchal and heterosexist system, famously termed *compulsory heterosexuality* by Adrienne Rich (1980). Finally, to argue that sexual orientation minorities were "born this way" assumes homosexuality as a natural state (just like heterosexuality) and obscures the politics of defining the very terms of the debate, maintaining a rigid system of codes of sexual behavior (e.g., if gays are just like heterosexuals, they should be able to marry and live like heterosexuals). Again, marriage may be a right, but it also keeps sexual minority people tied to relationship styles and mores created by a dominant group that may not fully reflect their unique needs or practices.

The thorny issue of how to advance an advocacy agenda for sexual minorities while also attempting to dismantle the categorical underpinnings that maintain their oppression may be addressed by distinguishing between individual and cultural levels of social constructionist formulations. Debates about whether sexual orientation and gender identity are essential or socially constructed are very different from arguments about whether individual people choose or are born with their sexual orientations or gender identities. That is, explaining how reality is culturally constructed does not deny that it is real to individuals living it, nor does it mean that the constructions, even when recognized as such, are easily modified (Broido, 2000; Vance, 1992). It is because the constructions are so deeply experienced as reality that they need to be simultaneously exposed, interrogated, and perhaps reimagined while protecting individuals who are victimized by a social hierarchy based on those constructions.

> Real live lesbians and gays need to be defended in an oppressive system, and the sexual hierarchy, which underlies that oppression, needs to be attacked on every level, particularly on the intellectual and conceptual levels where naturalized systems of domination draw so much of their energy. (Vance, 1992, p. 143)

The Place and Meaning of Science

According to the social constructionist stance, the scientific enterprise itself is socially constructed, existing in social and historical contexts. The ability to know cannot be separated from the beliefs, assumptions, and biases of the knower, and there is no objective reality unmediated by human experience and interpretation. Social constructionists are concerned about such issues as the role of power in meaning-making, narrative and rhetoric in science, reflexivity in theory and method, and the processes by which human experiences and scientific knowledge are both produced in, and reproduce, human communities (Gergen, 1985; Kitzinger, 1995).

Feminist and social constructionist scholars (e.g., Fausto-Sterling, 2000; Kitzinger, 1987; Tiefer, 2000) have observed how deeply the "science" of gender and sexuality, in particular, is grounded in essentialist ideas of "natural" markers of human difference within psychology. The ongoing effort, for example, to discover what causes homosexuality sits squarely in the essentialist camp, as do endless studies of gender differences between men and women (Hyde, 2005; Shields & Dicicco, 2011), as well as the current "TERF" wars between derisively labeled "trans exclusionary radical feminists" and transwomen over whether there exists a female essence that explains gender transitioning (Goldberg, 2014). But Kitzinger (1995) asserted that it is the fact that researchers set up social constructionist and essentialist stances as competing explanations for sexual identity that completely misses the point of social constructionist notions of science—that is, the conflict is based on a presumed essence (sexual orientation) that demands scientific evidence from both sides, and yet social constructionists already have pointed out that there is no real essence to debate. Thus, social constructionism does not provide

> alternative answers to questions posed by essentialism: it raises a wholly different set of questions. Instead of searching for "truths" about homosexuals [sic] and lesbians, it asks about the discursive practices, the narrative forms, within which homosexuals [sic] and lesbians are produced and reproduced. (Kitzinger, 1995, p. 150)

In summary, these theoretical positions represent fundamentally different epistemologies that should be made explicit in disseminating sexuality research (Tolman & Diamond, 2014).

Despite the scientific challenges, Kitzinger (1995) insisted almost two decades ago that the social constructionist–essentialist debate had invigorated the field of lesbian and gay psychology and that "the persistence and continuing parallel development of *both* logically incompatible theoretical frameworks is advantageous for the growth and vitality of both lesbian and gay psychology and the lesbian and gay movements" (p. 150; italics in original). Biological arguments of sexual minority development favor a moral neutrality (it is pointless to judge outcomes of a biological process), and demonstrations of sexual minority mental health are helpful to advancing these groups. Moreover, essentialism has had a firm foundation in research in lesbian, gay, bisexual, and transgender psychology, and to abandon it would be unwise, particularly in an era of attention to the brain and neurological processes. Indeed, a recent Gallup poll (McCarthy, 2014) illustrates the strong grip that essentialism has on the American psyche: Almost half (47%) of the U.S. population believes that people are born gay (up from 13% in 1977), and pollsters opine that the beliefs gap would disappear altogether if psychology ceased being "agnostic" about the origins question. The social constructionist contribution to science, on the other hand, offers caution in the uses of science and fosters healthy skepticism; indeed, Tolman and Diamond (2014) pointed out that failed attempts to integrate the two theoretical perspectives have served to underscore the critical role of theory in sexuality research—both to shape knowledge about sexuality itself and to shape knowledge about that knowledge and the social forces that produce and organize it.

The important point is not whether our identities are constructed or essential but how we understand our identities as both or neither. In everyday life, does the gender of the person you are holding hands with on the street matter? Of course it does, politically, psychologically, socially, legally, and to the law enforcement officers assigned to protect you. Do gender identity and expression matter? Of course they do—ask eminent transgender biologist Ben Barres, whose scientific reputation rose after he transitioned from female to male. In contemporary postmodern thought, there is a general recognition that dimensions termed "sexual orientation" and "gender identity" (and myriad other related labels) matter to people because of a science and a society that force that mattering. However, there remains a persistent, underlying, liberatory project rooted in social constructionism but positioning it into a more transformative, activist stance. This system of thought is aimed at casting off the shackles of a narrowly defined sex–gender system, challenging the "naturalness" of that system's organization of desire and conceptions of the self, interrogating desire and its relation to identity, theorizing how sexuality reproduces and reinforces social norms, and supporting a "politics of transgression" (Watson, 2005, p. 68) that transforms the status quo, both intellectual and social. This is the project of queer theory.

Queer Theory

Queer theory, a term coined by Teresa de Laurentis (1991) to title a scholarly conference, was an epistemological perspective that emerged from a linking of the emerging postpositivist views of science (catalyzed by social constructionist challenges embedded in the liberationist social movements of the 1960s and 1970s, particularly feminism) and the increasingly aggressive social activism of grass-roots organizations like ACT-UP and Queer Nation, which were finding radical ways to resist the status quo of sexual minority second class citizenship (Warner, 2012). "Queer" increasingly became associated with transgression as a means of resistance, as queer activists enacted a politics directed against shame and "normalization" (Warner, 2012), publicly breaking taboos and reclaiming the "neutralised heterosexual spaces of the everyday as legitimate queer spaces" (Watson, 2005, p. 73). Queer theory appropriates the formerly negative term *queer* to empower a multidisciplinary challenge to heterosexist hegemony and to transform society.

Queer theorizing interrogates the cultural and historical positioning of the "unified self" by scholars who increasingly were becoming interested in understanding why some differences in social location (e.g., gender, race, sexual orientation) matter more than others, pursuing the study of identity categories and how power is distributed among and between them (Minton,

1997; Watson, 2005). The project of queer theory, which is grounded in the intellectual traditions of feminism, psychoanalysis, Marxism, critical race theory, and cultural studies (Warner, 2012), is to subject texts, discourses, and practices to a range of strategies intended to disrupt, to question, to "render as strange" those that are "naturalized and neutralized" (i.e., taken for granted; Watson, 2005, p. 74). The ultimate goal is to transform the ways in which sexuality and gender—and their intersectionality with other identities, such as race and class—are addressed.

Queer theory emerged from the struggles of gay people to claim their voices and experiences: It

> represents a move away from a minoritizing position in which the rights and concerns of an oppressed minority are central . . . to a universalizing view that problematizes the sex/gender system and consequently becomes relevant for all people across the sexual spectrum. (Minton, 1997, p. 347)

Discursive strategies are central to effecting this shift from control by others to subjective agency that empowers a marginal positionality. That is, a de-essentialized queer identity takes power from its position of resistance against the discourse of homophobia, and, unlike a gay identity (which is grounded in an affirmative choice of homosexuality), a queer identity derives its meaning solely from its oppositional relation to the dominant, normative discourse. Moreover, queer identity as a marginal positionality "affords the opportunity to interrogate and resist all forms of hegemonic normativity, including patriarchy, racism, and elitism" and thus centralizes identity politics as a "theoretical and political strategy, making explicit the notion of a queer identity as the primary site of resistance" (Minton, 1997, p. 348).

Michel Foucault's work (e.g., 1978) constituted the genesis of queer theory. Foucault viewed power as relational—not something owned by one group or another, but enacted in human interactions. Of central importance is that political struggles are power relations in which resistance (opportunities for reverse discourses) can emerge. Watson (2005) summarized:

> by examining historical discourses, it was possible to understand how certain identities (such as the homosexual) were attached to individuals instead of acts/behaviours, and these individuals were then constituted as an object of knowledge. . . . It is this link between discourse and identity that queer theory takes up . . . the discourse speaks the object (i.e., sex/ sexuality) into being as well as its subject (the homosexual). By having a unified object (sex), diverse things like sensations, pleasures, biological functions, desires, etc. can be brought together. . . . So the idea that anything could potentially be identified as "sexual" . . . or everything that is

currently assigned to the realm of the sexual could *be re-assigned*, is an important idea. (p. 70)

Early queer theorists, building on Foucault's ideas, were concerned with the relationship between gender and sexuality as both categories and as day-to-day practices, analyzing sexuality in terms of power relations rather than individual identities and disputing societal processes that legitimize and support some forms of sexuality over others (Warner, 2012; Watson, 2005). Judith Butler (1990, 1993) and Eve Sedgewick (1990, 1993), foremost feminist queer theorists, offered important critiques of gender and heterosexism, Butler through her subversive "drag" parodies of heterosexual norms and Sedgewick through her persistent attacks on the cultural denial of same-sex eroticism, particularly between women. As these scholars revealed, queer theory opened myriad possibilities for reconsidering and reconceptualizing gender and sexuality.

Most contemporary queer theorists work to challenge and undermine attempts to render identity fixed, immutable, singular, or natural. Thus, queer theory–queer studies focuses on sexual categorization processes and their deconstruction rather than specific populations. However, because of its broad and comprehensive focus on gendered, sexualized systems of domination and control and its provocative intellectual energy, queer theory was quickly connected to other forms of domination in society (e.g., race, class, nationalism, capitalism), and subareas developed within queer studies that captured more focused interests such as post-Colonial queer studies and queer race studies. Indeed, Warner (2012) asserted that contemporary queer theory now represents so many branches in so many disciplines that it cannot easily be synthesized and summarized. Particularly relevant to psychologists is current queer scholarship in neoliberalism, homonormativity, intersectionality, and transgender studies (Grzanka, 2014).

Like the social constructionist paradigm with which it shares core challenges to science and society, queer theory is not without critique. Tensions have arisen around the theory–practice interface, with some viewing it as inaccessible in its language and too narrowly confined to apolitical, esoteric, reductionist deconstructions of text, whereas others claim that queer theory is too politicized and too connected to queer activism. Some are concerned that the queer focus obscures other important social categories such as gender, race, and class. Warner (2012) argued that queer theory and queer studies has led to the formation of a social space that queer people share as a "counterpublic," claiming that this space makes it possible

> to keep alive a political imagination of sexuality that is otherwise closed down by the dominant direction of gay and lesbian politics, which increasingly reduces its agenda to military service and marriage, and tends to remain locked in a national and even nationalist frame.

Queer theory has particular relevance for psychological theorizing and practice because it deliberately positions inquiry as decentered from normative assumptions, it challenges dominant discourse, and it is socially transgressive. Indeed, Watson (2005) asserted that the strength of queer theorizing is located in its possibilities for application to relational fields, in which the erotic can be reimagined and societally produced heteronormative assumptions about sex, gender, and sexuality can be disrupted. Similarly, Minton (1997) asserted that queer theory is concerned with "the agency of self-identities that reinvent themselves to effectively resist social regulation" (p. 349), thus linking queer theory to the psychology of subjective agency. This is of primary importance in conceptualizing therapy, the topic of this chapter's final section.

CONSTRUCTIONS AND AFFIRMATIVE THERAPY

In Alan Malyon's (1982) pioneering definition, *gay-affirmative therapy* is not an independent system of therapy but rather

> represents a special range of psychological knowledge which challenges the traditional view that homosexual desire and fixed homosexual orientations are pathological . . . This approach regards homophobia, as opposed to homosexuality, as a major pathological variable in the development of certain symptomatic conditions. (pp. 68–69)

The queer or social constructionist critique of gay-affirmative therapy is obvious: It presumes the existence of sexual identity categories, through which the erotic is viewed heteronormatively, with (narrowly) categorized sexual subjects interacting with their (binary-)gendered objects of desire. Once again we are faced with the conundrum of both affirming and deconstructing identities simultaneously.

In an unexpected and delightful metaphor, Watson (2005) likened being "queer" (in the queer theory sense) to being a person in therapy, "that is, to be a person in flux, contesting boundaries, eliding definition and exhibiting the constructedness of categorization. It is a process of problematizing and scrutinising the geneaology of categories" and a process of "self-constitution and self-transformation . . . anchored in the perilous and shifting sands of nonidentity, positionality, discursive reversibility, and . . . self-invention" (p. 75). Watson also noted that issues of power "cannot be underestimated with regard to the constitution of (sexual) identities" (p. 78). It is within systems of power that oppression and discrimination are enacted, leading to stress and compromised mental health, precisely the issues often presented by sexual minority individuals in therapy. Thus, even if sexual orientation and gender identity are socially constructed, stigma linked to these categories is real, and it exacts well-documented mental health costs (e.g., Cochran, Sullivan, & Mays, 2003; Herek, Gillis, & Cogan, 1999; Meyer, 2003; Pachankis, 2007), as Malyon (1982) recognized. This potentially queer reading of the therapy process may provide a useful way of conceptualizing "affirmative" therapy in a paradigm of denied fixed identity categories. Recent contributions by vocational psychologists in both social constructionism and constructivism offer promising possibilities for reimagining therapy.

Distinction Between Constructionist and Constructivist Stances

Although the terms *constructionist* and *constructivist stances* often are used interchangeably, greater specificity in our therapeutic thinking might be helpful, both to sharpen our own clinical formulations and to be consistent in the language we use with clients. Both stances rely on the assumption that external reality in an absolute sense does not exist but is constructed. However, reality is indeed constructed at the societal and individual levels, and this is where meaningful distinctions can be made. When society constructs, what results is called a *construction*, and it is based on a discursive process of naming and attributing qualities to the categories that are created. The theoretical system emanating from and describing this process is termed *social constructionism*, and it applies to both the process of constructing reality, to the resulting scientific paradigm, and to the discursive process that supports inquiries into constructed phenomena. However, individuals also construct their experience through the narratives or stories that they create, and this process is referred to as *constructivist*. Just as at the societal level, this constructivist process relies on discourses and narratives. It involves a process of considering, experimenting with, and discarding personal narratives until a coherent, satisfactory explanatory system has been created, with narratives constantly being reevaluated and rewritten to reflect progress in the overall narrative of the individual (see Young & Collin, 2004, for a similar articulation). Both constructionist and constructivist perspectives have been recognized within vocational psychology as useful ways of approaching the process of understanding work and careers and of intervening with individuals and groups when problems arise.

Constructionist–Constructivist Approach to Counseling and Therapy

Vocational theorist Mary Sue Richardson (2012) applied a social constructionist perspective to career counseling to present a new approach that she terms "counseling for work and relationship" (p. 190). Rejecting the traditional emphasis of vocational intervention on helping people to develop careers, her perspective is focused on helping people construct lives through both work and relationship. Life course trajectories consist of elements that are interdependent, fluid, permeable, and exist in dialectical relationships, and the individual constructs (indeed, coconstructs with others), in a social–relational context, a life that encompasses both paid/market work and unpaid (often invisible, e.g., child care and household) work. M. S. Richardson (2012) has posited that obviating the ways in which market work (i.e., career) trajectories are coconstructed just like other aspects of life helps people see how these paths are not determined by individual capacities, decisions, and behaviors alone, but rather are shaped by the interpersonal, social, economic, and political contexts in which people live.

In keeping with the social constructionist focus on discourse, M. S. Richardson (2012) deconstructed "career" discourse over the past century. Exhibiting interesting parallels to historical discourses around sexuality, her discursive interrogation deserves a bit of elaboration here. M. S. Richardson described how the conceptualization of career that began as "vocational choice" in the early 20th century (requiring "vocational guidance" from experts; Savickas, 2013) evolved to the idea of "career development" around mid-century (necessitating "career education"; Savickas, 2013); the term *career*, originally used broadly to represent any sort of developmental trajectory of a person in interaction with the environment (e.g., a "homosexual career"), came to be associated with paid work and became psychologized as a part of a person. M. S. Richardson (2012) asserted that both the choice and development career discourses are skewed toward a consideration of paid work only, a focus on internal processes, and a view of one's career as a linear, progressive move up a vertical hierarchy of status, pay, and advancement. This view promotes an individualistic, democratic view of people as able to assess themselves and the world of work, and choose work based on fulfillment of personal desires and needs that come to be self-evident over time based on an organic, stable developmental process—and that failure to do so indicates a weakness within that person. This is, of course, untrue for vast numbers of people who cannot freely choose work or are excluded from opportunities. There is a clear parallel here to the discourse of sexual orientation and gender diversity, which also implies an organic, predictable, developmental process of coming to know oneself in a gendered/sexual/relational sense, and then acting upon that knowledge in a "healthy" way—that is, within the constrained enactments of sexual (minority) identities deemed acceptable in present-day society.

M. S. Richardson (2012) argued that contextualism

reopens the distinction between personal and social levels of reality that was collapsed in the psychologized career . . . reposition[s] work as a context of development, rather than as an aspect of the self . . . [and] enables a shift in focus from how careers develop to how people develop in relation to the multiple social contexts in which they participate. (pp. 200–201)

This approach positions people to resist or challenge the "disruptive conditions of contemporary life" (p. 202)—for example, to recognize that lack of success in finding a job is rooted not in personal failure, but in a social context in which lack of power and resources, coupled with marginalization and oppression, severely compromise one's personal success. Again, the parallels to sexual orientation and gender diversity are striking, in that recognizing the contextualized nature of a social discourse positioning sexual orientation and gender identity as fixed, innate dimensions of selfhood can help gender and sexual minority individuals to resist narrow categories, experience less confusion and pain when labels don't fit, and embrace a more fluid, dynamic identity as sexual and relational beings.

Particularly applicable to therapy is M. S. Richardson's (2012) reliance on narrative theory as central for understanding how lives are constructed. According to narrative theory, we attempt to make sense of past experiences through constructing coherent narratives or stories about those experiences (using, of course, the story lines or roles or scripts available to us in our culture and time), and the constructed narratives influence and impel the actions we take; such actions are considered the leading edge of our stories of the future, which in turn require further construction of the narrative, and thus a recursive process is always occurring, coconstructed in social context. The specific kind of action M. S. Richardson focused on is *agentic action*, which is subjective, purposeful, and reflexive, in that people can evaluate and interpret their actions and then modify future actions as a result of this self-examination. In this perspective, agentic action is possible for anyone, and an inability to engage in agentic action may be helped by counseling/therapy, in which the central therapeutic task will be clients' construction of their lives going forward, with their capacity for agentic action strengthened and enhanced.

Narrative theorist George Howard once opined that "life is the story we live by, pathology is a story gone mad, and psychotherapy is an exercise in 'story repair'" (cited in Tavris, 1992, p. 301). The process of counseling/therapy from M. S. Richardson's (2012) social constructionist perspective is a process of helping people to recognize and come to terms with their personal narratives and to construct their futures (perhaps involving deconstructing and reconstructing earlier narratives), and taking agentic action toward those futures. As agentic action is culturally bound, the work of counselors and therapists is to help people identify both contextual and personal constraints that limit their possibilities for action and to support their challenge of and resistance to those parameters as they come to see that action "which seems to flow so naturally from subjective intentional states, is, in fact, shaped and informed by prevailing systems of power and hierarchy" (M. S. Richardson, 2012, p. 225). Especially important is to listen to client language and offer new, alternative language, thus empowering clients to reshape deeply engrained discourses that might limit their own imaginative constructions of their futures.

Another vocational theorist, Mark Savickas (2013), provided a concrete framework for assisting clients with the constructivist task of "life design" through narrative. The process is similar to that described by M. S. Richardson (2012), involving the examination of client stories, deconstructing and reconstructing those stories into a coherent identity narrative, and finally forming intentions and actions to be taken. Especially promising are five stimulus questions that Savickas has found effective in helping clients narrate their vocational stories, and I have adapted these for use in my own approach (described in the next section). Another notable contribution of Savickas's work is his observation that the counseling/therapy relationship is itself constructed through the use of language to describe the interaction (e.g., "guide," "counsel") and suggestion that the term *collaborative co-construction* (p. 660) better describes the process of the life design paradigm. This language shift is very consistent with the egalitarian approach of feminist therapy and offers a way to empower clients to find their own voices and directions.

Application to Affirmative Therapy

The work of M. S. Richardson (2012) and Savickas (2013) offers promise in conceptualizing counseling/therapy that is affirmative around issues of sexual orientation and gender diversity without relying on rigid, limited categories and labels. More specifically, it might be useful to distinguish between a sexual orientation–gender diversity discourse—which assumes enduring, innate characteristics of the individual determined early in life, in which "coming out" or "transitioning" in various ways is simply a behavioral enactment of one's true nature—and an identity construction and enactment discourse, which assumes a constructivist process whereby an individual creates and claims a gendered/sexual/relational identity through interpersonal and social interaction within a particular cultural and historical context, with coming out and transitioning as the articulation of that process (see D. Richardson, 1983–1984, for an earlier version of this argument). Although the idea of a fixed, immutable sexual orientation may provide a sense of comfort and stability to some clients, the capacity for self-exploration and experimentation—with the pressure to self-label removed—that is implicit in an identity construction approach also can be tremendously freeing for clients. Moreover, the latter approach appears to be more compatible with current conceptions of gender and sexuality, which are seen increasingly as subject to considerable fluidity, fluctuation, and change over time (particularly for women; see Diamond, 2008, 2014; Fassinger & Arseneau, 2008; Tiefer, 2000), with an ever-expanding variety of self-chosen labels to describe individual variations in people's lives.

To pull all of these strands (social constructionism and queer theory, construction of sexuality, affirmative therapy, and constructionist/constructivist vocational theory) together, I invoke here a model of identity enactment of gender-transgressive sexual minorities that I have presented previously (Fassinger & Arseneau, 2007). The term *gender-transgressive sexual minorities* is used as an inclusive term encompassing all manner of gender transgression inherent in sexual minority identities ("minorities" in that they do not belong to the heterosexual, cisgender, gender-conforming dominant group); this includes violation of societal gender norms (around identity, expression, and performance, as exemplified by transgender and gender nonconforming people), as well as partner preferences that transgress social norms around "opposite"-sex relationships (as exemplified by lesbian, gay, and bisexual people). Like the appropriation by sexual minorities of the word *queer* to denote defiance of negative labels, the word *transgression* is used deliberately here as an affirmation of strength in resisting social norms and of claiming the power to define and explain one's own life.

The model of enactment of transgressive sexual minority identities holds individual differences at its core and postulates a tripartite structure of interacting sexual, gender, and cultural orientations across four developmental trajectories: the personal arena of health (mental/physical/sexual); the interpersonal arena of relationships in families and communities; the social arena of education and work; and the sociopolitical arena of social structures, policies, and laws. I submit that these are relevant dimensions along which therapists and clients might coconstruct sexual minority clients' life narratives, and I propose a transgression-affirmative nested-narrative identity construction and enactment (NICE) model for therapy, focused on supporting transgression of social norms rather than specific identities or labels and using constructivist therapeutic activities.

The transgression-affirmative NICE approach overtly recognizes the constructed nature of identities within the context of life stories, as well as the egalitarian collaborative process to be undertaken in the relationship with the coconstructor–therapist. It begins with the story internal to the client (i.e., the client as a physical–sexual–relational being), and gradually moves outward to integrate the gender, sexual, and cultural stories learned in the family and community, in the educational and work institutions in which one has participated, and finally addresses the stories generated in the larger sociopolitical and legal arena that have been internalized to varying degrees by the client, often unconsciously. Table 1.1 contains five stimulus questions

TABLE 1.1
Questions for Transgression-Affirmative NICE Model

Question	Taps Into . . .
Who were your role models growing up—and into adulthood—and what did you learn from them about gender? About sexuality?	Client learning in the home and family, immediate community, schools (and teams, camps, etc.) and possibly workplaces, and in the social environment (via media); gives an idea of the development of self-concept around gender and sexuality (including attitudes about what is "healthy" or "normal"—physically, sexually, intimately) within the nested narratives of family, community, school, and larger society.
What are your favorite books, magazines, TV shows, movies, and electronic media (e.g., sites, games), and what are the images of gender and sexuality presented in these sources?	Client energies, interests, and motivational images; gives an idea of the cognitive influences on internal notions of sexuality and gender and forces articulation of unrecognized constructions, which can be interrogated using the nested narratives of family, community, school, the workplace, and the larger society.
Tell me a story about an important event from your past (can be distant past or more recent, a big or small event, something that happened or just a new way you suddenly began seeing things—the point is, it was important to you). Are there any aspects of this story that pertain to gender? To sexuality? How did these aspects affect you?	Client's narrative style and habits, as well as how she/he/they cognitively and affectively process(es) events; gives an idea of how best to guide and support collaborative revision of client stories, including affective and cognitive habits that might impede progress moving forward. To trace threads among nested narratives, queries can focus on a personal, physical or sexual event; a family or home event; a school or workplace event; and an event related to the larger social environment (e.g., social institutions such as laws, religion, media).
What are your earliest recollections about sexuality? About gender? How do you carry those recollections around with you in your daily life?	Primal responses to gender- and sexuality-related themes in the life story; gives a context for situating the current narrative into the client's overall life story. Again, question can be repeated within the nested narrative structures of the client's story and woven together to help the client build a coherent account of the client's life story and desired direction moving forward.
What is your favorite saying or motto?	Clients' own best "advice" for taking action; gives an idea of how a client might frame future actions and decisions (e.g., "carpe diem" may reflect a more impulsive behavioral style than "a stitch in time saves nine").

Note. NICE = nested-narrative identity construction and enactment. Data from Savickas (2013).

I adapted from Savickas (2013), which tap into various themes in clients' life stories, and can be useful in the process of coconstructing narratives.

These questions can be used as inquiry into any or all of the four developmental arenas (health, interpersonal relationships, education and work, and the sociopolitical environment) to help clients identify, articulate, examine, and revise the stories they live by. In the process of story creation and revisioning, the core aspects of self will become strengthened by examination. Moreover, the life story becomes more coherent, action to be taken is more clearly deliberate rather than a reaction to inculcated stories, and the way is paved for the client to engage self-confidently in a future of sustained story creation, examination, and adaptive revision. Clients recognize that identity labels may be self-chosen for a variety of personal reasons and are unceasingly open to re-evaluation and change as their stories demand.

The collaborative sharing of power between the client and therapist pays homage to the eschewal of hierarchy and privileged discourse that is core to the social constructionist stance and its feminist foundation. The influence of queer theory is evident in the radical movement of this approach beyond being "gay affirmative" to being "transgression affirmative," in that it consciously empowers clients to explore and redefine the meaning of transgression as it has been taught to them throughout the realms of social interaction, and to claim transgression of arbitrary, perhaps ill-fitting categories as positive action in their lives. The largely defensive discourses that predominate in both gender-transgressive sexual minority communities and the larger society (e.g., how-I-got-to-be-this-way, how-long-I've-been-this-way, I-can't-help-it-this-is-who-I-am, I-fell-in-love-with-someone-who-happened-to-be-a-man/woman, I-was-born-in-the-wrong-body) lose some of their authority to define experience. Rather, they are reconstructed into stories about how-I-came-to-think-about-transgression and how-I-found-it-in-myself-to-transgress-on-my-own-behalf. I view the latter as more compelling, empowering narratives for forging a secure and healthy identity. In addition, they are narratives that fit all kinds of transgression around gender and sexuality, including that of our allies in the liberatory process.

CONCLUSION: REVISITING THE CASE STUDY

How might the transgression-affirmative NICE approach improve therapeutic intervention? I return to the case of Shawna with which this chapter opened. The problems of essentialist conceptualizations are obvious in this case, and my client highlighted them. She was wed to the idea that there is one "true" sexual orientation that underlies sexual desire and that knowing what category one fits into simplifies one's life and promotes firm declarations of selfhood—particularly important if one needs a strong, coherent way to defend oneself against sexual prejudice in the dominant social group(s) in which one lives (the I-can't-help-it-this-is-who-I-am discourse). My notes from that time indicate that I was doing my best to be a good social constructionist, disabusing my client of constrictive notions of the self and pointing out their etiology in social institutions, teachings, and messages (including in her family and her religious community). I think I also did a reasonably good job of educating her, providing affirmative resources and connections, and helping her to open up to different possible ways of living her life than anything she had ever considered. But despite my regular revisiting of her goals and progress to obtain feedback from her about the extent to which our "time together" (my own term for counseling/therapy) was helping her (or not), I didn't have an end-point in mind, except for her to feel less stress and greater well-being. I took my usual feminist approach of shared power and collaboration, and although Shawna clearly liked thinking of me as a friend and equal, my feminist stance may have exacerbated her confusion, her demand for an external authoritative voice, and her desperation to figure herself out quickly.

In retrospect, I think that both my client and I might have benefitted from a deliberate application of the transgression-affirmative NICE approach, framing our work as collaborative coconstruction of a life story needing some deconstruction–examination and possible reconstruction/revision. This would have permitted Shawna more immediate authority and voice (it was her story, after all), and would have made clear right away that it was she (not I) who was the best expert on her life. Moreover, my feminist stance of collegiality and shared power, as well as my proactive addressing of our racial differences, might have induced less confusion in her if she viewed me as a corevisionist/coconstructor of a story that only she knew (and in her terms) until she made it known to me. In addition, the deconstruction of her nested narratives, particularly the narratives regarding family and religious community, might have felt less like everything she held dear was being challenged by an outsider (me) if we both had held constant the reminder that everything we were doing—including our time together itself—involved constructions to be examined collaboratively and considered for revisioning into a new story.

If I had used Savickas's (2013) questions regarding Shawna's career (recall that she presented with work-related issues initially), it is likely that the appeal and cognitive organizing function of sharing memories would have elicited her hidden sexual identity concerns more quickly, and I could easily have moved into broadening the focus of the questions to include gender and sexuality (as presented in Table 1.1). For example, the relatively recent loss of her mother had made her loathe to upset her father in any way, and she shared numerous anecdotes about his exacting standards for work and achievement, which contributed greatly to her job stress. However, she also felt constrained by (but was reluctant to discuss) his strict mores regarding physical appearance, social behavior, religious commitment, filial duty, and the like, where our focusing on the need to round out her story would have made the inclusion of gender transgression and sexuality concerns very natural and nonthreatening.

As another example, an event that she recounted many times (accompanied by photos) was a cotillionlike presentation party in her community, involving elegant dress, a male escort for the evening, and a public declaration of religious commitment. We discussed and deconstructed this event many times, of course, mining it for its meanings to her (e.g., psychologically, socially, sexually, religiously) and (later) comparing it to other forms of "coming out." However, I think that if we had been coconstructing Shawna's narrative in a more systematic way, consciously using the stimulus question about an important event to elaborate her emerging story, this singular event would have assumed the prominence it merited. In short, the use of stimulus questions might have tied together more effectively the strands of many seemingly disparate anecdotes into a more coherent narrative, which could have helped both of us to recognize the evolution of her reconstructed story more clearly and perhaps have helped to allay her ongoing anxiety about her lack of identity resolution.

Finally, I wonder if using this gender-transgressive NICE approach in a conscious way with Shawna might have helped me to be a better, more collaborative coconstructor than I was at the time, in that I might have remained more sharply focused on her narratives, rather than the social discourses I had in my head (and often assumed were in hers) and was eager to debunk. I believe that, initially, Shawna may have had difficulty with the concept of being deliberately "transgressive" because it was such a religiously loaded word for her, but given that her biggest fear was transgressing the boundaries that were being continually (re)established for her by others, I imagine that it also could have been liberating for her to claim transgression as a positive way of being. The fact that she became extraordinarily transgressive (e.g., being in a relationship with a couple rather than an individual) when she finally decided that she was ready, speaks to a strength in her that probably could have embraced transgression and even appreciated my affirmation of her social resistance, rather than expecting my identification and support of a specific identity (which, even years later, was not clear).

So, in the end, was I transgression affirmative with this client around her identity construction and enactment? Sort of. But there are so many ways that my work with Shawna might have been enhanced through the more systematic use of an overtly social constructionist and constructivist approach. It is my hope that this chapter encourages my colleagues to consider using the proposed transgression-affirmative, NICE perspective in their therapeutic work with clients, and that, together, we continue the critical work of shaping social and psychological discourse that ultimately liberates us.

REFERENCES

American Psychiatric Association. (1968). *Diagnostic and statistical manual of mental disorders* (2nd ed.). Washington, DC: Author.

American Psychiatric Association. (1987). *Diagnostic and statistical manual of mental disorders* (3rd ed., Rev.). Washington, DC: Author.

Bohan, J. S. (1996). *Psychology and sexual orientation: Coming to terms.* New York, NY: Routledge.

Boswell, J. (1980). *Christianity, social tolerance, and homosexuality.* Chicago, IL: University of Chicago Press.

Broido, E. M. (2000). Constructing identity: The nature and meaning of lesbian, gay, and bisexual identities. In R. M. Perez, K. A. DeBord, & K. J. Bieschke (Eds.), *Handbook of counseling and psychotherapy with lesbian, gay, and bisexual clients* (pp. 13–33). Washington, DC: American Psychological Association. http://dx.doi.org/10.1037/10339-001

Bullough, V. (2001). Step children of nature [Review of the book *Krafft-Ebing, psychiatry, and the making of sexual identity,* by H. Oosterhuis]. *Journal of Sex Research, 38,* 75–76.

Butler, J. (1990). *Gender trouble: Feminism and the subversion of identity.* London, England: Routledge.

Butler, J. (1993). *Bodies that matter: On the discursive limits of sex.* London, England: Routledge.

Cass, V. C. (1979). Homosexual identity formation: A theoretical model. *Journal of Homosexuality, 4,* 219–235. http://dx.doi.org/10.1300/J082v04n03_01

Cochran, S. D., Sullivan, J. G., & Mays, V. M. (2003). Prevalence of mental disorders, psychological distress, and mental health services use among lesbian, gay, and bisexual adults in the United States. *Journal of Consulting and Clinical Psychology, 71,* 53–61. http://dx.doi.org/10.1037/0022-006X.71.1.53

Coleman, E. (1982). Developmental stages of the coming out process. *Journal of Homosexuality, 7,* 31–43. http://dx.doi.org/10.1300/J082v07n02_06

Conger, J. (1975). Proceedings of the American Psychological Association, Incorporated, for the year 1974: Minutes of the annual meeting of the Council of Representatives. *American Psychologist, 30,* 620–651.

de Laurentis, T. (1991). Queer theory: Lesbian and gay sexualities. *Differences: A Journal of Feminist Cultural Studies, 3*(2), iii–xviii.

D'Emilio, J., & Freedman, E. B. (1988). *Intimate matters: A history of sexuality in America.* New York, NY: Harper & Row.

Diamond, L. M. (2008). *Sexual fluidity: Understanding women's love and desire.* Cambridge, MA: Harvard University Press.

Diamond, L. M. (2014). Gender and same-sex sexuality. In D. L. Tolman & L. M. Diamond (Eds.), *APA handbook of sexuality and psychology: Vol. 1. Person-based approaches* (pp. 629–652). Washington, DC: American Psychological Association.

Faderman, L. (1981). *Surpassing the love of men: Romantic friendship and love between women from the Renaissance to the present.* New York, NY: Morrow.

Faderman, L. (1991). *Odd girls and twilight lovers: A history of lesbian life in twentieth century America.* New York, NY: Columbia University Press.

Fassinger, R. E., & Arseneau, J. R. (2007). "I'd rather get wet than be under that umbrella": Differentiating the experiences and identities of lesbian, gay, bisexual, and transgender people. In K. J. Bieschke, R. M. Perez, & K. A. DeBord (Eds.), *Handbook of counseling and psychotherapy with lesbian, gay, bisexual, and transgender clients* (2nd ed., pp. 19–49). Washington, DC: American Psychological Association. http://dx.doi.org/10.1037/11482-001

Fassinger, R. E., & Arseneau, J. R. (2008). Diverse women's sexualities. In F. L. Denmark & M. A. Paludi (Eds.), *Psychology of women: A handbook of issues and theories* (pp. 484–508). Westport, CT: Praeger.

Fausto-Sterling, A. (2000). *Sexing the body: Gender politics and the construction of sexuality.* New York, NY: Basic Books.

Feinberg, L. (1996). *Transgender warriors: Making history from Joan of Arc to RuPaul.* Boston, MA: Beacon Press.

Foucault, M. (1978). *The history of sexuality: Vol. 1. An introduction* (R. Hurley, Trans.). New York, NY: Routledge.

Gagnon, J. H. (1990). Gender preference in erotic relations: The Kinsey Scale and sexual scripts. In D. P. McWhirter, S. A. Sanders, & J. M. Reinisch (Eds.), *Homosexuality/heterosexuality: Concepts of sexual orientation* (pp. 177–207). New York, NY: Oxford University Press.

Gagnon, J. H., & Simon, W. (1973). *Sexual conduct: The social sources of human sexuality.* Chicago, IL: Aldine.

Gavey, N. (1989). Feminist poststructuralism and discourse analysis: Contributions to feminist psychology. *Psychology of Women Quarterly, 13,* 459–475. http://dx.doi.org/10.1111/j.1471-6402.1989.tb01014.x

Gergen, K. J. (1973). Social psychology as history. *Journal of Personality and Social Psychology, 26,* 309–320. http://dx.doi.org/10.1037/h0034436

Gergen, K. J. (1985). The social constructionist movement in modern psychology. *American Psychologist, 40,* 266–275. http://dx.doi.org/10.1037/0003-066X.40.3.266

Gergen, M. M. (1988). Toward a feminist metatheory and methodology in the social sciences. In M. M. Gergen (Ed.), *Feminist thought and the structure of knowledge* (pp. 87–104). New York, NY: New York University Press.

Goldberg, M. (2014, August 4). *What is a woman? The dispute between radical feminism and transgenderism*. Retrieved from http://www.newyorker.com/magazine/2014/08/04/woman-2.

Greenberg, D. F. (1988). *The construction of homosexuality*. Chicago, IL: University of Chicago Press.

Grzanka, P. R. (Ed.). (2014). *Intersectionality: A foundations and frontiers reader*. Boulder, CO: Westview Press.

Guthrie, R. V. (1998). *Even the rat was white: A historical view of psychology* (2nd ed.). Boston, MA: Allyn & Bacon.

Harding, S. (1986). *The science question in feminism*. Ithaca, NY: Cornell University Press.

Hare-Mustin, R. T., & Marecek, J. (1988). The meaning of difference: Gender theory, postmodernism, and psychology. *American Psychologist, 43*, 455–464. http://dx.doi.org/10.1037/0003-066X.43.6.455

Herek, G. M., Gillis, J. R., & Cogan, J. C. (1999). Psychological sequelae of hate-crime victimization among lesbian, gay, and bisexual adults. *Journal of Consulting and Clinical Psychology, 67*, 945–951. http://dx.doi.org/10.1037/0022-006X.67.6.945

Hooker, E. (1957). The adjustment of the male overt homosexual. *Journal of Projective Techniques, 21*, 18–31. http://dx.doi.org/10.1080/08853126.1957.10380742

Hyde, J. S. (2005). The gender similarities hypothesis. *American Psychologist, 60*, 581–592. http://dx.doi.org/10.1037/0003-066X.60.6.581

Katz, J. N. (1995). *The invention of heterosexuality*. New York, NY: Penguin (Plume) Books.

Kinsey, A. C., Pomeroy, W. B., & Martin, C. E. (1948). *Sexual behavior in the human male*. Philadelphia, PA: Saunders.

Kinsey, A. C., Pomeroy, W. B., Martin, C. E., & Gebhard, P. H. (1953). *Sexual behavior in the human female*. Philadelphia, PA: Saunders.

Kitzinger, C. (1987). *The social construction of lesbianism*. London, England: Sage.

Kitzinger, C. (1995). Social constructionism: Implications for lesbian and gay psychology. In A. R. D'Augelli & C. J. Patterson (Eds.), *Lesbian, gay and bisexual identities over the lifespan: Psychological perspectives* (pp. 136–162). New York, NY: Oxford University Press. http://dx.doi.org/10.1093/acprof:oso/9780195082319.003.0006

Krafft-Ebing, R. von (1893). *Psychopathia sexualis, with especial reference to contrary sexual instinct: A medico-legal study* (Gilbert Chaddock, Trans.). Philadelphia, PA: F. A. Davis.

Malyon, A. K. (1982). Psychotherapeutic implications of internalized homophobia in gay men. In J. Gonsiorek (Ed.), *Homosexuality and psychotherapy: A practitioner's handbook of affirmative models* (pp. 59–69). New York, NY: Haworth Press. http://dx.doi.org/10.1300/J082v07n02_08

McCarthy, J. (2014, May 28). *Americans' views on origins of homosexuality remain split.* http:/www.gallup.com/poll/170753/americans-view-origins-homosexaulity-remain-split.aspx

McIntosh, M. (1968). The homosexual role. *Social Problems, 16,* 182–192. http://dx.doi.org/10.2307/800003

Meyer, I. H. (2003). Prejudice, social stress, and mental health in lesbian, gay, and bisexual populations: Conceptual issues and research evidence. *Psychological Bulletin, 129,* 674–697. http://dx.doi.org/10.1037/0033-2909.129.5.674

Minton, H. L. (1997). Queer theory: Historical roots and implications for psychology. *Theory & Psychology, 7,* 337–353. http://dx.doi.org/10.1177/0959354397073003

Minton, H. L., & McDonald, G. J. (1983–1984). Homosexual identity formation as a developmental process. *Journal of Homosexuality, 9*(2-3), 91–104.

Pachankis, J. E. (2007). The psychological implications of concealing a stigma: A cognitive-affective-behavioral model. *Psychological Bulletin, 133,* 328–345. http://dx.doi.org/10.1037/0033-2909.133.2.328

Prentice, D. A., & Miller, D. T. (2007). Psychological essentialism of human categories. *Current Directions in Psychological Science, 16,* 202–206. http://dx.doi.org/10.1111/j.1467-8721.2007.00504.x

Rich, A. (1980). Compulsory heterosexuality and lesbian existence. *Signs: Journal of Women in Culture and Society, 5,* 631–660. http://dx.doi.org/10.1086/493756

Richardson, D. (1983–1984). The dilemma of essentiality in homosexual theory. *Journal of Homosexuality, 9*(2-3), 79–90.

Richardson, M. S. (2012). Counseling for work and relationship. *The Counseling Psychologist, 40,* 190–242, 279–290. http://dx.doi.org/10.1177/0011000011406452

Savickas, M. L. (2013). The 2012 Leona Tyler Award address: Constructing careers—actors, agents, and authors. *The Counseling Psychologist, 41,* 648–662. http://dx.doi.org/10.1177/0011000012468339

Sedgewick, E. K. (1990). *The epistemology of the closet.* Berkeley: University of California Press.

Sedgewick, E. K. (1993). *Tendencies.* London, England: Duke University Press.

Selden, S. (1999). *Inheriting shame: The story of eugenics and racism in America.* New York, NY: Teacher's College Press.

Shields, S. A., & Dicicco, E. C. (2011). The social psychology of sex and gender: From gender differences to doing gender. *Psychology of Women Quarterly, 35,* 491–499. http://dx.doi.org/10.1177/0361684311414823

Szasz, T. (1970). *The manufacture of madness.* New York, NY: Delta.

Tavris, C. (1992). *The mismeasure of woman.* New York, NY: Simon & Schuster.

Tiefer, L. (2000). The social construction and social effects of sex research: The sexological model of sexuality. In C. B. Travis & J. W. White (Eds.), *Sexuality, society, and feminism* (pp. 79–107). Washington, DC: American Psychological Association. http://dx.doi.org/10.1037/10345-004

Tolman, D. L., & Diamond, L. M. (2014). Sexuality theory: A review, a revision, and a recommendation. In D. L. Tolman & L. M. Diamond (Eds.), *APA handbook of sexuality: Vol. 1. Person-based approaches* (pp. 3–27). Washington, DC: American Psychological Association.

Unger, R. K. (1983). Through the looking glass: No Wonderland yet! (The reciprocal relationship between methodology and models of reality). *Psychology of Women Quarterly, 8,* 9–32. http://dx.doi.org/10.1111/j.1471-6402.1983.tb00614.x

Unger, R. K. (2011). Through the looking glass once more. *Psychology of Women Quarterly, 35*(1), 180–182. http://dx.doi.org/10.1177/0361684310395919

Vance, C. S. (1992). Social construction theory: Problems in the history of sexuality. In H. Crowley & S. Hiummelweit (Eds.), *Knowing women: Feminism and knowledge* (pp. 132–145). London, England: Polity Press.

Warner, M. (2012, January 1). Queer and then? *Chronicle of Higher Education.* http://chronicle.com/article/QueerThen-/130161/

Watson, K. (2005). Queer theory. *Group Analysis, 38*(1), 67–81. http://dx.doi.org/10.1177/0533316405049369

West, C., & Zimmerman, D. H. (1987). Doing gender. *Gender & Society, 1*(2), 125–151. http://dx.doi.org/10.1177/0891243287001002002

Young, R. A., & Collin, A. (2004). Introduction: Constructivism and social constructionism in the career field. *Journal of Vocational Behavior, 64,* 373–388. http://dx.doi.org/10.1016/j.jvb.2003.12.005

2

ESSENTIALIST VIEWS ON SEXUAL ORIENTATION AND GENDER IDENTITY

FRANCISCO J. SÁNCHEZ AND TYSON PANKEY

"Being gay IS in your genes." (MacRae, 2014)
"Bisexuality passed on by 'hyper-heterosexuals'." (Osborne, 2008)
"'Transsexual gene' found by researchers." (Jenkins, 2008)

Often when biological reports are released on the genetics of sexual orientation and gender identity, the media sensationalizes the topic. The above titles are recent examples from articles on this hot-button topic. Even though these topics are relevant to everyone, including heterosexual and cisgendered people, research on the biological bases for these characteristics remains focused on sexual and gender minorities.

Certainly media exposure helps keep the topic at the forefront of social issues and can help familiarize the public with the lesbian, gay, bisexual, and transgender (LGBT) community. Yet the media can also spur misconceptions regarding such research, and the same scientific research can be misused to support opposing views. Some also believe that biological research is dehumanizing for LGBT people because it reduces their lived experience to mere biological mechanisms.

http://dx.doi.org/10.1037/15959-003
Handbook of Sexual Orientation and Gender Diversity in Counseling and Psychotherapy, K. A. DeBord, A. R. Fischer, K. J. Bieschke, and R. M. Perez (Editors)

Nevertheless, many LGBT people ask the same question early in their coming out process: "Why am I like this?" Inherent in the question is that something has "caused" them to feel the way that they do. To some degree, this is to be expected; this community has been historically marginalized for exhibiting characteristics that have often been labeled a "choice" and a "lifestyle." Thus, it is unsurprising that clients who present for therapy and who are struggling with their sexual orientation or gender identity may ask if there is a biological reason for their experience—a question that has yet to be fully answered.

In this chapter we focus on the idea that sexual orientation and gender identity are biologically determined and that variations in their expression are naturally occurring. Here we discuss what essentialism is, how essentialism can influence public opinion, whether there are scientific questions that are "off limits," what biological research has found, and how the idea of fixed identities has been challenged by newer research. It should be noted that most biological research has focused on the sexual orientation of gay men. Thus, we highlight research on lesbian women, bisexual people, and transgender people where possible.

ESSENTIALISM VERSUS CONSTRUCTIONISM

The "nature versus nurture" debate is a dated and oversimplistic dichotomy that, nevertheless, continues to be referenced (Tolman & Diamond, 2001). The study of human sexuality is one area in which this old debate persists when it comes to differences observed between cisgendered males and cisgendered females. For instance, women and men in general report different degrees of interest in casual sex, interest in multiple lifetime partners, interest in visual sexual stimuli (e.g., pornography), interest in younger sex partners, and interest in group sex (Okami & Shackelford, 2001). Some argue that such differences are due to evolved biological mechanisms and the influence of sex-specific hormones such as testosterone (Schmitt, Shackelford, & Buss, 2001). Others argue that such differences are due to socially constructed gender roles that influence sexual attitudes and behaviors (Fausto-Sterling, 2012; van Anders, 2013). Many scholars agree that the truth likely lies somewhere in between these polarized views (Tolman & Diamond, 2001).

Likewise, how and why people develop the sexual orientations and gender identities that they do can be rigidly viewed through these two lenses. On the one hand, some argue that sexual orientation and gender identity are essential and intrinsic traits or characteristics. This perspective, termed *essentialism* (Cartwright, 1968), suggests that biological mechanisms establish basic parameters that influence these traits. Thus, humans develop in predetermined and immutable ways, and these traits remain fixed throughout the life cycle. The labels used by different generations and the visibility of LGBT people may vary over time and across cultures, but the behaviors associated with each group have always existed. People who believe in this view may argue that being gay, for example, is innate rather than a choice (Breedlove, 1994).

On the other hand, some maintain that the concept of sexual orientation is the result of psychosocial and cultural processes aimed at making sense of human experiences. These processes include political contexts that privilege heteronormative behavior and oppress those who are not solely attracted to the "opposite" sex (see Chapter 1, this volume). This perspective, termed *social constructionism* (Berger & Luckmann, 1966), posits that any biological explanation of sexual orientation or gender identity is itself a social construction because few pure biological processes can be identified.

These dichotomous and singular views limit our understanding of these topics. Today, many researchers acknowledge that many biological (e.g., genetics, hormones) and sociocultural factors interact and influence sexual orientation and gender identity over the life course (e.g., Broido, 2000; Hines, 2011). These researchers adopt a *biopsychosocial model* (Engel, 1977) when considering complex behavioral traits. In this model, any biological predisposition likely interacts with environmental factors to influence the development of complex human traits.

BIOLOGICAL RESEARCH INFLUENCES PUBLIC OPINION

Public opinion regarding LGBT people has shifted over time. The Pew Research Center (Lipka, 2013), for instance, found that 51% of Americans believed that a gay or lesbian sexual orientation could not be changed, whereas 36% said it could be changed. This was a significant shift toward essentialism from 10 years earlier, when 42% fell on each side of the issue. Given the influence that public opinion has on public policy, how might essentialist findings and views influence this process?

One potential benefit of the essentialist perspective is that if biological mechanisms are found to influence sexual orientation and gender identity, then such findings may sway public opinion regarding these characteristics. In fact, research has shown that people are more accepting of gay men, lesbians, and transgender people if they believe there is evidence that the development of these identities is influenced by biology (Landén & Innala, 2000, 2002; Piskur & Degelman, 1992). For instance, Wood and Bartkowski (2004) found that people who believed that being gay was a biological phenomenon were more supportive of gay rights compared with those who believed that being gay was a choice. Similarly, Landén and Innala (2000) found that Swedish citizens who believed that being transsexual was caused by biological processes were more favorable about extending rights and providing support for transition-related procedures than were citizens who believed it was a choice.

At the same time, there is concern about how such information could be used to harm people. For instance, Sheldon, Pfeffer, Jayaratne, Feldbaum, and Petty (2007) conducted a qualitative analysis of 86 phone interviews in which participants were asked how the discovery of a genetic basis could harm gay and lesbian people. Themes that emerged from this question included increased hatred and discrimination (e.g., parents not wanting children carrying the gene and quarantining people), efforts to eliminate such genes, and stigmatization or discrimination against families with gay and lesbian offspring (e.g., viewing heterosexual siblings as carriers of the gene). Interestingly, when asked how the discovery of a genetic basis could help people, several participants stated that it would help lead to eliminating the gene, thus benefiting society. Others said that it would help parents in family planning (e.g., deciding whether they want to be parents knowing their offspring may inherit the gene). Sheldon et al. concluded that people's interpretation of the same results differed according to their biases.

Yet, even LGBT people disagree on how biological research will affect their communities. Some believe that finding a biological basis to explain sexual orientation and gender identity will help legitimize their experiences and provide an avenue for extending civil rights. Others, however, oppose biological research; they fear that, rather than viewing these characteristics as naturally occurring variations akin to eye color and hair color, such findings may instead be interpreted as a defect that can be prevented or "cured." Given that the history of scientific research on minority populations has at times been characterized by great deceit and prejudice (e.g., the Tuskegee Syphilis Study), it seems reasonable that critics worry about how such research may be used.

THE "GAY GENE": A FORBIDDEN KNOWLEDGE?

To what degree should scientists be allowed to study whatever piques their interest? Are some topics "off limits"? Should only research that potentially has a clear benefit to society be conducted?

In recent decades, sociopolitical factors have increasingly influenced the questions that scientists have pursued (Kempner, Perlis, & Merz, 2005). At the federal level, there are often debates regarding the value of providing funds for research, and politicians, on the basis of their personal beliefs, have made attempts to defund specific projects that have received federal funding (vs. accepting the peer-review process; Epstein, 2006; Grov, 2012). At the community level, opposing sides of a hot-button issue may spin scientific results to promote their interests; activists may even protest outside a scientist's laboratory and home, and some may engage in violent acts (Miller, 2007).

Such extreme sociopolitical responses have often revolved around what is termed *forbidden knowledge* or "knowledge considered too sensitive, dangerous, or taboo to produce" (Kempner, Merz, & Bosk, 2011, p. 476). Specific examples of this have included studies related to human cloning, embryonic stem cell creation, and group differences in intelligence. For some, the search for the biological factors that contribute to sexual orientation and gender identity may be considered forbidden knowledge because of the potential that such knowledge could be used to harm the LGBT community.

Yet, fears about what may occur should not halt the pursuit of knowledge. Knowledge itself is intended to inform and enlighten society. Moreover, knowledge is often sought because scientific discoveries (e.g., new technologies, safer medications, emerging psychotherapeutic interventions) can benefit society. Thus, it seems that *forbidden knowledge* refers to fears related to how knowledge is used versus the discovery of knowledge itself.

When it comes to historically marginalized groups, nevertheless, it is recommended that scientists remain mindful of how their published reports may be misrepresented or inadvertently harm the populations that they are studying. This is especially true for those engaged in *dual-use research* or research that can be used to both advance and harm human welfare (National Institutes of Health Office of Science Policy, 2012). Although dual-use research mainly refers to life science research that may inadvertently lead to biological weapons of mass destruction, it could also refer to genetic research that could "delete" genes associated with a specific community. Even if scientists do not intend their discoveries to be used to harm people, they still bear some responsibility for its outcome. As bioethicist Andrew Askland (2009) opined, "Science is answerable for the harms that it causes . . . science will not be absolved of the consequences of its actions because it is science" (p. 346).

Consequently, it is suggested that scientists remain transparent about their research and increase their engagement with society. This includes being open to close scrutiny of scientific behavior and to the examination of powerful technology. Furthermore, scientists are encouraged to engage with ethicists regarding controversial research and to engage with the public regarding their findings and what research should be prioritized. Institutional review boards can help by continuing to play an important role in maintaining ethical research practices, protecting vulnerable populations, and weighing trade-offs between potential harm and benefit to society. As bioethicist Paul Wolpe (2006) stated,

> Society invests scientists with public trust and privilege, granting them access to funds, materials, public institutions, and even their bodies as subjects for research. In return, society retains a right to set certain limits on the kind of scientific research that it believes is permissible. (p. 1025)

A BRIEF OVERVIEW OF BIOLOGICAL RESEARCH

Many clients in counseling often have questions regarding the biological basis for their experiences. The reasons for this are varied and can range from simple curiosity to a desire to have their experience normalized, especially for those who are being told that there is something "wrong" with them. How one chooses to approach such questions clearly depends on the specifics of each case (e.g., stage of identity development, degree of distress). For instance, it may be helpful to first explore the meaning of such questions for the client. Readers are referred to Chapters 5 and 6 of this volume for further ideas on therapeutic interventions.

Here we offer a brief overview of studies on the biological basis for sexual orientation and gender identity. This area of research has repetitively consisted of findings reported by one group that are not replicated by another group; to date, there are no definitive answers. As this line of research is considered essentialist, we briefly review the biological research related to hormones, genes, and the brain. Interested readers can find more extensive and thorough reviews elsewhere (e.g., Ngun, Ghahramani, Sánchez, Bocklandt, & Vilain, 2011; Sánchez, Bocklandt, & Vilain, 2009). Although some may be disappointed by the lack of consistent findings in this area of research, this "self-correcting" process is part of the nature of the scientific endeavor, especially when studying complex phenomena. Recent studies using emerging technologies are providing promising leads in solving this puzzle.

Hormones

Sex hormones (i.e., androgens and estrogens) play a critical role in human sex development, including the development of sex-specific organs during embryonic development and the maturation of the body during puberty. Research using animal models has found that manipulating sex hormones at different stages of development altered animals' sexual behavior (e.g., inducing receptivity in male rats and mounting behaviors by female rats; Davidson & Allinson, 1969; Larsson & Södersten, 1971; Paup, Mennin,

& Gorski, 1975; Phoenix, Goy, Gerall, & Young, 1959; Quadagno, Shryne, Anderson, & Gorski, 1972). Thus, one line of research has focused on the role of hormones in the development of sexual orientation. We highlight two main hypotheses in this area, which have yielded mixed scientific results.

First, it was incorrectly hypothesized that people attracted to the same sex had abnormal levels of sex hormones that caused their same-sex attraction or atypical gender identity (Meyer-Bahlburg, 1977). In fact, old clinical trials that attempted to induce heterosexual desire in gay men by administering testosterone resulted in the participants reporting greater instances of sex with other men than before the treatment (Glass & Johnson, 1944). The majority of research has instead found that the level of sex-specific hormones was similar between gay men and heterosexual men and between lesbian women and heterosexual women (e.g., Barlow, Abel, Blanchard, & Mavissakalian, 1974; Dancey, 1990; Downey, Ehrhardt, Schiffman, Dyrenfurth, & Becker, 1987; Gartrell, Loriaux, & Chase, 1977; Pillard, Rose, & Sherwood, 1974). Although one study found an increased likelihood of girls prenatally exposed to diethylstilbestrol, a synthetic nonsteroidal estrogen, identifying as lesbian or bisexual in adulthood (Ehrhardt et al., 1985), other researchers have not replicated the initial findings (Newbold, 1993; Titus-Ernstoff et al., 2003).

Likewise, there appear to be no significant differences in endogenous hormone levels between transgender and cisgender people (Meyer-Bahlburg, 2013). Although several small-scale studies found a higher prevalence of polycystic ovary syndrome (an endocrine disorder in which the ovaries secrete excess androgens) among female-to-male transsexual individuals compared with the general population (Baba et al., 2007; Balen, Schachter, Montgomery, Reid, & Jacobs, 1993; Bosinski et al., 1997; Futterweit, Weiss, & Fagerstrom, 1986), larger scale studies have not replicated these findings (Mueller et al., 2008).

Second, it has been hypothesized that hormonal disruptions during critical periods of in utero development affect sexual orientation and gender identity. Testing this hypothesis is difficult. The manipulation that is done on animal models to affect hormone levels during pregnancy would be unethical on humans. Extrapolations have, therefore, been made regarding this hypothesis. For instance, it has been reported that women diagnosed with congenital adrenal hyperplasia in which they were exposed to elevated levels of androgens during embryo development had an increased incidence of having sex with other women (Hines, Brook, & Conway, 2004; Johannsen, Ripa, Mortensen, & Main, 2006; Meyer-Bahlburg, Dolezal, Baker, & New, 2008; Money, Schwartz, & Lewis, 1984; Zucker et al., 1996).

There is also limited evidence that persons prenatally exposed to DES may exhibit fewer stereotypical gender-related interests and behaviors. That is, males prenatally exposed to DES report fewer stereotypically masculine interests and behaviors (e.g., contact sports) compared with males not exposed to DES; females prenatally exposed to DES exhibit more stereotypically masculine traits (e.g., aggression) compared with females not exposed (Reinisch, Ziemba-Davis, & Sanders, 1991; Yalom, Green, & Fisk, 1973). Thus, it is possible that exposure to significantly atypical hormone levels during critical periods of development may in rare cases contribute to feelings of same-sex attraction and to gender-related interests for some people.

Readers may be familiar with studies focused on finger-length ratio. Specifically, the ratio of the second finger (or "ring finger") and fourth finger (or "index finger") has been shown to be sexually dimorphic whereby males on average have a lower ratio compared with females. Some studies found atypical ratios for gay men and lesbians (Grimbos, Dawood, Burriss, Zucker, & Puts, 2010; Williams et al., 2000) and transgender people (Kraemer et al., 2009; Schneider, Pickel, & Stalla, 2006; Wallien, Zucker, Steensma, & Cohen-Kettenis, 2008). Although this ratio has been hypothesized to be a marker for androgen exposure in utero (Manning, Scutt, Wilson, & Lewis-Jones, 1998), there is limited evidence to support this claim. Thus, the link between early exposure to atypical hormone levels and either characteristic remains debatable.

As a whole, studies looking at the role that hormones play in human sexual orientation and gender identity have been inconsistent. The clearest evidence for a hormonal role comes from a few studies of women with congenital adrenal hyperplasia and persons prenatally exposed to DES. However, both these conditions create significantly atypical hormonal experiences in utero and are unlikely to apply to the general population of sexual minority individuals. Although this does not completely negate the role that hormones play in sexual orientation and gender identity, evidence has yet to show any clear causal connection in humans. Yet this may never be conclusively demonstrated given the ethical complexities of manipulating hormone levels in humans, especially during in utero development.

Genes

The phrase "gay gene" may play well in the media, but it has likely contributed to a misunderstanding of the role that genes play in our development in two key ways. First, few people are affected by *Mendelian traits*, or characteristics that are caused by the presence of a dominant gene or two recessive genes. Some examples include Huntington's disease and albinism. Thus, it is likely that several genetic factors influence sexual attraction as is true of other "complex traits" (e.g., diabetes, hypertension).

Second, what is being searched for is a set of genes that influence attraction toward males and a set of genes that influence attraction toward females.

Scholars have argued that everyone carries these genes (Bocklandt, Horvath, Vilain, & Hamer, 2006). Yet in most males and some females (i.e., lesbians) the genes for attraction toward males are hypothesized to be "turned off," and the genes for attraction toward female are hypothesized to be "turned on." The opposite is true for most women and some men (i.e., gay men). A parallel process can hypothetically be said to be true regarding gender identity whereby genes that influence male-typical and female-typical characteristics are being influenced. Several methodologies have been used to identify whether these traits are heritable and what genes may be involved. We highlight three common methods.

One method is *pedigree analysis* or the study of family trees to determine whether there is a mode of inheritance. The most publicized study using this method was related to sexual orientation among men: Hamer, Hu, Magnuson, Hu, and Pattatucci (1993) found an increased rate of gay men on the mother's side of the family compared with the father's side. This seemed to implicate the X chromosome given that males inherit the X chromosome from their mothers and the Y chromosome from their fathers.

This analysis was paired with a second method known as *genetic linkage analysis*. In this approach, researchers focus on relatives with a common characteristic and search for genetic regions that are shared by these specific relatives. Hamer et al. (1993) carried out a linkage scan of the X chromosome among a sample of gay men and found evidence of significant linkage to the Xq28 region. Although there were conflicting findings in subsequent studies (Hu et al., 1995; Rice, Anderson, Risch, & Ebers, 1999), a meta-analysis performed by Hamer et al. (1999) and a recent study of gay brothers (Sanders et al., 2015) provided further evidence that Xq28 holds genes related to sexual attraction, at least among men. Furthermore, other chromosomes have been found to likely influence sexual orientation (Mustanski et al., 2005). Nevertheless, 25 years have passed since the initial report and the exact genetic factors involved in sexual orientation have yet to be identified.

The third genetic methodology we highlight consists of studying twins. Monozygotic (MZ or identical) twins share the same DNA; thus, they develop very similar characteristics. For instance, the personalities of MZ twins are markedly more similar to each other compared with other relatives (e.g., fraternal twins, siblings, parents); this is true even among MZ twins who were raised apart (Bouchard & McGue, 2003). Yet when one member of a MZ twin pair is gay, the other twin is gay only 68% of the time (Kendler, Thornton, Gilman, & Kessler, 2000). One possible explanation for the discordance of sexual orientation among MZ twins may stem from *genomic imprinting* (Bocklandt & Hamer, 2003), an uncommon type of epigenetic process in which genes from one of the two parental chromosomes are "silenced," thus resulting in the expression of the corresponding "unsilenced" genes (see Duarte, 2013;

Tammen, Frisco, & Choi, 2013). If so, then some of the discordance in the sexual orientation of identical twins could be accounted for by epigenetic regulation. Even though identical twins inherit the same DNA sequence, unique biochemical processes (e.g., methylation and histone modification) may affect the DNA after the fertilized egg splits, thus leading to differences in gene expression during critical periods of development (Fraga et al., 2005). Furthermore, the earlier that MZ twins separate, the more likely it is that each will have unique biochemical environments, as each may have a placenta and may develop within an amniotic sac. Consequently, the observed discordance for homosexuality in twins, which is currently attributed to each twin's unique environment, could very well be caused by the "epigenetic environment."

Genetic studies of gender identity are particularly difficult to conduct because of the low co-occurrence rate of transgender identities within families (Green, 2000). The few genetic studies that have been conducted on transgender people have mainly looked at specific genes known or believed to influence characteristics (e.g., genes that affect hormone receptors; Hare et al., 2009), but findings have been inconsistent. It may be some time before sufficient sample sizes can be recruited for studies using other common genetic methodologies.

Overall, there is some evidence that sexual orientation is influenced by our genetic make-up. Specifically, a region of the X chromosome has been strongly implicated among gay men, although the exact genes involved have yet to be identified. Furthermore, emerging evidence suggests that genes located on other chromosomes may be involved in the development of sexual orientation. The evidence for a genetic influence on gender identity, however, is far more limited given the less common occurrence of this identity, limiting the ability to recruit sufficient number of participants needed for genetic analyses. Nevertheless, the elusive "gay gene" or genes involved in sexual orientation and gender identity are likely to be identified as technology continues to advance.

Neuroanatomy

The brain is the center of the nervous system, and it exerts control over the body. Its functioning and processes affect every aspect of our experience, including our feelings and our sense of self. Thus, researchers have sought to determine what role the brain may have in our sexual orientation and gender identity. Here we focus on autopsy studies and neuroimaging studies.

Brain Autopsies

In 1991, Simon LeVay published a widely publicized report suggesting that sexual orientation may be influenced by a specific brain region. LeVay compared three groups of autopsied brains: (a) 18 gay men and one bisexual man; (b) 16 presumed heterosexual men; and (c) six presumed heterosexual women. He reported that the first group of brains differed from their heterosexual counterparts. In particular, he found that the third interstitial nucleus of the anterior hypothalamus (INAH-3)—a sexually dimorphic brain structure shown to be significantly smaller in women when compared with men— was smaller in the first group of brains when compared with the heterosexual men's brains. LeVay's report was harshly criticized because all the gay men and the bisexual man had died of AIDS complications (although seven of the heterosexual men had also died of AIDS), because it was based on postmortem tissue and it included unsystematic variability caused by the participants' different lifestyles. A subsequent postmortem study found that the INAH-3 in homosexual men did not significantly differ from either heterosexual men or heterosexual women (Byne et al., 2001), even though INAH-3 has been found to significantly differ in size between the latter two groups.

LeVay's work was characteristic of the brain autopsy reports in the early 1990s, whereby one research group would provide initial data implicating specific regions as influencing sexual orientation and then a subsequent group would refute the original findings. These early brain studies were also criticized by other scholars, typically because of the cause of death of the cadavers. For instance, Allen and Gorski (1992) found that the anterior commissure (a smaller bundle of nerve fibers that, like the corpus callosum, connect the two hemispheres) was significantly larger in brains belonging to gay men compared with those belonging to heterosexual men. Two subsequent studies (Byne et al., 2001; Lasco, Jordan, Edgar, Petito, & Byne, 2002), however, did not replicate Allen and Gorski's findings. Likewise, Swaab and Hofman (1990) reported that the size of the suprachiasmatic nucleus of the hypothalamus (which regulates circadian rhythms) in gay men was found to be significantly larger compared with heterosexual men. Yet, as with LeVay's report, these two reports received substantial criticism because the gay men had all died of AIDS complications (Byne & Parsons, 1993).

Similarly, studies of autopsied brains of transsexual individuals (e.g., Garcia-Falgueras & Swaab, 2008; Kruijver et al., 2000) have been criticized for their flaws. One of the earliest reports by Zhou, Hofman, Gooren, and Swaab (1995) compared the autopsied brains of six male-to-female transsexual individuals to the brains of heterosexual and homosexual men and heterosexual women. The study found that the size of the sexually dimorphic bed nucleus of the stria terminalis of the hypothalamus among male-to-female transsexual individuals matched the size of cisgendered females. However, Zhou et al.'s findings were criticized because all of the autopsied male-to-female transsexual individuals had prolonged exposure to estrogen therapy, which has been found to alter neuroanatomy (Pol et al., 2006).

Overall, brain autopsy studies have generated more intrigue than clear answers, in part because of the vastly different lifestyles of the people who donated their bodies to science and in part because of the difficulty of obtaining sufficient number of brains to autopsy. Yet advances in technology provide great promise in understanding the role that our brains may play in sexual orientation and gender identity. We now turn to this topic.

Neuroimaging

Brain imaging techniques have offered a different way of measuring neuroanatomical differences. First, researchers have been able to use structural magnetic resonance imaging (MRI) and other techniques to study the structure of brain regions that may play a role in influencing sexual orientation and gender identity. For instance, women in general have greater global gray matter proportions and regional gray matter volumes and concentrations compared with men (Luders, Gaser, Narr, & Toga, 2009). Yet Ponseti et al. (2007) found that lesbian women had less gray matter concentration in the perirhinal cortex (involved in the processing of smells and sexual stimuli) compared with heterosexual women. Another example relates to hemispheric asymmetry and functional connectivity between the right and left amygdala, which have been found to be sexually dimorphic. However, Savic and Lindström (2008) found that these patterns were atypical among gay men (with more heterosexual female patterns) and lesbian women (with more heterosexual male patterns).

In terms of gender identity, some structural differences have been found when comparing transsexual individuals to nontranssexual controls. For instance, two different studies from Spain found that the white matter concentration—which plays an important role in electrical signals in axons—among female-to-male transsexual individuals was more similar to cisgendered males in several regions compared with cisgendered females (Rametti, Carrillo, Gómez-Gil, Junque, Segovia, et al., 2011). Yet white matter concentration among male-to-female transsexual individuals fell between cisgendered male and cisgendered female patterns (Rametti, Carrillo, Gómez-Gil, Junque, Zubiarre-Elorza, et al., 2011). Male-to-female transsexual individuals have also been found to have gray matter concentration more similar to cisgendered women than cisgendered men in the putamen, which plays a role in regulating movement (Luders, Sánchez, et al., 2009; Savic & Arver, 2011). Furthermore, male-to-female and female-to-male transsexual individuals have been found to have cortical thickness patterns in several brain regions consistent with the patterns found among the sex that they identify with versus the one they were assigned at birth (Luders et al., 2012; Rametti, Carrillo, Gómez-Gil, Junque, Segovia, et al., 2011; Rametti, Carrillo, Gómez-Gil, Junque, Zubiarre-Elorza, et al., 2011).

Second, researchers have been able to use functional MRI and other procedures to see how the brain functions in response to stimuli. For instance, researchers at the Karolinska Institute in Stockholm, Sweden, studied how the brain responded to smelling sex-specific putative-hormones or candidate compounds for human pheromones. They found that the hypothalamic activation of gay men was more similar to heterosexual women than to heterosexual men (Savic, Berglund, & Lindström, 2005); the hypothalamic activation of lesbian women was more similar to heterosexual men than to heterosexual women (Berglund, Lindström, & Savic, 2006); and the hypothalamic activation of male-to-female transsexual individuals was more similar to cisgendered, heterosexual control-women compared with cisgendered, heterosexual control-men (Berglund, Lindström, Dhejne-Helmy, & Savic, 2008). A subsequent functional MRI study also found that male-to-female transsexual individuals exposed to visual erotic stimuli exhibited cerebral activation more similar to cisgendered females versus cisgendered males (Gizewski et al., 2009).

Overall, brain studies—especially neuroimaging studies—have provided some of the more intriguing preliminary findings related to sexual orientation and gender identity. As this technology continues to advance, it is likely that more brain regions will be implicated. Nevertheless, it is important to keep in mind that neuroimaging technology has its limitations. These include sensitivity to movement that can create imaging artifacts, the stress of being in an MRI machine for extended periods of time (possibly influencing who chooses to participate), and the difficulty of controlling for individual lifestyles and experiences that may affect brain structure and functioning. MRI studies have also been criticized because of problematic statistical analyses (Vul, Harris, Winkielman, & Pashler, 2009). Thus, independent researchers must replicate these results before any firm conclusions can be drawn.

CHALLENGES TO ESSENTIALISM

Although biological research has begun to shed light on what factors may influence sexual orientation and gender identity, some findings challenge the idea that these characteristics are fixed or inflexible. Here we present three such examples.

One main challenge to the idea that sexuality is fixed for life is the fluidity that has been reported among women over the life course. Specifically, Diamond (2008) followed 79 women who identified as lesbian, bisexual, or "unlabeled" for 10 years beginning at late adolescence. She found that by the 10th year, 67% of the participants had changed their identities at least once (and 36% had changed their identities more than once). This phenomenon of fluidity seems to be far less common among men than among women (Mock & Eibach,

2012). Nevertheless, the self-reported sexual fluidity among women challenges the notion of sexuality being fixed for life and instead allows for the "capacity for context-specific flexibility in erotic response" (Diamond, 2008, p. 13).

Second, recent evidence has challenged two dominant views from the 20th century regarding neuroanatomy. One view was that all sex differences observed in the brain were solely due to the presence of hormones produced by the gonads (i.e., testes and ovaries) during critical periods of development, which initiates around 6 to 8 weeks after conception in humans. Yet emerging research has found that brain differentiation begins before the presence of hormones in response to sex-specific genomic-signals in individual tissues or brain regions (McCarthy & Arnold, 2011). Another view was that brain structure and function were essentially fixed throughout life. Newer research, however, has shown that the brain is actually a plastic organ that changes in response to environmental factors and life experiences. For instance, regions of the brain appear to be sensitive to practice and repetition of activities whereby the size of brain regions involved in the storage of "mental maps" has been found to be positively associated with the time spent as a taxicab driver (Maguire, Woollett, & Spiers, 2006); and the size of regions of the brain involved in auditory memory is associated with time spent as a piano tuner (Teki et al., 2012). Thus, our emerging understanding of neuroplasticity may influence our interpretation of the results of neuroimaging studies in ways we have yet to understand.

Third, emerging epigenetic research is challenging the once-held belief that the expression of our DNA is fixed throughout life. For instance, there is evidence that environmental factors, such as diet, exercise, and exposure to toxins, can alter how genes are expressed (Feil & Fraga, 2011). Even though the underlying DNA "blueprint" remains intact, biochemical anomalies impede the ability for certain genes to be "read." Consequently, simple inheritance of a genetic sequence does not mean that it will be permanently expressed throughout life. It is unclear how this may influence complex traits such as sexual orientation and gender identity. Yet epigenetics is a reminder that our biology does not necessarily determine our destiny for life.

CONCLUSION

In this chapter, we have provided a brief overview regarding essentialist concepts related to sexual orientation and gender identity. Many clients struggle with their sexual orientation and gender identity and often ask "why"; we hope that this chapter can help inform practitioners on some basic concepts related to the biology of sexual orientation and gender identity. We also hope that readers walk away with cautious optimism given the sociopolitical implications related to this type of research.

Biological research investigating the scientific underpinnings of both sexual orientation and gender identity greatly influences how people view these characteristics. Studies of hormones, genetics, and the brain each offer meaningful contributions to ongoing investigations into the hows and whys of sexual orientation and gender identity development. In particular, specific genetic regions (e.g., $Xq28$) and brain structures (e.g., the putamen) may play a key role in the development of these complex traits. Yet it is critical that we continue to not only scrutinize research findings but also to make ongoing efforts to replicate promising study designs and approaches.

Furthermore, scientists must remain mindful of the potential effect of their research findings on society. Although the pursuit of knowledge itself should not be prohibited, society does have a vested interest in how such knowledge is applied. Yet even when scientists believe that they have found some "truth," one should remain mindful that today's "truth" may be challenged in the future just as we now look at past scientific beliefs differently (e.g., that the brain is hardwired and inflexible throughout adulthood).

Ultimately, it is unlikely that either essentialism or social constructionism by itself provides a thorough understanding of sexual orientation and gender identity. Thus, additional efforts should be made to continue to promote biopsychosocial models that integrate these perspectives in order to give a more complete understanding of these critical self-defining traits.

It is our hope that every reader thinks critically about the sociopolitical forces present in our society and research institutions in order to better engage in scientific inquiry that respects and benefits all human beings.

REFERENCES

Allen, L. S., & Gorski, R. A. (1992). Sexual orientation and the size of the anterior commissure in the human brain. *Proceedings of the National Academy of Sciences of the United States of America, 89,* 7199–7202. http://dx.doi.org/10.1073/pnas.89.15.7199

Askland, A. (2009). Science and socially responsible freedom: Commentary on "Cognitive enhancement: Methods, ethics, regulatory challenges." *Science and Engineering Ethics, 15,* 343–349. http://dx.doi.org/10.1007/s11948-009-9132-7

Baba, T., Endo, T., Honnma, H., Kitajima, Y., Hayashi, T., Ikeda, H., . . . Saito, T. (2007). Association between polycystic ovary syndrome and female-to-male transsexuality. *Human Reproduction, 22,* 1011–1016. http://dx.doi.org/10.1093/humrep/del474

Balen, A. H., Schachter, M. E., Montgomery, D., Reid, R. W., & Jacobs, H. S. (1993). Polycystic ovaries are a common finding in untreated female to male transsexuals. *Clinical Endocrinology, 38,* 325–329. http://dx.doi.org/10.1111/j.1365-2265.1993.tb01013.x

Barlow, D. H., Abel, G. G., Blanchard, E. B., & Mavissakalian, M. (1974). Plasma testosterone levels and male homosexuality: A failure to replicate. *Archives of Sexual Behavior, 3*, 571–575. http://dx.doi.org/10.1007/BF01541139

Berger, P., & Luckmann, T. (1966). *The social construction of reality: A treatise in the sociology of knowledge.* Garden City, NY: Doubleday.

Berglund, H., Lindström, P., Dhejne-Helmy, C., & Savic, I. (2008). Male-to-female transsexuals show sex-atypical hypothalamus activation when smelling odorous steroids. *Cerebral Cortex, 18*, 1900–1908. http://dx.doi.org/10.1093/cercor/bhm216

Berglund, H., Lindström, P., & Savic, I. (2006). Brain response to putative pheromones in lesbian women. *Proceedings of the National Academy of Sciences of the United States of America, 103*, 8269–8274. http://dx.doi.org/10.1073/pnas.0600331103

Bocklandt, S., & Hamer, D. H. (2003). Beyond hormones: A novel hypothesis for the biological basis of male sexual orientation. *Journal of Endocrinological Investigation, 26*(Suppl.), 8–12.

Bocklandt, S., Horvath, S., Vilain, E., & Hamer, D. H. (2006). Extreme skewing of X chromosome inactivation in mothers of homosexual men. *Human Genetics, 118*, 691–694. http://dx.doi.org/10.1007/s00439-005-0119-4

Bosinski, H. A., Peter, M., Bonatz, G., Arndt, R., Heidenreich, M., Sippell, W. G., & Wille, R. (1997). A higher rate of hyperandrogenic disorders in female-to-male transsexuals. *Psychoneuroendocrinology, 22*, 361–380. http://dx.doi.org/10.1016/S0306-4530(97)00033-4

Bouchard, T. J., Jr., & McGue, M. (2003). Genetic and environmental influences on human psychological differences. *Journal of Neurobiology, 54*, 4–45. http://dx.doi.org/10.1002/neu.10160

Breedlove, S. M. (1994). Sexual differentiation of the human nervous system. *Annual Review of Psychology, 45*, 389–418. http://dx.doi.org/10.1146/annurev.ps.45.020194.002133

Broido, E. M. (2000). Constructing identity: The nature and meaning of lesbian, gay, and bisexual identities. In R. M. Perez, K. A. DeBord, & K. J. Bieschke (Eds.), *Handbook of counseling and psychotherapy with lesbian, gay, and bisexual clients* (pp. 13–33). Washington, DC: American Psychological Association. http://dx.doi.org/10.1037/10339-001

Byne, W., & Parsons, B. (1993). Human sexual orientation. The biologic theories reappraised. *Archives of General Psychiatry, 50*, 228–239. http://dx.doi.org/10.1001/archpsyc.1993.01820150078009

Byne, W., Tobet, S., Mattiace, L. A., Lasco, M. S., Kemether, E., Edgar, M. A., . . . Jones, L. B. (2001). The interstitial nuclei of the human anterior hypothalamus: An investigation of variation with sex, sexual orientation, and HIV status. *Hormones and Behavior, 40*, 86–92. http://dx.doi.org/10.1006/hbeh.2001.1680

Cartwright, R. L. (1968). Some remarks on essentialism. *The Journal of Philosophy, 65*, 615–626. http://dx.doi.org/10.2307/2024315

Dancey, C. P. (1990). Sexual orientation in women: An investigation of hormonal and personality variables. *Biological Psychology, 30,* 251–264. http://dx.doi.org/10.1016/0301-0511(90)90142-J

Davidson, J. M., & Allinson, P. A. (1969). Effects of estrogen on the sexual behavior of male rats. *Endocrinology, 84,* 1365–1372. http://dx.doi.org/10.1210/endo-84-6-1365

Diamond, L. M. (2008). Female bisexuality from adolescence to adulthood: Results from a 10-year longitudinal study. *Developmental Psychology, 44,* 5–14. http://dx.doi.org/10.1037/0012-1649.44.1.5

Downey, J., Ehrhardt, A. A., Schiffman, M., Dyrenfurth, I., & Becker, J. (1987). Sex hormones in lesbian and heterosexual women. *Hormones and Behavior, 21,* 347–357. http://dx.doi.org/10.1016/0018-506X(87)90019-5

Duarte, J. D. (2013). Epigenetics primer: Why the clinician should care about epigenetics. *Pharmacotherapy, 33,* 1362–1368. http://dx.doi.org/10.1002/phar.1325

Ehrhardt, A. A., Meyer-Bahlburg, H. F. L., Rosen, L. R., Feldman, J. F., Veridiano, N. P., Zimmerman, I., & McEwen, B. S. (1985). Sexual orientation after prenatal exposure to exogenous estrogen. *Archives of Sexual Behavior, 14,* 57–77. http://dx.doi.org/10.1007/BF01541353

Engel, G. L. (1977). The need for a new medical model: A challenge for biomedicine. *Science, 196,* 129–136. http://dx.doi.org/10.1126/science.847460

Epstein, S. (2006). The new attack on sexuality research: Morality and the politics of knowledge production. *Sexuality Research & Social Policy, 3,* 1–12. http://dx.doi.org/10.1525/srsp.2006.3.1.01

Fausto-Sterling, A. (2012). *Sex/gender: Biology in a social world.* New York, NY: Routledge.

Feil, R., & Fraga, M. F. (2011). Epigenetics and the environment: Emerging patterns and implications. *Nature Reviews. Genetics, 13,* 97–109.

Fraga, M. F., Ballestar, E., Paz, M. F., Ropero, S., Setien, F., Ballestar, M. L., . . . Esteller, M. (2005). Epigenetic differences arise during the lifetime of monozygotic twins. *Proceedings of the National Academy of Sciences of the United States of America, 102,* 10604–10609. http://dx.doi.org/10.1073/pnas.0500398102

Futterweit, W., Weiss, R. A., & Fagerstrom, R. M. (1986). Endocrine evaluation of forty female-to-male transsexuals: Increased frequency of polycystic ovarian disease in female transsexualism. *Archives of Sexual Behavior, 15*(1), 69–78. http://dx.doi.org/10.1007/BF01542305

Garcia-Falgueras, A., & Swaab, D. F. (2008). A sex difference in the hypothalamic uncinate nucleus: Relationship to gender identity. *Brain: A Journal of Neurology, 131*(Pt. 12), 3132–3146. http://dx.doi.org/10.1093/brain/awn276

Gartrell, N. K., Loriaux, D. L., & Chase, T. N. (1977). Plasma testosterone in homosexual and heterosexual women. *The American Journal of Psychiatry, 134,* 1117–1118. http://dx.doi.org/10.1176/ajp.134.10.1117

Gizewski, E. R., Krause, E., Schlamann, M., Happich, F., Ladd, M. E., Forsting, M., & Senf, W. (2009). Specific cerebral activation due to visual erotic stimuli in male-to-female transsexuals compared with male and female controls: An fMRI study. *Journal of Sexual Medicine, 6*, 440–448. http://dx.doi.org/10.1111/j.1743-6109.2008.00981.x

Glass, S. J., & Johnson, R. W. (1944). Limitations and complications of organo-therapy in male homosexuality. *The Journal of Clinical Endocrinology, 4*, 540–544. http://dx.doi.org/10.1210/jcem-4-11-540

Green, R. (2000). Family co-occurrence of "gender dysphoria": Ten sibling or parent–child pairs. *Archives of Sexual Behavior, 29*, 499–507. http://dx.doi.org/10.1023/A:1001947920872

Grimbos, T., Dawood, K., Burriss, R. P., Zucker, K. J., & Puts, D. A. (2010). Sexual orientation and the second to fourth finger length ratio: A meta-analysis in men and women. *Behavioral Neuroscience, 124*, 278–287. http://dx.doi.org/10.1037/a0018764

Grov, C. (2012). Dangerous politics and sex research: The example of "penis-gate 2011." *Sexuality Research & Social Policy, 9*, 95–98.

Hamer, D. H., Hu, S., Magnuson, V. L., Hu, N., & Pattatucci, A. M. (1993). A link-age between DNA markers on the X chromosome and male sexual orientation. *Science, 261*, 321–327. http://dx.doi.org/10.1126/science.8332896

Hamer, D. H., Rice, G., Risch, N., & Ebers, G. (1999). Genetics and male sexual orientation. *Science, 285*, 803. http://dx.doi.org/10.1126/science.285.5429.803a

Hare, L., Bernard, P., Sánchez, F. J., Baird, P. N., Vilain, E., Kennedy, T., & Harley, V. R. (2009). Androgen receptor repeat length polymorphism associated with male-to-female transsexualism. *Biological Psychiatry, 65*(1), 93–96. http://dx.doi.org/10.1016/j.biopsych.2008.08.033

Hines, M. (2011). Prenatal endocrine influences on sexual orientation and on sexu-ally differentiated childhood behavior. *Frontiers in Neuroendocrinology, 32*, 170–182. http://dx.doi.org/10.1016/j.yfrne.2011.02.006

Hines, M., Brook, C., & Conway, G. S. (2004). Androgen and psychosexual development: Core gender identity, sexual orientation and recalled child-hood gender role behavior in women and men with congenital adrenal hyper-plasia (CAH). *Journal of Sex Research, 41*, 75–81. http://dx.doi.org/10.1080/00224490409552215

Hu, S., Pattatucci, A. M., Patterson, C., Li, L., Fulker, D. W., Cherny, S. S., . . . Hamer, D. H. (1995). Linkage between sexual orientation and chromosome Xq28 in males but not in females. *Nature Genetics, 11*, 248–256. http://dx.doi.org/10.1038/ng1195-248

Jenkins, M. (2008, October 26). "Transsexual gene" found by researchers. *The Courier Mail.* Retrieved from http://www.couriermail.com.au/news/transsexual-gene-found/story-e6freoox-1111117863628?nk=d365b5539b7e29a17f312112fdb29aed

Johannsen, T. H., Ripa, C. P. L., Mortensen, E. L., & Main, K. M. (2006). Quality of life in 70 women with disorders of sex development. *European Journal of Endocrinology, 155*, 877–885. http://dx.doi.org/10.1530/eje.1.02294

Kempner, J., Merz, J. F., & Bosk, C. L. (2011). Forbidden knowledge: Public controversy and the production of nonknowledge. *Sociological Forum, 26*, 475–500. http://dx.doi.org/10.1111/j.1573-7861.2011.01259.x

Kempner, J., Perlis, C. S., & Merz, J. F. (2005). Forbidden knowledge [Editorial]. *Science, 307*, 854. http://dx.doi.org/10.1126/science.1107576

Kendler, K. S., Thornton, L. M., Gilman, S. E., & Kessler, R. C. (2000). Sexual orientation in a U.S. national sample of twin and nontwin sibling pairs. *The American Journal of Psychiatry, 157*, 1843–1846. http://dx.doi.org/10.1176/appi.ajp.157.11.1843

Kraemer, B., Noll, T., Delsignore, A., Milos, G., Schnyder, U., & Hepp, U. (2009). Finger length ratio (2D:4D) in adults with gender identity disorder. *Archives of Sexual Behavior, 38*, 359–363. http://dx.doi.org/10.1007/s10508-007-9262-4

Kruijver, F. P., Zhou, J. N., Pool, C. W., Hofman, M. A., Gooren, L. J., & Swaab, D. F. (2000). Male-to-female transsexuals have female neuron numbers in a limbic nucleus. *The Journal of Clinical Endocrinology and Metabolism, 85*, 2034–2041. http://dx.doi.org/10.1210/jcem.85.5.6564

Landén, M., & Innala, S. (2000). Attitudes toward transsexualism in a Swedish national survey. *Archives of Sexual Behavior, 29*, 375–388. http://dx.doi.org/10.1023/A:1001970521182

Landén, M., & Innala, S. (2002). The effect of a biological explanation on attitudes towards homosexual persons. A Swedish national sample study. *Nordic Journal of Psychiatry, 56*, 181–186. http://dx.doi.org/10.1080/080394802317607156

Larsson, K., & Södersten, P. (1971). Lordosis behavior in male rats treated with estrogen in combination with tetrabenazine and nialamide. *Psychopharmacologia, 21*, 13–16. http://dx.doi.org/10.1007/BF00403991

Lasco, M. S., Jordan, T. J., Edgar, M. A., Petito, C. K., & Byne, W. (2002). A lack of dimorphism of sex or sexual orientation in the human anterior commissure. *Brain Research, 936*, 95–98. http://dx.doi.org/10.1016/S0006-8993(02)02590-8

LeVay, S. (1991). A difference in hypothalamic structure between heterosexual and homosexual men. *Science, 253*, 1034–1037. http://dx.doi.org/10.1126/science.1887219

Lipka, M. (2013, August 20). *Half of Americans say sexual orientation cannot be changed.* Retrieved from http://www.pewresearch.org/fact-tank/2013/08/20/half-of-americans-say-sexual-orientation-cannot-be-changed/

Luders, E., Gaser, C., Narr, K. L., & Toga, A. W. (2009). Why sex matters: Brain size independent differences in gray matter distributions between men and women. *The Journal of Neuroscience, 29*, 14265–14270. http://dx.doi.org/10.1523/JNEUROSCI.2261-09.2009

Luders, E., Sánchez, F. J., Gaser, C., Toga, A. W., Narr, K. L., Hamilton, L. S., & Vilain, E. (2009). Regional gray matter variation in male-to-female transsexualism. *NeuroImage, 46*, 904–907. http://dx.doi.org/10.1016/j.neuroimage.2009.03.048

Luders, E., Sánchez, F. J., Tosun, D., Shattuck, D. W., Gaser, C., Vilain, E., & Toga, A. W. (2012). Increased cortical thickness in male-to-female transsexualism. *Journal of Behavioral & Brain Science, 2*, 357–362. http://dx.doi.org/10.4236/jbbs.2012.23040

MacRae, F. (2014, February 13). Being gay IS in your genes, say scientists in a controversial new DNA study. *DailyMail.com.* Retrieved from http://www.dailymail.co.uk/sciencetech/article-2559021/Being-gay-DNA-researchers-claim-controversial-new-study.html

Maguire, E. A., Woollett, K., & Spiers, H. J. (2006). London taxi drivers and bus drivers: A structural MRI and neuropsychological analysis. *Hippocampus, 16*, 1091–1101. http://dx.doi.org/10.1002/hipo.20233

Manning, J. T., Scutt, D., Wilson, J., & Lewis-Jones, D. I. (1998). The ratio of 2nd to 4th digit length: A predictor of sperm numbers and concentrations of testosterone, luteinizing hormone and oestrogen. *Human Reproduction, 13*, 3000–3004. http://dx.doi.org/10.1093/humrep/13.11.3000

McCarthy, M. M., & Arnold, A. P. (2011). Reframing sexual differentiation of the brain. *Nature Neuroscience, 14*, 677–683. http://dx.doi.org/10.1038/nn.2834

Meyer-Bahlburg, H. F. L. (1977). Sex hormones and male homosexuality in comparative perspective. *Archives of Sexual Behavior, 6*, 297–325. http://dx.doi.org/10.1007/BF01541203

Meyer-Bahlburg, H. F. L. (2013). Sex steroids and variants of gender identity. *Endocrinology and Metabolism Clinics of North America, 42*, 435–452. http://dx.doi.org/10.1016/j.ecl.2013.05.011

Meyer-Bahlburg, H. F. L., Dolezal, C., Baker, S. W., & New, M. I. (2008). Sexual orientation in women with classical or non-classical congenital adrenal hyperplasia as a function of degree of prenatal androgen excess. *Archives of Sexual Behavior, 37*, 85–99. http://dx.doi.org/10.1007/s10508-007-9265-1

Miller, G. (2007). Animal extremists get personal. *Science, 318*, 1856–1858. http://dx.doi.org/10.1126/science.318.5858.1856

Mock, S. E., & Eibach, R. P. (2012). Stability and change in sexual orientation identity over a 10-year period in adulthood. *Archives of Sexual Behavior, 41*, 641–648. http://dx.doi.org/10.1007/s10508-011-9761-1

Money, J., Schwartz, M., & Lewis, V. G. (1984). Adult erotosexual status and fetal hormonal masculinization and demasculinization: 46,XX congenital virilizing adrenal hyperplasia and 46,XY androgen-insensitivity syndrome compared. *Psychoneuroendocrinology, 9*, 405–414. http://dx.doi.org/10.1016/0306-4530(84)90048-9

Mueller, A., Gooren, L. J., Naton-Schötz, S., Cupisti, S., Beckmann, M. W., & Dittrich, R. (2008). Prevalence of polycystic ovary syndrome and hyperandrogenemia in female-to-male transsexuals. *The Journal of Clinical Endocrinology and Metabolism, 93,* 1408–1411. http://dx.doi.org/10.1210/jc.2007-2808

Mustanski, B. S., Dupree, M. G., Nievergelt, C. M., Bocklandt, S., Schork, N. J., & Hamer, D. H. (2005). A genomewide scan of male sexual orientation. *Human Genetics, 116,* 272–278. http://dx.doi.org/10.1007/s00439-004-1241-4

National Institutes of Health Office of Science Policy. (2012, March). *United States government policy for oversight of life sciences dual use research of concern.* Retrieved from http://www.phe.gov/s3/dualuse/Documents/us-policy-durc-032812.pdf

Newbold, R. R. (1993). Gender-related behavior in women exposed prenatally to diethylstilbestrol. *Environmental Health Perspectives, 101,* 208–213. http://dx.doi.org/10.1289/ehp.93101208

Ngun, T. C., Ghahramani, N., Sánchez, F. J., Bocklandt, S., & Vilain, E. (2011). The genetics of sex differences in brain and behavior. *Frontiers in Neuroendocrinology, 32,* 227–246. http://dx.doi.org/10.1016/j.yfrne.2010.10.001

Okami, P., & Shackelford, T. K. (2001). Human sex differences in sexual psychology and behavior. *Annual Review of Sex Research, 12,* 186–241.

Osborne, T. (2008, August, 15). Bisexuality passed on by "hyper-heterosexuals." *New Scientist.* Retrieved from http://www.newscientist.com/article/dn14543-bisexuality-passed-on-by-hyperheterosexuals.html#.VM0YucaFHG0

Paup, D. C., Mennin, S. P., & Gorski, R. A. (1975). Androgen- and estrogen-induced copulatory behavior and inhibition of luteinizing hormone (LH) secretion in the male rat. *Hormones and Behavior, 6,* 35–46. http://dx.doi.org/10.1016/0018-506X(75)90021-5

Phoenix, C. H., Goy, R. W., Gerall, A. A., & Young, W. C. (1959). Organizing action of prenatally administered testosterone propionate on the tissues mediating mating behavior in the female guinea pig. *Endocrinology, 65,* 369–382. http://dx.doi.org/10.1210/endo-65-3-369

Pillard, R. C., Rose, R. M., & Sherwood, M. (1974). Plasma testosterone levels in homosexual men. *Archives of Sexual Behavior, 3,* 453–458. http://dx.doi.org/10.1007/BF01541165

Piskur, J., & Degelman, D. (1992). Effect of reading a summary of research about biological bases of homosexual orientation on attitudes toward homosexuals. *Psychological Reports, 71,* 1219–1225. http://dx.doi.org/10.2466/PR0.71.8.1219-1225

Pol, H. E. H., Cohen-Kettenis, P. T., Van Haren, N. E. M., Peper, J. S., Brans, R. G. H., Cahn, W., . . . Kahn, R. S. (2006). Changing your sex changes your brain: Influences of testosterone and estrogen on adult human brain structure. *European Journal of Endocrinology, 155*(Suppl. 1), S107–S114. http://dx.doi.org/10.1530/eje.1.02248

Ponseti, J., Siebner, H. R., Klöppel, S., Wolff, S., Granert, O., Jansen, O., . . . Bosinski, H. A. (2007). Homosexual women have less grey matter in perirhinal cortex than heterosexual women. *PLoS ONE, 2,* e762.

Quadagno, D. M., Shryne, J., Anderson, C., & Gorski, R. A. (1972). Influence of gonadal hormones on social, sexual, emergence, and open field behaviour in the rat (*Rattus norvegicus*). *Animal Behaviour, 20,* 732–740. http://dx.doi.org/10.1016/S0003-3472(72)80145-3

Rametti, G., Carrillo, B., Gómez-Gil, E., Junque, C., Segovia, S., Gomez, Á., & Guillamon, A. (2011). White matter microstructure in female to male transsexuals before cross-sex hormonal treatment. A diffusion tensor imaging study. *Journal of Psychiatric Research, 45*(2), 199–204. http://dx.doi.org/10.1016/j.jpsychires.2010.05.006

Rametti, G., Carrillo, B., Gómez-Gil, E., Junque, C., Zubiarre-Elorza, L., Segovia, S., . . . Guillamon, A. (2011). The microstructure of white matter in male to female transsexuals before cross-sex hormonal treatment. A DTI study. *Journal of Psychiatric Research, 45,* 949–954. http://dx.doi.org/10.1016/j.jpsychires.2010.11.007

Reinisch, J. M., Ziemba-Davis, M., & Sanders, S. A. (1991). Hormonal contributions to sexually dimorphic behavioral development in humans. *Psychoneuroendocrinology, 16,* 213–278. http://dx.doi.org/10.1016/0306-4530(91)90080-D

Rice, G., Anderson, C., Risch, N., & Ebers, G. (1999). Male homosexuality: Absence of linkage to microsatellite markers at Xq28. *Science, 284,* 665–667. http://dx.doi.org/10.1126/science.284.5414.665

Sánchez, F. J., Bocklandt, S., & Vilain, E. (2009). The biology of sexual orientation and gender identity. In D. W. Pfaff, A. P. Arnold, A. M. Etgen, S. E. Fahrbach, & R. T. Rubin (Eds.), *Hormones, brain and behavior* (2nd ed., Vol. 4, pp. 1911–1929). San Diego, CA: Academic Press.

Sanders, A. R., Martin, E. R., Beecham, G. W., Guo, S., Dawood, K., Rieger, G., . . . Bailey, J. M. (2015). Genome-wide scan demonstrates significant linkage for male sexual orientation. *Psychological Medicine, 45,* 1379–1388. http://dx.doi.org/10.1017/S0033291714002451

Savic, I., & Arver, S. (2011). Sex dimorphism of the brain in male-to-female transsexuals. *Cerebral Cortex, 21,* 2525–2533. http://dx.doi.org/10.1093/cercor/bhr032

Savic, I., Berglund, H., & Lindström, P. (2005). Brain response to putative pheromones in homosexual men. *Proceedings of the National Academy of Sciences of the United States of America, 102,* 7356–7361. http://dx.doi.org/10.1073/pnas.0407998102

Savic, I., & Lindström, P. (2008). PET and MRI show differences in cerebral asymmetry and functional connectivity between homo- and heterosexual subjects. *Proceedings of the National Academy of Sciences of the United States of America, 105,* 9403–9408. http://dx.doi.org/10.1073/pnas.0801566105

Schmitt, D. P., Shackelford, T. K., & Buss, D. M. (2001). Are men really more "oriented" toward short-term mating than women? A critical review of theory and research. *Psychology, Evolution & Gender, 3,* 211–239. http://dx.doi.org/10.1080/14616660110119331

Schneider, H. J., Pickel, J., & Stalla, G. K. (2006). Typical female 2nd–4th finger length (2D:4D) ratios in male-to-female transsexuals-possible implications for prenatal androgen exposure. *Psychoneuroendocrinology, 31*, 265–269. http://dx.doi.org/10.1016/j.psyneuen.2005.07.005

Sheldon, J. P., Pfeffer, C. A., Jayaratne, T. E., Feldbaum, M., & Petty, E. M. (2007). Beliefs about the etiology of homosexuality and about the ramifications of discovering its possible genetic origin. *Journal of Homosexuality, 52*, 111–150. http://dx.doi.org/10.1300/J082v52n03_06

Swaab, D. F., & Hofman, M. A. (1990). An enlarged suprachiasmatic nucleus in homosexual men. *Brain Research, 537*, 141–148. http://dx.doi.org/10.1016/0006-8993(90)90350-K

Tammen, S. A., Frisco, S., & Choi, S. W. (2013). Epigenetics: The link between nature and nurture. *Molecular Aspects of Medicine, 34*, 753–764. http://dx.doi.org/10.1016/j.mam.2012.07.018

Teki, S., Kumar, S., von Kriegstein, K., Stewart, L., Lyness, C. R., Moore, B. C. J., . . . Griffiths, T. D. (2012). Navigating the auditory scene: An expert role for the hippocampus. *The Journal of Neuroscience, 32*, 12251–12257. http://dx.doi.org/10.1523/JNEUROSCI.0082-12.2012

Titus-Ernstoff, L., Perez, K., Hatch, E. E., Troisi, R., Palmer, J. R., Hartge, P., . . . Hoover, R. (2003). Psychosexual characteristics of men and women exposed prenatally to diethylstilbestrol. *Epidemiology, 14*, 155–160. http://dx.doi.org/10.1097/01.EDE.0000039059.38824.B2

Tolman, D. L., & Diamond, L. M. (2001). Desegregating sexuality research: Cultural and biological perspectives on gender and desire. *Annual Review of Sex Research, 12*, 33–74.

van Anders, S. M. (2013). Beyond masculinity: Testosterone, gender/sex, and human social behavior in a comparative context. *Frontiers in Neuroendocrinology, 34*, 198–210. http://dx.doi.org/10.1016/j.yfrne.2013.07.001

Vul, E., Harris, C., Winkielman, P., & Pashler, H. (2009). Puzzlingly high correlations in fMRI studies of emotion, personality, and social cognition. *Perspectives on Psychological Science, 4*, 274–290. http://dx.doi.org/10.1111/j.1745-6924.2009.01125.x

Wallien, M. S., Zucker, K. J., Steensma, T. D., & Cohen-Kettenis, P. T. (2008). 2D:4D finger-length ratios in children and adults with gender identity disorder. *Hormones and Behavior, 54*, 450–454. http://dx.doi.org/10.1016/j.yhbeh.2008.05.002

Williams, T. J., Pepitone, M. E., Christensen, S. E., Cooke, B. M., Huberman, A. D., Breedlove, N. J., . . . Breedlove, S. M. (2000, March 30). Finger-length ratios and sexual orientation. *Nature, 404*, 455–456. http://dx.doi.org/10.1038/35006555

Wolpe, P. R. (2006). Reasons scientists avoid thinking about ethics. *Cell, 125*, 1023–1025. http://dx.doi.org/10.1016/j.cell.2006.06.001

Wood, P. B., & Bartkowski, J. P. (2004). Attribution style and public policy attitudes toward gay rights. *Social Science Quarterly, 85*, 58–74. http://dx.doi.org/10.1111/j.0038-4941.2004.08501005.x

Yalom, I. D., Green, R., & Fisk, N. (1973). Prenatal exposure to female hormones. Effect on psychosexual development in boys. *Archives of General Psychiatry, 28*, 554–561. http://dx.doi.org/10.1001/archpsyc.1973.01750340080013

Zhou, J. N., Hofman, M. A., Gooren, L. J. G., & Swaab, D. F. (1995). A sex difference in the human brain and its relation to transsexuality. *Nature, 378*, 68–70. http://dx.doi.org/10.1038/378068a0

Zucker, K. J., Bradley, S. J., Oliver, G., Blake, J., Fleming, S., & Hood, J. (1996). Psychosexual development of women with congenital adrenal hyperplasia. *Hormones and Behavior, 30*, 300–318. http://dx.doi.org/10.1006/hbeh.1996.0038

3

CONTEXT, STIGMA, AND THERAPEUTIC PRACTICE

GLENDA M. RUSSELL AND CHRISTOPHER G. HAWKEY

Recent years have seen some dramatic and far-reaching changes in how sexual minority and gender-expansive (SMGE)[1] people are seen and treated and how their issues are addressed in the United States—indeed, in much of the Western world. The speed of this change prompted one pollster to opine, "Attitudes on this issue are changing faster than on any other issue in the history of public-opinion polling" (quoted in Clift, 2012). These changes

---

[1]Granting the lack of an ideal term inclusive of all members of the population of interest (especially a term that works well across geographical and temporal contexts), we have chosen to use the umbrella term *sexual minority and gender expansive (SMGE) persons*. The term *sexual minority* adequately encompasses people who express nonheterosexual orientations in their behavior and/or identity and/or social affiliations. We rejected *gender non-normative* because that term suggests that we actually know what gender normativity means and, furthermore, because the term privileges traditional gender norms as the standard against which all gender identities and expressions are measured. We prefer instead *gender expansive* to refer to individuals who, intentionally or not, experience and express themselves in ways that stand outside the framework of widely expected norms and roles. In general, in this chapter, we use SMGE to refer to the broad focus of our remarks. However, at times, we use other terms to refer to subgroups of larger SMGE communities, including when specific subgroups have been the subject of relevant research.

http://dx.doi.org/10.1037/15959-004
Handbook of Sexual Orientation and Gender Diversity in Counseling and Psychotherapy, K. A. DeBord, A. R. Fischer, K. J. Bieschke, and R. M. Perez (Editors)

influence the everyday lives of SMGE people, and as the lives of this far-flung and diverse population change, so do the stressors they encounter in the world, the complexity and degree of clarity associated with these stress-ors, the internal strengths that SMGE people have to draw upon, and the external resources they use. In short, context matters enormously in the lives of SMGE people and in their functioning in the world. In this chapter, we examine recent changes in the lives of SMGE people by considering changes in public policy and public attitudes that have affected—and continue to affect—SMGE lives. We then explore how these changes might affect the considerations that therapists and counselors should have in mind as they work with SMGE clients in therapy.

THE IMPORTANCE OF CONTEXT IN WORK WITH SMGE CLIENTS

Traditional discussions of clinical work with SMGE people have often relied on essentialist views of this population (Bohan & Russell, 1999). This approach assumes that all SMGE people experience more or less identical developmental trajectories in which intrinsic sexual orientation and gender identity unfold over time and move toward a uniform end point where indi-viduals fully integrate their sexual orientation and gender identity as core elements of their sense of self (e.g., Cass, 1979; Coleman, 1978; Troiden, 1989). Consistent with this essentialist view is the assumption that virtually all SMGE individuals encounter roughly the same sorts of stressors related to the emergence of their stigmatized identities.

However, more recent critiques of these essentialist developmental models, as well as research in related areas, have suggested that there is con-siderable variability in how minority orientations and gender identities are established and manifested over time. These critiques have addressed many factors that influence the development of nonheterosexual and noncisgender identities. For example, although Cass's (1979) early work is perhaps most frequently cited as the basis of the developmental trajectory described above, her later work drew from Berger and Luckmann (1975), Gergen (1984), and Shweder (1992) in emphasizing "reciprocal interaction," which she described as "an ongoing relationship between individuals and their sociocultural envi-ronments in which each *simultaneously* influences and is influenced by the other" (Cass, 1999, p. 115; italics in original).

Another body of work that has called into question the assumption of a universal end point in the emergence of sexual orientation and gender iden-tity is research demonstrating that many people who adopt nonheterosexual and noncisgender positions are increasingly drawing on novel and varied ideas regarding the meaning of those identities as well as the trajectories that lead to and the social significance of those identities (e.g., American Psychological Association [APA], 2008; Diamond, 2004, 2006). Another challenge to the notion of a fixed developmental progression comes from research on the consequences of anti–lesbian, gay, bisexual, and transgender (LGBT) political actions, which suggests that SMGE individuals who have apparently integrated their identities in terms of sexual orientation and gender identity may experience a disruption to that integration when faced with increased anti-LGBT rhetoric and negative electoral results (Russell, 2000, 2012; Russell & Richards, 2003).

Yet another critique has been put forth by researchers and clinicians who have elucidated the complex and unique experiences of SMGE people who occupy specific types of social positions, especially positions characterized by intersections between or among identities (Enns & Fischer, 2012). This work has highlighted especially those situations wherein people of color who are SMGE have the dual challenge of navigating sometimes-conflicting norms and expectations associated with membership in their various stigmatized groups (Chan, 1992; Manalansan, 1996; Rust, 1996). In their interactions with mainstream society, the individuals who occupy such positions have to deal with the stressors associated with two (or more) different types of stigma. Additionally, they often encounter anti-SMGE stigma within their racial–ethnic identity group and prejudice toward that group within the SMGE community (Díaz, Ayala, Bein, Henne, & Marin, 2001; Greene, 2007; Harper & Schneider, 2003). In such cases, people may call upon the skills learned in relation to one kind of stigma to manage another (Cochran, Mays, Alegria, Ortega, & Takeuchi, 2007).

Similar observations have been made with regard to identity development and the experience of stigma among people who are members of the SMGE community and who are also members of particular religious groups (APA, 2009b; Buchanan, Dzelme, Harris, & Hecker, 2001; Hammack & Cohler, 2011; Harris, Cook, & Kashubeck-West, 2008; Mann, 2013), belong to particular age groups and cohorts (D'Augelli, 2006; de Vries, 2014; Kimmel, 2003; Morgan, 2013; Russell & Bohan, 2005), are dealing with mental or physical disabilities (Löfgren-Mårtenson, 2009; Saad, 1997), and come from economically disadvantaged circumstances (APA, 2009a; Badgett, 2003). Additionally, the experience of SMGE identities and the stigma associated with those identities differ according to geographic region (Hatzenbuehler, 2010; Kosciw, Greytak, & Diaz, 2009) and rural versus urban residence (Hatzenbuehler, 2010; Oswald & Masciadrelli, 2008; Simpson, 2012; Smith & Mancoske, 1997; Stein, 2001).

STIGMA AND THE IMPACT OF SOCIAL
AND POLITICAL FORCES

Collectively, these challenges call into question traditional, essentialist notions of the uniformity of developmental pathways and experiences of SMGE people. They point instead to the influential role of context in shaping both the emergence of SMGE identities and the stigma associated with those identities. In light of this conclusion, research on stigma in general (Frost, 2011; Heatherton, Kleck, Hebl, & Hull, 2000; Levin & van Laar, 2006) and on stigma related to SMGE people in particular (Herek, 1998, 2007; Meyer, 2013) offers a useful framework for understanding the role of the contexts in which SMGE people live and work. This model can identify common threads that bind all SMGE people while also having room to encompass the striking variability among members of this population.

Goffman (1963), the sociologist who introduced the formal study of stigma, defined *stigma* as "an attribute that makes [a person] different from others in the category of persons available for him [sic] to be, and of a less desirable kind—in the extreme, a person who is quite thoroughly bad, or dangerous, or weak" (p. 3). Drawing from Frost's (2011) review, subsequent work in this area has elucidated a number of domains relevant to the broad topic of stigma, arenas ranging from structural inequalities through stereotypes and prejudice to discrimination. These dimensions, on which we elaborate later in this chapter, not only suggest the major areas of research productivity in stigma but also highlight the areas that clinicians would do well to consider when working with clients from stigmatized communities, including SMGE individuals. Attention to the role of stigma allows clinicians to keep in mind that all SMGE people have to contend with a particular kind of stigma, namely, the stigma associated with variations in the experience and expression of sex and gender and with (stigmatized) forms of their manifestation in identity and romantic relationships. The forms that such stigma takes are often referred to in the literature as homophobia, heterosexism, biphobia, transphobia, genderism, cisgenderism, and sexual prejudice.

In addition to allowing us to recognize the commonalities associated with the range of SMGE identities, the stigma model can also accommodate the enormous variety of forms in which stigma is manifested across individuals, locations, social positions, and historical time. As an example, this model allows us to identify and track both commonalities and differences between two people: a young adult African American cisgender, same-gender-loving, able-bodied man living in New York City who is in the professional class and well integrated into both the gay and African American communities and a White, late-middle-aged trans woman who lives with her female partner in the rural South, works at a minimum wage job, and is isolated from other SMGE people.

TEMPORAL CHANGES IN STIGMA RELATED TO SMGE PEOPLE

Here, we examine stigma as it relates to the lives of SMGE people and consider how it has changed over time. We start with some overarching descriptions and then move to more specific results of research on attitudes toward SMGE people and issues and findings from relevant polls. We can take the Stonewall uprising as a starting point. At this 1969 event, patrons at a New York City bar that catered to SMGE people resisted arrest, launching a several-day rebellion against anti-SMGE police harassment. The event is often seen as the beginning of the contemporary movement on behalf of equal rights for SMGE people. It is a reasonable place for us to begin because, although there was significant activity related to SMGE identity and rights prior to Stonewall (Katz, 1978; Miller, 1995), actual research and polling regarding SMGE identities and associated stigmas generally began after this. During the time since Stonewall, we have witnessed enormous change in all arenas, from micro to macro (Bronfenbrenner, 1979) and at personal, interpersonal, institutional, and cultural levels of analysis (Batts, 2002). Indeed, it is difficult to identify any domain in which some degree of change in the experiences of and attitudes toward SMGE individuals has not occurred.

Unlike many civil rights movements, which unfolded over many decades or even centuries, the struggle for equal rights for SMGE people has unfolded quite rapidly. Despite its youth, the movement for equality of SMGE people has catalyzed extraordinary changes in social attitudes and public policy in a relatively brief period. However, this movement for equality has at the same time evoked a great deal of highly publicized and well-financed opposition, much of which is very hostile and jeopardizes the safety and well-being of SMGE people throughout the country (Ball, 2010; Bull & Gallagher, 1996; Dugan, 2005; Fingerhut, Riggle, & Rostosky, 2011; Herman, 1997; Keen & Goldberg, 2001; Moats, 2004; Witt & McCorkle, 1997). It is in this overarchingly volatile landscape, which varies greatly from place to place and over time, that clinicians work with SMGE clients.

Quantitative and qualitative research—as well as everyday experience—strongly supports the notion that public attitudes and policies dramatically influence the well-being of marginalized populations (e.g., Hatzenbuehler, 2014; Riggle, Rostosky, & Horne, 2010). Thus, clinicians are well advised to maintain a working knowledge of the social factors that impact clients' lives. For groups of people currently engaged in a struggle for equal rights, this typically means analyzing multiple levels of social context, ranging from federal policies on the broadest end to implicit attitudes held by individuals in the client's social and occupational networks on the specific end. Keeping track of these multiple levels is not easy—not for counselors and therapists and not for their SMGE clients. Changes have been coming rapidly and through many avenues, including municipal, legislative, judicial, and corporate decisions. (A list of helpful Internet resources that track such changes on a regular basis is provided in Exhibit 3.1.)

Policy changes at these levels have varied widely and remain incomplete. For example, according to a 2013 Pew Research survey, the majority of SMGE people view equal employment rights as their "top priority" policy issue. The issue was first introduced in the early 1970s, but the proposed federal legislation that would provide such rights, the Employment Non-Discrimination Act of 2013, has eluded passage. Fewer than 20 states provide state-level nondiscrimination protection for SMGE people as of this writing, leaving more than one half of SMGE people without employment protection. A second "top priority" issue identified in the same Pew Research survey was marriage equality. In 2015, after that survey was published, the U.S. Supreme Court ruled that marriage was a constitutional right that could not be denied to same-sex couples, effectively legalizing same-sex marriage. Another important issue identified in the 2013 Pew

EXHIBIT 3.1
Internet Resources on the Changing Context for Sexual Minority
and Gender Expansive People

American Psychological Association Public Interest Directorate, Office of Lesbian, Gay, Bisexual, and Transgender Concerns: http://www.apa.org/pi/lgbt/index.aspx

Gallup Research: http://www.gallup.com

Website of Dr. Gregory Herek, a leading social psychologist interested in sexual prejudice: http://www.LGBpsychology.org

Human Rights Campaign, a civil rights organization working to achieve equality for lesbian, gay, bisexual and transgender Americans: http://www.HRC.org

Lambda Legal, a legal organization working for the civil rights of lesbians, gay men, and people with HIV/AIDS: http://www.lambdalegal.org

LGBT Movement Advancement Project, an independent nonprofit organization focusing on the effect of public policy on lesbian, gay, bisexual, and transgender people: http://www.LGBTmap.org

National Center for Transgender Equality, a social justice organization dedicated to advancing the equality of transgender people: http://transequality.org/

National LGBTQ Task Force, a national organization dedicated to building the grassroots power of the lesbian, gay, bisexual, transgender, and queer community: http://www.thetaskforce.org

Pew Research Center: http://www.pewsocialtrends.org

The Williams Institute, a think tank at UCLA Law dedicated to research on sexual orientation and gender identity law and public policy: http://williamsinstitute.law.ucla.edu

survey was adoption protection. According to Lambda Legal (2013), there are about 250,000 children in the United States who are being raised by same-sex couples. However, no federal adoption or fostering protections exist for families headed by same-sex couples. Thus, taken collectively, the status of rights for SMGE people in a range of significant life areas suggests an ever-changing and widely variable patchwork of laws, policies, and structural inequalities—to use Frost's (2011) term—that fosters uncertainty, limits practical planning, evokes worry, and reminds individuals in the affected group that they are still regarded as second-class members of society.

Beyond these concrete policies, attitudes are also in flux, albeit to differing degrees depending on a range of demographic and geographic variables (Horn, 2013). Recent polls have indicated majority voter support in general acceptance of gay and lesbian people (e.g., Greenberg Quinlan Rosner Research, 2014), although research specifically about bisexual and transgender communities is far more sparse (Horn, 2013). Polls also suggest a marked increase in people's contact with SMGE individuals. In 1985, only about 25% of Americans reported knowing a colleague, close friend, or relative who was gay or lesbian; by contrast, recent data indicate a reversal in the percentage, with 75% of Americans reporting that they know someone who is lesbian or gay (Greenberg Quinlan Rosner Research, 2014). Polls also indicate that the majority of Americans support marriage equality; polling surpassed the 50% mark in 2013 (Pew Research Center, 2015). However, that support was somewhat diminished after the U.S. Supreme Court legalized same-sex marriage in June 2015 (Associated Press, 2015).

Predecision polling data about the predicted impact of marriage equality were especially striking: "There will be less prejudice against gay people" (78%), "It will be easier to grow up gay" (76%), "Kids with gay parents will have more legal and social protections" (80%), and "Kids with gay parents will be less likely to be bullied" (60%; Greenberg Quinlan Rosner Research, 2014). Obviously, the respondents to the poll had no greater ability to predict the future than anyone else. Nonetheless, the high percentages of their responses suggest a strong and widespread belief that SMGE people in this country will continue to experience positive changes in a variety of spheres.

The remarkable changes that have occurred in recent years with regard to attitudes and practices related to SMGE people suggest not only how much change has occurred to date but also how much has not occurred. Even though same-sex marriage is now legal, the American electorate remains quite divided on the issue (Associated Press, 2015). There is still no federal employment protection for SMGE people anywhere in the country, and 52% of SMGE individuals are not protected from workplace discrimination even at the state level (Pew Research, 2013). The situation is even worse for transgender people than it is for lesbian, gay, and bisexual people. As examples, markedly fewer states and municipalities include protections based on gender identity and expression than based on sexual orientation, and the military is just beginning to consider open service by transgender persons, whereas such service is already available to lesbian, gay, and bisexual individuals. Furthermore, SMGE individuals can lose the limited rights they have simply by crossing state lines. In addition, for every index of positive change that has recently moved to a majority percentage, typically just under half of the population continue to hold SMGE people in lower and even disdainful regard.

There are many ways to frame the changes that have taken place over time with respect to the contexts in which SMGE people live and the effects of those changes on individuals' well-being. One way to conceptualize this change is to view it in terms of a movement from old-fashioned (overt, pervasive) to modern (subtler) forms of prejudice and oppression. Taken as a whole, attitudes and policies in the United States are currently characterized by less pervasive and less virulent forms of stigmatization than in the past (Andersen & Fetner, 2008; Hammack & Cohler, 2011). Additionally, positive resources for SMGE people have burgeoned in recent decades and are increasingly available to SMGE individuals in a range of settings. These include supportive institutional policies and practices, informal and formal community resources, increased range and depth of Internet resources, and the growing presence and visibility of heterosexual allies (Russell, 2011).

Despite this general trend toward greater acceptance and support, experiences with stigma and the availability of helpful resources both vary dramatically with geographic and social location. Two *New York Times* columnists observed,

> growing worry within the [LGBT] movement that recent legal and political successes have formed two quickly diverging worlds for lesbian, gay, bisexual or transgender Americans: one centered on the coasts and major cities, and another stretching across the South and up through the Rocky Mountains, in states where gays [sic] enjoy virtually no legal protections against discrimination. (Confessore & Peters, 2014)

To complicate matters even more, these differences are not consistently predictable. Although these variations can be understood as existing on a continuum from old-fashioned to modern stigmatization, in fact, old-fashioned homophobia (or biphobia, cisgenderism, etc.) can erupt under virtually any circumstances, even in an environment predominantly characterized by modern rather than old-fashioned prejudice and discrimination. Conversely, SMGE people living under conditions of generally high levels of old-fashioned stigma may encounter unexpected support and affirmation (Russell, 2011).

SMGE people are caught in a vortex of constant change, civil ambiguities, and attitudinal shifts. Changes of these sorts carry significant stress even as they appear to suggest movement in desirable directions. SMGE individuals frequently take these stressors for granted without regard to the toll the associated stress takes on their coping resources (Russell, 2000). It is incumbent upon counselors and therapists to assess the presence and impact of these stressors and to work with clients to identify them and develop appropriate coping strategies for ameliorating their impact.

IMPLICATIONS OF STIGMA FOR COUNSELING AND THERAPY WITH SMGE PEOPLE

We use Frost's (2011) model as a tool for framing our understanding of how stigma affects SMGE people and what counselors can do to assess and address these effects. Central to our analysis are two basic tenets of therapy with SMGE clients that are informed by research on stigma (Russell, 2012). The first tenet involves the importance of the client's appraisal of the stigma and its implications, a construct roughly equivalent to Frost's meaning-making strategies in response to stigma. We argue that what we describe as a *movement perspective* (Russell, 2000, 2012; Russell & Richards, 2003) represents a valuable key to a client's appraisal of stigma. The second tenet of a stigma-informed approach to therapy, which parallels Frost's coping and support strategies, entails the use of positive coping strategies that tend to be relevant for most people (Moos & Holahan, 2003). Although the latter tenet is familiar to most clinicians, the movement perspective requires some exposition. We describe this perspective in some detail next.

The Movement Perspective

The movement perspective represents a framework for understanding specific, time-limited events as elements of broad, long-term phenomena. Thus, it encourages those who are targeted by sociopolitically based forms of bias to see their experience in a broader context that stretches across social change movements and across time. In this framing, individual experiences are the consequence not of personal qualities but of sociopolitical acts that are indifferent to them as individuals. This allows clients to gain some cognitive distance from these acts—be they major anti-SMGE political campaigns or relatively minor interpersonal slights—by seeing them not as personal attacks but as manifestations of this broader sociopolitical context. This approach implicates SMGE persons not as flawed individuals but as members of a group that is unfairly targeted by an unjust social milieu. They can recognize themselves as individuals who have much in common not only with other SMGE people but also with members of other stigmatized groups in society and therefore as people who have much to gain from (and give to) collective work with other SMGE people and other justice-seeking people who fight against oppression in all its forms (Russell & Richards, 2003).

This perspective also has the advantage of framing political actions as part of a larger struggle for human rights. From this perspective, political victories are celebrated and political losses mourned, but both are seen as inevitable parts of how social change happens. In fact, losses are recognized as often serving very positive ends. They have the power to galvanize groups and inspire individuals, thus furthering movements toward positive social change. Clearly, this expansive vision grants clients a much more positive and empowering understanding of their experiences of stigma than they might construct if they frame that experience as evidence of their own inferiority or their own "overreaction." This sociopolitical movement perspective offers SMGE clients a tool for responding actively to stigmatizing actions of many types. It can be communicated to the client in a variety of ways, and it can be introduced into therapy in a manner that is consistent with client experiences and with virtually any theoretical and practice stance. It should be noted that although this perspective is rooted in a sociopolitical analysis, discussions with clients that introduce and explore the perspective do not necessarily rely on overtly political language. Therapists and counselors can talk of "bias" and "attitudes" and of "the LGBTQ [lesbian, gay, bisexual, transgender, and queer or questioning] community" as linguistic devices and generally avoid the language of politics. The importance of the approach is in setting up a cognitive appraisal that emphasizes a movement perspective, not (necessarily) in speaking in explicitly political terms.

Frost's Model of Stigma

Frost's (2011) process model of social stigma and its consequences begins from the presence of stigma that is rooted in structural inequalities and perpetrated through stereotypes, prejudice, and discrimination. From this grounding, the model addresses three overarching areas of significant concern: experiences of stigma, responses to stigma, and outcomes of stigma (see Figure 3.1). We explore these in some detail and then examine their implications for psychotherapy.

Each of the dimensions within this model represents an aspect of the potential experiences of SMGE people that derives from their stigmatized social positions and identities. As such, these dimensions provide a useful framework for the clinician who is assessing an SMGE client as a means of gaining a thorough and clear understanding of that client. Any of these dimensions may be relevant to a particular client at a particular time, and any of them may not. Some of the dimensions may be relevant at one time but not at

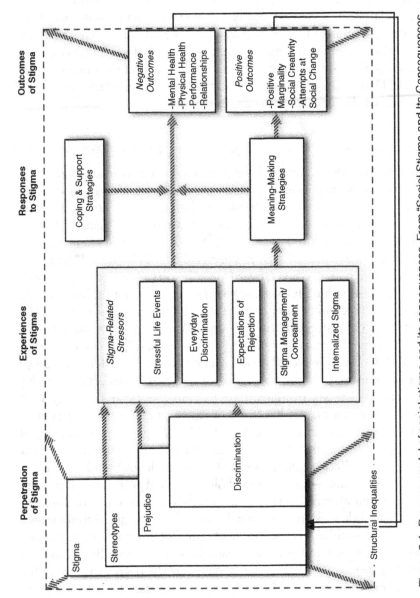

Figure 3.1. Process model of social stigma and its consequences. From "Social Stigma and Its Consequences for the Socially Stigmatized," by D. M. Frost, 2011, *Social and Personality Psychology Compass, 5,* p. 833. Copyright 2011 by D. M. Frost. Reprinted with permission.

another. Moreover, any of the dimensions may be relevant to a particular client at a particular time without that client's being aware of it. Clinicians can use these dimensions as a kind of checklist—or, better put, as "sensitizing devices" (Gergen, 1973, p. 317)—to help them to systematically attend to stigma-related processes that may be having an impact in terms of clients' presentation, their mix of stressors and sources of resilience, their social supports, and their ability to use therapy well. In the remainder of this chapter, we describe and comment on the clinical implications of the dimensions in Frost's (2011) model, paying particular attention to several of the dimensions that are likely to be especially relevant to therapy.

Stigma-Related Experiences: Stressful Life Events and Everyday Discrimination

Frost (2011) first addressed the experiences of stigma-related stress that SMGE people may encounter. In considering this element of the model, it is helpful to recognize the profound impact of changing social contexts on the stigma-related experiences of SMGE people. The nature of stigma for SMGE individuals was once relatively homogeneous. That is, most stigmatization targeting this group reflected what has been called "old fashioned" prejudice and discrimination. It was direct, overtly hostile, pervasive, and unrestrained by social norms—because it expressed dominant social norms. Many of the experiences included in Frost's notion of stressful life events are captured by the concept of old-fashioned prejudice and discrimination. Now, however, many SMGE people are as likely to encounter "modern" versions of stigma (Batts, 2002; Cowan, Heiple, Marquez, Khatchadourian, & McNevin, 2005; Eldridge & Johnson, 2011), which correspond to Frost's concept of everyday discrimination. This type of stigmatization is more subtle and is likely to be expressed in implicit rather than explicit ways. One of its forms has been referred to as *microaggressions* (Nadal et al., 2011), a term that encompasses both the apparent magnitude of these acts relative to overt bias and their damaging quality. Because many people (clients included) tend to think of prejudice and discrimination in terms of old-fashioned presentations that are overt, hostile, humiliating, and even violent, they may minimize or disregard the impact of subtle versions of stigma. Indeed, they may question their own judgment about such an experience, wondering whether it was, in fact, an expression of bias or whether they are simply over-reacting. By minimizing or dismissing these experiences, clients may deny the degree to which they rely on and expend psychic and social resources to adapt to or fight against these sorts of everyday expressions of bias and acts of discrimination (Charles, Piazza, Mogle, Sliwinski, & Almeida, 2013). Indeed, clients may be mystified by the effects of these experiences on their mood and other aspects of mental health and well-being (e.g., Russell, 2012). Lacking a framework for understanding these events, clients may not be as adept as they otherwise could be at generating intentional responses to these impacts. Over time, this situation can lead to increased symptoms, including a sense of powerlessness and lack of self-efficacy that Ginges and Atran (2008) called the *inertia effect*.

The combination of the dramatic heterogeneity of these experiences and the variability in their severity suggests that SMGE people would benefit from two sets of skills: skills for recognizing and describing their encounters with stigma and skills for responding to expressions of bias in ways that promote health and well-being. Both of these skills derive from the aforementioned movement perspective. The ability to discern and describe experiences with modern forms of prejudice and discrimination constitutes an important basis for managing the stress that such events engender. Stress of any type requires adaptation, and the ability to identify a stressor and pinpoint its source facilitates more appropriate styles of adaptation. In the absence of an accurate label, clients are in danger of regarding the impact of stigma as a purely personal problem, which carries the potential not only for mystification but also for a sense of isolation and self-blame. By contrast, being able to identify the problem as a reflection of stigma effectively defines the problem as residing in the social system, that is, as a social and political phenomenon. This analysis is more accurate and thereby facilitates demystification. Additionally, this framework recognizes that the problem is a collective one, which, in turn opens the possibility of a collective solution (Russell & Bohan, 2007). Such an understanding serves to reduce the sense of isolation and also points to the value of external as well as internal resources for ameliorating the consequences.

Expectation of Rejection

One dimension of stigma-related experiences highlighted by Frost (2011) is the expectation of rejection, a topic that has received a good deal of attention in the literature on minority stress (e.g., Meyer, 2013). *Rejection* refers to a process or event in which a stigmatized individual is made to feel different, set aside, or excluded. Rejection can occur at psychological as well as at social and other practical levels. The literature on social rejection suggests that being excluded can engender a variety of negative consequences (e.g., Williams, Forgas, & von Hippel, 2013). People in stigmatized groups may be called upon to expend energy in coping with rejection. They also expend energy in worrying about and trying to avoid rejection and in preparing themselves for the possibility of being rejected despite their efforts. This expenditure of energy might occur at a psychological level only, in anxiety about the possibility of rejection and trying to figure out how to avoid it. Additionally, energy may also be expended at a practical level; this can occur in virtually any context—in the family, in broader social contexts, in employment contexts, in nonwork institutional contexts, and so on. It may entail efforts to conceal one's status from others and a tendency to avoid occupational and social contexts where one's identity might be revealed (Frable, Platt, & Hoey, 1998; Frable, Wortman, & Joseph, 1997). It may also involve ingratiating oneself to others and working diligently to be above reproach in an effort to disguise or counterbalance the stigmatized identity (Russell, Bohan, & Lilly, 2000).

Often, SMGE people's efforts to avoid rejection have continued for so long that aspects of the pattern have become habitual, automatic, and unrecognized (Bargh & Chartrand, 1999; Bargh, Chen, & Burrows, 1996). In this case, individuals may be actively trying to avoid rejection without recognizing that they are doing so. This process is further complicated by the rapid change in attitudes about SMGE people. When dealing with persons and situations where rejection might be an issue, one size does not fit all; the same strategy may be necessary and effective in one situation and useless or unnecessary in another. Yet, the requirement to change approaches from one situation to the next requires a good deal of ongoing assessment and cognitive flexibility. Given the limited potential for always getting it "right," the danger of energy depletion and self-blame is high (Downie, Mageau, Koestner, & Liodden, 2006).

The issue of energy depletion carries significant therapeutic implications. It is important that the therapist or counselor encourage clients' awareness of their concerns about rejection and foster a realistic assessment of both the psychological and practical effects that rejection might bring, because both are important. Appropriate questions for the therapy to explore might include the issue of what is the root cause of rejection and what is the cost to the client of avoiding rejection. The discussion should also address the question of what might help the client to defend against rejection, with appropriate areas for exploration including social support and the movement perspective discussed earlier.

Stigma Management and Concealment

Another type of stigma-related experience mentioned by Frost (2011) is the need for stigma management. Goffman (1963) suggested two broad types of identity that may be associated with stigma. A *discredited* (and stigmatized) identity is one in which the stigmatizing condition is readily observable. Certain racial identities are often given as an example of discredited identities. A *discreditable* (and stigmatized) identity, on the other hand, is one in which the stigmatized characteristic is not readily observable and can thus often be concealed. A nonheterosexual orientation is frequently offered as an example of a discreditable (concealable) identity, although this is not the case for all nonheterosexual people. In the case of a discredited identity, individuals cannot hide their identity, which may expose them to danger in situations where their identity is highly stigmatized. This may apply to some lesbian, gay, and bisexual (LGB) individuals, although sexual orientation is often concealable. Transgender people, especially while they are transitioning and especially some male-to-female individuals, are more likely to encounter the dangers associated with a discredited identity.

When a discreditable identity can be concealed, the individual may make choices about when to disclose the stigmatizing characteristic (Downie et al., 2006). However, although this identity appears preferable in terms of day-to-day physical and psychological safety, it engenders a new task: actively managing information about the discreditable identity. This means making frequent decisions, often very quickly, about whether to disclose the stigmatized identity in a particular situation. Furthermore, individuals have to make this decision while also considering whether disclosing in a given situation risks information diffusion that may place them at risk in other situations. A great deal of psychic energy can be spent in the act of concealment, in decisions about whether to disclose, and in the anxiety over whether disclosure may result in loss of control over this personal information. Given these difficulties, it is easy to understand why people may choose not to disclose, even when the immediate circumstances may seem safe. Yet, withholding information about one's SMGE identity creates fertile ground for the emergence of internalized stigma (Herek & Garnets, 2007). It is easy to frame nondisclosure as a secret and to associate this secret with the idea that something is wrong or bad. The fear of self-disclosure can also thwart the individual's efforts to enter into community with other people in the stigmatized group, which can be important to positive coping (Russell, 2000; Russell & Richards, 2003).

The question of disclosure is an important one in therapy, as SMGE people regularly struggle with questions of stigma management, whether in terms of staying safe with a discredited identity (Hendricks & Testa, 2012) or in terms of information management in the case of a discreditable identity. One useful strategy is to assume a position of "rational outness" (Bradford & Ryan, 1987), which entails being as "out" as one can safely be. It is important for therapists to recognize that what constitutes rational outness may be influenced by race–ethnicity, class, ability status, religion, and other factors. Following this strategy requires a careful assessment of the relative levels of safety and danger in one's environment, as well as a recognition that those may change over time and across circumstances.

This task may be made more difficult by the variability of contexts as a function of rapid social change, discussed above. It has been pointed out, for example, that court victories with regard to marriage equality leave members of same-sex couples in some states "mired in a legal paradox": They "might be free to marry but could still lose their jobs in the 29 states where it remains legal to fire employees for their sexual orientation" (Confessore & Peters, 2014). This variability likely makes it more difficult to predict the response that one might receive to self-disclosure than in earlier times when a more homogeneous response would have been expected across situations. Furthermore, as SMGE individuals move between and among different geographic locales, it may be difficult for them to keep up with the changing nature and intensity of stigma directed at their group. They may even be able to articulate that the place where they now live is more (or less) homophobic than the place where they lived before but still be unable to use that cognitive awareness to adjust the disclosure aspects of their lives accordingly. Concerns and behaviors around safety can take on an automatic quality (Bargh & Chartrand, 1999; Bargh et al., 1996) that is independent of current circumstances. For all of these reasons, clients may find it difficult to understand the relative levels of risk and danger in order to practice rational outness. Relatedly, the degree to which some of the stigma associated with SMGE people has in recent times become more subtle—that is, modern as opposed to old-fashioned heterosexism—makes it possible that the client will encounter stigma at very subtle levels. Research suggests that such encounters, though not immediately dangerous, can take a significant toll over time (Nadal et al., 2011).

One aspect of the therapy for this question entails a simple exposure paradigm, helping the SMGE client to face fears associated with increased outness in a variety of situations while attending to the realistic dangers involved. The benefits of this approach may be especially clear when working with clients who are unable to make adjustments that seem appropriate in new or changing contexts. The therapist can rely on an exposure paradigm to help clients to gradually move toward a more appropriate balance between their concerns and actions, on the one hand, and the environment, on the other. Therapy of this sort generally starts with clients' focusing on past experiences that might have suggested current fears, and these fears are then examined with an eye toward how realistic they are, what might have generated them initially, and what maintains them now. Therapy then moves to imagined disclosures of sexual orientation or gender identity in a hierarchically arranged sequence starting from those that generate the least fear. Clients move toward enactment of this disclosure at a pace that ensures that no disclosure is experienced as overwhelming and that none exceeds the client's capacity to deal with the reactions that it might evoke. One complication of the exposure approach in the current context is that it is not always possible to predict whether a situation will be safe. It is important to acknowledge this to the client and to work on tolerating ambiguity as a part of the exposure paradigm. Such ambiguity also opens the way for considering coping strategies appropriate to those situations where safety may be uncertain.

Additionally, it is important to reduce the potential for self-blame on those occasions where the client does not predict outcomes accurately. The movement perspective is a useful tool in this arena. The therapist can point out that homophobia and heterosexism are not rational; they are products of conscious and nonconscious biases that are not grounded in logic. Given that it is very difficult to predict irrational phenomena, it can be expected that clients' predictions are sometimes wrong, not because of faulty reasoning by the client but because of the very nature of such bias. Again, this approach has the benefit of underscoring where the problem lies—not in the client or in SMGE identity but in persons who hold irrational stigmatizing attitudes toward SMGE people.

Internalized Stigma

The next dimension of stigma-related experience noted by Frost (2011) has to do with the internalization of stigma. *Internalized stigma* is a collective term incorporating internalized homophobia, heterosexism, biphobia, genderism, and transphobia. The term is used to denote SMGE individuals' internalization of the negative and stigmatizing messages about their identities that they have been exposed to as members of society. Internalized stigma is usually discussed as an internal trait of the individual, and it is typically framed as a negative quality. In recent years, however, new understandings have framed internalized stigma as a state, rather than a trait (Russell & Bohan, 2006, 2007). It is a reflection of the individual's immediate context, especially with regard to the nature and severity of the stigma that exists in that context. Furthermore, internalized stigma can only be understood in terms of its coexistence and interaction with external stigma. Thus, if the level of stigma in an individual's environment increases, we can expect that internalized stigma will rise as well. More precisely, it is likely to rise unless it is interrupted by the individual (e.g., confronting internalized messages) or by some external variable (e.g., social support) that challenges the stigma. If we ignore the level and severity of the external stigma and focus only on its internalization, we are in danger of overpathologizing the person or of blaming the victim (Batts, 2002).

Therapy concerning internalized stigma must be carried out with a delicate balance in focus between external stigma and its internalized manifestations. Internalized stigma cannot be understood without reference to external stigma. But sole attention to external stigma carries the danger of rendering the individual passive and powerless with no possibility for agency in personal or social change (Lamb, 1996). As we emphasized earlier, the nature of the individual's appraisal of most problems is important in dealing with internalized stigma. In this regard, the movement perspective (Russell & Bohan, 2007;

Russell & Richards, 2003) may help the client to see the relationship between internal and external stigma and to see that internalized stigma is, at its root, largely a reflection of external stigma. This, in turn, locates the problem as bias in the real world—as a collective problem rather than an individual problem. This appraisal allows the individual to interrupt the internalizing pull of the cycle that defines the relationship between external and internal stigma.

The focus of therapy, then, is looking at the messages, both explicit and implicit (Banse, Seise, & Zerbes, 2001; Greenwald et al., 2002; Herek, Gillis, & Cogan, 1999), about SMGE people, their lives, and their relationships that the client is likely to encounter in everyday interactions with the social world. These messages are expressions of attitudes. Like all attitudes, they have cognitive and affective components that together predispose people to behave in particular ways—namely, a way that is consistent with the thoughts and feelings associated with the attitude. When viewed this way, it is possible to dismantle messages and analyze their components. Sometimes, countering the cognitive aspect by challenging misinformation is helpful. The therapist may work to expose beliefs that are rooted in prejudice: stereotypes, half-truths, and outright lies. Often, it is helpful to learn where and how stigmatizing messages were learned, especially since many may have been learned from important relationships in a person's life, such as parents, religious leaders, teachers, and so on. At other times, it may be helpful to consider the affective components of stigmatizing messages. Many faulty beliefs are instated and reinforced by association with fear and other strong emotions. Additionally, it may be helpful to employ counter stereotypes (Blair, 2002) as a tool for demonstrating problems with faulty images. Counselors can, for example, recommend that a client use the Internet to search for narratives of SMGE people that counter specific negative images that the client has internalized. This practice has been particularly useful for some SMGE people who are members of conservative faith communities and who have regarded the idea that persons might be members of both SMGE and faith communities as a virtual impossibility. Thus, both cognitions and emotions associated with stigma can be exposed to scrutiny in therapy, much like any faulty or dysfunctional attitude can be. In this case, it is important for the therapist and the client to keep in mind both that these particular attitudes have social origins and that they receive a fair amount of ongoing social reinforcement, some of it obvious and some more subtle.

Through all of this runs the underlying emphasis on the movement perspective and the intrinsically interrelated nature of external stigma and internalized stigma. A part of deploying the movement perspective in therapy is its psychoeducational value in understanding the nature of stigma: how it works, what its consequences may be, how it can be undone, and why active coping is an important response to stigma. We address these issues in the next section.

NEGATIVE CONSEQUENCES OF STIGMA

As Frost's (2011) model suggests, stigma can have consequences at many levels. It can affect mental health, physical health, individuals' performance in a variety of domains, and their interpersonal relationships. Sometimes these consequences are acute, as in the case of hate crimes (Balsam & Hughes, 2013; Garnets, Herek, & Levy, 1992). More often, the consequences of stigma emerge over time, possibly as a result of the cumulative effects of stressful experiences and the erosion of coping skills under continued stress. In some cases, the impact of stigma in the form of microaggressions can go unnoticed. People often become so habituated to a certain level of day-to-day stress associated with a stigmatized identity that they do not notice the toll it is taking on their well-being (Russell, 2000).

With respect to health consequences, some are the direct result of stigmatization, whereas some may be related to difficulties in access to quality mental or physical health care. Risk behaviors, including those associated with HIV/AIDS, may be complicating factors. There is considerable research on the physical health impacts of other forms of stigma, especially racism, but research on the health consequences of stigma based on sexual orientation and gender identity is limited (but see Hatzenbuehler, 2014; Hatzenbuehler, Phelan, & Link, 2013; Meyer & Frost, 2013). Cochran and Mays (2013) summarized the somewhat more extensive line of research on the mental health consequences of anti-SMGE stigma. Among their most relevant conclusions is the observation that sexual minority men and sexual minority women evidenced elevated levels of depressive, anxiety, and substance abuse disorders and that "the elevated risk is on the order of the size of differences seen commonly between men and women, between people of varying racial/ethnic backgrounds, or among people reporting different income levels" (Cochran & Mays, 2013, p. 212). Cochran and Mays also made the point that, across the relevant studies they reviewed, most sexual minority individuals (like most heterosexual individuals) do not demonstrate recent clinical problems.

Very limited research has been carried out examining the consequences of SMGE stigma for performance. Hence, we are forced to draw inferences from parallel research on groups facing other types of stigma. Most of that research has addressed performance in academic and employment domains, and much of the more recent literature focuses on the experience of stereotype threat. The findings suggest that members of stigmatized groups often expend energy in activities such as worrying about how they are judged (specifically, as members of a social group) or trying to avoid confirming negative stereotypes (Schmader, 2010). For SMGE individuals, a good part of this energy may be expended in concealment efforts. Such concerns detract from energy that could be better invested in task performance. The impact of stigma on relationships can also be significant, and this issue needs to be part of the therapeutic exploration of internalized stigma. For example, internalized stigma can foster ambivalence about one's own relationship or partner as well as stereotypes about bad or short-lived relationships. The effects of stigma may be especially problematic when either real or feared situations create a discrepancy between partners in how open or closeted each wants to be. This is not uncommon, given that partners often come from different backgrounds, and, as discussed earlier, the context in which one lives has a dramatic impact on how much negative stigma may have been internalized and on how safe the world seems. Such discrepancies can create conflict that is challenging to resolve.

Any of these domains is ripe for discussion in therapy. In the case of acute outcomes, therapy employs an acute stress model or, when necessary, a trauma model (Russell & Hawkey, 2013). For more erosive experiences, therapy focuses on encouraging the client to identify the nature and intensity of stressors in the environment and on their efforts to cope with these stressors over time. In each case, a realistic appraisal of external stigma and a careful exploration of internalized stigma are required.

RESPONSES TO STIGMA: COPING AND BEYOND

SMGE persons, like members of other stigmatized groups, draw on both personal and community resources in their efforts to cope with stigma (e.g., DeBlaere & Bertsch, 2013). And SMGE people manage to do well despite the frequency with which they contend with stigma (Cochran & Mays, 2013). Years ago, D'Augelli (1994) introduced the notion of the *affirmative assumption*. Speaking specifically about lesbians and gay men, D'Augelli noted that most of these individuals manage to navigate the process of coming out and develop a healthy sense of self despite the difficulties inherent in their stigmatized status. Clinicians would do well to approach their SMGE clients with this assumption as a baseline expectation, while remaining aware of the very real possibility that some of their SMGE clients will express challenges associated with their stigmatized identity as well as any of the difficulties that befall people in general. Furthermore, therapists and counselors should remain open to the possibility that their SMGE clients have met with stigma in such a way that they have not only avoided long-term negative consequences but have also developed successful coping skills in the process, skills that Kimmel (1978/1993) referred to as *crisis competence*.

Effective coping in people from any group generally draws on both personal and community resources (Moos & Holahan, 2003). As the status of SMGE people in the United States has improved over time, albeit in varying degrees in various places, SMGE people have experienced greater access to and a wider variety of internal and external coping resources. Recent literature has highlighted some of the coping strategies that can be of use to SMGE individuals. Calling upon results from a study on LGB people who were the target of antigay political initiatives, Russell and Richards (2003) suggested that LGB people facing such stigmatization may profitably draw upon a range of strategies. The first of these is an appraisal that emphasizes the sociopolitical nature of the stressors they are facing and the potential for collective action as a coping (as well as a political) strategy—the movement perspective that we have already discussed. Additional coping techniques include efforts to confront signs of internalized stigma in themselves and active management of affective responses to being targeted. Finally, coping strategies that call upon social support systems are helpful, including acknowledging the presence of heterosexual allies; welcoming their support; and drawing upon the SMGE community for information, practical resources, and social support. Other research has suggested the value of adopting a group identity, working actively against prejudice and discrimination in the world, confronting internalized stigma, striving for self-identity, challenging identity labels, and seeking social change in the context of a larger movement (Bohan, Russell, & Montgomery, 2002; Russell, Bohan, & Lilly, 2000). Clinicians can integrate an understanding of all of these coping strategies in their work with members of the SMGE community (see especially Russell, 2012).

Some research has moved beyond matters of merely ameliorating the impact of stressors to fostering resilience. Of particular note here is work that emphasizes the positive aspects of SMGE identities. This approach, which was introduced early on by Brown (1989), has been elaborated in recent research. Frost (2011) emphasized Unger's (2002) contention that stigmatized individuals often display agency and resilience in their responses to marginalized statuses as well as other work highlighting social creativity and social change efforts as positive outcomes of some responses to stigma. Another example of this research on resilience is found in Riggle and Rostosky's (2012) work, which employed an online open-ended survey asking a large sample of LGBT people to describe positive aspects of their respective identities. Their analysis identified eight general themes in respondents' comments: living an authentic life; having increased awareness and self-insight; feeling free to create flexible roles for varied meanings and expressions of gender; creating supportive families of support; exploring expressions of sexuality and creating intimate relationships with new rules; having a unique perspective on life, with empathy and compassion for others; being a positive role model, mentor, and activist working for social change; and belonging to the LGBT community. Clinicians would do well to pay heed to the importance of helping their clients to recognize the potential for these characteristics and to develop them in their lives. The mere existence of these findings has surprised and delighted some SMGE clients, who are accustomed to knowing what is difficult about their own lives and those of other SMGE people, but who rarely ask themselves what is rewarding and meaningful about this aspect of their lives.

BY WAY OF SUMMARY

The rapid changes that have occurred for SMGE people in a relatively brief period of time have often been a mark of successful social change efforts and a source of great excitement. These changes have not been equally (or equitably) distributed among all SMGE people in the United States, not to mention elsewhere in the world. In addition, pushbacks and backlashes of varying types and degrees have typically followed closely on the heels of such changes. Both the positive and the negative circumstances in which SMGE people find themselves require adaptation.

Therapists and counselors working with members of this population can draw from stigma theory as well as a number of specific empirically and clinically derived tools that are useful in countering the negative impact of stigma and fostering resilience at both individual and community levels. Central among these tools is a movement perspective, which allows therapist and client alike to use context, with its differing and shifting manifestations, as a touchstone for understanding and ameliorating problems and for creating positive individual and social change.

We would be remiss if we ended this chapter without acknowledging that much of what we have said can be used outside the boundaries of counseling and therapy (Russell & Bohan, 2007). The value of a movement perspective in particular and of good coping skills in general can be taught and modeled in any number of contexts, including workshops, talks, political campaigns, and movement organizations. The potential for mental health professionals to offer this information to SMGE communities exists virtually anywhere, including online (see Lin & Israel, 2012). It is information that can be tailored to particular times, places, and political circumstances. The information can be of significant value to SMGE people, whether it comes in the context of therapy sessions or through nontherapy contexts. We invite you to pass it on.

REFERENCES

American Psychological Association. (2008). *Report of the Task Force on Gender Identity and Gender Variance*. Retrieved from http://www.apa.org/pi/lgbt/resources/policy/gender-identity-report.pdf

American Psychological Association. (2009a). *Lesbian, gay, bisexual, and transgender persons and socioeconomic status.* Retrieved from http://www.apa.org/pi/ses/resources/publications/factsheet-lgbt.pdf

American Psychological Association. (2009b). *Report of the APA Task Force on Appropriate Therapeutic Responses to Sexual Orientation.* Retrieved from http://www.apa.org/pi/lgbt/resources/therapeutic-response.pdf

Andersen, R., & Fetner, T. (2008). Cohort differences in tolerance of homosexuality: Attitude change in Canada and the United States, 1981–2000. *Public Opinion Quarterly, 72,* 311–330. http://dx.doi.org/10.1093/poq/nfn017

Associated Press. (2015, July 18). Poll shows slight differences in gay marriage support since Supreme Court rulings. *USA Today.* Retrieved from http://www.usatoday.com/story/news/nation/2015/07/18/ap-poll-sharp-divisions-after-high-court-backs-gay-marriage/30341661

Badgett, M. V. L. (2003). *Money, myths, and change: The economic lives of lesbians and gay men.* Chicago, IL: University of Chicago Press.

Ball, C. A. (2010). *From the closet to the classroom: Five LGBT lawsuits that have changed our nation.* Boston, MA: Beacon.

Balsam, K., & Hughes, T. (2013). Sexual orientation, victimization, and hate crimes. In C. J. Patterson & A. R. D'Augelli (Eds.), *Handbook of psychology and sexual orientation* (pp. 267–280). New York, NY: Oxford University Press.

Banse, R., Seise, J., & Zerbes, N. (2001). Implicit attitudes towards homosexuality: Reliability, validity, and controllability of the IAT. *Zeitschrift für Experimentelle Psychologie, 48,* 145–160. http://dx.doi.org/10.1026//0949-3946.48.2.145

Bargh, J. A., & Chartrand, T. L. (1999). The unbearable automaticity of being. *American Psychologist, 54,* 462–479. http://dx.doi.org/10.1037/0003-066X.54.7.462

Bargh, J. A., Chen, M., & Burrows, L. (1996). Automaticity of social behavior: Direct effects of trait construct and stereotype-activation on action. *Journal of Personality and Social Psychology, 71,* 230–244. http://dx.doi.org/10.1037/0022-3514.71.2.230

Batts, V. (2002). *Is reconciliation possible? Lessons from combating "modern racism."* Retrieved from http://sph.unc.edu/files/2013/07/ditf_is_reconciliation_possible.pdf

Berger, P., & Luckmann, T. (1975). *The social construction of reality: A treatise in the sociology of knowledge.* New York, NY: Penguin.

Blair, I. V. (2002). The malleability of automatic stereotypes and prejudice. *Personality and Social Psychology Review, 6,* 242–261. http://dx.doi.org/10.1207/S15327957PSPR0603_8

Bohan, J. S., & Russell, G. M. (Eds.). (1999). *Conversations about psychology and sexual orientation.* New York: New York University Press.

Bohan, J. S., Russell, G. M., & Montgomery, S. (2002). Gay youth and gay adults: Bridging the generation gap. *Journal of Homosexuality, 44,* 15–41. http://dx.doi.org/10.1300/J082v44n01_02

Bradford, J., & Ryan, C. (1987). *The national lesbian health care survey.* Washington, DC: National Lesbian Health Fund.

Bronfenbrenner, U. (1979). *The ecology of human development: Experiments by nature and design.* Cambridge, MA: Harvard University Press.

Brown, L. S. (1989). New voices, new visions: Toward a lesbian/gay paradigm for psychology. *Psychology of Women Quarterly, 13,* 445–458. http://dx.doi.org/10.1111/j.1471-6402.1989.tb01013.x

Buchanan, M., Dzelme, K., Harris, D., & Hecker, L. (2001). Challenges of being simultaneously gay or lesbian and spiritual and/or religious: A narrative perspective. *The American Journal of Family Therapy, 29,* 435–449. http://dx.doi.org/10.1080/01926180127629

Bull, C., & Gallagher, J. (1996). *Perfect enemies: The religious right, the gay movement, and the politics of the 1990s.* New York, NY: Crown.

Cass, V. C. (1979). Homosexual identity formation: A theoretical model. *Journal of Homosexuality, 4,* 219–235. http://dx.doi.org/10.1300/J082v04n03_01

Cass, V. C. (1999). Bringing psychology in from the cold: Framing psychological theory and research within a social constructionist psychology approach. In J. S. Bohan & G. M. Russell (Eds.), *Conversations about psychology and sexual orientation* (pp. 106–128). New York: New York University Press.

Chan, C. (1992). Asian–American lesbians and gay men. In S. Dworkin & F. Gutierrez (Eds.), *Counseling gay men and lesbians: Journey to the end of the rainbow* (pp. 115–124). Alexandria, VA: American Association for Counseling and Development.

Charles, S. T., Piazza, J. R., Mogle, J., Sliwinski, M. J., & Almeida, D. M. (2013). The wear and tear of daily stressors on mental health. *Psychological Science, 24,* 733–741. http://dx.doi.org/10.1177/0956797612462222

Clift, E. (2012, July 31). Why the Democrats backed a gay-marriage plank for the party convention. *The Daily Beast.* Retrieved from http://www.thedailybeast.com/articles/2012/07/31/why-the-democrats-backed-a-gay-marriage-plank-for-the-party-convention.html

Cochran, S. D., & Mays, V. M. (2013). Sexual orientation and mental health. In C. J. Patterson & A. R. D'Augelli (Eds.), *Handbook of psychology and sexual orientation* (pp. 204–222). New York, NY: Oxford University Press.

Cochran, S. D., Mays, V. M., Alegria, M., Ortega, A. N., & Takeuchi, D. (2007). Mental health and substance use disorders among Latino and Asian American lesbian, gay, and bisexual adults. *Journal of Consulting and Clinical Psychology, 75,* 785–794. http://dx.doi.org/10.1037/0022-006X.75.5.785

Coleman, E. (1978). Toward a new model of treatment of homosexuality: A review. *Journal of Homosexuality, 3,* 345–359. http://dx.doi.org/10.1300/J082v03n04_03

Confessore, N., & Peters, J. W. (2014, April 27). Gay rights push shifts its focus south and west. *The New York Times.* Retrieved from http://www.nytimes.com/2014/04/28/us/politics/gay-rights-push-shifts-its-focus-south-and-west.html

Cowan, G., Heiple, B., Marquez, C., Khatchadourian, D., & McNevin, M. (2005). Heterosexuals' attitudes toward hate crimes and hate speech against gays and lesbians: Old-fashioned and modern heterosexism. *Journal of Homosexuality, 49,* 67–82. http://dx.doi.org/10.1300/J082v49n02_04

D'Augelli, A. R. (1994). Lesbian and gay male development: Steps toward an analysis of lesbians' and gay men's lives. In B. Greene & G. M. Herek (Eds.), *Lesbian and gay psychology: Theory, research, and clinical applications* (pp. 118–132). Thousand Oaks, CA: Sage. http://dx.doi.org/10.4135/9781483326757.n7

D'Augelli, A. R. (2006). Developmental and contextual factors and mental health among lesbian, gay, and bisexual youths. In A. M. Omoto & H. S. Kurtzman (Eds.), *Sexual orientation and mental health: Examining identity and development in lesbian, gay, and bisexual people* (pp. 37–53). Washington, DC: American Psychological Association. http://dx.doi.org/10.1037/11261-002

DeBlaere, C., & Bertsch, K. (2013). Perceived sexist events and psychological distress of sexual minority women of color: The moderating role of womanism. *Psychology of Women Quarterly, 37,* 167–178. http://dx.doi.org/10.1177/0361684312470436

de Vries, B. (2014). LG(BT) persons in the second half of life: The intersectional influences of stigma and cohort. *LGBT Health, 1,* 18–23. http://dx.doi.org/10.1089/lgbt.2013.0005

Diamond, L. M. (2004). Emerging perspectives on distinctions between romantic love and sexual desire. *Current Directions in Psychological Science, 13,* 116–119. http://dx.doi.org/10.1111/j.0963-7214.2004.00287.x

Diamond, L. M. (2006). Careful what you ask for: Reconsidering feminist epistemology and autobiographical narrative in research on sexual identity development. *Signs: Journal of Women in Culture and Society, 31,* 471–491. http://dx.doi.org/10.1086/491684

Díaz, R. M., Ayala, G., Bein, E., Henne, J., & Marin, B. V. (2001). The impact of homophobia, poverty, and racism on the mental health of gay and bisexual Latino men: Findings from 3 US cities. *American Journal of Public Health, 91,* 927–932. http://dx.doi.org/10.2105/AJPH.91.6.927

Downie, M., Mageau, G. A., Koestner, R., & Liodden, T. (2006). On the risk of being a cultural chameleon: Variations in collective self-esteem across social interactions. *Cultural Diversity & Ethnic Minority Psychology, 12,* 527–540.

Dugan, K. B. (2005). *The struggle over gay, lesbian, and bisexual rights: Facing off in Cincinnati.* New York, NY: Routledge.

Eldridge, J., & Johnson, P. (2011). The relationship between old-fashioned and modern heterosexism to social dominance orientation and structural violence. *Journal of Homosexuality, 58,* 382–401. http://dx.doi.org/10.1080/00918369.2011.546734

Employment Non-Discrimination Act of 2013, S. 815, 113th Cong. (2013). Retrieved from https://www.govtrack.us/congress/bills/113/s815/text

Enns, C. Z., & Fischer, A. R. (2012). On the complexity of multiple feminist identities. *The Counseling Psychologist, 40,* 1149–1163. http://dx.doi.org/10.1177/0011000012439477

Fingerhut, A. W., Riggle, E. D. B., & Rostosky, S. S. (2011). Same-sex marriage: The social and psychological implications of policy and debates. *Journal of Social Issues, 67*, 225–241. http://dx.doi.org/10.1111/j.1540-4560.2011.01695.x

Frable, D. E. S., Platt, L., & Hoey, S. (1998). Concealable stigmas and positive self-perceptions: Feeling better around similar others. *Journal of Personality and Social Psychology, 74*, 909–922. http://dx.doi.org/10.1037/0022-3514.74.4.909

Frable, D. E. S., Wortman, C., & Joseph, J. (1997). The importance of cultural stigma, personal visibility, community networks, and positive multiraciality. In M. P. P. Root (Ed.), *The multiracial experience: Racial blenders as the news frontier* (pp. 79–97). Newburg Park, CA: Sage.

Frost, D. M. (2011). Social stigma and its consequences for the socially stigmatized. *Social and Personality Psychology Compass, 5*, 824–839. http://dx.doi.org/10.1111/j.1751-9004.2011.00394.x

Garnets, L., Herek, G. M., & Levy, B. (1992). Violence and victimization of lesbians and gay men: Mental health consequences. In G. M. Herek & K. T. Berrill (Eds.), *Hate crimes: Confronting violence against lesbians and gay men* (pp. 207–226). London, England: Sage.

Gergen, K. J. (1973). Social psychology as history. *Journal of Personality & Social Psychology, 26*, 309–320.

Gergen, K. J. (1984). Theory of the self: Impasse and evolution. *Advances in Experimental Social Psychology, 17*, 49–115. http://dx.doi.org/10.1016/S0065-2601(08)60118-5

Ginges, J., & Atran, S. (2008). Humiliation and the inertia effect: Implications for understanding violence and compromise in intractable intergroup conflicts. *Journal of Cognition and Culture, 8*, 281–294. http://dx.doi.org/10.1163/156853708X358182

Goffman, E. (1963). *Stigma: Notes on the management of spoiled identity.* Englewood Cliffs, NJ: Prentice-Hall.

Greenberg Quinlan Rosner Research. (2014, March 27). *Survey charts dramatic change toward marriage equality.* Retrieved from http://www.gqrr.com/articles/2014/03/27/survey-reveals-dramatic-change-toward-marriage-equality

Greene, B. (2007). Delivering ethical psychological services to lesbian, gay, and bisexual clients. In K. J. Bieschke, R. M. Perez, & K. A. DeBord (Eds.), *Handbook of counseling and psychotherapy with lesbian, gay, bisexual, and transgender clients* (2nd ed., pp. 181–199). Washington, DC: American Psychological Association. http://dx.doi.org/10.1037/11482-007

Greenwald, A. G., Banaji, M. R., Rudman, L. A., Farnham, S. D., Nosek, B. A., & Mellott, D. S. (2002). A unified theory of implicit attitudes, stereotypes, self-esteem, and self-concept. *Psychological Review, 109*, 3–25.

Hammack, P. L., & Cohler, B. J. (2011). Narrative identity and the politics of exclusion: Social change and the gay and lesbian life course. *Sexuality Research & Social Policy, 8*, 162–182. http://dx.doi.org/10.1007/s13178-011-0060-3

Harper, G. W., & Schneider, M. (2003). Oppression and discrimination among lesbian, gay, bisexual, and transgendered people and communities: A challenge for community psychology. *American Journal of Community Psychology, 31*, 243–252. http://dx.doi.org/10.1023/A:1023906620085

Harris, J. I., Cook, S. W., & Kashubeck-West, S. (2008). Religious attitudes, internalized homophobia, and identity in gay and lesbian adults. *Journal of Gay & Lesbian Mental Health, 12*, 205–225. http://dx.doi.org/10.1080/19359700802111452

Hatzenbuehler, M. L. (2010). Social factors as determinants of mental health disparities in LGB populations: Implications for public policy. *Social Issues and Policy Review, 4*, 31–62. http://dx.doi.org/10.1111/j.1751-2409.2010.01017.x

Hatzenbuehler, M. L. (2014). Structural stigma and the health of lesbian, gay, and bisexual populations. *Current Directions in Psychological Science, 23*, 127–132. http://dx.doi.org/10.1177/0963721414523775

Hatzenbuehler, M. L., Phelan, J. C., & Link, B. G. (2013). Stigma as a fundamental cause of population health inequalities. *American Journal of Public Health, 103*, 813–821. http://dx.doi.org/10.2105/AJPH.2012.301069

Heatherton, T. F., Kleck, R. E., Hebl, M. R., & Hull, J. G. (Eds.). (2000). *The social psychology of stigma*. New York, NY: Guilford Press.

Hendricks, M. L., & Testa, R. J. (2012). A conceptual framework for clinical work with transgender and gender nonconforming clients: An adaptation of the minority stress model. *Professional Psychology: Research and Practice, 43*, 460–467. http://dx.doi.org/10.1037/a0029597

Herek, G. M. (Ed.). (1998). *Stigma and sexual orientation: Understanding prejudice against lesbians, gay men, and bisexuals*. Thousand Oaks, CA: Sage.

Herek, G. M. (2007). Confronting sexual stigma and prejudice: Theory and practice. *Journal of Social Issues, 63*, 905–925. http://dx.doi.org/10.1111/j.1540-4560.2007.00544.x

Herek, G. M., & Garnets, L. D. (2007). Sexual orientation and mental health. *Annual Review of Clinical Psychology, 3*, 353–375. http://dx.doi.org/10.1146/annurev.clinpsy.3.022806.091510

Herek, G. M., Gillis, J. R., & Cogan, J. C. (1999). Psychological sequelae of hate-crime victimization among lesbian, gay, and bisexual adults. *Journal of Consulting and Clinical Psychology, 67*, 945–951. http://dx.doi.org/10.1037/0022-006X.67.6.945

Herman, D. (1997). *The antigay agenda: Orthodox vision and the Christian right*. Chicago, IL: University of Chicago Press. http://dx.doi.org/10.7208/chicago/9780226327693.001.0001

Horn, S. S. (2013). Attitudes about sexual orientation. In C. J. Patterson & A. R. D'Augelli (Eds.), *Handbook of psychology and sexual orientation* (pp. 240–251). New York, NY: Oxford University Press.

Katz, J. N. (1978). *Gay American history: Lesbians and gay men in the U.S.A.* New York, NY: Avon.

Keen, L., & Goldberg, S. B. (2001). *Strangers to the law: Gay people on trial*. Ann Arbor: University of Michigan Press.

Kimmel, D. C. (1978). Adult development and aging: A gay perspective. *Journal of Social Issues, 34,* 113–130. [Reprinted in L. D. Garnets & D. C. Kimmel (Eds.) (1993). *Psychological perspectives on lesbian and gay male experiences* (pp. 517–534). New York, NY: Columbia University Press.

Kimmel, D. C. (2003). Identifying and addressing health issues of gay, lesbian, bisexual, transgender (LGBT) populations in rural communities: Psychological perspectives. In L. D. Garnets & D. C. Kimmel (Eds.), *Psychological perspectives on lesbian, gay, and bisexual experiences* (2nd ed., pp. 435–440). New York, NY: Columbia University Press.

Kosciw, J. G., Greytak, E. A., & Diaz, E. M. (2009). Who, what, where, when, and why: Demographic and ecological factors contributing to hostile school climate for lesbian, gay, bisexual, and transgender youth. *Journal of Youth and Adolescence, 38,* 976–988. http://dx.doi.org/10.1007/s10964-009-9412-1

Lamb, S. (1996). *The trouble with blame: Victims, perpetrators, and responsibility.* Cambridge, MA: Harvard University Press.

Lambda Legal. (2013). *Davenport v. Little-Bowser.* Retrieved from http://www.lambda legal.org/in-court/cases/davenport-v-little-bowser

Levin, S., & van Laar, C. (Eds.). (2006). *Stigma and group inequality: Social psychological perspectives.* Mahwah, NJ: Erlbaum.

Lin, Y.-J., & Israel, T. (2012). A computer-based intervention to reduce internalized heterosexism in men. *Journal of Counseling Psychology, 59,* 458–464. http://dx.doi.org/10.1037/a0028282

Löfgren-Mårtenson, L. (2009). The invisibility of young homosexual women and men with intellectual disabilities. *Sexuality and Disability, 27*(1), 21–26.

Manalansan, M. (1996). Double minorities: Latino, Black, and Asian men who have sex with men. In R. Savin-Williams & K. Cohen (Eds.), *The lives of lesbians, gays, and bisexuals: Children to adults* (pp. 393–415). Fort Worth, TX: Harcourt Brace.

Mann, M. J. (2013). The nexus of stigma and social policy: Implications for pastoral care and psychotherapy with gay, lesbian, bisexual, and transgender persons and their families. *Pastoral Psychology, 62,* 199–210. http://dx.doi.org/10.1007/s11089-012-0460-1

Meyer, I. H. (2013). Prejudice, social stress, and mental health in lesbian, gay, and bisexual populations: Conceptual issues and research evidence. *Psychology of Sexual Orientation and Gender Diversity, 1,* 3–26. http://dx.doi.org/10.1037/2329-0382.1.S.3

Meyer, I. H., & Frost, D. M. (2013). Minority stress and the health of sexual minorities. In C. J. Patterson & A. R. D'Augelli (Eds.), *Handbook of psychology and sexual orientation* (pp. 252–266). New York, NY: Oxford University Press.

Miller, N. (1995). *Out of the past: Gay and lesbian history from 1869 to the present.* New York, NY: Vintage Books.

Moats, D. (2004). *Civil wars: A battle for gay marriage.* Orlando, FL: Harcourt.

Moos, R. H., & Holahan, C. J. (2003). Dispositional and contextual perspectives on coping: Toward an integrative framework. *Journal of Clinical Psychology, 59,* 1387–1403. http://dx.doi.org/10.1002/jclp.10229

Morgan, E. M. (2013). Contemporary issues in sexual orientation and identity development in emerging adulthood. *Emerging Adulthood, 1,* 52–66. http://dx.doi.org/10.1177/2167696812469187

Nadal, K. L., Issa, M.-A., Leon, J., Meterko, V., Wideman, M., & Wong, Y. (2011). Sexual orientation microaggressions: "Death by a thousand cuts" for lesbian, gay, and bisexual youth. *Journal of LGBT Youth, 8,* 234–259. http://dx.doi.org/10.1080/19361653.2011.584204

Oswald, R. F., & Masciadrelli, B. P. (2008). Generative ritual among nonmetropolitan lesbians and gay men: Promoting social inclusion. *Journal of Marriage and Family, 70,* 1060–1073. http://dx.doi.org/10.1111/j.1741-3737.2008.00546.x

Pew Research Center. (2013, June 13). *A survey of LGBT Americans.* Retrieved from http://www.pewsocialtrends.org/2013/06/13/a-survey-of-lgbt-americans/

Pew Research Center. (2015, July 29). *Changing attitudes on gay marriage.* Retrieved from http://www.pewforum.org/2015/07/29/graphics-slideshow-changing-attitudes-on-gay-marriage/

Riggle, E. D. B., & Rostosky, S. S. (2012). *A positive view of LGBTQ: Embracing identity and cultivating well-being.* Lanham, MD: Rowman & Littlefield.

Riggle, E. D. B., Rostosky, S. S., & Horne, S. (2010). Does it matter where you live? Nondiscrimination laws and the experience of LGB residents. *Sexuality Research and Social Policy: A Journal of the NSRC, 7*(3), 168–175.

Russell, G. M. (2000). *Voted out: Psychological consequences of anti-gay politics.* New York: New York University Press.

Russell, G. M. (2011). Motives of heterosexual allies in collective action for equality. *Journal of Social Issues, 67,* 376–393. http://dx.doi.org/10.1111/j.1540-4560.2011.01703.x

Russell, G. M. (2012). When the personal and the political collide: LGBT people as political targets. In S. H. Dworkin & M. Pope (Eds.), *A casebook of counseling with lesbian, gay, bisexual, and transgender persons and their families* (pp. 329–339). Alexandria, VA: American Counseling Association.

Russell, G. M., & Bohan, J. S. (2005). The gay generation gap: Communicating across the LGBT generational divide. *Angles: The Policy Journal of the Institute for Gay and Lesbian Strategic Studies, 8*(1), 1–8.

Russell, G. M., & Bohan, J. S. (2006). The case of internalized homophobia: Theory and/as practice. *Theory & Psychology, 16,* 343–366. http://dx.doi.org/10.1177/0959354306064283

Russell, G. M., & Bohan, J. S. (2007). Liberating psychotherapy: Liberation psychology and psychotherapy with LGBT clients. *Journal of Gay & Lesbian Psychotherapy, 11,* 59–75. http://dx.doi.org/10.1300/J236v11n03_04

Russell, G. M., Bohan, J. S., & Lilly, D. (2000). Queer youth: Old stories, new stories. In S. Jones (Ed.), *A sea of stories: The shaping power of narrative in gay and lesbian culture* (pp. 69–92). New York, NY: Haworth.

Russell, G. M., & Hawkey, C. G. (2013). Therapy with victims of hate crimes. In G. P. Koocher, J. C. Norcross, & B. A. Greene (Eds.), *Psychologists' desk reference* (3d ed., pp. 323–327). New York, NY: Oxford University Press. http://dx.doi.org/10.1093/med:psych/9780199845491.003.0067

Russell, G. M., & Richards, J. A. (2003). Stressor and resilience factors for lesbians, gay men, and bisexuals confronting antigay politics. *American Journal of Community Psychology, 31*, 313–328. http://dx.doi.org/10.1023/A:1023919022811

Rust, P. (1996). Managing multiple identities: Diversity among bisexual women and men. In B. Firestein (Ed.), *Bisexuality: The psychology and politics of an invisible minority* (pp. 53–83). Thousand Oaks, CA: Sage.

Saad, C. (1997). Disability and the lesbian, gay man, or bisexual individual. In M. Sipski & S. C. Alexander (Eds.), *Sexual function in people with disability and chronic illness: A health professional's guide* (pp. 413–427). Gaithersburg, MD: Aspen.

Schmader, T. (2010). Stereotype threat deconstructed. *Current Directions in Psychological Science, 19*, 14–18. http://dx.doi.org/10.1177/0963721409359292

Shweder, R. (1992). Cultural psychology: What is it? In J. Stigler, R. Shweder, & G. Herdt (Eds.), *Cultural psychology: Essays on comparative human development* (pp. 1–46). Cambridge, England: Cambridge University Press.

Simpson, P. (2012). Perils, precariousness and pleasures: Middle-aged gay men negotiating urban heterospaces. *Sociological Research Online, 17*, 23. Retrieved from http://www.socresonline.org.uk/17/3/23.html. http://dx.doi.org/10.5153/sro.2665

Smith, D. S., & Mancoske, R. J. (Eds.). (1997). *Rural gays and lesbians: Building on the strengths of communities*. Binghamton, NY: Harrington Park Press.

Stein, A. (2001). *The stranger next door: The story of a small community's battle over sex, faith, and civil rights*. Boston, MA: Beacon.

Troiden, R. R. (1989). The formation of homosexual identities. *Journal of Homosexuality, 17*, 43–74. http://dx.doi.org/10.1300/J082v17n01_02

Unger, R. K. (2002). The 1999 SPSSI Presidential Address: Outside inside—Positive marginality and social change. *Journal of Social Issues, 56*, 163–179. http://dx.doi.org/10.1111/0022-4537.00158

United States v. Windsor 570 U.S. 12 (2013).

Williams, K. D., Forgas, J. P., & von Hippel, W. (Eds.). (2013). *The social outcast: Ostracism, social exclusion, rejection, and bullying*. New York, NY: Psychology Press.

Witt, S. L., & McCorkle, S. (Eds.). (1997). *Anti-gay rights: Assessing voter initiatives*. Westport, CT: Praeger.

4

(RE)FOCUSING INTERSECTIONALITY: FROM SOCIAL IDENTITIES BACK TO SYSTEMS OF OPPRESSION AND PRIVILEGE

BONNIE MORADI

The concept of intersectionality is rooted in the work of many Black feminist scholars and activists (e.g., Collins, 1989; Combahee River Collective, 1977–1983; Crenshaw, 1989) who have offered thoughtful critiques of sociopolitical movements that focused narrowly on single dimensions of oppression (e.g., racism, sexism). In response to such critiques, feminist scholars and activists adopted the intersectionality perspective to address the ways in which sociopolitical systems involving multiple forms of oppression and privilege shape people's experiences. Indeed, the intersectionality perspective has been described as "the most important theoretical contribution that women's studies, in conjunction with other related fields, has made so far" (McCall, 2005, p. 1771). In her widely viewed TED talk on feminism, the blogger and

http://dx.doi.org/10.1037/15959-005
Handbook of Sexual Orientation and Gender Diversity in Counseling and Psychotherapy, K. A. DeBord, A. R. Fischer, K. J. Bieschke, and R. M. Perez (Editors)

activist Courtney Martin (2010) described the centrality of intersectionality in feminist movements as follows:

> [M]y feminism is very indebted to my mom's, but it looks very different. My mom says, "patriarchy." I say, "intersectionality." So race, class, gender, ability, all of these things go into our experiences of what it means to be a woman. Pay equity? Yes. Absolutely a feminist issue. But for me, so is immigration.

In recent years, the concept of intersectionality has gained popularity beyond feminist scholarship and activism. This growing influence is evident in calls for integrating an intersectionality perspective in fields ranging from health and health disparities (Rogers & Kelly, 2011; Weber & Parra-Medina, 2003) to global inequality and human rights (Bond, 2003; Verloo, 2006; Yuval-Davis, 2006). Within psychology, an intersectionality lens has been used for some time (e.g., Greene, 1994; K. R. King, 2003; Landrine, Klonoff, Alcaraz, Scott, & Wikins, 1995; Moradi & Subich, 2003) but is gaining momentum with recent articulations of its value for the field (e.g., Cole, 2009; Shields, 2008; Warner, 2008; Warner & Shields, 2013) and with several special issues of psychological journals dedicated to the topic (Moradi, DeBlaere, & Huang, 2010; Parent, DeBlaere, & Moradi, 2013; Shields, 2008).

With growing interest in intersectionality, some are cautioning that intersectionality has become a buzzword, with much confusion about what it means or how it should be applied (Choo & Ferree, 2010; K. Davis, 2008; Nash, 2008). These cautions suggest that scholars are falling short of fully realizing the promise of intersectionality. My aim in this chapter is to articulate some of these concerns and to offer some thought questions for mitigating these limitations when translating intersectionality into clinical practice. I begin by returning to the roots of intersectionality and its original conceptualizations. I then unpack how intersectionality has been used in psychological research along three themes: Whose experiences are at the center of analysis? How is intersectionality conceptualized and examined? What are the "things" considered to be intersecting? Within the sections focusing on each of these themes, I offer a set of questions to promote reflection about that theme in clinical practice. I end with some concluding thoughts about the promise of intersectionality for research and clinical practice. Throughout this chapter, I attend to research with sexual minority and trans and gender nonconforming populations.[1]

---

[1] I use the term *sexual minority* to refer to lesbian, gay, bisexual, queer, and other nonheterosexual sexual orientations and identities and the phrase *trans and gender nonconforming* to refer to transgender, transsexual, woman, man, gender queer, and other binary and nonbinary gender identities and expressions for people whose sex assigned at birth differs from their gender identity or expression.

However, I believe that there is value in considering this discussion and the thought questions for clinical practice with all clients.

ROOTS OF INTERSECTIONALITY IN BLACK FEMINIST THOUGHT

Conceptualizations of intersectionality in the United States are rooted in Black feminist activism and scholarship. In 1851, at a women's rights convention in Akron, Ohio, Sojourner Truth famously asked "Ain't I a Woman?" With this question, she challenged the neglect of slavery and African American women's experiences in conventional notions of women's rights. This sentiment has been echoed by authors and activists, including bell hooks (1981), Patricia Hill Collins (1989), Angela Davis (1981), Audre Lorde (1984), and the Combahee River Collective (1977–1983). These Black feminist scholars and activists, many of whom also identified as lesbian, challenged feminist and civil rights scholars and movements to address ageism, classism, heterosexism, racism, sexism, and other forms of oppression. Thus, the earliest steps in the evolution of the concept of intersectionality involved heterosexual and sexual minority Black feminist scholars and activists highlighting the simple but radical point that women of color's experiences of the confluence of multiple oppressions were omitted from but are critical to knowledge production and to movements for social and political justice.

The next steps in the evolution of intersectionality involved articulating how multiple forms of oppression combined to shape people's experiences. Concepts of double jeopardy and multiple jeopardy (Beale, 1970; Jeffries & Ransford, 1980; D. K. King, 1988) were introduced to describe the additive and multiplicative roles of forces of oppression. In these conceptualizations, racism, sexism, and other forces of oppression and privilege have separate and unique roles that combine in additive ways (e.g., racism plus sexism) or interactive ways (e.g., racism magnifies the impact of sexism). These additive and interactive effects result in stratification of power and resources, with White men at the top, women of color at the bottom, and men of color and White women in between.

Such additive and multiplicative perspectives were critical advancements in conceptualizations of intersectionality. However, one limitation of such perspectives is the assumption that different forms of oppression are independent enough that people can separate their experiences into component oppressions, allowing researchers to analyze additive and interactive effects. For example, Black lesbian women's experiences of oppression can be divided into the additive and interactive effects of heterosexism, racism, and sexism. My own research on intersectionality reflected, and to some extent continues to reflect, this approach and its limitations (e.g., Moradi & Subich, 2003).

To address the shortcomings of the assumption of independence in additive and multiplicative approaches, Kimberle Crenshaw (1989) and Patricia Hill Collins (2000) provided alternative conceptualizations. Crenshaw (1989) introduced the term *intersectionality* to express how the separate treatment of race and sex discrimination in U.S. law and judicial decisions, as well as in feminist and antiracist political activism, rendered Black women's experiences invisible:

> Black women sometimes experience discrimination in ways similar to white women's experiences; sometimes they share very similar experiences with Black men. Yet often they experience double-discrimination—the combined effects of practices which discriminate on the basis of race, and on the basis of sex. And sometimes, they experience discrimination as Black women—not the sum of race and sex discrimination, but as Black women . . . Yet the continued insistence that Black women's demands and needs be filtered through categorical analyses that completely obscure their experiences guarantees that their needs will seldom be addressed. (p. 149)

Crenshaw's (1989) analysis acknowledged the potentially separate roles of racism and sexism captured in additive and multiplicative perspectives, but she also called for attention to manifestations of discrimination that are directed distinctively at Black women. Terms such as *ethgender* (Johnson-Bailey & Cervero, 1996) and *gendered racism* (Essed, 1991; St. Jean & Feagin, 1997) have been offered to capture these distinctive experiences, but use of these terms has not gained much ground beyond academia.

Patricia Hill Collins (2000) extended the notion of intersectionality by describing it as a structural matrix of domination. Specifically, she noted that multiple forces of oppression are mutually dependent in shaping people's experiences and are situated within various cultural and historical matrices of domination. For example, constructions of sexuality involve the mutual dependence of heterosexism, neocolonialism, racism, sexism, and other forms of oppression intersecting to construct different groups of people (e.g., men from developed countries, trans and gender nonconforming people, White women, women of color) as agents, consumers, objects, and commodities in relation to one another within current U.S. and global matrices of domination.

As this overview suggests, the concept of intersectionality is rooted in critical analysis of sociopolitical movements that focused on single dimensions of oppression, in calls to acknowledge women of color's experiences as a valuable source of knowledge and activism, and in a focus on structural sociopolitical forces that oppress and privilege people. In the remainder of this chapter, I encourage readers to keep these themes in mind and to use as a frame of reference the following question: What might the founders of intersectionality say about this research and its translation into clinical practice?

TRANSLATIONS OF INTERSECTIONALITY IN RESEARCH AND PRACTICE

In this section, I build on considerations for integrating intersectionality into the process of psychological research (e.g., Cole, 2009; DeBlaere, Brewster, Sarkees, & Moradi, 2010; Shields, 2008; Warner, 2008; Warner & Shields, 2013) by unpacking how intersectionality has been used in psychological research along three themes: Whose experiences are at the center of analysis? How is intersectionality conceptualized and examined? What are the "things" considered to be intersecting? In each section, I discuss where we are and how we can move closer to the original spirit of intersectionality. I end each section with some questions to help translate these themes into reflective thinking in clinical practice. I offer reflection questions because there is evidence that simple priming of intersectionality considerations can promote intersectional thinking and more positive perceptions of groups with intersecting minority statuses (Greenwood & Christian, 2008).

Whose Experiences Are at the Center of Analysis?

In much of the foundational theory, research, and practice in psychology, the answer to the question "Whose experiences are at the center of analysis" was decidedly (though implicitly) White, heterosexual, middle and upper class, college men. The experiences of other groups (e.g., women, sexual minority people, people of color, poor and working class people, people with disabilities) were considered anomalies or departures from these norms and were often explicitly excluded from sampling frames. These practices have waned. Nevertheless, ubiquitous and often implicit biases continue to define whose experiences are at the center of analysis, even when the analysis focuses on minority populations.

Purdie-Vaughns and Eibach (2008) suggested that androcentric, ethnocentric, and heterosexist biases combine to define an implicit prototype or reference group for various minority groups. For example, when we consider racial–ethnic minority issues, the experiences of racial–ethnic minority heterosexual men serve as the implicit reference point; when we consider sexual minority issues, the experiences of White gay men serve as the implicit reference point; and when we consider gender and sexism, the experiences of White heterosexual women serve as the implicit reference point. These implicit prototypes result in intersectional invisibility—that is, they render invisible people who experience several forms of minority status. For example, Black women's experiences become invisible in discussions of Black people's experiences and in discussions of women's experiences. Similarly, lesbian and bisexual women's experiences become invisible in discussions of sexual minority people's experiences and in discussions of women's experiences.

There is evidence of such intersectional invisibility in people's perceptions and in psychological research. For example, in two experimental studies, Goff, Thomas, and Jackson (2008) demonstrated that people's perceptions of "Blackness" and "maleness" overlapped. That is, participants rated Black women and men (images of faces or video clip characters) as more masculine than White women and men. Moreover, this overlap resulted in more errors in categorizing Black women as women (relative to categorizing White women as women or categorizing Black or White men as men). Some scholars (e.g., Boehmer, 2002; Greene, 1994; Moradi, DeBlaere, & Huang, 2010) have noted that the intersectional invisibility of sexual minority people of color is reinforced when research participants' sexual orientation characteristics are omitted in studies with racial–ethnic minority people and participants' racial–ethnic characteristics are omitted in studies with sexual minority people. The picture is bleaker if we consider substantive attention to sexual minority people of color in research. In a content analysis, Huang et al. (2010) found that less than 4% of abstracts for research on sexual orientation and less than 1% of abstracts for research on race–ethnicity attended substantively to sexual minority people of color. An important contribution of the intersectionality perspective is to make explicit the existence of implicit prototypes and to encourage intentional efforts to mitigate intersectional invisibility in research and practice.

Purdie-Vaughns and Eibach's (2008) analysis also encourages a broadening of the intersectionality lens. For example, the intersection of gender–sexism and race–racism, typically in Black women's experiences, has been formative in intersectionality scholarship (e.g., K. R. King, 2003; Moradi & Subich, 2003; Yoder & Aniakudo, 1997). However, focusing narrowly on this intersection can result in overlooking questions about the roles of ability status, sexual orientation, social class, and other dimensions in Black women's experiences (Nash, 2008). Similarly, attention to the experiences of sexual minority men of color has advanced understanding of the confluence of racism and heterosexism in relation to psychological symptomatology (Huang et al., 2010). However, this research tends to be conducted with Latino and African American young adult to middle aged men recruited from large metropolitan areas, and it tends to focus on risky sexual behaviors and substance use (Huang et al. 2010). Thus, experiences such as those of sexual minority women and trans or gender nonconforming people of color and experiences beyond sexual behaviors and substance use may be overlooked. Creating prototypes of intersectionality can limit our understanding of the experiences of the prototypic groups themselves and also constrain our understanding of the full breadth of intersectionalities.

An important contribution of intersectionality is its call for placing the experiences of nonprototype groups at the center of analysis (Choo & Ferree, 2010; Collins, 1989, 2000). Such practice is a contrast to the typical approach of generating knowledge and practice from the experiences of prototype groups and evaluating (or assuming) the generalizability of these experiences to other groups (e.g., Moradi & DeBlaere, 2010; Moradi, Mohr, Worthington, & Fassinger, 2009). An example of centralizing nonprototype intersectionalities is Hurtado and Sinha's (2008) analysis of the narratives of feminist identified working class Latino heterosexual and sexual minority men, a group that is not a prototype of any of the component categories of feminist, working class, Latino, or men. This analysis revealed definitions of "manhood" that were shaped by race, ethnicity, social class, and sexual orientation; were relational and reflected connections to family and community; emphasized ethics and equity; and challenged hegemonic masculinity including its construction through heteronormativity, patriarchy, and dominance.

As this example illustrates, research on nonprototypic intersections elucidates the experiences of the understudied groups themselves, challenges stereotypes about each of the component categories and their intersections (e.g., that Latino men are gender traditional, that feminists are middle to upper class White women), and produces novel conceptualizations of human experiences (e.g., manhood). Following this example, we might ask what kinds of questions and experiences would become evident if we attended to nonprototype intersectionalities such as the experiences of sexual minority women with disabilities, gender queer people of color, or sexual minority people residing in rural settings.

In clinical practice, integrating the following questions into our repertoire of reflective thinking may help to identify sexual minority (or any other group) prototypes and challenge intersectional invisibility when working with all clients:

- When I think about sexual minority, trans, and gender nonconforming people, what prototype comes to mind automatically for me? Based on this prototype, what kinds of experiences am I likely to attend to and to overlook? With which clients am I likely to attend to (or to overlook) issues of sexual orientation and gender identity and expression? How can I promote consideration of these issues with all clients, including clients who are not sexual minority, trans, or gender nonconforming prototypes? How can I broaden the range of experiences that I consider with sexual minority, trans, and gender nonconforming clients?

- When I think about intersectionality, what is the prototype that comes to mind automatically for me? Based on this prototype, which dimensions of intersectionality am I likely to attend to and to overlook? With which clients am I likely to attend to (or to overlook) considerations of intersectionality? How can I promote consideration of intersectionality with all clients, including clients who are not intersectionality prototypes? How can I promote consideration of intersectionality across dimensions, including dimensions that are not intersectionality prototypes (e.g., ability status)?

How Is Intersectionality Conceptualized and Examined?

Leslie McCall (2005) classified analyses of intersectionality into three approaches: anticategorical, intracategorical complexity, and intercategorical complexity. These three approaches share in common the aim of complicating social categories and systems of inequality, either by fundamentally questioning and subverting those categories (anticategorical) or by revealing the complexities within those categories (intracategorical complexity) and in their interrelations (intercategorical complexity). However, the different approaches involve different points of emphasis.

Anticategorical approaches challenge the very validity of social categories and the systems of inequality that produce them; for example, deconstructing essentialist notions of gender binaries, sexual orientation categories, and racial categories and articulating how these categories are constructed in specific social, historical, and political contexts. The *intracategorical complexity* and *intercategorical complexity* approaches acknowledge the social construction of categories but also use the categories in analyses based on the notion that the categories reflect meaningful, and sometimes durable, aspects of people's experiences in a given context. Intracategorical complexity approaches tend to focus on the experiences of single understudied groups (e.g., Black lesbian women) and how multiple categories of oppression intersect to shape that group's experiences. Intercategorical complexity approaches use group comparisons to reveal how multiple categories, including both privilege and oppression along those categories, combine to shape structural inequalities. For example, people of different gender, ethnic–racial, and sexual orientation groups and the resultant intersecting subgroups (e.g., heterosexual Asian American men, sexual minority White women) may be compared to understand how gender, ethnic–racial, and sexual orientation oppression and privilege combine to shape inequalities in various outcomes. Research on intersectionality and mental health with sexual minority and trans and gender nonconforming people largely takes an intracategorical complexity approach. Several themes emerge from this research: (a) intersectionality and distress, (b) questioning our questions about intersectionality, and (c) intersectionality and resilience.

Intersectionality and Distress

Many intracategorical complexity studies focus on a particular subgroup with multiple minority statuses and examine whether various forms of oppression (e.g., heterosexism, racism) account for additive unique variance in mental health and whether there are significant interactions such that one form (e.g., heterosexism) intensifies the deleterious link of the other form (e.g., racism) with criterion variables. For example, heterosexist and racist discrimination had unique additive relations with depression for African American and multiracial sexual minority adolescents (Thoma & Huebner, 2013). Internalized heterosexism and internalized racism had unique additive relations with low self-esteem for sexual minority African American people (Szymanski & Gupta, 2009a). Racist discrimination and internalized heterosexism had unique additive links with psychological distress for Asian American sexual minority people and African American sexual minority women (Szymanski & Gupta, 2009b; Szymanski & Meyer, 2008). Internalized heterosexism, internalized sexism, heterosexist victimization, and sexist discrimination had unique additive relations with psychological distress in samples comprising predominantly White sexual minority women (Szymanski, 2005; Szymanski & Kashubeck-West, 2008). Across these studies with various sample sizes and statistical power, interactions of the two forms of oppression were generally not significant. Thus, in clinical practice, these studies suggest exploring potential additive relations of multiple forms of discrimination or internalized prejudice with mental health in case conceptualization and treatment planning. However, the notion that one form of oppression exacerbates the link of another form of oppression with poor mental health is generally not supported.

One limitation of the aforementioned studies is that they may not fully capture the unique experiences of intersectionality for the populations of interest. For example, in qualitative studies, trans and gender nonconforming women of color described experiencing transphobia, racism, sexual objectification, and poverty as sources of stress that increased intrapersonal risk factors (e.g., internalized transphobia, self-objectification, high need for gender identity affirmation) that ultimately promoted engagement in high-risk sexual contexts and behaviors (Sevelius, 2013). Black sexual minority men described experiences of racism, heterosexism, and pressures to perform traditional masculinity as sources of stress (Bowleg, 2013). Black/African American sexual minority women described racism, sexism, and heterosexism as sources of stress; noted the primacy of racism; and described these stressors as inextricably linked and sometimes difficult to separate (Bowleg, Huang, Brooks, Black, & Burkholder, 2003).

Building on such findings, some studies use qualitative data on the unique experiences of the populations of interest, along with traditional quantitative approaches, to assess experiences of intersectionality. Examples of studies using this approach reveal that for Latino American gay and bisexual men, social isolation, low self-esteem, and experiences of homophobia and poverty but not racism or resilience factors were associated uniquely with psychological distress (Díaz, Ayala, Bein, Henne, & Marin, 2001). For Latina/o American sexual minority men and trans women (male-to-female), racist discrimination and internalized heterosexism, but not heterosexist discrimination or internalized racism, were associated uniquely with having sex under the influence of drugs and alcohol (Ramirez-Valles, Kuhns, Campbell, & Díaz, 2010). For sexual minority and trans and gender nonconforming people of color, heterosexism in racial–ethnic minority communities and racism in dating and close relationships were correlated positively with psychological distress, but racism in lesbian, gay, bisexual and transgender communities was not correlated with distress (Balsam, Molina, Beadnell, Simoni, & Walters, 2011). Collectively, these studies offer some support for additive intersectionality while also capturing some of the unique intersectional experiences of the populations of interest. These findings illustrate that different groups can have shared experiences (e.g., experience of racism across these samples), additive experiences (e.g., additional experiences of sexism for sexual minority women of color), and unique experiences shaped by particular intersections (e.g., intersection of sexual orientation and gender oppression and privilege manifested as pressures to perform traditional masculinity for Black sexual minority men). Translated into clinical practice, these studies are a helpful reminder of the importance of assessing unique experiences of intersectionality from the client's perspective.

Questioning Our Questions About Intersectionality

The importance of attending to the client's perspective is underscored by another theme in qualitative studies: researchers' discussions of a disconnect between their request for participants to describe conflict, ranking, and compartmentalization of their identities on the one hand, and participants' confusion and difficulty with doing so on the other hand. For example, Meyer (2010) described asking Black sexual minority people about conflict between sexual orientation identity and racial–ethnic identity, Yoder and Aniakudo (1997) described asking African American women firefighters to distinguish between their experiences of racism and sexism, and Bowleg (2008, 2013) described asking Black sexual minority women and men to describe if and how they rank the importance of their race, gender, and sexual orientation. In each case, the authors noted research participants' confusion, ambivalence, and rejection of the meaning and relevance of such probes.

Such participant reactions are consistent with the intersectionality perspective that different forms of oppression are interconnected. These reactions are also consistent with quantitative evidence that reports of racist, sexist, and heterosexist discrimination are correlated significantly, with effect sizes ranging from .18 to .54 in studies that used traditional measures (e.g., DeBlaere et al., 2014; Szymanski & Gupta, 2009b; Szymanski & Meyer, 2008; Thoma & Huebner, 2013; Velez, Moradi, & DeBlaere, 2015) and from .52 to .64 in a study that used measures of lesbian, gay, bisexual, and transgender people of color's intersectional experiences (Balsam et al., 2011).

The thoughtful reflections that Bowleg (2008, 2013), Meyer (2010), and Yoder and Aniakudo (1997) provided on the methodologies they used, and their research participants' responses, illustrate the powerful influence of the additive frame in limiting the nature of the questions we ask and the answers we receive about intersectionality, even in relatively flexible and open-ended interview questions. Although it is valuable to acknowledge potential experiences of cultural conflict or differential identity salience, research participants' responses to researchers' queries suggest the need to attend to intersectionality as involving identity cohesion, interconnection, and resilience.

Intersectionality and Resilience

A number of studies have probed strength, resilience, and coping associated with intersectionality for sexual minority and trans and gender nonconforming people of color. For example, Bowleg (2013) asked Black sexual minority men about the benefits of their intersecting identities. They described introspection and psychological growth, freedom from restrictive cultural norms, and openness to exploring new opportunities and strengths. Bowleg et al.'s (2003) sample of Black/African American sexual minority women described resilience factors, including external sources of support (e.g., Black communities, Black lesbian literature, Internet resources), intrapersonal strengths (e.g., sense of unique identity as a Black lesbian, self-esteem, sense of freedom from restrictive cultural norms), and interpersonal relationships. A notable coping strategy that emerged from Bowleg et al.'s interviews with Black/African American sexual minority women and Wilson and Miller's (2002) interviews with African American sexual minority men was role flexing; that is, managing and reducing exposure to discrimination by reorienting oneself to the aspect of identity (e.g., race–ethnicity, sexual orientation) that is less stigmatized or garners more support in a particular context. Singh (2013) found that trans and gender nonconforming youth of color described their gender and racial–ethnic identities as evolving and fused or interconnected. They pursued community connections, social media, and self-advocacy to protect themselves in the face of oppression.

Consistent with these themes from qualitative data, quantitative data with sexual minority women of color suggest that political activism around sexual minority issues buffered the link between heterosexist discrimination and psychological distress (DeBlaere et al., 2014) and that womanist consciousness (recognition of the intersections of racism and sexism) buffered the association between sexist discrimination and psychological distress (DeBlaere & Bertsch, 2013). Moreover, one novel though nascent area of support for multiplicative relations is the finding that for Latina/o sexual minority people, low internalized racism buffered the negative link between heterosexist discrimination and self-esteem and that low internalized heterosexism buffered the negative link between racist discrimination and self-esteem (Velez et al., 2015). Such synthesized interactions suggest that resisting internalization of one form of oppression may protect self-esteem when faced with high levels of another form of oppression.

These findings underscore the value of attending to ways in which individuals may draw upon intersectionality as a source of strength and resilience. Some of these resilience factors (e.g., freedom from restrictive cultural norms, openness to exploring new opportunities) echo those found in qualitative studies with samples of predominantly White sexual minority people (Riggle, Whitman, Olson, Rostosky, & Strong, 2008; Rostosky, Riggle, Pascale-Hague, & McCants, 2010). Other resilience factors and approaches to coping draw explicitly from interconnections among intersecting identities and the dynamic nature of identity construction; for example, role flexing to reorient to less stigmatized identities in a given context (e.g., Bowleg et al., 2003; Wilson & Miller, 2002), pursuing activism and connections with different communities (e.g., Bowleg et al., 2003; Singh, 2013), or drawing resilience from low internalized prejudice of one form when faced with high discrimination of another form (Velez et al., 2015). Moreover, findings on the strengths of intersectionality can be helpful in working with all clients, whether or not they are intersectionality prototypes. For example, White gay men may benefit from considering the value of role flexing or connections with different communities as ways to mitigate exposure to discrimination and resist oppression. However, the research described here also suggests that strength and resilience processes are easy to overlook when the implicit frame of intersectionality assumes identity conflict and distress.

The patterns of findings across the studies reviewed in this section point to a number of questions to help integrate empirical findings into clinical practice and also to help clarify and expand how we as clinicians conceptualize intersectionality in our work with clients:

- Which formulations of intersectionality come to the foreground for me, and which am I likely to overlook (e.g., additive, interactive, unique manifestations)? What are my assumptions about the consequences of intersectionality (e.g., risk and distress, identity conflict and cohesion, strength and resilience)?
- What language do I use to ask clients about intersectionality and its consequences (e.g., identity conflict, ranking, cohesion, strength)? How might the questions I ask limit the answers I get about my clients' experiences? What questions can I ask to explore a fuller picture of how intersectionality operates in my clients' experiences?

What Are the "Things" Considered to Be Intersecting?

In the research described thus far, several implicit themes operate about the things that are considered to be intersecting. The intersecting things are often framed as characteristics of minority people or their experiences (e.g., minority identity, perceived discrimination) rather than as sociocultural systems and contexts; are often multiple forms of oppression or minority status rather than forms of privilege (e.g., White identity, experiences of heterosexual privilege); and often involve gender, ethnicity–race, and sexual orientation with other dimensions (e.g., ability status, social class) receiving less attention. Disrupting and expanding our vision of intersectionality to address contexts, privilege, and less examined dimensions is critical to realizing the promise of intersectionality.

Research taking an anticategorical approach has been particularly helpful in this regard. For example, Valentine (2007) took a feminist geography approach to analyzing a case study. In a categorical approach, we might label Jeanette, the subject of the case study, as a White, lesbian, Deaf, woman. However, the focus of Valentine's analysis on time and place, rather than on categories as intrapersonal factors, demonstrated that Jeanette's experiences of gender, sexual orientation, social class, disability, and Deaf identity were context dependent and evolving. Specifically, Jeanette's adoption and disclosure of identity categories shaped and were shaped by the time period of her life and by each specific context in her life (e.g., family, workplace, Deaf community). Thus, Valentine's (2007) analysis underscored the experience of intersectionality not as static and dispositional to Jeanette, but as dynamic and both shaping and shaped by context.

As another example, Diamond and Butterworth's (2008) analysis of four trans and gender nonconforming people's narratives illustrated participants' flexibility, change, and resistance in relation to gender categories and to essentialist biological notions of gender. These participants' descriptions of dynamic identity construction also pointed to novel notions of sexual orientation. Specifically, as these participants shifted from identifying as lesbian or bisexual women toward a male or masculine gender identity, they also became more sexually attracted to and involved with men. The participants explained that these shifts did not reflect greater attraction to traitlike characteristics of men or masculinity. Rather, these shifts reflected changing interpersonal power dynamics—as men, they experienced more equal power with other men and therefore were more open to sexual relationships with men. This is a fundamentally different view from prevailing notions of sexual orientation and suggests that sexual orientation could involve attraction to equal power.

Both of these examples reveal the value of questioning the fundamental essence of categories in research and in clinical practice. In both cases, categories typically discussed as aspects of people (e.g., gender identity, disability, sexual orientation) are reconsidered as aspects of social context. Both analyses reveal the dynamic process of identity construction across time and place and how recognizing this dynamism could yield fundamentally new ways of thinking about human experience—for example, viewing interpersonal power as central to sexual orientation. In clinical practice, this shift can be subtle but powerful: Instead of asking how clients' gender, ethnicity–race, and sexual orientation influence their presenting concerns, one might ask: How do my clients construct themselves in various interpersonal, structural, historical, and other power dynamics; how do these dynamics shape my clients; and how do these patterns of coconstruction shape clients' presenting concerns?

Such a shift in perspective can be challenging in the context of the deeply rooted tradition in psychology to think in terms of group differences. Choo and Ferree (2010) described the danger of a group differences frame: It reduces intersectionality's focus on inequality to a focus on diversity. In such a frame, diversity becomes a euphemism for how nonprototype groups diverge from implicit prototypes, and differences are often attributed to unique (or problematic) cultural characteristics of the nonprototype groups. Thus, in a circular logic, sociodemographic group differences are sought and then explained by the original sociodemographic categories of analysis. Group similarities are often ignored and assumptions about group differences can persist despite evidence to the contrary (e.g., Helms, Jernigan, & Mascher, 2005; Hyde, 2005; Moradi & DeBlaere, 2010; Moradi, Wiseman, et al., 2010).

One example of this pattern is discussions of Latina/o cultures as particularly homophobic despite recent evidence to the contrary. For example, a national survey found that similar percentages of Latina/o American people (59%) and the general U.S. population (58%) believed that homosexuality should be accepted by society (Pew Hispanic Center, 2012). In this example, the focus on how nonprototype groups differ from the norm (even when data are inconsistent with such a focus) makes invisible the need to address heterosexism in over 40% of the U.S. population, Latina/o or not. The point is not to suggest that heterosexism is not prevalent among Latina/o people. Rather, it is important to note that similarly high levels of heterosexist attitudes in the general U.S. population do not result in problematizing White or U.S. culture as particularly heterosexist. In this way, the focus on group differences can promote a pattern of scrutinizing minority identities and cultures but not applying a parallel critical lens to dominant identities and cultures.

Illustrating this point, Meyer (2010) noted that terms such as *machismo* and *down low* are used specifically to signal areas of identity conflict for Latino and Black men, but parallel espousal of traditional gender role ideology or concealment of sexual orientation among White sexual minority people are not framed as uniquely characteristic of White culture or identity conflict. In other words, culture-specific factors (e.g., Latino culture, Black churches) are invoked as explanatory forces when minority statuses are involved, but cultural factors escape scrutiny when dominant statuses are involved (Moradi & DeBlaere, 2010). Similarly, identity conflict and rankings are probed when minority statuses are involved but not when privileged identities are involved (e.g., How does your gay identity conflict with your White cultural background? How does your high socioeconomic status rank relative to your identity as a man?).

Applying parallel scrutiny and asking questions about privileged statuses may help deepen understanding of participants' confusion and ambivalence when they are asked to compartmentalize their minority identities. Such practice also promotes the use of intersectional analysis to understand not only minority statuses but also how privileged statuses shape people's experiences. Indeed, in a study unique for its examination of the interplay between privileged and oppressed statuses, Croteau, Talbot, Lance, and Evans (2002) interviewed 18 higher education professionals (who were heterosexual people of color, White sexual minority people, or White heterosexual women) about how their privileged and oppressed statuses affected each other. One theme that emerged from these interviews was that participants readily identified their privileged and oppressed statuses but had difficulty staying focused on the mutual influence of these statuses. Instead, participants frequently slipped into discussing one dimension at a time. This pattern attests to the challenge of naming and probing privilege. Croteau et al.'s study also underscores the need for intentional reflection on privilege and the interplay of privilege and oppression. When encouraged to focus on the interplay, participants claimed that privilege sometimes reduced the effects of oppression, masked recognition of their oppressed statuses, or lessened their acceptance by other oppressed group members. However, having an oppressed status also promoted empathy and connections with others who had different oppressed statuses. Such empathy can be the groundwork for coalition building, discussed in the concluding section of this chapter.

These themes suggest the importance of attending to intersections, not as a few specific characteristics of people or groups but as structures that give rise to privilege and oppression. In this frame, people shape and are shaped by interpersonal, situational, historical, and other dynamic systems of power. Against the powerful backdrop of the group differences tradition, the following reflection questions may help to encourage clinicians to attend to structures of privilege and oppression and their interplay:

- With which clients do I attend to group differences and culture as explanatory factors for presenting concerns? How does my attention to group differences or similarities fit with empirical evidence and with my clients' experiences? How do I promote naming culture and power when my clients' minority statuses are involved as well as when their privileged statuses are involved?
- What are my assumptions about where intersectionality is located (e.g., in person, in context)? What does the language I use with my clients suggest about my emphasis on individual characteristics (e.g., gender, ethnicity, sexual orientation) versus sociocultural systems (e.g., cisgenderism, heterosexism, racism, and sexism); about my emphasis on identity as static versus shifting in the context of interpersonal, structural, historical, and other power dynamics?

POLITICAL INTERSECTIONALITY: THE ROOTS AND THE PROMISE OF INTERSECTIONALITY

Focusing on implicit prototypes, the tendency to compartmentalize experiences, seek differences, and explain differences as rooted in characteristics of individuals fits comfortably within the typical lens of psychology research and practice—how is this group or client different from what is normative (closely aligned with what is healthy), what about this group or client (or the group or client's culture or identities) explains this difference, and how can this group or client change to become healthier (more normative)? This frame focuses on the individual's sociodemographic characteristics, which can be readily operationalized and used as explanatory factors in hypothesis testing or case conceptualization. What is left out of this frame, however, is a major underpinning of intersectionality as a tool for recognizing structural and political forces that oppress and privilege people, identifying how those systems create shared concerns, and building political coalitions to combat those systems (e.g., Collins, 2000; Crenshaw, 1989).

Cole (2008) described this as *political intersectionality*. As an example of political intersectionality, Hancock (2007) described indigenismo movements that involve the political collaboration of Native American and Latino people in the United States with indigenous people in Guatemala, Mexico, Peru, and other countries to fight for civil rights and equality. Political intersectionality challenges traditional identity politics whereby single identity categories (e.g., gay, women) are the foundation for political groups (Hancock, 2007). These single identity categories are presumed to represent shared experiences within the group but often reflect the experiences of the implicit prototypes. The roots of intersectionality—from Sojourner Truth's declaration of "Ain't I a Woman?" to Crenshaw's (1989) explicit discussion of intersectionality—were to reveal precisely this limitation of identity politics in feminist and antiracist political activism.

The shift from focusing on individual characteristics and individual change to attending to systems of power and forming coalitions reflects both the roots and the promise of intersectionality. In part, this shift involves intentional reflection and reframing. For example, Walby, Armstrong, and Strid (2012) suggested that terms such as *categories* be replaced with terms such as *set of unequal social relations, inequality,* and *social system* to underscore the structural interrelatedness of oppression and privilege. Following this example, we might replace language about ability status, gender, race, class, and sexual orientation with language capturing ableism, sexism, racism, classism, heterosexism or, more broadly oppression, injustice, and privilege. The reflection questions I have offered thus far may also facilitate intentional reframing.

However, the shift toward building coalitions to challenge systems of power ultimately requires action outside of reflection, reframing, and the therapy room. Here, it seems appropriate to quote Crenshaw's (1991) vision of the promise of intersectionality:

> organized identity groups in which we find ourselves are in fact coalitions, or at least potential coalitions waiting to be formed . . . With identity thus reconceptualized, it may be easier to understand the need for and to summon the courage to challenge groups that are after all, in one sense, "home" to us, in the name of the parts of us that are not made

at home. This takes a great deal of energy and arouses intense anxiety. The most one could expect is that we will dare to speak against internal exclusions and marginalization, that we might call attention to how the identity of "the group" has been centered on the intersectional identities of a few. Recognizing that identity politics takes place at the site where categories intersect thus seems more fruitful than challenging the possibility of talking about categories at all. Through an awareness of intersectionality, we can better acknowledge and ground the differences among us and negotiate the means by which these differences will find expression in constructing group politics. (p. 1299)

In this excerpt, Crenshaw (1991) articulated the key points about the who, the how, and the what of intersectionality that I have attempted to elaborate on. Crenshaw's (1991) description underscores that intersectionality is more than a call for attention to multiple identities, group differences, or within-group diversity. Intersectionality invites us to think beyond aspects of identity that feel intrinsic to us. Intersectionality invites us to consider systems that give rise to inequality and to apply equal scrutiny to oppression and privilege. Intersectionality invites us to attend to shared experiences around which we can build coalitions to challenge systems of inequality. This shift from identities to systems may be challenging, uncomfortable, and outside of the traditional box of research and clinical practice. I believe that Crenshaw's (1991) vision, articulated over two decades ago, that remains an important compass for realizing the promise of intersectionality. Realizing the promise of intersectionality ultimately requires power-disrupting collective action by clients, clinicians, scholars, and the coalitions that they build.

REFERENCES

Balsam, K. F., Molina, Y., Beadnell, B., Simoni, J., & Walters, K. (2011). Measuring multiple minority stress: The LGBT People of Color Microaggressions Scale. *Cultural Diversity and Ethnic Minority Psychology, 17*, 163–174. http://dx.doi.org/10.1037/a0023244

Beale, F. M. (1970). Double jeopardy: To be Black and female. In T. Cade Bambara (Ed.), *The Black woman: An anthology* (pp. 109–122). New York, NY: Washington Square Press.

Boehmer, U. (2002). Twenty years of public health research: Inclusion of lesbian, gay, bisexual, and transgender populations. *American Journal of Public Health, 92*, 1125–1130. http://dx.doi.org/10.2105/AJPH.92.7.1125

Bond, J. E. (2003). International intersectionality: A theoretical and pragmatic exploration of women's international human rights violations. *Emory Law Journal, 52*, 71–186.

Bowleg, L. (2008). When Black + lesbian + woman ≠ Black lesbian woman: The methodological challenges of qualitative and quantitative intersectionality research. *Sex Roles, 59,* 312–325. http://dx.doi.org/10.1007/s11199-008-9400-z

Bowleg, L. (2013). "Once you've blended the cake, you can't take the parts back to the main ingredients": Black gay and bisexual men's descriptions and experiences of intersectionality. *Sex Roles, 68,* 754–767. http://dx.doi.org/10.1007/s11199-012-0152-4

Bowleg, L., Huang, J., Brooks, K., Black, A., & Burkholder, G. (2003). Triple jeopardy and beyond: Multiple minority stress and resilience among Black lesbians. *Journal of Lesbian Studies, 7,* 87–108. http://dx.doi.org/10.1300/J155v07n04_06

Choo, H. Y., & Ferree, M. M. (2010). Practicing intersectionality in sociological research: A critical analysis of inclusions, interactions, and institutions in the study of inequalities. *Sociological Theory, 28,* 129–149. http://dx.doi.org/10.1111/j.1467-9558.2010.01370.x

Cole, E. R. (2008). Coalitions as a model for intersectionality: From practice to theory. *Sex Roles, 59,* 443–453. http://dx.doi.org/10.1007/s11199-008-9419-1

Cole, E. R. (2009). Intersectionality and research in psychology. *American Psychologist, 64,* 170–180. http://dx.doi.org/10.1037/a0014564

Collins, P. H. (1989). The social construction of Black feminist thought. *Signs: Journal of Women in Culture and Society, 14,* 745–773. http://dx.doi.org/10.1086/494543

Collins, P. H. (2000). *Black feminist thought: Knowledge, consciousness, and the politics of empowerment.* New York, NY: Routledge.

Combahee River Collective. (1977–1983). The Combahee River Collective statement. In B. Smith (Ed.), *Homegirls: A Black feminist anthology* (pp. 264–274). New York, NY: Kitchen Table, Women of Color Press.

Crenshaw, K. (1989). Demarginalizing the intersection of race and sex: A Black feminist critique of antidiscrimination doctrine, feminist theory and antiracist politics. *University of Chicago Legal Forum, 1989,* 139–167.

Crenshaw, K. (1991). Mapping the margins: Intersectionality, identity politics, and violence against women of color. *Stanford Law Review, 43,* 1241–1299. http://dx.doi.org/10.2307/1229039

Croteau, J. M., Talbot, D. M., Lance, T. S., & Evans, N. J. (2002). A qualitative study of the interplay between privilege and oppression. *Journal of Multicultural Counseling and Development, 30,* 239–258. http://dx.doi.org/10.1002/j.2161-1912.2002.tb00522.x

Davis, A. Y. (1981). *Women, race, and class.* New York, NY: Random House.

Davis, K. (2008). Intersectionality as a buzzword: A sociology of science perspective on what makes a feminist theory successful. *Feminist Theory, 9,* 67–85. http://dx.doi.org/10.1177/1464700108086364

DeBlaere, C., & Bertsch, K. N. (2013). Perceived sexist events and psychological distress of sexual minority women of color: The moderating role of womanism. *Psychology of Women Quarterly, 37*, 167–178. http://dx.doi.org/10.1177/0361684312470436

DeBlaere, C., Brewster, M. E., Bertsch, K. N., DeCarlo, A. L., Kegel, K. A., & Presseau, C. D. (2014). The protective power of collective action for sexual minority women of color: An investigation of multiple discrimination experiences and psychological distress. *Psychology of Women Quarterly, 38*, 20–32. http://dx.doi.org/10.1177/0361684313493252

DeBlaere, C., Brewster, M. E., Sarkees, A., & Moradi, B. (2010). Conducting research with LGB people of color: Methodological challenges and strategies. *The Counseling Psychologist, 38*, 331–362. http://dx.doi.org/10.1177/0011000009335257

Diamond, L. M., & Butterworth, M. (2008). Questioning gender and sexual identity: Dynamic links over time. *Sex Roles, 59*, 365–376. http://dx.doi.org/10.1007/s11199-008-9425-3

Díaz, R. M., Ayala, G., Bein, E., Henne, J., & Marin, B. V. (2001). The impact of homophobia, poverty, and racism on the mental health of gay and bisexual Latino men: Findings from 3 US cities. *American Journal of Public Health, 91*, 927–932. http://dx.doi.org/10.2105/AJPH.91.6.927

Essed, P. (1991). *Understanding everyday racism: An interdisciplinary theory.* Newbury Park, CA: Sage.

Goff, P., Thomas, M. A., & Jackson, M. (2008). "Ain't I a woman?": Towards an intersectional approach to person perception and group-based harms. *Sex Roles, 59*, 392–403. http://dx.doi.org/10.1007/s11199-008-9505-4

Greene, B. (1994). African American women. In L. Comas-Díaz & B. Greene (Eds.), *Women of color: Integrating ethnic and gender identities in psychotherapy* (pp. 10–29). New York, NY: Guilford Press.

Greenwood, R., & Christian, A. (2008). What happens when we unpack the invisible knapsack? Intersectional political consciousness and inter-group appraisals. *Sex Roles, 59*, 404–417. http://dx.doi.org/10.1007/s11199-008-9439-x

Hancock, A. M. (2007). When multiplication doesn't equal quick addition: Examining intersectionality as a research paradigm. *Perspectives on Politics, 5*, 63–79. http://dx.doi.org/10.1017/S1537592707070065

Helms, J. E., Jernigan, M., & Mascher, J. (2005). The meaning of race in psychology and how to change it: A methodological perspective. *American Psychologist, 60*, 27–36.

hooks, b. (1981). *Ain't I a woman: Black women and feminism.* Boston, MA: South End Press.

Huang, Y. P., Brewster, M. E., Moradi, B., Goodman, M. B., Wiseman, M. C., & Martin, A. (2010). Content analysis of literature about lesbian, gay, and bisexual people of color: 1998–2007. *The Counseling Psychologist, 38*, 363–396. http://dx.doi.org/10.1177/0011000009335255

Hurtado, A., & Sinha, M. (2008). More than men: Latino feminist masculinities and intersectionality. *Sex Roles, 59*, 337–349. http://dx.doi.org/10.1007/s11199-008-9405-7

Hyde, J. S. (2005). The gender similarities hypothesis. *American Psychologist, 60,* 581–592. http://dx.doi.org/10.1037/0003-066X.60.6.581

Jeffries, V., & Ransford, E. H. (1980). *Social stratification: A multiple hierarchy approach.* Wellesley, MA: Allyn & Bacon.

Johnson-Bailey, J., & Cervero, R. M. (1996). An analysis of the educational narratives of reentry Black women. *Adult Education Quarterly, 46,* 142–157. http://dx.doi.org/10.1177/074171369604600302

King, D. K. (1988). Multiple jeopardy, multiple consciousness: The context of a Black feminist ideology. *Signs: Journal of Women in Culture and Society, 14,* 42–72. http://dx.doi.org/10.1086/494491

King, K. R. (2003). Do you see what I see? Effects of group consciousness on African American women's attributions to prejudice. *Psychology of Women Quarterly, 27,* 17–30. http://dx.doi.org/10.1111/1471-6402.t01-2-00003

Landrine, H., Klonoff, E. A., Alcaraz, R., Scott, J., & Wikins, P. (1995). Multiple variables in discrimination. In B. Lott & D. Maluso (Eds.), *The social psychology of interpersonal discrimination* (pp. 183–224). New York, NY: Guilford Press.

Lorde, A. (1984). *Sister outsider.* Berkeley, CA: Crossing Press.

Martin, C. (2010). *Courtney Martin: This isn't her mother's feminism* [Video file]. Available from http://www.ted.com/talks/courtney_martin_reinventing_feminism.html

McCall, L. (2005). The complexity of intersectionality. *Signs: Journal of Women in Culture and Society, 30,* 1771–1800. http://dx.doi.org/10.1086/426800

Meyer, I. H. (2010). Identity, stress, and resilience in lesbians, gay men, and bisexuals of color. *The Counseling Psychologist, 38,* 442–454. http://dx.doi.org/10.1177/0011000009351601

Moradi, B., & DeBlaere, C. (2010). Replacing either/or with both/and: Illustrations of perspective alternation. *The Counseling Psychologist, 38,* 455–468. http://dx.doi.org/10.1177/0011000009356460

Moradi, B., DeBlaere, C., & Huang, Y. P. (2010). Centralizing the experiences of LGB people of color in counseling psychology. *The Counseling Psychologist, 38,* 322–330. http://dx.doi.org/10.1177/0011000008330832

Moradi, B., Mohr, J. J., Worthington, R. L., & Fassinger, R. E. (2009). Counseling psychology research on sexual (orientation) minority issues: Conceptual and methodological challenges and opportunities. *Journal of Counseling Psychology, 56,* 5–22. http://dx.doi.org/10.1037/a0014572

Moradi, B., & Subich, L. (2003). A concomitant examination of the relations of perceived racist and the sexist events to psychological distress for African American women. *The Counseling Psychologist, 31,* 451–469. http://dx.doi.org/10.1177/0011000003031004007

Moradi, B., Wiseman, M. C., DeBlaere, C., Goodman, M. B., Sarkees, A., Brewster, M. E., & Huang, Y. P. (2010). LGB of color and White individuals' perceptions of heterosexist stigma, internalized homophobia, and outness: Comparisons of levels and links. *The Counseling Psychologist, 38,* 397–424. http://dx.doi.org/10.1177/0011000009335263

Nash, J. C. (2008). Re-thinking intersectionality. *Feminist Review, 89*, 1–15. http:// dx.doi.org/10.1057/fr.2008.4

Parent, M. C., DeBlaere, C., & Moradi, B. (2013). Approaches to research on inter- sectionality: Perspectives on gender, LGBT, and racial/ethnic identities. *Sex Roles, 68*, 639–645. http://dx.doi.org/10.1007/s11199-013-0283-2

Pew Hispanic Center. (2012, April 4). *When labels don't fit: Hispanics and their views of identity.* Washington, DC: Author.

Purdie-Vaughns, V., & Eibach, R. P. (2008). Intersectional invisibility: The distinc- tive advantages and disadvantages of multiple subordinate-group identities. *Sex Roles, 59*, 377–391. http://dx.doi.org/10.1007/s11199-008-9424-4

Ramirez-Valles, J., Kuhns, L. M., Campbell, R. T., & Díaz, R. M. (2010). Social inte- gration and health: Community involvement, stigmatized identities, and sexual risk in Latino sexual minorities. *Journal of Health and Social Behavior, 51*, 30–47. http://dx.doi.org/10.1177/0022146509361176

Riggle, E. D. B., Whitman, J. S., Olson, A., Rostosky, S. S., & Strong, S. (2008). The positive aspects of being a lesbian or gay man. *Professional Psychology: Research and Practice, 39*, 210–217. http://dx.doi.org/10.1037/0735-7028.39.2.210

Rogers, J., & Kelly, U. A. (2011). Feminist intersectionality: Bringing social justice to health disparities research. *Nursing Ethics, 18*, 397–407. http://dx.doi.org/ 10.1177/0969733011398094

Rostosky, S. S., Riggle, E. D. B., Pascale-Hague, D., & McCants, L. E. (2010). The positive aspects of a bisexual identification. *Psychology and Sexuality, 1*, 131–144. http://dx.doi.org/10.1080/19419899.2010.484595

Sevelius, J. M. (2013). Gender affirmation: A framework for conceptualizing risk behavior among transgender women of color. *Sex Roles, 68*, 675–689. http:// dx.doi.org/10.1007/s11199-012-0216-5

Shields, S. A. (2008). Gender: An intersectionality perspective. *Sex Roles, 59*, 301–311. http://dx.doi.org/10.1007/s11199-008-9501-8

Singh, A. A. (2013). Transgender youth of color and resilience: Negotiating oppres- sion and finding support. *Sex Roles, 68*, 690–702. http://dx.doi.org/10.1007/ s11199-012-0149-z

St. Jean, Y., & Feagin, J. R. (1997). Racial masques: Black women and subtle gen- dered racism. In N. V. Benkraitis (Ed.), *Subtle sexism* (pp. 179–200). Thousand Oaks, CA: Sage.

Szymanski, D. M. (2005). Heterosexism and sexism as correlates of psychological distress in lesbians. *Journal of Counseling & Development, 83*, 355–360. http:// dx.doi.org/10.1002/j.1556-6678.2005.tb00355.x

Szymanski, D. M., & Gupta, A. (2009a). Examining the relationship between mul- tiple internalized oppressions and African American lesbian, gay, bisexual, and questioning persons' self-esteem and psychological distress. *Journal of Counseling Psychology, 56*, 110–118. http://dx.doi.org/10.1037/a0013317

Szymanski, D. M., & Gupta, A. (2009b). Examining the relationships between mul- tiple oppressions and Asian American sexual minority persons' psychological distress. *Journal of Gay & Lesbian Social Services, 21*, 267–281. http://dx.doi.org/10.1080/10538720902772212

Szymanski, D. M., & Kashubeck-West, S. (2008). Mediators of the relationship between internalized oppressions and lesbian and bisexual women's psychological distress. *The Counseling Psychologist, 36*, 575–594. http://dx.doi.org/10.1177/0011000007309490

Szymanski, D. M., & Meyer, D. (2008). Racism and heterosexism as correlates of psychological distress in African American sexual minority women. *Journal of LGBT Issues in Counseling, 2*, 94–108. http://dx.doi.org/10.1080/15538600802125423

Thoma, B. C., & Huebner, D. M. (2013). Health consequences of racist and antigay discrimination for multiple minority adolescents. *Cultural Diversity and Ethnic Minority Psychology, 19*, 404–413. http://dx.doi.org/10.1037/a0031739

Valentine, G. (2007). Theorizing and researching intersectionality: A challenge for feminist geography. *The Professional Geographer, 59*, 10–21. http://dx.doi.org/10.1111/j.1467-9272.2007.00587.x

Velez, B. L., Moradi, B., & DeBlaere, C. (2015). Multiple oppressions and the mental health of sexual minority Latina/o individuals. *The Counseling Psychologist, 43*, 7–38.

Verloo, M. (2006). Multiple inequalities, intersectionality and the European Union. *European Journal of Women's Studies, 13*, 211–228.

Walby, S., Armstrong, J., & Strid, S. (2012). Intersectionality: Multiple inequalities in social theory. *Sociology, 46*, 224–240. http://dx.doi.org/10.1177/0038038511416164

Warner, L. R. (2008). A best practices guide to intersectional approaches in psychological research. *Sex Roles, 59*, 454–463. http://dx.doi.org/10.1007/s11199-008-9504-5

Warner, L. R., & Shields, S. A. (2013). The intersections of sexuality, gender, and race: Identity research at the crossroads. *Sex Roles, 68*, 803–810. http://dx.doi.org/10.1007/s11199-013-0281-4

Weber, L., & Parra-Medina, D. (2003). Intersectionality and women's health: Charting a path to eliminating health disparities. *Gender Perspectives on Health and Medicine, 7*, 181–230. http://dx.doi.org/10.1016/S1529-2126(03)07006-1

Wilson, B. D. M., & Miller, R. L. (2002). Strategies for managing heterosexism used among African-American gay and bisexual men. *Journal of Black Psychology, 28*, 371–391.

Yoder, J. D., & Aniakudo, P. (1997). "Outsider within" the firehouse: Subordination and difference in the social interactions of African American women firefighters. *Gender & Society, 11*, 324–341. http://dx.doi.org/10.1177/089124397011003004

Yuval-Davis, N. (2006). Intersectionality and feminist politics. *European Journal of Women's Studies, 13*, 193–209. http://dx.doi.org/10.1177/1350506806065752

II

AFFIRMATIVE COUNSELING WITH SEXUAL MINORITY, TRANSGENDER, AND GENDER NONCONFORMING CLIENTS

5

AFFIRMATIVE COUNSELING WITH SEXUAL MINORITY CLIENTS

PARRISH L. PAUL

When I was first asked to write this chapter, I found myself wondering what affirmative counseling for sexual minority clients means in today's world. Bieschke, Perez, and DeBord (2007) argued that despite the best intentions of many mental health professionals, being meaningfully and inclusively affirmative is a complex process: "We believe that the path to affirmation begins with the realization that as members of a heterosexist society, all of us, regardless of sexual orientation, bring our heterosexual biases into our work as counselors and therapists" (p. 5). How far have we come in the affirmation of sexual minority persons and in regard to societal heterosexism? Social support for sexual minority persons appears to be growing. For example, public endorsement of marriage equality has increased in recent years, particularly in younger generations ("Growing Support," 2014), and the 2015 United States Supreme Court ruling allowing same-sex couples to marry (de Vogue & Diamond, 2015) changed the legal and civil rights landscape for same-sex

http://dx.doi.org/10.1037/15959-006
Handbook of Sexual Orientation and Gender Diversity in Counseling and Psychotherapy, K. A. DeBord, A. R. Fischer, K. J. Bieschke, and R. M. Perez (Editors)

couples. Affirmation of sexual minority persons is not consistent or necessarily commonplace, however. In the last several years, some trainees in mental health fields have argued that because of their religious beliefs, they should not be required to provide clinical services to sexual minority clients or they should not provide services that are affirmative of sexual minority identity (Bieschke & Mintz, 2012). I see these recent events as examples of a societal tension that includes growing social support for sexual minority persons alongside the continued existence of an oppressive heteronormative system. This is the context and experience of sexual minority individuals today.

A brief clinical example illustrates this point. (Details have been changed to protect confidentiality, but the spirit of the case has been maintained.) A client once told me about how she carried a great stone on her back. She could explain in detail about the size and weight of the stone, the meaning it held for her, and the pain she felt with this burden. At first I thought the psychotherapeutic work would be focused primarily on releasing this weight. Later I realized that as heavy as the stone was to bear, as difficult as it was for her to be reminded of what it meant, and as many times as it dragged my client into self-doubt, the stone also served a valuable purpose for her. This client wanted to remember, every day, that she should not allow herself to "just relax." She guarded against trusting relationships, and she had tired of hoping for her life to change. Over the years, it had become more painful to forget that the world she lived in was not a safe and trusting place, so the pain of the burden became easier to bear than the pain of losing faith in the world all over again. For this client, the heterosexist social system not only was oppressive, but it also weighed her down and made her doubt and accuse herself severely. What I had not understood at first was how she would use this burden to guard herself. Because she had a fundamental fear that she could never be truly accepted and loved as a "gay woman," the stone served as a protector and reminder. Carrying this weight seemed easier to her than feeling disappointed and hurt once again when experiencing the heterosexism or homophobia that she encountered.

I tell this story as an example of the ways in which systems of oppression live in the experiences of our clients and can coalesce into mental health concerns over time. Clinicians can help clients to see the ways these systems of power and privilege may label the client as pathological or somehow broken, when perhaps it would be more appropriate to name oppression as the real issue. Because we as clinicians grow up in these same systems and can also be blind to how they have shaped or wounded us, we may also bring heterosexist biases into our work and potentially recreate the wounding that brought clients to our doors in the first place. In this chapter, I review the ways in which minority stress delivered through systemic heterosexism can have an impact on mental health for sexual minority persons. I also consider guidelines and competencies that have been recently published and how these may be applied in a case example. Finally I consider how clinicians can be meaningfully affirmative in work with sexual minority persons, when some practitioners may continue to struggle to do so. First, however, I situate the following chapter in terms of my own assumptions, biases, social locations, and influences.

MY CONTEXT: INFLUENCES ON THIS CHAPTER

I am a gay, White male, born in the southern United States. I have cisgender and White male privilege. I do not currently experience outwardly negative reactions to my sexual minority identity. However, I have grown up in a society that normalizes heterosexual identity and behavior and oppresses sexual minority persons. I feel the effects of oppression and the fears that can accompany it in some moments. I believe that I may experience discomfort, judgment, hate, or other negative reactions because of my sexual minority identity. Sometimes when I cannot explain a difficult or hurtful situation and have exhausted other ways to understand what is happening, I wonder whether there is homophobia occurring. I have been treated pretty well in life compared to the experiences of many of my clients, but my experiences as a gay man can make me wonder how I will be treated by others.

I have other intersections of identity that are important. I have been partnered for 16 years at the time of this writing. I grew up Christian, though it would likely be better to describe me as a spiritual person now. I am fortunate to have held several different types of positions in the field of psychology, though I have maintained an overall focus on work as a practitioner (who also values some scholarly, training, and administrative roles in my work). Other intersections of identity wax and wane in importance during different periods of my life. I share all of this so that readers understand my lens. For some people, this will make my writing mean more, whereas others may determine that I am too biased by my own experience to be a trusted voice.

THE CONTEXT FOR SEXUAL MINORITY PERSONS

Sexual minorities comprise approximately 3% to 8% of the U.S. population, depending on the source (Graham, Carney, & Kluck, 2012). Does this range of percentages really capture the population and experience of sexual minority persons? Does it include only those who identify in a particular way, such as lesbian, gay, and bisexual, or those who are comfortable enough to participate in research? Does it also include those for whom the current definitions of identity are less clear or appropriate? According to the Williams Institute (Gates, 2011), an estimated 3.5% of U.S. adults identify as lesbian, gay, or bisexual; 8.2% of people reported same-sex sexual experience; and 11% reported at least some same-sex attraction. Perhaps including sexual experience and attraction better describes the percentage range of sexual minority persons in the population, at least in some ways. However, for some people, it is extremely difficult to first recognize and then name a sexual minority identity to others; they fear they will not be accepted or loved by family, by their experience of God(s), religious communities, friends, coworkers, or others. For all the recent positive societal changes that suggest increasing acceptance, a heterosexist system of power and privilege remains, and the oppressive messages of that system remain strong (e.g., Brewster, Moradi, DeBlaere, & Velez, 2013; Brown, 2008; G. W. Harper, Brodsky, & Bruce, 2012; Lick, Durso, & Johnson, 2013; Meyer, 2013). For some sexual minority persons, living in such a system could be traumatizing.

Sexual Minority Oppression as Trauma

Brown (2008) conceptualized minority sexual orientation as a potential risk factor for trauma, created from ongoing exposure to discrimination and oppression. Many sexual minority persons experience negative consequences from families, friends, and communities. They may feel discomfort or lose valued relationships or social supports. They may be viewed as uncaring about certain cultural beliefs or practices by attempting to integrate a sexual minority identity. A heterosexist privilege is interwoven in our society that oppresses, judges, or second-guesses others (Croteau, Lark, Lidderdale, & Chung, 2005). As an example, I ask readers to abandon professional distance for a moment to try on the lived experiences of some of our clients. How would it feel to live inside a societal discourse that communicates messages that you are somehow less than others, wrong, or bad? Consider how hard it may be to develop ways to support and soothe yourself in the face of oppressive messages. Can you imagine how it feels when the people who raised you say painful things about you, or when the people and groups you have come to love exclude you? I ask you to envision how tired you may become with the effort and how sometimes you may not quite be able to remember that you are okay and the system of oppression is what is broken. These are the experiences that many of our clients bring with them to our sessions. As difficult and painful as many individual stories may be, I do not mean to imply that there is not beauty and support in being a sexual minority person.

Positive Aspects of Sexual Minority Identity

Sexual minority individuals also experience great resilience and agency, coping effectively within the current heterosexist system (e.g., A. Harper et al., 2013; G. W. Harper et al., 2012; Kertzner, Meyer, Frost, & Stirratt, 2009; Russell

& Richards, 2003; Saewyc, 2011). Many individuals describe a profound sense of acceptance and community, and they are active and engaged in meaningful ways. Riggle, Whitman, Olson, Rostosky, and Strong (2008) qualitatively analyzed online survey data on perceptions of the positive aspects of being gay or lesbian. Their 553 participants described positive features including having community; constructing families of choice and other strong relational connections; being a positive role model; having authenticity and honesty; participation in social justice and activism; exploring multiple expressions of sexuality and relationship; and developing insight, a sense of self, and increased empathy and compassion. Lesbian participants also described egalitarian relationships. However, these positive aspects may not sustain all sexual minority persons, particularly given varying individual experience and changes in social acceptance over time that could be experienced differently across sexual minority age cohorts. The stress created by minority status in the societal discourse is considered in the section that follows.

MINORITY STRESS

Sexual minority status has not been viewed as a mental disorder in and of itself for more than 40 years. In the majority of existing sexual minority research, participants have been described by specific identity labels (most frequently lesbian, gay, and bisexual). For clarity, I use the identity labels named by researchers when describing specific research examples. Research evidence suggests that sexual minority populations experience mental disorders at higher rates than heterosexual persons (Meyer, 2013), with gay men and lesbians about 2.5 times more likely than heterosexual persons to have experienced a mental health diagnosis of some kind over their lifetimes. Lesbian, gay, and bisexual individuals appear to have a higher risk for suicidal ideation and attempts than heterosexual persons, with data suggesting that gay men may demonstrate the most suicidal risk (Meyer, 2013). As noted earlier, individual resilience and agency abound (e.g., G. W. Harper et al., 2012; Riggle et al., 2008), along with research participants describing many positive experiences of community and authenticity in living. However, the context of heterosexism remains, with discrimination, prejudice, and violence disproportionately experienced by many lesbian, gay, and bisexual clients, leading to increases in psychological distress (Garnets, Herek, & Levy, 1990; Mays & Cochran 2001; Meyer, 2013).

Minority Stress as Psychological Distress

Meyer (2003, 2013) has argued that a minority stress model may help to explain the increased incidence of mental disorders in sexual minority populations. In brief, the stress that results from marginalized status creates psychological distress that can reach debilitating levels for some people. Discrimination, prejudice, and stigma, the inter- and intra-personal difficulties that tend to accompany such struggles, and other stressors that any sexual majority or minority person may experience can combine to increase the risk for psychological illness. Furthermore, Meyer (2013) argued that minority stress is not only the experience of stressful events themselves, it is also tied to the phenomenological and existential meaning of oppression, the increased stress related to the meaning we make of our situations, how this affects our personal control and our relationships with ourselves and others, and so on.

Researchers have explored tenets of minority stress theory with sexual minority persons in increasing specificity over time. Specifically attending to issues of minority stress with bisexual persons, Brewster et al. (2013) studied the relationship between minority stressors and mechanisms promoting mental health. The researchers found that greater psychological distress and lower psychological well-being were consistent with high perceived antibisexual prejudice, expectations of stigma, and internalized biphobia. Velez, Moradi, and Brewster (2013) extended minority stress theory to the experiences of lesbian, gay, and bisexual persons in the workplace, researching relationships between minority stress (operationalized as heterosexist discrimination in the workplace, expectations of stigma, internalized heterosexism in the individual, and identity management strategies) and psychological distress and job satisfaction. Participants who experienced minority stress reported increased psychological stress and less job satisfaction. Lick, Durso, and Johnson (2013) further argued that minority stress affects both the mental health and the physical health of sexual minority persons. These authors noted that there is growing research evidence suggesting that sexual minority persons suffer more acute and chronic physical health concerns than heterosexual persons; they suggested that this disparity is due to negative social experiences and the internalized homophobia that results from oppression and stigmatization.

Resilience and Coping With Minority Stress

Meyer (2013) noted that stressful situations can at times lead to increased resilience and development of coping skills. L. Carter, Mollen, and Smith (2014) examined components of minority stress theory with a sample of 165 lesbian, gay, and bisexual persons. These researchers found that locus of control moderated the relationship between prejudice that participants experienced in the workplace and overall psychological distress. In other words, participants with more internalized locus of control (or more personal sense of control) were more buffered from distress or perhaps more resilient in the face of distress.

More research is needed on the ways sexual minority persons with other inter-sections of oppressed identities as well could be at risk for more distress, but may also have increased opportunities for sources of support in communities tied to their multiple identities (Meyer, 2010).

Individuals in stress may find affirmative communities and group connec-tions that are meaningful (Meyer, 2013). However, they must be able to allow themselves membership in an oppressed group to enable themselves to receive support from that group—a challenge for some people. The intersections of identity that are valued by a person may increase the challenge. When an iden-tity is oppressed or stigmatized, there is the potential for impact on the well-being of the person (Meyer, 2013). Minority identity may weaken the impact of stress when there is community or support, or it may increase the distress when that identity mirrors the message of a heterosexist society.

When I stop to reflect on minority stress theory, it resonates with the stories of my clients. Clients have tended to respond to the aggressions and microaggressions they experience and have what I see as humanly under-standable reactions of becoming stuck, depressed, or anxious. They may face other concerns as well. They try to soothe the pain in whatever ways they can—sometimes coping beautifully, with much support, community, fam-ily, or faith, and sometimes perhaps not coping as well, with substance use, sexual behavior they later regret, or in many other ways that may result in symptoms of depression, anxiety, or other concerns. Systemic heterosexism would then allow those with the most power and privilege to observe those individuals who are struggling and say how it all makes sense, because the people who were called "less than" or "sick" would now be viewed through a lens of psychopathology. Instead, in my understanding of the minority stress model, the stress that sexual minority persons experience is added to normal human stress, is "supported" by the heterosexist messages of society, is chronic and ongoing, and may coalesce into serious concerns, depending on the resources of the individual.

GUIDELINES, COMPETENCIES, AND CONSIDERATIONS FOR AFFIRMATIVE PRACTICE

How can practitioners address these deeply seated societal messages with clients? In this section, I review considerations in developing affirma-tion in clinical practice, along with several recent guidelines and competen-cies. To begin, what does affirmative practice mean? Perez (2007) offered the following definition of *affirmative therapy*:

the integration of knowledge and awareness by the therapist of the unique development and cultural aspect of [lesbian, gay, bisexual, and transgender] individuals, the therapist's own self-knowledge, and the translation of this knowledge and awareness into effective and helpful therapy skills at all stages of the therapeutic process. (p. 408)

Kort (2008) added that clinicians should not only work with clients to address internalized homophobia but, to limit potential bias, clinicians must also address their own heterosexual privilege. Pope, Mobley, and Myers (2010) reminded practitioners that a therapist's value for affirmation of sexual minorities is vital in counseling but that value is not to be applied in such a way that clients' other cultural and social identities should be missed or lessened in some way.

Development of an Affirmative Practice

It is beyond the scope of this chapter to provide a detailed review of the literature on developing affirmative practice; here I give some highlights. Matthews (2007) addressed ways in which heterosexism may function in the therapeutic relationship and called for counselors to examine their own attitudes and potential biases and to develop their knowledge, skills, and awareness. Among other issues, Matthews noted the value of active avoidance of heterosexism in paperwork, communications, and office spaces, along with the importance of creating an embracing environment for sexual minority clients (Matthews, 2007). Pachankis and Goldfried (2013) reviewed clinical issues, including attention to potential clinician bias, affirmative practices, issues with underrepresented populations, and other sexual minority-related concerns. Readers are also encouraged to consider the work of Bieschke, Hardy, Fassinger, and Croteau (2008), who explore intersections of identity for lesbian, gay, bisexual, or transgender persons, gender expression and gender transgression, and age cohort differences in experience and how issues such as disability, race–ethnicity, social class and socioeconomic status, and religious or spiritual experience intertwine for individual clients.

Major mental health organizations (e.g., American Counseling Association, 2013; American Psychiatric Association, 1998, 2000; Anton, 2010; National Association of Social Workers, 2000) view attempts to alter sexual orientation as likely unsuccessful and potentially harmful to clients (American Psychological Association [APA] Task Force, 2009). For more about clients who have more severe conflicts with accepting their sexual minority orientations or who may even wish to seek change in their sexual orientations because of their struggle with these issues, see Ariel Shidlo and John C. Gonsiorek (Chapter 11, this volume), Beckstead and Israel (2007), and the Report of the APA Task Force on Appropriate Therapeutic

Responses to Sexual Orientation (2009), which includes "A Framework for the Appropriate Application of Affirmative Therapeutic Interviews" (p. 63; see also Anton, 2010).

Microaggressions in Clinical Practice

Research and theory on microaggressions that occur in the clinical setting are also important in considering affirmative practice. *Microaggressions* are interactions that on the surface may seem to be harmless or have no deeper meaning but actually are discriminatory, oppressive, or prejudicial in their message or content (Nadal et al., 2011; Shelton & Delgado-Romero, 2013). Because these communications tend to be indirect or subtle, sexual minority individuals may be unsure if some comment was negative or aggressive. They may feel that something they cannot define occurred, rather than initially realizing a microaggression or microinsult was presented. Furthermore, the individual who delivered the aggression may not be fully aware of it—that person may be well-intentioned and acting out of a heterosexist social experience rather than intending harm. For people who have been oppressed and have experienced direct messages of hatred or intolerance, these subtle messages may be specifically hard to recognize but also deeply troubling and uncomfortable.

Shelton and Delgado-Romero (2013) qualitatively explored the phenomenon of sexual orientation microaggressions with 16 psychotherapy clients who were identified as sexual minorities. Participants reported experiencing microaggressions in therapy and described the following themes: therapists' assumptions that sexual orientation is the cause of presenting issues; therapists avoiding or minimizing sexual orientation issues; therapists overidentifying with clients; communication of stereotypes; heteronormative bias; feeling pressured to remain in therapy when clients felt they were done, which communicated to clients an idea that sexual minority persons needed treatment; and therapists giving the message that clients should expect to deal with ongoing struggle if they claim a sexual minority identity. For participants, sexual orientation microaggressions left clients with negative emotional reactions; they felt mistrustful of therapists and wondered whether therapy would be effective (Shelton & Delgado-Romero, 2011).

Nadal and colleagues (2011) used a qualitative focus group approach with 26 lesbian, gay, and bisexual participants to explore how microaggressions affected mental health and how participants coped with these experiences. Participants noted that they had experienced microaggressions from family, media, religious, government, and educational institutions and from within the sexual minority community. They reported feeling emotionally unsafe and uncomfortable, along with feeling anger, confusion, and sadness, in reaction to the microaggressive events. Some participants acknowledged that microaggressions have led to or added to mental health concerns, including depression, anxiety, and posttraumatic stress (according to participant self-report). More research is needed on the ways in which microaggressions could contribute to mental health concerns. Helms, Nicolas, and Green (2012) recommended that practitioners and researchers must further consider the ways racism and ethnoviolence can be traumatizing and affect mental health. I argue that a similar consideration of sexual orientation micro- and macro-aggressions may be useful in understanding the experiences and struggles of sexual minority clients. I now turn to recent guidelines and competencies that further describe affirmative practices for clinicians.

Recent Guidelines and Competencies for Affirmative Practice

Major mental health organizations (e.g., American Association for Marriage and Family Therapy, 1991; American Counseling Association, 1998; American Psychiatric Association, 1974, 1998; APA, 2012; Association for Lesbian, Gay, Bisexual, and Transgender Issues in Counseling [A. Harper et al., 2013]; Canadian Psychological Association, 1995; National Association of Social Workers, 1996) have issued policies stating that sexual minority identity and expression are not indicative of mental illness. It is not within the scope of this chapter to review all position statements and recommendations for practice with sexual minority clients. However, two national organizations (i.e., APA and the Association for Lesbian, Gay, Bisexual, and Transgender Issues in Counseling [ALGBTIC]) have recently created specific guidelines or competencies for practice, and those documents are reviewed here and used in the case discussion in the following section.

Guidelines for Psychological Practice With Lesbian, Gay, and Bisexual Clients (APA, 2012) provides practice recommendations in regard to treatment of sexual minority clients, along with information on applying the guidelines in practice and providing references for further study. The 2012 revision of these practice guidelines was drafted in response to changes in the field, including developments in research and theory. Important additions to the current version of the guidelines reflect increasingly complex and thorough understandings of practice with sexual minority clients, including specific attention to distinguishing between sexual orientation and gender identity; how attempts to change sexual orientation have not been demonstrated as safe or effective; the influences of religion and spirituality over the lifespan; the impact of HIV/AIDS, with attention to how these issues have been misunderstood at times in relation to sexual orientation; the impact of socioeconomic status; and the misuse or misrepresentation of research related to the lives of sexual minority persons (APA, 2012).

The ALGBTIC, a division of the American Counseling Association, published *Competencies for Counseling With Lesbian, Gay, Bisexual, Queer, Questioning, Intersex, and Ally Individuals* (A. Harper et al., 2013). Though similar to APA guidelines in their aim to create supportive and safe practice relationships with sexual minority individuals, the ALGBTIC competencies are written from the perspective of what is expected of counselors rather than in language that is aspirational in nature. The ALGBTIC competencies offer instruction to clinicians not only in working with sexual minority persons and those who may be questioning their sexual orientations, but also in work with allies and intersex individuals. The competencies focus on domains of developmental issues, social and cultural concerns, group work, professional and ethical practice, vocational and lifestyle issues, assessment, research, and program evaluation (A. Harper et al., 2013).

Case Study

The following case study[1] illustrates how selected guidelines may be applied in clinical practice.

> Carl is a 37-year-old White gay man. He entered therapy with concerns related to maintaining sobriety after several years of considerable alcohol abuse. He also described a struggle related to accepting his disability status—after a car wreck a little more than one year ago, Carl was no longer able to walk and now uses a wheelchair. He had loved running (which had been a primary source of stress relief), and he feared that he would not find a romantic partner. Carl stated that his former romantic partners (whom he saw as highly attractive and physically active) would not want a relationship with "someone in a wheelchair." Furthermore, Carl was concerned that his struggle with physical health and his alcohol use in the last several years had led to trouble at work—he was on probation after missing work repeatedly when he had been hungover or actively drinking.
>
> After several months of treatment, Carl revealed that he had been driving drunk when he had the accident that led to the loss of use of his legs. He was nearly inconsolable in session as he mourned his actions and his loss. Over several sessions, Carl revealed that he had been drinking on the day of the car wreck after receiving some bad news—his physician told him that he had contracted a sexually transmitted disease (STD). As Carl talked about this news, he was highly self-condemning. He described contracting this STD in terms such as "sinful" or "dirty" and called himself a "stupid faggot," which was surprising and difficult to hear. Carl seemed to not respond well when offered kind and supportive words that day.

---

[1]Client identifiers have been changed to protect confidentiality.

When asked, Carl revealed that he had followed a course of medication and the STD was no longer an issue. However, he explained that before the accident, he tended to abuse alcohol before he would feel comfortable having sex with other men. In a quiet voice, he recounted how inebriation led him to participate in some sexual situations that he later regretted. Carl went on to explain that after the accident he began drinking alcohol most days and that only recently when he entered treatment (which was approximately one year from the date of the car wreck) did he stop drinking alcohol altogether.

In the last year, Carl reconnected with his family because he had needed physical and logistical support. He described this as wonderful but also often talked about how misunderstood he felt. He explained his family's conservative Christian beliefs and how they have never accepted his sexual identity. He relayed that though the family "does not believe in" sexual minority identities, they seem more comfortable spending time with him when he is single than they did in the past when he was in a relationship. Carl acknowledged how important his own Christian identity was when he was younger, but he claimed that in recent years it has not been a central identity for him. Over time he revealed that he fears not only that his family will never accept him but also that God could never actually love him. When asked directly if he fears that everything he has suffered is punishment for being gay, Carl said quietly and tearfully, "Yes."

Many guidelines and competencies are relevant in work with Carl, and I will review several selected items from each document. For the sake of brevity, I refer to the documents as APA Guidelines (APA, 2012) and ALGBTIC Competencies (A. Harper et al., 2013), respectively. Practitioners might employ a variety of techniques and conceptualizations with Carl, which cannot be reviewed exhaustively in the following case discussion. I first list key guidelines and competencies relevant to a particular theme in Carl's work, followed by a description of therapeutic conceptualizations.

Heterosexism and Oppression

APA Guideline 1: Psychologists strive to understand the effects of stigma (i.e., prejudice, discrimination, and violence) and its various contextual manifestations in the lives of lesbian, gay, and bisexual people.

APA Guideline 10: Psychologists strive to understand the ways in which a person's lesbian, gay, or bisexual orientation may have an impact on his or her family of origin and the relationship with that family of origin.

ALGBTIC Competency C.5: Acknowledge the physical (e.g., access to health care, HIV, and other health issues), social (e.g., family/partner relationships), emotional (e.g., anxiety, depression, substance abuse), cultural (e.g., lack of support from others in their racial/ethnic group), spiritual (e.g., possible conflict between their spiritual values and those of their family's), and/or other stressors (e.g., financial problems as a result of employment discrimination) that may interfere with sexual minority individuals' ability to achieve their goals.

Stigma, prejudice, and discrimination, particularly as related to the family's lack of support, have been experienced as traumatic by Carl (Brown, 2008; Meyer, 2013). In my opinion, the central issue in Carl's work is an inability to accept and embrace his sexual identity, leading to many of the struggles he described. These guidelines and competencies encourage practitioners to see the ways in which stigma, prejudice, and lack of support are the underlying issues for Carl. This conceptualization allows the clinician to view the heterosexist system as pathological and traumatizing and see Carl's strengths in his attempts to cope over time (Pachankis & Goldfried, 2013).

Religion–Spirituality and Intersections of Identity

APA Guideline 12: Psychologists are encouraged to consider the influences of religion and spirituality in the lives of lesbian, gay, and bisexual persons.

ALGBTIC Competency B.12: Recognize that spiritual development and religious practices may be important for LGBQQ [lesbian, gay, bisexual, questioning, queer] individuals, yet they may also present a particular challenge given the limited LGBQQ positive religious institutions that may be present in a given community, and that many LGBQQ individuals may face personal struggles related to their faith and their identity.

ALGBTIC Competency B.7: Recognize how internalized prejudice, including heterosexism, racism, classism, religious/spiritual discrimination, ableism, adultism, ageism, and sexism may influence the counselor's own attitudes as well as those of LGBQQ individuals, resulting in negative attitudes and/or feelings towards LGBQQ individuals.

ALGBTIC Competency E.4: Seek consultation and supervision from an individual who has knowledge, awareness, and skills working with LGBQQ individuals for continued self-reflection and personal growth to ensure that their own biases, skill, or knowledge deficits about LGBQQ persons do not negatively affect the helping relationships.

As deeper issues were explored over time with Carl, perhaps the fundamental concern that led to his difficulty in accepting himself was his desire for a meaningful "relationship with God" and his fear that God would never fully love him (Haldeman, 2004). As with any ongoing treatment, over time Carl provided more information. He shared that a religious identity had been central for him, and he had struggled with a sense of isolation and grief as he pursued a meaningful "relationship with God" while he concurrently felt he could never be fully loved in return. He struggled to find a religious community that was accepting and also felt similar to the faith community he grew up with and valued.

Clinicians could struggle with this issue. Some may not feel competent to discuss Christianity at all or in any depth (Vieten et al., 2013). Others may struggle to integrate their own religious beliefs related to sexual minority persons and feel unsure how to fully engage in this work with Carl. I encourage consultation in an ongoing way, which I believe is important in any clinical work that touches areas that feel unresolved or difficult for the clinician (Borders, 2012; Greenburg, Lewis, & Johnson, 1985). It would be a disservice to Carl if the clinician's discomfort or unease somehow allowed avoidance of this central issue. My work with Carl would not be as a theologian. It would be to help him challenge his assumptions, cognitive distortions, and his fears and feelings and to consider his meaning making around these issues in deep and complex ways. It could be important for Carl to find trusted and affirmative religious leaders to speak with outside of our sessions, while we could continue to explore areas I was competent to explore with him (Milstein, Manierre, & Yali, 2010).

Disability Status and Intersections of Identity

APA Guideline 15: Psychologists are encouraged to recognize the particular challenges that lesbian, gay, and bisexual individuals with physical, sensory, and cognitive-emotional disabilities experience.

Carl's disability status added to his overall sense of stigma and disenfranchisement (Esmail, Darry, Walter & Knupp, 2010; Sakellariou, 2006). How he viewed himself and how he perceived that others viewed him as a disabled person were particularly painful for him. It would be important to explore his sense of loss related to no longer identifying as a runner and his past use of running as a stress relief activity. Furthermore, it would be valuable to consider accessibility problems that he might have experienced as he attempted to find support and to discuss concerns related to physical changes and losses Carl experienced, along with how both identifying as a sexual minority and his bodily changes may or may not link to how he feels broken and unlovable. A support group related to his disability status could be an important resource over time (APA, 2012; Williams, 2007).

Many other issues are likely to surface in this case, and the clinician's own struggles or reactions could limit objectivity.

AFFIRMATIVE COUNSELING: A NEW PARADIGM

Some may ask whether these guidelines and competencies are enough. Are individuals in the field adequately prepared to work affirmatively with sexual minority clients? Most mental health professionals have knowingly worked with sexual minority persons (Graham et al., 2012), and we know that many sexual minority clients and professionals themselves consider the extent to which therapists are affirmative (Liddle, 1996; Lyons, 2010). Without doubt, there is increasing social acceptance and legal recognition today for sexual minority persons. Yet, sexual minority clients continue to enter treatment struggling with issues of self-esteem, proneness to shame, and concerns related to forgiveness (Greene & Britton, 2013), and some continue to seek sexual orientation change, which has not been demonstrated to be effective (APA Task Force on Appropriate Therapeutic Responses to Sexual Orientation, 2009; Flentje, Heck, & Cochran, 2013). In the end, many mental health professionals report little to no formal training in working with this population (Lyons, 2010) and may find it difficult to fully take on professional training related to these issues because of personal bias (Worthington, 2010).

One goal in this chapter was to encourage a dialogue about potential personal tensions or conflicts for clinicians. Clinician biases and belief systems have been shaped by a culture of heterosexism. How do clinicians achieve an affirmative stance then, particularly for those whose biases or belief systems make affirmation a challenge? My hope is that a deep and complex conversation on these issues will explore how affirmative practice can occur. This conversation requires ongoing consideration of the oppressive nature of a heteronormative system and the limits of technical skill alone within such a powerful system. The belief systems of all practitioners should be respected in a way that limits the oppression experienced by sexual minority individuals.

Heterosexism as Power and Oppression

If we did not still live in a heterosexist system, I wonder if we would still have to consider *affirmative* counseling for sexual minorities as the topic of this chapter. For many other aspects of diversity and intersections of identity, we assume that good counseling will at a minimum include sensitivity to issues of difference and culture (APA, 2003). We expect clinicians to be aware of personal biases, develop relevant skills, gain needed knowledge about the people they are working with, and deepen their insight and self-knowledge, so that they can deliver services in a sensitive, ethical, and competent way. Therefore, in some ways, I believe that the first step in being affirmative in practice is to be what we are asked to be by the field: ethical, competent, and skilled clinicians.

However, because we do not live in a society that is neutral around issues of sexuality, and unlike many other expressions of cultural diversity, there is an element imposed on these identities that implies right or wrong, good or bad, sinful or not (if you are religious, perhaps). Therefore, I suggest that it cannot be enough to simply ask clinicians to be caring and competent. Because of the societal messages, some clinicians will have conflicting beliefs about these issues. Furthermore, because of the affirmative stance of the field, these conflicting beliefs may not fully emerge, or they may not be shared or processed openly. Bieschke and Dendy (2010) suggested that the field of psychology may have foreclosed on an affirmative stance without a thorough consideration of the ways in which cultural and religious values may compete with a full and deep affirmation. This could lead to marginalization or silencing of professionals who find it difficult to reconcile their own values with sexual minority affirmation, perhaps not providing support for such persons to develop competence over time.

Other professionals who do not have conflicting religious beliefs may still have personal reactions to the idea of sexual minority identity or experience that are less clear and may feel confusing or difficult to explain. For example, I have heard some people say that imagining same-sex sexual behavior "just feels gross." For some people, this negative response seems to be tied to a lifetime of heterosexist societal messages, rather than to a belief system they can name. Therapists have not grown up in a vacuum, separate from these powerful messages (APA, 2012). Even sexual minority therapists and allies may struggle at times with the ways in which these messages may color therapeutic conceptualizations or interpretations.

Technical Skill and Competence

Is good technique enough? Is it possible for clinicians to hold personal conflicts about this issue and still treat clients competently? Is it possible for any researcher or theorist to suggest an approach that would somehow address all these concerns? Bieschke and Dendy (2010) suggested that the process of becoming affirmative may be more akin to an acculturation process, and they used Berry's (1980) model of acculturation to ethics training as a framework for developing competence in working with sexual minorities. Furthermore, they suggested that a "minimum level" (p. 430) of affirmation is necessary for competence in working with sexual minority persons because otherwise homophobia and heterosexism would color their clinical judgment. I agree with Bieschke and Dendy that there likely must be some amount of affirmation for competence. Though some may disagree, I believe that personal experience and the resulting bias (positive or negative) influence our perceptions, views, and conceptualizations in therapeutic encounters. It is my contention that without some degree of insight into this process for oneself, clinicians would be too biased to provide competent treatment. Furthermore, I believe that this small amount of affirmation is what would allow someone with conflicted feelings on these issues to challenge themselves to do competent work. There is a danger of following only the letter of the law, a kind of checklist approach to guidelines or competencies. I hope clinicians follow affirmative practice guidelines and are culturally competent in working with sexual minority clients. However, I am unsure that a mandate to do so would be well received by all or would be necessarily meaningful; guidelines that are followed reflexively cannot do enough to counter systemic heterosexism.

Minority Stress and the Impact on the Therapy Relationship

An important addition to this process is the experience of sexual minority clients themselves. The weight of minority stress has created discomfort at a minimum, with potential for trauma or ongoing mental health concerns related to the cumulative experience of oppression in each client (Meyer, 2013). Sexual minority people tend to have plenty of relationships that feel complicated by lack of affirmation from family, coworkers, and others (Pachankis & Goldfried, 2013). Is it appropriate to ask them to navigate this with their therapist as well, particularly when the therapist has power to diagnose and may or may not have insight into personal biases? In the end, I believe that your sexual minority clients will know if there is some lack of support in the therapeutic relationship. They may not always have the words for it, and it may take some time for clients to identify (depending on the weight of the presenting issues and other issues relevant to the client or situation). Yet, I believe that clients will eventually know on some level if they are not supported meaningfully by a therapist, and there is risk that such a lack of support will add to minority stress and may even be traumatizing (Brown, 2008; Meyer, 2013).

Reexamining an Affirmative Approach

Given the above arguments, this is what I say to practitioners today: Competence is necessary, and multicultural competence is part of this (APA, 2003, 2010, 2012; Hancock, 2014). I do not believe it is meaningful to demand affirmation in a way that asks a professional to devalue or somehow ignore personal beliefs. However, if this is an issue of conflict for you, I ask you to sit full in the tension of the conflict. Our sexual minority clients deserve ethical and competent treatment, which involves clinicians ensuring that our biases do not cloud our judgment. Competence with sexual minority persons also demands that I not see their sexuality as pathology, but the heterosexist system creates potential difficulty in this regard. I ask you to consider how you would want to be treated by a therapist—and to provide this to your clients. I even ask us all to go further and change the system of heterosexism that sustains minority stress for sexual minority persons.

How do we do this? First, it is important for trainees to receive training around working with sexual minority clients (APA Board of Educational Affairs, 2013; Bieschke & Mintz, 2012). It is essential that clinicians have sufficient knowledge and skill to handle situations that may arise without causing harm to clients. Trainees could benefit from ongoing consideration of ways in which any established approach to counseling can be applied with an affirmative stance. This issue is not settled when a clinician leaves trainee status, however. Many professionals will eventually work in institutions or systems that do not allow for transfer of clients because of personal belief systems. Issues of abandonment are raised when therapy with long-term clients is terminated (APA, 2010), which in turn raises the potential for recreating some clients' trauma or wounding (Brown, 2008).

I am not suggesting that clinicians be insensitive to religious beliefs. I have great respect for professionals who take on the potentially painful task of exploring these issues to such an extent that they could work affirmatively, despite personal reservations. Hancock (2014) asserted that it may be possible to refer a sexual minority client in an attempt to address clinical issues. However, she questions the ethics of referring a client because of his or her membership in a particular population. It may be that a referral to an outside practitioner while a clinician is exploring these issues is the most ethical thing to do during a time of deep consideration of these issues. It may be that for some clinicians, the personal tensions they experience are so great that they must find a way to not include sexual minority clients in their practice. However, this should only occur after long and thoughtful deliberation; professionals should make such decisions only after fully engaging in the process. I agree with the position of Bieschke and Mintz (2012), who argued that demographic competence and dynamic inclusivity are necessary to ensure that referrals of sexual minority clients and other practice decisions are not discriminatory.

This issue cannot be as simple as clinicians being affirmative or referring out. This is not an issue without valence in society. When a clinician refers a client because of overall discomfort with sexual minority persons, that clinician is participating in and continuing the oppression of heterosexism in society. I do not say this with accusation or without kindness; I ask myself about how I could contribute to other oppressions in the world in my own ways, and I ask this of all of us. I also ask for a deeper move toward affirmation and for us to challenge the current heterosexist system, because the current paradigm must change.

When I entered this field, there was more of what I call a well-intended apologetic stance toward sexual minority persons than there is today. The message that I experienced was that even if you are a sexual minority person, you are still valuable. I am grateful for the intention of these messages. However, the paradigm needs to change so that sexual minority persons do not start at a ground of forgiveness or being "loved anyway." The field needs to communicate that sexual minority persons start on the same ground as anyone—with a validation of normality, acceptableness, and value that is not dependent on another's forgiveness or magnanimity. The way to do this is to allow ourselves to cognitively, affectively, and experientially be affected by the stories and experiences of our sexual minority clients and friends (e.g., Bieschke, Croteau, Lark, & Vandiver, 2005).

The old paradigm seems to be changing, but we still live in a system with complicated messages for sexual minority persons. I hope that as mental health professionals, we can be an active part of ending those messages and the minority stress and psychological distress that they create. As much as I hope for a uniformly affirmative stance in mental health practice, this approach cannot be mandated or implemented through a checklist and still have meaning. I do not believe it is particularly helpful or effective to simply demand that my colleagues who feel conflicted about affirmation "just get over it." It seems more likely that the real struggles these colleagues experience, and the possible resulting bias that could be harmful to clients, would only go underground as a result, rather than be explored and challenged. In my experience, the more we attempt to force a change in someone's belief, the more resistance grows. Instead, I hope to create relationships with trainees and colleagues that encourage hard discussions as a way to encourage development of affirmative practice. Just as I do with clients, I want to hold colleagues' "feet to the fire" in a real way with these issues, but in a way that demonstrates kindness, invites dialogue, and creates opportunity for meaningful change.

REFLECTIONS AND FUTURE DIRECTIONS

Like other contributors to this volume, I have been asked to comment about what the process of writing this chapter was like, what questions remain, and what discussions are needed. I am honored to have been asked to contribute, and there are several areas that I hope people will continue to discuss. I have described tensions in affirmative practice with issues of competence and the ways our own belief systems could inform our work. I believe there are more conversations to have about how we can honor the beliefs of people in the field in a meaningful way and also find a path toward deeper affirmation. This cannot be lip service to religious or other beliefs that may find sexual minority affirmation a challenge. However, I hope we can also continue to ask about ways to lessen the power and oppression of the heterosexist system. Furthermore, I suggest that we continue to find ways to integrate training on these issues more fully. High rates of sexual minority individuals tend to participate in treatment and also eventually tend to report disappointment of some kind with treatment more often than sexual majority clients (Lyons, 2010), and it is unclear if professionals feel they have been appropriately trained for this work.

Some people in the field do not believe that the discrimination of the past exists today; I respectfully disagree. While I was writing this chapter, legislation in several states has been introduced or voted into law which asserts that trainees in mental health fields can opt out of treating certain clients because of a sincerely held religious belief (APA Board of Educational Affairs, 2013; Hancock, 2014; "The 'Conscience Clause' in Professional Training," 2015). Though sexual minority issues are not specifically identified in the written or suggested state codes, the legal cases thus far have focused on refusal to treat a sexual minority client (Bieschke & Mintz, 2012). Also, several states have introduced legislation that would allow business owners to refuse services based on their sincerely held religious beliefs (C. J. Carter, Brumfield, & Watkins, 2014; Wilson, 2014). Though no specific language in these bills names sexual minority individuals for specific exclusion, opponents to these bills have argued that it is sexual minority clients who are actually refused business services (Shoichet & Abdullah, 2014). Currently, there are seven countries in the world in which it is possible to receive the death penalty for same-sex sexual behavior; in 70 other countries, citizens can receive prison sentences for their sexual orientation ("Where Is it Illegal to be Gay?," 2014).

These issues of oppression and discrimination remain within the field itself as well. In my doctoral cohort, one person had the courage to admit struggling with integrating Christian beliefs with full affirmation of sexual minority persons. We had some painful talks about this, and I am thankful for a doctoral program and an environment that would allow such discussion. I am hopeful as well, because after our ongoing discussions, I would refer a sexual minority client to my old friend today because I trust my friend's willingness and ability to hold these issues complexly and with empathy.

I was initially concerned in writing this chapter about communicating compassion with gentleness while also saying what has felt important to say. Later, I became aware that some readers could view my approach as too understanding or patient with those who struggle to be affirmative. In the end, I do not know if it is possible to inspire people to be affirmative. I do not know how to work with some of the political voices in this country that seem uninterested in at least considering sexual minority persons as having the same rights as others. I do have hope, though, that despite ongoing oppression and discrimination of sexual minorities, there is also real and growing support within the field (APA, 2012) and in the larger society (Simpson, 2014). For practitioners, I encourage a consideration of the ways in which minority stress, microaggressions, and other challenges described in this chapter are relevant to your work. Guidelines, competencies, and affirmative approaches are valuable contributions to the field. However, my challenge to readers is to participate in a deep and full affirmation with clients who challenge your experience or viewpoints (Bieschke & Mintz, 2012). My respectful call to us all is to shift the paradigm so that sexual minority clients can begin at a ground of full acceptance. If we offer less, then on some level we offer or participate in oppression and harm.

REFERENCES

American Association for Marriage and Family Therapy. (1991). AAMFT code of ethics. Washington, DC: Author.

American Counseling Association. (1998, March 27). On appropriate counseling responses to sexual orientation. Adopted by the American Counseling Association Governing Council.

American Counseling Association. (2013). Ethical issues related to conversion or reparative therapy. Retrieved from http://www.counseling.org/news/updates/2013/01/16/ethical-issues-related-to-conversion-or-reparative-therapy

American Psychiatric Association. (1974). Position statement on homosexuality and civil rights. The American Journal of Psychiatry, 131, 497.

American Psychiatric Association. (1998). Position statement on psychiatric treatment and sexual orientation. Retrieved from https://www.camft.org/ias/images/PDFs/SOCE/APA_Position_Statement.pdf

American Psychiatric Association. (2000). Position statement on therapies focused on attempts to change sexual orientation (reparative or conversion therapies). Retrieved from http://www.psychiatry.org/file%20library/about-apa/organization-documents-policies/policies/position-2000-therapies-change-sexual-orientation.pdf

American Psychological Association. (2003). Guidelines on multicultural education, training, research, practice, and organizational change for psychologists. American Psychologist, 58, 377–402.

American Psychological Association. (2010). Ethical principles of psychologists and code of conduct (2002, Amended June 1, 2010). Retrieved from http://www.apa.org/ethics/code/index.aspx

American Psychological Association. (2012). Guidelines for psychological practice with lesbian, gay, and bisexual clients. American Psychologist, 67, 10–42. http://dx.doi.org/10.1037/a0024659

American Psychological Association Board of Educational Affairs. (2013). Preparing processional psychologists to serve a diverse public. Retrieved from http://www.apa.org/pi/lgbt/resources/policy/diversity-preparation.aspx

Anton, B. S. (2010). Proceedings of the American Psychological Association for the legislative year 2009: Minutes of the annual meeting of the Council of Representatives and minutes of the meetings of the Board of Directors. American Psychologist, 65, 385–475. http://dx.doi.org/10.1037/a0019553

APA Task Force on Appropriate Therapeutic Responses to Sexual Orientation. (2009). Report of the APA Task Force on Appropriate Therapeutic Responses to

Sexual Orientation. Washington, DC: American Psychological Association. Retrieved from http://www.apa.org/pi/lgbt/resources/therapeutic-response.pdf

Beckstead, L., & Israel, T. (2007). Affirmative counseling and psychotherapy focused on issues related to sexual orientation conflicts. In K. J. Bieschke, R. M. Perez, & K. A. DeBord (Eds.), *Handbook of counseling and psychotherapy with lesbian, gay, bisexual, and transgender clients* (2nd ed., pp. 221–244). Washington, DC: American Psychological Association. http://dx.doi.org/10.1037/11482-009

Berry, J. W. (1980). Acculturation as a variety of adaptation. In A. M. Padilla (Ed.), *Acculturation: Theory, models, and some new findings* (pp. 17–37). Washington, DC: American Psychological Association.

Bieschke, K. J., Croteau, J. M., Lark, J. S., & Vandiver, B. J. (2005). Toward a discourse of sexual orientation equity in the counseling professions. In J. M. Croteau, J. S. Lark, M. Lidderdale, & Y. B. Chung (Eds.), *Deconstructing heterosexism in the counseling professions: Multicultural narrative voices* (pp. 189–210). Thousand Oaks, CA: Sage. http://dx.doi.org/10.4135/9781452204529.n22

Bieschke, K. J., & Dendy, A. K. (2010). Using the Ethical Acculturation Model as a framework for attaining competence to work with clients who identify as sexual minorities. In H. Z. Lyons, K. J. Bieschke, A. K. Dendy, R. L. Worthington, & R. Georgemiller (2010), Psychologists' competence to treat lesbian, gay and bisexual clients: State of the field and strategies for improvement. *Professional Psychology: Research and Practice, 41,* 424–434.

Bieschke, K. J., Hardy, J. A., Fassinger, R. E., & Croteau, J. M. (2008). Intersecting identities of gender-transgressive sexual minorities: Toward a new paradigm of affirmative psychology. In W. Walsh (Ed.), *Biennial review of counseling psychology* (Vol. 1, pp. 177–207). New York, NY: Routledge/Taylor & Francis Group.

Bieschke, K. J., & Mintz, L. B. (2012). Counseling psychology model training values statement addressing diversity: History, current use, and future directions. *Training and Education in Professional Psychology, 6,* 196–203. http://dx.doi.org/10.1037/a0030810

Bieschke, K. J., Perez, R. M., & DeBord, K. A. (2007). Introduction: The challenge of providing affirmative psychotherapy while honoring diverse contexts. In K. J. Bieschke, R. M. Perez, & K. A. DeBord (Eds.), *Handbook of counseling and psychotherapy with lesbian, gay, bisexual, and transgender clients* (2nd ed., pp. 3–11). Washington, DC: American Psychological Association. http://dx.doi.org/10.1037/11482-000

Borders, L. (2012). Dyadic, triadic, and group models of peer supervision/consultation: What are their components, and is there evidence of their effectiveness? *Clinical Psychologist, 16*(2), 59–71. http://dx.doi.org/10.1111/j.1742-9552.2012.00046.x

Brewster, M. E., Moradi, B., DeBlaere, C., & Velez, B. L. (2013). Navigating the borderlands: The roles of minority stressors, bicultural self-efficacy, and cognitive flexibility in the mental health of bisexual individuals. *Journal of Counseling Psychology, 60,* 543–556. http://dx.doi.org/10.1037/a0033224

Brown, L. S. (2008). *Cultural competence in trauma therapy: Beyond the flashback*. Washington, DC: American Psychological Association. http://dx.doi.org/10.1037/11752-000

Canadian Psychological Association. (1995). *Canadian code of ethics for psychologists*. Ottawa, Ontario, Canada: Author.

Carter, C. J., Brumfield, B., & Watkins, T. (2014, February 27). *Arizona's anti-gay bill veto unlikely to end "religious freedom" movement*. Retrieved from http://www.cnn.com/2014/02/26/politics/religious-freedom-states/

Carter, L., Mollen, D., & Smith, N. (2014). Locus of control, minority stress, and psychological distress among lesbian, gay, and bisexual individuals. *Journal of Counseling Psychology, 61*, 169–175.

Croteau, J. M., Lark, J. S., Lidderdale, M., & Chung, Y. B. (2005). *Deconstructing heterosexism in the counseling professions: Multicultural narrative voices*. Thousand Oaks, CA: Sage.

de Vogue, A., & Diamond, J. (2015, June 27). Supreme Court rules in favor of same-sex marriage nationwide. Retrieved from http://www.cnn.com/2015/06/26/politics/supreme-court-same-sex-marriage-ruling

Esmail, S., Darry, K., Walter, A., & Knupp, H. (2010). Attitudes and perceptions towards disability and sexuality. *Disability and Rehabilitation, 32*, 1148–1155.

Flentje, A., Heck, N. C., & Cochran, B. N. (2013). Sexual reorientation therapy interventions: Perspectives of ex-ex-gay individuals. *Journal of Gay & Lesbian Mental Health, 17*, 256–277. http://dx.doi.org/10.1080/19359705.2013.773268

Garnets, L. D., Herek, G. M., & Levy, B. (1990). Violence and victimization of lesbians and gay men: Mental health consequences. *Journal of Interpersonal Violence, 5*, 366–383. http://dx.doi.org/10.1177/088626090005003010

Gates, G. J. (2011, April). *How many people are lesbian, gay, bisexual, and transgender?* Retrieved from http://williamsinstitute.law.ucla.edu/wp-content/uploads/Gates-How-Many-People-LGBT-Apr-2011.pdf

Graham, S. R., Carney, J. S., & Kluck, A. S. (2012). Perceived competency in working with LGB clients: Where are we now? *Counselor Education and Supervision, 51*(1), 2–16. http://dx.doi.org/10.1002/j.1556-6978.2012.00001.x

Greenburg, S. L., Lewis, G. J., & Johnson, M. (1985). Peer consultation groups for private practitioners. *Professional Psychology: Research and Practice, 16*, 437–447.

Greene, D. C., & Britton, P. J. (2013). The influence of forgiveness on lesbian, gay, bisexual, transgender, and questioning individuals' shame and self-esteem. *Journal of Counseling & Development, 91*(2), 195–205. http://dx.doi.org/10.1002/j.1556-6676.2013.00086.x

Growing support for same-sex marriage across generations. (2014, March 5). Retrieved from Pew Research Center website: http://www.pewsocialtrends.org/2014/03/07/millennials-in-adulthood/sdt-next-america-03-07-2014-2-01/

Haldeman, D. C. (2004). When sexual and religious orientations collide: Considerations in working with conflicted same-sex attracted male clients. *The Counseling Psychologist, 32*, 691–715. http://dx.doi.org/10.1177/0011000004267560

Haldeman, D. C. (2004). When sexual and religious orientations collide: Considerations in working with conflicted same-sex attracted male clients. *The Counseling Psychologist, 32*, 691–715. http://dx.doi.org/10.1177/0011000004267560

Hancock, K. A. (2014). Student beliefs, multiculturalism, and client welfare. *Psychology of Sexual Orientation and Gender Diversity, 1*(1), 4–9. http://dx.doi.org/10.1037/sgd0000021

Harper, A., Finnerty, P., Martinez, M., Brace, A., Crethar, H. C., Loos, B., . . . the ALGBTIC LGBQQIA Competencies Taskforce. (2013). Association for lesbian, gay, bisexual, and transgender issues in counseling competencies for counseling with lesbian, gay, bisexual, queer, questioning, intersex, and ally individuals. *Journal of LGBT Issues in Counseling, 7*(1), 2–43. http://dx.doi.org/10.1080/15538605.2013.755444

Harper, G. W., Brodsky, A., & Bruce, D. (2012). What's good about being gay? Perspectives from youth. *Journal of LGBT Youth, 9*(1), 22–41. http://dx.doi.org/10.1080/19361653.2012.628230

Helms, J. E., Nicolas, G., & Green, C. E. (2012). Racism and ethnoviolence as trauma: Enhancing professional and research training. *Traumatology, 18*(1), 65–74. http://dx.doi.org/10.1177/1534765610396728

Kertzner, R. M., Meyer, I. H., Frost, D. M., & Stirratt, M. J. (2009). Social and psychological well-being in lesbians, gay men, and bisexuals: The effects of race, gender, age, and sexual identity. *American Journal of Orthopsychiatry, 79*, 500–510. http://dx.doi.org/10.1037/a0016848

Kort, J. (2008). *Gay affirmative therapy for the straight clinician: The essential guide.* New York, NY: Norton.

Lick, D. J., Durso, L. E., & Johnson, K. L. (2013). Minority stress and physical health among sexual minorities. *Perspectives on Psychological Science, 8*, 521–548. http://dx.doi.org/10.1177/1745691613497965

Liddle, B. J. (1996). Therapist sexual orientation, gender, and counseling practices as they relate to ratings on helpfulness by gay and lesbian clients. *Journal of Counseling Psychology, 43*, 394–401. http://dx.doi.org/10.1037/0022-0167.43.4.394

Lyons, H. Z. (2010). Ethical practice with lesbian, gay, and bisexual clients: A focus on psychologist competence. In H. Z. Lyons, K. J. Bieschke, A. K. Dendy, R. L. Worthington, & R. Georgemiller (2010), Psychologists' competence to treat lesbian, gay and bisexual clients: State of the field and strategies for improvement. *Professional Psychology: Research and Practice, 41*, 424–434. http://dx.doi.org/10.1037/a0021121

Matthews, C. R. (2007). Affirmative lesbian, gay, and bisexual counseling with all clients. In K. J. Bieschke, R. M. Perez, & K. A. DeBord (Eds.), *Handbook of counseling and psychotherapy with lesbian, gay, bisexual, and transgender clients* (2nd ed., pp. 201–219). Washington, DC: American Psychological Association. http://dx.doi.org/10.1037/11482-008

Mays, V. M., & Cochran, S. D. (2001). Mental health correlates of perceived discrimination among lesbian, gay, and bisexual adults in the United States. *American Journal of Public Health, 91*, 1869–1876. http://dx.doi.org/10.2105/AJPH.91.11.1869

Meyer, I. H. (2003). Prejudice as stress: Conceptual and measurement problems. *American Journal of Public Health, 93*, 262–265. http://dx.doi.org/10.2105/AJPH.93.2.262

Meyer, I. H. (2010). Identity, stress, and resilience in lesbians, gay men, and bisexuals of color. *The Counseling Psychologist, 38*, 442–454. http://dx.doi.org/10.1177/0011000009351601

Meyer, I. H. (2013). Prejudice, social stress, and mental health in lesbian, gay, and bisexual populations. *Psychology of Sexual Orientation and Gender Diversity, 1*(S), 3–26. http://dx.doi.org/10.1037/2329-0382.1.S.3

Milstein, G., Manierre, A., & Yali, A. M. (2010). Psychological care for persons of diverse religions: A collaborative continuum. *Professional Psychology: Research and Practice, 41*, 371–381. http://dx.doi.org/10.1037/a0021074

Nadal, K. L., Wong, Y., Isse, M.-A., Meterko, V., Leon, J., & Wideman, M. (2011). Sexual orientation microaggressions: Processes and coping mechanisms for lesbian, gay, and bisexual individuals. *Journal of LGBT Issues in Counseling, 5*(1), 21–46. http://dx.doi.org/10.1080/15538605.2011.554606

National Association of Social Workers. (1996). *Code of ethics of the National Association of Social Workers.* Retrieved from http://www.naswdc.org/code.htm

National Association of Social Workers. (2000). *"Reparative" and "conversion" therapies for lesbians and gay men.* Retrieved from http://www.naswdc.org/diversity/lgb/reparative.asp

Pachankis, J. E., & Goldfried, M. R. (2013). Clinical issues in working with lesbian, gay, and bisexual clients. *Psychology of Sexual Orientation and Gender Diversity, 1*(S), 45–48. doi:10.1037/2329-0382.1.S.45

Perez, R. M. (2007). The 'Boring' State of Research and Psychotherapy With Lesbian, Gay, Bisexual, and Transgender Clients: Revisiting Barón (1991). In K. J. Bieschke, R. M. Perez, & K. A. DeBord (Eds.), *Handbook of counseling and psychotherapy with lesbian, gay, bisexual, and transgender clients* (2nd ed., pp. 399–418). Washington, DC: American Psychological Association. http://dx.doi.org/10.1037/11482-017

Pope, A. L., Mobley, A. K., & Myers, J. E. (2010). Integrating identities for same-sex attracted clients: Using developmental counseling and therapy to address sexual orientation conflicts. *Journal of LGBT Issues in Counseling, 4*(1), 32–47. http://dx.doi.org/10.1080/15538600903552749

Riggle, E. D. B., Whitman, J. S., Olson, A., Rostosky, S. S., & Strong, S. (2008). The positive aspects of being a lesbian or gay man. *Professional Psychology: Research and Practice, 39*, 210–217. http://dx.doi.org/10.1037/0735-7028.39.2.210

Russell, G. M., & Richards, J. A. (2003). Stressor and resilience factors for lesbians, gay men, and bisexuals confronting antigay politics. *American Journal of Community Psychology, 31*(3-4), 313–328. http://dx.doi.org/10.1023/A:1023919022811

Saewyc, E. M. (2011). Research on adolescent sexual orientation: Development, health disparities, stigma, and resilience. *Journal of Research on Adolescence, 21*(1), 256–272. http://dx.doi.org/10.1111/j.1532-7795.2010.00727.x

Shelton, K., & Delgado-Romero, E. A. (2011). Sexual microaggressions: The experience of lesbian, gay, bisexual and queer clients in psychotherapy. *Journal of Counseling Psychology, 58*, 210–221.

Shelton, K., & Delgado-Romero, E. A. (2013). Sexual orientation microaggressions: The experience of lesbian, gay, bisexual, and queer clients in psychotherapy. *Psychology of Sexual Orientation and Gender Diversity, 1*(S), 59–70. http://dx.doi.org/10.1037/2329-0382.1.S.59

Shoichet, C. E., & Abdullah, H. (2014, February 26). "Arizona's gov. Jan Brewer vetoes controversial anti-gay bill, SB 1062." CNN Politics. Retrieved from http://www.cnn.com/2014/02/26/politics/arizona-brewer-bill/

Simpson, I. (2014, February 26). Majority of Americans now support gay marriage, survey finds. Reuters. Retrieved from http://www.reuters.com/article/2014/02/26/us-usa-gay-survey-idUSBREA1P07020140226

The "conscience clause" in professional training. (2015). American Psychological Association. Retrieved from http://www.apa.org/ed/graduate/conscience-clause-brief.aspx

Velez, B. L., Moradi, B., & Brewster, M. E. (2013). Testing the tenets of minority stress theory in workplace contexts. *Journal of Counseling Psychology, 60*, 532–542. http://dx.doi.org/10.1037/a0033346

Vieten, C., Scammell, S., Pilato, R., Ammondson, I., Pargament, K. I., & Lukoff, D. (2013). Spiritual and religious competencies for psychologists. *Psychology of Religion and Spirituality, 5*(3), 129–144. http://dx.doi.org/10.1037/a0032699

Where is it illegal to be gay? (2014, February 10). BBC News. Retrieved from http://www.bbc.com/news/world-25927595

Williams, J. (2007). Review of "Gay, lesbian, bisexual, and transgender people with developmental disabilities and mental retardation: Stories of the Rainbow Support Group." *Sexuality Research & Social Policy: A Journal of the NSRC, 4*(1), 108–109. doi:10.1525/srsp.2007.4.1.108

Wilson, R. (2014, April 1). Mississippi passes Arizona-style religious freedom bill. *Washington Post.* Retrieved from http://www.washingtonpost.com/blogs/govbeat/wp/2014/04/01/mississippi-passes-arizona-style-religious-freedom-bill/

Worthington, R. L. (2010). Ethical training and practice with LGB-identified clients: Self-efficacy, competencies, and evidence-based practice. In H. Z. Lyons, K. J. Bieschke, A. K. Dendy, R. L. Worthington, & R. Georgemiller (2010), Psychologists' competence to treat lesbian, gay and bisexual clients: State of the field and strategies for improvement. *Professional Psychology: Research and Practice, 41*, 431–433.

6

AFFIRMATIVE COUNSELING WITH TRANSGENDER AND GENDER NONCONFORMING CLIENTS

ANNELIESE A. SINGH AND LORE M. DICKEY

As transgender and gender nonconforming (TGNC) clients have increasingly organized and advocated for their human rights around the world, there have been changes in counseling and psychological practice with TGNC people as well. In this chapter, we use *TGNC* as an umbrella term to denote people whose gender identity or gender expression does not align with the sex they were assigned at birth (American Psychological Association [APA], 2015). We define *TGNC-affirmative counseling* as counseling approaches that provide empowering environments for TGNC clients, are culturally responsive to TGNC clients' needs, and help address the impacts of societal oppression on TGNC mental health. TGNC-affirmative counselors, therefore, have the awareness, knowledge, and skills to not only affirm TGNC clients in their gender journeys but also to address the multicultural and social justice issues influencing a client's overall well-being (APA, 2015).

http://dx.doi.org/10.1037/15959-007
Handbook of Sexual Orientation and Gender Diversity in Counseling and Psychotherapy, K. A. DeBord, A. R. Fischer, K. J. Bieschke, and R. M. Perez (Editors)

A starting point in becoming a TGNC-affirmative counselor is to understand that TGNC identities are not a recent occurrence in the world. TGNC people have existed throughout numerous cultures over a long period of time (Namaste, 2000). As a result of colonization practices, however, many TGNC communities and cultures that were indigenously viewed as valuable were destroyed or damaged (Lev, 2004). In addition to being knowledgeable of this TGNC history, affirmative counseling includes attention to the risk and resilience factors of TGNC clients. TGNC people, for instance, face societal barriers in the form of transgender oppression (also termed *transpreju-dice*) that influence the access they have to resources to support healthy lives (Harper & Schneider, 2003; Institute of Medicine, 2011). Simultaneously, TGNC people also develop resilience strategies that allow them to navigate this oppression in their lives, which is an important area for TGNC-affirmative counselors and psychologists to explore (Singh, 2013; Singh & McKleroy, 2011). TGNC-affirmative counseling often involves the mental health practitioner serving in the role of consultant in order to educate people in a TGNC person's life (e.g., family members, work supervisor) about concerns and needs, potentially coordinating care with health care providers, and advising clients regarding identity (Bockting, Knudson, & Goldberg, 2006).

We begin this chapter with a review of the definitions, language use, and theoretical frameworks and competencies that counselors and psychologists should have knowledge of in order to provide TGNC-affirmative counseling. We then discuss the history of counseling practice and treatment of TGNC people, followed by specific strategies for developing TGNC-affirmative counseling practice and environments. We review counseling issues affecting those TGNC people for whom a social transition is a goal (see Chapter 16 for the physical components of medical transition). We then discuss the common concerns clients have across their lifespan, as well as the major components TGNC-affirmative counseling. The chapter ends with a clinical intake example with a TGNC client. The first author identifies as a South Asian queer person, whose gender identity is genderqueer femme and who is perceived as cisgender, and thus is able to access cisgender privilege. The second author identifies as a White trans man with a lesbian history.

DEFINITIONS, LANGUAGE USE, AND THEORETICAL FRAMEWORKS IN TGNC-AFFIRMATIVE COUNSELING

Foundational information for TGNC-affirmative counseling rests on a strong knowledge base of and language use in working with TGNC people that is respectful and empowering, as well as theoretical frameworks that can assist counselors and psychologists in conceptualizing TGNC mental health. Definitions are covered extensively in the introduction to this book.

TGNC Language

Because language is continuously evolving in TGNC communities, TGNC-affirmative counseling requires that counselors and psychologists be knowledgeable about the various words and expressions TGNC clients use to describe themselves and are prepared to use these words and understand their meanings. When a TGNC client uses a term that the practitioner does not understand, he or she should ask for clarification in a respectful manner. Affirmative counseling also involves using pronouns or words that TGNC clients express as being important to them (see the section "Preparing to be a TGNC-Affirmative Practitioner" for more details). There are helpful glossaries of TGNC terms that can be found online and are listed in the Appendix (see, e.g., Lambda Legal's *Bending the Mold*).

Diverse TGNC people may use language that is unique to their cultural background. For instance, the use of the phrase *masculine of center* has increased recently in TGNC communities of color, as people wanted to develop terms that were not as closely associated with White, Western, and academic terms (Brown Boi Project, 2012). TGNC youth may use words such as *gender blender*, *gender bender*, and other creative words to describe themselves. Regardless of the age and racial–ethnic identity of a TGNC client, affirmative practitioners endeavor to use these terms and language in respectful ways that empower clients and support them on their gender journey (Gonzalez & McNulty, 2010).

Helpful TGNC-Affirmative Theoretical Frameworks and Competencies

TGNC-affirmative counselors should use intersectionality as a theoretical framework in order to attend to the confluence of a client's gender identity with other identities that could influence the presenting issue and their overall mental health and well-being (Warner, 2008; see also Chapter 4, this volume). These multiple identities include race–ethnicity, sexual orientation, age, class, disability, religion–spiritual affiliation, migration status, and education status among others. A TGNC client living with a disability, for example, may present for counseling seeking assistance with securing a letter for hormone therapy but may also have concerns about transportation. Attention to how intersectionality of identities influences TGNC client health and well-being can also affect the extent to which clients feel empowered or safe in their gender journeys (Burnes & Chen, 2012). A TGNC high school student, for instance, may want her parents to use female pronouns and a female name she has identified but might be facing her parents' refusal to do so; therefore, she could use assistance connecting with other TGNC young people. (We discuss lifespan issues for young TGNC people in a later section of this chapter.) Intersectionality theory can help provide a foundation that enables counselors to conduct a thorough intake, as well as help identify potential barriers (e.g., racism, ableism, adultism) and supports that TGNC clients have in their lives that help them be resilient (Burnes & Chen, 2012; for further information on intersectionality and lesbian, gay, bisexual, transgender, and queer clients, see Chapter 4, this volume).

In addition to intersectionality, TGNC-affirmative counselors and psychologists should be aware of and be able to apply the minority stress model (Meyer, 2003) in their case conceptualization and intervention strategies. The minority stress model has typically been used with sexual minority client conceptualization and assessment (see Chapter 3); however, the model has recently been applied to the lived experiences of TGNC people (Hendricks & Testa, 2012). In the original minority stress model, Meyer described distal and proximal stressors that influence mental health. Distal factors include discrimination events, where, for example, a TGNC person experiences prejudice at work or in public regarding gender identity (Hendricks & Testa, 2012). Proximal factors include the anticipation of discrimination, concealment of one's gender identity, and internalization of transgender oppression (Hendricks & Testa, 2012). Both proximal and distal factors influence health outcomes in a positive or negative manner (Institute of Medicine, 2011). For instance, the more a TGNC person experiences discrimination and internalizes transgender oppression, the greater the potential negative health outcomes could be (Grant et al., 2011). Using intersectionality theory described above in tandem with the minority stress model helps clinicians address the experiences TGNC people of diverse backgrounds face. TGNC people of color, for example, may face additional challenges, such as high rates of poverty (Grant et al., 2011) and HIV/AIDS (Nemoto, Operario, Keatley, Han, & Soma, 2004).

Evolving History of Counseling and Psychological Practice With TGNC People

A major component of TGNC-affirmative counseling is to have knowledge of the history and evolution of counseling and psychological practices with TGNC clients. This knowledge is important because for many years practitioners have worked with TGNC identity and expression from a pathological framework (and still do to some extent) rather than as an affirmed identity. In this manner, counselors and psychologists served as gatekeepers and worked primarily with TGNC people who identified as transsexuals seeking medical interventions such as hormone therapy and surgery (Singh & Burnes, 2010).

The practice of TGNC counseling and therapy has a long history of patholo-gizing TGNC through diagnostic practices (see Chapter 16, this volume, for a history of diagnosis with TGNC people).

The recent movement toward TGNC-affirmative counseling calls for counselors and psychologists to enter the roles of supporter and advocate, rather than as merely gatekeeper and diagnostician (Singh & Burnes, 2010). This change in role has been precipitated by TGNC activism advocating for more responsive health care environments. There have also been profes-sional documents in the field that have helped shift this practitioner role. For instance, the World Professional Association of Transgender Health (WPATH) released its seventh version of its *Standards of Care for the Health of Transsexual, Transgender, and Gender-Nonconforming People* in 2012 (Coleman et al., 2012). The WPATH *Standards of Care* describes standards for health care professionals working across a variety of fields (e.g., mental health, endo-crinology, surgery) with TGNC clients. In the new *Standards of Care*, the WPATH explicitly states that gender dysphoria is not a mental illness, in addi-tion to emphasizing the negative health outcomes for TGNC people related to societal oppression they face:

> Thus, transsexual, transgender, and gender-nonconforming individuals are not inherently disordered. Rather, the distress of gender dysphoria, when present, is the concern that might be diagnosable and for which various treatment options are available. The existence of a diagnosis for such dysphoria often facilitates access to health care and can guide further research into effective treatments. (Coleman et al., 2012, p. 169)

The *Standards of Care* also describes the tasks the mental health practitioner has in working with TGNC people over their lifespan in terms of assessment of gender dysphoria. There is extensive discussion of the assessment of gender dysphoria and its diagnosis in terms of the criteria of *Diagnostic and Statistical Manual of Mental Disorders* (fifth ed.; American Psychiatric Association, 2013) in Chapter 16.

Whereas the WPATH *Standards of Care* (Coleman et al., 2012) discusses treatment standards for TGNC people, the American Counseling Association (ACA) released *Competencies for Counseling With Transgender Clients* in 2010. Although these are primarily training competencies for counselors working with TGNC people, the competencies provide helpful information for under-standing TGNC-affirming counseling approaches and interventions. The com-petencies cover the following areas: human growth and development, social and cultural foundations, helping relationships, group work, professional ori-entation, appraisal, and research. The ACA competencies are grounded in strengths-based, multicultural, advocacy, resilience, and feminist theoretical frameworks, which the authors encourage as part of TGNC-affirmative prac-tice. Whereas the ACA competencies are primarily geared toward working with

TGNC adults, the APA (2015) developed guidelines for TGNC-affirmative psychological practice for TGNC clients across the lifespan. These guidelines are also grounded in strengths-based, multicultural, and advocacy theoretical frameworks. The guidelines also address issues of family building and sexuality, in addition to more general psychological practice.

DEVELOPING TGNC-AFFIRMATIVE COUNSELING ENVIRONMENTS

Because TGNC people may have experienced a range of transgender oppression in various domains of their lives (e.g., school, employment, family, relationships, health care), they may experience distrust of mental health practitioners. Some of this distrust is also rooted in the history of TGNC counseling, which has included mental health practitioner gatekeeping. In addition, TGNC people commonly experience microaggressions in society (Nadal, Rivera, & Corpus, 2010). Mental health counselors and psychologists, therefore, should strive to develop and ensure that the counseling environment is a safe place for TGNC clients to explore gender identity and gender expression (Nadal, Skolnik, & Wong, 2012). In this section, we discuss how to develop TGNC-affirmative counseling environments, including aspects of becoming a TGNC-affirmative practitioner, designing inclusive paperwork and marketing materials, using thorough individual counseling and assessment, and conducting inclusive group counseling.

Preparing to be a TGNC-Affirmative Practitioner

Often in the scholarship on TGNC counseling, the emphasis is on the personhood of TGNC clients and their gender identity (Bockting et al., 2006). The challenge for counselors and psychologists, however, is that little has been written on the influence of the practitioner's gender identity on practice with TGNC clients. Practitioners should develop awareness about their own gender journeys because their gender is not only consistently evolving over the lifespan but is also influenced by culture (APA, 2015). They can begin to develop self-awareness by reflecting on the cultural message they have received over their lives about their own gender identity and gender expression. For instance, what gender roles, norms, and socialization have they experienced in their lives? Counselors and psychologists can also ask themselves what the consequences have been for stepping outside of gender identity and gender expression norms for their assigned sex at birth.

As counselors and psychologists explore their own gender histories, they should consider connecting gender roles, norms, and socialization to the potential intersections with their identities of race–ethnicity, disability, and social class among others (Burnes & Chen, 2012). As practitioners examine their own gender journeys, they should identify the privilege and oppression experiences associated with the intersection of their identities. Reflecting on their gender journeys not only helps them develop awareness of the societal and cultural influences on their gender but also encourages them to refrain from imposing their views of gender (whether they are cisgender or TGNC) on TGNC people in counseling (Singh & Burnes, 2010). This is especially true because the counseling relationship is a hierarchical one, even if practitioners endeavor to share power with their clients.

TGNC-affirmative providers should be attentive to the paperwork and marketing materials they use. For example, intake forms may be the first signal to a prospective client that a provider is or is not TGNC-affirming in their practice. Keeping in mind the intersection of identities TGNC people may have, counselors and psychologists should ensure their paperwork and materials signal an open and affirmative stance to working with clients of diverse cultural backgrounds (ACA, 2010).

During the counseling intake, practitioners should collect basic demographic data while also ensuring that these explorations are respectful and focused (Lev, 2004). For instance, the most basic area of concern for the TGNC client might be in identifying the name and gender they would like the counselor to use (Bockting et al., 2006). This name, gender, and related pronouns may or may not be the same as that shown on identity documents, including insurance cards (Coleman et al., 2012). Counselors and psychologists are encouraged to explore this with clients in a way that is accepting and affirming (Singh & Burnes, 2010). Practitioners may provide a fill-in-the-blank option that asks for the client's gender and for the pronoun that the counselor should use (APA, 2015).

The next area of concern on most intake forms relates to relationship status, which is another situation to which TGNC-affirmative providers should use flexibility and open-mindedness. Some TGNC clients may present with what appears to be a complex relationship history. For example, a trans woman may be married to her wife whom she has known for many years, predating her social and medical transition. Most providers will find that their standard intake form does not address this type of relationship configuration, and a fill-in-the-blank option can be used to address this under "significant relationship(s) status."

For counselors and psychologists who work in settings that use electronic records, there are additional concerns that may need to be addressed. Changing a paper-based intake is relatively simple and inexpensive. However, changing an electronic record can be both time-consuming and expensive. Counselors are encouraged to advocate on behalf of their clients for the use of an electronic record that is flexible enough to meet the needs of TGNC clients. The Fenway Institute and Center for American Progress (2013) recently published a resource that addresses the use of electronic health records in a manner that is TGNC-affirmative.

When developing marketing materials for clinical or educational services, practitioners are encouraged to use inclusive language (APA, 2015). This language addresses not only gender identity but also intersecting identities that many people possess. It might be useful to test marketing materials with local, regional, or national TGNC providers to determine whether the target audience can "see themselves" in the materials.

Individual Counseling

Counseling and assessment services are often required for TGNC clients (Coleman et al., 2012). The WPATH *Standards of Care* revised the requirement for TGNC counselors and psychologists working with TGNC clients so that a master's-level counselor is able to write letters of referral. TGNC people may seek counseling and assessment services specifically in order to procure a letter of support to access medical transition. However, it is becoming increasingly common in the United States for medical providers to use an informed consent model for care for hormone therapy (Deutsch, 2012; see also Chapter 16, this volume).

Historically, TGNC clients were required to complete a "real life experience" or see a mental health provider for a specific length of time (e.g., 12 months). These requirements no longer exist, and counselors and psychologists are encouraged to dispel these commonly held beliefs among their colleagues or clients (Coleman et al., 2012). Although it is important to address co-occurring mental health concerns, these are not necessarily reasons to delay a person's request to make a medical or social transition (Coleman et al., 2012).

Mental health practitioners are often called upon to conduct a clinical assessment of a client. This might be true for TGNC clients as well. Practitioners should be aware that there are no published assessments that are designed to clinically assess a person's gender identity. Psychologists are reminded of the ethical responsibility to use assessment tools only for their intended purpose (APA, 2010). For example, using a personality assessment to determine transition readiness is not consistent with the original purpose of the assessment.

Group Counseling Considerations

Group counseling can be an affordable way to address the needs of TGNC clients, and there are several considerations that should be addressed (dickey

& Loewy, 2010). The first consideration a provider might make is how the group will be led. Will a practitioner lead the group or will it be a peer-led group? There are advantages and drawbacks to either type of leadership. An advantage of having a mental health professional lead the group is that significant clinical concerns for one or more of the group members can be more easily addressed by the practitioner. The largest challenge in having a practitioner lead the group relates to cost. Peer-led groups are typically made available for little to no cost (e.g., $5–$10 a session), whereas a practitioner might charge a significant fee (e.g., $50 or more per session).

Another consideration relates to the format of the group (dickey & Loewy, 2010). Will the group be a drop-in group with an open-ended time frame, or will it be a closed group that meets for a set number of sessions? Many TGNC support groups use a drop-in model that is open-ended (no set end date). The benefit of these types of groups is that TGNC people may have more or less need to access the group for support across their social and medical transition. A disadvantage of a drop-in group is that the group members may change from one session to the next. Therefore, some practitioners prefer to use a close-ended time frame, especially with groups geared toward family members and partners of TGNC people, which may benefit from having a predetermined group membership. A group might take a variety of formats, and the practitioner needs to be sure that the format supports the goals of the group.

Location is a final consideration. Counselors and psychologists should consider whether the group could meet in the practitioner's office and whether this location would feel welcoming to the TGNC clients. The same is true for groups that are held in religious facilities. Because TGNC people experience discrimination from conservative religious organizations, it may be wise to avoid using such facilities even if a particular facility is welcoming (dickey & Loewy, 2010).

Social Transition and TGNC-Affirmative Counseling

In the United States, it is becoming more common for TGNC people to make a social transition. In general, a social transition might include some combination of the following: (a) name change, (b) pronoun change, and (c) change in manner of dress or gender expression. In some ways, making a social transition can be more challenging than a medical transition for a TGNC client and the people they interact with on a daily basis (Bockting et al., 2006). However, for adolescents and youth, this may be the only option available, as they are unlikely to find a medical provider who will assist in a medical transition.

Some of the challenges that TGNC people face when making a social transition include addressing this decision with the people with whom they interact on a daily basis (Lev, 2004). For example, a school-age person may need to discuss a name change with school administrators and with each teacher (Gonzalez & McNulty, 2010). If the teachers and the administration are supportive, this may not cause any difficulty. In the State of California, legislation was passed in 2013 that requires school districts to provide TGNC-affirmative spaces for their students. However, practitioners outside of California should be knowledgeable about the extent to which their school jurisdictions are responsive in how they address the needs of TGNC students. The majority of U.S. school facilities and programs are designed to focus on cisgender boys or girls with a heavy investment in the gender binary, which creates barriers for TGNC students (Gonzalez & McNulty, 2010).

TGNC adults may have similar issues in colleges and universities (Beemyn, 2005). For TGNC people who are employed, a host of workplace issues might need to be addressed. Provided that a person has had a legal name change, the process of updating personnel records should be relatively straightforward; however, encouraging colleagues and supervisors to use the correct name and pronoun may be more of a challenge (Beemyn, 2005). In Chapter 16 of this book, the physical components and considerations of medical transition are addressed.

TGNC-affirmative counselors and psychologists may commonly be asked to consult about a TGNC client, and this consultation often centers on the need for coordination of care (APA, 2015). Psychologists are encouraged to develop a wide network of TGNC-affirmative providers in the fields of medicine (e.g., endocrinology, primary care, gynecology), social work, and law. Developing this network ensures that practitioners have access to a variety of providers who can address the needs of their TGNC clients.

TGNC-AFFIRMATIVE COUNSELING ACROSS THE LIFESPAN

There are developmental concerns and contexts to keep in mind when working with TGNC people, even if they are not engaging in a social or medical transition. Lifespan concerns for young TGNC people are different than for TGNC people in middle or late adulthood. Lifespan contexts are also influenced by the interaction of TGNC people with significant others, family, friends, and allies in their lives, and these interactions can help determine whether TGNC people have positive or negative health outcomes. In this section, we discuss the major aspects of TGNC-affirmative counseling with people in the stages of childhood, adolescence, middle adulthood, and late adulthood.

Practice Concerns With TGNC Children

Typically with children, the terms *gender nonconforming*, *gender variant*, *gender diverse*, *gender expansive*, or *gender creative* are used. One of the reasons for using these phrases is that although gender identity is fluid throughout the lifespan (Kohlberg, 1966), gender identity and gender expression are especially fluid in children. For instance, gender play can vary widely, as well as the choices regarding clothing and peer groups, depending on whether a child identifies as TGNC (Edwards-Leeper & Spack, 2012).

When assessing gender dysphoria, counselors and psychologists may notice that counseling approaches in the field vary, and there is a significant lack of professional consensus about how to work with TGNC children, accompanied by a lack of research on outcomes (Edwards-Leeper & Spack, 2012). Practitioners should work closely with TGNC children and families to normalize all gender play and help parents understand their child's needs related to their gender or gender dysphoria (Adelson & the American Academy of Child and Adolescent Psychiatry Committee on Quality Issues, 2012).

Counselors and psychologists working with TGNC children should assess for co-occurring mental health conditions. This assessment should not be conducted to restrict the gender identity and gender expression of a TGNC child but to identify any additional barriers the child may face. A thorough suicide and trauma history assessment is important to conduct with TGNC children as well (Liu & Mustanski, 2012). Using art and play therapy to conduct these assessments and using these modalities during ongoing counseling can be very helpful. Having a range of clothing and toys across genders is also important so that TGNC children can select the ones that feel best to them. Because TGNC children have increased gender fluidity, practitioners must have the skill to support families in allowing their child to decide to return to a previous gender identity that is aligned with their assigned birth sex. Counselors and psychologists may notice that parents have a more challenging time with this situation than their child (Edwards-Leeper & Spack, 2012). In these instances, affirmative counseling with children entails continuing to support them in exploring their gender identity and gender expression in a way that is congruent with how they feel, as well as validating their thoughts and feelings about their gender. In other instances, children may express gender fluidity and a nonbinary identity where they may not identify with a consistent gender. In these situations, affirmative counseling includes also validating a child's gender identity and gender expression during the transition from childhood to adulthood.

When working with TGNC children, practitioners may also work with caregivers, schools, and extended family. Caregivers (e.g., parents, guardians) may not have the education they need to understand the fluidity of gender identity and gender expression. Counselors and psychologists, therefore, begin consultations with families by normalizing not only the child's gender fluidity, but also the resulting concerns caregivers may have. A helpful way of normalizing gender fluidity is to provide psychoeducation on gender fluidity in children in the counseling session and through brochures that families may read (see the entries "American Psychological Association" and "Trans Youth and Family Allies" in the websites section of the Appendix). Even as they keep the best interest of the TGNC child in mind, practitioners often are also working to dispel myths about gender nonconformity and conducting a careful family assessment of the safety of the child in the family, social, and school settings.

One of the common fears that families hold is related to the oppression they anticipate their child facing in school, community, and extended family settings (Edwards-Leeper & Spack, 2012). Counselors and psychologists should be able to not only help identify what these fears are but also provide collaborative solutions (Gonzalez & McNulty, 2010). For instance, if caregivers are concerned that their child may experience discrimination in schools, practitioners can brainstorm with them about the range of options available to them such as educating school administrators and teachers or changing schools. Caregivers may not know that school counselors are required to advocate for the needs of all students and can be helpful in facilitating a TGNC-affirming environment within the school (Gonzalez & McNulty, 2010).

A focus of all TGNC-affirming counseling should include sharing with families the research findings that TGNC youth have more positive health outcomes when there is family support. For instance, levels of self-esteem are greater and levels of depression, suicide ideation, and suicide attempts for TGNC youth decrease when there is family acceptance (Ryan, Russell, Huebner, Diaz, & Sanchez, 2010). In addition, counselors and psychologists should understand and educate their TGNC children and adolescent clients and their families about the ethical and legal protections for TGNC youth in schools. For example, school personnel are bound by the ethical mandates of their related professions to provide supportive environments for TGNC people, and there is extensive case law and legislation protecting TGNC youth rights so that they are safe in their school settings (Gonzalez & McNulty, 2010).

Other ethical concerns when working with TGNC children include endeavoring to support the best welfare of the child while also supporting parents who may not be affirming of their child. In these instances, the practitioner should continuously be guided by best practices with TGNC mental health (e.g., APA *Guidelines for Psychological Practice With Transgender and*

Gender Nonconforming, WPATH *Standards of Care*, American Counseling Association *Competencies for Counseling With Transgender Clients*). In these documents guiding TGNC mental health practice, there is a recommendation for ongoing consultation and supervision to support practitioner interventions in these instances. Practitioners should be mindful that affirmative counseling of TGNC children places the child at the center of interventions, while simultaneously educating and supporting parents in accessing TGNC-affirmative resources. Practitioners should also be aware of the laws in their particular state; mental health care for TGNC people differs from state to state. For example, in Washington, a 13-year-old can consent to counseling without parental permission, and there is a similar law in California. Additionally, some states have outlawed the use of reparative or conversion therapy with sexual and gender minority minors. A recent publication from the U.S. Substance Abuse Mental Health Services Administration (USSAMHSA, 2015) and Shidlo and Gonsiorek (Chapter 11, this volume) cover the dangers of this approach to clinical work.

Working With TGNC Adolescents

Adolescence can be a challenging developmental period, and for TGNC adolescents it can bring additional struggles and barriers. In addition to assessing co-occurring mental health concerns, exploring internalized negative belief systems about TGNC people that adolescents have allows practitioners to examine and confront negative stereotypes and myths about TGNC people. Assessing for suicide ideation and attempts as well as self-injury and trauma is important because of high rates among TGNC adolescents (Liu & Mustanski, 2012). In addition, counselors and psychologists should assess TGNC adolescents for resilience, strengths, and competencies, ranging from peer and parental support to positive belief systems about their gender identity and gender expression.

When working with TGNC adolescents who want a medical transition and are supported by their caregivers, practitioners often refer to and work collaboratively with their physical health care providers. For instance, counselors and psychologists may refer TGNC people in early to middle adolescence to a pediatric endocrinologist who can prescribe puberty-suppressing treatment in order to delay body development associated with their assigned birth sex (Hembree et al., 2009). This medical treatment can provide TGNC adolescents and their families with time to explore the adolescent's gender identity and gender expression should they decide to pursue hormone therapy in the future (Edwards-Leeper & Spack, 2012). In addition, for some TGNC adolescents the idea of puberty in their assigned birth sex may cause extreme duress in their life (Brill & Pepper, 2008). With

TGNC people in later adolescence, practitioners may make referrals for hormone therapy for a person who is 16 years old or an emancipated minor (Coleman et al., 2012). Before a TGNC adolescent is referred to hormone therapy, it is important to collaboratively assess the client's potential family building goals because hormone therapy affects fertility. Counselors and psychologists should be able to address and explore these questions as well as normalize the early nature of these discussions considering their life stage. Practitioners should be prepared to make referrals to fertility specialists should TGNC adolescents or their parents want to gain additional information about family building with biological family ties in mind (Singh & Sangganjanavanich, 2015).

As with TGNC children, counselors and psychologists often work closely with families, providing education on TGNC adolescence, addressing myths, and connecting families with online and in-person support groups and information (e.g., PFLAG, Trans Youth and Family Allies; Gonzalez & McNulty, 2010). Family therapy is therefore a common modality of treatment, and practitioners must be skilled in addressing conflict that may exist within the family (Brill & Pepper, 2008; Lev, 2004). For instance, one parent or legal guardian may be supportive of a TGNC adolescent's gender identity and gender expression, whereas another may express not only a lack of support but also open hostility. Educating families about the stages of coming out can help families understand that the emotions they are experiencing are common. Using her experience of counseling TGNC people across the lifespan, Lev (2004) identified the stages of coming out for families of TGNC people on. These stages may not apply to all families, but counselors and psychologists working with families who have little to no previous information or education on TGNC identities may find that these stages are typical. The first stage, discovery and disclosure of TGNC status to family, includes feelings of shock and betrayal. In the second stage, turmoil, families experience denial and conflict. In the third stage, negotiation, family members explore the degree to which they can accept and support their transgender family member. The fourth stage, balance, refers to the balance that family members must strike as they face the everyday challenges and opportunities related to having a family member who is TGNC; it does not necessarily imply that family members have resolved their concerns about their family member's TGNC identity. Counselors and psychologists should continue to balance information giving, respect, and value for the TGNC person's autonomy and TGNC identity and acknowledge the challenges and opportunities that each of these coming out stages entails. In addition, practitioners should explicitly explore how culturally informed family values influence their experiences in each of these stages.

With TGNC adolescent clients, practitioners must explore peer relationships and the timing of social transition (if desired). TGNC adolescents report experiences of frequent bullying in school settings and a lack of support from school personnel (Kosciw, Greytak, Bartkiewicz, Boesen, & Palmer, 2012). Collaboratively identifying the steps that TGNC adolescents should take in case they are bullied is therefore critical. Counselors and psychologists can address these concerns through the use of role plays. These explorations of bullying should include cyberbullying that may occur on social networks and other sites. Designing a safety plan is also helpful with TGNC adolescents so they are aware of what to do if, for instance, they experience bullying in a restroom from peers or in class from a teacher. For a more extensive discussion of working with TGNC children, see Brill and Pepper's (2008) *The Transgender Child*.

Counseling TGNC People in Middle Adulthood

The WPATH *Standards of Care* offers a listing of tasks that mental health professionals should attend to when working with adults (Coleman et al., 2012). These tasks include making a diagnosis (as indicated), assessing for co-occurring mental health concerns, making a referral to medical treatment (e.g., hormone and surgical care), and providing psychoeducation regarding the options a TGNC client might consider. One of these tasks relates to assessment of the client. Accordingly, the WPATH *Standards of Care* states,

> The evaluation includes, at a minimum, assessment of gender identity and gender dysphoria, history and development of gender dysphoric feelings, the impact of stigma attached to gender nonconformity on mental health, and the availability of support from family, friends, and peers. (Coleman et al., 2012, p. 180)

As a part of this assessment process, the provider is charged not only with determining the presence of clinical concerns that might lead to a diagnosis of gender dysphoria but also with understanding how these symptoms might be better accounted for by a different diagnosis or by increased attention to the social context and environment. Providers are encouraged to complete assessments in a timely manner (Lev, 2004). This helps to speed the process of accessing necessary care without any undue delays. Providers are also cautioned to be sensitive with regard to making decisions based on assessments that force the use of the gender binary. Research has shown that results of assessments fluctuate for TGNC people over the course of their transition (Keo-Meier et al., 2014); this is also true for most individuals.

Regardless of the age at which a person becomes aware of their TGNC identity, the impact on their life can quite disruptive. This is especially true for people in middle adulthood. If a TGNC person has established a family and a career, it is likely that their decision to explore their gender identity affects all aspects of their life (APA, 2015). People come out as TGNC individuals later in life for a variety of reasons (Cook-Daniels, 2006; Samons, 2009). For some, they may not have realized until later in life that such a transition was even possible. Others may have known at an earlier age but suppressed the feelings in hopes that they might pass. As they established their families and careers, they may have felt the need to wait until their children were grown.

Families can be a tremendous source of support, and they can also be a source of stress for a TGNC person. Family support for the TGNC person's decision to transition provides a buffer of support that can ease the process on many levels (Moody & Smith, 2013; Ryan et al., 2010). However, not all families are supportive. Difficulties that TGNC people might face with their family include separation and divorce. They may also, as a result of the separation and divorce, be challenged with custody battles for the children (Flynn, 2006). Adding this layer of complexity and legal challenge to a TGNC person's life can be daunting. Providers are encouraged to gain a full understanding of the family dynamics in an effort to assure that clients have the support they need to address these concerns.

Coming out to family members can be difficult. Middle-aged adults may be unsure about how and when to come out to their partners and children. Depending on their age, children may have little to no difficulty understanding the changes their parent is considering. Prior to puberty, children seem to be fairly resilient in understanding their parent's transition process (Lev, 2004). This also tends to be the case for children who are young adults. The children who seem to have the largest struggle are those who are in puberty, as they are also trying to understand the changes that are happening in their own body (Lev, 2004). Several resources are available to help TGNC clients understand the impact on their family members; the Appendix lists some of them.

Not unlike the TGNC person, family members have a transition process of their own to complete. Family members are likely to receive questions from friends and acquaintances about the TGNC person. These challenges might be compounded by a lack of understanding and willingness to be supportive. Providers should be prepared to help their clients navigate these challenges.

Working With TGNC People in Late Adulthood

Older TGNC people can have some of the same challenges that middle-aged adults face. An area that can be unique to older adults is the need for care as they age. If older adults do not have family to care for them later in life, they may face difficulties finding TGNC-affirmative care. The film *Gen Silent* (Maddux, 2011) is an excellent depiction of the challenges faced by lesbian, gay, bisexual, and transgender (LGBT) older adults who are out but then find that they are suddenly forced to go back in the closet to receive care (Maddux, 2011). Providers are encouraged to assist TGNC clients with locating care facilities that provide TGNC-affirmative care, which may include sharing online resources with them about how to select a provider (see the Appendix).

THE PRACTITIONER ROLE OF ADVOCACY IN TGNC-AFFIRMATIVE COUNSELING

The role of advocacy in TGNC-affirmative counseling can be important whether working in short-term or long-term counseling with TGNC clients (Singh & Burnes, 2010). Practitioners may be the only source of support in these clients' lives about their gender identity and gender expression; therefore, being prepared to engage in advocacy is critical. In this section, we discuss ethical issues, legal issues and protections, and policy change.

Ethical Issues in TGNC-Affirmative Counseling

A common ethical concern in TGNC-affirmative counseling is the scope of the practitioner's training. Practitioners should be careful to not work outside the boundaries of their training while simultaneously seeking continuing education on TGNC-affirmative counseling (APA, 2010). Just as there are constantly evolving terms that TGNC people use to describe their gender identity and gender expression, there are also constantly evolving ethics, laws, and policies related to TGNC people that counselors and psychologists should be aware of, in addition to research that informs TGNC-affirmative counseling.

Because of the lack of TGNC-affirmative training models preparing practitioners to work with TGNC people and because many counselors and psychologists have not received continuing education on TGNC-affirmative counseling, a major ethical issue in the field is the lack of well-prepared practitioners (Jensen, 2010). Therefore, even in large, urban cities, there may be a limited range of TGNC-affirmative counselors and psychologists who are available to TGNC clients; practitioners who are well-trained may have a caseload of TGNC clients who have many intersecting and overlapping social and work lives. TGNC-affirmative counselors and psychologists who live in an area where there is restricted access to TGNC counseling can work with local and state professional associations to conduct TGNC-affirmative continuing education or meet in consulting groups on TGNC counseling where practitioners can discuss TGNC-affirmative counseling. Counselors and psychologists with a large caseload of TGNC clients working in a small community or rural setting should be prepared to discuss confidentiality in an ongoing manner in order to remind clients of their legal right of privacy.

Legal Issues and Protections for TGNC People

Despite some changes in recent years, TGNC people have few to no legal protections in the United States. In 2014, President Barack Obama issued an executive order banning TGNC employment discrimination at the federal level and signed an executive order making it illegal to discriminate against federal employees or contractors (National Center for Transgender Equality [NCTE], 2014). Nevertheless, TGNC people are often apprehensive about coming out in the workplace for fear of losing their jobs. According to the National Gay & Lesbian Task Force (NGLTF), only 17 states and the District of Columbia have laws protecting TGNC people from discrimination (NGLTF, 2013b). As a result, TGNC people are at risk of discrimination in most U.S. states.

TGNC people have federal protection from hate crimes, but state-level protection is similar to nondiscrimination protection (NCTE, 2011a). Fifteen states and the District of Columbia designate penalties for hate crimes (NGLTF, 2013a). TGNC people are often victims of hate crimes, the worst of which result in the death of the TGNC person (NCTE, 2011b). These losses are often devastating for members of the TGNC community. In 1998, members of the TGNC community began to commemorate these losses by establishing the Transgender Day of Remembrance (TDOR; GLAAD, 2013).

Another area where TGNC people are often at a disadvantage is related to institutional care, including prisons, jails, and shelters. These facilities are often segregated by sex, and TGNC people are often forced to either be located with people of the same birth sex or are placed in solitary confinement, which ensures that the inmate is in protective custody but is also unduly punitive. Placing TGNC people in facilities with others who have the same sex assigned at birth can lead to increased risk of violence toward the TGNC person. NCTE has been working to change the regulations in the U.S. federal prison system and has identified four key areas for policy change: access to health care, classification of prisoners, safe housing of prisoners, and Prison Rape Elimination Act requirements (NCTE, 2011a).

Advocating for TGNC-Affirmative Policy Change

Psychologists and other mental health providers are encouraged to advocate for the needs of their TGNC clients. Policies and practices in a variety of areas impact the lives of TGNC people, including simple changes such as assuring that TGNC people have access to restrooms. The Transgender Law Center has published a resource titled *Peeing in Peace* (2005), an activist's guide for addressing basic needs of TGNC people.

Providers can take simple steps to help make safe restrooms available for their TGNC clients. Some buildings have single stall restrooms that are designed to be accessible for people with disabilities. Providers are encouraged to work with administrators to remove signs that indicate the restrooms are for women or men. These single stall restrooms can easily be made into gender-neutral facilities. If the facilities are such that there are only women's and men's restrooms, providers should not assume the client's preference for which facility to access; rather they should make keys to either facility available and let users make their own decision. Lack of access to restrooms can exacerbate health problems for TGNC people (Transgender Law Center, 2005). Providers can help to ease that by assuring the restrooms are accessible and gender neutral when possible.

Another area where people often need support with regard to policy change includes educational institutions. Accommodations in the education setting vary based on the level of the institution. For instance, the needs of a gender nonconforming first grader will be different from those of a first-year college student. What is similar is that both students deserve to be treated respectfully and to be provided with a safe learning environment. Establishing a safe learning environment can start with updating nondiscrimination policies to ensure they are inclusive of TGNC individuals. This simple effort signals to TGNC people that there are allies in the organization who will be supportive. Space limitations preclude a detailed discussion of the full breadth of interventions that might be considered in the educational system. Readers are encouraged to explore the resources in the Appendix for more ideas about how to address the needs of students.

A final area that psychologists and counselors should be aware of relates to the logistics of changing the name and gender marker on various legal documents, including a driver's license and birth certificate. The rules and laws that govern how these changes are made vary from state to state. For instance, most states require some form of genital surgery to change the gender marker on a birth certificate. However, three states (Idaho, Ohio, and Tennessee) currently will not make a change. Additionally, some states amend the birth certificate rather than correcting the gender marker. The result is that a TGNC person who needs to use a birth certificate as a form of identification is unnecessarily outed. One of the best resources for understanding the nuanced differences in state regulations for birth certificate changes is Lambda Legal (2014). See the resources in the Appendix for more information about this process.

Case Study of TGNC-Affirmative Counseling and Therapy

The following case study provides a snapshot of a TGNC-affirmative counseling intake session. Lee[1] is a psychologist who is 36 years old, White, and Christian and who identifies as cisgender and as a man. A client, Ayn, who is 22 years old, identifies as a male-to-female person, and is Korean American, contacted Lee to seek "gender counseling and needs a letter for hormones."

Lee has previously attended several continuing education workshops on TGNC-affirmative counseling and participates in a peer consultation group of fellow practitioners working with TGNC people. Lee has extensively reflected on his own gender journey and his Whiteness. He has identified several stereotypes he internalized based on the intersection of being White and cisgender. These stereotypes included assumptions that men should not display emotions and that TGNC people were "born in the wrong body." Lee has discussed his gender journey reflections and assumptions about TGNC people with his peer consultation group, and he has learned to refrain from using pathologizing statements ("born in the wrong body") and assuming that a TGNC person must identify as TGNC early on in life. He also has learned to intentionally explore race–ethnicity as a White person himself and with clients in order to understand how race–ethnicity and other identities may influence the client–therapist relationship.

Lee shares with Ayn on the phone that he looks forward to seeing Ayn and asks about the pronouns Ayn uses. Ayn shares that she uses the pronouns *her* and *she* and that *Ayn* is the name she would like other people to use. Lee does not use the word *preferred* when speaking about the name and pronouns Ayn would like Lee to use. When Ayn comes to the intake session, she completes paperwork that is TGNC affirming. She is able to write in her gender identity (male-to-female) and her sexual orientation (lesbian) in response to fill-in-the-blank items, in contrast to paperwork that might ask her to check a gender box with only "male" and "female" options. Ayn is also able to do the same with her race–ethnicity (Korean American) and her religion–spiritual affiliation status (agnostic).

As Lee explores Ayn's paperwork in the first session and gathers additional intake and demographic information, he asks her to describe how she experiences the intersection of her identities. Lee also conducts a thorough trauma and resilience assessment with her. Ayn shares that she feels proud of being Korean American now but that she did not feel this way earlier in life. She reports that she was bullied verbally with racist epithets. Ayn also shares that she was physically harassed in high school because she had a more feminine

---

[1] Identifiers have been changed to protect confidentiality.

appearance. Lee asks about other trauma Ayn has experienced during her life, and she shares that she experienced violence in her first relationship with a cisgender woman. Lee explores the resilience and coping strategies that Ayn used during her lifetime to navigate challenging times. She shares that she has a strong social support system of people who are her "family of choice." Lee also explores the degree of support she has within her family, friendships, and work relationships. He also assesses other sources of resilience and coping, such as typical stress management techniques and religious–spiritual identity. Because TGNC people often experience suicidal ideation in response to societal discrimination (Grant et al., 2011), Lee conducts a thorough suicide assessment in addition to a thorough assessment of resilience and coping. Included in this assessment is an exploration of potential school and workplace harassment and any co-occurring conditions such as depression, anxiety, and disordered eating (Effrig, Bieschke, & Locke, 2011).

Lee assesses how much Ayn knows about hormone therapy (because this is the primary reason she is seeking counseling at this time). Ayn shares that she does not know much. Lee provides an overview of the steps involved in procuring a letter. He also shares an overview of the TGNC-affirming endocrinologists that he typically refers to, as well as sharing the content of what is shared in a letter, and the important role of her confidentiality ensuring that the minimal amount of information is contained in the letter of referral. Lee ensures that there is time for Ayn to ask questions and collaboratively explores how long Ayn will be in therapy before a letter is written. Lee concludes the session by emphasizing his role as supporter and advocate for Ayn. He also explores what the session has been like for Ayn and what it will be like to be in counseling specifically to access a letter of referral.

CONCLUSION

As the above case study indicates, being able to provide TGNC-affirmative counseling begins with ensuring that one has current information and training on TGNC-affirmative approaches. This also includes self-reflection on the gender identity of the counselor or psychologist and the use of respectful language when interacting with TGNC clients. TGNC clients are often aware of the history of pathology in counseling and psychology, so they may anticipate discrimination from their providers. Use of TGNC-affirmative paperwork is therefore vital to demonstrate that a counseling office will be responsive and affirming to TGNC client needs. The extensive resilience and trauma assessment includes exploration of coping, suicidality, and trauma in order to address the traumatic experiences they may have and the resilience strategies they may have developed in response to societal oppression. Finally, the mental health provider is continually conscious to limit the amount of information that they disclose when called to collaborate with other health care professionals in order to protect client confidentiality and rights.

In this chapter, we discussed the foundational components of TGNC-affirmative counseling. Because of the rapidly changing field of TGNC health and the increase of TGNC-affirmative laws and policies, counselors and psychologists should strive to stay current. When TGNC-affirmative psychologists connect with other TGNC-affirmative service providers across disciplines, these connections facilitate awareness and knowledge of TGNC-affirming resources.

REFERENCES

Adelson, S. L., & the American Academy of Child and Adolescent Psychiatry Committee on Quality Issues. (2012). Practice parameter on gay, lesbian, or bisexual sexual orientation, gender nonconformity, and gender discordance in children and adolescents. *Journal of the American Academy of Child & Adolescent Psychiatry, 51*, 957–974. http://dx.doi.org/10.1016/j.jaac.2012.07.004

American Counseling Association. (2010). *Competencies for counseling with transgender clients*. Retrieved from http://www.counseling.org/Resources/Competencies/ALGBTIC_Competencies.pdf

American Psychiatric Association. (2013). *Diagnostic and statistical manual of mental disorders* (5th ed.). Arlington, VA: Author.

American Psychological Association. (2010). *Ethical principles of psychologists and code of conduct (2002, amended June 1, 2010)*. Retrieved from http://www.apa.org/ethics/code/principles.pdf

American Psychological Association. (2015). Guidelines for psychological practice with transgender and gender nonconforming people. *American Psychologist, 79*, 832–864. http://dx.doi.org/10.1037/a0039906

Beemyn, G. (2005). Making campuses more inclusive of transgender students. *Journal of Gay & Lesbian Issues in Education, 3*(1), 77–87. http://dx.doi.org/10.1300/J367v03n01_08

Bockting, W. O., Knudson, G., & Goldberg, J. M. (2006). Counseling and mental health care for transgender adults and loved ones. *International Journal of Transgenderism, 9*, 35–82. http://dx.doi.org/10.1300/J485v09n03_03

Brill, S., & Pepper, R. (2008). *The transgender child: A handbook for families and professionals*. San Francisco, CA: Cleis.

Brown Boi Project. (2012). *Freeing ourselves: A guide to health and self love for brown bois*. Oakland, CA: Author.

Burnes, T. R., & Chen, M. M. (2012). The multiple identities of transgender individuals: Incorporating a framework of intersectionality to gender crossing. In

R. Josselson & M. Harway (Eds.), *Navigating multiple identities: Race, gender, culture, nationality, and roles* (pp. 113–128). New York, NY: Oxford University Press. http://dx.doi.org/10.1093/acprof:oso/9780199732074.003.0007

Coleman, E., Bockting, W., Botzer, M., Cohen-Kettenis, P., DeCuypere, G., Feldman, J., . . . Zucker, K. (2012). Standards of care for the health of transsexual, transgender, and gender-nonconforming people, 7th version. *International Journal of Transgenderism, 13*(4), 165–232. http://dx.doi.org/10.1080/15532739.2011.700873

Cook-Daniels, L. (2006). Trans aging. In D. Kimmel, T. Rose, & S. David (Eds.), *Lesbian, gay, bisexual, and transgender aging: Research and clinical perspectives* (pp. 20–35). New York, NY: Columbia University Press.

Deutsch, M. B. (2012). Use of the Informed Consent Model in the provision of cross-sex hormone therapy: A survey of the practices of selected clinics. *International Journal of Transgenderism, 13*, 140–146. http://dx.doi.org/10.1080/15532739.2011.675233

dickey, l. m., & Loewy, M. I. (2010). Group work with transgender clients. *Journal for Specialists in Group Work, 35*, 236–245. http://dx.doi.org/10.1080/01933922.2010.492904

Edwards-Leeper, L., & Spack, N. P. (2012). Psychological evaluation and medical treatment of transgender youth in an interdisciplinary "Gender Management Service" (GeMS) in a major pediatric center. *Journal of Homosexuality, 59*, 321–336. http://dx.doi.org/10.1080/00918369.2012.653302

Effrig, J. C., Bieschke, K. J., & Locke, B. D. (2011). Examining victimization and psychological distress in transgender college students. *Journal of College Counseling, 14*, 143–157. http://dx.doi.org/10.1002/j.2161-1882.2011.tb00269.x

Fenway Institute & Center for American Progress. (2013). *Asking patients questions about sexual orientation and gender identity in clinical settings: A study in four health centers*. Retrieved from http://thefenwayinstitute.org/wp-content/uploads/COM228_SOGI_CHARN_WhitePaper.pdf

Flynn, T. (2006). The ties that [don't] bind: Transgender family law and the unmaking of families. In P. Currah, R. M. Juang, & S. P. Minter (Eds.), *Transgender rights* (pp. 32–50). Minneapolis: University of Minnesota Press.

GLAAD. (2013). *Transgender day of remembrance #TDOR—November 20*. Retrieved from http://www.glaad.org/tdor

Gonzalez, M., & McNulty, J. (2010). Achieving competency with transgender youth: School counselors as collaborative advocates. *Journal of LGBT Issues in Counseling, 4*, 176–186. http://dx.doi.org/10.1080/15538605.2010.524841

Grant, J. M., Mottet, L. A., Tanis, J., Harrison, J., Herman, J. L., & Kiesling, M. (2011). *Injustice at every turn: A report of the national transgender discrimination survey*. Washington, DC: National Center for Transgender Equality & National Gay and Lesbian Task Force.

Harper, G. W., & Schneider, M. (2003). Oppression and discrimination among lesbian, gay, bisexual, and transgendered people and communities: A challenge for community psychology. *American Journal of Community Psychology, 31,* 243–252. http://dx.doi.org/10.1023/A:1023906620085

Hembree, W. C., Cohen-Kettenis, P., Delemarre-van de Waal, H. A., Gooren, L. J., Meyer, W. J., III, Spack, N. P., . . . Montori, V. M. (2009). Endocrine treatment of transsexual persons: An Endocrine Society clinical practice guideline. *The Journal of Clinical Endocrinology and Metabolism, 94,* 3132–3154. http://dx.doi. org/10.1210/jc.2009-0345

Hendricks, M. L., & Testa, R. J. (2012). A conceptual framework for clinical work with transgender and gender nonconforming clients: An adaptation of the minority stress model. *Professional Psychology: Research and Practice, 43,* 460–467. http://dx.doi.org/10.1037/a0029597

Institute of Medicine. (2011). *The health of lesbian, gay, bisexual, and transgender people: Building a foundation for better understanding.* Washington, DC: National Academy of Sciences.

Jensen, L. L. (2010). *Training experiences as predictors of affirming attitudes toward trans clients* (Unpublished thesis). Southern Illinois University, Carbondale.

Keo-Meier, C. L., Herman, L. I., Reisner, S. L., Pardo, S. T., Sharp, C., & Babcock, J. C. (2014). Testosterone treatment and MMPI–2 improvement in transgender men: A prospective controlled study. *Journal of Consulting and Clinical Psychology, 83,* 143–156. http://dx.doi.org/10.1037/a0037599

Kohlberg, L. (1966). A cognitive-developmental analysis of children's sex-role concepts and attitudes. In E. E. Maccoby (Ed.), *The development of sex differences* (pp. 82–173). Stanford, CA: Stanford University Press.

Kosciw, J. G., Greytak, E. A., Bartkiewicz, M. J., Boesen, M. J., & Palmer, N. A. (2012). *The 2011 National School Climate Survey: The experiences of lesbian, gay, bisexual, and transgender youth in our nation's schools.* New York, NY: Gay, Lesbian, & Straight Education Network.

Lambda Legal. (2014). *Sources of authority to amend sex designation on birth certificates.* Retrieved from http://www.lambdalegal.org/publications/sources-of-authority-to-amend

Lev, A. I. (2004). *Transgender emergence: Therapeutic guidelines for working with gender-variant people and their families.* New York, NY: Haworth Clinical Practice.

Liu, R. T., & Mustanski, B. (2012). Suicidal ideation and self-harm in lesbian, gay, bisexual, and transgender youth. *American Journal of Preventive Medicine, 42,* 221–228. http://dx.doi.org/10.1016/j.amepre.2011.10.023

Maddux, S. (Producer & Director). (2011). *Gen silent* [Motion Picture]. Glendale, AZ: Interrobang Productions.

Meyer, I. H. (2003). Prejudice, social stress, and mental health in lesbian, gay, and bisexual populations: Conceptual issues and research evidence. *Psychological Bulletin, 129,* 674–697. http://dx.doi.org/10.1037/0033-2909.129.5.674

Moody, C., & Smith, N. G. (2013). Suicide protective factors among trans adults. *Archives of Sexual Behavior, 42,* 739–752. http://dx.doi.org/10.1007/s10508-013-0099-8

Nadal, K. L., Rivera, D. P., & Corpus, M. J. H. (2010). Sexual orientation and transgender microaggressions: Implications for mental health and counseling. In D. W. Sue (Ed.), *Microaggressions and marginality: Manifestations, dynamics, and impact* (pp. 217–240). Hoboken, NJ: John Wiley & Sons.

Nadal, K. L., Skolnik, A., & Wong, Y. (2012). Interpersonal and systemic microaggressions toward transgender people: Implications for counseling. *Journal of LGBT Issues in Counseling, 6,* 55–82. http://dx.doi.org/10.1080/15538605.2012.648583

Namaste, V. K. (2000). *Invisible lives: The erasure of transsexual and transgendered people.* Chicago, IL: University of Chicago.

National Center for Transgender Equality. (2011a). *Federal prisons.* Retrieved from http://transequality.org/Issues/prisons.html

National Center for Transgender Equality. (2011b). *Hate crimes.* Retrieved from http://transequality.org/Issues/issues_hate_crimes.html

National Center for Transgender Equality. (2014). *NCTE applauds the signing of LGBT workers executive order.* Retrieved from http://transequality.org/news.html#2014ExectuiveOrderSigning

National Gay & Lesbian Task Force. (2013a). *Hate crime laws in the U.S.* Retrieved from http://www.thetaskforce.org/downloads/reports/issue_maps/hate_crimes_06_13_color.pdf

National Gay & Lesbian Task Force. (2013b). *State nondiscrimination laws in the U.S.* Retrieved from http://www.thetaskforce.org/downloads/reports/issue_maps/non_discrimination_6_13_color.pdf

Nemoto, T., Operario, D., Keatley, J., Han, L., & Soma, T. (2004). HIV risk behaviors among male-to-female transgender persons of color in San Francisco. *American Journal of Public Health, 94,* 1193–1199. http://dx.doi.org/10.2105/AJPH.94.7.1193

Ryan, C., Russell, S. T., Huebner, D., Diaz, R., & Sanchez, J. (2010). Family acceptance in adolescence and the health of LGBT young adults. *Journal of Child and Adolescence and the Health of LGBT Young Adults, 23,* 205–213.

Samons, S. L. (2009). *When the opposite sex isn't: Sexual orientation in male-to-female transgender people.* New York, NY: Routledge.

Singh, A. A. (2013). Transgender youth of color and resilience: Negotiating oppression and finding support. *Sex Roles, 68,* 690–702.

Singh, A. A., & Burnes, T. R. (2010). Shifting the counselor role from gatekeeping to advocacy: Ten strategies for using the ACA *Competencies for Counseling Transgender Clients* for individual and social change. *Journal of LGBT Issues in Counseling, 4*(3-4), 241–255. http://dx.doi.org/10.1080/15538605.2010.525455

Singh, A. A., & McKleroy, V. S. (2011). "Just getting out of bed is a revolutionary act": The resilience of transgender people of color who have survived traumatic life events. *Traumatology, 17*(2), 34–44. http://dx.doi.org/10.1177/1534765610369261

Singh, A. A., & Sangganjanavanich, V. (2015). Gender dysphoria. In B. Flamez & J. C. Watson (Eds.), *Diagnosing and treating children and adolescents: A guide for mental health professionals* (pp. 366–385). New York, NY: John Wiley & Sons.

Transgender Law Center. (2005). *Peeing in peace*. Retrieved from http://transgenderlawcenter.org/issues/public-accomodations/peeing-in-peace

U.S. Substance Abuse Mental Health Services Administration. (2015). *Ending conversion therapy: Supporting and affirming LGBTQ youth*. Retrieved from http://store.samhsa.gov/product/SMA15-4928?WT.ac=AD_20151026_EndConversionTherapy

Warner, L. R. (2008). A best practices guide to intersectional approaches in psychological research. *Sex Roles, 59*, 454–463. http://dx.doi.org/10.1007/s11199-008-9504-5

7

WORKING WITH SURVIVORS OF TRAUMA IN THE SEXUAL MINORITY AND TRANSGENDER AND GENDER NONCONFORMING POPULATIONS

DAVID W. PANTALONE, SARAH E. VALENTINE, AND JILLIAN C. SHIPHERD

In this chapter, we review the literature on treating trauma in sexual minority (SM) and transgender and gender nonconforming (TGNC) populations and describe some treatment strategies, based on the most up-to-date scientific and professional literatures, for addressing trauma exposure and its sequelae. We begin by (a) briefly defining some important terms and relations (i.e., trauma vs. posttraumatic stress disorder [PTSD]) and (b) presenting epidemiologic data showing that trauma—especially in the form of interpersonal victimization—is an unfortunately common experience in the lives of SM and TGNC individuals. Then, we (c) discuss Meyer's (1995) minority stress theory, a well-supported and useful model for understanding the intersections between identity and exposure to potentially traumatic interpersonal

This chapter was coauthored by an employee of the United States government as part of official duty and is considered to be in the public domain. Any views expressed herein do not necessarily represent the views of the United States government, and the author's participation in the work is not meant to serve as an official endorsement.

http://dx.doi.org/10.1037/15959-008
Handbook of Sexual Orientation and Gender Diversity in Counseling and Psychotherapy, K. A. DeBord, A. R. Fischer, K. J. Bieschke, and R. M. Perez (Editors)

and structural experiences. Finally, we (d) present some empirically informed suggestions about how to work with SM and TGNC survivors of interpersonal victimization, including assessment and intervention strategies, and (e) showcase detailed case studies presenting the conceptualization and course of treatment for two different evidence-based approaches.

TERMINOLOGY

What counts as a *traumatic event*? Even on this basic point, there has been considerable disagreement. The most straightforward way to understand a traumatic event is that it is a highly stressful experience (or series of experiences) that may cause PTSD, the name given to the constellation of symptoms that follow a traumatic event for some trauma survivors. The trauma is the antecedent, and the set of symptoms that ensue (PTSD) is the consequence. Not every traumatic event results in PTSD, but every case of PTSD is the result of exposure to a traumatic event. It is important for clinicians to remember that most individuals exposed to a potentially traumatic event do not go on to develop PTSD—in fact, most individuals experience a natural recovery, characterized by dissipation of acute stress symptoms, without the need for formal treatment (e.g., Keane, Marshall, & Taft, 2006).

Some important, formative work by Rothbaum, Foa, Riggs, Murdock, and Walsh (1992) provided clarity to the relation between trauma and PTSD. In their sample of 95 female rape victims reporting to an emergency room, 94% met the severity criteria for PTSD at the time of the initial assessment (M = 12 days postassault) and, over time, the majority of the women no longer met criteria (65% met criteria at 35 days postassault, 47% met criteria at 12 weeks postassault, and so forth). This finding has been replicated by other researchers and with other types of trauma exposure (e.g., Riggs, Rothbaum, & Foa, 1995). These studies demonstrate that a natural recovery process occurs for most people who experience a traumatic event, typically in the first 3 or 4 months. Thus, a diagnosis of PTSD and, therefore, PTSD treatment, are only warranted for those individuals who do not recover naturally on their own without intervention.

In the fifth edition of the *Diagnostic and Statistical Manual of Mental Disorders* (DSM–5; American Psychiatric Association, 2013), traumatic events (Criterion A for PTSD) are defined as exposure to an actual or threatened death, serious injury, or sexual violence—direct, witnessed, or learned of, occurring to close family member or friend. Traumatic events can also include repeated or extreme exposure to aversive details of traumatic events; this type of presentation is most commonly seen in first responders, such as police officers. Some traumatologists have argued that the definition of a traumatic event must necessarily remain broad, and they are loathe to draw rigid boundaries on the construct; others appear to take the position that any given event could be traumatizing to any given individual (e.g., McNally, 2003). Many trauma researchers have criticized this latter definition of trauma for being overly inclusive and, thus, introducing unnecessary heterogeneity into the diagnostic pool of what constitutes PTSD. Across studies, though, it appears that a high magnitude stressor, coupled with a perception of danger in the context of genuine threat, is the combination that most predictably results in PTSD. The symptom criteria for PTSD in the *DSM–5* are defined by reexperiencing the traumatic event(s) (i.e., spontaneous memories of the specific event, recurrent dreams or nightmares, flashbacks); avoidance of distressing memories, thoughts, feelings, or external reminders of the traumatic event; negative cognitions and mood (i.e., persistent and distorted sense of blame, estrangement or detachment from others, diminished interest or pleasure in activities, inability to remember key aspects of the event); and arousal (appearance of aggressive, reckless, or self-destructive behavior, sleep disturbances, hypervigilance, exaggerated startle). A diagnosis of PTSD is assigned only if symptoms across all categories persist 1 month after exposure to a potentially traumatic event.

PREVALENCE OF TRAUMATIC EVENTS

Available data indicate that SM and TGNC individuals have high rates of exposure to traumatic stressors of all types (e.g., Corliss et al., 2009; Friedman et al., 2011; Goldberg & Meyer, 2013; Lehavot & Simpson, 2013; Shipherd, Maguen, Skidmore, & Abramovitz, 2011; Sweet & Welles, 2012). Indeed, SM and TGNC individuals face many types of potentially traumatic events, including car accidents, natural disasters, and combat—however, addressing the unique intricacies of each of these types of experiences for SM or TGNC would be outside the scope of this chapter. Chief in the literature, and in our own shared experience as psychologists who treat SM and TGNC individuals, is the ubiquity of interpersonal victimization of this population.

Interpersonal victimization experiences, such as violent rape, are the type of traumatic experiences most likely to result in PTSD (e.g., Schumm, Briggs-Phillips, & Hobfoll, 2006). Epidemiologic data clearly indicate that SM and TGNC individuals experience high rates of exposure to potentially traumatic interpersonal victimization experiences. For example, a large systematic review of 75 studies on SM health published between 1989 and 2009 indicated that 12% to 54% of gay or bisexual men and 15% to 85% of lesbian or bisexual women reported having an experience of sexual assault (Rothman, Exner, & Baughman, 2011). In a national study comparing lifetime rates of interpersonal violence experienced by SM individuals (Balsam, Rothblum,

& Beauchaine, 2005), researchers found that SM individuals experienced higher victimization rates across all types of interpersonal violence (childhood physical and sexual abuse, partner violence, adult physical and sexual assault) compared to their same-sex heterosexual siblings. Although epidemiologic data on rates of interpersonal violence among TGNC individuals is sparse, a recent study found that TGNC individuals were more likely (54.8% vs. 19.5%) to have experienced childhood abuse compared to cisgender individuals (Reisner, White, Bradford, & Mimiaga, 2014). Together, these studies indicate that SM and TGNC individuals may be especially vulnerability to interpersonal victimization and, thus, to PTSD.

GUIDING FRAMEWORK

One of the main points we make when teaching various audiences about how to work clinically with SM or TGNC individuals is to remember that they are "just regular people" first and that their sexual orientation or gender identity are additional aspects of their background to consider—just like other aspects of their background, including their race, ethnicity, socioeconomic status, and disability status. It is essential that clinicians not overvalue or undervalue the role of a person's sexual orientation or gender identity in their assessment of any clinical problem, including exposure to potentially traumatic events or PTSD. Teaching about general cultural competence in working with SM or TGNC clients is beyond the scope of this chapter; however, there are numerous resources available, including the other chapters in this volume, other volumes (e.g., Lev, 2003; Martell, Safren, & Prince, 2003), other chapters (e.g., Pantalone, Iwamasa, & Martell, 2009; Pantalone, Pachankis, Rood, & Bankoff, 2014), and clinically relevant peer-reviewed journal articles (e.g., Carroll & Gilroy, 2002; Maguen, Shipherd, & Harris, 2005). In addition, the journal *Clinical Psychology: Science and Practice* has devoted a special issue to this topic, synthesizing the literature on training in health of lesbian, gay, bisexual, and transgender individuals, including cultural competence, published in summer 2015 (Volume 22).

One theoretical model, with growing empirical support for some SM and TGNC subgroups, maintains a similar focus. Psychologist Ilan Meyer (1995, 2003) described a *minority stress model* (see Figure 7.1) that has primarily been used as a framework for understanding the presence of health disparities between SM and heterosexual populations; this framework has been used to examine within-group differences among various SM groups. The minority stress model purports that (a) SM individuals represent a disadvantaged social group that is frequently subjected to stigma and discrimination in the form of proximal (internal) and distal (external) stressors, including interpersonal

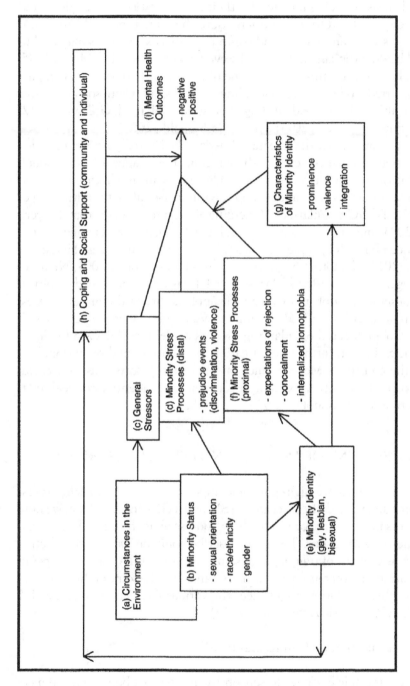

Figure 7.1. Meyer's minority stress model. From "Prejudice, Social Stress, and Mental Health in Lesbian, Gay, and Bisexual Populations: Conceptual Issues and Research Evidence," by I. H. Meyer, 2003, *Psychological Bulletin, 129*, p. 679. Copyright 2003 by the American Psychological Association.

victimization generally and adverse events that individuals experience specifically because of being targeted for their SM identities; (b) proximal and distal stressors related to sexual orientation, then, predispose SM individuals to excess stress and PTSD; and (c) in turn, this excess stress may lead to physical health problems and, thus, observed health disparities (Meyer, 1995, 2003). The minority stress model is one of the most established and empirically supported models for understanding the impact of psychosocial stressors on the health of SM individuals (e.g., Feinstein, Goldfried, & Davila, 2012; Kamen, Burns, & Beach, 2011; Kimmel & Mahalik, 2005).

Readers may notice that the model, as described initially, has not included TGNC populations specifically, although gender does appear in the model. There is no reason to believe that this model, with some modifications, would not also be a useful way to understand the interpersonal victimization experiences of TGNC populations. Emerging literature suggests that Meyer's (1995, 2003) minority stress model can likely be adapted and applied to the experience of TGNC people with regard to mental health (e.g., Hendricks & Testa, 2012; Nemoto, Operario, Keatley, Han, & Soma, 2004; Nemoto, Sausa, Operario, & Keatley, 2006), although there are no published empirical studies designed a priori to evaluate the applicability of the minority stress model in an exclusively TGNC sample. We also know of several research groups who are focused on adapting Meyer's model for TGNC individuals, specifically, through further investigation, explication, and operationalization of the constructs Meyer termed *minority stress processes*, as they correspond to gender identity, expectations of rejection, identity concealment, and internalized transphobia (e.g., Rood et al., 2015).

ASSESSMENT OF TRAUMA AND RELATED DISORDERS

In this section, we highlight some important considerations for assessing trauma and related disorders among SM and TGNC clients. First, we note how clients may be more or less likely to endorse abuse based on how assessment questions are asked. Then, we describe common barriers to effective therapist assessment of trauma, note some SM- and TGNC-specific types of victimization that therapists should assess, and describe some of the ways that clients in this population might meet the various PTSD criteria in DSM–5 (American Psychiatric Association, 2013).

Client Identification of Trauma and PTSD

There is ample evidence to support the notion that both validated measures and a high degree of clinical skill are required to accurately assess trauma exposure and traumatic sequelae, such as PTSD (e.g., Weathers, Keane, & Foa, 2008). Furthermore, clients who have experienced interpersonal victimization may not label their experiences as "abuse" per se and, thus, questions such as "Have you ever been abused?" may not identify true cases of trauma exposure or trauma-related distress (Hardt & Rutter, 2004; Littleton, Rhatigan, & Axsom, 2007). In one study of HIV-positive gay and bisexual men (N = 166) conducted by our research group, we found that only 54% of the men who endorsed behavioral indicators of childhood physical abuse (65% of the total sample) responded yes to the statement "In my opinion, I was physically abused" (Valentine & Pantalone, 2013). Furthermore, we found no differences in mental health symptoms across groups; that is, victimized men who affirmatively labeled their victimization experiences as "abuse," and those who did not, endorsed the same high levels of mental health problems, suggesting that it is the experience of and response to victimization itself that is associated with poor mental health, and not how clients label their experiences. These findings provide an important reminder that behaviorally anchored questions (e.g., "Has your partner hurt you physically or tried to hurt you physically, by slapping, punching, or kicking you?") should be used to screen for victimization history, rather than perceptually based questions.

Therapist Assessment of Trauma

There is a common misconception that talking about trauma is itself traumatic for clients. Typically, this misconception is due to lack of experience working with trauma survivors or a lack of conceptual understanding of the benefits of reducing avoidance of the trauma and associated memories. Individuals living with PTSD spend a considerable amount of time thinking about their traumatic event and, thus, many find relief in talking about it in therapy rather than to have to mask thinking about it as they often do (or try to do) at other times. Cognitive behavioral models, which have resulted in the leading evidence-based treatments for PTSD, offer one approach for conceptualizing this discussion. Indeed, there is evidence to support the notion that asking clients about past abuse experiences can be beneficial (e.g., Dyregrov, Dyregrov, & Raundalen, 2000; Griffin, Resick, Waldrop, & Mechanic, 2003; Johnson & Benight, 2003).

Furthermore, unidentified trauma responses may distort case conceptualization and hamper subsequent treatment planning. Omitting a thorough trauma assessment may, in fact, cause harm to the patient, by virtue of misdiagnosis and incorrectly targeted treatment. Indeed, there is evidence that PTSD treatment should be prioritized, because of the generalized benefits of treatment to both comorbid mental health conditions such as depression and also to physical health problems such as chronic pain (e.g., Shipherd,

Clum, Suvak, & Resick, 2014). Multiple studies have examined the emotional and cognitive effect of assessments that require a client to describe vivid details of the traumatic event (including early childhood victimization as well as rape) on client distress or harm (Dyregrov et al., 2000; Griffin et al., 2003; Johnson & Benight, 2003). In each of these studies, the majority of participants reported that they gained something therapeutic from the assessment, even prior to receiving any formal treatment, including increased insight regarding their experience and reduced stigma about their symptoms. Although some clients reported feeling distressed as a result of being asked such questions, most clients stated that they would still be willing to talk further about their experiences; in other words, these clients found talking about trauma helpful even though doing so caused them distress in the moment (Griffin et al., 2003). The importance of conducting a culturally competent assessment with SM or TGNC individuals cannot be overstated, particularly when the trauma was in some way related to the client's minority status. Offering a skillful and validating assessment of sexual orientation and gender identity, along with other individual difference variables (such as race–ethnicity) as part of routine assessment, can help create an environment of trust and open discussion (Bradford, Cahill, Grasso, & Makadon, 2012; Sherman, Kauth, Shipherd, & Street, 2014).

Given the high rates of multiple types of trauma in sexual and gender minority populations (e.g., Ard & Makadon, 2011; Corliss et al., 2009; Friedman et al., 2011; Goldberg & Meyer, 2013; Lehavot & Simpson, 2013; Mattocks et al., 2013; Mimiaga et al., 2009; Rothman et al., 2011; Shipherd et al., 2011; Sweet & Welles, 2012), it is essential that clinicians assess directly for exposure to potentially traumatic events, as well as clients' responses to these events. In accordance with the minority stress model (Meyer, 2003), experiences of discrimination and microaggressions may exacerbate negative trauma sequelae and shape posttraumatic responses. Thus, any assessment of trauma conducted with SM or TGNC clients should also include probing questions about these additional types of victimization—especially as these experiences may have a cumulative, negative effect on the client's psychosocial functioning. For example, clinicians may ask broad, open-ended questions regarding any additional adverse life experiences that *the client* believes were a result of their SM or TGNC identity (e.g., wondering generally about bullying, discrimination, social isolation, hate crimes). It is essential for clinicians to validate the client's lived experience by normalizing the range of responses that trauma exposure can produce and the client as the one who determines the relevance of sexual orientation or gender identity to these responses. (For a clinical example of trauma treatment following an antigay physical assault, see the case study in Kaysen, Lostutter, and Goines, 2005.) Clinicians should not make assumptions about the relevance of these aspects of a client's identity to their experience of or responses to trauma. Furthermore, clients who believe that their SM or TGNC status is irrelevant may feel invalidated if a clinician were to draw such connections. In all cases, we recommend asking open-ended questions (i.e., *Why do you think you were bullied?*) rather than leading with the provision of an interpretation; doing so can increase validation of the client's personal experience, and glean clinically useful data on the client's values and belief systems.

Of note, the *DSM–5* definition of PTSD explicitly includes engagement in reckless or self-destructive behaviors. This can provide an important context for the high incidence of a range of health risk behaviors, including sexual risk taking, heavy or problematic drinking, tobacco use, and polysubstance use that have been observed among SM and TGNC groups (Blosnich, Lee, & Horn, 2011; Boroughs, Valentine, et al., 2015; Cochran, Ackerman, Mays, & Ross, 2004; Drabble, Midanik, & Trocki, 2005; Green & Feinstein, 2012; J. G. Lee, Griffin, & Melvin, 2009; Lehavot & Simoni, 2011; Marshal et al., 2008; McCabe, Hughes, Bostwick, West, & Boyd, 2009; Woodford, Krentzman, & Gattis, 2012). SM women, specifically, are at higher risk of medical comorbidity associated with binge-eating, low exercise, and poor diet (Bankoff & Pantalone, 2014; Blosnich, Foynes, & Shipherd, 2013; see also Chapter 15, this volume). Although these have not been systematically linked to the new *DSM–5* criteria on risk behaviors, it could be that health risk behaviors reflect clients' attempts to modulate their PTSD symptoms.

Developing evidence supports the relation between co-occurring psychosocial problems and sexual risk taking in both SM men (e.g., Mustanski, Garofalo, Herrick, & Donenberg, 2007; Stall et al., 2003) and transgender women (Brennan et al., 2012). In one study, SM men with histories of childhood sexual abuse and partner abuse were more likely to engage in unprotected sex (e.g., O'Cleirigh, Safren, & Mayer, 2012), and these same men were more likely to report comorbid substance abuse and depression. These findings support a syndemics framework, whereby co-occurring psychosocial problems common among SM and TGNC individuals produce an adverse synergistic effect on health (Stall et al., 2003). In Valentine et al.'s (2015) study of SM women, co-occurring psychosocial problems (i.e., childhood sexual abuse, partner violence, substance use, mental health distress) produced a syndemic (additive) effect on 7-year medical costs and utilization, as well as mental health utilization, suggesting that syndemic conditions may help to explain increased morbidity and higher health care costs in this population. Overall, the literature strongly indicates that standard assessments for SM and TGNC clients should include screening for common psychosocial problems (i.e., substance use, depression, suicide risk) among SM and TGNC, especially because they often co-occur with trauma.

TREATMENT OF TRAUMA AND RELATED DISORDERS

For the purpose of this chapter, we decided to focus on PTSD in our clinical examples; this lets us provide clear recommendations from the empirical literature using evidence-based treatments (as this literature has consistently used *DSM* criteria to characterize their samples). To date, prolonged exposure (Foa, Hembree, & Rothbaum, 2007), cognitive therapies (e.g., cognitive processing therapy, Resick & Schnicke, 1992; trauma-focused cognitive behavior therapy, Cohen, Mannarino, & Deblinger, 2006), and reprocessing therapies (eye-movement desensitization and reprocessing [EMDR], Shapiro, 1989) have garnered the most empirical support, with several randomized controlled trials reporting on the results of prolonged exposure and cognitive processing therapy (for a review, see Foa, 2000, 2006), including a head-to-head comparison (e.g., Resick, Nishith, Weaver, Astin, & Feuer, 2002). The developers of each of these therapies have published manuals and created extensive training programs for clinicians; therefore, it is beyond the scope of this chapter to provide in-depth training to readers in these various treatments. Instead, we highlight key differences in case conceptualization and corresponding treatment targets, and we encourage clinicians who are interested in learning more about those treatments to find local resources.

Cognitive and behavioral protocols draw on four core components: psychoeducation, anxiety reduction and management, exposures, and cognitive restructuring. In these therapies, the aim of cognitive restructuring is to identify thoughts and beliefs that resulted from (or were reinforced by) the trauma, including assumptions of blame and distorted cognitions about self, others, and the world. Common themes that emerge from processing of trauma (through written accounts in cognitive processing therapy or client-driven discussion following imaginal exposures in prolonged exposure) include exaggerated beliefs about safety, trust, power and control, intimacy, and self-esteem. Exposures help clients habituate to trauma cues, including the trauma memory and real-life trauma reminders. EMDR is also a structured psychotherapy approach that aims to improve information processing of trauma stimuli by having the client engage in hand movements or tapping while revisiting a memory, image, or belief about the trauma. Conceptually, prolonged exposure, cognitive processing therapy, and EMDR can be understood as "processing models," although there is no agreed-upon mechanism of change behind EMDR (for a full review of evidence-based treatments for PTSD, see Bisson, Roberts, Andrew, Cooper, & Lewis, 2013). In a review of 70 studies that assessed treatment outcome for trauma-focused interventions, Bisson and colleagues (2013) found that the trauma-focused cognitive behavior therapy treatments (prolonged exposure and cognitive processing therapy) and EMDR had the best evidence for efficacy.

SM AND TGNC CULTURAL ADAPTATION
OF EVIDENCE-BASED TREATMENTS

To our knowledge, there have been no randomized controlled trials of evidence-based treatments for PTSD specifically targeting SM or TGNC individuals or specifically targeting gay- or trans-related traumatic events such as hate crimes. Furthermore, we could find no studies that piloted a culturally adapted treatment for PTSD for any SM or TGNC groups. It could, however, be argued that quality therapy for PTSD by a culturally competent therapist who is trained in empirically supported treatments would be sufficient (Boroughs, Bedoya, O'Cleirigh, & Safren, 2015). The tenets of evidence-based treatments are consistent with SM and TGNC-affirmative practices (e.g., allows client to define their own values and beliefs in their own words; patient-centered and collaborative client–clinician relationship). Thus, the most important task is for clinicians to engage in high-quality, evidence-based practices. These treatments have not been systematically tested in SM or TGNC populations; however, there is no reason to believe that they would not work just as well given, for example, that cognitive processing therapy has been implemented in diverse groups with much success (e.g., Schulz, Resick, Huber, & Griffin, 2006).

Researchers studying cultural adaptations of evidence-based treatments have identified the importance of modifications that (a) account for social context and (b) enhance treatment engagement and relevance. These types of adaptations help clinicians to provide culturally competent care without reducing treatment fidelity (Lau, 2006). In this chapter, we highlight aspects of the social context as well as methods of reducing stigma (to improve engagement) when working with SM or TGNC clients receiving trauma-focused therapy. This section is not meant to be an exhaustive list of the complex and nuanced ways in which trauma and identity contribute to distress; rather, we aim to provide a glimpse into some recurrent themes that have emerged in the literature, as well as our clinical experiences with SM and TGNC clients. Also, it is worth noting that many SM and TGNC individuals have other intersectional identities and characteristics that influence their experience of the world—for example, being a racial–ethnic minority or having a medical condition like HIV—and that it is important for skilled therapists to tailor their intervention approach accordingly, to acknowledge and demonstrate respect for the whole of the individual, whatever their identities.

What follow are typical beliefs about sexual orientation or gender identity and specific suggestions for cultural adaptations that might be useful for therapists to keep in mind when treating SM or TGNC clients for PTSD.

- *"Abuse made me gay."* Clients who had early sexual trauma experiences often express the belief that abuse made them gay. For instance, some gay men may believe that their sexual orientation was altered as a result of their "enjoyment" of male-perpetrated childhood sexual abuse. Some men even describe being sexually attracted (in the present) to men who resemble their past abuser(s). Alternately, some lesbian women may use the converse logic, that is, they purport that they are sexually attracted to women as a result of their traumatic experiences of male-perpetrated sexual abuse. Traumatic early sexual experiences are formative, regardless of the sexual orientation of the victim or the gender of the perpetrator (for an overview, see Browne & Finkelhor, 1986). It is important to remember that sexual abuse occurs within a complex system that can create confusion about the meaning associated with sexual attention and intimacy. This complexity is heightened when the abuse occurs in childhood, before an individual has the chance to develop healthy conceptualizations of sex and love. Moreover, hard-wired biologic responses such as sexual arousal can occur even in the context of abuse and are often misinterpreted, both by perpetrators and survivors, as evidence that the abuse was actually desired or enjoyable. Therefore, clinicians should respond by normalizing these trauma responses, providing psychoeducation that sexual arousal is a learned and involuntary response and does not necessarily reflect an indication of desire, attraction, or consent. Responding to clients in this manner can reduce the shame that may be elicited about these normative responses. A direct way to challenge the accuracy of the belief that "abuse made me gay" is to ask clients if they believe that all people who identify as gay were sexually abused. Often clients can identify other SM individuals without an abuse history or note that they have heterosexual friends who experienced sexual abuse. If clients cannot generate examples of nonabused SM individuals, then the clinician can provide psychoeducation on the relations between sexual and gender minority identity and victimization (i.e., not *all* victims of abuse are SM–TGNC, not *all* SM–TGNC people have been abused).

- "*I was romantically (or sexually) drawn to my perpetrator before the abuse, so the abuse is my fault.*" Clients may describe that their response to the attention of the perpetrator was originally positive, particularly in the context of dating or marital relationships. In our experiences, SM and TGNC clients often describe a broader social context of isolation, rejection, and marginalization. As a result, these clients sometimes describe initially positive responses to the attention they received from their perpetrator. Indeed, there is a literature that documents "grooming" behaviors by perpetrators that include offering love, encouragement, and support to otherwise lonely or disenfranchised individuals (e.g., Sullivan & Beech, 2004). This desire for positive social interaction is a vulnerability for abuse—and one that is not limited to SM and TGNC clients, of course—but for any person who experiences interpersonal rejection by family, social isolation, or societal stress. A direct way to challenge this unhelpful belief is to ask about the client's intentions for responding to the perpetrator in an open and curious way (e.g., "Did you intend for the abuse to happen?"). This line of questioning can help the client to arrive at the conclusion that curiosity and desire for attention did not cause abuse. Moreover, it can be helpful to explore with clients the idea that having had prior consensual sex, particularly in the context of a relationship, does not revoke one's right to say no to future sexual encounters.

Clinicians should attempt to assess and conceptualize the effect of minority stress on client adjustment following trauma; the following areas can be explored:

- *Experiences of discrimination, hate crimes, or bullying.* The degree to which clients perceive their victimization experiences as being related to their sexual orientation or gender expression varies widely across individuals and instances of abuse. Clinicians should take time to assess the degree to which clients believe that any aspect of their identity may have either contributed to the trauma itself or to their posttrauma adjustment. Clinicians should also ask clients about additional types of victimization related to minority stress that may have influenced their emotional responses and beliefs about the traumatic event. For example, understanding past and current experiences of discrimination can help the clinician assess the client's safety and determine whether beliefs about safety are realistic or distortions. These experiences can also have an effect on the client's ability to trust others, as having experienced hate crimes and discrimination can reinforce such beliefs as "I can't trust anyone." In addition, these experiences of discrimination or bullying may interfere with help-seeking behavior, because the client may expect negative reactions from peers, family, police, and medical/mental health providers (Roberts, Watlington, Nett, & Batten, 2010).

- *Family and peer responses to the coming out process, and disclosure of abuse.* As with all clients who experience trauma, SM and TGNC clients may describe early family environments as formative in the development of beliefs about themselves, others, and the world. Depending on the nature and timing of the traumatic experiences, they can "shatter" prior positive beliefs (Janoff-Bulman, 1992), reinforce prior negative beliefs, or (if the abuse is early enough) actually serve as foundational beliefs. Early rejection and abuse from family members is developmentally disruptive for any child, and familial rejection and abuse are unfortunately common among SM and TGNC children (e.g., Balsam et al., 2005; D'Augelli & Hershberger, 1993). If a client has disclosed his or her SM or TGNC identity to others, the clinician should ask about these coming out experiences, to better understand the presence or absence of affirming relationships and support from the client's social network. Presumably, clients who describe positive reactions from family members during the coming out process may be more likely to disclose trauma, because these clients have gathered evidence that they can safely disclose emotionally charged content. Positive family responses to prior disclosure of sexual orientation or gender identity may facilitate disclosure of and recovery from trauma, because these affirmative relationships may help the client to counter distorted cognitions about oneself, others, and the world.
- *Internalized homophobia.* Often clients with PTSD endorse negative cognitions about the self that may have predated the specific traumatic event targeted in treatment. Some clients describe experiences of interpersonal abuse as reinforcing long-held beliefs associated with internalized homophobia or transphobia (e.g., "I am evil"; "I am a bad person, therefore, I deserve punishment"; "I am unlovable"; e.g., Meyer, 2003). Clinicians can respond by validating that these beliefs may have predated abuse experiences and that these have become "unhealthy thinking habits," and, potentially, habits that have been around for so long that the client can no longer remember a time when they did not seem true. Given that internalized homophobia or transphobia are so deeply engrained, a clinician may gain more traction by challenging the utility, rather than the accuracy, of these beliefs. For example, one could ask, "How does it help you to believe that you are unlovable?" Typically, the client's response will be, "It doesn't help, but it's still true." Such responses allow the therapist room to identify the negative effects of the belief. A

client may describe several consequence of this belief, including social isolation, engaging in anonymous (nonemotionally intimate) sex, or feelings of hopelessness around future intimate relationships. If negative consequences of the belief can be identified, this opens the door for hypothesis testing the distorted belief. A therapist might suggest, "Given all the negative effects of this belief, are you willing to consider the possibility of thinking differently? Sounds to me like things couldn't get worse and might even get a little better . . ."

- *Social context of trauma: Seeking partners outside of one's peer group.* Because of social isolation, rejection, or a perceived lack of available dating partners in their peer groups, some younger SM and TGNC individuals may seek friends or sex partners who are significantly older. Many adult SM and TGNC individuals, in retrospect, describe these as positive and healthy experiences that decreased their sense of social isolation and gave them practice at adult relationships (e.g., Bruce, Harper, Fernández, Jamil, & the Adolescent Medicine Trials Network for HIV/AIDS Interventions, 2012). Although these are not inherently problematic, this scenario increases a young person's risk for abuse, given the inherent power differential between dating or sexual partners of disparate ages. Clinicians should be sensitive to how clients describe these experiences; for instance, clients may not label such relationships as coercive. Sometimes clients revise their definitions of abuse over the course of treatment, as they begin to process the impact of the trauma. For example, clients may become better at recognizing jealous or controlling behaviors in their consensual partners, or they may come to view as exploitation what they initially considered "harmless exploration" with an older individual.

- *Sexual stereotypes and beliefs about victimization.* Some clients, particularly SM men, describe disclosing sexual trauma to SM male peers and having that abuse dismissed as normative (e.g., Todahl, Linville, Bustin, Wheeler, & Gau, 2009), that is, being told that early sexual debut is a "rite of passage" into gay male culture. In the case of TGNC individuals, perpetrators may use gender nonconformity as an excuse for the abuse (Grossman, D'Augelli, Howell, & Hubbard, 2006), with abuse used as a way of "teaching you to be a woman," as personified in the film *Boys Don't Cry* (Sharp, Hart, Kolodner, Vachon, & Peirce, 1999) and, in the case of lesbian victims, "showing them what they are missing" with male perpetrators (Little & Terrance, 2010). In our experience, some clients describe these types of responses when they disclosed abuse experiences even to SM or TGNC friends, which demonstrates the pervasive nature of our homophobic and transphobic culture. Some clients subsequently internalized the notion that abuse is a minority sociocultural norm and, thus, it is to be expected in relationships. For example, some clients express stereotypical beliefs about male gender roles (i.e., men are aggressive–violent; therefore, aggression–violence in same-sex relationships between men should be expected) that dismiss or glorify violence. In addition, lesbians may underidentify partner abuse, as women are stereotypically portrayed as potentially victims of abuse only at the hands of men (Little & Terrance, 2010). In reality, people of any gender can be perpetrators or victims. What can be more challenging is to report and obtain treatment for partner violence when also trying to overcome societal expectations and personal views about sex-based roles in relationships defined by power, such as abusive relationships.

CASE EXAMPLES

In this section, we present case examples based on clients we have actually treated and using evidence-based treatment paradigms with which we have expertise: prolonged exposure and cognitive processing therapy. All patient identifiers have been changed to mask client identities.

Case Example 1: Prolonged Exposure

Background

Prior to the initiation of treatment, the therapist attended a 4-day workshop to learn prolonged exposure therapy and then received weekly consultation by a prolonged exposure expert, as well as regular clinical supervision on the case. Emily (a pseudonym) was a 54-year-old, bisexual-identified, African American veteran who served as an engineer in the army during the post-Vietnam (noncombat) era. At intake, she reported having several experiences of physical and sexual violence—including persistent physical abuse in childhood and rape during her military service—as well as discrimination based on race and gender, generally during her life and especially during her military service. Emily met *DSM* criteria for PTSD and major depressive disorder based on the relevant Structured Clinical Interview for DSM Disorders modules (First, Spitzer, Gibbon, & Williams, 2012).

As part of her initial evaluation, the therapist approached the intersectionality of various aspects of her identity (such as her sexual orientation, gender, and race) as well as the influences of these identities on how she understood the etiology of her mental health problems and coping responses. Emily also reported that her role as a mother was central to her identity and that she had a strong sense of self-efficacy regarding her ability to parent. She noted several intersectional aspects of her identity (race, gender and gender role, sexual orientation) as contributing to her trauma and the associated depression and PTSD. During repeated revisiting and processing of her military sexual assault, she described nuanced ways in which these aspects of her identity served as both strengths and vulnerabilities over the years.

Emotional Processing: Emergent Themes From the Imaginal Exposure

Following the first imaginal exposure (i.e., revisiting of the memory in session), Emily highlighted beliefs about self-blame and the desire to socially isolate in order to protect herself from emotional pain caused by others. Emily also reflected on how feelings of loneliness and isolation predated the rape and that she felt like an "outsider" as a result of her race and sexual orientation. The experience of rape only exacerbated these thoughts and feelings. She noted how her behaviors (i.e., choosing to date men) were strongly influenced by the military's then-current policy, "Don't Ask, Don't Tell" (J. L. Lee, 2013). There were several themes that emerged in the processing discussion following imaginal exposures that were associated with aspects of her identity. Emily described how the assault occurred in the context of months of verbal threats from African American men and women on her base in response to Emily dating a White service member. She expressed self-blaming thoughts such as, "If I had just not dated a White guy, then they would have left me alone. None of this would ever have happened." Her self-blaming thoughts were reinforced by her perception that nonconformity to gender role expectations in her job as an engineer may have further provoked men's violence. As a result of being victimized by multiple male perpetrators, both while in the service and previously during her childhood, Emily described a generalized fear of men and reported how she avoided being alone with men. She described various consequences of this avoidance over the years, including limitations in access to health care and employment options and increased social isolation. Emily also believed that her sexual attractions and behaviors were altered as a result of male-perpetrated violence, in that she chose to date only women after the sexual assault. Emily reported feeling comfortable with her sexuality and considered the shift to dating women as "adaptive," in that she did not have the physiological reactivity and pain during intercourse that she experienced with men after the assault. Processing this memory also brought forth some significant thoughts associated with previous traumas. For instance, she reported that she "should have learned" from her early experiences of abuse and therefore could have been able to prevent victimization as an adult.

In Vivo Exposure Assignments

In vivo exposure assignments focused on reducing avoidance behaviors as well as increasing social connections. These included riding the elevator to and from her appointments (regardless of whether men were present); going through checkout lines with male cashiers; asking a man for directions; sitting in a waiting room with men; talking about her assaults with close friends and her adult daughter; going to restaurants with friends; inviting friends to her house for dinner; driving alone at night; attending a women's support group; and hugging male family members (who had not been abuse perpetrators).

Clinical Relevance of SM or TGNC Identity

Emily expressed long-standing, pervasive, negative beliefs about herself and other people that stemmed from her early experiences of physical abuse by her father and were later reinforced by her military service sexual assault. Emily did not believe that her sexual orientation contributed to current distress. Instead, she expressed that the experiences of abuse and discrimination during her military service were related to her lack of conformity to social norms about interracial dating and gender role expectations. Note that clients may interpret the associations between their SM or TGNC identity and their victimization experiences in many ways. For one, clients may self-blame, suggesting that violence was in some way provoked by aspects of their identity. This was Emily's initial interpretation; she had the thought, "I deserved the assault because I was dating outside my race." Second, clients can adopt a more balanced interpretation of the trauma and acknowledge the context of abuse, such as how nonconformity led to social marginalization, thus increasing one's vulnerability to abuse. Over the course of treatment, Emily adopted a new way of thinking; she stated, "The men who did this to me knew that I did not have many friends, and that I probably would not talk to anyone about what happened." This second way of thinking shifts blame away from the victim by acknowledging societal and perpetrator factors that contributed to the assault.

An additional consideration for Emily was the way that being perceived as "other" had, in some ways, been protective over her lifetime. Across settings and over time, Emily described a history of nonconformity to social norms within her family, school, and military contexts. For example, she reported that her personal values of educational and professional achievement contrasted with her societal gender role expectations, as well as her family's expectations, during her youth. Deciding not to be limited by these expectations, Emily excelled as an Army engineer and moved away from the lifelong poverty and substance abuse experienced by members of her nuclear and extended families. This is just one example of why it was important to ask open-ended questions about her minority identities and their relations to the trauma: These associations are often complex and multifaceted.

By revisiting the memory repeatedly, both in-session and by completing in vivo assignments outside of her sessions, Emily gained a sense of mastery over the thoughts and emotions associated with the trauma. Over the course of treatment, Emily displayed a significant decrease in PTSD symptoms and reached subclinical PTSD symptoms after eight sessions of prolonged exposure therapy. At termination, she expressed optimism about future relationships, particularly with her partner, daughter, and foster children.

Case Example 2: Cognitive Processing Therapy

Background

Prior to the initiation of treatment, the therapist attended a 2-day workshop to learn cognitive processing therapy and received ongoing peer consultation and supervision on the case. Steve was a 39-year-old gay-identified White man who lived with his partner of 7 years and worked as a computer scientist. At baseline, Steve endorsed a history of depression and PTSD, but he did not meet diagnostic criteria for either disorder. Despite endorsing subclinical PTSD symptoms, Steve wished to start PTSD treatment to "understand my past experiences and how they shape my sexual behavior now"—a wise motivation for treatment, especially since he was HIV-negative and engaging in a significant amount of condomless anal sex with casual partners, making his risk for acquiring HIV quite high.

Steve's first experience of childhood sexual abuse was at age 10 when he was approached by a man while on vacation with his family. This man asked Steve to meet him in the bathroom near the amusement park. The abuse involved touching and attempted (but not completed) intercourse. Also, around this age, Steve experienced genital touching from a friend's older brother, which involved force and coercion. In his teenage years, Steve had multiple sexual partners who were more than 10 years older than he was. Although, at the time of the initial assessment, he did not perceive these teenage experiences as abuse, his thoughts about these experiences became increasingly upsetting to him over the course of therapy, as he more fully recognized the contextual factors operating (i.e., the power dynamics inherent in relationships with significant age discrepancies).

In cognitive processing therapy, clients are coached to write an impact statement that describes the ways that their past traumatic experiences continue to affect their present functioning. A segment of Steve's impact statement (again, we have altered aspects to preserve confidentiality) follows:

> I got myself into a situation that I ended up not wanting. I invited the situation with nonverbal cues, due to my curiosity. I am an open and trusting person from the get-go. I am independent and adventurous. I was sexually curious at a young age. I knew I was "different" from other kids that age, and this was the first person to look at me the way I looked at them. I am spontaneous. I am attractive (to some people). "They" [perpetrators] found me attractive. I was mature at a young age and very intuitive to situations. I was aware of my sexual feelings towards men and frustrated and alone with these thoughts. For the first time, I didn't feel alone, so I jumped at the opportunity to get more experience, to better understand my sexuality. An adult took advantage of this situation by seeking sexual activities with me, as a child, who did not know better. I trusted an adult, and he broke that trust. I felt pressure to do things I didn't want to do. I wasn't a consenting adult.

Steve's impact statement revealed several adaptive and balanced beliefs about the meaning of his sexual trauma that likely prevented him from meeting full PTSD (e.g., "An adult took advantage of this situation by seeking sexual activities with me, as a child, who did not know better. I trusted an adult, and he broke that trust"; "I wasn't a consenting adult"). However, the impact statement lacked emotional content and, when reviewing the impact statement in session, the therapist asked about underlying thoughts. Through that discussion, Steve shared some extreme, rigid beliefs ("stuck points" in cognitive processing therapy parlance) that likely were maintaining his intrusive and avoidant PTSD symptoms. Some of these stuck points include the following beliefs: "I am bad," "I am worthless," "I am broken," "The abuse was my fault," "I am powerless in sexual situations," "If I assert my own needs, I will be rejected," "My sexual needs are not important," "I am only good for sex," and "Sex is the only way for me to connect with other men."

Clinical Relevance of SM or TGNC Identity

Steve endorsed cognitions consistent with the just-world hypothesis, which states that good things happen to good people and bad things happen to bad people (Vogt, Shipherd, & Resick, 2012). Therefore, when he experienced abuse at age 10, he adjusted his beliefs such that "this bad thing happened to me and, therefore, I must a bad person." Believing that he was a "bad person" was ego-syntonic with his increasing awareness that his attractions to men were not acceptable to society (i.e., internalized homophobia). Steve also endorsed significant shame about his current practice of having anonymous sex in public bathrooms—which was, indeed, the context of his first abuse experience. The therapist directly targeted Steve's shame-inducing cognitions through cognitive restructuring exercises (i.e., formal handouts practiced as homework and reviewed in session) and Socratic questioning (i.e., clinician's open-ended questioning to guide the client toward more balanced thinking). Steve's beliefs about his powerlessness in sexual situations, and prioritization of his partner's pleasure and preferences for condom use over his own, were directly related to HIV risk. With HIV risk reduction as Steve's primary treatment goal, the therapist targeted these cognitions repeatedly and consistently in session. Steve engaged in homework to improve communication and condom negotiation with his sexual partners and, in doing so, began to value and prioritize his own needs and health in all of his sexual relationships.

SUMMARY AND CONCLUSION

Overall, the published clinical and research literature indicates that SM and TGNC individuals experience a significant burden of trauma throughout their lives, especially interpersonal victimization related to their (potentially multiple) minority status(es). Thus, screening for traumatic events and potential sequelae is a critical component of competent psychotherapy with SM and TGNC individuals. There are no published, evidence-based treatments for addressing trauma or PTSD in SM and TGNC populations, specifically. However, in this chapter, we presented an overview of empirically supported assessment and intervention techniques for PTSD (prolonged exposure and cognitive processing therapy) with some suggestions for ways that clinicians might culturally tailor existing approaches for SM and TGNC clients. Despite the lack of clinical trials of SM and TGNC culturally adapted trauma treatments, there is no reason to believe that such treatments would be harmful. Rather, it is highly likely that these same treatments—that have been beneficial for other diverse groups—are also beneficial for SM and TGNC clients.

We all really enjoyed working together on this chapter, despite the emotionally heavy content. We three have worked together in dyads in various capacities over the years, but never all together on a writing project like this. It was so gratifying for me (DWP) to see the deep clinical and research knowledge brought to bear on this chapter by my first-ever doctoral student mentee (SEV), and by my dear friend and colleague of many years (JCS). Together, we noted our collective surprise, dismay, and hope regarding the state of the literature on working with SM or TGNC survivors of trauma. We hope that our thoughts on this topic, shared here in this chapter, are helpful to practitioners looking for guidance about how to go about doing this important work. We also hope to inspire researchers who are curious about what the next steps are in advancing the literature in the field.

REFERENCES

American Psychiatric Association. (2013). *Diagnostic and statistical manual of mental disorders* (5th ed.). Arlington, VA: Author.

Ard, K. L., & Makadon, H. J. (2011). Addressing intimate partner violence in lesbian, gay, bisexual, and transgender patients. *Journal of General Internal Medicine, 26,* 930–933. http://dx.doi.org/10.1007/s11606-011-1697-6

Balsam, K. F., Rothblum, E. D., & Beauchaine, T. P. (2005). Victimization over the life span: A comparison of lesbian, gay, bisexual, and heterosexual siblings. *Journal of Consulting and Clinical Psychology, 73,* 477–487. http://dx.doi.org/10.1037/0022-006X.73.3.477

Bankoff, S. M., & Pantalone, D. W. (2014). Patterns of disordered eating behavior in women by sexual orientation: A review of the literature. *Eating Disorders, 22,* 261–274.

Bisson, J. I., Roberts, N. P., Andrew, M., Cooper, R., & Lewis, C. (2013). Psychological therapies for chronic post-traumatic stress disorder (PTSD) in adults. *Cochrane Database of Systematic Reviews, 12,* CD003388.

Blosnich, J., Foynes, M. M., & Shipherd, J. C. (2013). Health disparities among sexual minority women veterans. *Journal of Women's Health, 22,* 631–636. http://dx.doi.org/10.1089/jwh.2012.4214

Blosnich, J., Lee, J. G., & Horn, K. (2011). A systematic review of the aetiology of tobacco disparities for sexual minorities. *Tobacco Control, 22*(2), 66–73. http://dx.doi.org/10.1136/tobaccocontrol-2011-050181

Boroughs, M. S., Bedoya, C. A., O'Cleirigh, C., & Safren, S. A. (2015). Toward defining, measuring, and evaluating LGBT cultural competence for psychologists. *Clinical Psychology: Science and Practice, 22,* 151–171. http://dx.doi.org/10.1111/cpsp.12098

Boroughs, M. S., Valentine, S. E., Ironson, G. H., Shipherd, J. C., Safren, S. A., Taylor, S. W., . . . O'Cleirigh, C. (2015). Complexity of childhood sexual abuse: Predictors of current post-traumatic stress disorder, mood disorders, substance use, and sexual risk behavior among adult men who have sex with men. *Archives of Sexual Behavior, 44,* 1891–1902. http://dx.doi.org/10.1007/s10508-015-0546-9

Bradford, J. B., Cahill, S., Grasso, C., & Makadon, H. J. (2012). *How to gather data on sexual orientation and gender identity in clinical settings.* Boston, MA: The Fenway Institute.

Brennan, J., Kuhns, L. M., Johnson, A. K., Belzer, M., Wilson, E. C., Garofalo, R., & the Adolescent Medicine Trials Network for HIV/AIDS Interventions. (2012). Syndemic theory and HIV-related risk among young transgender women: The role of multiple, co-occurring health problems and social marginalization. *American Journal of Public Health, 102,* 1751–1757. http://dx.doi.org/10.2105/AJPH.2011.300433

Browne, A., & Finkelhor, D. (1986). Initial and long-term effects: A review of the research. In D. Finkelhor (Ed.), *Sourcebook on child sexual abuse* (pp. 143–179). Beverly Hills, CA: Sage.

Bruce, D., Harper, G. W., Fernández, M. I., Jamil, O. B., & the Adolescent Medicine Trials Network for HIV/AIDS Interventions. (2012). Age-concordant and age-discordant sexual behavior among gay and bisexual male adolescents. *Archives of Sexual Behavior, 41,* 441–448. http://dx.doi.org/10.1007/s10508-011-9730-8

Carroll, L., & Gilroy, P. J. (2002). Transgender issues in counselor preparation. *Counselor Education and Supervision, 41,* 233–242. http://dx.doi.org/10.1002/j.1556-6978.2002.tb01286.x

Cochran, S. D., Ackerman, D., Mays, V. M., & Ross, M. W. (2004). Prevalence of non-medical drug use and dependence among homosexually active men and women in the US population. *Addiction, 99,* 989–998. http://dx.doi.org/10.1111/j.1360-0443.2004.00759.x

Cohen, J. A., Mannarino, A. P., & Deblinger, E. (2006). *Treating trauma and traumatic grief in children and adolescents.* New York, NY: Guilford Press.

Corliss, H. L., Cochran, S. D., Mays, V. M., Greenland, S., & Seeman, T. E. (2009). Age of minority sexual orientation development and risk of childhood maltreatment and suicide attempts in women. *American Journal of Orthopsychiatry, 79,* 511–521. http://dx.doi.org/10.1037/a0017163

D'Augelli, A. R., & Hershberger, S. L. (1993). Lesbian, gay, and bisexual youth in community settings: Personal challenges and mental health problems. *American Journal of Community Psychology, 21,* 421–448. http://dx.doi.org/10.1007/BF00942151

Drabble, L., Midanik, L. T., & Trocki, K. (2005). Reports of alcohol consumption and alcohol-related problems among homosexual, bisexual and heterosexual respondents: Results from the 2000 National Alcohol Survey. *Journal of Studies on Alcohol, 66,* 111–120. http://dx.doi.org/10.15288/jsa.2005.66.111

Dyregrov, K., Dyregrov, A., & Raundalen, M. (2000). Refugee families' experience of research participation. *Journal of Traumatic Stress, 13,* 413–426. http://dx.doi.org/10.1023/A:1007777006605

Feinstein, B. A., Goldfried, M. R., & Davila, J. (2012). The relationship between experiences of discrimination and mental health among lesbians and gay men: An examination of internalized homonegativity and rejection sensitivity as potential mechanisms. *Journal of Consulting and Clinical Psychology, 80,* 917–927. http://dx.doi.org/10.1037/a0029425

First, M. B., Spitzer, R. L., Gibbon, M., & Williams, J. B. (2012). *Structured Clinical Interview for DSM–IV Axis I Disorders (SCID-I), clinician version, administration booklet*. Washington, DC: American Psychiatric Publishing.

Foa, E. B. (2000). Psychosocial treatment of posttraumatic stress disorder. *Journal of Clinical Psychiatry, 61*(Suppl. 5), 43–48.

Foa, E. B. (2006). Psychosocial therapy for posttraumatic stress disorder. *The Journal of Clinical Psychiatry, 67*(Suppl. 2), 40–45.

Foa, E. B., Hembree, E. A., & Rothbaum, B. O. (2007). *Prolonged exposure therapy for PTSD: Emotional processing of traumatic experiences therapist guide (treatments that work)*. New York, NY: Oxford University Press. http://dx.doi.org/10.1093/med:psych/9780195308501.001.0001

Friedman, M. S., Marshal, M. P., Guadamuz, T. E., Wei, C., Wong, C. F., Saewyc, E., & Stall, R. (2011). A meta-analysis of disparities in childhood sexual abuse, parental physical abuse, and peer victimization among sexual minority and sexual nonminority individuals. *American Journal of Public Health, 101,* 1481–1494. http://dx.doi.org/10.2105/AJPH.2009.190009

Goldberg, N. G., & Meyer, I. H. (2013). Sexual orientation disparities in history of intimate partner violence: Results from the California health interview survey. *Journal of Interpersonal Violence, 28,* 1109–1118. http://dx.doi.org/10.1177/0886260512459384

Green, K. E., & Feinstein, B. A. (2012). Substance use in lesbian, gay, and bisexual populations: An update on empirical research and implications for treatment. *Psychology of Addictive Behaviors, 26,* 265–278. http://dx.doi.org/10.1037/a0025424

Griffin, M. G., Resick, P. A., Waldrop, A. E., & Mechanic, M. B. (2003). Participation in trauma research: Is there evidence of harm? *Journal of Traumatic Stress, 16,* 221–227. http://dx.doi.org/10.1023/A:1023735821900

Grossman, A. H., D'Augelli, A. R., Howell, T. J., & Hubbard, S. (2006). Parents' reactions to transgender youth's gender nonconforming expressions and identity. *Journal of Gay & Lesbian Social Services, 18,* 3–16.

Hardt, J., & Rutter, M. (2004). Validity of adult retrospective reports of adverse childhood experiences: Review of the evidence. *Journal of Child Psychology and Psychiatry, and Allied Disciplines, 45,* 260–273. http://dx.doi.org/10.1111/j.1469-7610.2004.00218.x

Hendricks, M. L., & Testa, R. J. (2012). A conceptual framework for clinical work with transgender and gender nonconforming clients: An adaptation of the minority stress model. *Professional Psychology: Research and Practice, 43,* 460–467. http://dx.doi.org/10.1037/a0029597

Janoff-Bulman, R. (1992). *Shattered assumptions: Towards a new psychology of trauma*. New York, NY: Free Press.

Johnson, L. E., & Benight, C. C. (2003). Effects of trauma-focused research on recent domestic violence survivors. *Journal of Traumatic Stress, 16,* 567–571. http://dx.doi.org/10.1023/B:JOTS.0000004080.50361.f3

Kamen, C., Burns, M., & Beach, S. R. (2011). Minority stress in same-sex male relationships: When does it impact relationship satisfaction? *Journal of Homosexuality, 58*, 1372–1390. http://dx.doi.org/10.1080/00918369.2011.614904

Kaysen, D., Lostutter, T. W., & Goines, M. A. (2005). Cognitive processing therapy for acute stress disorder resulting from an anti-gay assault. *Cognitive and Behavioral Practice, 12*, 278–289. http://dx.doi.org/10.1016/S1077-7229(05)80050-1

Keane, T. M., Marshall, A. D., & Taft, C. T. (2006). Posttraumatic stress disorder: Etiology, epidemiology, and treatment outcome. *Annual Review of Clinical Psychology, 2*, 161–197. http://dx.doi.org/10.1146/annurev.clinpsy.2.022305.095305

Kimmel, S. B., & Mahalik, J. R. (2005). Body image concerns of gay men: The roles of minority stress and conformity to masculine norms. *Journal of Consulting and Clinical Psychology, 73*, 1185–1190. http://dx.doi.org/10.1037/0022-006X.73.6.1185

Lau, A. (2006). Making the case for selective and directed cultural adaptations of evidence-based treatments: Examples from parent training. *Clinical Psychology: Science and Practice, 13*, 295–310. http://dx.doi.org/10.1111/j.1468-2850.2006.00042.x

Lee, J. G., Griffin, G. K., & Melvin, C. L. (2009). Tobacco use among sexual minorities in the USA, 1987 to May 2007: A systematic review. *Tobacco Control, 18*, 275–282. http://dx.doi.org/10.1136/tc.2008.028241

Lee, J. L. (2013). The comprehensive review working group and don't ask, don't tell repeal at the department of defense. *Journal of Homosexuality, 60*, 282–311. http://dx.doi.org/10.1080/00918369.2013.744673

Lehavot, K., & Simoni, J. M. (2011). The impact of minority stress on mental health and substance use among sexual minority women. *Journal of Consulting and Clinical Psychology, 79*, 159–170. http://dx.doi.org/10.1037/a0022839

Lehavot, K., & Simpson, T. L. (2013). Incorporating lesbian and bisexual women into women veterans' health priorities. *Journal of General Internal Medicine, 28*(Suppl. 2), S609–S614. http://dx.doi.org/10.1007/s11606-012-2291-2

Lev, A. I. (2003). *Transgender emergence: Therapeutic guidelines for working with gender-variant people and their families*. Binghamton, NY: Haworth Press.

Little, B., & Terrance, C. (2010). Perceptions of domestic violence in lesbian relationships: Stereotypes and gender role expectations. *Journal of Homosexuality, 57*, 429–440. http://dx.doi.org/10.1080/00918360903543170

Littleton, H., Rhatigan, D. L., & Axsom, D. (2007). Unacknowledged rape: How much do we know about the hidden rape victim? *Journal of Aggression, Maltreatment & Trauma, 14*, 57–74. http://dx.doi.org/10.1300/J146v14n04_04

Maguen, S., Shipherd, J. C., & Harris, H. N. (2005). Providing culturally sensitive care for transgender patients. *Cognitive and Behavioral Practice, 12*, 479–490. http://dx.doi.org/10.1016/S1077-7229(05)80075-6

Marshal, M. P., Friedman, M. S., Stall, R., King, K. M., Miles, J., Gold, M. A., . . . Morse, J. Q. (2008). Sexual orientation and adolescent substance use: A meta-analysis and methodological review. *Addiction, 103*, 546–556. http://dx.doi.org/10.1111/j.1360-0443.2008.02149.x

Martell, C. R., Safren, S. A., & Prince, S. E. (2003). *Cognitive behavioral therapy with gay, lesbian, and bisexual clients.* New York, NY: Guilford Press.

Mattocks, K. M., Sadler, A., Yano, E. M., Krebs, E. E., Zephyrin, L., Brandt, C., . . . Haskell, S. (2013). Sexual victimization, health status, and VA healthcare utilization among lesbian and bisexual OEF/OIF veterans. *Journal of General Internal Medicine, 28*(Suppl. 2), S604–S608. http://dx.doi.org/10.1007/s11606-013-2357-9

McCabe, S. E., Hughes, T. L., Bostwick, W. B., West, B. T., & Boyd, C. J. (2009). Sexual orientation, substance use behaviors and substance dependence in the United States. *Addiction, 104*, 1333–1345. http://dx.doi.org/10.1111/j.1360-0443.2009.02596.x

McNally, R. J. (2003). Progress and controversy in the study of posttraumatic stress disorder. *Annual Review of Psychology, 54*, 229–252. http://dx.doi.org/10.1146/annurev.psych.54.101601.145112

Meyer, I. H. (1995). Minority stress and mental health in gay men. *Journal of Health and Social Behavior, 36*, 38–56. http://dx.doi.org/10.2307/2137286

Meyer, I. H. (2003). Prejudice, social stress, and mental health in lesbian, gay, and bisexual populations: Conceptual issues and research evidence. *Psychological Bulletin, 129*, 674–697. http://dx.doi.org/10.1037/0033-2909.129.5.674

Mimiaga, M. J., Noonan, E., Donnell, D., Safren, S. A., Koenen, K. C., Gortmaker, S., . . . Mayer, K. H. (2009). Childhood sexual abuse is highly associated with HIV risk-taking behavior and infection among MSM in the EXPLORE Study. *Journal of Acquired Immune Deficiency Syndromes, 51*, 340–348. http://dx.doi.org/10.1097/QAI.0b013e3181a24b38

Mustanski, B., Garofalo, R., Herrick, A., & Donenberg, G. (2007). Psychosocial health problems increase risk for HIV among urban young men who have sex with men: Preliminary evidence of a syndemic in need of attention. *Annals of Behavioral Medicine, 34*(1), 37–45. http://dx.doi.org/10.1007/BF02879919

Nemoto, T., Operario, D., Keatley, J., Han, L., & Soma, T. (2004). HIV risk behaviors among male-to-female transgender persons of color in San Francisco. *American Journal of Public Health, 94*, 1193–1199. http://dx.doi.org/10.2105/AJPH.94.7.1193

Nemoto, T., Sausa, L. A., Operario, D., & Keatley, J. (2006). Need for HIV/AIDS education and intervention for MTF transgenders: Responding to the challenge. *Journal of Homosexuality, 51*(1), 183–202. http://dx.doi.org/10.1300/J082v51n01_09

O'Cleirigh, C., Safren, S. A., & Mayer, K. H. (2012). The pervasive effects of childhood sexual abuse: Challenges for improving HIV prevention and treatment interventions. *Journal of Acquired Immune Deficiency Syndromes, 59*, 331–334. http://dx.doi.org/10.1097/QAI.0b013e31824aed80

Pantalone, D. W., Iwamasa, G. Y., & Martell, C. R. (2009). Adapting cognitive–behavioral therapies to diverse populations. In K. S. Dobson (Ed.), *Handbook of cognitive–behavioral therapies* (3d ed., pp. 445–464). New York, NY: Guilford Press.

Pantalone, D. W., Pachankis, J. E., Rood, B. A., & Bankoff, S. M. (2014). The health and wellness of sexual and gender minorities. In R. A. R. Gurung (Ed.), *Multicultural approaches to health and wellness in America* (pp. 195–224). New York, NY: Praeger.

Reisner, S. L., White, J. M., Bradford, J. B., & Mimiaga, M. J. (2014). Transgender health disparities: Comparing full cohort and nested matched-pair study designs in a community health center. *LGBT Health, 1*, 177–184. http://dx.doi.org/10.1089/lgbt.2014.0009

Resick, P. A., Nishith, P., Weaver, T. L., Astin, M. C., & Feuer, C. A. (2002). A comparison of cognitive-processing therapy with prolonged exposure and a waiting condition for the treatment of chronic posttraumatic stress disorder in female rape victims. *Journal of Consulting and Clinical Psychology, 70*, 867–879. http://dx.doi.org/10.1037/0022-006X.70.4.867

Resick, P. A., & Schnicke, M. K. (1992). Cognitive processing therapy for sexual assault victims. *Journal of Consulting and Clinical Psychology, 60*, 748–756. http://dx.doi.org/10.1037/0022-006X.60.5.748

Riggs, D. S., Rothbaum, B. O., & Foa, E. B. (1995). A prospective examination of symptoms of posttraumatic stress disorder in victims of nonsexual assault. *Journal of Interpersonal Violence, 10*, 201–214. http://dx.doi.org/10.1177/0886260595010002005

Roberts, S. T., Watlington, C. G., Nett, S. D., & Batten, S. V. (2010). Sexual trauma disclosure in clinical settings: Addressing diversity. *Journal of Trauma & Dissociation, 11*(2), 244–259. http://dx.doi.org/10.1080/15299730903502961

Rood, B. R., Puckett, J. A., Surace, F. I., Berman, A. K., Maroney, M. R., & Pantalone, D. W. (2015, November). Concealment and expecting rejection: Exploring how transgender individuals respond to threat. In M. S. Boroughs (Chair), *Traumatic life experiences among sexual and gender minorities: Implications for the development and dissemination of evidence-based assessment and intervention.* Symposium conducted at the 49th Annual Convention of the Association for Behavioral and Cognitive Therapies, Chicago, IL.

Rothbaum, B. O., Foa, E. B., Riggs, D. S., Murdock, T., & Walsh, W. (1992). A prospective examination of post-traumatic stress disorder in rape victims. *Journal of Traumatic Stress, 5*, 455–475. http://dx.doi.org/10.1002/jts.2490050309

Rothman, E. F., Exner, D., & Baughman, A. L. (2011). The prevalence of sexual assault against people who identify as gay, lesbian, or bisexual in the United States: A systematic review. *Trauma, Violence, & Abuse, 12*(2), 55–66. http://dx.doi.org/10.1177/1524838010390707

Schulz, P. M., Resick, P. A., Huber, L. C., & Griffin, M. G. (2006). The effectiveness of cognitive processing therapy for PTSD with refugees in a community setting. *Cognitive and Behavioral Practice, 13*, 322–331. http://dx.doi.org/10.1016/j.cbpra.2006.04.011

Schumm, J. A., Briggs-Phillips, M., & Hobfoll, S. E. (2006). Cumulative interpersonal traumas and social support as risk and resiliency factors in predicting PTSD and depression among inner-city women. *Journal of Traumatic Stress, 19*, 825–836. http://dx.doi.org/10.1002/jts.20159

Shapiro, F. (1989). Eye movement desensitization: A new treatment for post-traumatic stress disorder. *Journal of Behavior Therapy and Experimental Psychiatry, 20*, 211–217. http://dx.doi.org/10.1016/0005-7916(89)90025-6

Sharp, J., Hart, J., Kolodner, C., Vachon, C. (Producers), & Peirce, K. (Director). (1999). *Boys don't cry* [Videocassette]. Farmington Hills, MI: CBS/Fox Home Video.

Sherman, M. D., Kauth, M. R., Shipherd, J. C., & Street, R. L. (2014). Provider beliefs and practices about assessing sexual orientation in two VHA hospitals. *LGBT Health, 1*, 185–191. http://dx.doi.org/10.1089/lgbt.2014.0008

Shipherd, J. C., Clum, G., Suvak, M., & Resick, P. A. (2014). Treatment-related reductions in PTSD and changes in physical health symptoms in women. *Journal of Behavioral Medicine, 37*, 423–433. http://dx.doi.org/10.1007/s10865-013-9500-2

Shipherd, J. C., Maguen, S., Skidmore, W. C., & Abramovitz, S. M. (2011). Potentially traumatic events in a transgender sample: Frequency and associated symptoms. *Traumatology, 17*(2), 56–67. http://dx.doi.org/10.1177/1534765610395614

Stall, R., Mills, T. C., Williamson, J., Hart, T., Greenwood, G., Paul, J., . . . Catania, J. A. (2003). Association of co-occurring psychosocial health problems and increased vulnerability to HIV/AIDS among urban men who have sex with men. *American Journal of Public Health, 93*, 939–942. http://dx.doi.org/10.2105/AJPH.93.6.939

Sullivan, J., & Beech, A. (2004). A comparative study of demographic data relating to intra-and extra-familial child sexual abusers and professional perpetrators. *Journal of Sexual Aggression, 10*(1), 39–50. http://dx.doi.org/10.1080/13552600410001667788

Sweet, T., & Welles, S. L. (2012). Associations of sexual identity or same-sex behaviors with history of childhood sexual abuse and HIV/STI risk in the United States. *Journal of Acquired Immune Deficiency Syndromes, 59*, 400–408. http://dx.doi.org/10.1097/QAI.0b013e3182400e75

Todahl, J. L., Linville, D., Bustin, A., Wheeler, J., & Gau, J. (2009). Sexual assault support services and community systems: Understanding critical issues and needs in the LGBTQ community. *Violence Against Women, 15*, 952–976. http://dx.doi.org/10.1177/1077801209335494

Valentine, S. E., Elsesser, S., Grasso, C., Safren, S. A., Bradford, J. B., Mereish, E., & O'Cleirigh, C. (2015). The predictive syndemic effect of multiple psychosocial problems on health care costs and utilization among sexual minority women.

Journal of Urban Health, 92, 1092–1104. http://dx.doi.org/10.1007/s11524-015-9989-5

Valentine, S. E., & Pantalone, D. W. (2013). Correlates of perceptual and behavioral definitions of abuse in HIV-positive sexual minority men. *Psychological Trauma: Theory, Research, Practice, and Policy, 5,* 417–425. http://dx.doi.org/10.1037/a0029094

Vogt, D. S., Shipherd, J. C., & Resick, P. A. (2012). Posttraumatic maladaptive beliefs scale: Evolution of the personal beliefs and reactions scale. *Assessment, 19,* 308–317. http://dx.doi.org/10.1177/1073191110376161

Weathers, F. W., Keane, T., & Foa, E. B. (2008). Assessment and diagnosis of adults. In E. B. Foa, T. M. Keane, M. J. Friedman, & J. A. Cohen (Eds.), *Effective treatments for PTSD* (2nd ed., pp. 23–61). New York, NY: Guilford Press.

Woodford, M. R., Krentzman, A. R., & Gattis, M. N. (2012). Alcohol and drug use among sexual minority college students and their heterosexual counterparts: The effects of experiencing and witnessing incivility and hostility on campus. *Substance Abuse Rehabilitation, 3,* 11–23. http://dx.doi.org/10.2147/SAR.S26347

8

CONFLICTING IDENTITIES: SEXUAL MINORITY, TRANSGENDER, AND GENDER NONCONFORMING INDIVIDUALS NAVIGATING BETWEEN RELIGION AND GENDER–SEXUAL ORIENTATION IDENTITY

SUSAN KASHUBECK-WEST, AMBER M. WHITELEY,
TARA VOSSENKEMPER, CAROL ROBINSON, AND CORI DEITZ

In the United States, the majority of people identify as religious or spiritual and almost 90% of people indicate that they engage in various personal acts of faith (Halkitis et al., 2009). Surveys indicate that 76% of individuals identify as Christian, and Christianity is a major socializing force in the United States (Dahl & Galliher, 2012). For many people in the United States, religion serves as a source of strength, promotes community and cultural functions, and helps in developing self-identity and values (García, Gray-Stanley, & Ramirez-Valles, 2008). As a central societal institution, religion plays a large role in shaping the trajectories and transitions of people's lives (García et al., 2008).

An obstacle faced by numerous sexual minority and transgender and gender nonconforming (TGNC) individuals is that of reconciling their desire for self-acceptance with the negative messages that are conveyed by a number of faith institutions. Although some Judeo–Christian religious institutions

http://dx.doi.org/10.1037/15959-009
Handbook of Sexual Orientation and Gender Diversity in Counseling and Psychotherapy, K. A. DeBord,
A. R. Fischer, K. J. Bieschke, and R. M. Perez (Editors)

in the United States are openly supportive of sexual and gender minorities (e.g., Alliance of Baptists, Unitarian Universalist, Episcopal, United Church of Christ), many other mainstream religions are not supportive, and some actively promote negative and hostile views. Porter, Ronneberg, and Witten (2013) reported that only 39% of the 46 Christian denominations that currently are active in the United States allow sexual minority and TGNC members, only 20% allow ordination of sexual minority and TGNC individuals, and less than 9% allow same-sex couples to marry within the church. Levy and Lo (2013) noted that many religious denominations rely on biblical teachings about gender and gender roles, resulting in very strict views on gender. For individuals who belong to nonaffirming faith traditions, the conflict between deeply held religious values and one's gender–sexual identity can be very deep.

Sexual minority and TGNC individuals may find the discrimination and negative messages from religious institutions to be so intolerable that they abandon these religions altogether. For example, Schuck and Liddle (2001) found that many sexual minority individuals left their religions of origin in search of more affirming spiritual practices. Similarly, Sheridan (2001) noted that many TGNC people move toward individualized relationships with God, especially as they encounter barriers to church participation. Kidd and Witten (2008) found that many TGNC people worked to develop faith systems (different religious traditions or alternative interpretations of religious teachings) that helped them accept their transgender identities. Witten and Eyler (2012) reported that more than half of the participants in the TranScience Longitudinal Aging Research Study moved from traditional Western religions to a more personalized spiritual practice. However, some individuals desire to remain in their faith traditions; such a choice can lead to intense feelings of personal conflict between gender–sexual identity and religious identity (Rodriguez & Ouellette, 2000).

In the first section of this chapter, we briefly explore a handful of faith traditions commonly found in the United States. Our intent is to provide a quick snapshot of current perspectives on sexual minorities and TGNC people from scholarly writing on those faith traditions as well as what their online presence suggests. Dramatic increases in Internet access and usage make the web an important resource. It is important to understand the kinds of messages and information our clients may be accessing. Indeed, Levy and Lo (2013) reported that their TGNC participants found the use of the Internet for research to be especially helpful. The second section provides an overview of the scholarly literature on religious stigma and mental health outcomes for sexual minority and TGNC individuals. From there we move into the third section, a discussion of options for conflict resolution. Finally, a case study provides an illustration of the material presented in this chapter.

We identified two potential biases that we wish to bring to readers' attention: (a) it is very difficult for individuals to reconcile their sexual or gender identities with their religious identities if they come from nonaffirming faith traditions; and (b) mental health fields sometimes have discounted the importance of religious identity to sexual minority and TGNC people and underestimated the amount of loss people might experience if asked to give up their religion. An assumption we had was that changing someone's sexual orientation or gender identity is not an appropriate goal of counseling (see Chapter 11, this volume). In terms of our social locations, all of the authors of this chapter identify as cisgendered females; one of us is African American and Native American and the rest are White. Our social class backgrounds range from working class to upper middle class. Three authors identify as heterosexual, and two identify as lesbian. All were raised Christian; currently two authors identify as spiritual, one as atheist, one as Buddhist, and one as liberal Mormon.

RELIGIOUS PERSPECTIVES

Some faith traditions are affirming of sexual minority and TGNC individuals. For example, Buddhism and Hinduism often embrace a third sex, and a number of Native American religions are gender inclusive (Porter et al., 2013). At the same time, many religious institutions are aligned with perspectives that portray these individuals as immoral, unnatural, and sinful. Notably, there is much more discussion of sexual orientation by religious traditions than discussion of gender identity. For example, Levy and Lo (2013) reported that their TGNC participants did not recall any overt mention of gender identity, although they heard many messages about sexual orientation. Within oppressive faith traditions one often finds movements and individuals that are more liberal in their views on sexual minority and TGNC individuals, and they can be important resources for individuals struggling to resolve conflicts between religious and sexual–gender identities. Resources are available online that provide information and community for individuals who want to explore issues related to faith and sexual–gender identity. Campbell (2012) described the ways in which online spaces can assist individuals in creating a sense of personal identity and group belonging that may otherwise be very difficult to cultivate. For example, http://www.whosoever.org is an online community with a focus on helping sexual minority and TGNC individuals who identify as Christian to have a safe place to grow in their faith by connecting with others and accessing resources for spiritual learning. Another online community, http://www.transfaithonline.com, is led by TGNC individuals and focuses on providing a safe space to discuss faith and spirituality.

In the following sections, we review the positions of several major faith traditions in the United States on sexual minority and TGNC individuals. We chose three Christian denominations on the basis of popularity (Catholic), racial and ethnic minority representation (Baptist), and recent news coverage with regard to sexual minority and TGNC issues (Latter-Day Saints). Two other faith traditions, Judaism and Islam, are covered because of their prominence in the United States. According to the U.S. Census Bureau (2012) *Statistical Abstract*, in 2008 about 173.4 million U.S. citizens described their religious identification as Christian (including 57.2 million Catholics, 36.1 million Baptists, and 3.2 million Mormons), 2.7 million identified as Jewish, and 1.3 million as Muslim.

Catholicism

Historically and currently, the official position of the Catholic Church is that enactment of a same-sex orientation is a sin, based on natural law (the idea that men and women are naturally made to fit each other for sex and procreation) and scripture (Hunt, 2006; McGinniss, 2010). In addition, Catholicism takes a largely negative and discriminatory position on TGNC individuals. According to Bordeyne (2006), public proponents (i.e., bishops, priests, Catholic politicians) are required to oppose same-sex unions and marriages. Indeed, the Church has sanctioned discrimination against sexual minority and TGNC individuals in areas such as adoptions, teaching, the military, and coaching youth athletic teams (Hunt, 2006). At the same time, the Catholic Church views same-sex-oriented individuals as deserving to be treated with respect, compassion, and sensitivity and as being called to chastity (Catholic Answers, 2004). Thus, the only acceptable option for same-sex-oriented individuals is sexual abstinence. Official positions aside, over the past 30 years there have been numerous individual clergy, Catholic organizations, and U.S. dioceses that have acted pastorally toward sexual minority and TGNC individuals and that have voiced disagreement with the official Catholic position (Hunt, 2006). Notably, Pope Francis stated that "if a person is gay and seeks God and has good will, who am I to judge?" (BBC News, 2013). In the fall of 2014, the Vatican appeared to be softening its stance on homosexuality, although interpretations of the Vatican statements seemed to vary widely; the Vatican appeared to back away from affirmation after a backlash (Gallagher & Burke, 2014).

A search of web content using the terms *Catholic* and *homosexuality* revealed a plethora of sites. The Vatican site publishes a series of documents outlining the position of the Church on "persons with homosexual tendencies" (e.g., Congregation for Catholic Education, 2005). Affirming websites for organizations such as DignityUSA and New Ways Ministry that work for social justice for all sexual orientations and gender identities within the Catholic Church provide helpful resources for sexual minority and TGNC Catholics.

Baptist

The largest Protestant faith tradition in the United States is Baptist, including congregations that belong to the American Baptist Association (more liberal), the National Baptist Convention (seen as moderate), and the Southern Baptist Convention (more conservative). The Southern Baptist convention has issued several resolutions over the decades rejecting homosexuality as a "lifestyle." For example, the convention issued a resolution in 1988 blaming homosexual activity for the spread of AIDS to "innocent victims" and calling homosexuality a "perversion of divine standards and as a violation of nature and natural affections" and "an abomination in the eyes of God" (Southern Baptist Convention, 1988). It opposes same-sex marriages and equivalent unions (Southern Baptist Convention, 2008). In 2014, the Southern Baptist Convention approved a resolution stating that "gender identity is determined by biological sex, not one's self-perception" and opposing any types of therapy that might "alter one's bodily identity." Similarly, the American Baptist Churches USA (a smaller conservative convention) indicated that "God's design for sexual intimacy places it within the context of marriage between one man and one woman, and acknowledge that the practice of homosexuality is incompatible with Biblical teaching" (American Baptist Churches USA, n.d.).

The National Baptist Convention, USA, Inc. is predominantly African American and the second largest Baptist denomination globally. According to its website (http://www.nationalbaptist.com), the denomination holds no official view on homosexuality and leaves the issue to individual congregations to address. However, in a position letter written in response to President Obama's declaration of support for same-sex marriage, the convention stated that marriage was a "sacred biblical covenant between a man and a woman" (Scruggs, 2012).

The American Baptist denomination has several alliances and associations within it that are affirming of all sexual orientations and gender identities. For example, the small, theologically progressive Alliance of Baptists supports "full inclusion of women and [lesbian, gay, bisexual, and transgender] persons in congregational life, including their ordination and marriage equality" (Covenant of the Alliance of Baptists, 2012). Similarly, the Association of Welcoming and Affirming Baptists (http://www.awab.org) is an affirming group of about 50 churches and organizations that supports and advocates for the inclusion of sexual minority and TGNC individuals within Baptist faith communities.

The online presence for Baptists reflects the diverse perspectives that span the Baptist convention. Resolutions on homosexuality from the Southern Baptist Convention are available, as are a variety of affirming resources from the Alliance of Baptists (http://www.allianceofbaptists.org) and Association of Welcoming and Affirming Baptists.

Latter-Day Saints (Mormon)

Historically, the Mormon Church and its followers have ostracized same-sex couples. Under Mormon teaching, Mormon couples must be married in a Mormon Temple to earn exaltation (i.e., spiritual growth ultimately resulting in becoming one with God), but only heterosexual couples can be married in the temple (McConkie, 1966). According to Mormon doctrine, same-sex orientation "is a choice that leads to sickness, depression, and poor spiritual mental health" (Johns & Hanna, 2011, p. 205). At the same time, the Church released a statement indicating that same-sex attraction, in and of itself, is not a sin, but to act on that attraction is a sin (http://www.mormonsandgays. org). Additionally, the Church advocates for its members to be accepting and kind to all of God's children, including those who are same-sex oriented. A recent statement by a church elder reiterated the Church's position on same-sex marriage: "While many governments and well-meaning individuals have redefined marriage, the Lord has not" (Pearce, 2014).

In 1995, the Latter-Day Saints (LDS) released an official statement declaring that "gender is an essential characteristic of individual pre-mortal, mortal, and eternal identity and purpose" (Hinkley, 1995, para. 2). More recently, TGNC persons have been accepted in the church and may be baptized, although those who have undergone gender affirmation surgery may not receive the priesthood or enter the temple (LDS Church, 2010). An Internet search on Mormon and homosexuality revealed a variety of sites, some promoted by the LDS Church (e.g., http://MormonsandGays.org, http://Northstarlds.org) and some not (e.g., No More Strangers: LGBT Mormon Forum [http://www.nomorestrangers. org], LDS Family Fellowship [http://www.ldsfamilyfellowship.org], Mormons for Equality [http://www.mormonsformarriage.com], Affirmation [http://www. affirmation.org]). Those promoted by the Church provide information and resources consistent with Church policy, whereas the other groups provide resources designed to support sexual minority and TGNC Mormons.

Judaism

Historically, Jewish law has condemned same-sex attraction, although lesbian behavior was seen as less offensive than gay male behavior (Morris, 1987). Within the four broad branches of Judaism there are differences in perspectives on same-sex sexual orientations and TGNC issues. For example, within the Orthodox branch, attitudes vary from benevolence to disgust and advocacy for reparative therapy (Davis, 2008). Modern Orthodox communal leaders released a statement in 2010 that affirmed support for the fair treatment of lesbian and gay individuals and, at the same time, reaffirmed the prohibition of homosexual acts ("Statement of Principles," 2010). Some Orthodox leaders recognize the efficacy of gender affirmation surgery in changing a person's gender according to Jewish law (Waldenberg, n.d.). In addition, in 2007 Joy Ladin became the first openly transgender professor at an Orthodox institution (Ladin, 2012).

Conservative Judaism is often portrayed as the branch occupying a middle ground between Orthodox and Reform Judaism; its rulings on same-sex attraction have been viewed as contradictory (Wertheimer, 2007). In June 2012, guidelines were established within the Conservative tradition for the marriage of same-sex couples. At the same time, Conservative rabbis and clergy were told they were not forced to perform same-sex marriage ceremonies and could opt to refrain from doing so (Markoe, 2012). In 2003, the Committee on Jewish Law and Standards of the Rabbinical Assembly approved a rabbinic rule that concluded that gender affirmation surgery was permissible as a treatment of gender dysphoria and that complete gender affirmation surgery resulted in a change in the person's sex status (Rabinowitz, 2003).

Reform Judaism is grounded in *halakhah* (Jewish law) but also stresses the importance of justice, personal autonomy, and individual rights (Davis, 2008). Since the 1970s, Reform rabbis have performed same-sex ceremonies, and in 1990, the Reform movement began ordaining openly out rabbis. In 2000, the Reform movement passed a resolution that permitted rabbis in the Reform tradition to officiate at same-sex ceremonies (Moss & Ulmer, 2008). Similarly, Reform Judaism has been open to TGNC individuals since the late 1970s (Jewish Telegraphic Agency, 2007). Initially, acceptance centered on those persons who had undergone gender affirmation surgery; over time the Union for Reform Judaism pronounced clear support for all TGNC persons and in 2007 included a blessing sanctifying the sex-change process (Eskenazi & Harris, 2007). Reconstructionist Judaism is quite liberal with regard to support for same-sex sexual orientations, as rabbis practicing this branch of Judaism have been officiating same-sex couples' rituals, including wedding ceremonies, since the early 1990s (Davis, 2008). Similarly, positive views on TGNC people are a part of Reconstructionist Jewish ideology (Ott, 2009). One important website in the United States is the Institute for Judaism and Sexual Orientation (http://huc.edu/ijso/inclusion/) where an extensive list of articles and texts on the subjects of Judaism and sexual orientation/gender identity is provided.

Islam

Historically, male homosexuality was openly practiced and tolerated from the 7th century to the 20th century (Eidhamar, 2014). As views toward sexual minorities became more liberal in the 20th century in the West, views in Muslim societies shifted to become more oppressive. The religion focuses primarily on male homosexuality—women's same-sex behavior is ignored. The practice of Islam can be separated into two broad approaches: traditional and progressive (Eidhamar, 2014), including variations within each perspective with regard to views on same-sex attraction. The traditional approach views the Quran in a literal manner, sees it as condemning of same-sex orientations, and makes no differentiation between attraction and behavior (Eidhamar, 2014). According to this approach, same-sex orientation is learned (not innate), is sinful, and is punished both in this life and in eternity. However, a moderate traditional view exists wherein same-sex-oriented individuals are viewed with compassion and encouraged to seek help, accept themselves, and see their orientations as a test from God, rather than as a punishment (Mission Islam, n.d.). This approach differentiates between attraction and behavior, such that lesbian, gay, and bisexual (LGB) Muslims are respected as humans who must refrain from same-sex sexual behaviors (Eidhamar, 2014).

Progressive perspectives have pushed for reform, questioning whether the Qur'an should dictate current practice and asserting that same-sex-oriented individuals are a part of the divine plan (Jamal, 2001; Kugle, 2010). These progressive stances are often perceived as being influenced by Western cultures. Overall, Eidhamar (2014) suggested that there is more support and practice of traditional Islamic stances and very little support for progressive stances. Indeed, homosexuality is punished by death in several Islamic countries (Kligerman, 2007).

Searching for material online related to Islam and sexual orientation and gender identity was more difficult; some websites crashed repeatedly, and others had viruses associated with them. The Al-Fatiha Foundation is noted as a primary affirming resource for sexual minority and TGNC Muslims, yet its website was not accessible. Muslims for Progressive Values (http://mpvusa.org) has a section of their website devoted to resources and information for lesbian, gay, bisexual, transgender, questioning, and intersex (LGBTQI) individuals that includes websites from around the world.

RELIGIOUS STIGMA AND MENTAL HEALTH

For many people, increased religiosity is associated with less psychological distress and with greater life satisfaction, happiness, and well-being (e.g., Chatters et al., 2008; Ellison, Boardman, Williams, & Jackson, 2001; Krause,

2004). However, these findings do not extend to many sexual minority and TGNC individuals (e.g., Barnes & Meyer, 2012; Lease, Horne, & Noffsinger-Frazier, 2005). When religious institutions convey that sexual minority and TGNC individuals are immoral and second-class, these messages often are internalized. Indeed, heterosexist messages from religious sources have been associated with shame, guilt, and internalized heterosexism (Ream & Savin-Williams, 2005; Sherry, Adelman, Whilde, & Quick, 2010). Although religious institutions in the United States have been less likely to discuss TGNC issues, most religions identify a deity with a specific sex (and can be described as either patriarchal or matriarchal), have sex-based rules that define power and authority, and have hierarchies and belief systems about gender roles (Porter et al., 2013).

Schuck and Liddle (2001) reported that the experience of religious conflict was related to increased challenges in coming out among LGB individuals and suggested that religious conflicts may affect LGB identity formation. For example, a number of participants reported fearing that they had been rejected by God or would go to hell. Many participants reported feeling guilt and shame about their sexual orientation; such feelings can make it very difficult to develop a positive sexual identity. Several other authors have argued that participating in conservative religious traditions can be detrimental to the psychological health and identity development of sexual minority and TGNC individuals (e.g., Hagen, Arczynski, Morrow, & Hawxhurst, 2011; Rodriguez & Ouellette, 2000). Lease et al. (2005) suggested that disaffirming religious environments may result in sexual minority individuals feeling self-blame, greater internalized heterosexism, isolation, depression, and suicidal thinking. Szymanski, Kashubeck-West, and Meyer (2008) reviewed the literature on religiosity and internalized heterosexism and reported that adherence to conservative religious beliefs was associated with increased levels of internalized stigma, whereas involvement in affirmative faith organizations and independent religious decision making were associated with less internalized stigma.

More recently, Page, Lindahl, and Malik (2013) reported that involvement with religious or spiritual belief systems that spread rejecting and condemning messages about sexual minorities was related to more internalized negative self-messages and greater challenges in developing and accepting one's sexual identity in a sample of adolescents and young adults. Wagner et al. (2013) found that gay and bisexual male participants who indicated inner battles between their religious beliefs and sexual orientation had significant levels of religious guilt and felt social pressure to adapt to the heteronormative culture. Barnes and Meyer (2012) reported that participants in nonaffirming religious settings had higher internalized heterosexism than sexual minority individuals who participated in affirming religions and those who did not attend any religious institutions. Finally, compared with sexual minority individuals who attended accepting–affirming religious institutions, sexual minority individuals who participated in rejecting–disaffirming religious institutions reported less emotional well-being, less social support, and greater identity conflict (Hamblin & Gross, 2013).

In addition to associations with internalized heterosexism, the religious climate around sexual minority youths may be related to their health risk behaviors. Hatzenbuehler, Pachankis, and Wolff (2012) reported that their survey data from 1,400 sexual minority youth indicated that the religious climate was more strongly associated with their alcohol abuse and sexual behavior than it was for heterosexually identified youth. LGB youth living in counties with a religious climate that was supportive of sexual minorities reported fewer symptoms of alcohol abuse and fewer sexual partners. Interestingly, the gender differences found by Eliason, Burke, van Olphen, and Howell (2011) suggested that religiosity operates as a protective factor for sexual minority female college students with regard to alcohol, tobacco, and other drug use and operates as a risk factor for sexual minority men. Eliason et al. indicated that potential differences in types of religious affiliation (e.g., nonaffirming vs. affirming) across men and women may have played a role; the sample size was too small to investigate such possibilities. Clearly, religion appears to be an important factor in understanding the psychological well-being of many sexual minority individuals.

Rodriguez and Follins (2012) reported that few studies in the psychological literature address the role of religion and spirituality in the lives of TGNC individuals. Although many articles use acronyms such as LGBT, LGBTQ, and LGBTQIAA (to refer to groups consisting of lesbian, gay, bisexual, transgender, queer, intersex, asexual, or ally individuals), seldom has there been any particular focus on TGNC experiences. Golub, Walker, Longmire-Avital, Bimbi, and Parsons (2010) studied relations between religious behaviors, social support, and risky sexual behavior in transgender women. Their results indicated that women with low levels of religious behaviors were less likely to engage in risky sexual behavior than women with high levels of religiosity. According to Abu-Raiya and Pargament (2015), 20 years of empirical study have demonstrated that positive religious coping practices have been associated with positive health behaviors; however, this relationship might not hold for transgender women. Much more focused research on the experiences of TGNC individuals is needed. The limited research that has been conducted has been primarily with White individuals with a Christian background; the experiences of TGNC people of color and of other religious traditions are missing (Rodriguez & Follins, 2012).

CONFLICT RESOLUTION

Given the conflict that many religious sexual minority and TGNC clients have felt between their religious identity and their sexual orientation–gender identity, it is not surprising that they have sought counseling for assistance. Beckstead and Morrow (2004) indicated that when faced with this conflict, clients and therapists often feel there are only two polarizing choices available— leave one's religion or renounce one's sexuality. Similarly, Whitehead and Whitehead (2014) noted that many TGNC individuals struggle to identify ways to live life openly and fully, rather than in the disguise that church communities often demand. Such a perspective suggests there is no middle ground and no way out of this conflict without losing an important part of one's identity. However, Bartoli and Gillem (2008) noted that clients experience this conflict in a variety of ways and resolve it differently; sometimes resolution involves privileging one identity over another, and sometimes it does not. Indeed, there may be within-community differences; Fredriksen-Goldsen et al. (2011) reported that TGNC individuals have higher levels of engagement in religious–spiritual activities than their non-TGNC sexual minority counterparts. Finally, Levy and Lo (2013) found that questioning their gender identity led TGNC participants to further develop their faith; thus, these conflicts can result in much personal growth. Indeed, Whitehead and Whitehead (2014) noted that resolving the dilemma between gender identity and religious faith can become a journey of faith. This growth can be possible for clients, therapists, and trainees who struggle to reconcile internal conflicts related to sexual orientation, gender identity, and religious faith.

An examination of the literature suggests that there have been three main approaches to dealing with the conflict between sexual orientation and religious faith: (a) change one's sexual orientation (e.g., Yarhouse, 1998); (b) leave one's current faith tradition, perhaps joining an affirming faith tradition (Barret & Barzan, 1996); and (c) engage in psychotherapy centered on integration of religion and sexual orientation (e.g., Haldeman, 2004). We could not find literature specifically related to psychotherapy to help TGNC individuals resolve conflicts between gender identity and religious faith. Thus, this section focuses primarily on sexual orientation.

Change One's Sexual Orientation

Therapeutic interventions that aim to change, modify, or manage undesirable nonheterosexual orientations are described as *sexual orientation change efforts* (SOCE; APA Task Force on Appropriate Therapeutic Responses to Sexual Orientation, 2009, pg. v; see also Chapter 11, this volume). Clients who seek to change their sexual orientation have done so mostly through religion-based programs or ministries (Dehlin, Galliher, Bradshaw, Hyde, & Crowell, 2015; Haldeman, 2004; Tozer & Hayes, 2004). Emphasizing the power of prayer and belief in God as behaviors designed to strengthen willpower against same-sex attractions, many clients are told that change in orientation is achievable. SOCE approaches are seen as ethical by their proponents, in that they do not force clients into accepting a sexual minority identity that conflicts with deeply held religious beliefs (Yarhouse, 1998). However, Serovich et al. (2008) reported that the empirical literature on SOCE had a number of methodological problems that indicated an overall lack of scientific rigor, resulting in a research base that was not sound. Similarly, the 2009 APA Task Force on Appropriate Therapeutic Responses to Sexual Orientation reported that no firm conclusions about the effectiveness of SOCE could be drawn because of a lack of methodologically sound research, and it identified some evidence (cf. Haldeman, 2002; Shidlo & Schroeder, 2002) that SOCE might be harmful. More important, the APA Task Force stated that any benefits resultant from SOCE could be accomplished using affirmative and multiculturally appropriate therapeutic approaches, thus avoiding the harm that SOCE might engender. A recent study by Dehlin et al. (2015) with a large sample ($N = 1,612$) of LDS participants found that SOCE was viewed as ineffective or damaging.

Leave One's Religion of Origin

For many clients, leaving their religion becomes a natural choice for them as they begin to embrace their sexual identity. For example, Sherry et al. (2010) found that nearly 40% of LGB individuals either rejected religion altogether or converted to a more affirming faith. Some clients who leave religion altogether replace it with some form of spirituality; 17% of the sample in Sherry et al.'s study reported that they were spiritual but not religious. Moving toward a form of spirituality that is separate from formal organized religion can be good for mental health and can assist clients with reconciling past negative religious experiences (Lease et al., 2005; Sherry et al., 2010). Moreover, moving away from a dichotomous belief that one's sexuality is in direct conflict with one's faith can help a client regain self-confidence and trust in past spiritual experiences (Super & Jacobson, 2011). Barret and Barzan (1996) noted that leaving one's religion may enable sexual minority individuals to think critically about their faith experiences and define an affirming spiritual reality for themselves. According to Hagen et al. (2011), participation in spiritually affirming communities has several benefits. For example, Lease et al. (2005) reported that sexual minority individuals who belonged to affirming religious organizations reported less internalized heterosexism. Similarly, Smith and Home (2008) found that spiritual wellness was associated with greater sexual satisfaction in sexual minority women.

Clients who choose to leave their religion may experience powerful feelings of grief and loss, not only from a loss of faith but also from a potential loss of culture, identity, and family. Leaving one's religion can feel like experiencing a divorce or a death (Hattie & Beagan, 2013). For counselors working with clients who choose to leave their religion of origin, addressing the experience of grief and loss is important. Moreover, as Hagan et al. noted, religion and culture are often inseparable for sexual minority individuals of color, making it difficult to challenge a nonaffirming religious environment when that community is also a person's primary social network and source of support.

Unfortunately, the mental health profession has at times minimized the religious identity of persons experiencing conflict between sexual identity and religious identity. Indeed, sexual minority clients have reported facing blatant counselor biases regarding their religious identities. For example, Shelton and Delgado-Romero (2011) found that clients reported that previous therapists had devalued nonaffirming religious traditions or had assumed clients experienced religious discord. Similarly, Buser, Goodrich, Luke, and Buser (2011) quoted a participant who reported that his therapist saw his Catholicism as incompatible with his sexual identity and that mental health would involve leaving this faith tradition, even though the participant did not experience conflict between his faith and sexuality. Buser et al. noted the following experiences: therapists who did not understand how much grief clients experienced around losing a faith tradition; therapists who minimized the painful impact of religious teachings on clients' sense of themselves as damaged or flawed; and clients who felt misunderstood, unheard, and angry. It is vital that counselors understand that for many clients, leaving their religion might be equivalent to losing much of what has made up their world, including a major source of identity and community.

INTEGRATION OF CONFLICTING IDENTITIES

Working toward integration of conflicting sexual orientation–gender identities and religious identities is a complicated endeavor. Many clients have experiences of shame and guilt from their religious upbringing (Super & Jacobson, 2011), and extending those experiences into the counseling setting can be damaging. Haldeman (2004) noted that for some clients, their religious identity is so strongly important that it appears to be more realistic for them to contemplate changing their sexual orientation than to leave their religion of origin. Understanding models of religious or spiritual identity development and sexual identity development can be helpful for counselors as they conceptualize how these client identities may intersect in unique ways (Kocet, Sanabria, & Smith, 2011). Therapists need to remember that some sexual minority and

TGNC people may experience psychological health and well-being even when participating in oppressive religious institutions, whereas others may not be able to maintain their conservative religious beliefs and embrace their sexual–gender identities (Rodriguez & Ouellette, 2000). Several approaches have been suggested for assisting clients with integration of their religious and sexual–gender identities (e.g., Bozard & Sanders, 2011; Buchanan, Dzelme, Harris, & Hecker, 2001; Haldeman, 2004; Morrow & Hawxhurst, 1998). We briefly describe a few of these approaches next.

Haldeman (2004) noted that some clients felt irreconcilable conflicts between their religious identities and their sexual orientations and that neither SOCE nor affirmative therapy was an appropriate option. For those clients, he advocated for a person-centered approach to psychotherapy that avoided these polarized approaches. Haldeman's person-centered approach to reconciling conflict involved three stages: assessment, intervention, and integration. Assessment is a time for the client to evaluate current sexual behaviors and desires and to explore how his or her religious culture affects views of sexual identity. Based on a thorough understanding of the existential and psychosocial forces at play, the therapist and client collaborate in choosing goals for therapy and interventions for reaching those goals. Thus, the strategies used in the intervention phase are derived from the specific goals of the client. The third stage, integration, reflects the resolution of the conflict the client experiences between religion and sexual identity. This resolution will look different for each client, because it reflects the client's contexts and goals.

In 1998, Morrow and Hawxhurst put forward a model for empowerment of clients in feminist multicultural counseling that Hagen et al. (2011) identified as useful for integrating spirituality into the therapy process with sexual minority women. We believe the model would be helpful for TGNC clients and sexual minority men as well. This model draws from the major components of feminist multicultural counseling, recognizes that client concerns occur within a sociocultural context, and focuses on the importance of intersections of oppression. Morrow and Hawxhurst emphasized the importance of exploring intersecting identities related to sexual orientation, gender, religion and spirituality, social class, race, disability, age, and ethnicity. By doing so, their framework has a goal of providing clients with an opportunity to feel whole and that each identity is respected.

Bozard and Sanders (2011) identified an affirmative approach to conflict resolution with religiously identified sexual minority and TGNC clients that they named the GRACE model, an acronym for *goals, renewal, action, connection,* and *empowerment.* The GRACE model is seen as particularly applicable to clients who wish to explore religiously based spirituality.

- The first step is to work with the client to establish the *goals* of therapy. Goal exploration involves four components: (a) examining the client's religious history, (b) assessing how the client feels about religion, (c) identifying the client's goals with regard to a religious life, and (d) assessing the client's level of readiness for a new kind of religious life.

- *Renewal of hope* involves creating awareness of places where one can belong and of religion as a positive dimension in one's life. This step involves exploring past beliefs regarding religion and new possibilities, such as turning toward spirituality (Bozard & Sanders, 2011; Ginicola & Smith, 2011). Without hope, it is unlikely that clients could get past their experience of negative judgments from religious authorities (Bozard & Sanders, 2011).
- The third step in the GRACE model is *action*, where the client transitions from deliberation to forward movement (Bozard & Sanders, 2011). Integral aspects of this step include discussion of issues such as how the client might connect with religion, how the client wants to handle the issue of presentation of sexual–gender identity, readiness for connecting with religion, prioritizing what the client wants to achieve first, and resources the client has and needs in order to take action (Bozard & Sanders, 2011).
- The *connection* component of the GRACE model involves exploration of possible connections with God and with religious communities. Connecting with affirmative religious communities and with the possibility of reconciliation with God can be an important but challenging aspect of this step. Counselors are not expected to be religious experts; they can use bibliotherapy and introduction to affirming religious and spiritual leaders who can talk with clients.
- The final step is *empowerment*, wherein the counselor works to process client experiences and emotions, especially as they encounter social resistance. Clients can find strength and encouragement by keeping in mind the positive motivating factors underlying their pursuit of religious connection (Bozard & Sanders, 2011).

Although there is a growing body of literature around approaches to rectifying dissonance between a person's religious/spiritual identity and sexual orientation/gender identity, there is not enough research to recommend one "right" approach. The SOCEs clearly are not recommended; research suggests that they do more harm than good (Dehlin et al., 2015; Haldeman, 2002; Shidlo & Schroeder, 2002; see also Chapter 11, this volume). However, with regard to the approaches that advocate for integrating conflicting identities, none have been empirically tested to date.

Another problem with many of these approaches to handling conflicting identities is that with the exception of Morrow and Hawxhurst (1998), they focus primarily on religion/spirituality and sexual orientation/gender identity, without acknowledgment and discussion of how other identities, such as race and ethnicity, social class, and disability, may intersect with these two identities and affect how the conflict is experienced. The importance of understanding intersecting identities is receiving attention in the literature in general (e.g., Cole, 2009; see also Chapter 4, this volume), yet our understanding of how various therapeutic approaches work with regard to clients with different combinations of identities is in its infancy.

In the case example that follows, we draw most heavily on the GRACE model of Bozard and Sanders (2011) because we find it to be a comprehensive method for approaching the deep conflict that religious sexual minority and TGNC clients might face. At the same time, Bozard and Sanders do not discuss explicitly the ways in which multiple and intersecting identities create a unique cultural context that is important for understanding each client. Thus, as Morrow and Hawxhurst (1998) advised, we include material related to cultural context.

CASE EXAMPLE

Janelle[1] is a 35-year-old, middle-class, African American female currently living in a metropolitan Midwestern city. Originally from a Southern city she describes as "culturally limited," she was drawn to the new area by greater employment opportunities. Janelle's family of origin includes her father, who died of cancer when she was in middle school, her mother, and a brother who is 3 years older. She reports having limited contact with her brother at this time; Janelle is in regular contact with her mother.

After her father's death, her mother felt suddenly cut off from his professional community, which had been the primary social outlet for the entire family. Although religious involvement had been minimal during their marriage, Janelle's mother sought support from the Southern Baptist church of her youth, and over time the church became the predominant factor in her social and emotional life. For Janelle, the family reliance on the church was increasingly problematic, particularly in relation to the development of her own growing same-sex sexual attractions. Overhearing church gossip regarding specific individuals involved in "shameful sin" led Janelle to understand that same-sex relationships were not acceptable and were wrong in the eyes of God. This left her feeling intimidated, angry, and very confused; she had

---

[1]Client identifiers have been changed to protect confidentiality.

no peers or adults with whom she could talk in order to better understand her attractions and how she might fit into the local social world. Fitting in was complicated by the fact that Janelle's father had had a prominent position in both the professional and African American social communities, leading to a pervasive awareness of the possible impact of any family member's personal behavior on the family's position in the community. Intellect and a "big smile" were discussed in the family as the best ways to withstand social assaults during the racially turbulent period of Janelle's childhood.

Janelle did not date anyone in high school or in college, even though she did meet women to whom she felt attractions. She reported that too many people knew her family and dating women would have become a matter of gossip and intense social judgment. In addition, she "felt within her bones" that her same-sex attraction was wrong in the eyes of God. After a few years of postcollege employment, a move to a larger city with a greater variety of professional opportunities was appealing to her. At the same time, the decision to relocate was "extremely difficult"; she had never lived far from her mother, who feared for her safety in a big city. Janelle was also terrified to meet other lesbians, feeling that to do so might lead her down a path that involved "selling her soul to the devil." Before she moved, she disclosed her sexual orientation to her mother, who reacted with both discomfort and some support.

Janelle found acclimating to the new area particularly difficult. She was afraid to connect with other African American individuals for fear of rejection because of her sexual orientation, and at the same time the idea of socializing in the lesbian community was quite anxiety provoking. Although her Southern Baptist church at home had offered a sense of community (provided that she not disclose her sexuality), she was hesitant to search for a faith community here, even though the absence of worship in her life was a loss. After confiding these issues to a work friend, Janelle eventually began to consider the friend's advice to speak with a counselor. Janelle agreed that this might be helpful, but only if the counselor were "just normal," meaning not a part of any minority community.

Janelle was pleased to find a counselor named Barbara, originally from England, who described herself as interested in helping all clients understand what they would like to create in life and assisting them in pursuing that. After several months of working together on stressors related to the move to this new city and her new job, Janelle confided her same-sex attractions to Barbara and the difficulty this issue continued to present in her life. She expressed her feelings of shame, immorality, and sense of uncleanliness related to her sexual minority status. It was clear to Barbara that these feelings stemmed from negative messages put forward by Janelle's faith of origin and that they were deeply rooted. At the same time, Barbara could see the significant loss that Janelle was experiencing by not having a faith community in her life.

Barbara began working with Janelle to understand what her faith and religion meant to her, both throughout her life, and currently. She asked Janelle to detail the messages that she had received about nonheterosexuality and how she understood them in relation to her own sexual orientation. Barbara also asked Janelle questions to elicit her feelings about religion, the issues of loss that Janelle has experienced, and what kind of religious life Janelle would have in an ideal world. Barbara wove this into this discussion her understanding of the other identity contexts of Janelle's life and asked Janelle for more information and clarification when it was needed. For example, Barbara and Janelle discussed the role of African American women in her church and community, the importance of having children for many African Americans, and how her family and community at home would react to her having children in a relationship with a woman. Part of this discussion centered on the increasing pressures Janelle was facing from her family because of her age and perceptions that she was running out of time to bear children.

From the understanding that Barbara was developing of Janelle, she felt Janelle might benefit from exploring various Baptist denominations to gain awareness of how these different Baptist traditions understand same-sex attraction. Barbara hoped that this exploration might create possibilities within Janelle to feel more positively about her sexual orientation and a possible reconnection with religion. In discussing this potential action with Janelle, it was clear that she was both scared and excited about the possibility of learning new viewpoints. Janelle preferred to do this exploration online, and Barbara referred her to several websites.

As Janelle was doing her online exploration, she and Barbara spent several sessions imagining her life as it would be if she decided (a) to prioritize her religion and remain in the closet, (b) to prioritize her sexual orientation and leave religion altogether, (c) to be open about her sexual orientation and remain in her Southern Baptist denomination, (d) to be open about her sexual orientation but join a more affirming faith tradition, and (e) to not make a decision. Deep exploration of how she imagined her life, her relationships, her future about 10 years down the road, and her feelings and thoughts about each possibility led Janelle to realize that she needed to make a decision sooner rather than later. Learning about different Baptist denominations that were affirming of same-sex sexual attraction helped her identify what felt the most important to her about religion, which was her connection to God and to a community of like-minded people. Recognizing this led Janelle to eventually seek out and attend services at a liberal Baptist congregation. Fearing she might be the only African American person in attendance, she was pleased to see that the congregation was quite diverse and welcoming.

As Janelle continued to attend her new church, she and Barbara continued to explore her feelings about her sexual orientation, how they developed, how they were reinforced throughout her life, and how her new experiences at church were opening her up to the possibility that she might be worthy of love in both God's eyes and the eyes of her family and community. Barbara encouraged her to speak with leaders of her church for assistance with navigating the chasm between the old religious messages she grew up hearing and these new interpretations. Thinking about herself in new ways was somewhat strange to Janelle, and it would require more time and experience before she felt a more integrated and positive self-concept.

CONCLUSION

Although many religious traditions continue to promote negative messages about sexual minority and TGNC people that may result in harmful outcomes, we found that some nonaffirming religions had branches that were more supportive and affirming. Several models for resolving the conflict between religious identity and sexual–gender identity were identified; none have been empirically tested to date. Research on these models is sorely needed. These models potentially have broad utility for helping all people, not just sexual minority and TGNC individuals, resolve internal conflicts and promote more inclusive communities. Not surprisingly, the literature focused primarily on majority culture clients (White, middle-class, male, Christian); there is a great need for scholarship on sexual minority and TGNC people of color and on conflicts associated with other religious faiths. Additionally, little research has focused specifically on TGNC individuals; more research is needed. Finally, as society continues to move toward more acceptance of sexual minority and TGNC people, the intensity of some of these conflicts may lessen. In our view, hope is warranted.

REFERENCES

Abu-Raiya, H., & Pargament, K. I. (2015). Religious coping among diverse religions: Commonalities and divergences. *Psychology of Religion and Spirituality, 7,* 24–33. http://dx.doi.org/10.1037/a0037652

American Baptist Churches USA. (n.d.). *Responses/actions pertaining to homosexuality.* Retrieved from http://www.abc-usa.org/wp-content/uploads/2012/06/homosexuality.pdf

APA Task Force on Appropriate Therapeutic Responses to Sexual Orientation. (2009). *Report of the task force on appropriate therapeutic responses to sexual orientation.* Washington, DC: American Psychological Association.

Barnes, D. M., & Meyer, I. H. (2012). Religious affiliation, internalized homophobia, and mental health in lesbians, gay men, and bisexuals. *American Journal of Ortho-psychiatry, 82*, 505–515. http://dx.doi.org/10.1111/j.1939-0025.2012.01185.x

Barret, R., & Barzan, R. (1996). Spiritual experiences of gay men and lesbians. *Counseling and Values, 41*, 4–15. http://dx.doi.org/10.1002/j.2161-007X.1996.tb00858.x

Bartoli, E., & Gillem, A. R. (2008). Continuing to depolarize the debate on sexual orientation and religion: Identity and the therapeutic process. *Professional Psychology: Research and Practice, 39*, 202–209. http://dx.doi.org/10.1037/0735-7028.39.2.202

BBC News. (2013, July 29). *Pope Francis: Who am I to judge gay people?* Retrieved from http://www.bbc.com/news/world-europe-23489702

Beckstead, A. L., & Morrow, S. L. (2004). Mormon clients' experiences of conversion therapy: The need for a new treatment approach. *The Counseling Psychologist, 32*, 651–690.

Bordeyne, P. (2006). Homosexuality, seen in relation to ecumenical dialogue: What really matters to the Catholic Church. *New Blackfriars, 87*, 561–577. http://dx.doi.org/10.1111/j.1741-2005.2006.00116.x

Bozard, R. J., & Sanders, C. J. (2011). Helping Christian lesbian, gay, and bisexual clients recover religion as a source of strength: Developing a model for assessment and integration of religious identity in counseling. *Journal of LGBT Issues in Counseling, 5*, 47–74. http://dx.doi.org/10.1080/15538605.2011.554791

Buchanan, M., Dzelme, K., Harris, D., & Hecker, L. (2001). Challenge of being simultaneously gay or lesbian and spiritual and/or religious: A narrative perspective. *The American Journal of Family Therapy, 29*, 435–449. http://dx.doi.org/10.1080/01926180127629

Buser, J. K., Goodrich, K. M., Luke, M., & Buser, T. J. (2011). A narratology of lesbian, gay, bisexual, and transgender clients' experiences addressing religious and spiritual issues in counseling. *Journal of LGBT Issues in Counseling, 5*, 282–303. http://dx.doi.org/10.1080/15538605.2011.632395

Campbell, H. A. (2012). Understanding the relationship between religion online and offline in a networked society. *Journal of the American Academy of Religion, 80*, 64–93. http://dx.doi.org/10.1093/jaarel/lfr074

Catholic Answers to Explain and Defend the Faith. (2004). *Homosexuality*. Retrieved from http://www.catholic.com/tracts/homosexuality

Chatters, L. M., Bullard, K. M., Taylor, R. J., Woodward, A. T., Neighbors, H. W., & Jackson, J. S. (2008). Religious participation and *DSM–IV* disorders among older African Americans: Findings from the National Survey of American Life. *The American Journal of Geriatric Psychiatry, 16*, 957–965. http://dx.doi.org/10.1097/JGP.0b013e3181898081

Cole, E. R. (2009). Intersectionality and research in psychology. *American Psychologist, 64*, 170–180. http://dx.doi.org/10.1037/a0014564

Congregation for Catholic Education. (2005, November 4). *Instruction concerning the criteria for the discernment of vocations with regard to persons with homosexual tendencies in view of their admission to the seminary and to Holy Orders.* Retrieved from http://www.vatican.va/roman_curia/congregations/ccatheduc/documents/rc_con_ccatheduc_doc_20051104_istruzione_en.html

Covenant of the Alliance of Baptists. (2012, April 14). *A statement on lifelong sexual education, sexual & reproductive rights, and opposing sexual injustice and violence.* Retrieved from http://allianceofbaptists.org/documents/LifelongSexual Education2012.pdf

Dahl, A. L., & Galliher, R. V. (2012). LGBTQ adolescents and young adults raised within a Christian religious context: Positive and negative outcomes. *Journal of Adolescence, 35*(6), 1611–1618. http://dx.doi.org/10.1016/j.adolescence.2012.07.003

Davis, D. S. (2008). Religion, genetics, and sexual orientation: The Jewish tradition. *Kennedy Institute of Ethics Journal, 18,* 125–148. http://dx.doi.org/10.1353/ken.0.0008

Dehlin, J. P., Galliher, R. V., Bradshaw, W. S., Hyde, D. C., & Crowell, K. A. (2015). Sexual orientation change efforts among current or former LDS church members. *Journal of Counseling Psychology, 62,* 95–105. http://dx.doi.org/10.1037/cou0000011

Eidhamar, L. G. (2014). Is gayness a test from Allah? Typologies in Muslim stances on homosexuality. *Islam & Christian–Muslim Relations, 25,* 245–266. http://dx.doi.org/10.1080/09596410.2013.869882

Eliason, M. J., Burke, A., van Olphen, J., & Howell, R. (2011). Complex interactions of sexual identity, sex/gender, and religious/spiritual identity on substance use among college students. *Sexuality Research & Social Policy, 8,* 117–125. http://dx.doi.org/10.1007/s13178-011-0046-1

Ellison, C. G., Boardman, J. D., Williams, D. R., & Jackson, J. S. (2001). Religious involvement, stress, and mental health: Findings from the 1995 Detroit Area Study. *Social Forces, 80,* 215–249. http://dx.doi.org/10.1353/sof.2001.0063

Eskenazi, J., & Harris, B. (2007). *Blessed are the transgendered, say S.F. rabbi and the Reform movement.* Retrieved from http://www.jweekly.com/article/full/33139/blessed-are-the-transgendered-say-s-f-rabbi-and-the-reform-movement/

Fredriksen-Goldsen, K. I., Kim, H.-J., Emlet, C. A., Muraco, A., Erosheva, E. A., Hoy-Ellis, C. P., Goldsen, J., & Petry, H. (2011). *The aging and health report: Disparities and resilience among lesbian, gay, bisexual, and transgender older adults.* Seattle, WA: Institute for Multigenerational Health.

Gallagher, D., & Burke, D. (2014, October 14). *Under conservative assault, Vatican backtracks on gay comments.* Retrieved from http://www.cnn.com/2014/10/14/world/vatican-backtrack-gays/index.html

García, D. I., Gray-Stanley, J., & Ramirez-Valles, J. (2008). "The priest obviously doesn't know that I'm gay": The religious and spiritual journeys of Latino gay men. *Journal of Homosexuality, 55,* 411–436. http://dx.doi.org/10.1080/00918360802345149

Ginicola, M. M., & Smith, C. (2011). The church, the closet, and the couch: The counselor's role in assisting clients to integrate their sexual orientation and religious identity. *Journal of LGBT Issues in Counseling, 5*, 304–326. http://dx.doi.org/10.1080/15538605.2011.632309

Golub, S. A., Walker, J. J., Longmire-Avital, B., Bimbi, D. S., & Parsons, J. T. (2010). The role of religiosity, social support, and stress-related growth in protecting against HIV risk among transgender women. *Journal of Health Psychology, 15*, 1135–1144. http://dx.doi.org/10.1177/1359105310364169

Hagen, W. B., Arczynski, A. V., Morrow, S. L., & Hawxhurst, D. M. (2011). Lesbian, bisexual, and queer women's spirituality in feminist multicultural counseling. *Journal of LGBT Issues in Counseling, 5*, 220–236. http://dx.doi.org/10.1080/15538605.2011.633070

Haldeman, D. C. (2002). Gay rights, patient rights: The implications of sexual orientation conversion therapy. *Professional Psychology: Research and Practice, 33*, 260–264. http://dx.doi.org/10.1037/0735-7028.33.3.260

Haldeman, D. C. (2004). When sexual and religious orientation collide: Considerations in working with conflicted same-sex attracted male clients. *The Counseling Psychologist, 32*, 691–715. http://dx.doi.org/10.1177/0011000004267560

Halkitis, P. N., Mattis, J. S., Sahadath, J. K., Massie, D., Ladyzhenskaya, L., Pitrelli, K., . . . Cowie, S. E. (2009). The meanings and manifestations of religion and spirituality among lesbian, gay, bisexual, and transgender adults. *Journal of Adult Development, 16*, 250–262. http://dx.doi.org/10.1007/s10804-009-9071-1

Hamblin, R., & Gross, A. M. (2013). Role of religious attendance and identity conflict in psychological well-being. *Journal of Religion and Health, 52*, 817–827. http://dx.doi.org/10.1007/s10943-011-9514-4

Hattie, B., & Beagan, B. L. (2013). Reconfiguring spirituality and sexual/gender identity: "It's a feeling of connection to something bigger, it's part of a wholeness." *Journal of Religion & Spirituality in Social Work: Social Thought, 32*, 244–268. http://dx.doi.org/10.1080/15426432.2013.801733

Hatzenbuehler, M. L., Pachankis, J. E., & Wolff, J. (2012). Religious climate and health risk behaviors in sexual minority youths: A population-based study. *American Journal of Public Health, 102*, 657–663. http://dx.doi.org/10.2105/AJPH.2011.300517

Hinkley, G. B. (1995). *The family: A proclamation to the world.* Retrieved from http://www.lds.org/topics/family-proclamation

Hunt, M. E. (2006). Catholic pride . . . and prejudice. *Conscience, 5*, 11–16. Retrieved from http://www.catholicsforchoice.org/topics/sexuality/documents/prideandprej.pdf

Jamal, A. (2001). The story of Lot and the Qur'an's perception of the mortality of same-sex sexuality. *Journal of Homosexuality, 41*, 1–88. http://dx.doi.org/10.1300/J082v41n01_01

Jewish Telegraphic Agency. (2007). *Reform devises sex-change blessings*. Retrieved from http://www.forward.com/articles/11403/reform-devises-sex-change-belssings-/#ixzz2FRMb98N7

Johns, R. D., & Hanna, F. J. (2011). Peculiar and queer: Spiritual and emotional salvation for the LGBTQ Mormon. *Journal of LGBT Issues in Counseling, 5,* 197–219. http://dx.doi.org/10.1080/15538605.2011.633157

Kidd, J. D., & Witten, T. M. (2008). Understanding spirituality and religiosity in the transgender community: Implications for aging. *Journal of Religion, Spirituality & Aging, 20,* 29–62. http://dx.doi.org/10.1080/15528030801922004

Kligerman, N. (2007). Homosexuality in Islam: A difficult paradox. *Macalester Islam Journal, 2,* 52–64. Retrieved from http://digitalcommons.macalester.edu/islam/vol2/iss3/8

Kocet, M. M., Sanabria, S., & Smith, M. R. (2011). Finding the spirit within: Religion, spirituality, and faith development in lesbian, gay, and bisexual individuals. *Journal of LGBT Issues in Counseling, 5,* 163–179. http://dx.doi.org/10.1080/15538605.2011.633060

Krause, N. (2004). Common facets of religion, unique facets of religion, and life satisfaction among older African Americans. *Journal of Gerontology: Social Sciences, 59B,* S109–S117. http://dx.doi.org/10.1093/geronb/59.2.S109

Kugle, S. S. (2010). *Homosexuality in Islam: Critical reflection on gay, lesbian, and transgender Muslims.* Oxford, England: Oneworld.

Ladin, J. (2012). *Through the door of life: A Jewish journey between genders.* Madison: University of Wisconsin Press.

LDS Church. (2010). *Handbook 1: Bishops and stake presidents.* Salt Lake City, UT: Author.

Lease, S. H., Horne, S. G., & Noffsinger-Frazier, N. (2005). Affirming faith experiences and psychological health for Caucasian lesbian, gay, and bisexual individuals. *Journal of Counseling Psychology, 52,* 378–388. http://dx.doi.org/10.1037/0022-0167.52.3.378

Levy, D. L., & Lo, J. R. (2013). Transgender, transsexual, and gender queer individuals with a Christian upbringing: The process of resolving conflict between gender identity and faith. *Journal of Religion & Spirituality in Social Work: Social Thought, 32,* 60–83. http://dx.doi.org/10.1080/15426432.2013.749079

Markoe, L. (2012). *Conservative Jews' shift on gay rites causes no stir.* Retrieved from http://www.christiancentury.org/article/2012-06/conservative-jews-gay-wedding-rules-mostly-met-shrug

McConkie, B. (1966). *Mormon doctrine* (2nd ed.). Salt Lake City, UT: Bookcraft.

McGinniss, M. (2010). The church's response to the homosexual. *The Journal of Ministry & Theology, 14,* 129–163.

Mission Islam. (n.d.). *Islam and homosexuality.* Retrieved from http://www.missionislam.com/knowledge/homosexuality.htm

Morris, B. (1987). Challenge, criticism and compassion: Modern Jewish responses to Jewish homosexuals. *Jewish Social Studies, 49*, 283–292.

Morrow, S. L., & Hawxhurst, D. M. (1998). Feminist therapy: Integrating political analysis in counseling and psychotherapy. *Women & Therapy, 21*, 37–50. http://dx.doi.org/10.1300/J015v21n02_03

Moss, J. A., & Ulmer, R. B. (2008). "Two men under one cloak"—the Sages permit it: Homosexual marriage in Judaism. *Journal of Homosexuality, 55*, 71–105. http://dx.doi.org/10.1080/00918360802129337

Ott, K. M. (2009). *Sex and the seminary: Preparing ministers for sexual health and justice*. Retrieved from http://www.religiousinstitute.org/sex-and-the-seminary-preparing-ministers-for-sexual-health-and-justice/

Page, M. J. L., Lindahl, K. M., & Malik, N. M. (2013). The role of religion and stress in sexual identity and mental health among LGB youth. *Journal of Research on Adolescence, 23*, 665–677. http://dx.doi.org/10.1111/jora.12025

Pearce, M. (2014, April 6). Mormon Church: Same-sex marriage and gay sex are still not OK. *Los Angeles Times*. Retrieved from http://articles.latimes.com/2014/apr/06/nation/la-na-nn-mormon-same-sex-marriage-20140406

Porter, K. E., Ronneberg, C. R., & Witten, T. M. (2013). Religious affiliation and successful aging among transgender older adults: Findings from the Trans MetLife survey. *Journal of Religion, Spirituality & Aging, 25*, 112–138. http://dx.doi.org/10.1080/15528030.2012.739988

Rabinowitz, M. E. (2003). *Status of transsexuals*. Retrieved from http://keshet.wpengine.netdna-cdn.com/wp-content/uploads/2012/02/Status-of-Transsexuals.pdf

Ream, G. L., & Savin-Williams, R. C. (2005). Reconciling Christianity and positive non-heterosexual identity in adolescence, with implication for psychological well-being. *Journal of Gay & Lesbian Issues in Education, 2*(3), 19–36. http://dx.doi.org/10.1300/J367v02n03_03

Rodriguez, E. M., & Follins, L. D. (2012). Did God make me this way? Expanding psychological research on queer religiosity and spirituality to include intersex and transgender individuals. *Psychology and Sexuality, 3*, 214–225. http://dx.doi.org/10.1080/19419899.2012.700023

Rodriguez, E. M., & Ouellette, S. C. (2000). Gay and lesbian Christians: Homosexual and religious identity integration in the members and participants of a gay-positive church. *Journal for the Scientific Study of Religion, 39*, 333–347. http://dx.doi.org/10.1111/0021-8294.00028

Schuck, K. D., & Liddle, B. J. (2001). Religious conflicts experienced by lesbian, gay, and bisexual individuals. *Journal of Gay & Lesbian Psychotherapy, 5*(2), 63–82. http://dx.doi.org/10.1300/J236v05n02_07

Scruggs, J. R. (2012). *A statement on the same-sex marriage issue, voting and Christian responsibility*. Retrieved from National Baptist Convention website: http://www.nationalbaptist.com/about-us/news--press-releases/the-same-sex-marriage-issue,-voting-and-christian-responsibility.html

Serovich, J. M., Craft, S. M., Toviessi, P., Gangamma, R., McDowell, T., & Grafsky, E. L. (2008). A systematic review of the research base on sexual reorientation therapies. *Journal of Marital and Family Therapy, 34*, 227–238. http://dx.doi.org/10.1111/j.1752-0606.2008.00065.x

Shelton, K., & Delgado-Romero, E. A. (2011). Sexual orientation microaggressions: The experience of lesbian, gay, bisexual, and queer clients in psychotherapy. *Journal of Counseling Psychology, 58*, 210–221. http://dx.doi.org/10.1037/a0022251

Sheridan, V. (2001). *Crossing over: Liberating the transgendered Christian.* Cleveland, OH: Pilgrim Press.

Sherry, A., Adelman, A., Whilde, M. R., & Quick, D. (2010). Competing selves: Negotiating the intersection of spiritual and sexual identities. *Professional Psychology: Research and Practice, 41*, 112–119. http://dx.doi.org/10.1037/a0017471

Shidlo, A., & Schroeder, M. (2002). Changing sexual orientation: A consumers' report. *Professional Psychology: Research and Practice, 33*, 249–259. http://dx.doi.org/10.1037/0735-7028.33.3.249

Smith, B. L., & Home, S. G. (2008). What's faith got to do with it? The role of spirituality and religion in lesbian and bisexual women's sexual satisfaction. *Women & Therapy, 31*, 73–87. http://dx.doi.org/10.1300/02703140802145243

Southern Baptist Convention. (1988). *Resolution on homosexuality.* Retrieved from http://www.sbc.net/resolutions/610/resolution-on-homosexuality

Southern Baptist Convention. (2008). *On the California Supreme Court decision to allow same-sex marriage.* Retrieved from http://www.sbc.net/resolutions/1190/on-the-california-supreme-court-decision-to-allow-samesex-marriage

Southern Baptist Convention. (2014). *On transgender identity.* Retrieved from http://www.sbc.net/resolutions/2250/on-transgender-identity

Statement of Principles on the Place of Jews With a Homosexual Orientation in Our Community. (2010, July). Retrieved from http://www.statementofprinciplesnya.blogspot.com

Super, J. T., & Jacobson, L. (2011). Religious abuse: Implications for counseling lesbian, gay, bisexual, and transgender individuals. *Journal of LGBT Issues in Counseling, 5*(3-4), 180–196. http://dx.doi.org/10.1080/15538605.2011.632739

Szymanski, D. M., Kashubeck-West, S., & Meyer, J. (2008). Internalized heterosexism: Measurement, psychosocial correlates, and research directions. *The Counseling Psychologist, 36*, 525–574. http://dx.doi.org/10.1177/0011000007309489

Tozer, E. E., & Hayes, J. A. (2004). Why do individuals seek conversion therapy? The role of religiosity, internalized homonegativity, and identity development. *The Counseling Psychologist, 32*, 716–740. http://dx.doi.org/10.1177/0011000004267563

U.S. Census Bureau. (2012). *Statistical Abstract of the United States: 2012.* Retrieved from http://www2.census.gov/library/publications/2011/compendia/statab/131ed/2012-statab.pdf

Wagner, G. J., Aunon, F. M., Kaplan, R. L., Karam, R., Khouri, D., Tohme, J., & Mokhbat, J. (2013). Sexual stigma, psychological well-being and social engagement among men who have sex with men in Beirut, Lebanon. *Culture, Health & Sexuality, 15,* 570–582. http://dx.doi.org/10.1080/13691058.2013.775345

Waldenberg, E. Y. (n.d.). *About the responsa of Rabbi Eliezer Yehuda Waldenberg, author of the Tzitz Eliezer, which are relevant to the status of transsexuals.* Retrieved from http://www.starways.net/beth/tzitz.html

Wertheimer, J. (2007, September 1). *The perplexities of Conservative Judaism.* Retrieved from http://www.commentarymagazine.com/article/the-perplexities-of-conservative-judaism/

Whitehead, J. D., & Whitehead, E. E. (2014). Transgender lives: From bewilderment to God's extravagance. *Pastoral Psychology, 63,* 171–184. http://dx.doi.org/10.1007/s11089-013-0543-7

Witten, T. M., & Eyler, A. E. (Eds.). (2012). *Gay, lesbian, bisexual and transgender aging: Challenges in research practice and policy.* Baltimore, MD: Johns Hopkins University Press.

Yarhouse, M. A. (1998). When clients seek treatment for same-sex attraction: Ethical issues in the "right to choose" debate. *Psychotherapy: Theory, Research Practice, Training, 35,* 248–259. http://dx.doi.org/10.1037/h0087753

9

SPECIAL ISSUES IN PSYCHOTHERAPY WITH SEXUAL MINORITY AND TRANSGENDER AND GENDER NONCONFORMING ADOLESCENTS

TYREL J. STARKS AND BRETT M. MILLAR

During the developmental stage known as adolescence, a number of major life events and factors—such as puberty, transitioning into high school, and an increasing autonomy from parents—coincide to mark the teenage years (roughly ages 12–13 to 17–18) as a period of significant physical, psychological, and social changes. Some of these changes arrive abruptly and are keenly felt, while others exert their influence more gradually and subtly. For many adolescents, these changes are accompanied by expanding opportunities for autonomy. In part because of this, the period of adolescence has been characterized by the challenge of establishing one's identity (Erikson, 1980).

In recent decades, the view of adolescence as the brief timespan that bridges childhood to adulthood has been superseded by the view that the tasks of identity exploration and transformation continue well beyond the age of 18. The period from age 18 to 29 is now seen as a distinct developmental stage, termed *emerging adulthood* (Arnett, 2000). For the purposes of this chapter,

http://dx.doi.org/10.1037/15959-010
Handbook of Sexual Orientation and Gender Diversity in Counseling and Psychotherapy, K. A. DeBord, A. R. Fischer, K. J. Bieschke, and R. M. Perez (Editors)

we focus specifically on the developmental context of adolescence. We begin by situating sexual minority and transgender and gender nonconforming (TGNC) adolescents within the context of recent sociopolitical changes and identity development theories.

In recent years there have been major advances for sexual minority and TGNC people in the Western world: in legislation, in politics, and visibility in mainstream media and sports. The Internet has also vastly increased access to role models, social support, and information—for example, the Trevor Project (http://www.trevorproject.org) and the It Gets Better Project (http://www.itgetsbetter.org). These sources of legitimizing support and acknowledgment were simply not part of the landscape for sexual minority and TGNC youth until very recently.

However, such progress does not evenly trickle down. Access to its benefits can greatly vary and depends on numerous factors including: where sexual minority and TGNC adolescents live; whether their family and friends are religiously, culturally, or socially conservative; what kind of environment is created within their school; and whether the adolescent is exploring their sexual identity, their gender identity, or both. Determining how to handle the concealment of one's sexual identity, braving negative responses to nonconforming gender expression, persevering through disruptions in important interpersonal relationships, experiencing elevated rates of health-risk behavior, and enduring high levels of emotional distress are challenges that continue to significantly burden these youth. To better understand this constellation of factors, we first consider adolescence in the context of sexual and gender development. Next, we review physical and mental health disparities frequently encountered by sexual minority and TGNC adolescents. Finally, we present recommendations for addressing these challenges in psychotherapy with sexual minority and TGNC adolescents.

ADOLESCENCE IN THE CONTEXT OF SEXUAL AND GENDER DEVELOPMENT

The exploration of sexual identity and gender identity constitutes a substantial part of the identity development process for sexual minority and TGNC youth; however, individuals can vary greatly in the timing and trajectory of this identity development process (Rosario, Schrimshaw, Hunter, & Braun, 2006). In a sample of 133 gay or lesbian youth (D'Augelli, Rendina, Sinclair, & Grossman, 2008), the average age of first awareness of same-sex attraction was 9.3 years; self-identification as gay or lesbian, however, occurred more than 4 years later, at 13.8 years. Disclosing to a friend occurred at 14.5 years and disclosing to a parent occurred at 14.7 years. These data suggest that a sexual minority adolescent may, on average, experience 5 years of being aware of same-sex attraction before seeking support from friends or family.

Developmental research conducted in the past decade has highlighted the fluid nature of sexual identity processes. While approximately 70% of adolescents and college-age respondents who identified as gay, lesbian, or bisexual retained this identity (Diamond, 2000; Rosario et al., 2006), approximately half of those reporting some level of same-sex attraction did not, in the long term, identify as gay, lesbian, or bisexual. In sum, many people self-report some level of same-sex attraction; however, substantial within-person variability in attraction, behavior, and identity means that not all same-sex attraction leads to subsequent behavior or integration into a sexual minority identity.

The available literature suggests that adolescence is also a pivotal time for gender identity development among TGNC youth, as early experiences of dissonance between felt gender identity and physiological sex are made more acute with the onset of puberty (Devor, 2004; Morgan & Stevens, 2008). In their study of 55 TGNC youth, Grossman, D'Augelli, and Frank (2011) found that the average age of "feeling different from others" was 8 years old. Meanwhile, on average, the male-to-female TGNC youth identified as transgender at age 13 and disclosed to parents at age 14, while the female-to-male TGNC youth identified as transgender at age 15 and disclosed to parents at age 17. Other developmental work is beginning to examine intersections between gender and sexual identity development by exploring the unique experiences of such development for transgender-identified individuals (Bockting, Benner, & Coleman, 2009). However, it is vital that counselors take care to not automatically lump issues of sexual orientation in with gender identity, as many transgender individuals may not identify as gay, lesbian, or bisexual (Clements-Nolle, Marx, Guzman, & Katz, 2001). The continuation of such work, and the translation of findings into comprehensive developmental theory, will be critical in enhancing our understanding of the experiences of TGNC adolescents.

MENTAL AND PHYSICAL HEALTH DISPARITIES

The cultural context for sexual minority and TGNC adolescents in the United States has changed rapidly in recent years. The research literature is not yet able to confirm whether and how these most recent sociocultural changes have impacted the lived experience and health of sexual minority and TGNC youth; however, some evidence of change is emerging within academic discourse in which sexual minority and TGNC issues are increasingly being framed in terms of resilience and strengths rather than focusing solely on deficits and psychopathology (e.g., Harper, Brodsky, & Bruce, 2012; Singh,

Hays, & Watson, 2011). Despite these promising trends, there is ample evidence that sexual minority and TGNC youth continue to experience health disparities compared with their heterosexual counterparts. In this section, we highlight some of these, including disruptions in interpersonal relationships, substance use, sexually transmitted infection risk, anxiety, and depression.

Disruptions in Interpersonal Relationships

Adolescence is commonly characterized by an expansion of one's social universe and an increase in the salience of peer relationships (Erikson, 1980). Both peer and parental support and acceptance are powerful determinants of outcomes for sexual minority and TGNC youth (Henrich, Brookmeyer, Shrier, & Shahar, 2006). In this section, we briefly review literature examining peer and parental relationship factors among sexual minority and TGNC youth. The section ends with a focus on emerging romantic relationships—a unique form of peer relationship.

Both general parent–adolescent relationship quality and parental acceptance of their adolescent's sexual minority and TGNC identity are significantly associated with positive outcomes, such as greater self-esteem, perceived social support, and general health, while parental rejection is strongly associated with adverse outcomes (Ryan, 2010). Rejected youth reported significantly higher rates of depression, suicide attempts, illicit substance use, risky sex, and safety issues involved in running away and homelessness (Saewyc, 2011). Importantly, prior to coming out, a majority of sexual minority and TGNC adolescents anticipated that their parents would react negatively to the disclosure (D'Augelli et al., 2008). This anticipated fear is associated with increased levels of anxiety, increased substance use, and decreased assertiveness in relationships (Pachankis, Goldfried, & Ramrattan, 2008).

It is unfortunate that many sexual minority and TGNC youth do not just anticipate negative reactions from family members, they also experience them. For example, 52% of sexual minority individuals reported parental rejection during the initial stages of coming out (D'Augelli et al., 2008). Baiocco and colleagues (2014) cited findings that parents are more likely to react negatively to their child's coming out if the parent is of older age, more religious, less educated, or more traditional in their values regarding family, marriage, and gender roles. Furthermore, a father is more likely to react negatively if the child is male, while a mother is more likely to react negatively if the child is female (D'Augelli, 2006). A negative coming out process may create additional stressors such as verbal and physical confrontation, the loss of support, increased social isolation, and the reinforcement of negative self-image (Rosario, Schrimshaw, & Hunter, 2009). Because of their status as legal minors, adolescents have relatively few resources to respond to severe forms of parental rejection. Not surprisingly, sexual minority and TGNC youth are overrepresented in the population of homeless youth, and these youth are incredibly vulnerable (National Coalition for the Homeless, 2009).

Similar to parental rejection, peer rejection has been connected to adverse outcomes for sexual minority and TGNC youth, including increased substance use, trauma symptoms (see Chapter 7, this volume), and suicidal ideation and behaviors (D'Augelli, 2002). Research indicates that experiences of social rejection, teasing, and bullying are all too common. In a recent study of more than 8,000 sexual minority and TGNC students ages 13 through 20, eight in 10 reported recent verbal victimization, four in 10 reported physical harassment, six in 10 felt unsafe at school, and more than half had experienced cyberbullying (Kosciw, Greytak, Bartkiewicz, Boesen, & Palmer, 2012).

Taken together, these results suggest that psychotherapy with sexual minority and TGNC adolescents should incorporate a thorough evaluation of how culture, religion, and immediate social environment may present additional challenges, as increased victimization has been observed in numerous ethnic and cultural communities (Moradi et al., 2010). The consequences of peer rejection may be particularly potent in the school setting. In a study by Grossman and D'Augelli (2006), one TGNC participant described school as "the most traumatic aspect of growing up" (p. 122). Bullying and victimization have been associated with lower grades, fewer plans for postsecondary school education, higher levels of depression, and increased rates of absenteeism, jeopardizing opportunities for both academic and social development among sexual minority and TGNC adolescents (Kosciw et al., 2012).

As sexual minority and TGNC adolescents explore the prospect of dating, they are confronted with unique barriers and challenges that their heterosexual peers are far less likely to encounter. For example, not all sexual-health programs offered in public schools provide information relevant to same-sex sexual behavior or integrate information about diverse sexual and gender identities (Formby, 2011). At the same time, sexual minority and TGNC youth typically have fewer potential partners from which to choose, and may not receive the social validation and support for their relationship generally given to heterosexual couples. Same-sex attracted youth are also more likely to have their romantic hopes dashed by the realization that the person they desire does not share the same sexual orientation, and the possible backlash from approaching a peer with an incompatible sexual orientation is much greater. In addition, public interaction with a same-sex partner, such as going out on a date or public displays of affection, may bring a risk of disclosure that not all sexual minority and TGNC youth are prepared to handle.

Cutting across various interpersonal relationships, Starks, Newcomb, and Mustanski (2015) examined associations among parental attachment, peer attachment, and romantic relationship quality. Their research was guided by attachment theory (Ainsworth, 1985), which posits that individuals formulate internal working models of the self and of others through initial interactions with caregivers. These models in turn shape subsequent interactions with important others. Starks et al. (2015) found that peer and parental attachment were positively associated with one another and both contributed uniquely to the prediction of global mental health. In turn, stronger peer attachments earlier in adolescence were indirectly associated with later romantic relationship quality through a pathway mediated by global mental health functioning.

Substance Use

Rates of substance use, particularly heavy drinking and marijuana use, among adolescents in general in the United States are high. Results from the Youth Risk Behavior Surveillance (YRBS; Kann et al., 2014) indicate that 23.1% of ninth through 12th graders used marijuana and 21.9% engaged in heavy drinking. Higher rates of substance use among sexual minority individuals compared with their heterosexual counterparts are also well documented (Austin & Bozick, 2011), and evidence suggests that these disparities in substance use prevalence emerge during adolescence (Marshal et al., 2008).

Substance use among TGNC youth has received much less attention. The YRBS does not provide data specifically related to substance use among TGNC youth. In their community sample of TGNC female youth between the ages of 16 and 25, Garofalo, Deleon, Osmer, Doll, and Harper (2006) observed rates of alcohol (65%), marijuana (71%), ecstasy (23%), and cocaine (21%) use that were somewhat higher than the estimated rates of alcohol (43.7%) and marijuana (20.2%) use provided by Herbst et al. (2008) based on the results of 29 studies of TGNC people. This combination of findings across studies suggests that TGNC adolescents and young adults may be even more likely to use substances than older TGNC people.

The use of substances may serve a range of functions for sexual minority and TGNC youth not commonly shared by their heterosexual counterparts. Substance use may serve to help cope with feelings of anxiety, depression, or other experiences of stigma. Recent research has indicated that the link between rejection sensitivity and alcohol consumption is stronger among those sexual minority men who were exposed to higher levels of structural stigma during adolescence (Pachankis, Hatzenbuehler, & Starks, 2014). In addition, substance use may alleviate social anxiety and facilitate interaction with peers and potential sexual or romantic partners, and may also be used to reduce anxiety or enhance feelings of closeness during sex (Brennan & Shaver, 1995; Feeney, Peterson, Gallois, & Terry, 2000).

Sexual Health Risk Behavior

Substance use and sexual health risk-taking behavior are health challenges that commonly occur together (Poulin & Graham, 2001). It is therefore not surprising that many sexual minority and TGNC youth face elevated risk of sexually transmitted infections (STIs; CDC, 2012b), as well as increased risk of substance use (Marshal et al., 2008). Rates of new HIV infections among many of these adolescents are of particular concern (CDC, 2014).

Recent data on HIV incidence highlighted the vulnerability of sexual minority and TGNC youth, particularly youth of color. While HIV infection rates in the United States have either remained steady or declined over the past 10 years, rates of HIV infection among sexual minority men rose 12% in 2010 (CDC, 2013b). Infection rates were highest in the youngest age group, ages 13 to 24, where new infections increased 22% (CDC, 2012a). Significant racial disparities were observed in this age group, with African American and Latino youth comprising the majority of those infected (CDC, 2012a, 2013b). While lesbian and bisexual women are generally at lower risk of HIV infection than men who have sex with men, they are more likely than heterosexual women to contract and transmit STIs such as bacterial vaginosis, chlamydia, HPV, and herpes via vaginal fluid and skin contact (Office of Women's Health, 2012). When lesbian, bisexual, and other women who have sex with women also have sex with men, their risk of STI infection is increased (Bailey, 2004; Office of Women's Health, 2012).

The CDC does not provide specific information on rates of HIV infection among TGNC youth; however, incidence data suggest that the transgender community bears a disproportionate burden of HIV infection. In 2010, national incidence rates for HIV infection were 2.1% among transgender individuals compared with 0.4% among females in general and 1.2% among males in general in the United States. Transgender women are at a greater risk for HIV infection than transgender men (CDC, 2013a), and significant racial disparities in infection rates have been documented in this population. For example, the prevalence of HIV infection among African American transgender women (56.3%) is significantly higher than among their White (16.7%) and Latina (16.1%) counterparts (CDC, 2013a).

Several factors may compound HIV and STI risk for sexual minority and TGNC youth. Rates of HIV testing and condom use among high school students are low, even for those who are sexually active (CDC, 2014), and accessing medical care independent of their parents may be very difficult. Adolescents generally perceive themselves to be at lower risk of HIV infection (CDC, 2014). They may be less skillful in discussing the issue of STI risk and less effective at negotiating condom use with partners (CDC, 2011). Younger partners, particularly sexual minority men, are more likely to get HIV from older partners, and this risk increases with age disparity (CDC, 2014; Sullivan, Salazar, Buchbinder, & Sanchez, 2009) and with perceptions of the relationship as serious (Mustanski, Newcomb, & Clerkin, 2011).

Studies of sexual risk-taking with casual partners suggest that concerns about emotional closeness and intimacy are also relevant to the sexual health of young sexually active gay and bisexual men (Golub, Starks, Payton, & Parsons, 2011; Starks, Payton, Golub, Weinberger, & Parsons, 2014). The belief that condoms interfere with intimacy predicts sexual risk-taking with casual partners above and beyond the beliefs that condoms decrease sexual pleasure and reduce HIV risk (Golub et al., 2011). The association between the belief that condoms reduce intimacy and the likelihood of sexual risk-taking is greater for youth who have also experienced high levels of sexual identity-related stigma (Starks et al., 2014). While these relational factors are understudied among both those who are heterosexual and many who identify as sexual minorities in the United States, their salience for young gay and bisexual men would suggest that they may potentially be more broadly relevant to sexual health for sexual minority and TGNC youth.

Emotional Challenges and Psychological Consequences of Stigma

Sexual minority and TGNC youth face an extensive list of mental health disparities: increased rates of anxiety disorders, depression, posttraumatic stress symptoms, self-harming, and suicidal ideation and behaviors (Liu & Mustanski, 2012; Ryan, Huebner, Diaz, & Sanchez, 2009). Contrary to outdated claims that sexual minority and TGNC individuals are somehow inherently prone to psychopathology, research overwhelmingly supports the position that socially-created or external stressors are the cause of these mental health disparities (see Chapter 3, this volume, for more details). For example, Safren and Heimberg (1999) found that the significant differences in rates of depression, hopelessness, and suicidality reported by sexual minority adolescents compared with their heterosexual counterparts disappeared after statistically controlling for stress experiences. Furthermore, experiences of co-occurring sexuality-based and race-based discrimination have been shown to be strongly associated with increased rates of depression in sexual minority men of color (Bostwick, Boyd, Hughes, West, & McCabe, 2014).

Hatzenbuehler (2009) outlined a psychological mediation framework examining causal pathways linking experiences of stigma and psychopathology in sexual minority populations. This framework suggests that experiences of stigma lead to disruptions in interpersonal/social relationships, emotional dysregulation, and cognitive processing, which are implicated in the association between stigma experiences and mental health outcomes. Consistent with a psychological mediation framework, Pachankis (2007) offered a cognitive–affective–behavioral model describing the mental health effects of concealing a stigmatized identity. This work identified considerable costs associated with the salience of a concealable stigma like sexual identity, including disturbances of thought (e.g., hypervigilance, suspicion, preoccupation), mood (e.g., anxiety, depression, shame, guilt), and behavior (e.g., social isolation, impression management, impaired close relationships).

Developmental research has shown that many TGNC youth delay the full expression of their gender identity. This may take the form of wearing gender-conforming clothing or engaging in gender-conforming activities in response to social pressure or avoid stigma (Devor, 2004). Recent research has also explored how TGNC individuals face similar pressures in the workplace (Mizock & Mueser, 2014). The 2009 National Transgender Discrimination Report (Grant et al., 2010) found that experiences of discrimination were particularly prevalent for TGNC of color, again highlighting the importance of intersectionality.

The emotional experience of sexual minority and TGNC identity-related stress is unique from stress associated with other identities (e.g., race, religion, culture). Unlike these other kinds of minority identities, which are usually shared by one's parents and siblings, the sexual minority and TGNC adolescent is often the only sexual minority individual within their family home. As such, they may not have the benefit of being able to learn from how their family members deal with sexual minority stress—and as discussed earlier, instead of being a protective buffer or "shelter against the storm outside," one's family may become a major source of proximal stress, or the storm itself.

IMPLICATIONS FOR PSYCHOTHERAPY

In this section, we recommend some intervention strategies to address the challenges discussed in the previous section. First, we introduce the case of Juan, an example that illustrates salient issues in the treatment of adolescents. Then, using existing intervention research as a starting point, we describe intervention approaches to address substance use, sexual health, and mental health in an integrated manner; recommend strategies for engaging parents and addressing family factors during the informed consent process and throughout the course of treatment; and discuss the incorporation of peer and romantic relationships.

Juan[1] is a 16-year-old male-identified high school junior. He lives in a town of about 40,000 people with his parents (still married), and his two younger siblings (a brother, age 12, and a sister, age 11). His father is of

---

[1]This case example is based on fictional characters.

Dominican descent—the first generation born in the United States—and is a maintenance worker at an elementary school. Juan's mother is a nurse at the local hospital. Her family, of Irish and German descent, is five generations postimmigration.

Juan has always vaguely felt like he wasn't quite the son his father wanted. He has more in common with his mother and the two have always been close. During elementary school, Juan's father would often accuse his mother of "coddling him" and treating him like a "little girl," but Juan enjoyed helping her with his younger siblings. Since middle school, things have become somewhat more difficult. Juan's father had hoped that Juan would develop more athletic interests as he grew older. When Juan didn't, his father began focusing on Juan's younger brother and now mostly ignores Juan. Things became even harder for Juan when he didn't show the interest in girls that his father expected. While not being athletic made him invisible, not having a girlfriend made him a target. His parents had several fights over comments his father made about Juan being "a little queer."

As things became more difficult at home, Juan spent more time out of the house. He made friends with a group of kids in high school who were considered "alternative" by most. None of them were "popular" kids, but together they at least formed a group of their own, and this offered Juan some protection from the popular kids who had started calling him a "fag." Most of the kids in his group smoked marijuana, and Juan found that it helped him relax in social situations. Juan now smokes two or three days a week after school.

For the past few years, Juan has felt like he is keeping a secret—that his father is actually right: He does like boys. The problem is his secret has become harder to keep as his attraction to guys has become clearer. Unable to think of another way to meet guys, Juan has gone online a couple of times to find partners. Last weekend, Juan had sex for the first time with a 17-year-old guy who lives in a nearby town. It was the second time they had hung out, and Juan couldn't help but feel that he really liked this guy. He told Juan that he was also a virgin, so they didn't use a condom. Afterward, Juan was a little worried about whether that was such a good idea, but finally being with a guy was amazing.

During a recent parent-teacher conference, Juan's teacher expressed to Juan's mother concerns about Juan's academic performance. His teacher believed that he may be feeling depressed and recommended that she take Juan to see a counselor. Juan's father raised no objection but desired no involvement in Juan's counseling process. While Juan was annoyed with his teacher for talking about him and resented his mother for treating him "like he was crazy," he didn't mind the idea of talking with someone. His main concern was that the counselor would tell his parents everything he said. He felt torn between finally sharing his feelings with someone and keeping information secret that he believes would upset his parents, particularly his father.

Integrate Sexual Health, Mental Health, and Substance Use Interventions

The emotional and sexual lives of adolescents, as illustrated in Juan's case, are interrelated. Some innovative intervention-development research conducted specifically with youth, including sexual minority youth (D'Amico, Miles, Stern, & Meredith, 2008; Naar-King et al., 2006; Parsons, Lelutiu-Weinberger, Botsko, & Golub, 2014), has suggested that motivational interviewing (MI; Miller & Rollnick, 2013) can provide a useful framework for counselors working with adolescents in discussing interrelated substance use and sexual health factors. Parsons et al. (2014) found empirical support for the efficacy of a four-session MI-based intervention to reduce both substance use and HIV-transmission-risk behavior among young gay and bisexual men. Research with HIV-positive youth found that similar integrated approaches improved self-esteem and reduced depressive symptoms while achieving reductions in condomless sex and improved medication adherence (Chen, Murphy, Naar-King, & Parsons, 2011; Naar-King, Parsons, Murphy, Kolmodin, & Harris, 2010).

MI is a client-centered approach for discussing a target issue; understanding that issue in relation to a client's broader goals, values, and context; and subsequently developing plans to help a client achieve identified goals (Miller & Rollnick, 2013). Naar-King and Suarez (2010) wrote a book dedicated to the application of MI specifically with adolescents and young adults. They suggested that MI may be a particularly useful frame to guide work with adolescents and young adults, who may at times present for treatment because of parental insistence (rather than personal interest). They may also be experiencing behavioral pressure and influence from multiple sources (e.g., school, family, peers). Naar-King and Suarez pointed out that certain aspects of MI are particularly applicable to these types of developmental challenges. Inherent in MI is an attention to multiple agendas, an emphasis on understanding client concerns, and a focus on building personal motivation to proceed toward self-identified goals. A number of additional resources are available to counselors who wish to incorporate MI into their intervention repertoire through the MI Network of Trainers at http://www.motivationalinterviewing.org.

Juan's marijuana use, heightened anxiety around peer relationships at school, difficulty meeting romantic partners, and concealed sexual risk-taking are interconnected. He is also ambivalent about engaging in the counseling process, in part because he feels he has been mandated to come by his mother.

This kind of presentation is well suited to the use of MI. The counselor may begin by explaining that the purpose of sessions is to explore Juan's values, goals, feelings, and ideas around specific behaviors rather than to mandate or instruct him on how to behave. Through the flexible use of basic MI techniques, such as open questions and reflections, the counselor may proceed to invite Juan to describe and reflect on his current sexual behavior and substance use. As this conversation unfolds, the counselor may also elicit information about Juan's broader goals, values, and social identities. Using summaries and reflections as well as structured activities—such as the personal values card sort—the counselor may highlight ways in which Juan's substance use and high-risk sexual behavior are inconsistent with, or potentially compromise, salient goals, values, and identities. To the extent that Juan identifies ways in which he could modify his behavior to better reflect his goals, values, and sense of identity, the process of change-planning (Miller & Rollnik, 2013) may become more prominent.

Engaging Parents and Addressing Family Factors With Sexual Minority and TGNC Youth

There are a number of ways in which providers of individual psychotherapy can incorporate attention to parental relationships and related factors into their intervention work with sexual minority and TGNC adolescents. This section discusses two specific recommendations. First, we describe how parents may be engaged during the informed consent process. Second, we discuss strategies for involving family members and addressing relationships with family members during the course of treatment.

Engaging Parents Within the Informed Consent Process

Counselors working with adolescents may benefit from adopting an informed consent process that engages the adolescent and their caregiver (where applicable) in a discussion to clarify the kinds of information to which the parent will (or will not) have access. This conversation offers counselors the opportunity to differentiate between behaviors that carry clear legal mandates for disclosure (e.g., imminent danger to self or others) and those that may involve risk taking but do not clearly invoke a legal duty to warn (e.g., consensual sexual activity, substance use, truancy). These more ambiguous domains of privacy are potentially the most important to discuss with caregivers and adolescents during the informed consent process. Caregivers may have differing expectations regarding what information a counselor will, or must, share with them, and some guardians may have attitudes or beliefs that do not permit discussions of sexual behavior or sexuality.

By making the subject of sexuality routine and clearly establishing expectations about confidentiality with all clients, therapists reduce stigma and establish sexuality as a normative aspect of adolescence. The utility of this kind of approach to the informed consent process is illustrated in Juan's case. Clearly addressing the limits of confidentiality related to sexual behavior, substance use, and other risk-taking behavior permits Juan to enter the counseling process with a clearer understanding of how and when his parents may access information about his disclosures in therapy. The counselor can also explain to Juan and his mother how disclosures of risk-taking behavior would be made should Juan bring up information of which his mother wishes to be informed. Failure to establish clear expectations about the limits of parent–adolescent confidentiality and the process of disclosure before the intervention's start could result in breaches of the therapeutic relationship with both Juan and Juan's parents.

Engaging Parents and Parent–Adolescent Relationship Factors Throughout Treatment

Beyond informed consent, the importance of providing support, information, and mentorship to parents who are in the process of accepting their child's sexual identity has been well documented in the literature (Saltzburg, 2004). In recent years, novel strategies for providing support and addressing parental perceptions about raising a sexual minority and TGNC adolescent have been proposed within the framework of narrative therapy (Saltzburg, 2007). Narrative therapy (see Chapter 1, this volume) posits that clients both construct and communicate the meaning of events through the telling and retelling of stories (Gonçalves & Stiles, 2011). In the process of psychotherapy, client stories are elicited and engaged in a manner that may lead to the evolution of the narrative—a transformation of meaning (Pennebaker, 1993)—thereby initiating change outside of psychotherapy (Gonçalves & Stiles, 2011). Similarly, interventions focused on helping parents accept, affirm, and support the healthy adjustment of their gender nonconforming children and adolescents have demonstrated potential to improve parent–child relationships as well as youth mental health outcomes (Hill, Menvielle, Sica, & Johnson, 2010; Rosenberg & Jellinek, 2002). The Children's Gender and Sexual Advocacy Center at Children's National Medical Center offers online resources for youth and the parents of gender nonconforming children (see http://childrensnational.org/gendervariance).

Other intervention strategies exist to improve parent–adolescent communication, reduce confrontation, and enhance emotional connections. The foundations for innovative intervention strategies with sexual minority and TGNC youth and their families may be found within existing counselor skill sets, provided these extant strategies are adapted to address the unique needs and circumstances of this population. For example, LaSala (2000) provided a series of case examples in which family psychotherapy interventions around planned engagement and communication were utilized in the context of psychotherapy to support sexual minority clients during the coming out process. Meanwhile, preliminary results of attachment-based family interventions show early evidence that they may be effective in improving parent–adolescent relationship quality and reducing depression in sexual minority and TGNC youth (Diamond et al., 2012).

These narrative approaches to therapy may be particularly useful when working with sexual minority or TGNC adolescents in situations where one parent (or both) is difficult or impossible to engage in the process of psychotherapy. While Juan has maintained a good relationship with his mother, his relationship with his father is markedly strained. Addressing the relationship between Juan and his father is complicated in part by the fact that his father does not wish to be engaged by Juan's counselor or participate jointly in sessions. A narrative approach, in which Juan has the opportunity to tell the story of his relationship with his father, may be useful in helping Juan to clarify what this relationship means for him and what his goals are in resurrecting, maintaining, or improving it. This may help Juan reframe his father's behavior as a reflection of cultural values, beliefs, and behavioral choices as opposed to a reflection of Juan's intrinsic worth. In particular, there may be opportunity for Juan to reflect on how his father's attitudes about masculinity might have been shaped by the experience of growing up the child of immigrant Dominican parents in ways that Juan may not realize and with which Juan does not identify.

Addressing Peer and Relationship Factors

Peer-Relationship Factors

The universe of resources available to counselors, educators, and associated professionals invested in improving the social climate for sexual minority and TGNC adolescents has expanded. Specific resources intended to help enact structural interventions that improve the safety and support experienced by sexual minority and TGNC youth in schools (MacGillivray, 2014) and athletic activities (e.g., Griffin, Perrotti, Priest, & Muska, 2002) are now available. While counselors providing individual psychotherapy may not always be positioned to directly utilize these types of resources, they may enhance counselors' abilities to provide specific recommendations to youth, parents, and other professionals.

Experiences of rejection, and anxiety associated with the anticipation of possible rejection, may suppress the ability of sexual minority and TGNC adolescents to practice and develop social skills necessary to navigate peer relationships. This has the potential to initiate a cycle in which social isolation leads to diminished social skills, which leads to further isolation and withdrawal. Intervention may therefore be substantially enhanced through the incorporation of social-skills-training interventions, which have demonstrated modest effects (of small to moderate size) in reducing emotional and behavioral disorders in youth (Cook et al., 2008; Maag, 2006). Interventions typically focus on developing social perception as well as problem-solving skills (Spence, 2003). They also often incorporate components focused on reducing anxiety, avoidance of social interactions, and practicing adaptive social behaviors (e.g., rehearsal with feedback and coaching; Spence, 2003).

Despite evidence that social-skills training is a component of many effective cognitive behavioral therapy (CBT) interventions with adolescents (Spence, 2003), the use of social-skills training specifically with sexual minority and TGNC youth has received little to no attention. Several aspects of Juan's case point to the utility of social-skills training: He uses substances to relax in social situations; he has struggled to establish a friend network; and he has a limited repertoire of behaviors for interacting with potential sexual and romantic partners. After using an MI approach to elaborate and clarify Juan's goals and values related to sexual partners, romantic relationships, and friendships, a counselor might then work with him to identify deficits in perception, emotion regulation, and behavior skills that inhibit his accomplishment of these goals. Subsequently, the counselor may use a mixture of role-playing, coaching, and problem-solving strategies with Juan to develop alternative skills that he could use outside of session.

Notably, social skills interventions have been shown effective in conjunction with group (e.g., Herbert et al., 2005) as well as individual CBT. Group delivery may be particularly helpful for sexual minority and TGNC adolescents, given that it simultaneously facilitates social modeling and the development of peer relationships while reducing social isolation and cultivating new behavioral skills. In a group setting, Juan might have the opportunity to benefit from the experiences and expertise of other youth and in turn serve as a source of information to them. This would afford him the opportunity to receive and provide support and feedback to peers facing similar challenges, while he also expands his own behavioral repertoire.

Romantic Partners

Romantic relationships present a context similar to, but distinct from, peer relationships. While some studies point to primary, main, or established relationships as the primary context for HIV-transmission risk (Goodreau et al., 2012; Sullivan et al., 2009), others indicate that being partnered is associated with improved mental health and social outcomes (Bauermeister et al., 2010; Russell & Consolacion, 2003). The mental health field must confront the challenge of disentangling the individual and dyadic factors that confer risk versus resilience in relationships. Meanwhile, providers must assist individual sexual minority and TGNC adolescents in negotiating the social challenges associated with romantic and sexual pursuits: finding partners, dating, and carrying on successful intimate relationships.

One avenue for intervention is to focus on the development of interpersonal skills associated with healthy relationships in adolescents who are not currently dating or partnered. Communication skills and sexual assertiveness have been associated with reduced sexual health risk-taking with casual and dating partners for heterosexual adolescents and young adults (Rickert, Sanghvi, & Wiemann, 2002; Widman, Welsh, McNulty, & Little, 2006). Cognitive–behavioral couples therapy typically incorporates communication skill-building components (Sher, 2011), and may provide a starting point for counselors to use relationship skill-building interventions to address the unique needs of sexual minority and TGNC youth.

In addition to thinking about relationship skill-building with individual adolescents, counselors should begin to consider whether and how to engage relationship partners for sexual minority and TGNC adolescents who are in relationships. Admittedly, the joint treatment of two minor children would be potentially complicated by informed consent and confidentiality laws. However, given the salience of relationship factors for outcomes with sexual minority youth, the potential utility of such strategies should not be overlooked. Where consent issues can be navigated, these kinds of interventions may provide clinicians with useful strategies which may benefit sexual minority and TGNC youth in their current and future relationships.

Even when counselors are unable to engage with relationship partners directly, HIV-testing procedures developed specifically for couples may be accessible. These services may serve as a useful adjunct to individual psychotherapy for sexual minority and TGNC adolescents who are in relationships. Couples HIV testing and counseling interventions have been endorsed by the CDC and are currently being disseminated nationwide. In these interventions, both members of the couple complete an HIV test together, receive their results together as a couple, and engage in a conversation about their sexual health goals and behaviors.

CONCLUSION

Counseling with sexual minority and TGNC adolescents brings with it a range of challenges. Evolving identities may lead to intense and sometimes conflicting emotions, and expanding individual freedoms associated with self-awareness may lead to adolescents' engagement in risk behaviors and behavioral choices that are at odds with the values and preferences of parents and guardians. Peer and family relationships may change accordingly—and dramatically—over relatively brief periods of time, emphasizing the need for sensitive, integrated, and inclusive interventions. It is our view that the interrelated nature of relationships, emotions, and health-related behaviors like substance use and sexual risk-taking, represents both a challenge and an opportunity. While the overlapping and connected nature of these factors may sometimes make it difficult to know where to start, it also means that movement in one area may potentiate movement in others. Counselors are challenged to develop effective strategies to target specific treatment foci, and also to engage adolescents in innovative ways that allow them to represent themselves fully in the therapeutic process.

REFERENCES

Ainsworth, M. D. (1985). Attachments across the life span. *Bulletin of the New York Academy of Medicine, 61*, 792–812.

Arnett, J. J. (2000). Emerging adulthood. A theory of development from the late teens through the twenties. *American Psychologist, 55*, 469–480. http://dx.doi.org/10.1037/0003-066X.55.5.469

Austin, E. L., & Bozick, R. (2011). Sexual orientation, partnership formation, and substance use in the transition to adulthood. *Journal of Youth and Adolescence, 41*, 167–178. http://dx.doi.org/10.1007/s10964-011-9653-7

Bailey, J. V. (2004). Sexually transmitted infections in women who have sex with women. *Sexually Transmitted Infections, 80*, 244–246. http://dx.doi.org/10.1136/sti.2003.007641

Baiocco, R., Fontanesi, L., Santamaria, F., Ioverno, S., Marasco, B., Baumgartner, E., . . . Laghi, F. (2014). Negative parental responses to coming out and family functioning in a sample of lesbian and gay young adults. *Journal of Child and Family Studies, 24*, 1490–1500. http://dx.doi.org/10.1007/s10826-014-9954-z

Bauermeister, J. A., Johns, M. M., Sandfort, T. G. M., Eisenberg, A., Grossman, A. H., & D'Augelli, A. R. (2010). Relationship trajectories and psychological well-being among sexual minority youth. *Journal of Youth and Adolescence, 39*, 1148–1163. http://dx.doi.org/10.1007/s10964-010-9557-y

Bockting, W., Benner, A., & Coleman, E. (2009). Gay and bisexual identity development among female-to-male transsexuals in North America: Emergence of a transgender sexuality. *Archives of Sexual Behavior, 38*, 688–701. http://dx.doi.org/10.1007/s10508-009-9489-3

Bostwick, W. B., Boyd, C. J., Hughes, T. L., West, B. T., & McCabe, S. E. (2014). Discrimination and mental health among lesbian, gay, and bisexual adults in the United States. *American Journal of Orthopsychiatry, 84*, 35–45. http://dx.doi.org/10.1037/h0098851

Brennan, D. J., & Shaver, P. R. (1995). Dimensions of adult attachment, affect regulation, and romantic relationship functioning. *Personality and Social Psychology Bulletin, 21*, 267–283. http://dx.doi.org/10.1177/0146167295213008

Centers for Disease Control and Prevention. (2011). *HIV among youth*. Atlanta, GA: U.S. Department of Health and Human Services. Retrieved from http://www.cdc.gov/hiv/group/age/youth

Centers for Disease Control and Prevention. (2012a). *New HIV infections in the United States*. Atlanta, GA: U.S. Department of Health and Human Services. Retrieved from http://www.cdc.gov/nchhstp/newsroom/docs/2012/hiv-infections-2007-2010.pdf

Centers for Disease Control and Prevention. (2012b). *Sexually Transmitted Disease Surveillance 2008*. Atlanta, GA: U.S. Department of Health and Human Services. Retrieved from http://www.cdc.gov/std/stats12/default.htm

Centers for Disease Control and Prevention. (2013a). *HIV among transgender people in the United States*. Atlanta, GA: U.S. Department of Health and Human Services. Retrieved from http://www.cdc.gov/hiv/group/gender/transgender/index.html

Centers for Disease Control and Prevention. (2013b). *HIV in the United States: At a glance*. Atlanta, GA: U.S. Department of Health and Human Services. Retrieved from http://www.cdc.gov/hiv/pdf/statistics_basics_factsheet.pdf

Centers for Disease Control and Prevention. (2014). *HIV among youth*. Atlanta: U.S. Department of Health and Human Services. Atlanta, GA: U.S. Department of Health and Human Services. Retrieved from http://www.cdc.gov/hiv/pdf/library_factsheet_HIV_amongYouth.pdf

Chen, X., Murphy, D. A., Naar-King, S., & Parsons, J. T. (2011). A clinic-based motivational intervention improves condom use among subgroups of youth living with HIV. *Journal of Adolescent Health, 49*, 193–198. http://dx.doi.org/10.1016/j.jadohealth.2010.11.252

Clements-Nolle, K., Marx, R., Guzman, R., & Katz, M. (2001). HIV prevalence, risk behaviors, health care use, and mental health status of transgender persons: Implications for public health intervention. *American Journal of Public Health, 91*, 915–921. http://dx.doi.org/10.2105/AJPH.91.6.915

Cook, C. R., Gresham, F. M., Kern, L., Barreras, R. B., Thornton, S., & Crews, S. D. (2008). Social skills training for secondary students with emotional and/or behavioral disorders: A review and analysis of the meta-analytic literature. *Journal of Emotional and Behavioral Disorders, 16*, 131–144. http://dx.doi.org/10.1177/1063426608314541

D'Amico, E. J., Miles, J. N. V., Stern, S. A., & Meredith, L. S. (2008). Brief motivational interviewing for teens at risk of substance use consequences: A randomized pilot study in a primary care clinic. *Journal of Substance Abuse Treatment, 35*, 53–61. http://dx.doi.org/10.1016/j.jsat.2007.08.008

D'Augelli, A. R. (2002). Mental health problems among lesbian, gay, and bisexual youth ages 14 to 21. *Clinical Child Psychology and Psychiatry, 7*, 433–456. http://dx.doi.org/10.1177/1359104502007003039

D'Augelli, A. R. (2006). Developmental and contextual factors and mental health among lesbian, gay and bisexual youths. In A. M. Omoto & H. S. Kurtzman (Eds.), *Sexual orientation and mental health: Examining identity and development in lesbian, gay, and bisexual people* (pp. 37–53). Washington, DC: American Psychological Association. http://dx.doi.org/10.1037/11261-002

D'Augelli, A. R., Rendina, H. J., Sinclair, K. O., & Grossman, A. H. (2008). Lesbian and gay youth's aspirations for marriage and raising children. *Journal of LGBT Issues in Counseling, 1*, 77–98. http://dx.doi.org/10.1300/J462v01n04_06

Devor, A. H. (2004). Witnessing and mirroring: A fourteen stage model of transsexual identity formation. *Journal of Gay & Lesbian Psychotherapy, 8*, 41–67.

Diamond, G. M., Diamond, G. S., Levy, S., Closs, C., Ladipo, T., & Siqueland, L. (2012). Attachment-based family therapy for suicidal lesbian, gay, and bisexual adolescents: A treatment development study and open trial with preliminary findings. *Psychotherapy, 49*, 62–71. http://dx.doi.org/10.1037/a0026247

Diamond, L. M. (2000). Sexual identity, attractions, and behavior among young sexual-minority women over a 2-year period. *Developmental Psychology, 36*, 241–250. http://dx.doi.org/10.1037/0012-1649.36.2.241

Erikson, E. H. (1980). *Identity and the life cycle.* New York, NY: Norton.

Feeney, J. A., Peterson, C., Gallois, C., & Terry, D. J. (2000). Attachment style as a predictor of sexual attitudes and behavior in late adolescence. *Psychology & Health, 14*, 1105–1122. http://dx.doi.org/10.1080/08870440008407370

Formby, E. (2011). Sex and relationships education, sexual health, and lesbian, gay and bisexual sexual cultures: Views from young people. *Sex Education, 11*, 255–266. http://dx.doi.org/10.1080/14681811.2011.590078

Garofalo, R., Deleon, J., Osmer, E., Doll, M., & Harper, G. W. (2006). Overlooked, misunderstood and at-risk: Exploring the lives and HIV risk of ethnic minority male-to-female transgender youth. *Journal of Adolescent Health, 38*, 230–236. http://dx.doi.org/10.1016/j.jadohealth.2005.03.023

Golub, S. A., Starks, T. J., Payton, G., & Parsons, J. T. (2011). The critical role of intimacy in the sexual risk behaviors of gay and bisexual men. *AIDS and Behavior, 16*, 626–632. http://dx.doi.org/10.1007/s10461-011-9972-4

Gonçalves, M. M., & Stiles, W. B. (2011). Narrative and psychotherapy: Introduction to the special section. *Psychotherapy Research, 21*, 1–3. http://dx.doi.org/10.1080/10503307.2010.534510

Goodreau, S. M., Carnegie, N. B., Vittinghoff, E., Lama, J. R., Sanchez, J., Grinsztejn, B., . . . Buchbinder, S. P. (2012). What drives the US and Peruvian HIV epidemics in men who have sex with men (MSM)? *PLoS ONE, 7*, e50522. http://dx.doi.org/10.1371/journal.pone.0050522

Grant, J. M., Mottet, L. A., Tanis, J., Herman, J. L., Harrison, J., & Keisling, M. (2010). *National Transgender Discrimination Survey Report on health and health care* (pp. 1–23). Washington, DC: National Center for Transgender Equality and National Gay and Lesbian Task Force.

Griffin, P., Perrotti, J., Priest, L., & Muska, M. (2002). *It takes a team! Making sports safe for lesbian, gay, bisexual and transgender athletes and coaches: An educational kit for athletes, coaches, and athletic directors*. Retrieved from http://www.promotion-plus.org/Images/New%20publications%202005/EliminateHomophobiaKit.pdf

Grossman, A. H., & D'Augelli, A. R. (2006). Transgender youth. *Journal of Homosexuality, 51*, 111–128. http://dx.doi.org/10.1300/J082v51n01_06

Grossman, A. H., D'Augelli, A. R., & Frank, J. A. (2011). Aspects of psychological resilience among transgender youth. *Journal of LGBT Youth, 8*, 103–115. http://dx.doi.org/10.1080/19361653.2011.541347

Harper, G. W., Brodsky, A., & Bruce, D. (2012). What's good about being gay? Perspectives from youth. *Journal of LGBT Youth, 9*, 22–41. http://dx.doi.org/10.1080/19361653.2012.628230

Hatzenbuehler, M. L. (2009). How does sexual minority stigma "get under the skin"? A psychological mediation framework. *Psychological Bulletin, 135*, 707–730. http://dx.doi.org/10.1037/a0016441

Henrich, C. C., Brookmeyer, K. A., Shrier, L. A., & Shahar, G. (2006). Supportive relationships and sexual risk behavior in adolescence: An ecological-transactional approach. *Journal of Pediatric Psychology, 31*, 286–297. http://dx.doi.org/10.1093/jpepsy/jsj024

Herbert, J., Gaudiano, B., Rheingold, A., Myers, V., Dalrymple, K., & Nolan, E. (2005). Social skills training augments the effectiveness of cognitive behavioral group therapy for social anxiety disorder. *Behavior Therapy, 36*, 125–138. http://dx.doi.org/10.1016/S0005-7894(05)80061-9

Herbst, J. H., Jacobs, E. D., Finlayson, T. J., McKleroy, V. S., Neumann, M. S., Crepaz, N., & HIV/AIDS Prevention Research Synthesis Team. (2008). Estimating HIV prevalence and risk behaviors of transgender persons in the United States: A systematic review. *AIDS and Behavior, 12*, 1–17. http://dx.doi.org/10.1007/s10461-007-9299-3

Hill, D. B., Menvielle, E., Sica, K. M., & Johnson, A. (2010). An affirmative intervention for families with gender variant children: Parental ratings of child mental health and gender. *Journal of Sex & Marital Therapy, 36*, 6–23. http://dx.doi.org/10.1080/00926230903375560

Kann, L., Kinchen, S., Shanklin, S. L., Flint, K. H., Kawkins, J., Harris, W. A., . . . Zaza, S. (2014). Youth risk behavior surveillance—United States, 2013. *MMWR Surveillance Summaries, 63*, 1–168.

Kosciw, J. G., Greytak, E. A., Bartkiewicz, M. J., Boesen, M. J., & Palmer, N. A. (2012). *The 2011 National School Climate Survey: The experiences of lesbian, gay, bisexual, and transgender youth in our nation's schools*. New York, NY: Gay, Lesbian and Straight Education Network.

LaSala, M. C. (2000). Lesbians, gay men, and their parents: Family therapy for the coming-out crisis. *Family Process, 39*, 67–81. http://dx.doi.org/10.1111/j.1545-5300.2000.39108.x

Liu, R. T., & Mustanski, B. (2012). Suicidal ideation and self-harm in lesbian, gay, bisexual, and transgender youth. *American Journal of Preventive Medicine, 42*, 221–228. http://dx.doi.org/10.1016/j.amepre.2011.10.023

Maag, J. W. (2006). Social skills training for students with emotional and behavioral disorders: A review of reviews. *Behavioral Disorders, 31*, 5–17.

MacGillivray, I. K. (2014). *Gay-straight alliances: A handbook for students, educators, and parents.* New York, NY: Routledge.

Marshal, M. P., Friedman, M. S., Stall, R., King, K. M., Miles, J., Gold, M. A., . . . Morse, J. Q. (2008). Sexual orientation and adolescent substance use: A meta-analysis and methodological review. *Addiction, 103*, 546–556. http://dx.doi.org/10.1111/j.1360-0443.2008.02149.x

Miller, W. R., & Rollnick, S. (2013). *Motivational interviewing* (3rd ed.). New York, NY: Guilford Press.

Mizock, L., & Mueser, K. T. (2014). Employment, mental health, internalized stigma, and coping with transphobia among transgender individuals. *Psychology of Sexual Orientation and Gender Diversity, 1*, 146–158. http://dx.doi.org/10.1037/sgd0000029

Moradi, B., Wiseman, M. C., DeBlaere, C., Goodman, M. B., Sarkees, A., Brewster, M. E., & Huang, Y. P. (2010). LGB of color and White individuals' perceptions of heterosexist stigma, internalized homophobia, and outness: Comparisons of levels and links. *The Counseling Psychologist, 38*, 397–424. http://dx.doi.org/10.1177/0011000009335263

Morgan, S. W., & Stevens, P. E. (2008). Transgender identity development as represented by a group of female-to-male transgendered adults. *Issues in Mental Health Nursing, 29*, 585–599. http://dx.doi.org/10.1080/01612840802048782

Mustanski, B., Newcomb, M. E., & Clerkin, E. M. (2011). Relationship characteristics and sexual risk-taking in young men who have sex with men. *Health Psychology, 30*, 597–605. http://dx.doi.org/10.1037/a0023858

Naar-King, S., Parsons, J. T., Murphy, D., Kolmodin, K., & Harris, D. R. (2010). A multisite randomized trial of a motivational intervention targeting multiple risks in youth living with HIV: Initial effects on motivation, self-efficacy, and depression. *Journal of Adolescent Health, 46*, 422–428. http://dx.doi.org/10.1016/j.jadohealth.2009.11.198

Naar-King, S., & Suarez, M. (2010). *Motivational interviewing with adolescents and young adults.* New York, NY: The Guilford Press.

Naar-King, S., Wright, K., Parsons, J. T., Frey, M., Templin, T., Lam, P., & Murphy, D. (2006). Healthy choices: Motivational enhancement therapy for health risk behaviors in HIV-positive youth. *AIDS Education and Prevention, 18*, 1–11. http://dx.doi.org/10.1521/aeap.2006.18.1.1

National Coalition for the Homeless. (2009). *LGBT Homeless: Factsheet.* Retrieved from http://www.nationalhomeless.org/factsheets/lgbtq.html

Office of Women's Health. (2012). *Lesbian and bisexual health fact sheet.* Washington, DC: U.S. Department of Health and Human Services. Retrieved from http://womenshealth.gov/publications/our-publications/fact-sheet/lesbian-bisexual-health.html#e

Pachankis, J. E. (2007). The psychological implications of concealing a stigma: A cognitive-affective-behavioral model. *Psychological Bulletin, 133*, 328–345. http://dx.doi.org/10.1037/0033-2909.133.2.328

Pachankis, J. E., Goldfried, M. R., & Ramrattan, M. E. (2008). Extension of the rejection sensitivity construct to the interpersonal functioning of gay men. *Journal of Consulting and Clinical Psychology, 76*, 306–317. http://dx.doi.org/ 10.1037/0022-006X.76.2.306

Pachankis, J. E., Hatzenbuehler, M. L., & Starks, T. J. (2014). The influence of structural stigma and rejection sensitivity on young sexual minority men's daily tobacco and alcohol use. *Social Science & Medicine, 103*, 67–75. http://dx.doi.org/ 10.1016/j.socscimed.2013.10.005

Parsons, J. T., Lelutiu-Weinberger, C., Botsko, M., & Golub, S. A. (2014). A randomized controlled trial utilizing motivational interviewing to reduce HIV risk and drug use in young gay and bisexual men. *Journal of Consulting and Clinical Psychology, 82*, 9–18. http://dx.doi.org/10.1037/a0035311

Pennebaker, J. W. (1993). Putting stress into words: Health, linguistic, and therapeutic implications. *Behaviour Research and Therapy, 31*, 539–548. http://dx.doi.org/ 10.1016/0005-7967(93)90105-4

Poulin, C., & Graham, L. (2001). The association between substance use, unplanned sexual intercourse and other sexual behaviours among adolescent students. *Addiction, 96*, 607–621. http://dx.doi.org/10.1046/j.1360-0443.2001.9646079.x

Rickert, V. I., Sanghvi, R., & Wiemann, C. M. (2002). Is lack of sexual assertiveness among adolescent and young adult women a cause for concern? *Perspectives on Sexual and Reproductive Health, 34*, 178–183. http://dx.doi.org/10.2307/3097727

Rosario, M., Schrimshaw, E. W., & Hunter, J. (2009). Disclosure of sexual orientation and subsequent substance use and abuse among lesbian, gay, and bisexual youths: Critical role of disclosure reactions. *Psychology of Addictive Behaviors, 23*, 175–184. http://dx.doi.org/10.1037/a0014284

Rosario, M., Schrimshaw, E. W., Hunter, J., & Braun, L. (2006). Sexual identity development among lesbian, gay, and bisexual youths: Consistency and change over time. *Journal of Sex Research, 43*, 46–58. http://dx.doi.org/10.1080/ 00224490609552298

Rosenberg, M., & Jellinek, M. S. (2002). Children with gender identity issues and their parents in individual and group treatment. *Journal of the American Academy of Child & Adolescent Psychiatry, 41*, 619–621. http://dx.doi.org/10.1097/ 00004583-200205000-00020

Russell, S. T., & Consolacion, T. B. (2003). Adolescent romance and emotional health in the United States: Beyond binaries. *Journal of Clinical Child and Adolescent Psychology, 32*, 499–508. http://dx.doi.org/10.1207/S15374424JCCP3204_2

Ryan, C. (2010). Engaging families to support lesbian, gay, bisexual, and transgender youth: The Family Acceptance Project. *Prevention Researcher, 17*, 11–13.

Ryan, C., Huebner, D., Diaz, R. M., & Sanchez, J. (2009). Family rejection as a predictor of negative health outcomes in white and Latino lesbian, gay, and bisexual young adults. *Pediatrics, 123*, 346–352. http://dx.doi.org/10.1542/ peds.2007-3524

Saewyc, E. M. (2011). Research on adolescent sexual orientation: Development, health disparities, stigma, and resilience. *Journal of Research on Adolescence, 21,* 256–272. http://dx.doi.org/10.1111/j.1532-7795.2010.00727.x

Safren, S. A., & Heimberg, R. G. (1999). Depression, hopelessness, suicidality, and related factors in sexual minority and heterosexual adolescents. *Journal of Consulting and Clinical Psychology, 67,* 859–866. http://dx.doi.org/10.1037/0022-006X.67.6.859

Saltzburg, S. (2004). Learning that an adolescent child is gay or lesbian: The parent experience. *Social Work, 49,* 109–118. http://dx.doi.org/10.1093/sw/49.1.109

Saltzburg, S. (2007). Narrative therapy pathways for re-authoring with parents of adolescents coming-out as lesbian, gay, and bisexual. *Contemporary Family Therapy, 29,* 57–69. http://dx.doi.org/10.1007/s10591-007-9035-1

Sher, T. G. (2011). Cognitive behavioral couples therapy. In J. S. Kreutzer, B. Caplan, & J. DeLuca (Eds.), *Encyclopedia of clinical neuropsychology* (pp. 618–619). New York, NY: Springer. http://dx.doi.org/10.1007/978-0-387-79948-3_415

Singh, A. A., Hays, D. G., & Watson, L. S. (2011). Strength in the face of adversity: Resilience strategies of transgender individuals. *Journal of Counseling & Development, 89,* 20–27. http://dx.doi.org/10.1002/j.1556-6678.2011.tb00057.x

Spence, S. H. (2003). Social skills training with children and young people: Theory, evidence and practice. *Child and Adolescent Mental Health, 8,* 84–96. http://dx.doi.org/10.1111/1475-3588.00051

Starks, T. J., Newcomb, M. E., & Mustanski, B. (2015). A longitudinal study of interpersonal relationships among lesbian, gay, and bisexual adolescents and young adults: Mediational pathways from attachment to romantic relationship quality. *Archives of Sexual Behavior, 44,* 1821–1831. http://dx.doi.org/10.1007/s10508-015-0492-6

Starks, T. J., Payton, G., Golub, S. A., Weinberger, C. L., & Parsons, J. T. (2014). Contextualizing condom use: Intimacy interference, stigma, and unprotected sex. *Journal of Health Psychology, 19,* 711–720. http://dx.doi.org/10.1177/1359105313478643

Sullivan, P. S., Salazar, L., Buchbinder, S., & Sanchez, T. H. (2009). Estimating the proportion of HIV transmissions from main sex partners among men who have sex with men in five US cities. *AIDS, 23,* 1153–1162. http://dx.doi.org/10.1097/QAD.0b013e32832baa34

Widman, L., Welsh, D. P., McNulty, J. K., & Little, K. C. (2006). Sexual communication and contraceptive use in adolescent dating couples. *Journal of Adolescent Health, 39,* 893–899. http://dx.doi.org/10.1016/j.jadohealth.2006.06.003

10

SPECIAL ISSUES RELATED TO AGING ADULTS

TAMMI VACHA-HAASE AND WESTON V. DONALDSON

Older adults who identify as lesbian, gay, or bisexual (LGB) or as transgender and gender nonconforming (TGNC) have often been considered an "invisible minority." Historically, research and clinical literature on aging has not typically acknowledged diversity in sexual orientation and gender identity. In turn, LGBT-related written work has not classically considered the experiences of LGBT adults in later life. Although recent years have brought about some progress, the older-adult LGBT population continues to be veiled throughout the literature, with neither clear identification or inclusion in aging publications nor direct recognition of their presence represented in the literature focusing on LGBT people.

This increasingly growing group, however, can no longer be concealed, as current demographics project a significant growth in numbers for this population in coming decades. When looking at the most recent population-based Gallup survey of LGBT individuals, 3.4% of Americans overall identified as

http://dx.doi.org/10.1037/15959-011
Handbook of Sexual Orientation and Gender Diversity in Counseling and Psychotherapy, K. A. DeBord, A. R. Fischer, K. J. Bieschke, and R. M. Perez (Editors)

LGBT, with only 1.9% of those ages 65 and older self-identified as LGBT (Gates & Newport, 2012). The difference among age groups may have been due to the difficulty in sampling from the LGBT older-adult population, or those individuals may identify differently based on continued stigma from generational-cohort norms (Kimmel, 2014). With 40 million adults currently over the age of 65 in the United States, this would suggest that there are currently about 765,000 older LGBT Americans. By 2030, estimates predict that one in five people in the United States will be age 65 or older (U.S. Census Bureau, 2008), with projections indicating there may be as many as two million to seven million people in their later years who identify as LGBT (Grant, Koskovich, Frazer, & Bjerk, 2010). Referred to as the "Silver Tsunami," the surge of older adults in the United States' population will have an immense impact on health care, social services, economic growth, and policy development, including those sexual minority and gender nonconforming people over the age of 65 who, compared with their peers, reported lower income, lower education, and being a person of color (Gates & Newport, 2012).

Given the increasing prevalence of older adults who identify as LGBT, the goal of this chapter is to identify the increasing need to understand how LGBT identities and the aging process intersect. This chapter is written with the understanding that although the visibility of LGBT people has increased in the past decade, it is still likely that aging-services providers are unaware of them to an extent; and even well-meaning, informed practitioners may be unsure of how to work effectively with LGBT individuals in their later years.

The authors have approached the discussion of sexuality and gender from a social constructivist paradigm (see Chapter 1, this volume), acknowledging the contemporary context and constructed meanings of sexual and gender identities and gender variance. For practitioners, it is important when talking with older LGBT individuals to realize that, to them, current terms may not apply or may feel foreign given their life histories and generational cohort. The authors have attempted to present the information contained in this chapter in a way that incorporates the social context and complex intersection of multiple identities of older LGBT people.

A secondary intention of this chapter, which draws from the authors' personal values of social justice and advocacy work, is to provide practitioners with tools and strategies for becoming LGBT allies in their work with older adults. It is hoped that by becoming more informed, practitioners can have a greater empathy for the experience of older LGBT adults, as well as a better idea of their particular needs at this stage of their life.

We focus first on intersecting identities for older LGBT adults, including those related to generational cohort, age, sexuality, and gender. Attention is then given to spirituality and religious beliefs, followed by a discussion of family systems and social support, including family of origin, family of choice, caregiving, and residential decisions. Overall health and well-being are explored, highlighting the areas of sexual and mental health. The financial and legal issues faced by older LGBT adults are explored, with attention directed toward the challenges of end-of-life planning. Finally, we emphasize clinical practice, providing recommendations for working as a culturally competent provider and creating a culturally affirming environment. Integrated throughout the chapter is the discussion of Betty, a member of the older LGBT population. Betty's intersecting identities and current experience are explored in relationship to key concepts, and in hopes of offering ideas of how to work with an older adult who is part of an invisible minority.

CASE STUDY

Betty[1] is a 72-year-old African American cisgender woman who identifies as gay. She lives in a large city in the southeastern United States. Six months ago, Betty lost her partner of 32 years, Doris, to cancer, and finds herself frightened by being on her own. The state where she lives does not offer legal protections for same-sex couples, so she and Doris were compelled to draft advance directives and other paperwork to ensure that their possessions would be retained in the case of death. Betty now lives in low-income housing, and her only source of income is Social Security. Her health is poor, as she suffers from diabetes, chronic obstructive pulmonary disease (COPD), and arthritis. Betty worked for 27 years as an office manager for a legal firm but was forced to retire early at age 61 due to medical reasons. Since the age of 18, she had smoked a pack of cigarettes daily, until she quit approximately 15 years ago following the COPD diagnosis. Betty identifies as Christian but has not attended church for several decades. She was heterosexually married for 4 years when she was much younger, and she has one daughter, who now lives in another state. When Betty came out in her late 30s, this strained her relationship with her daughter and other family members, and they rarely speak. Betty eventually met and fell in love with Doris, a White European American woman who had also been previously heterosexually married. Although they were supportive of the relationship, since her death, Doris's children tend to contact Betty only around holidays and birthdays. Betty is hesitant to reach out to Doris's family, as she knows they are busy with their own careers and family; she does not want to be a burden to them. The close friendships that Betty and Doris enjoyed when they were younger have disappeared in recent years, as many friends have moved away or died. Serving as Doris's primary caregiver during the last year of her illness, Betty lost contact

---

[1]This case example is based on fictional characters.

with many of her friends, as she either felt guilty leaving Doris at home or was worried that Doris would become jealous knowing that she was enjoying lunch with another woman. Doris, who was more than 20 years older than Betty, believed that it was important to not share their relationship with even their closest heterosexual friends. Now, even though Betty believes these friends would be accepting and supportive, out of respect for Doris's wishes, she is hesitant to share her love for Doris and the grief she is experiencing. Although Betty understands she is grieving, she does not trust that anyone else could understand. She feels depressed and anxious almost every day; she dreads facing the future alone and is unsure where she can go for help.

Betty's current situation illustrates many themes that are common to LGBT older adults. Her story shows a complex interaction between health problems, poverty, bereavement, social stigma, the sociopolitical context of her state of residence, racial identity, and family dynamics. The information contained in this chapter is intended to highlight these issues, illustrating ways that practitioners could help a client such as Betty.

IDENTITY AND INTERSECTIONALITY

LGBT older adults do not belong solely to social categories based on their sexual orientation or gender identity, but have membership in other social groups such as age, race, ethnicity, gender, class, ability, and a host of other identities. Using the lens of intersectionality is beneficial to best describe and understand the experiences of older adults, acknowledging the combined effect of both privileged and marginalized identities on an individual's life experience (Cole, 2009; see also Chapter 4, this volume). Stoller and Gibson (2000) proposed a model of aging that looks at "different worlds in aging," based on individuals' race, ethnicity, social class, and gender. From this perspective, the experience of aging exists within stratifications of privilege and marginalization. For example, although TGNC people are among the most marginalized groups in the United States and are at risk for poverty and chronic health problems, this is even truer for TGNC people of color, who are also more likely to live in poverty (Fredriksen-Goldsen et al., 2011). This perspective points to the importance of considering intersecting identities of older people when describing their aging processes and experiences. Knowing that an individual is TGNC is only partially useful, as societal inequalities related to additional social identities will likely impact the person's access to health care, access to support for their gender expression and the transitioning process (if applicable), potential for poverty, and probability for developing medical and psychiatric conditions.

Thus, when considering the diverse experiences of older LGBT people, it is useful to use theoretical frameworks that encompass not only the dimensions of age and sexual and gender identity but also social class, race/ethnicity, and other social identities. When first meeting Betty, the woman in the case study, the practitioner would benefit from recognizing all her various social identities and group memberships. She cannot be fully appreciated as only a woman, or an African American, or an older adult, or a lesbian, or even as a widow. Practitioners are encouraged to focus on an integrative conceptualization of Betty's multiple identities and life experiences, within the context of understanding the impact of a lifetime of racism, sexism, heterosexism, and now, ageism. Although a complicated process, it is the approach necessary to truly provide Betty with the best care.

The *double jeopardy hypothesis*, which proposes that older racial-ethnic minority adults experience greater disadvantages from aging because of the existing stress and discrimination associated with being a person of color (Markides & Black, 1995), may be useful in understanding Betty based on her age and ethnicity. Intersectional invisibility theory (Purdie-Vaughns & Eibach, 2008) would suggest that Betty does not fit the prototype of her constituent subordinate groups given that she has several multiple-subordinate identities (e.g., she may not be seen as a prototypical "African American person," who is assumed to be male and heterosexual; she may not be seen as a prototypical "lesbian," who is assumed to be White).

However, all of the above frameworks lack consideration of intersection among Betty's many membership groups. Perhaps a more encompassing theoretical perspective is the proposition of a "multifarious jeopardy" hypothesis that includes intersection of her age, cohort, race-ethnicity, gender identity, sexual orientation, social class, and disability (Vacha-Haase, Donaldson, & Foster, 2014). Betty faces what might be considered a multidimensional phenomenon as she must integrate gender-role messages with cultural values and continuing experiences with racism at the same time she experiences the aging process, while also grieving the loss of her partner. Depending on her own awareness of the multiplicity of identities and her internalization of the larger society's constructions about issues such as sexual orientation, as well as her own beliefs, norms, and expectations, the potential for internal conflict is heightened, and the difficulty of moving forward with changes in her life is made increasingly challenging.

Generational Cohort and Self-Identification

The generational cohort to which one belongs contributes to a collective identity that is also individually salient, as identification with one's generation or cohort is often a more meaningful experience than identification with one's age group (Weiss & Lang, 2009). For example, those currently over the age of 85 experienced World War II, the popularization of owning a television in the United States, and crooners like Frank Sinatra, in comparison with the baby boomers (65–74 years old), who came of age during the Vietnam War, space flights to the moon, and the Beatles.

When discussing any subpopulation of people, it is important to acknowledge the impact that historical and generational influences may have on their interpretations of experience. This is all the more true for older LGBT people, who have seen vast changes in society's approach to sexual and gender minorities over the past century. Based on the cohort group to which they belong, distinct historic, social, religious, and economic factors have dictated social and familial norms in the lives of older LGBT people. They have lived within contexts of unique prejudicial and societal views that pathologized and marginalized key parts of their identity. The oldest-old lived much of their lives in a time when homosexuality was a criminal offense and was considered a mental illness (Morrow, 1998). No doubt this had a significant impact on the way many LGBT people expressed their sexuality, and on their understanding of their own attractions and behaviors. There are some older adults who underwent treatments to change their sexual identity or gender nonconformity (see Chapter 11, this volume). These individuals describe horrific experiences in aversion therapy using chemical- or electrical-aversive techniques (Dickinson, Cook, Playle, & Hallett, 2012). Even for those who have since gone on to live openly as LGBT adults, the memories and experiences from their treatment may continue to haunt them (Dickinson et al., 2012).

In the case study at the beginning of this chapter, it appears that Doris's cohort group clearly affected her views on the safety of sharing that she was in a same-sex relationship. Given she was in her 90s when she passed away, her cohort group would have experienced very different societal views and values than younger cohorts. For example, the cohort group one has membership in most likely would influence one's experience of the 1969 Stonewall riots. Although they both experienced these spontaneous, violent demonstrations through the lens of lesbian women, given the 20 years' age difference between Betty and Doris in the case example, the understanding, meaning, and impact of this event most likely would have been different for each woman. Betty and Doris were also an interracial couple, which adds another layer of complexity to the intersecting identities and generational experiences. Interracial heterosexual marriage was illegal until 1967 with the *Loving v. Virginia* ruling and has continued to be met with intolerance in the ensuing decades. Given the region of the country in which Betty and Doris lived, along with their racial and sexual identities, the possible reasons that they likely felt a need to protect themselves and stay in the closet are multifaceted and interwoven.

Ageism and Age Identity

Ageism, perhaps one of the most socially condoned forms of prejudice (Nelson, 2005), mistakenly views old age as involving feeble minds and weak bodies living in nursing homes and draining the national budget. Unfortunately, very little attention has been given to age-related biases and the intersection of gender, sexual orientation, and race-ethnicity, with the majority of the research on stereotypes focusing on ageism regarding the "generic" older adult, most typically assumed to be White, cisgender, and heterosexual—the default societal standard. Little research is available to shed light on the differences between stereotypes, or on how ageism may appear for a 72-year-old African American lesbian woman such as Betty in comparison with others her age. Regardless, Betty must be aware of society's tendency toward ageism, as well as how this might promote the internalization of ageist beliefs about herself and her abilities. Although she experiences a degree of physical limitation, the ageist stereotypes described above realistically describe neither Betty nor the majority of LGBT individuals in their later years.

Attitudes toward aging range from negative to positive, but they are more likely negative given cultural stigma in the United States (Logan, Ward, & Spitze, 1992). This may be intensified for LGBT older adults. For example, due to the intense focus on youth among gay males, a phenomenon called *accelerated aging* has been hypothesized, whereby gay men tend to identify themselves as old at a much younger age than their heterosexual male counterparts (David & Knight, 2008; Friend, 1987). Although the idea is controversial and the results are mixed regarding this trend, there is evidence that this may also apply to older single gay and bisexual men, particularly those who are more involved in the "bar scene" (Hostetler, 2012). Potential effects of this form of ageism can lead to loneliness, depression, isolation, and suicide among some middle-aged and older gay and bisexual men (Hostetler, 2012). This negativity toward aging has been demonstrated to be greater among gay men than lesbians, even when men's attitudes about their own age are more positive (Schope, 2005).

However, in contrast, it should be noted that older LGBT people may also demonstrate greater resiliency when facing late life and its challenges (Orel, 2004). For example, when older LGBT people were asked to define *successful aging*, few were able to do so without acknowledging the challenges they currently faced, implying that successful aging was not an absence of problems but having the means to cope with problems associated with being an older LGBT person (Van Wagenen, Driskell, & Bradford, 2013). This ability to cope with negative associations of aging may be derived from their life experience as people who have faced prejudice and discrimination as sexual minorities, gender minorities, racial minorities, and other marginalized, intersecting identities (Hash & Rogers, 2013; Morrow, 1998). For example, although Betty in the case study is currently struggling, she may be able to maintain hope by employing the coping mechanisms she developed over her lifetime; that is, perhaps the resolve she utilized to help her succeed as an African American, gay woman working in the business world years ago may strengthen her ability to move forward at this point in her life.

In one sample of LGBT baby boomers, a majority (74%) of respondents said that being LGBT better prepared them for aging, although 54% also indicated that being LGBT made aspects of aging more challenging (MetLife Mature Market Institute [MetLife], 2010). Because of their particular life experiences, LGBT older adults may show increased self-advocacy, gender role flexibility, interdependence, self-reliance, and ability to handle stress and crisis situations, all of which may contribute to successful aging (Hash & Rogers, 2013; MetLife, 2010; Morrow, 1998).

Although Betty may already identify herself as old given that she is in her 70s, with current life expectancy projections, she may live another 10 to 20 years (U.S. Department of Health and Human Services, Centers for Disease Control and Prevention, National Center for Health Statistics, 2014). Helping her to identify her strengths, including the resiliency she has fostered through life experiences and the coping mechanisms she developed, may allow Betty to remember her abilities and potential, regardless of her current age or situation. She may be empowered by realizing that although Doris was a significant part of her life, Betty "is still Betty" and has a number of intrapersonal resources on which she can rely.

Sexual Identity

Another important aspect to consider as part of older adulthood is *sexual identity*—that is, how people self-identify based on their sexual attractions, relationships, and behaviors (Cass, 1979). The sexual identities of older adults may not be synonymous with their sexual orientation or sexual behavior, however, as self-identification is key. In this chapter, the focus is on the identities of older people who identify as nonheterosexual.

Sexual identity development has been conceptualized as a lifelong process through which individuals become aware of their sexual attractions, explore the meaning of such attractions, accept the attractions and their implications, and integrate sexuality into their life (Cass, 1979). Although there are several well-known models, perhaps the framework described by Friend (1991), suggesting sexual identity is developed based on individual psychology and social construction, is most relevant to older LGBT individuals. This model embraces how socially constructed ideas of sexuality and identity may have largely been shaped by the various historical and political contexts individuals have lived within. Friend (1991) also proposed a theory of aging that is specific to sexual orientation, acknowledging that older LGB adults coconstruct their sexual and aging identities, drawing from their previous experiences of marginalization as well as the resiliency that they have amassed over their lifetimes.

Borrowing from Friend's (1991) model, it is easy to understand why Doris and Betty espoused differences in their willingness to be open about their relationship. In the 1940s, Doris would have been very aware of the possibility that others' knowing she was gay could possibly lead to being charged with a crime or diagnosed with a disease where she could be medically incarcerated for openly showing affection toward another woman. In contrast, Betty's young adulthood was full of counterculture movements, with the first made-for-television documentary about homosexuality being broadcast on American television and the passing of the Sexual Offences Bill in 1967, which decriminalized homosexuality in England. Based on their cognitive, behavioral, and affective responses to their sexual orientation, it is understandable that Betty and Doris, as well as other older LGBT adults, develop a range of responses to their sexuality as well as their age (Friend, 1991; Kolb, 2004).

Gender Identity

All older adults, not just TGNC individuals, have a rich gender identity. Gender identities are fluid, socially constructed, and culturally understood ways in which many people personally experience gender (Persson, 2009). Gender identity begins forming in early childhood, and can continue to change and develop over the lifespan. For TGNC older adults, gender identity development is unique in that it often does not conform to the traditional male–female/masculine–feminine gender binary. Part of the life experience for some older TGNC individuals is the process of transitioning, which involves many combinations of social, biological, relational, and personal changes so that a person's gender presentation is consistent with their gender identity, regardless of natal sex (Cook-Daniels, 2006; Persson, 2009).

Transitioning in Late Life

Unlike the coming out process that many LGBT individuals go through to accept and live comfortably with their sexual identity, the transitioning process for TGNC individuals is one that sometimes may be visible to others (Cook-Daniels, 2006). Therefore, older TGNC individuals need to navigate the changes associated with transitioning in their relationships with family, friends, health care providers, and social services providers. With greater visibility and discussion about TGNC people in current society, many middle-aged and older TGNC adults are now deciding to come out as being TGNC people and to begin living in gender-congruent ways, including pursuing hormonal and surgical modification (Cook-Daniels, 2006; Persson, 2009). Transitioning may bring with it additional health risks due to complications from hormonal therapies and surgeries, changes in social roles and relationships, loss of legal protections and access to benefits, and risk of losing employment, all of which may be more difficult to confront in later life (Cook-Daniels, 2002; see also Chapter 16, this volume). For those who transitioned in early life, or who have chosen to not transition, they may experience even more distrust of health care professionals, who were the "gatekeepers" of the transitioning process that would have allowed them to live in ways that affirm their gender identity (Cook-Daniels, 2006). Indeed, it is important to acknowledge that older TGNC adults may or may not have received hormonal or surgical alterations as part of their transition; moreover, there is great variability in individuals' specific experiences before, during, and after transition. There is evidence that for TGNC older adults, undergoing gender affirmation (previously known as *sex reassignment*) surgery or other means of transitioning marks a significant milestone that may lead them to think about their remaining lifetime in a different, often more positive, way (Fabbre, 2014).

SPIRITUALITY AND RELIGIOUS BELIEFS

Understanding how older LGBT adults' religious beliefs interfaces with their gender and sexual identity will be beneficial for practitioners, as it may uncover another layer of LGBT individuals' cultural identity, their intrapersonal strengths, and challenges they have faced. For many, the importance of spirituality and religious adherence increases with age, probably in relationship to a parallel increase in introspection or interiority that has been identified with later phases of the life cycle (Orel, 2004). However, this may not be true for all LGBT older adults. For example, Betty's Christian upbringing, in contrast with her nonattendance of church for several decades, may provide practitioners with areas for further exploration to better understand her views and experience of the death of her partner. Perhaps, like some other older African American LGBT people, she has become alienated from her church due to discrimination and prejudice (Woody, 2014). Attention may be given to how this is a part of the loss and grief that she is feeling, as well as an opportunity to further explore the extent to which she wants spirituality, religious beliefs, and religious community to play a role in her life in the future. See Chapter 8, this volume, for more on spiritual and religious issues and LGBT individuals.

FAMILY SYSTEMS AND SOCIAL SUPPORT

Research evidence for the benefit of social support and community on physical and mental health is extensive and reliable (Cornwell & Waite, 2009). The heteronormative assumption is that older adults can turn to family for help and support; however, this may not be the case when there are strained relationships, such as with Betty in the case study example. Betty has been estranged from her family for many years and appears to be unable to turn to her daughter even after the loss of her partner. Although Doris's family was supportive of their relationship, and viewed Betty as a part of the family while Doris was alive, it may be difficult to know what role they believe Betty should play now in the family. Rarely are these type of issues discussed openly amongst family members, and little is known about how to move forward in these uncharted territories across multigenerational-family relationships. It may be that Doris's family believes their relationship with Betty ended when Doris's life ended. That is, they may consider their obligation to Betty having been only in relation to their mother or grandmother Doris; and with her death, they no longer consider Betty a member of the family. Or it is possible that including her as a family member causes what they consider to be embarrassing questions, or places more focus on a part of their mother's life that they accepted but never totally agreed with. However, it may also be the case that Doris's family mistakenly believes that Betty no longer wishes to be a part of their family unit. Given that she has not contacted them, they may assume that she has moved on with her life and no longer has room for them in what she is now doing. They may also believe they are being respectful of Betty, allowing her to grieve, and then move forward with another relationship, without the constraints of her previous partner's family. Although in the case study Betty does not have a current relationship with her family of origin, this is not the norm for the majority of older LGBT adults (Brennan-Ing, Karpiak, & Seidel, 2011; Shippy, Cantor, & Brennan, 2004).

Family of Origin

Older LGBT adults are also likely to have been heterosexually partnered or married, and may have children from those relationships. Individuals who come out later in life likely have to go through the process of coming out to a spouse and children, and reactions among family members can vary from rejection to acceptance (Heaphy, Yip, & Thompson, 2004). Even when LGBT individuals have strained or ruptured relationships with parents, siblings, and/or other close family members, they consistently rate family relationships as being important (Heaphy et al., 2004).

Family of Choice

Given that some LGBT people may lack support from their family of origin and children, they have often turned to a *family of choice*, which may refer to a range of people including close friends, current and former spouses and partners, and accepting blood relatives (Weeks, Heaphy, & Donovan, 2001). Friendship is identified as one of the most important aspects of life among older LGBT people (Heaphy et al., 2004). Recent research on the social support networks of older LGBT people showed that they were more likely to reach out to a partner first, then to friends, and finally to kin—even though a majority of them were still connected in some way to their families of origin (Brennan-Ing et al., 2011; Shippy, Cantor, & Brennan, 2004).

Unfortunately for Betty, her family of choice was limited by her older partner's fears about discrimination and not being accepted even amongst their closest friends. With Doris's death, Betty finds herself estranged from her family of origin, as well as lacking the social support network that a family of choice might provide. In addition, because Betty remains sensitive to how strongly Doris felt about not living openly as partners, she is torn between seeking the social support she so needs and her desire to maintain respect for Doris's wishes. Clinicians might consider helping Betty process the ambivalence she feels about seeking support, while fearing negative reactions from others based on her sexual identity. This may also include connecting Betty to social groups for older LGBT people in her area, if such exist, in order to help her build a friend network (see the list of resources at the end of the chapter for examples of community organizations for older LGBT adults).

The idea of *community* is an important concept for older LGBT people, referring to their participation in their greater community where they live, or more specifically to the nonheterosexual and gender nonconforming communities in which they feel they belong. LGBT individuals are often involved in their local communities, even though they may not be out to neighbors or other community members (Heaphy et al., 2004). However, involvement in the LGBT community has been described as both a boon and a burden to the well-being of older LGBT adults (Hostetler, 2012). Continued involvement in the LGBT community provides social support and connections, opportunities to give back, and a greater sense of meaning or purpose. In contrast, gay men who are more involved in the bar and club scene may be at increased risk for feelings of isolation and stigma due to their advancing age (Hostetler, 2012). Unfortunately, the understanding of the effects community involvement has on older LGBT adults is limited, as studies have generally tended to draw from urban samples from areas where there are larger populations of LGBT people (Hostetler, 2012).

When working with older LGBT individuals, the meanings and effects of being involved with other LGBT people in the community should be considered with sensitivity, and on an individual basis, as people might react very differently to interactions within LGBT communities. In the case study with Betty, her involvement in the community was not identified, and may be an area for further exploration. Serving as Doris's caregiver for a year, Betty may have dropped many of her outside activities. She may now benefit from being encouraged to consider reengaging with her community, possibly as a way of contributing or adding purpose in her life, while also beginning to cultivate a much-needed support system.

Caregiving

Empirical literature has shown that 40% to 80% of lesbians and 40% to 60% of gay men are in couple relationships (Cahill, South, & Spade, 2000). Many partnered LGBT individuals live with their partners, but surveys show that there are a significant proportion of people in relationships who live alone (Heaphy et al., 2004). Regardless of their relationship status or living arrangements, many older adults will become the primary caregiver for a loved one. Like Betty in the case study, LGBT older adults often find themselves in the role of being a caregiver to a partner, friend, or other community member. LGBT individuals who are partnered are most likely to turn to their partner in the case of financial or health crises (Heaphy et al., 2004). However, because older LGBT people are less likely to rely on family of origin for caregiving needs and support, many must seek long-term care in community-based or institutional facilities (SAGE, 2010) when another caregiving option is not available.

While juggling multiple roles and responsibilities, LGBT caregivers face many of the same challenges experienced by their heterosexual peers (Coon, 2003, 2007). However, they often face additional barriers on a number of levels, including fear of discrimination and provider lack of sensitivity (Coon & Zeiss, 2003). Given that caregivers are at an increased likelihood of experiencing depression and physical disability (Fredriksen-Goldsen et al., 2011), caregivers should be encouraged to seek out needed support and professional services. The National Resource Center on LGBT Aging offers a resource center on LGBT caregiving, including information on the Family and Medical Leave Act (1993) and tips for finding LGBT-affirming services.

Residential Decisions

As they age, older LGBT adults will likely find that they need to change their place of residence due to retirement, functional limitations, or increased need for assistance and supportive health care. Numerous studies have identified the concerns of LGBT older adults with respect to entering postretirement care facilities (Brotman, Ryan, & Cormier, 2003; Smith, McCaslin, Chang, Martinez, & McGrew, 2010; Stein, Beckerman, & Sherman, 2010), with many older LGBT adults indicating a preference for LGBT-friendly or LGBT-specific housing facilities (Grant et al., 2010; Stein, Beckerman, & Sherman, 2010). Unfortunately, there are too few of these options currently available, and such facilities may not exist in the region individuals live in, leading them to rely on facilities that are geographically close and financially feasible (Grant et al., 2010).

In comparison with their heterosexual counterparts, older LGBT individuals are likely to have additional concerns about long-term-care facilities, as they face unique challenges in these living situations (Shankle, Maxwell, Katzman, & Landers, 2003). For example, LGBT residents who were out for several decades may feel they need to go "back in the closet" due to fears of being denied care or being mistreated (Stein, Beckerman, & Sherman, 2010). Indeed, existing research shows that older LGBT adults often expect to face discrimination in long-term-care settings (N. C. Jackson, Johnson, & Roberts, 2008). Because of this, approximately one third of individuals say they are willing to hide their sexual orientation (Smith et al., 2010). Older LGBT adults may also fear being separated from their partner, or needing to hide the nature of their relationship from facility staff and other residents (Hash & Cramer, 2003; Smith et al., 2010). TGNC individuals often fear being in a long-term-care setting where they require intimate caregiving tasks, as they do not know how staff members would react to gender nonconforming bodies, or scars from gender affirmation surgeries (Cook-Daniels, 2006; Witten & Eyler, 2012).

There is evidence of mistreatment, discrimination, and denial of care to LGBT older adults in long-term-care facilities. In addition, LGBT residents also face heteronormative policies and homophobic attitudes that impact their daily life (Hash & Cramer, 2003; Tolley & Ranzijn, 2006). Even if residents and staff are not overtly homophobic, they most likely make heteronormative assumptions about others (S. Jackson, 2006). For example, a staff member might assume that a same-sex partner is a sibling or other relative, and not the resident's significant other. Some partners of LGBT residents have experienced hostility in facilities, and others seek to prevent it and protect themselves by creating legal documents such as advance directives (Hash & Cramer, 2003). Even when heterosexual residents are not homophobic, they are likely to hold a "live and let live" attitude that would prevent them from specifically reaching out to their sexual minority peers, thus creating barriers to social engagement, emotional support, and friendship (Donaldson, Asta, & Vacha-Haase, 2014).

OLDER LGBT HEALTH AND WELL-BEING

Overall, a majority of older LGBT people rate their health as "good" or "excellent" (Brennan-Ing et al., 2011). However, health disparities among LGBT people are well-documented, and range from negative effects of stigmatization to reduced access to health care services (Dean et al., 2000). See Chapters 15 and 16, this volume.

Financial barriers continue to lead to poor health outcomes among older LGBT individuals (Brennan-Ing et al., 2011; Fredriksen-Goldsen et al., 2011), as does a lack of knowledge of available services. Many have reported feeling that if they did try to access community services, they would be discriminated against or denied services (Brennan-Ing et al., 2011). This was even more common among HIV-positive individuals, due to the stigma they felt was associated with their serostatus. TGNC older adults likely face significant barriers to proper health care, including poverty, disability, lack of insurance coverage, and a dearth of health care providers who are aware of trans aging issues (Finkenauer, Sherratt, Marlow, & Brodey, 2012). LGBT older adults have identified needs for increased social interaction, transportation to medical appointments, mental health counseling, regular calls or visits, and support during posthospital recovery (Brennan-Ing et al., 2011).

Practitioners can make a significant difference in the older adult's quality of life by being familiar with the resources for older LGBT people that are available in the community. In the case study, Betty's prior experiences with health care, whether good or bad, will most likely affect her willingness to seek help for her medical as well as her emotional needs. In working with Betty, the daily effect of her diabetes, COPD, and arthritis should be attended to, and the extent to which she is obtaining medical care explored.

Sexual Health

Although older adults are generally desexualized and sexually disempowered by negative stereotypes of aging and ageist dialogues in current United States society (Adams et al., 2003), the sexual health of the older LGBT individual is an important area to be addressed. Research has shown that many older adults remain sexually active, and seek companionship through dating; however, such discussions are largely focused on heterosexual populations (Adams et al., 2003). Older gay men tended to report an overall lowered frequency of sexual activity, but this may possibly be due to the devastating impact of HIV/AIDS over their lifetime (Brown, Alley, Sarosy, Quarto, & Cook, 2002).

The Internet provides affordable, easy access to sexual content, along with anonymity, which may make it attractive to older users (Cooper, 1998).

Older LGBT adults have access to websites and phone apps catering to social and sexual connection. One examination of LGBT online dating profiles showed that older individuals tended to play the "age game," whereby age is a salient factor in self-presentations and interactions (Jönson & Siverskog, 2012). People seem to use self-deprecating humor when talking about their age, as a means of acknowledging their age but also focusing on desirable qualities.

Mental Health

The mental health of older LGBT people is affected not only by current stressors and mental illness but also by lifelong experiences of oppression, stigma, minority stress, and discrimination (Grant et al., 2010; Kimmel, 2014). A recent national survey indicated that older LGBT adults reported a higher incidence of depression and substance use/abuse, in addition to obesity and physical disability (Fredriksen-Goldsen et al., 2011). Given that Betty is reporting anxiety and depression, a thorough assessment of her current symptoms would be recommended. Diagnostic differentiation would be useful, helping to distinguish whether Betty was suffering from an anxiety and/ or depressive disorder, or if the symptoms could be better accounted for by grief, or potentially the stress she is experiencing due to financial limitations and health concerns, as well as loneliness. Additional considerations would be the potential for substance use or abuse, as well as medical concerns or issues. Attention would also be directed toward the subtleness of the possible added distress of lifelong membership in a multitude of marginalized groups. For more on the consequences of stigma, see Chapter 3, this volume.

Many older LGBT adults may have experienced violence, rape, or other threats over their lifetime, resulting in higher rates of anxiety, posttraumatic stress disorder, or other reactions to trauma (Fredriksen-Goldsen et al., 2011). This may be particularly salient for TGNC individuals, who have been shown to have a significantly high rate of trauma exposure (Finkenauer et al., 2012). However, because they are often required to enter mental health care as part of the transitioning process, TGNC older adults may feel wary of utilizing mental health services for other purposes (Cook-Daniels, 2006).

As individuals age, death of family and friends becomes more common, and with that comes loss and bereavement. Given the significant losses of those who lived through the AIDS crisis, many older LGBT people may have experience in losing someone they loved, including lovers and friends. People in committed partnerships or marriages feel the same grief as their heterosexual counterparts do when their loved one passes away, but their grief may not be seen as equal or as significant by those who are not LGBT affirmative. This can create a sense of "disenfranchised grief," whereby the

LGBT bereaved have fewer avenues of emotional support following the death of a partner or spouse (Blevins & Werth, 2006).

Betty's experience with losing her partner, Doris, provides almost a textbook example of disenfranchised grief, as the stigma surrounding her samesex relationship may prevent her from speaking about Doris's death and from being able to access the support she needs. Without being able to talk about her love for her partner, and her feelings of loss, sadness, and hopelessness about the future, Betty continues to experience significant symptoms of grief and increasing warning signs of depression and anxiety. Betty's loss of her partner of over 30 years appears to be overwhelming and may lead her to feel as though she is in limbo regarding how to proceed and cope, along with challenging her sense of identity. A skilled practitioner may be able to help Betty face these challenges, supporting her as she navigates the grief process and begins healing, with a focus that must also include rebuilding a new life without her partner.

FINANCIAL AND LEGAL ISSUES

LGBT older adults are subject to inadequate protection and unequal benefits through Social Security, Medicare/Medicaid, pension plans, and tax-qualified retirement plans (Services and Advocacy for Gay, Lesbian, Bisexual, and Transgender Elders and LGBT Movement Advancement Project, 2010). These benefits, along with survivor's benefits, inheritance rights, and hospital visitation rights, may be denied due to being TGNC or part of a same-sex couple, as to be eligible to receive any of the benefits the individual's name and gender must match other records used for identity verification (Cook-Daniels, 2006).

Prior to *Obergefell v. Hodges* (2015) and legalization of same-sex marriage in the United States in June 2015, many states did not recognize same-sex partnerships, providing little to no protection for the surviving loved one. Now, same-sex marriage is legal in the United States and many other countries, such as Canada, New Zealand, South Africa, Uruguay, and the United Kingdom. Prohibitions set forth by the Defense of Marriage Act (DOMA) were struck down in 2013, thereby giving same-sex couples equal access to Medicare benefits and allowing active-duty military personnel and veterans and their partners to receive military/veteran's benefits (Kimmel, 2014).

Although these changes may be viewed as moving in a positive direction for granting LGBT people and their relationships more protection, it may be difficult for older adults to adjust to the openness with which such topics are discussed, and they may display a range of reactions to these developments. People like Betty may regret not being able to have had their relationships recognized by the government during their lifetime.

Mental health practitioners who encounter the psychosocial distress caused by such legal and financial issues in the lives of their older LGBT clients can provide not only psychological intervention and support but also referral to local, regional, and national organizations that assist older adults. Organizations such as AARP and MetLife have developed services and resources to assist older LGBT people; LGBT-oriented organizations like Lambda Legal, SAGE, and the National Resource Center on LGBT Aging offer advocacy, support, and information on LGBT nondiscrimination rights, advance-care planning, estate planning, and Medicare coverage (see the list of resources at the end of the chapter for information on the above-mentioned organizations).

End-of-Life Planning and Care

The current literature suggests that LGBT people, much like their heterosexual and cisgender counterparts, may not plan extensively for their end-of-life care, which leaves them with fewer choices when the need does arise for social services and long-term care (Clark, Boehmer, Rogers, & Sullivan, 2010; Croghan, Moone, & Olson, 2014). Advance directives (e.g., living wills, "Do Not Resuscitate" orders), while necessary and often a person's best hope of having her or his wishes carried out at end of life, are sometimes not communicated between patients and providers, or are even ignored (Blevins & Werth, 2006). In this documentation it is important that directives clearly state that the person's partner can participate in end-of-life decisions as a nonfamily member, which is a significant issue of concern among many LGBT individuals.

CLINICAL PRACTICE

Similar to many individuals in minority groups, older LGBT adults who seek mental health services have likely been affected by complex interactions of intersecting stigmas and lifetime histories of hiding, trauma, and fear. Sensitive and skilled practitioners must consider all of these pieces in conceptualizing and interacting with the older adult LGBT population. Depending on the context, older LGBT clients may understandably feel some level of fear or mistrust in a mental health or health care setting (Hash & Cramer, 2003). The responsibility falls upon the practitioner to convey an LGBT-affirmative approach, remaining open to discussing issues of sexual minority and TGNC identity and providing a welcoming, supportive environment. Offering cues that indicate an LGBT-affirming stance can enhance the provider-patient relationship (Wilkerson, Rybicki, Barber, & Smolenski, 2011).

The Culturally Competent Provider

LGBT older adults have identified important areas for recognition by culturally competent practitioners, including knowledge about the importance of relationships to LGBT people, the importance of preferred gender pronouns and gender expression, the diversity that exists in the LGBT community, the effects of HIV/AIDS on that community, and the impact of religious and societal oppression on LGBT experiences (Jihanian, 2013). Competent providers tend to be described as holding open, welcoming, nonjudgmental, and compassionate attitudes.

Practitioners can help to demonstrate they are affirmative of their older LGBT clients by addressing sexual needs and desires, and acknowledging the impact of technology on their ability to connect with sexual partners (Adams et al., 2003). Part of this affirmative stance could be conveyed by addressing dating and sexuality with older clients, including a discussion of safe-sex practices, phone apps, websites, and other forms of sexual connection and expression that may be important to older LGBT people.

In addition, a significant part of working with older LGBT adults is self-awareness, in particular, being conscious of one's own biases regarding age, as well as recognizing one's own gender and sexual identities and how those might influence work with older LGBT and TGNC people. Skilled clinicians are aware of personal preconceptions, while being sensitive to the within-group differences of older adults (Crowther & Zeiss, 2003). Even in today's society, many myths and stigmas are attached to growing older, leading to misinformation and ageism as well as homophobia and transphobia.

Practitioners are encouraged to explore how they might react to having Betty as a client. How does her age affect how one might work with her? How about her identity as an African American? A woman? A lesbian? What might be most difficult to truly understand or accept? Which aspects are easier to connect with? Clinicians are encouraged to reflect on these questions and the meanings of their answers.

A Culturally Affirming Environment

A culturally affirming environment includes structural components (e.g., gender-inclusive bathrooms and smooth interactions with staff) and systemic factors (e.g., using intake forms that do not rely on heteronormative or binary gender assumptions). Asking about (but not requiring) minority sexual orientation and gender identities on intake paperwork, displaying written nondiscrimination policies including gender identity, sexual orientation, and gender presentation, or having LGBT-related magazines or newspapers in the waiting area (Travis, 2011) or other explicit visual cues related to LGBT people in the office or on websites are all indicative of a welcoming environment where the older client can feel accepted. The intention is to demonstrate to LGBT older clients that the practitioner and/or agency is aware that they exist and matter, which is an important first step in building clients' trust.

Those practicing in rural areas should keep in mind that older LGBT adults are less likely to be out and more likely to have a lower income and feel guarded around family and friends (Lee & Quam, 2013). These practitioners should be sensitive to the logistical issues specific to a small community and particularly aware of LGBT-oriented community resources (Lee & Quam, 2013).

CONCLUSION

LGBT individuals in their later years should not continue to be an invisible minority, as they deserve respectful, competent, and compassionate care from insightful and dedicated professionals. In working with Betty, the woman in the case study at the beginning of this chapter, a practitioner would be able to identify a number of issues of concern related to her situation. Her experience as a woman, as a woman of color, as a gay woman, as a primary caregiver for a loved one, as a person of lower socioeconomic status, as a person disabled by health problems, as someone bereaved of a loved one—all are vital in understanding her, and each aspect should be addressed by culturally competent interventions and offerings of support.

Research questions related to older LGBT people must continue to become more complex, more nuanced, and more relevant to their lives in contemporary society. The past decade has shown a magnificent growth of research and writing on a spectrum of topics related to older LGBT adults, such that this area is shifting from an invisible topic to one that is appreciated by researchers and practitioners in multiple disciplines. However, much more remains to be done, particularly when it comes to applying empirical knowledge, changing attitudes, and promoting awareness regarding issues of salience for the older LGBT population.

RELEVANT RESOURCES

Alzheimer's Association LGBT Caregiver Concerns pamphlet: https://www.alz.org/national/documents/brochure_lgbt_caregiver.pdf
GenSilent: http://stumaddux.com/GEN_SILENT.html

Guidelines for Psychological Practice with Older Adults: http://www.apa.org/
practice/guidelines/older-adults.aspx

Lambda Legal: Trans Aging: We're Still Here! Transgender Rights Toolkit: A Legal
Guide for Trans People and Their Advocates: http://www.lambdalegal.org/
publications/trt_trans-aging-were-still-here

Lambda Legal for Seniors: http://www.lambdalegal.org/issues/seniors

LGBT Aging Project: http://www.lgbtagingproject.org/

Movement Advancement Project, LGBT Older Adults (MAP): http://www.lgbtmap.org/
policy-and-issue-analysis/lgbt-older-adults

National Resource Center on LGBT Aging: http://www.lgbtagingcenter.org/

Older Lesbians Organizing for Change (OLOC): http://www.oloc.org/

Outing Age 2010: http://www.thetaskforce.org/downloads/reports/reports/outingage_
final.pdf

Project Visibility (Boulder, CO): http://www.bouldercounty.org/family/seniors/pages/
projvis.aspx

Services & Advocacy for GLBT Elders (SAGE): http://www.sageusa.org/about/
index.cfm

The Fenway Institute, Caring for the Older LGBT Adult: http://www.
lgbthealtheducation.org/wp-content/uploads/Module-6-Caring-for-
Older-LGBT-Adults.pdf

Transgender Aging Network: http://forge-forward.org/aging/

What Mental Health Providers Should Know About Working With Older
Adults: http://www.apa.org/pi/aging/resources/guides/practitioners-should-
know.aspx

REFERENCES

Adams, M. S., Oye, J., & Parker, T. S. (2003). Sexuality of older adults and the
Internet: From sex education to cybersex. *Sexual and Relationship Therapy, 18,*
405–415.

Blevins, D., & Werth, J. L. (2006). End-of-life issues for LGBT older adults. In
D. Kimmel, T. Rose, & S. David (Eds.), *Lesbian, gay, bisexual, and transgender
aging: Research and clinical perspectives* (pp. 206–226). New York, NY: Columbia
University Press.

Brennan-Ing, M., Karpiak, S. E., & Seidel, L. (2011). *Health and psychosocial needs
of LGBT older adults.* Retrieved from http://www.lgbtagingcenter.org/resources/
pdfs/COH%20Study%20Final%20Report%20091911.pdf

Brotman, S., Ryan, B., & Cormier, R. (2003). The health and social service needs
of gay and lesbian elders and their families in Canada. *Gerontologist, 43,*
192–202.

Brown, L. B., Alley, G. R., Sarosy, S., Quarto, G., & Cook, T. (2002). Gay men. *Journal of Gay & Lesbian Social Services, 13*, 41–54. http://dx.doi.org/10.1300/J041v13n04_06

Cahill, S., South, K., & Spade, J. (2000). Outing age: Public policy issues affecting gay, lesbian, bisexual and transgender elders. Washington, DC: National Gay and Lesbian Task Force.

Cass, V. C. (1979). Homosexuality identity formation. *Journal of Homosexuality, 4*, 219–235. http://dx.doi.org/10.1300/J082v04n03_01

Clark, M. A., Boehmer, U., Rogers, M. L., & Sullivan, M. (2010). Planning for future care needs: Experiences of unmarried heterosexual and sexual minority women. *Women & Health, 50*, 599–617. http://dx.doi.org/10.1080/03630242.2010.522476

Cole, E. R. (2009). Intersectionality and research in psychology. *American Psychologist, 64*, 170–180. http://psycnet.apa.org/doi/10.1037/a0014564

Cook-Daniels, L. (2002). *Transgender elders and SOFFAs: A primer.* Retrieved from https://forge-forward.org/wp-content/docs/TransEldersPrimer_REV_3hole_2009-04-12.pdf

Cook-Daniels, L. (2006). Trans aging. In D. Kimmel, T. Rose, & S. David (Eds.), *Lesbian, gay, bisexual and transgender aging: Research and clinical perspectives* (pp. 21–35). New York, NY: Columbia University Press.

Coon, D. W. (2003). *Lesbian, gay, bisexual and transgender (LGBT) issues and family caregiving.* Retrieved from https://www.caregiver.org/sites/caregiver.org/files/pdfs/op_2003_lgbt_issues.pdf

Coon, D. W. (2007). Exploring interventions for LGBT caregivers. *Journal of Gay & Lesbian Social Services, 18*, 109–128. http://dx.doi.org/10.1300/J041v18n03_07

Coon, D. W., & Zeiss, L. M. (2003). Caring for families we choose: Intervention issues with LGBT caregivers. In D. W. Coon, D. Gallagher-Thompson, & L. Thompson (Eds.), *Innovative interventions to reduce dementia caregiver distress: A clinical guide* (pp. 267–295). New York, NY: Springer.

Cooper, A. (1998). Sexuality and the Internet: Surfing into the new millennium. *CyberPsychology & Behavior, 1*, 187–193. http://dx.doi.org/10.1089/cpb.1998.1.187

Cornwell, E. Y., & Waite, L. J. (2009). Social disconnectedness, perceived isolation, and health among older adults. *Journal of Health and Social Behavior, 50*, 31–48. http://dx.doi.org/10.1177/002214650905000103

Croghan, C. F., Moone, R. P., & Olson, A. M. (2014). Friends, family, and caregiving among midlife and older lesbian, gay, bisexual, and transgender adults. *Journal of Homosexuality, 61*, 79–102. http://dx.doi.org/10.1080/00918369.2013.835238

Crowther, M. R., & Zeiss, A. M. (2003). Aging and mental health. In J. S. Mio & G. Y. Iwamasa (Eds.), *Culturally diverse mental health: The challenge of research and resistance* (pp. 309–322). New York, NY: Brunner-Routledge.

David, S., & Knight, B. G. (2008). Stress and coping among gay men: Age and ethnic differences. *Psychology and Aging, 23,* 62–69.

Dean, L., Meyer, I. H., Robinson, K., Sell, R. L., Sember, R., Silenzio, V. M. B., . . . Xavier, J. (2000). Lesbian, gay, bisexual, and transgender health: Findings and concerns. *Journal of the Gay and Lesbian Medical Association, 4,* 102–151.

Dickinson, T., Cook, M., Playle, J., & Hallett, C. (2012). "Queer" treatments: Giving a voice to former patients who received treatments for their "sexual deviations." *Journal of Clinical Nursing, 21,* 1345–1354.

Donaldson, W. V., Asta, E. L., & Vacha-Haase, T. (2014). Attitudes of heterosexual assisted living residents toward gay and lesbian peers. *Clinical Gerontologist, 37,* 167–189. http://dx.doi.org/10.1080/07317115.2013.868849

Fabbre, V. D. (2014). Gender transitions in later life: The significance of time in queer aging. *Journal of Gerontological Social Work, 57,* 161–175. http://dx.doi.org/10.1080/01634372.2013.855287

Family and Medical Leave Act, 29 U.S.C. § 2601 (1993).

Finkenauer, S., Sherratt, J., Marlow, J., & Brodey, A. (2012). When injustice gets old: A systematic review of trans aging. *Journal of Gay & Lesbian Social Services, 24,* 311–330. http://dx.doi.org/10.1080/10538720.2012.722497

Fredriksen-Goldsen, K. I., Kim, H. J., Emlet, C. A., Muraco, A., Erosheva, E. A., Hoy-Ellis, C. P., . . . Petry, H. (2011). *The aging and health report: Disparities and resilience among lesbian, gay, bisexual, and transgender older adults.* Seattle, WA: Institute for Multigenerational Health.

Friend, R. A. (1987). The individual and social psychology of aging: Clinical implications for lesbians and gay men. *Journal of Homosexuality, 14,* 307–331. http://dx.doi.org/10.1300/J082v14n01_22

Friend, R. A. (1991). Older lesbian and gay people: A theory of successful aging. *Journal of Homosexuality, 20,* 99–118. http://dx.doi.org/10.1300/J082v20n03_07

Gates, G. J., & Newport, F. (2012). *Gallup special report: The U.S. adult LGBT population.* Retrieved from http://www.gallup.com/poll/158066/special-report-adults-identify-lgbt.aspx

Grant, J. M., Koskovich, G., Frazer, M. S., & Bjerk, S. (2010). *Outing age 2010: Public policy issues affecting lesbian, gay, bisexual, and transgender elders.* Washington, DC: National Gay and Lesbian Task Force Policy Institute.

Hash, K. M., & Cramer, E. P. (2003). Empowering gay and lesbian caregivers and uncovering their unique experiences through the use of qualitative methods. *Journal of Gay & Lesbian Social Services, 15,* 47–63.

Hash, K. M., & Rogers, A. (2013). Clinical practice with older LGBT clients: Overcoming lifelong stigma through strength and resilience. *Clinical Social Work Journal, 41,* 249–257. http://dx.doi.org/10.1007/s10615-013-0437-2

Heaphy, B., Yip, A. K. T., & Thompson, D. (2004). Ageing in a non-heterosexual context. *Ageing and Society, 24,* 881–902. http://dx.doi.org/10.1017/S0144686X03001600

Hostetler, A. J. (2012). Community involvement, perceived control, and attitudes toward aging among lesbians and gay men. *The International Journal of Aging & Human Development, 75*, 141–167. http://dx.doi.org/10.2190/AG.75.2.c

Jackson, N. C., Johnson, M. J., & Roberts, R. (2008). The potential impact of discrimination fears of older gays, lesbians, bisexuals and transgender individuals living in small- to moderate-sized cities on long-term health care. *Journal of Homosexuality, 54*, 325–339.

Jackson, S. (2006). Gender, sexuality and heterosexuality: The complexity (and limits) of heteronormativity. *Feminist Theory, 7*, 105–121.

Jihanian, L. J. (2013). Specifying long-term care provider responsiveness to LGBT older adults. *Journal of Gay & Lesbian Social Services, 25*, 210–231. http://dx.doi.org/10.1080/10538720.2013.782834

Jönson, H., & Siverskog, A. (2012). Turning vinegar into wine: Humorous self-presentations among older GLBTQ online daters. *Journal of Aging Studies, 26*, 55–64.

Kimmel, D. (2014). Lesbian, gay, bisexual, and transgender aging concerns. *Clinical Gerontologist, 37*, 49–63. http://dx.doi.org/10.1080/07317115.2014.847310

Kolb, P. J. (2004). Theories of aging and social work practice with sensitivity to diversity. *Journal of Human Behavior in the Social Environment, 9*, 2–24. http://dx.doi.org/10.1300/J137v09n04_01

Lee, M. G., & Quam, J. K. (2013). Comparing supports for LGBT aging in rural versus urban areas. *Journal of Gerontological Social Work, 56*, 112–126. http://dx.doi.org/10.1080/01634372.2012.747580

Logan, J. R., Ward, R., & Spitze, G. (1992). As old as you feel: Age identity in middle and later life. *Social Forces, 71*, 451–467.

Loving v. Virginia, 388 U.S. 1, 87 S. Ct. 1817, 18 L. Ed. 2d 1010, 1967 U.S. 1082. (1967).

Markides, K. S., & Black, S. A. (1995). Race, ethnicity, and aging: The impact of inequality. In R. H. Binstock & L. K. George (Eds.), *Handbook of aging and the social sciences* (pp. 153–167). San Diego, CA: Academic Press.

MetLife Mature Market Institute. (2010). *Still out, still aging: The MetLife study of lesbian, gay, bisexual, and transgender baby boomers.* New York, NY: Metropolitan Life Insurance Company.

Morrow, S. L. (1998). Toward a new paradigm in counseling psychology training and education. Invited reaction to Major Contribution on Lesbian, Gay, and Bisexual Affirmative Training. *The Counseling Psychologist, 26*, 797–808.

Nelson, T. D. (2005). Ageism: Prejudice against our feared future self. *Journal of Social Issues, 61*, 207–221.

Obergefell v. Hodges, No. 14-556, slip op. at 23 (U.S. June 26, 2015).

Orel, N. A. (2004). Gay, lesbian, and bisexual elders. *Journal of Gerontological Social Work, 43*, 57–77. http://dx.doi.org/10.1300/J083v43n02_05

Persson, D. I. (2009). Unique challenges of transgender aging: Implications from the literature. *Journal of Gerontological Social Work, 52,* 633–646. http://dx.doi.org/10.1080/01634370802609056

Purdie-Vaughns, V., & Eibach, R. P. (2008). Intersectional invisibility: The distinctive advantages and disadvantages of multiple subordinate-group identities. *Sex Roles, 59,* 377–391.

Schope, R. D. (2005). Who's afraid of growing old? *Journal of Gerontological Social Work, 45,* 23–39. http://dx.doi.org/10.1300/J083v45n04_03

Services and Advocacy for Gay, Lesbian, Bisexual, and Transgender Elders (SAGE) and LGBT Movement Advancement Project. (2010). *Improving the lives of LGBT older adults.* Retrieved from http://www.lgbtmap.org/file/improving-the-lives-of-lgbt-older-adults.pdf

Shankle, M. D., Maxwell, C. A., Katzman, E. S., & Landers, S. (2003). An invisible population: Older lesbian, gay, bisexual, and transgender individuals. *Clinical Research and Regulatory Affairs, 20,* 159–182.

Shippy, R. A., Cantor, M. H., & Brennan, M. (2004). Social networks of aging gay men. *The Journal of Men's Studies, 13,* 107–120. http://dx.doi.org/10.3149/jms.1301.107

Smith, L. A., McCaslin, R., Chang, J., Martinez, P., & McGrew, P. (2010). Assessing the needs of older gay, lesbian, bisexual, and transgender people: A service-learning and agency partnership approach. *Journal of Gerontological Social Work, 53,* 387–401. http://dx.doi.org/10.1080/01634372.2010.486433

Stein, G. L., Beckerman, N. L., & Sherman, P. A. (2010). Lesbian and gay elders and long-term care: Identifying the unique psychosocial perspectives and challenges. *Journal of Gerontological Social Work, 53,* 421–435.

Stoller, E. P., & Gibson, R. C. (2000). Introduction: Different worlds in aging: Gender, race, and class. In E. Stoller & R. Gibson (Eds.), *Worlds of difference: Inequality in the aging experience* (pp. 1–16). Thousand Oaks, CA: Sage. http://dx.doi.org/10.4135/9781483328539.n1

Tolley, C., & Ranzijn, R. (2006). Predictors of heteronormativity in residential aged care facilities. *Australasian Journal on Ageing, 25,* 209–214.

Travis, L. A. (2011, May). *Elder care: A resource for interprofessional providers: What you should know about LGBT older adults.* Retrieved from https://www.pogoe.org/productid/20939

U.S. Census Bureau. (2008). *2008 national population projections.* Retrieved from http://www.census.gov/population/projections/data/national/2008.html

U.S. Department of Health and Human Services, Centers for Disease Control and Prevention, National Center for Health Statistics. (2014). *Health, United States, 2013: With special feature on prescription drugs.* Retrieved from http://www.cdc.gov/nchs/data/hus/hus13.pdf#018

Vacha-Haase, T., Donaldson, W. V., & Foster, A. (2014). Race-ethnicity and gender in older adults. In M. L. Miville & A. D. Ferguson (Eds.), *Handbook of race-ethnicity and gender in psychology* (pp. 65–83). New York, NY: Springer. http://dx.doi.org/10.1007/978-1-4614-8860-6_4

Van Wagenen, A., Driskell, J., & Bradford, J. (2013). "I'm still raring to go": Successful aging among lesbian, gay, bisexual, and transgender older adults. *Journal of Aging Studies, 27*, 1–14. http://dx.doi.org/10.1016/j.jaging.2012.09.001

Weeks, J., Heaphy, B., & Donovan, C. (2001). *Same sex intimacies.* London, England: Routledge. http://dx.doi.org/10.4324/9780203167168

Weiss, D., & Lang, F. R. (2009). Thinking about my generation: Adaptive effects of a dual age identity in later adulthood. *Psychology and Aging, 24*, 729–734.

Wilkerson, J. M., Rybicki, S., Barber, C. A., & Smolenski, D. J. (2011). Creating a culturally competent clinical environment for LGBT patients. *Journal of Gay & Lesbian Social Services, 23*, 376–394.

Witten, T. M., & Eyler, A. E. (2012). Transgender and aging: Beings and becomings. In T. M. Witten & A. E. Eyler (Eds.), *Gay, lesbian, bisexual & transgender aging: Challenges in research, practice, and policy* (pp. 187–269). Baltimore, MD: The Johns Hopkins University Press.

Woody, I. (2014). Aging out: A qualitative exploration of ageism and heterosexism among aging African American lesbians and gay men. *Journal of Homosexuality, 61*, 145–165. http://dx.doi.org/10.1080/00918369.2013.835603

III

ESSENTIAL AREAS FOR PRACTICE, RESEARCH, TRAINING, AND HEALTH

11

PSYCHOTHERAPY WITH CLIENTS WHO HAVE BEEN THROUGH SEXUAL ORIENTATION CHANGE INTERVENTIONS OR REQUEST TO CHANGE THEIR SEXUAL ORIENTATION

ARIEL SHIDLO AND JOHN C. GONSIOREK

My psychologist took the position that he was neutral about [whether a homosexual orientation was normal]. He took a position that he was neutral about something that you can't be neutral. About two-thirds of the way into therapy I decided to stop trying to be heterosexual and found a boyfriend and came out. . . . I asked [my therapist] if he thought he could help me still. . . . He implied that he could help me just as easily become . . . a gay-adjusted person as a well-adjusted heterosexual person. At the time I bought that at face value. [Now] I see the false neutrality that existed. I don't think you can believe in a pathological and a normative view of homosexuality at the same time. I don't think that being neutral exists as a compromise between these two states.
—Male consumer of a sexual orientation change intervention
(Shidlo & Schroeder, 2001)

The first author would like to thank the Research Institute Without Walls interns, Eliza Dudelzak, Ali Ehteshami, Christie Julien, Lucy Moore, Erica Tanne, and coordinator, Elizabeth Vento, for their help.

http://dx.doi.org/10.1037/15959-012
Handbook of Sexual Orientation and Gender Diversity in Counseling and Psychotherapy, K. A. DeBord, A. R. Fischer, K. J. Bieschke, and R. M. Perez (Editors)

In this chapter, we first describe the sociopolitical context of sexual orientation change interventions (SOCIs), and the nomenclature issues that arise when discussing these interventions. We then examine the core tenets of SOCIs, the motivations of those who seek such interventions, the special case of SOCIs with minors, and the ethical problems and iatrogenic effects of these interventions. We conclude with two sections on clinical approaches: one on alternatives to SOCIs for clients seeking sexual orientation change, and the other on working with clients who have experienced failed SOCIs.

SOCIOPOLITICAL CONTEXT OF SOCIs

SOCIs need to be understood in the sociopolitical context of lesbian, gay, bisexual, or transgender (LGBT) communities. In the United States, Canada, and many other countries, civil rights and legal protections for LGB individuals continue to make strides toward equality. In some countries, there is a countermovement of escalating legal penalties and violent, state-condoned persecution against sexual minorities (e.g., Gettleman, 2010; Hauser, 2014). In the United States, while anti-LGB prejudice, discrimination, and violence exist, a growing majority of the population is adopting accepting attitudes toward lesbians and gay men (Art, 2014; Gallup, n.d.). In tandem with mainstream social changes, psychology and other mental health disciplines have shifted from a focus on trying to rid lesbians and gay men of their same-sex sexual orientation to recognizing their unique mental health needs (e.g., American Psychiatric Association, 2013; American Psychological Association [APA], 2012).

Psychologist Gerald C. Davison was an early critic of SOCIs. In 1974, he called on clinicians to stop offering SOCIs and to recognize the social oppression that leads clients to seek these treatments. Speaking in the 1970s climate of widespread antigay prejudice, he said, "The very existence of change-of-orientation programs strengthens societal prejudices against homosexuality and contributes to the self-hate . . . that [is one of the] . . . determinants of the 'voluntary' desire by some homosexuals to become heterosexual" (Davison, 1976, p. 157). Not until the late 1990s did professional associations catch up with Davison's pioneering efforts and begin to speak out against SOCIs (American Psychiatric Association, 2000; APA, 1998; National Association of Social Workers, 2010; Pan American Health Organization & World Health Organization, 2012; United Kingdom Council for Psychotherapy, 2014).

In 2009, the APA adopted the recommendations of the Task Force on Appropriate Therapeutic Responses to Sexual Orientation[1] (APA, 2009).

---

[1]Hereinafter, this document is referred to as the APA Task Force.

After reviewing 83 studies, the APA Task Force found that claims for the efficacy and safety of SOCIs are not supported by research and there does not exist compelling evidence that SOCIs reliably increase heterosexual attraction or decrease homosexual attraction.[2] APA has encouraged "mental health professionals to avoid misrepresenting the efficacy of sexual orientation change efforts by promoting or promising change in sexual orientation" (Anton, 2010, p. 31).

NOMENCLATURE

The APA Task Force distinguished between sexual orientation and sexual orientation identity. *Sexual orientation* is defined as

> an individual's patterns of sexual, romantic, and affectional arousal and desire for other persons based on those persons' gender and sex characteristics. Sexual orientation is tied to physiological drives and biological systems that are beyond conscious choice and involve profound emotional feelings, such as "falling in love." (APA, 2009, p. 30)

Sexual orientation identity

> refers to acknowledgment and internalization of sexual orientation and reflects self-exploration, self-awareness, self-recognition, group membership and affiliation, and culture. Sexual orientation identity involves private and public ways of self-identifying and is a key element in determining relational and interpersonal decisions, as it creates a foundation for the formation of community, social support, role models, friendship, and partnering. (APA, 2009, p. 30; see also Worthington, Savoy, Dillon, & Vernaglia, 2002)

SOCI practitioners have often confounded the constructs of sexual orientation and sexual orientation identity. Many of these practitioners disrupt clients' sexual orientation identity and erroneously posit this as change in sexual orientation. For example, if a SOCI client eliminates or reduces same-sex sexual behavior, initiates heterosexual sexual behavior, and rejects a gay identity, these do not indicate a change in sexual orientation but rather changes in sexual orientation identity and behavioral expression without altering core components of sexual orientation. The term *same-sex attraction* is used by SOCI clinicians to underlie their view that sexual and romantic attraction to persons of the same sex are malleable and symptomatic of psychopathology rather than stable characteristics of a same-sex

---

[2]The reader is invited to read the APA Task Force report for a detailed examination of the empirical evidence.

sexual orientation (e.g., National Association for Research and Therapy of Homosexuality [NARTH], 2010). Similarly, peer SOCIs use the term *ex-gay* to denote their rejection not only of a same-sex sexual orientation but also of LGB communities and at times even civil rights for LGB persons (Besen, 2015).

WHAT ARE SOCIs AND THEIR CORE TENETS?

A wide variety of clinical interventions, including psychoanalysis, behavior therapy, cognitive behavior therapy, hypnosis, eye-movement desensitization and reprocessing, psychotropic medications, couples therapy, family therapy, group therapy, and inpatient psychiatric treatment have all been used as SOCIs, whether or not such use is consistent with the standards of care of these techniques. Additionally, peer and religious interventions, including religious counseling, Homosexuals Anonymous (http://www.homosexuals-anonymous.com), fasting, praying, exorcism, and residential programs, have also been used (Shidlo & Schroeder, 2002). Most consumers of SOCIs pursue multiple courses of clinical, peer, and religious interventions over many years (APA, 2009). For example, in the Shidlo and Schroeder (2002) sample, 43% of participants reported two interventions; the median number of sessions was 72. The mean number of years that persons pursue SOCIs appears to range from 2 to at least 6 years (A. L. Beckstead & Morrow, 2004; Rix, 2013; Shidlo & Schroeder, 2002).

There are significant similarities among current clinical, peer, and religious SOCIs. These interventions are based upon discredited and erroneous assumptions, especially that same-sex sexual orientations are developmental disorders caused by poor relationships with parents, defective gender identity, social rejection, trauma, and sexual abuse. These approaches are typically derived from a religious belief that same-sex sexual orientations, sexual expression, and relationships are sinful (Drescher, 2002).

Peer SOCIs peaked in the 1990s. At that time, Exodus International—a network of ex-gay peer-religious groups—had 120 local ministries in the United States and Canada, and 150 ministries in 17 other countries (Exodus International, n.d.). Exodus International disbanded in 2012—its last president apologized for harming ex-gays and their families:

> I am sorry that some of you spent years working through the shame and guilt you felt when your attractions didn't change. I am sorry we promoted . . . change efforts . . . that stigmatized parents. (Schlanger & Wolfson, 2014)

Precisely because SOCIs fabricate alleged psychopathologies that blame parents for their children becoming homosexual, it is important to keep in mind that the harm caused by SOCIs can involve both primary (LGB individuals) and secondary (their families, spouses) victims.

As mental health professionals have increasingly abandoned and rejected SOCIs, the overtly religious character of many SOCI practitioners has increasingly predominated. NARTH was founded in 1992 in response to the marginalization of SOCI practitioners by mental health professionals. Concurrently, survivors of ex-gay groups and other SOCIs have formed social networks to assist healing and reintegration into the LGB community (e.g., http://www.beyondexgay.com).

Much of the SOCI literature is characterized by profound abhorrence toward LGB persons, relationships, and communities (e.g., Byrd, 2013; Satinover, 1996; Socarides, 1995).[3] SOCI writings transform social prejudice into psychological language without empirical support. For example, Nicolosi (1993) stated, "Homosexual relationships are so characteristically volatile because the homosexual hates what he loves" (p. 152). SOCI writers have used militant and apocalyptic language: "It is not a battle over mere sexuality, but rather over which spirit shall claim our allegiance, the cultural and political battle over homosexuality [is] . . . the defining moment of our society" (Satinover, 1996, p. 250).

Members of NARTH and their allies in the Family Research Council, the primary organization of SOCI practitioners, have fought the repeal of sodomy laws and the extension of antidiscrimination laws, adoption rights, and marriage for lesbians and gay men (Drescher, 1998; Lenz, 2012; Terkel, 2010). NARTH recently invited to its annual conference the leader of Family Watch International (FWI), listed by the Southern Poverty Law Center (SPLC) as a group that lobbies globally to criminalize LGB persons (Throckmorton, 2011a; SPLC, 2013). The NARTH website also links to an FWI video that is promoted by NARTH as featuring interviews with their members (NARTH, 2010).[4] NARTH's claim to being a scientific organization has been compromised by endorsing antigay theological positions (Throckmorton, 2012a). Consistent with their essentially conservative-religious basis, SOCIs circumvent the core fiduciary duty of health care professionals to operate in the best interests of clients by focusing on the rights of SOCI clinicians. Nicolosi, a cofounder of NARTH, described it as "the only secular group in the United States which protects *the rights of therapists* [emphasis added] to counsel clients with unwanted homosexuality" (Nicolosi, n.d.). It is not coincidental that NARTH statements

---

[3]Notable exceptions include Yarhouse and Throckmorton (2002) and Throckmorton (2002); these authors have become critical of traditional clinical SOCIs.
[4]The FWI film "Understanding Same Sex Attraction" and its companion policy brief on SOCI are forceful political statements on the fight against global LGB civil and human rights (Family Watch International, n.d.).

on the rights of individuals who are distressed by their same-sex sexual orientation are made in the context of defending the rights of SOCI *clinicians*.

In recent decades, the predominant clinical SOCI has been the neo-psychoanalytic reparative therapy championed by Nicolosi (1991; Drescher, 2002). *Reparative therapy* claims that sexual attraction to and falling in love with same-sex partners are generated by deficits in gender identification caused by poor relationships with a same-sex parent, same-sex peers, and trauma. This therapy emphasizes the questioning of what motivates sexual or romantic feelings toward persons of the same sex, with an eye toward identifying an underlying pathological causation. The inconsistent reasoning behind this is revealed when the reasons for opposite-sex desire—a goal of reparative therapy—are not subject to such scrutiny. Reparative therapy engages in a tenacious search for intrapsychic and interpersonal difficulties that demonstrate how they ostensibly cause homosexual desire, and it teaches clients to disrupt same-sex desire by pathologizing it as a symptom.

Reparative therapy and most current SOCIs posit that a defective gender identity underlies same-sex desire, and therefore attempt to bolster gender identity by encouraging conforming-to-gender stereotypes. As the APA Task Force (APA, 2009) detailed, there is no empirical basis for the assumptions made by reparative therapy and other SOCIs; in fact, many of their constructs are flatly contradicted by the empirical literature. While some SOCIs target lesbian women (e.g., Harren Hamilton, 2011), the overwhelming focus is on gay men. Many of these interventions are characterized by profound sexism. For example, SOCI literature gives scant attention to the impact on women who are partners of male SOCI clients who struggle with their sexual orientation while maintaining a heterosexual relationship.

In summary, SOCIs fabricate a scientific-sounding theoretical base, but one without empirical support; instead, they are based on a particular and narrow set of theological ideas that do not represent a full spectrum of theological perspectives, Christian perspectives, or even conservative Christian perspectives. This disinformation then serves as a springboard for a range of SOCIs that are often labeled with familiar mental health intervention labels but that bear scant resemblance to the original therapeutic models or to the standards of care they require.

CLIENT MOTIVATIONS FOR SOCIs

Most SOCI consumers in the United States appear to be Caucasian men of conservative religions (APA, 2009). There are limited data on involvement with SOCIs on the parts of women and ethnic minorities. SOCI clients are distressed by same-sex desire and love, and sexual behavior and relationships with same-sex partners, and they do not want to view themselves or be seen by others as lesbian or gay. The Ex-Gay Survivor's Survey (Rix, 2013) found that the most frequent reasons for seeking SOCIs were religious beliefs, the desire to fit in socially, the wish to please family and friends, the fear of losing family and friends, and misinformation on what it means to be gay.

L. Beckstead and Israel (2007) distinguished between *intrinsic* and *extrinsic* motivations for SOCI. One can further differentiate intrinsic factors between those not based on shame, such as religious beliefs and emotional commitment to a heterosexual spouse, versus those driven by internalized homonegativity. Homonegative beliefs include viewing lesbians and gay men overall as having unhappy lives, dysfunctional relationships, and suffering from sexual addiction, substance abuse, violence, and disease (Shidlo, 1994). A former male consumer of SOCI reported that he "wanted to . . . be attracted to women because . . . [he] believed that was the only way that . . . [he] would find happiness and love and have a family, and escape . . . a . . . frightening fate" (Shidlo & Schroeder, 2001).

Persons who pursue peer and religious SOCIs may also be motivated by the desire for social connectedness. Shidlo and Schroeder (2002) found that some SOCI consumers had been out as lesbian or gay pre-SOCI but felt alienated from lesbians and gay men and blamed their sexual orientation for their failure to connect with their peers. Their same-sex sexual orientation served as an explanatory mechanism for their unhappiness, a belief encouraged by SOCIs.

Extrinsic reasons for SOCI include external pressure or coercion by one's family of origin, heterosexual spouse, and church (APA, 2009; A. L. Beckstead & Morrow, 2004; Shidlo & Schroeder, 2002). Schroeder and Shidlo (2002) found that some persons had been forced by religious universities to pursue SOCIs. The penalty for not complying with SOCI was expulsion or loss of student financial aid. For many who seek SOCIs, social support systems overlap heavily with religious community. Implicit or explicit threats of loss of such community provide powerful external pressure, especially if no support system in LGB communities has yet been developed.

SOCI consumers do not always enter psychotherapy with the intention of changing their sexual orientation. Their presenting complaint may be depression or anxiety, low self-esteem, guilt about their homosexual orientation, and difficulties with a same-sex relationship. SOCI clinicians frame these difficulties as *the result* of a homosexual orientation and prescribe changing sexual orientation. In the Shidlo and Schroeder (2002) study, 25% of SOCIs were clinician-initiated—the client did not ask for SOCI. It is contrary to APA LGB Guidelines (APA, 2012) and APA Task Force (APA,

2009) recommendations for clinicians to offer SOCI to clients who have not requested help to change their homosexual orientation.

Davison (2001) wrote on the critical role the clinician has in helping the client construct an understanding of the relationship of sexual orientation to distress:

> People seldom go to mental health clinicians with [clearly delineated] problems. . . . A person . . . consults a therapist because he or she is unhappy. . . . The clinician *transforms* these often vague and complex complaints into a conceptualization of . . . what the causes are, and what might be done to alleviate the suffering. . . . Psychological problems are for the most part *constructions* of the clinician. (p. 696, emphases in original)

SOCI clinicians teach clients to interpret same-sex desire and love as symptoms that need to be disrupted. They reinforce the problematization of desire and encourage clients to judge their self-esteem, self-mastery, and mental health by how successfully they derail same-sex desire (Shidlo & Schroeder, 2002).

SOCI WITH MINORS AND YOUTH

SOCI clinicians offer advice to parents on how to prevent their children from becoming homosexual, and NARTH warned against helping LGB youth accept their sexual orientation. For example, in *A Parent's Guide to Preventing Homosexuality*, Nicolosi and Nicolosi (2002) focused on correcting purported gender nonconformity as a strategy to prevent and eliminate same-sex attraction. The APA Task Force (APA, 2009) found only a handful of clinical reports and no empirical research on SOCI with teens. It expressed concern about forced residential and inpatient SOCIs with minors in light of the burgeoning movement to recognize the rights and capacity of many adolescents to consent to treatment. The APA Task Force concluded that the use of residential and inpatient SOCIs with youth is not recommended. Some minors and youth participate in SOCIs under coercion by parents, schools, and religious institutions.[5] In the United States there are two states, California and New Jersey, that have banned the use of clinical SOCIs with minors; others are working on getting similar bills passed (Reuters, 2014).

---

[5]A CNN report on gender nonconforming boys forced into SOCI is available on YouTube (Savvas Tappi, 2011a, 2011b, 2011c).

Distortion of Empirical Findings

SOCIs are rife with ethical problems (APA, 2009; Schroeder & Shidlo, 2002). A central ethical problem is that these interventions typically ignore or misrepresent empirical research on LGB mental health. For example, Shidlo and Schroeder's research (2002) has been misrepresented repeatedly in NARTH documents by the erroneous claim that the researchers did not recruit participants who perceived that SOCI was helpful. Throckmorton (2011b, 2012b) and Kincaid (2011) have described other instances in which NARTH leaders have misrepresented researchers' findings.

SOCI clinicians provide misinformation that results in negative and long-lasting effects on the self-image of clients (American Psychiatric Association, 2000; A. L. Beckstead & Morrow, 2004; Haldeman, 2002; Rix, 2013; Schroeder & Shidlo, 2002; Shidlo & Schroeder, 2002). Participants in the Schroeder and Shidlo (2002) study reported misinformation asserted by their SOCI practitioners. Some of the more noteworthy included the following:

- *Ignoring or distorting APA and American Psychiatric Association's positions on LGB mental health.* This typically involves SOCI clinicians not discussing with clients the 1970s depathologizing of same-sex sexual orientations, or claiming that these diagnostic changes were based on political pressure, not the consensus of scientific findings.
- *Claiming same-sex sexual orientations are psychological disorders, symptoms of another disorder, and socially destructive.* SOCIs commonly include an exhaustive search for life events that demonstrate the pathology of same-sex desire, regardless of whether there is empirical or theoretical support for such assertions and regardless of the damage done to client self-esteem and relationships.
- *Asserting that lesbian and gay lives and relationships are characterized by unhappiness.* Most SOCIs involve indoctrination of clients into the belief that same-sex relationships never succeed and that gay and lesbian individuals are invariably unhappy. Since disruption of connection with lesbian and gay communities is a common SOCI strategy, SOCI clients have limited opportunities to challenge such misrepresentations.

On a more basic level of health care standards, therapeutic interventions that lack an empirical basis and whose assumptions are contradicted by scientific information, such as SOCIs, invariably violate informed consent requirements unless practitioners tell clients that their recommendation is not an accepted standard of care and is potentially dangerous. It is of interest to note that SOCI practitioners often sidestep this significant ethical problem by actively distorting ideas of informed consent and client choice (e.g., Rosik, 2001).

Gonsiorek (2004) critiqued "the assumption of unlimited client choice in therapeutic goals and methodologies" (p. 754). In discussing the duty of psychologists to refuse certain client requests, he stated,

> Clients . . . make requests of psychologists to engage in . . . treatment activities that are unsubstantiated, . . . unethical, . . . or . . . ill-advised. They may make such requests on the basis of naiveté, . . . social pressure, . . . [and] misinformation. . . . There is no . . . impropriety in their making such requests; they do not have psychologists' fiduciary duty. . . . Clients are basing the understanding of their distress and symptomatology on [SOCI] constructs that are not known to have either validity or any reliable relationship to their symptoms. . . . They are also requesting treatment[s] . . . whose . . . ethical basis . . . [is] questionable and are known to pose substantial risk of harm. (pp. 754–755)

He further added that

> when clients make inappropriate requests, psychologists are required to provide informed consent about . . . options and to educate clients about professional standards and appropriate practice . . . *Client choice properly functions as an aspect of informed consent and not as a substitute for ethical decision making and practice standards.* A client's request for conversion therapy is a questionable request . . . in terms of ethics, efficacy, and possible harm. . . . It is nonsense to assert that in requests for conversion therapy, respect for diversity requires that psychologists abdicate these complex duties. (pp. 754–755, emphasis added)

When clients experience conflict between their homosexual orientation and religious values, Gonsiorek (2004) called on psychologists not to "rescue clients from grappling with their own existential, spiritual, and philosophical dilemmas when the various components of who they are in their human fullness do not easily coexist" (p. 753).

As this overview of ethical problems suggests, SOCIs are inconsistent with APA LGB Guidelines (APA, 2012) that state the following:

> APA's (1998) "Resolution on Appropriate Therapeutic Responses to Sexual Orientation" offers a framework for psychologists working with clients who are concerned about the implications of their sexual orientation. [It] . . . highlights . . . sections of the APA Ethics Code that apply to all psychologists working with lesbian, gay, and bisexual older adults, adults, and youths. These sections include prohibitions against

discriminatory practices (e.g., basing treatment upon pathology-based views of homosexuality or bisexuality); the misrepresentation of scientific or clinical data (e.g., the unsubstantiated claim that sexual orientation can be changed); and a clear mandate for informed consent (APA, 1992). Informed consent would include a discussion of the lack of empirical evidence that SOCE [sexual orientation conversion efforts] are effective and their potential risks to the client (APA, 2009b) and the provision of accurate information about sexual orientation to clients who are misinformed or confused. (p. 14)

It is difficult to adequately convey the pervasive disrespect and at times overt scorn toward gay and lesbian individuals in SOCI writings. This is a central ethical problem with SOCIs: We cannot think of another purported psychotherapeutic endeavor for any group of clients that is characterized by such contempt. Indeed, health care professions, in their ethical guidelines, uniformly view disrespect of clients as incompatible with service provision. We invite readers to peruse the SOCI literature and judge for themselves.

Iatrogenic Effects of SOCIs

Adverse iatrogenic effects of SOCIs constitute a particular class of ethical problems in that causing no harm is a core ethical principle of health care professions. The APA Task Force (APA, 2009) determined that empirical data on the harmfulness of SOCIs have methodological limitations that do not allow for interpretation of causality. Nonetheless, the Task Force concluded that the data are sufficiently strong to state that SOCIs pose iatrogenic risks. Consumers' reports of harm include confusion about sexual orientation, anxiety, depression, grief, guilt, hopelessness, poor self-image, suicidal ideation, self-hatred, sexual dysfunction, intrusive imagery while having sex, deteriorated relationships with family, loss of social support, loss of faith, and intimacy difficulties (APA, 2009; A. L. Beckstead & Morrow, 2004; Haldeman, 2002; Rix, 2013; Schroeder & Shidlo, 2002; Shidlo & Schroeder, 2002).

We conceptualize four features of SOCIs as likely to be involved in iatrogenic effects: clients are told that (a) their homosexual orientation and same-sex desire are signs of a mental disorder; (b) SOCI can change their sexual orientation if they are highly motivated; (c) when SOCIs fail, clients are left to blame themselves; and (d) clients are then left with an intensification of contempt toward their homosexual orientation and LGB persons. Once a SOCI fails, there is no mechanism to help clients evict the misinformation and heightened self-contempt that typically results. Although some SOCI clinicians have begun to acknowledge that their work fails with some clients (Rosik, 2003), they have yet to demonstrate effective tools to process iatrogenic effects. Shidlo and Schroeder's (2002; Schroeder & Shidlo, 2002) finding that self-blame is common in failed SOCIs was confirmed by A. L. Beckstead and Morrow (2004):

> Harms [that] participants experienced seemed to rest on their . . . reliance on a paradigm that proclaimed that homosexuality or being LGB was evil and needed to be "repaired" or avoided. Most . . . participants [who did not succeed in SOCI] described how this reinforcement of their previous stereotypes caused more confusion, problems with intimacy, and hopelessness about their . . . options. (p. 672)

PSYCHOTHERAPY WITH CLIENTS WHO REQUEST TO CHANGE THEIR SEXUAL ORIENTATION: ALTERNATIVES TO SOCIs

The APA Task Force (APA, 2009) recommended that clients who request to change their homosexual orientation be offered alternatives to SOCIs based on the empirical evidence that a homosexual orientation is not a sign of a mental illness. SOCI clinicians have rejected this position and countered that consumers are entitled to choose therapeutic goals, and clinicians should be unconstrained to tell clients that they view a homosexual orientation as a treatable disorder (NARTH, 2010).

There are SOCI alternatives consistent with the recommendations of the APA Task Force (APA, 2009) and APA LGB Guidelines (APA, 2012). For example, Throckmorton and Yarhouse's (2006) sexual identity therapy does not focus on changes in sexual orientation as a sign of success or failure:

> Some religious individuals will determine that their religious identity is the preferred organizing principle for them, even if it means choosing to live with sexual feelings they do not value. Conversely, some religious individuals will determine that their religious beliefs may become modified to allow integration of same-sex eroticism within their valued identity. (p. 7)

L. Beckstead and Israel's (2007) approach goes further: It counteracts heterosexism, confronts internalized homonegativity, and encourages clients to explore conflict between sexual orientation and religious or other beliefs without a rush to foreclose. They remind clinicians not to value resolution of conflict about sexual orientation but remain supportive of clients who value their religious identity above a conventional adoption of an LGB identity.

Similarly, Bartoli and Gillem (2008) provided a useful framework for working with clients who believe that "the solution to their dilemma is to privilege or deny either [their religious or sexual orientation] identity" (p. 204). They encouraged therapists to explore fears of modifying religious beliefs or mourn the impossibility of integrating a homosexual orientation with a heterosexual relationship. When it is impossible to avoid compromise in religious or sexual orientation identity, they suggest that clinician and client view

> each solution as flexible and impermanent . . . [to] minimize the anxiety of both therapist and client about finding the "perfect" solution. . . . Temporary solutions . . . [are not] an indication of failure on the part of the therapist, the client, or the treatment. [They] do . . . justice to the fluidity and complexity of human beings' needs, identities, and beliefs. (p. 205)

These approaches offer guidance for working with clients whose beliefs preclude an acceptance of a homosexual orientation identity. Some clients need to grieve the incompatibility of sexual orientation and their values. At the same time, clinicians can help differentiate between religious beliefs about same-sex desire, sex, relationships, and marriage, versus unsubstantiated views that violations of these beliefs are signs of psychological disorder.

POST-SOCI INTERVENTIONS

Given the misinformation with which SOCI clients have been indoctrinated and the likelihood of some degree of iatrogenic effects, working with clients after SOCI is clinically challenging. Post-SOCI clients may benefit from exploring how shame toward their same-sex sexual orientation and contempt toward LGB persons may have been exacerbated by SOCI and may have been the motivation to seek SOCI. Haldeman (2002) noted that clinicians need to

> reinforce the notion that post-conversion therapy . . . does not require the client to switch to a pro-gay perspective. . . . ambivalence about his sexual identity . . . need not be hidden to please the . . . therapist. It should be treated as a welcome element in the treatment. (p. 122)

The invitation to express internalized homonegativity can be accompanied by a joint questioning of the accuracy of these attitudes and identifying the emotions and sensations they evoke.

Clinicians can educate post-SOCI clients on empirical evidence that (a) homosexual and bisexual orientations are normal variants of sexual expression, (b) determinants of all sexual orientations remain unknown, (c) SOCI misinformation that same-sex couples are psychologically dysfunctional has no basis in fact, (d) same-sex couples' parenting abilities are no different from heterosexuals' (Goldberg & Allen, 2013; Patterson, 2009), and (e) the effectiveness of SOCIs is unsubstantiated and their theories are erroneous (A. L. Beckstead & Israel, 2007). For some post-SOCI clients, the outcome of psychotherapy can be ambiguous: neither a conflict-free sexual orientation identity, nor coming out and forming same-sex relationships.

Clients who reject the help of clinicians who do not offer SOCI and insist on seeking SOCIs need to be encouraged by clinicians to monitor in their future SOCIs the development of a sense of failure, shame, hopelessness, and internalized homonegativity (L. Beckstead & Israel, 2007). Clients should also be encouraged to ask SOCI clinicians, as part of informed consent, for information on how failure to change sexual orientation will be dealt with and how termination will be managed.

Overall, post-SOCI interventions are clinically demanding. In addition to the unresolved tensions between sexual orientation, religious beliefs, and other aspects of identity that are not integrated by SOCIs, a variety of adverse sequelae are created that often require clinical attention. Clinicians treating post-SOCI clients may want to be alert to particular negative effects that merit assessment and intervention:

- *Muddled thinking about sexual orientation.* Because SOCIs provide a dizzying array of explanations of homosexual orientation and how it is to be changed, clients are often left confused about what their homosexual orientation means and how it relates to other aspects of their identity (Schroeder & Shidlo, 2002; Shidlo & Schroeder, 2002). SOCIs overemphasize sexual orientation as a larger-than-life aspect of identity and of psychological and social functioning. Clients may need help in bringing down to size the importance of sexual orientation in proportion to interpersonal and vocational life challenges.
- *Poor differentiation of sexual orientation identity from other identity areas.* Clients may need help to recognize that many aspects of their psychological and interpersonal functioning are independent of sexual orientation. They often find that preoccupation with changing sexuality has left other aspects of their lives neglected. After clients have processed internalized homonegativity and the possibly traumatic effects of SOCIs, clinicians can gently encourage them to conceive of a future in which the preoccupation with sexual orientation decreases in its salience. In the words of a former SOCI consumer, "It took me a while to realize that there is more to life than sexuality" (Shidlo & Schroeder, 2001).
- *Mistrust of sexual arousal and romantic love feelings.* One common SOCI intervention is to teach clients to interrupt sexual arousal and feelings of love toward same-sex persons. SOCI derails spontaneous same-sex sexual and love responses by teaching clients that these are destructive desires that are not

to be trusted (Schroeder & Shidlo, 2002; Shidlo & Schroeder, 2002). Many post-SOCI clients are left with a long-lasting mistrust of their feelings toward same-sex partners and intrusive imagery, and may need help in processing contempt and fear in response to same-sex desire and love.

- *Gender nonconforming behavior.* SOCIs link gender non-conforming behavior to sexual orientation (NARTH, 2010). After the failure of SOCI, clients may experience shame about gender-related behavior and fear behaving in ways that unintentionally out them as lesbian or gay. Some clients may benefit from help to accept gender nonconforming behavior.
- *Depression, anxiety, and suicidal ideation.* SOCI clients who failed to change may experience a resurgence of depression, anxiety, and suicidal ideation (APA, 2012; A. L. Beckstead & Morrow, 2004; Shidlo & Schroeder, 2002). They may struggle with a disruption of sense of identity and need help in redefining themselves. Clients may benefit from framing this period as necessitating grieving and recovery from LGB-related traumatic events that they experienced growing up, and during and after their SOCIs.
- *Grieving lost time and developmental challenges.* Many SOCI clients spend years, sometimes decades, attempting to change their sexual orientation (A. L. Beckstead & Morrow, 2004; Shidlo & Schroeder, 2002). One of the more pernicious effects of failed SOCIs is that the time lost—spent trying to change—cannot be retrieved. Post-SOCI, clients may need to grieve that they lag behind their peers in forming a same-sex relationship or marriage. Clients may suffer from social anxiety, social skill deficits, and untreated characterological issues that interfere with forming new friendships and relationships.
- *Multiple social losses.* Persons who fail SOCIs, especially those in peer and religious counseling, may experience a series of social losses. SOCI clients are encouraged to give up LGB relationships and friendships, similar to the way in which 12-Step group members are advised to distance themselves from active substance abusers. New ex-gay networks may be lost when the client abandons SOCI. Post-SOCI clients may face challenges in forming friendships with LGB persons. Clinicians can encourage clients to access LGB community resources as well as ex-ex-gay groups (http://www.lgbtcenters.org/localstatenational-groups.aspx; http://www.beyondexgay.com; http://www.jqyouth.org; http://gottagivemhope.blogspot.com). APA LGB Guidelines' (APA,

2012) Appendices A and B provide resources for clients, families, and clinicians.

- *Relational refugees*. Similar to refugees who flee anti-LGBT persecution (Shidlo & Ahola, 2013), post-SOCI clients may become *relational refugees* who fall in between LGB, ex-gay, ex-ex-gay, and heterosexual communities.[6] Clients may benefit from addressing the shame and secrecy that they feel about having participated in SOCI and their alienation from LGB peers. Some clients may not benefit—early in the therapy—from encouragement to connect with the LGB community. They may need to first grieve lost time and overcome contempt toward themselves and LGB persons (Haldeman, 2002).

- *Damage to the client's relationship with family of origin, and secondary harm to heterosexual spouses and the client's parents*. SOCIs indoctrinate clients to believe that relationships with parents are to blame for a homosexual orientation. Clinicians can assess whether a client's relationship and feelings about his or her parents have been derailed by SOCI. A decision to abandon SOCIs, whether or not an LGB identity is adopted, may test clients' relationships with their parents, heterosexual spouses, children, and extended family. Heterosexual spouses and partners may experience a sense of deception and sexual rejection when attempts to change a homosexual orientation unravel (Buxton, 1994, 2004). Not sufficiently recognized as negatively impacted by SOCIs, parents may be harmed by feeling blamed by SOCI doctrines; they may benefit from clinical and peer interventions that normalize having children who are LGB. Clinicians can recommend couple and family therapy, and support groups for heterosexual spouses in mixed orientation relationships and parents of LGB children (http://www.straightspouse.org and http://www.pflag.org).

- *Religious and spiritual harm*. Clients may experience harm to their religious identity. They may feel angry with God and struggle to reconcile religious beliefs with SOCI failure and a homosexual orientation identity (Shidlo & Schroeder, 2002). Clinicians can refer to literature in this area for therapeutic guidelines (Bartoli & Gillem, 2008; A. L. Beckstead & Morrow, 2004; Gonsiorek, Richards, Pargament, & McMinn, 2009; Haldeman, 2002, 2004; Yarhouse & Beckstead, 2011).

---

[6]The term *relational refugees* was introduced by Wimberly (2000, 2001) to describe African Americans who are not grounded in nurturing and liberating relationships. It provides a powerful metaphor for what some LGB persons may experience—especially those who find themselves between LGB and heterosexual identities and communities.

SUMMARY

This chapter has examined the impact of SOCIs and the challenges experienced by clients after their sexual orientation fails to change. The APA Task Force (APA, 2009) found that SOCIs are not effective and have iatrogenic effects. Nonetheless, for some clients, the acceptance of a homosexual orientation may not be a possible outcome. This chapter provides guidance for psychotherapy with persons who have difficulties integrating their sexual orientation identity with other identities. Clinicians can utilize interventions that honor the conflict between religious beliefs and a homosexual orientation, remain in their role as evidence-based practitioners, and yet not collude in an iatrogenic pathologizing of a homosexual orientation. Readers are encouraged to read APA LGB Guidelines (APA, 2012), the report of the APA Task Force (APA, 2009), and other chapters in this volume for more detailed guidance about evidence-based clinical practice with clients with a homosexual or bisexual orientation.

REFERENCES

American Psychological Association. (1998). Resolution on appropriate therapeutic responses to sexual orientation. *American Psychologist, 53*, 934–935.

American Psychological Association. (2009). *Report of the American Psychological Association's Task Force on Appropriate Therapeutic Responses to Sexual Orientation*. Retrieved from http://www.apa.org/pi/lgbt/resources/therapeutic-response.pdf

American Psychological Association. (2012). Guidelines for psychological practice with lesbian, gay, and bisexual clients. *American Psychologist, 67*, 10–42. http://dx.doi.org/10.1037/a0024659

American Psychiatric Association. (2000). *Committee on Psychotherapy by Psychiatrists (COPP) position statement on therapies focused on attempts to change sexual orientation (reparative or conversion therapies)*. Retrieved from http://www.aglp.org/pages/position.html#Anchor-55000

American Psychiatric Association. (2013). *Position statement on issues related to homosexuality. Approved December 2013 by the APA Board of Trustees*. Retrieved from http://www.aglp.org/pages/LGBTPositionStatements.php

Anton, B. S. (2010). Proceedings of the American Psychological Association for the legislative year 2009: Minutes of the annual meeting of the Council of Representatives and minutes of the meetings of the Board of Directors. *American Psychologist, 65*, 385–475. http://dx.doi.org/10.1037/a0019553

Art, S. (2014). *Most Americans say same-sex couples entitled to adopt*. Retrieved from http://www.gallup.com/poll/170801/americans-say-sex-couples-entitled-adopt.aspx

Bartoli, E., & Gillem, A. R. (2008). Continuing to depolarize the debate on sexual orientation and religion: Identity and the therapeutic process. *Professional Psychology: Research and Practice, 39,* 202–209. http://dx.doi.org/10.1037/0735-7028.39.2.202

Beckstead, A. L., & Morrow, S. L. (2004). Mormon clients' experiences of conversion therapy: The need for a new treatment approach. *The Counseling Psychologist, 32,* 651–690. http://dx.doi.org/10.1177/0011000004267555

Beckstead, L., & Israel, T. (2007). Affirmative counseling and psychotherapy focused on issues related to sexual orientation conflicts. In K. J. Bieschke, R. M. Perez, & K. A. DeBord (Eds.), *Handbook of counseling and psychotherapy with lesbian, gay, bisexual, and transgender clients* (2nd ed., pp. 221–244). Washington, DC: American Psychological Association. http://dx.doi.org/10.1037/11482-009

Besen, W. (2015). *Why former 'ex-gay' Randy Thomas' coming out is a huge deal.* Retrieved from http://www.truthwinsout.org/opinion/2015/01/40517/

Buxton, A. P. (1994). *The other side of the closet: The coming-out crisis for straight spouses and families.* New York, NY: John Wiley & Sons.

Buxton, A. P. (2004). Paths and pitfalls: How heterosexual spouses cope when their husbands or wives come out. *Journal of Couple & Relationship Therapy, 3,* 95–109. http://dx.doi.org/10.1300/J398v03n02_10

Byrd, A. D. (2013). *Pediatrics group endorses homosexual adoption . . . but new policy places children at risk.* Retrieved from http://www.narth.org/docs/endorses.html

Davison, G. C. (1976). Homosexuality: The ethical challenge. *Journal of Consulting and Clinical Psychology, 44,* 157–162.

Davison, G. C. (2001). Conceptual and ethical issues in therapy for the psychological problems of gay men, lesbians, and bisexuals. *Journal of Clinical Psychology, 57,* 695–704. http://dx.doi.org/10.1002/jclp.1038

Drescher, J. (1998). I'm your handyman: A history of reparative therapies. *Journal of Homosexuality, 36,* 19–42.

Drescher, J. (2002). I'm your handyman: A history of reparative therapies. In A. Shidlo, M. Schroeder, & J. Drescher (Eds.), *Sexual conversion therapy: Ethical, clinical, and research perspectives* (pp. 5–24). New York, NY: Haworth Press.

Exodus International. (n.d.). In *Wikipedia.* Retrieved from http://en.wikipedia.org/wiki/Exodus_International

Family Watch International. (n.d.). *Understanding same-sex attraction.* Retrieved from http://www.familywatchinternational.org/fwi/documentary.cfm

FWI (n.d.). *Understanding same-sex attractions* [Videofile]. Retrieved from the NARTH website: http://www.narth.com

Gallup. (n.d.). *Gay and lesbian rights.* Retrieved from http://www.gallup.com/poll/1651/gay-lesbian-rights.aspx

Gettleman, J. (2010, January 4). Gay in Uganda, and feeling hunted. *The New York Times.* Retrieved from http://www.nytimes.com/2010/01/04/world/africa/04gay.html

Goldberg, A. E., & Allen, K. R. (Eds.). (2013). *LGBT-parent families: Innovations in research and implications for practice*. New York, NY: Springer. http://dx.doi.org/ 10.1007/978-1-4614-4556-2

Gonsiorek, J. C. (2004). Reflections from the conversion therapy battlefield. *The Counseling Psychologist, 32*, 750–759. http://dx.doi.org/10.1177/0011000004267621

Gonsiorek, J. C., Richards, P. S., Pargament, K. I., & McMinn, M. R. (2009). Ethical challenges and opportunities at the edge: Incorporating spirituality and religion into psychotherapy. *Professional Psychology: Research and Practice, 40*, 385–395. http://dx.doi.org/10.1037/a0016488

Haldeman, D. C. (2002). Therapeutic antidotes: Helping gay and bisexual men recover from conversion therapies. In A. Shidlo, M. Schroeder, & J. Drescher (Eds.), *Sexual conversion therapy: Ethical, clinical, and research perspectives* (pp. 117–130). New York, NY: Haworth Press. http://dx.doi.org/10.1300/J236v05n03_08

Haldeman, D. C. (2004). When sexual and religious orientation collide: Considerations in working with conflicted same-sex attracted male clients. *The Counseling Psychologist, 32*, 691–715. http://dx.doi.org/10.1177/0011000004267560

Harren Hamilton, J. (Producer). (2011). *Dr. Julie Harren Hamilton - Homosexuality 101 part 2* [Video file]. Retrieved from http://www.youtube.com/watch? v=1pR7uCJwvP0

Hauser, C. (2014, February 4). Rights group releases video of LGBT attacks in Russia. *The New York Times*. Retrieved from http://thelede.blogs.nytimes.com/2014/02/04/ rights-group-releases-video-of-lgbt-attacks-in-russia/

Kincaid, T. (2011). Mormon Reorientation [sic] group fraudulently misquotes Collins [Blog post]. Retrieved from http://www.boxturtlebulletin.com/tag/a-dean-byrd

Lenz, R. (2012). *NARTH becomes main source for anti-gay 'junk science.'* Retrieved from https://www.splcenter.org/fighting-hate/intelligence-report/2012/narth-becomes-main-source-anti-gay-%E2%80%98junk-science%E2%80%99

NARTH. (2010). *Task Force on Practice Guidelines for the Treatment of Unwanted Same-Sex Attractions and Behavior*. Retrieved from http://www.scribd.com/doc/ 115508811/NARTH-Practice-Guidelines

National Association of Social Workers. (2010). *"Reparative" and "conversion" therapies for lesbians and gay men: Position statement by the National Committee on Lesbian, Gay, and Bisexual Issues, NASW*. Retrieved from http://www.naswdc.org/diversity/ lgb/reparative.asp

Nicolosi, J. (1991). *Reparative therapy of male homosexuality: A new clinical approach*. Northvale, NJ: Jason Aronson Inc.

Nicolosi, J. (1993). *Healing homosexuality: Case stories of reparative therapy*. New York, NY: Jason Aronson Inc.

Nicolosi, J. (n.d.). *What is reparative therapy? Examining the controversy*. Retrieved from http://josephnicolosi.com/what-is-reparative-therapy-exa/

Nicolosi, J., & Nicolosi, L. A. (2002). *A parent's guide to preventing homosexuality*. Downers Grove, IL: InterVarsity Press.

Pan American Health Organization & World Health Organization. (2012, May 17). *"Therapies" to change sexual orientation lack medical justification and threaten health.* Retrieved from http://www.paho.org/hq/index.php?option=com_content&view=article&id=6803&Itemid=1

Patterson, C. J. (2009). Children of lesbian and gay parents: Psychology, law, and policy. *American Psychologist, 64,* 727–736. http://dx.doi.org/10.1037/0003-066X.64.8.727

Reuters. (2014). *N.Y. lawmakers consider ban on gay "conversion therapy" for minors.* Retrieved from http://news.yahoo.com/n-y-lawmakers-consider-ban-gay-conversion-therapy-202156656.html

Rix, J. (2013). *400 Ex-gay survivors document harm of reparative therapy: Beyond Ex-Gay announces the results of extensive survivor surveys.* Retrieved from http://www.beyondexgay.com/survey/results.html

Rosik, C. H. (2001). *Conversion therapy revisited: Parameters and rationale for ethical care.* Retrieved from http://www.narth.org/docs/conversiontherapy.html

Rosik, C. H. (2003). Motivational, ethical, and epistemological foundations in the treatment of unwanted homoerotic attraction. *Journal of Marital and Family Therapy, 29,* 13–28. http://dx.doi.org/10.1111/j.1752-0606.2003.tb00379.x

Satinover, J. (1996). *Homosexuality and the politics of truth.* Grand Rapids, MI: Baker.

Savvas Tappi. (2011a). *"Sissy" boy experiment part 1* [Video file]. Retrieved from http://www.youtube.com/watch?v=CJ7VigOWm_M

Savvas Tappi. (2011b). *"Sissy" boy experiment part 2* [Video file]. Retrieved from http://www.youtube.com/watch?v=YtUes86A378

Savvas Tappi. (2011c). *"Sissy" boy experiment part 3* [Video file]. Retrieved from http://www.youtube.com/watch?v=eHOvP6tMhEg

Schlanger, Z., & Wolfson, E. (2014, May 1). Ex-ex-gay pride. *Newsweek.* Retrieved from http://www.newsweek.com/ex-ex-gay-pride-249282

Schroeder, M., & Shidlo, A. (2002). Ethical issues in sexual orientation conversion therapies: An empirical study of consumers. In A. Shidlo, M. Schroeder, & J. Drescher (Eds.), *Sexual conversion therapy: Ethical, clinical, and research perspectives* (pp. 131–166). New York, NY: Haworth Press. http://dx.doi.org/10.1300/J236v05n03_09

Shidlo, A. (1994). Internalized homophobia: Conceptual and empirical issues in measurement. In B. Greene & G. Herek (Eds.), *Lesbian and gay psychology: Theory, research, and clinical applications* (pp. 176–205). Thousand Oaks, CA: Sage. http://dx.doi.org/10.4135/9781483326757.n10

Shidlo, A., & Ahola, J. (2013). Mental health challenges of LGBT forced migrants. *Forced Migration Review, 42,* 9–11. http://www.fmreview.org/en/fmr42full.pdf

Shidlo, A., & Schroeder, M. (2001). [Data collected in the study "Changing sexual orientation: A consumer's report" but not published in Shidlo & Schroeder (2002)]. Unpublished raw data.

Shidlo, A., & Schroeder, M. (2002). Changing sexual orientation: A consumer's report. *Professional Psychology: Research and Practice, 33,* 249–259. http://dx.doi.org/10.1037/0735-7028.33.3.249

Socarides, C. (1995). *Homosexuality: A freedom too far.* Phoenix, AZ: Adam Margrave Books.

Southern Poverty Law Center. (2013). *Criminalizing sex: Six U.S. anti-gay groups abroad.* Retrieved from https://www.splcenter.org/20130709/dangerous-liaisons#criminalizing-sex

Terkel, A. (2010). *How the Rekers 'rent boy' scandal could undermine Prop. 8 supporters' court battle.* Think Progress. Retrieved from http://thinkprogress.org/politics/2010/05/19/98027/rekers-prop8/

Throckmorton, W. (2002). Initial empirical and clinical findings concerning the change process for exgays. *Professional Psychology: Research and Practice, 33,* 242–248. http://dx.doi.org/10.1037/0735-7028.33.3.242

Throckmorton, W. (2011a). NARTH features leader of international efforts to keep homosexuality illegal [Blog post]. Retrieved from http://www.patheos.com/blogs/warrenthrockmorton/2011/10/31/narth-features-leader-of-international-efforts-to-keep-homosexuality-illegal/

Throckmorton, W. (2011b). University of Utah professor: NARTH article "unscientific and irresponsible" [Blog post]. Retrieved from http://www.patheos.com/blogs/warrenthrockmorton/2011/12/06/university-of-utah-professor-narth-article-irresponsible-and-unscientific/

Throckmorton, W. (2012a). NARTH burnishes science credentials by promoting Torah Declaration [Blog post]. Retrieved from http://www.patheos.com/blogs/warrenthrockmorton/2012/01/03/narth-burnishes-science-credentials-by-promoting-torah-declaration/

Throckmorton, W. (2012b). *Seton Hall professor: NARTH member "misreported and misrepresented" my research.* Retrieved from http://www.patheos.com/blogs/warrenthrockmorton/2012/01/05/sirotafitzgibbons/

Throckmorton, W., & Yarhouse, M. A. (2006). *Sexual identity therapy: Practice framework for managing sexual identity conflicts.* Retrieved from http://www.sitframework.com/wp-content/uploads/2009/07/sexualidentitytherapyframeworkfinal.pdf

United Kingdom Council for Psychotherapy. (2014). *Conversion therapy consensus statement.* Retrieved from http://www.psychotherapy.org.uk/index.php?id=528

Wimberly, E. P. (2000). *Relational refugees: Alienation and re-incorporation in African American churches and communities.* Nashville, TN: Abingdon Press.

Wimberly, E. P. (2001). Pastoral care of sexual diversity in the Black church. *American Journal of Pastoral Counseling, 3*, 45–58. http://dx.doi.org/10.1300/J062v03n03_04

Worthington, R. L., Savoy, H., Dillon, F. R., & Vernaglia, E. R. (2002). Heterosexual identity development: A multidimensional model of individual and group identity. *The Counseling Psychologist, 30*, 496–531. http://dx.doi.org/10.1177/0010000203030004002

Yarhouse, M. A., & Beckstead, A. L. (2011). Using group therapy to navigate and resolve sexual orientation and religious conflicts. *Counseling and Values, 56*, 96–120. http://dx.doi.org/10.1002/j.2161-007X.2011.tb01034.x

Yarhouse, M. A., & Throckmorton, W. (2002). Ethical issues in attempts to ban reorientation therapies. *Psychotherapy: Theory, Research, Practice, Training, 39*, 66–75. http://dx.doi.org/10.1037/0033-3204.39.1.66

12

LESBIAN, GAY, BISEXUAL, AND TRANSGENDER FAMILY ISSUES IN THE CONTEXT OF CHANGING LEGAL AND SOCIAL POLICY ENVIRONMENTS

CHARLOTTE J. PATTERSON

How do the legal and social policy contexts in which lesbian, gay, bisexual, and transgender (LGBT) Americans live influence their day-to-day experiences? The current historical moment is an exciting time to consider this question. At the time of this writing, many important legal and policy changes that affect sexual minorities are occurring in the United States (Boies & Olson, 2014; Klarman, 2013). After many years of hostility from the legal system (Murdoch & Price, 2001; Rubenstein, 1996), LGBT Americans' struggle for equal rights under the law is gathering momentum. As a result, lesbian and gay lives in particular are changing, and an unusual opportunity to observe the impact of legal and policy change upon human behavior is before us (Patterson, 2009, 2013b). Although bisexual and transgender issues

This work is based substantially on a chapter published by the author in *Handbook of Counseling and Psychotherapy With Lesbian, Gay, Bisexual, and Transgender Clients, Second Edition*, K. J. Bieschke, R. M. Perez, and K. A. DeBord (Editors). Copyright 2007 by the American Psychological Association.

http://dx.doi.org/10.1037/15959-013
Handbook of Sexual Orientation and Gender Diversity in Counseling and Psychotherapy, K. A. DeBord, A. R. Fischer, K. J. Bieschke, and R. M. Perez (Editors)

are beginning to receive more attention, change is most noticeable for lesbian and gay people (Ball, 2012; Rivers, 2013).

This chapter begins with an overview of the legal and policy environments in which LGBT Americans live today and then explores some of the ways in which issues of couples, parents, and families are influenced by these contexts. Throughout the chapter, the primary focus is on lesbian and gay couples, parents, and families in the contemporary United States, and the main concern is to identify ways in which changing legal and policy environments affect their experiences. Some attention will also be devoted to bisexual and transgender experiences. Since there is tremendous variability in both environments and experiences, a key theme will be diversity. Diversity in legal and policy climates on the one hand, and diversity among LGBT Americans on the other, are at the center of the discussion.

LEGAL AND SOCIAL POLICY CONTEXTS OF LGBT FAMILY ISSUES

The legal and ideological landscapes in which LGBT Americans live are shifting in many significant ways (Patterson, Fulcher, & Wainright, 2002). Big legal changes have occurred together with major shifts in public opinion about homosexuality during recent years. In the 1990s, polls revealed that most Americans were opposed to legal recognition for the marriages of same-sex couples. By 2015, however, a Gallup Poll reported that 60% of Americans were in favor of such legal recognition (Gallup Organization, 2015). This trend is also evident in public opinion about employment discrimination. Prior to 1980, only 56% of Americans favored equal rights in job opportunities; but by 2008, fully 89% favored such equal rights, and the question was no longer even being asked in Gallup Polls (Gallup Organization, 2015; Herek, 2003). These changes in attitudes took place in the context of changes in experiences. In 1985, only 24% of Americans reported that they had lesbian or gay friends or relatives, but by 2013, fully 75% reported this (Gallup Organization, 2015). Whether changes in public opinion have caused policy changes or vice versa, sizeable shifts in law, policy, and public opinion have taken place over the same period of time.

A number of important legal changes relevant to lesbian and gay people have taken place in recent years. Some have occurred at the federal level and affect all Americans. Others have occurred at state or local levels and affect only those living in a particular jurisdiction. Other policy changes have been made in business or educational settings and affect different numbers of people, depending upon the size of the organizations in question. The result is a patchwork of legal and policy environments that vary in significant ways from one part of the country to another (National LGBTQ Task Force, 2011; Patterson, 2013a, 2013b).

Legal Situation of LGBT Individuals and Couples

One act of Congress and three U.S. Supreme Court rulings have been particularly important to LGBT individuals and couples in recent years. The first of these developments involved the repeal of a federal law (nicknamed "Don't Ask, Don't Tell") that prevented lesbian women and gay men from serving openly in the armed forces of the United States. In 2010, Congress voted to repeal the Don't Ask, Don't Tell law, and by 2011, gay and lesbian members of the armed services were allowed to serve openly. Considering that the armed services have long been the nation's largest employer, this was an important step in the direction of equality for lesbians and gay men.

The first of the court rulings was *Lawrence v. Texas* (2003), which struck down laws criminalizing oral or anal sexual practices between consenting adults (i.e., the so-called sodomy laws). Although sodomy laws had rarely been enforced, when they were, their enforcement was often specifically targeted at gay men, and the laws were also used to justify various kinds of discrimination against lesbians and gay men. For example, sodomy laws were invoked to justify employment discrimination (Badgett, 2001, 2003) and to justify discrimination against lesbian, gay, and bisexual parents in the context of child-custody proceedings (Swisher & Cook, 2001). The *Lawrence* decision had the effect of ensuring that consensual sexual behavior of same-sex couples was accorded the same fundamental privacy status as that of other Americans. The demise of sodomy laws across the country meant that these could no longer be used to justify discriminatory policies, and so it was an important step toward recognition of lesbian, gay, and bisexual Americans as equal citizens.

A second major U.S. Supreme Court decision was handed down in *United States v. Windsor* (2013), which struck down part of the federal law that defined marriage as being between a man and a woman. As a result of the *Windsor* decision, same-sex couples who had married in any jurisdiction that recognized their marriage were regarded as married in federal law and in policy. Thus, married same-sex couples became eligible for the rights and responsibilities of marriage under federal law. The *Windsor* decision also opened the door for additional challenges to statewide bans on legal recognition for the marriages of same-sex couples.

The third and most significant of the U.S. Supreme Court rulings relevant to LGBT rights of recent years was *Obergefell v. Hodges* (2015), which made marriage equality the law of the land. Based on ideas about fundamental rights and on those about guarantees of equal protection, the ruling gave the right to marry to same-sex as well as to different-sex couples. The right to have their marriages recognized by law opened up many rights and responsibilities to same-sex couples, including those relevant to issues such as immigration, inheritance, Social Security, taxation, and veterans' benefits.

In addition to these alterations in federal law, there have been many changes in state and local laws and in employment policies that are relevant to lesbian, gay, and bisexual individuals. For instance, many states and the District of Columbia now have in place laws (and others have executive orders) that prohibit workplace discrimination on the basis of sexual orientation, and some of these also include protections for gender identity (Grant et al., 2011). In addition, many cities and counties have instituted nondiscrimination policies that include sexual orientation and gender identity. Numerous employers have adopted nondiscrimination policies that include both sexual orientation and gender identity, including more than 375 of Forbes 500 companies (Human Rights Campaign, 2015). Such policies vary dramatically in their nature, with some proving to be more meaningful than others, but the trend toward increasing recognition of equal employment rights is clear.

Protections against employment discrimination may be especially important to transgender individuals. Many LGBT people report that they receive unfair treatment at work (Pew Research Center, 2013), and transgender people are especially likely to report such problems. In one survey, 90% of transgender respondents said that they had experienced difficulties at work due to gender identity; almost half said that they had been fired, not hired, or denied a promotion due to their gender identity (National LGBTQ Task Force, 2011).

One result of recent changes in law and policy is that what was once a unitary experience of discrimination and oppression for many LGBT individuals and couples in the United States has now been transformed. A same-sex couple in Iowa, who have married and are recognized as a couple in law and practice, may well be open about their couple status and be recognized as a married couple by friends, neighbors, and family members. A same-sex couple in Kentucky, on the other hand, now has the right to marry, but they may be aware of local opposition to their marriage and may feel the need to hide their sexual identity and relationship status from many important people in their environment. As a result, they may encounter a variety of problems with friends, neighbors, and family members. Thus, even in the face of real progress in the federal courts, the uneven pace of change in different parts of the United States means that same-sex couples who live in different jurisdictions may also live in different circumstances.

Legal Situation of LGBT Parents and Their Children

The legal and policy situation with regard to issues of lesbian and gay parents also remains variable across the United States today, with some states providing more favorable environments than others. Automatic legal recognition of parent–child bonds for all children born into a marriage is now available to married same-sex couples throughout the country; this is a major development attributable to the *Obergefell* decision.

The legal situation of children born to unmarried same-sex couples is less certain, and legal recognition of a second parent in an unmarried same-sex couple may be difficult to obtain. Second-parent adoptions, in which a coparent adopts his or her partner's child without terminating the partner's parental rights, can be used in these situations. Second-parent adoptions by unmarried couples are, however, prohibited in Nebraska, North Carolina, Ohio, and Wisconsin (National Center for Lesbian Rights [NCLR], 2015). Regardless of sexual orientation, Utah also prohibits anyone who is living with an unmarried partner from adopting a child. Thus, legal recognition of parent–child bonds is still limited for some same-sex couples (NCLR, 2015).

Most states do not prohibit discrimination in foster care or adoption on the basis of gender identity. Currently, only six states bar discrimination on the basis of gender identity by law or by regulation (Stotzer, Herman, & Hasenbush, 2014). Thus, adoption and foster-care options may not be open to transgender individuals in many jurisdictions (Downing, 2013).

Custody and visitation arrangements, especially after the separation and/or divorce of parenting couples, are another area of concern for lesbian, gay, and transgender parents. Couples who divorce after one person declares a nonheterosexual identity may turn to the courts to create custody and visitation plans for their minor children. For many years, courts across the country were hostile to the interests of lesbian and gay parents and their children, even going so far in some cases as to hold the parents unfit as a result of their sexual orientation (Maggiore, 1992; Swisher & Cook, 2001). In recent years, such blatant discrimination has become less common, although egregious decisions do still occur (Ball, 2012). Most common now is the so-called nexus standard, holding that a parent's sexual orientation should be presumed irrelevant to custody proceedings unless it can be shown to have had a negative effect upon the children (Patterson, 2009). Problems with custody and/or visitation after divorce are, however, still reported by many transgender individuals (Grant et al., 2011; Stotzer, Herman, & Hasenbush, 2014).

Overall, the legal and policy landscape for lesbian and gay parents and their children is undeniably improved, but it still varies in significant ways from one jurisdiction to another (Ball, 2012). Throughout the country, a same-sex couple who marries and then has children will both be considered legal parents of those children. In cases where one already had children at the time of marriage, the couple may often be able to complete a second-parent adoption, and in this way achieve many of the benefits and protections afforded to married heterosexual couples and their children. In a handful of states, however, and especially for transgender individuals, family relationships may be more difficult to protect.

LGBT INDIVIDUALS AND THEIR FAMILIES OF ORIGIN

Against the landscape of varied laws and policies across the United States, LGBT peoples' issues as members of families can often be complex (Downing, 2013; Patterson, 2013a, 2013b; Ross & Dobinson, 2013). In addition to the usual issues of young adults that involve renegotiation of family roles as they transition into adult work, couple relationships, and parenthood, LGBT young adults often face a number of additional concerns. The establishment of work and career patterns, the creation and recognition of sexual and romantic relationships, and decisions about transition to parenthood (all normative tasks of early adulthood) may well pose special concerns for LGBT young adults, especially in their extended families.

Consider first the young adult's employment concerns (Badgett, 2003). Antigay and antitransgender prejudice and discrimination may be on the wane overall, but both are believed to remain common in some lines of work (Human Rights Campaign, 2014; Mohr & Fassinger, 2013). For this reason, openly LGBT adults may see their options in some occupations as limited by attitudes toward sexual orientation and gender identity (Badgett, 2003; Mohr & Fassinger, 2013). Consider also the fact that family businesses may be controlled by relatives whose attitudes about sexual orientation and gender identity can vary across the spectrum of opinion. Other things being equal, LGBT people are unlikely to seek out—and likely to leave—situations in which they will work for employers who are known to hold negative attitudes about them. In a recent survey, almost one in 10 LGBT respondents said that a negative atmosphere with regard to sexual orientation and/or gender diversity had caused them to leave a job (Human Rights Campaign, 2014).

How will these issues be discussed within families, if at all? Depending upon the degree to which nonheterosexual or gender nonconforming identities have been disclosed in the family, these discussions may be open and clear, on the one hand, or limited (even nonexistent), on the other. Those who do not feel safe disclosing their identities to members of their extended families are also going to experience difficulty explaining why their career choices are more constrained than those of their heterosexual or cisgender siblings. One result may often be an emotional distancing of LGBT young adults from members of the extended family to whom nonheterosexual and/or transgender identities have not been disclosed (Savin-Williams, 2003).

If a young adult has kept his or her sexual orientation or gender identity secret from some or all of his or her extended family members, then this will almost certainly decrease the degree to which it is possible to share information about sexual and romantic dimensions of his or her life (Cohler & Michaels, 2013; Savin-Williams, 2003). Even if LGBT individuals have disclosed their identities to members of their extended families, they still may encounter reluctance on the part of family members to entertain any real discussion of romantic interests. Again, one result may be the emotional distancing of LGBT young adults from members of the extended family who feel unable or unwilling to acknowledge the sexual or romantic interests in their lives; such distancing has been found to be associated with depressive symptoms and with substance abuse among LGBT young adults (e.g., Ryan, Huebner, Diaz, & Sanchez, 2009). As more and more LGBT individuals come out to family members and as negative attitudes fade, these issues will recede in importance. In some parts of the United States today, however, such issues remain very much in the forefront of consciousness for LGBT young adults.

Another process that necessitates renegotiation of roles in families involves a young adult's transition to parenthood. This process may be especially challenging for LGBT individuals and couples (Goldberg, 2010; Patterson, 2013a, 2013b). If nonheterosexual identities remain undisclosed in the context of transitions to parenthood, problems in family communication are almost certain to arise. Even when nonheterosexual identities are acknowledged by all members of an extended family, however, heterosexual family members may express surprise or disapproval at the thought of a lesbian or gay person wishing to become a parent (Patterson, 1996). Especially since the legal and policy contexts in some jurisdictions fail to provide recognition for same-sex parents' relationships with one another and with children, members of the extended family may find themselves entertaining questions that would not be raised for heterosexual siblings. Indeed, in many situations, prospective grandparents may be puzzled about the extent to which they should view themselves as grandparents at all (Patterson, 1996). When a birth occurs for a lesbian couple, usually only one of them is biologically linked to the child. While that partner's parents are likely to see themselves as grandparents, the parents of her partner, who are not biologically linked with the child, may be less sure of their role. All these and many related issues are likely to provide challenges as families seek to renegotiate roles and relationships upon the birth or adoption of a child.

Depending upon the family's response, challenges of these kinds can bring widely different outcomes (Patterson, 1996). The failure to acknowledge and accept a family member's nonheterosexuality or gender nonconformity can result in distancing and other failures of communication and in this way work against family cohesion. On the other hand, when families respond successfully to such challenges by acknowledging and including nonheterosexual family members, their partners, and children, families may grow closer.

When a family is flexible enough to meet these kinds of challenges, real benefits may ensue for the entire family (Patterson, 2013b).

These processes are deeply affected by the legal and policy contexts in which they take place. Family members may have attended a couple's marriage, and they may have become aware of its legal force. Members of a couple's extended family may also recognize the impact of second-parent adoptions that legalize bonds between children and their same-sex parents. In some areas, such conditions have long favored the extended family's ability to acknowledge and even embrace the LGBT family member, his or her partner, and their children. In other states, where these options are newer, families have had fewer supports as they seek to accommodate LGBT family members. Thus, to the extent that legal and policy environments are influential, the experiences of same-sex couples and their families in different jurisdictions have been likely to diverge.

At present, we know little about the extent to which family members' attitudes are affected by the legal contexts in which they are situated. To what degree does the extent of legal recognition offered to same-sex couples affect the attitudes of their family members? Might family attitudes change as legal recognition has become available for same-sex couples? And how do the answers to such questions vary among sexual minority individuals of varying ethnic and racial groups and among individuals in different socioeconomic strata of society? Questions like these are ripe for research.

Psychosocial Issues for Couples

All couples must navigate issues of work, sexuality, and power; and all must decide how to build and maintain social networks of friends and family members. In addition, however, special issues arise for same-sex couples (Fingerhut & Peplau, 2013), and it is on these special issues that the current discussion is focused. Instead of attempting an exhaustive treatment, this discussion focuses on selected issues that exemplify differences in the experience of same-sex and different-sex couples, as well as those among same-sex couples living in different jurisdictions.

A central issue for same-sex couples and for couples that contain at least one transgender partner is the question of how open to be with regard to these minority identities. How safe is it, in various settings, for members of a couple to be open about LGBT identities as individuals or as members of a couple? Different environments may provide markedly different kinds of incentives and disincentives for disclosure. Individuals in some employment settings may be subject to job discrimination or even loss of employment if they are open about their sexual orientation or gender identity (Badgett, 2003). In other jobs, it may feel safe to disclose nonheterosexual and/or transgender identities. Likewise, family, neighborhood, and community environments vary widely in their treatment of LGBT individuals (Oswald & Holman, 2013). The costs and benefits of disclosure may therefore differ from one setting to another.

If members of a couple see costs and benefits of disclosure in the same terms and if their respective work and social environments afford the same patterns of incentives and disincentives for openness, then they are likely to reach similar decisions about disclosure (Fingerhut & Peplau, 2013). It is, however, often the case that members of a couple experience different environments in this respect. For instance, one person's parents may be welcoming, while the other's parents may have difficulty accepting nonheterosexual or transgender identities. One person's employment setting may welcome diversity, while the other's job environment may reject or stigmatize those with LGBT identities. In such cases, partners may disagree about the appropriate degree of openness with regard to their sexual identities and their couple status. When there is disagreement within a couple, negotiation of issues surrounding disclosure of LGBT identities is likely to be difficult.

Another issue worth highlighting is that of division of labor (Fingerhut & Peplau, 2013; Patterson, 2013a, 2013b). How does a couple divide the paid and unpaid labor involved in their everyday lives? And how does this differ for same-sex and different-sex couples? It is well-known that many different-sex couples adopt specialized divisions of labor, in which husbands devote themselves more to paid employment and wives spend more time in unpaid household labor and childcare. In dual-earner families, the pattern is often less pronounced, but even among two-career heterosexual couples, patterns of specialization can often be observed. The divisions of labor adopted by same-sex couples, however, appear to be quite different (Farr, Forssell, & Patterson, 2010; Goldberg, Smith, & Perry-Jenkins, 2012; Patterson, Sutfin, & Fulcher, 2004).

Same-sex couples are much more likely than heterosexual couples to adopt egalitarian patterns, with both members of the couple equally participating in both paid and unpaid labor (Farr et al., 2010; Farr & Patterson, 2013; Goldberg et al., 2012; Patterson, 2013b). For example, in a study of lesbian and heterosexual couples, all of whom were rearing young children, lesbian mothers each reported spending about 35 hours per week, on average, in paid employment, and they reported evenly sharing childcare (Patterson et al., 2004). In contrast, heterosexual husbands reported averaging 45 or more hours per week in paid employment, while heterosexual wives reported averaging about 25 hours per week in paid employment but were primarily responsible for childcare (Patterson et al., 2004). A striking aspect of the results was that, when hours of paid employment for the two members of a couple were summed, they reached about 70 hours per week for both family types; family incomes were likewise similar across family type. In other words, given about the same amount of overall labor to divide, lesbian couples were more likely than heterosexual couples to report that they do so in an egalitarian fashion. This result is consistent with a wide array of data from studies conducted both in the United States and abroad, and similar findings have been reported for gay male as well as lesbian couples (e.g., Farr et al., 2010; Golombok et al., 2014; Tornello, Sonnenberg, & Patterson, 2015).

Why do same-sex couples seem so much more likely than different-sex couples to describe themselves as adopting egalitarian divisions of labor? The legal and policy environments in which same-sex couples have lived may be a factor in these decisions (Farr et al., 2010; Goldberg, 2013; Patterson et al., 2004). Given their relative lack of access to legal protections, health insurance, and other financial benefits for a nonemployed partner, same-sex couples may in the past have favored egalitarian divisions of labor because these help to protect both partners in the event of relationship dissolution. Without legal protections, same-sex partners who gave up paid employment in order to devote themselves to the unpaid labor at home may have become more vulnerable economically than their heterosexual peers.

If the economic vulnerabilities of same-sex couples were once an important factor in determining their division of labor, then same-sex couples might be expected to shift their divisions of labor now that law and policies have changed (Patterson, 2004). Now that legal recognition of their marriages has become available to same-sex couples, some of the economic vulnerabilities of a stay-at-home partner might be reduced. Will the opportunity for same-sex couples to undertake legal marriages result in their adoption of more specialized divisions of labor? Or will other factors such as ideological commitments dominate such decision-making processes? Just as they do for different-sex couples, legal and policy contexts provide the background against which decisions about division of labor are made by same-sex couples. What we do not yet know, however, is how decisive these have been for decision making about division of labor among lesbian and gay couples (Goldberg, 2013; Patterson et al., 2004).

Another area for negotiation among couples is how they will manage sexuality (Fingerhut & Peplau, 2013). Like heterosexual women, lesbian women most often favor monogamy as a standard for coupled relationships (Solomon, Rothblum, & Balsam, 2005). Gay male couples, on the other hand, seem to be much less committed to monogamy, and some make explicit agreements about the place of nonmonogamy in the context of their coupled relationships (Huebner, Mandic, Mackaronis, Beougher, & Hoff, 2012). In general, such agreements have been found to be unrelated to relationship quality (Parsons, Starks, Gamarel, & Grov, 2012). It is not yet known to what extent the nature and impact of any such agreements is affected by the legal context of a relationship (i.e., whether or not a couple is legally married).

These and related issues are in need of further study. Issues of outness, division of labor, and management of sexuality are all important to same-sex couples, and responses to them may vary as a function of the legal and policy contexts in which couples live. Also in need of study, however, are the issues of bisexual and transgender individuals and couples, especially as these intersect with other identities, such as those associated with race, ethnicity, and socioeconomic status. Future research that examines such issues could contribute greatly to the understanding of same-sex couples' lives.

Psychosocial Issues for Parents

Just as legal and policy contexts affect decisions made by couples, they also provide the background against which LGBT parents make decisions relevant to their children. As parents, LGBT individuals and couples must take law and policy into account as they attempt to create, maintain, and protect their families. Issues that couples must grapple with about whether, when, and how to become parents are resolved in the context of existing law and policy (Patterson, 1994; Patterson et al., 2002). One approach is to move to jurisdictions with favorable laws. Lesbian couples who are expecting to give birth have been known to travel across state lines during labor in order for the child to be born in a state with favorable legal precedents. Lesbian couples have likewise been known to move their homes across county or state lines in order to complete a second-parent adoption. Gay male couples may travel to jurisdictions with favorable laws about surrogacy. Same-sex couples routinely seek out neighborhoods and schools that they believe will provide safe environments in which to rear and educate their children (Casper & Schultz, 1999). On the other hand, in matters that concern adoption, foster care, custody, and visitation, LGBT parents have many times run afoul of discriminatory legal policies and precedents (Ball, 2012; Patterson et al., 2002).

One important area in which law and policy must be considered concerns family formation (Buell, 2001; Patterson, 1994, 2013a, 2013b). In addition to all the usual concerns of prospective parents (e.g., Will we able to support a child? Will we be good parents?), LGBT prospective parents must consider additional questions that focus on the legal climate. For example, lesbian couples who wish to have a child via donor insemination may discover that not every clinic or sperm bank is willing to work with them, though many are (Chan, Raboy, & Patterson, 1998; Patterson, 1994). A study of the screening practices of assisted reproductive technology programs in the United States (Gurmankin, Caplan, & Braverman, 2005) found that 82% of these programs were willing to work with lesbian couples seeking donor insemination and 44% were willing to work with gay male couples seeking to make surrogacy arrangements. Prospective LGBT parents must identify facilities and services that are open to them.

In a similar vein, gay male couples who wish to adopt a child may discover that not every adoption agency is willing to work with gay men, though many are. In a national survey of agencies in the United States (Brodzinsky, Patterson, & Vaziri, 2002), 63% of respondents indicated willingness to work with lesbian and gay applicants, and more than a third reported having completed a recent adoption placement with a lesbian or gay adult. Little information is available for transgender individuals in this area (Stotzer et al., 2014). It is clear, however, that decisions about adoption take place in the varied legal and policy contexts in which LGBT people live (Patterson, 2009).

Even after becoming parents, lesbian and gay couples may find many of their choices constrained by the legal and policy situation in the area where they live (Patterson, 1994). In making decisions about parental employment options, for example, unmarried couples may find that health insurance coverage for children is available through one but not the other partner's employer, and may thus be forced to make decisions about division of labor that are different than the ones they would select on other grounds. Even though children may live with two same-sex parents, only one of the adults may be accorded parental status in law. In some jurisdictions, the status of transgender parents may remain uncertain, or the possibility of second-parent adoptions may not exist. A parent who has been excluded from legal standing may also be barred from decision making about medical or educational matters for children, and the family's decisions about allocation of many tasks may be constrained by these and related forms of discrimination. Issues such as these can generate considerable stress in otherwise well-functioning families (Goldberg, 2010).

One specific form that such challenges can take, especially in jurisdictions that do not allow second-parent adoptions, involves boundary issues (Patterson, 2000, 2013b). When one parent does and the other parent does not have parental rights and responsibilities in the eyes of the law, it can raise questions in the minds of school and medical personnel, friends, neighbors, and members of the extended family about whether both partners are "real" parents. For example, taking up the law's failure to legitimize familial links, extended family members can find themselves questioning the depth and extent of parent–child bonds or may fail to recognize them altogether. When this happens, couples may have to work to clarify the situation and to advocate for recognition of important family relationships (Johnson & O'Connor, 2001).

The ways in which family lives are affected by their legal and policy contexts were investigated by Shapiro, Peterson, and Stewart (2009), who studied mental health among divorced lesbian and divorced heterosexual mothers living in Canada or in the United States. The international contrast was of interest because, despite many similarities between the two countries, Canada provided a more supportive legal climate for lesbian mothers and their children. For example, adoption and marriage rights were available to all lesbian mothers in Canada, but these rights were not available to lesbian mothers in most parts of the United States at the time the study was conducted. Shapiro et al. found that lesbian mothers in the United States reported more concern about legal problems and about discrimination based on sexual orientation—but not more general family worries—than did lesbian mothers in Canada. Among heterosexual mothers whose family relationships enjoyed protection of the law in both countries, there were no differences across national boundaries. These results suggest that contextual factors may be important influences on mental health among lesbian mothers, gay fathers, and their offspring.

CONCLUSION

Legal and social policy contexts of LGBT Americans' lives have changed dramatically over recent years. Real progress against many forms of discrimination has taken place. At the national level, decriminalization of private consensual sexual behavior between same-sex partners (i.e., the demise of the sodomy laws) has been an important development, as has the advent of marriage equality. On the other hand, the legal context still varies between jurisdictions. It is still true that many lesbian and gay Americans live in jurisdictions that may not recognize their parent–child relationships and that do not protect them from employment discrimination based on sexual orientation. The issues of bisexual and transgender individuals and couples have scarcely been addressed at all by law and policy in many parts of the country. Despite tremendous progress, full equality under the law still eludes sexual minority citizens in every corner of the United States.

In view of rapidly shifting legal and social policy environments, social scientists are faced with unusual opportunities to study the impact of such changes upon human behavior (Patterson, 2013b). For example, how are relationships affected when legal recognition for them becomes available? Researchers have begun to study this question among same-sex couples who have undertaken marriages and civil unions (Balsam, Beauchaine, Rothblum, & Solomon, 2008; Rothblum, Balsam, & Solomon, 2011). Results thus far suggest that, at least in some cases, when the marriages of same-sex couples are recognized, the health of sexual minority populations improves. For instance, Hatzenbuehler et al. (2012) studied medical and mental health care costs among gay men in Massachusetts before and after same-sex marriages were legalized. They found that numbers of health-care visits and also costs of mental-health care decreased among gay men after enactment of same-sex marriage laws. Research in this area is just beginning, and much remains to be learned, but findings like those of Hatzenbuehler and his colleagues suggest that policies like legalization of same-sex marriage may be helpful in reducing health-care costs among members of sexual minorities.

From the standpoint of clinical and counseling practice, a number of considerations emerge from this review. First, it is essential to be aware of the diversity that characterizes experiences of lesbian and gay individuals, especially as a function of the fit between their identities and their social and legal environments. A lesbian woman who is parenting children in the context of a long-term-couple relationship is likely to have very different issues than a young gay man who has no children and who is not currently involved in a romantic relationship, even if they live in the same neighborhood. The very same people may have different experiences if laws and policies in their jurisdiction change or if they move from one jurisdiction to another. Each person's individual experiences should be examined in light of the relevant social, legal, and policy contexts, and at this moment in history, these are likely to show considerable variation.

It is also worth considering the ways that race and ethnicity are likely to interact with legal and policy concerns. For example, an analysis of data from the 2000 United States Census suggests that same-sex couples who are Black are much more likely than those who are White to be parents of minor children (Dang & Frazer, 2004). In fact, 61% of Black female couples and 46% of Black male couples reported children under 18 years of age living in their households, whereas only 38% of White female couples and only 24% of White male couples reported this (Dang & Frazer, 2004). Thus, variations in law that disadvantage parents and their children (e.g., foster parenting laws, adoption laws) can be expected to have greater impact on Black than on White lesbian- and gay-parented families (Moore & Brainer, 2013). Moreover, variations among racial groups in pathways to parenthood and in attitudes about lesbian and gay parenting may affect experiences of family life across racial groups (Moore & Brainer, 2013).

Second, it is valuable for clinicians to become aware of legal and policy realities in their own area, insofar as these may be relevant to experiences among their clients. Do applicable laws and policies permit adoption, foster care, and second-parent adoption by nonheterosexual and noncisgender prospective parents? Does the jurisdiction in question have laws prohibiting employment discrimination on the basis of sexual orientation and gender identity? LGBT clients' struggles with financial and emotional issues associated with couple relationships and parenting are best understood against the background of their social, legal, and policy environments.

Third, it can also be useful to assess clients' own levels of knowledge about relevant legal and policy issues. If clients are not well-informed about a particular issue, practitioners can help by offering accurate information. In this way, practitioners can serve educational functions by directing clients' attention to relevant aspects of their environments. It is also the case that LGBT clients are likely to feel more comfortable with practitioners who demonstrate knowledge of laws and policies of importance to them.

Fourth, it can be valuable to assess LGBT clients' current state of mind with regard to the legal and policy context in which they are living. When high-profile cases yield substantial public debate, this can be stressful for many LGBT adults (Rostosky, Riggle, Horne, & Miller, 2009). The advent of marriage equality may have different meanings for different clients, depending upon relationship status, family support, and so forth. Legal and policy issues may loom larger in the lives of some clients than others.

In summary, there has been tremendous change, but there is still considerable variability in the contexts of LGBT family lives in the United States today. Some LGBT people live openly among supportive family members, work as openly LGBT employees in businesses that welcome diversity, and have their family relationships recognized by all applicable laws. Others still experience stigma in the context of their extended families and suffer discrimination at work and under law. As attitudes and laws become more accepting, more LGBT people across the country will be able to live in supportive social climates. Looking ahead, one can imagine a day when lesbian, gay, bisexual, and transgender Americans will truly be equal citizens under the law.

REFERENCES

Badgett, M. V. L. (2001). Money, myths, and change: The economic lives of lesbians and gay men. Chicago, IL: University of Chicago Press.

Badgett, M. V. L. (2003). Employment and sexual orientation: Disclosure and discrimination in the workplace. In L. D. Garnets & D. C. Kimmel (Eds.), Psychological perspectives on lesbian, gay and bisexual experiences (2nd ed., pp. 327–348). New York, NY: Columbia University Press.

Ball, C. A. (2012). The right to be parents. New York, NY: New York University Press.

Balsam, K. F., Beauchaine, T. P., Rothblum, E. D., & Solomon, S. E. (2008). Three-year follow-up of same-sex couples who had civil unions in Vermont, same-sex couples not in civil unions, and heterosexual married couples. Developmental Psychology, 44, 102–116. http://dx.doi.org/10.1037/0012-1649.44.1.102

Boies, D., & Olson, T. B. (2014). Redeeming the dream: The case for marriage equality. New York, NY: Viking Penguin.

Brodzinsky, D. M., Patterson, C. J., & Vaziri, M. (2002). Adoption agency perspectives on lesbian and gay prospective parents: A national study. *Adoption Quarterly, 5,* 5–23. http://dx.doi.org/10.1300/J145v05n03_02

Buell, C. (2001). Legal issues affecting alternative families: A therapist's primer. *Journal of Gay & Lesbian Psychotherapy, 4,* 75–90. http://dx.doi.org/10.1300/J236v04n03_06

Casper, V., & Schultz, S. B. (1999). *Gay parents, straight schools.* New York, NY: Columbia University Teacher's College Press.

Chan, R., Raboy, B., & Patterson, C. J. (1998). Psychosexual adjustment among children conceived via donor insemination by lesbian and heterosexual mothers. *Child Development, 69,* 443–457.

Cohler, B. J., & Michaels, S. (2013). Emergent adulthood in lesbian and gay lives: Individual development, life course, and social change. In C. J. Patterson & A. R. D'Augelli (Eds.), *Handbook of psychology and sexual orientation* (pp. 102–117). New York, NY: Oxford University Press.

Dang, A., & Frazer, S. (2004). *Black same-sex households in the United States.* Washington, DC: National Gay and Lesbian Task Force.

Downing, J. B. (2013). Transgender-parent families. In A. E. Goldberg & K. R. Allen (Eds.), *LGBT-parent families: Innovations in research and implications for practice* (pp. 105–115). New York, NY: Springer. http://dx.doi.org/10.1007/978-1-4614-4556-2_7

Farr, R. H., Forssell, S. L., & Patterson, C. J. (2010). Parenting and child development in adoptive families: Does parental sexual orientation matter? *Applied Developmental Science, 14,* 164–178. http://dx.doi.org/10.1080/10888691.2010.500958

Farr, R. H., & Patterson, C. J. (2013). Coparenting among lesbian, gay, and heterosexual couples: Associations with adopted children's outcomes. *Child Development, 84,* 1226–1240. http://dx.doi.org/10.1111/cdev.12046

Fingerhut, A. W., & Peplau, L. A. (2013). Same-sex romantic relationships. In C. J. Patterson & A. R. D'Augelli (Eds.), *Handbook of psychology and sexual orientation* (pp. 165–178). New York, NY: Oxford University Press.

Gallup Organization. (2015). *Gay and lesbian rights.* Retrieved from http://www.gallup.com/poll/1651/Gay-Lesbian-Rights.aspx

Goldberg, A. E. (2010). *Lesbian and gay parents and their children: Research on the family life cycle.* Washington, DC: American Psychological Association. http://dx.doi.org/10.1037/12055-000

Goldberg, A. E. (2013). "Doing" and "undoing" gender: The meaning and division of housework in same-sex couples. *Journal of Family Theory & Review, 5,* 85–104. http://dx.doi.org/10.1111/jftr.12009

Goldberg, A. E., Smith, J. Z., & Perry-Jenkins, M. (2012). The division of labor in lesbian, gay, and heterosexual new adoptive parents. *Journal of Marriage and Family, 74,* 812–828. http://dx.doi.org/10.1111/j.1741-3737.2012.00992.x

Golombok, S., Mellish, L., Jennings, S., Casey, P., Tasker, F., & Lamb, M. E. (2014). Adoptive gay father families: Parent–child relationships and children's psychological adjustment. *Child Development, 85,* 456–468. http://dx.doi.org/10.1111/cdev.12155

Grant, J. M., Mottet, L. A., Tanis, J., Harrison, J., Herman, J. L., & Keisling, M. (2011). *Injustice at every turn: A report of the National Transgender Discrimination Survey.* Washington, DC: National Center for Transgender Equality and National Gay and Lesbian Task Force.

Gurmankin, A. D., Caplan, A. L., & Braverman, A. M. (2005). Screening practices and beliefs of assisted reproductive technology programs. *Fertility and Sterility, 83,* 61–67.

Hatzenbuehler, M. L., O'Cleirigh, C., Grasso, C., Mayer, K., Safren, S., & Bradford, J. (2012). Effect of same-sex marriage laws on health care use and expenditures in sexual minority men: A quasi-natural experiment. *American Journal of Public Health, 102,* 285–291. http://dx.doi.org/10.2105/AJPH.2011.300382

Herek, G. W. (2003). *Sexual prejudice: Prevalence.* Retrieved from http://psc.dss.ucdavis.edu/rainbow/HTML/prej_prev.html

Huebner, D. M., Mandic, C. G., Mackaronis, J. E., Beougher, S. C., & Hoff, C. C. (2012). The impact of parenting on gay male couples' relationships, sexuality, and HIV risk. *Couple and Family Psychology: Research and Practice, 1,* 106–119. http://dx.doi.org/10.1037/a0028687

Human Rights Campaign. (2014). *The cost of the closet and the rewards of inclusion.* Washington, DC: Author.

Human Rights Campaign. (2015). *Corporate Equality Index.* Washington, DC: Author.

Johnson, S. M., & O'Connor, E. (2001). *For lesbian parents: Your guide to helping your family grow up happy, healthy, and proud.* New York, NY: Guilford Press.

Klarman, M. J. (2013). *From the closet to the altar: Courts, backlash, and the struggle for same-sex marriage.* New York, NY: Oxford University Press.

Lawrence v. Texas, 123 S. Ct. 2472, 2480 (2003).

Maggiore, D. J. (Ed.). (1992). *Lesbians and child custody: A casebook.* New York, NY: Garland.

Mohr, J. J., & Fassinger, R. E. (2013). Work, career, and sexual orientation. In C. J. Patterson & A. R. D'Augelli (Eds.), *Handbook of psychology and sexual orientation* (pp. 151–164). New York, NY: Oxford University Press.

Moore, M. R., & Brainer, A. (2013). Race and ethnicity in the lives of sexual minority parents and their children. In A. E. Goldberg & K. R. Allen (Eds.), *LGBT-parent families: Innovations in research and implications for practice* (pp. 133–148). New York, NY: Springer. http://dx.doi.org/10.1007/978-1-4614-4556-2_9

Murdoch, J., & Price, D. (2001). *Courting justice: Gay men and lesbians v. the Supreme Court.* New York, NY: Basic Books.

National Center for Lesbian Rights. (2015). *Adoption by LGBT Parents.* Retrieved from http://www.nclrights.org

National LGBTQ Task Force. (2011). *Injustice at every turn: A Report of the National Transgender Discrimination Survey.* Washington, DC: Author.

Obergefell v. Hodges, 576 U.S. _____ (2015).

Oswald, R. F., & Holman, E. G. (2013). Place matters: LGB Families in community context. In A. E. Goldberg & K. R. Allen (Eds.), *LGBT-parent families: Innovations in research and implications for practice* (pp. 193–208). New York, NY: Springer. http://dx.doi.org/10.1007/978-1-4614-4556-2_13

Parsons, J. T., Starks, T. J., Gamarel, K. E., & Grov, C. (2012). Non-monogamy and sexual relationship quality among same-sex male couples. *Journal of Family Psychology, 26,* 669–677. http://dx.doi.org/10.1037/a0029561

Patterson, C. J. (1994). Lesbian and gay couples considering parenthood: An agenda for research, service, and advocacy. *Journal of Gay & Lesbian Social Services, 1,* 33–55. http://dx.doi.org/10.1300/J041v01n02_03

Patterson, C. J. (1996). Contributions of lesbian and gay parents and their children to the prevention of heterosexism. In E. D. Rothblum & L. A. Bond (Eds.), *Preventing heterosexism and homophobia* (pp. 184–202). Thousand Oaks, CA: Sage. http://dx.doi.org/10.4135/9781483327655.n10

Patterson, C. J. (2000). Family relationships of lesbians and gay men. *Journal of Marriage and the Family, 62,* 1052–1069. http://dx.doi.org/10.1111/j.1741-3737.2000.01052.x

Patterson, C. J. (2004). What difference does a civil union make? Changing public policies and the experiences of same-sex couples: Comment on Solomon, Rothblum, and Balsam (2004). *Journal of Family Psychology, 18,* 287–289. http://dx.doi.org/10.1037/0893-3200.18.2.287

Patterson, C. J. (2009). Children of lesbian and gay parents: Psychology, law, and policy. *American Psychologist, 64,* 727–736. http://dx.doi.org/10.1037/0003-066X.64.8.727

Patterson, C. J. (2013a). Family lives of lesbian and gay adults. In G. W. Peterson & K. R. Bush (Eds.), *Handbook of marriage and the family* (pp. 659–681). New York, NY: Springer. http://dx.doi.org/10.1007/978-1-4614-3987-5_27

Patterson, C. J. (2013b). Sexual orientation and family lives. In C. J. Patterson & A. R. D'Augelli (Eds.), *Handbook of psychology and sexual orientation* (pp. 223–236). New York, NY: Oxford University Press.

Patterson, C. J., Fulcher, M., & Wainright, J. (2002). Children of lesbian and gay parents: Research, law, and policy. In B. L. Bottoms, M. B. Kovera, & B. D. McAuliff (Eds.), *Children, social science and the law* (pp. 176–200). New York, NY: Cambridge University Press. http://dx.doi.org/10.1017/CBO9780511500114.008

Patterson, C. J., Sutfin, E. L., & Fulcher, M. (2004). Division of labor among lesbian and heterosexual parenting couples: Correlates of specialized versus shared patterns. *Journal of Adult Development, 11,* 179–189. http://dx.doi.org/10.1023/B:JADE.0000035626.90331.47

Pew Research Center. (2013). *A survey of LGBT Americans: Attitudes, experiences, and values in a changing time.* Washington, DC: Author.

Rivers, D. W. (2013). *Radical relations: Lesbian mothers, gay fathers, and their children in the United States since World War II.* Chapel Hill: University of North Carolina Press.

Ross, L. E., & Dobinson, C. (2013). Where is the "B" in LGBT parenting? A call for research on bisexual parenting. In A. E. Goldberg & K. R. Allen (Eds.), *LGBT-parent families: Innovations in research and implications for practice* (pp. 87–103). New York, NY: Springer. http://dx.doi.org/10.1007/978-1-4614-4556-2_6

Rostosky, S. S., Riggle, E. D. B., Horne, S. G., & Miller, A. D. (2009). Marriage amendments and psychological distress in lesbian, gay, and bisexual adults. *Journal of Counseling Psychology, 56,* 56–66. http://dx.doi.org/10.1037/a0013609

Rothblum, E. D., Balsam, K. F., & Solomon, S. E. (2011). Narratives of same-sex couples who had civil unions in Vermont: The impact of legalizing relationships on couples and social policy. *Sexuality Research and Social Policy, 8,* 183–191. http://dx.doi.org/10.1007/s13178-011-0054-1

Rubenstein, W. B. (1996). Lesbians, gay men, and the law. In R. C. Savin-Williams & K. M. Cohen (Eds.), *The lives of lesbians, gays, and bisexuals: Children to adults* (pp. 331–344). New York, NY: Harcourt Brace.

Ryan, C., Huebner, D., Diaz, R. M., & Sanchez, J. (2009). Family rejection as a predictor of negative health outcomes in White and Latino lesbian, gay, and bisexual young adults. *Pediatrics, 123,* 346–352. http://dx.doi.org/10.1542/peds.2007-3524

Savin-Williams, R. C. (2003). Lesbian, gay and bisexual youths' relationships with their parents. In L. D. Garnets & D. C. Kimmel (Eds.), *Psychological perspectives on lesbian, gay and bisexual experiences* (2nd ed., pp. 299–326). New York, NY: Columbia University Press.

Shapiro, D. N., Peterson, C., & Stewart, A. J. (2009). Legal and social contexts and mental health among lesbian and heterosexual mothers. *Journal of Family Psychology, 23,* 255–262. http://dx.doi.org/10.1037/a0014973

Solomon, S. E., Rothblum, E. D., & Balsam, K. F. (2005). Money, housework, sex, and conflict: Same-sex couples in civil unions, those not in civil unions, and heterosexual married siblings. *Sex Roles, 52,* 561–575. http://dx.doi.org/10.1007/s11199-005-3725-7

Stotzer, R. L., Herman, J. L., & Hasenbush, A. (2014). *Transgender parenting: A review of existing research.* Los Angeles, CA: Williams Institute, UCLA School of Law.

Swisher, P. N., & Cook, N. D. (2001). Bottoms v. Bottoms: In whose best interest? Analysis of a lesbian mother child custody dispute. In J. M. Lehmann (Ed.), *The gay and lesbian marriage and family reader* (pp. 251–299). Lincoln: University of Nebraska Press.

Tornello, S. L., Sonnenberg, B., & Patterson, C. J. (2015). Division of labor among gay fathers: Associations with parent, couple, and child adjustment. *Psychology of Sexual Orientation and Gender Diversity, 2,* 365–375. http://dx.doi.org/10.1037/sgd0000109

United States v. Windsor 570 U.S. 12 (2013).

13

ADDRESSING THE NEEDS OF LESBIAN, GAY, BISEXUAL, TRANSGENDER, AND QUEER CLIENTS: AN ANALYSIS OF RECENT RESEARCH AND SCHOLARSHIP

ROGER L. WORTHINGTON AND JENNAH N. STRATHAUSEN

In the last several years, the American Psychological Association (APA) published the *Report of the APA Task Force on Gender Identity and Gender Variance* (2009), the American Counseling Association (ACA) produced a new set of *Competencies for Counseling With Transgender Clients* (Burnes et al., 2010), and the APA updated the *Guidelines for Psychological Practice With Lesbian, Gay and Bisexual Clients* (APA, 2012). In addition, the *Report of the American Psychological Association Task Force on Appropriate Therapeutic Responses to Sexual Orientation* (APA Task Force on Appropriate Therapeutic Responses to Sexual Orientation, 2009) was also published, providing a comprehensive review of the literature and recommendations regarding sexual orientation change efforts (SOCEs), otherwise known as *reparative therapies, conversion therapies,* or *reorientation therapies.* These broad practice guidelines provide sound recommendations regarding counseling and psychotherapy based on substantive empirical research.

http://dx.doi.org/10.1037/15959-014
Handbook of Sexual Orientation and Gender Diversity in Counseling and Psychotherapy, K. A. DeBord, A. R. Fischer, K. J. Bieschke, and R. M. Perez (Editors)

Research regarding counseling services with lesbian, gay, bisexual, transgender, and queer (LGBTQ) clients has expanded in frequency and scope over the last few decades (e.g., Alessi, 2013; Cabaj, 2008; Diamond, 2007; Huang et al., 2010; Moradi, Mohr, Worthington, & Fassinger, 2009; Patterson, 1995), providing a robust literature that addresses a large number of clinical issues. Despite this comparatively rapid increase in scholarship about sexual orientation, sexual identity development, gender identity and expression, and the life experiences of sexual minority individuals, there remain long-standing misconceptions, stereotypes, and biases about LGBTQ individuals (Frost, 2011; Meyer, 2013; Worthington, Dillon, & Becker-Schutte, 2005). In addition, the vast majority of research in this area continues to perpetuate past biases inherent to other forms of research about sexual orientation and gender identity: (a) trans* populations continue to receive peripheral attention within the broader literature that is otherwise portrayed as inclusive of LGB and T individuals (e.g., Israel, 2005); (b) research focused on sexual orientation continues to rely heavily on a *cisgender* (i.e., an adjective for people whose gender corresponds to their assigned sex) binary when participants are divided into sexual orientation identity groups, such that lesbians and bisexual or queer-identified women tend to be collapsed into a single group, whereas gay, bisexual, and queer-identified men tend to be collapsed into another group; (c) definitions of sexual orientation and sexual identity development continue to evolve, which results in problems when various studies define these constructs differently (or fail to define them at all); and (d) assumptions about sexual orientation identities or dependence on self-report measures of sexual orientation identities remain prevalent in the literature, and adequate measurement of sexual orientation or sexual identity development is rare (Worthington & Navarro, 2003; Worthington & Reynolds, 2009). Whereas past chapters on counseling research in the *Handbook of Counseling and Psychotherapy With Lesbian, Gay, Bisexual, and Transgender Clients* have focused exclusively on working with LGB clients (Bieschke, McClanahan, Tozer, Grzegorek, & Park, 2000; Bieschke, Paul, & Blasko, 2007), this chapter provides additional information derived from current literature about working with trans* clients as well.

The purpose of this chapter is to provide readers with an overview of the research and scholarly literature since the printing of the 2007 *Handbook of Counseling and Psychotherapy With Lesbian, Gay, Bisexual, and Transgender Clients* (with some overlap to provide context where necessary). The chapter begins with a brief discussion of the importance of conceptualizing client issues from an approach that accounts for intersecting identities. The bulk of the chapter provides an analysis of the literature on a broad range of counseling and clinical issues, at times extrapolating from research not directly tied to counseling and psychotherapy to assist readers in understanding psychological issues relevant to working with LGBTQ clients. We conclude the chapter with an analysis and discussion of recent research and scholarship on counseling issues related to sexual orientation and gender identity.

INTERSECTIONALITY

Consideration of intersecting identities is crucial for the advancement of our understanding of clinical work with LGBTQ clients. Race, class, ethnicity, gender, religion/spirituality, disability, and age are interdependent, overlapping, and mutually constitutive (Bowleg, 2013). A significant amount of literature on intersectionality highlights the extent to which multiple minority statuses may increase and compound experiences of stigma and minority stress (Cochran, Mays, Alegria, Ortega, & Takeuchi, 2007; McCabe, Bostwick, Hughes, West, & Boyd, 2010; Moradi, DeBlaere, & Huang, 2010; Szymanski & Sung, 2010). On the basis of this literature, it has been observed that institutionalized forms of bias and discrimination may increase the impact of multiple experiences of marginalization (Balsam, Molina, Beadnell, Simoni, & Walters, 2011). Issues of intersectionality have been integrated throughout the various chapters of this handbook (see, e.g., Chapter 4, this volume). For the purposes of this chapter, we address how intersectionality has been addressed in the empirical literature about clinical issues with LGBTQ populations.

LGBT people share similar experiences based on gender transgression and societal sexual prejudice (Fassinger & Arseneau, 2008). Conflation of gender expression with sexual orientation identity (e.g., the assumption that transgression of gender norms implies a same-sex sexual orientation) can be tied to the fundamental presumptive binaries related to sexual orientation and gender. However, the associations among sexual orientation identity and gender identity and expression are complex and at times divergent (dickey, Burnes, & Singh, 2012). For example, trans* individuals often face unique developmental processes (e.g., gender transition for some) and medical issues (e.g., medical and psychological misdiagnosis and mistreatment, denial of access to qualified care). In addition, there are critical connections between LGBQ and trans* individuals based on stigma, discrimination, and oppression, resulting in considerable overlap among trans* issues and LGBQ issues on the basis of law and public policy (e.g., legal discrimination, social marginalization, hate incidents), identity development (e.g., self-stigma, self-expression), and relationships (e.g., conflict, loss; Moradi et al., 2009). Nevertheless, most people experience gender identity and sexual orientation as separate phenomena (e.g., dickey et al., 2012), meaning that (a) trans* people can identify as asexual, polysexual (e.g., does not limit affection, romance, or attraction to a single gender or sex, and does not subscribe to the cisgender binary), transsensual (e.g., primarily attracted to transgender or transsexual people), heterosexual, gay, lesbian, bisexual, or queer; and (b) lesbian, gay, bisexual, and queer individuals are not constrained in their orientations toward people solely within the cisgender binary (APA Task Force on Gender Identity and Gender Variance, 2009). Thus, the term *transgender* represents a broad group of identities with a variety of gender identities (e.g., gender queer, genderblend, drag king, drag queen, transsexual, androgyne) with separate and distinct sexual orientation identities (e.g., heterosexual, lesbian or gay, bisexual, queer, polysexual, asexual).

The perpetuation of the cisgender binary in research and scholarship with LGBTQ populations continues to complicate our understanding of counseling and training. A preponderance of the literature on clinical issues for LGBTQ individuals contains implicitly normative assumptions regarding a cisgender binary in which current gender identity and sex assignment at birth are confounded (e.g., males are boys and men, and females are girls and women). For our purposes, the problem of this set of cisgender normative assumptions is twofold: (a) LGB identities are privileged over trans* identities when issues described as LGBT are addressed and (b) samples within research focused on LGB issues tend to be constrained by the cisgender binary (e.g., lesbian, gay, and bisexual individuals as considered to be either men or women, or trans* individuals are dropped from samples during analysis). As such, the research literature continues to perpetuate assumptions of normative cisgender identities within samples otherwise presumed to be of diverse sexual orientation identities.

COUNSELING ISSUES

Our review of the literature uncovered empirical research in four broad categories: (a) counseling issues with trans* clients; (b) training, competencies, self-efficacy, and effectiveness with LBG clients; (c) SOCEs; and (d) special populations and focal clinical issues.

Counseling Issues With Trans* Clients

The *Report of the APA Task Force on Gender Identity and Gender Variance* (APA Task Force on Gender Identity and Gender Variance, 2009) in part emphasized the important shifts in conceptualization of gender identity and gender variance in the professional literature, treatment standards, and society at large. For example, whereas the historical paradigm for treatment of individuals who experience incongruity or distress included some form or combination of hormone therapy and/or surgery, current professional standards emphasize concerns over issues of power, privilege, and oppression, along with corresponding issues of stigma and minority stress (ALGBTIC LGBQQIA Competencies Taskforce et al., 2013). Thus, a significant shift has occurred away from surgical and/or hormonal transitions toward the exploration of a variety of available pathways and transitional options in the context of the best interests of the individual (APA Task Force on Gender Identity and Gender Variance, 2009). To date there has been no published research to document the impact of the change in the *Diagnostic and Statistical Manual of Mental Disorders (DSM)* terminology from *gender identity disorder* to *gender dysphoria*; however, earlier research showed that although gender-variant behavior is more common among girls than among boys, mental health referrals for gender-atypical behavior have been historically more common among boys than among girls, at least until high school (APA Task Force on Gender Identity and Gender Variance, 2009).

The debate about the nature of gender dysphoria is beyond the scope of this chapter; however, it is important to highlight the prevalent features of the opposing viewpoints. On one side of the debate are proponents of treatments focused on the assumption that cross-gender identification and behaviors are inherently distressful for the children, adolescents, and adults who experience them. On the other side of the debate are proponents of the social construction of gender and a conceptualization of gender dysphoria as arising primarily from social stigma, rejection, and distress resulting as a natural response to oppression and discrimination (APA Task Force on Gender Identity and Gender Variance, 2009; Brewster, Velez, DeBlaere, & Moradi, 2012; Burnes et al., 2010; Cruz, 2014; Israel, 2005; Levitt & Ippolito, 2014a, 2014b). Nevertheless, there appears to be agreement that "children and adolescents who are extreme in wishing for or adopting a cross-gender role need assistance to avoid the negative impact of stigmatization" (APA Task Force on Gender Identity and Gender Variance, 2009, p. 46) and that the best interests of each individual will be taken into account in any decisions made about interventions regarding gender identity and expression. Ultimately, part of the debate centers on the appropriate focus of treatments or interventions toward (a) a focus on reducing environmental conditions that result in shame and self-stigma as a consequence of cross-gender identification and behavior versus (b) alleviating cross-gender behaviors with the intent of reducing ostracism and rejection (APA Task Force on Gender Identity and Gender Variance, 2009). The ALGBTIC Transgender Committee (2010) took a stronger stance on the identification of competencies designed to advance advocacy, stigma reduction, and transpositive (trans* affirming) approaches to counseling with trans* clients. Singh and Burnes (2010), for example, recommended that the values of feminism, social justice, multiculturalism, advocacy, and wellness can be leveraged along with a strengths-based approach and increased counselor competency to create and maintain counseling spaces that are transpositive and facilitative of resilience.

When working with clients who belong to marginalized communities, it is sometimes challenging to recognize and acknowledge resilience in the face of harsh discriminatory treatment. Cerezo, Morales, Quintero, and Rothman (2014) provided findings that highlight the resilience of 10 transgender women who emigrated from Latin America to the United States by describing the positive impact of social support and community-based resources on their mental health, despite experiences of physical and sexual assault, educational and occupational discrimination, and loss of social and familial relationships. Stigma and discrimination are among the many challenges faced by trans* individuals within the health care system, which often results in the postponement of ameliorative care, which is often due to a lack of training (Cruz, 2014; Heck, Croot, & Robohm, 2015). Hiestand, Horne, and Levitt (2008) reported results from a survey of 516 butch-identified ($n = 220$) or femme-identified ($n = 296$) women regarding their health care and mental health experiences, in which butch-identified women perceived poorer treatment, had fewer routine gynecological exams, were more likely to be out in their health care settings, expressed greater importance on securing LGBTQ-positive practitioners, and had more difficulty finding LGBTQ-positive medical doctors. Bess and Stabb (2009), however, reported a qualitative study of seven trans* clients about their satisfaction with the therapeutic alliance with their therapists and found that participants described positive experiences overall, "although many reported less positive experiences with previous therapists and others in social service agencies that did not specialize in gender diversity" (p. 280). Budge, Adelson, and Howard (2013) reported that self-identified transgender men and women in their sample reported high rates of depression and anxiety, which were both positively related to avoidant coping and negatively related to social support. Avoidant coping was less prevalent among those who were further along in their transition process. Although all of these issues are not directly related to counseling and psychotherapy, counseling professionals should remain aware of the various forms of marginalization and stigma encountered by trans* people in a variety of contexts.

Levitt and Ippolito (2014a, 2014b) provided two qualitative companion studies using grounded theory analysis to assess transgender identity development and navigating minority stressors in an effort to develop an authentic self-presentation. Levitt and Ippolito (2014a) provided a rich analysis of the experiences of participants across time (retrospectively) in arriving at their gender identity in a description of common processes of transgender identity development by "(1) developing constructs to represent one's gender authentically; (2) finding ways to communicate one's gender to others and be seen; and (3) balancing these needs with one's need to survive under discriminatory political, social, and economic conditions" (p. 1736). The authors described three clusters of themes, each containing two categories that highlight the process of development from childhood experiences of danger, isolation, turmoil, and trauma through the discovery of language of acceptance and the discovery of affirming communities toward the recognition of identity as an ongoing process of balancing authenticity with safety and change. These authors also addressed minority stress challenges related to understanding gender differently, vocational and economic concerns, health, educational and social supports related to safe spaces, and intimate relationships (Levitt & Ippolito, 2014b).

There are an increasing number of articles dealing with employment issues, workplace experiences, and career development for trans* individuals. Brewster et al. (2012) reported that more supportive and less discriminatory workplace environments and explicit identity disclosure (within the context of supportive environments) are associated with greater job satisfaction. Budge, Tebbe, and Howard (2010) conducted a grounded theory investigation of the work experiences of transgender individuals in which two work experience models emerged: (a) the process of gender transitioning at work (e.g., preparation, coming out, presentation and appearance at work, others' reactions, affective/coping) and (b) the career decision-making process (e.g., barriers, prospects, aspirations, actions, gratification, contextual influences). Key areas of stress associated with transitioning at work included hostile coworkers, gendered spaces, and lack of employee protection policies, whereas strategies for preparing to transition at work included informing human resources and identifying allies (Brewster, Velez, Mennicke, & Tebbe, 2014). Counseling professionals are encouraged to inquire about workplace stress and job satisfaction in the context of psychotherapy.

Given the inherent oversimplification of trans* issues within a brief section of this chapter, we encourage readers interested in greater depth to more substantive work contained in or cited by the documents produced by the APA Task Force on Gender Identity and Gender Variance (2009) and the ALGBTIC Transgender Committee (2010). Trans* issues are largely ignored in the literature, which may be reflective of discrimination from both the heterosexual and LGB communities. Though the field recognizes important changes in clinical language, the effects of stigma and marginalization, and the importance of resiliency when working with trans* individuals, more research needs to be conducted with regards to intersecting identities. Trans* and bisexual issues are often "tacked on" to LGB research (O'Shaughnessy & Spokane, 2013).

Competencies, Training, Self-Efficacy, and Effectiveness With LGB Clients

By far the largest number of studies on a particular topic were focused on improving the competencies, effectiveness, and self-efficacy of practicing therapists and counselors-in-training (see Chapter 14, this volume). Although not every study included trans* or bisexual individuals, several did. Generally, research has consistently indicated that interpersonal characteristics (e.g., personal relationships with LGBT individuals), sexual identity (e.g., LGBT identities, sexual identity development), focused training about LGBT issues, personality characteristics (e.g., openness), and clinical experiences working with LGBT clients are associated with greater LGB-affirmative counseling self-efficacy (Bidell, 2013; Dillon & Worthington, 2003; Dillon, Worthington, Soth-McNett, & Schwartz, 2008; Grove, 2009; O'Shaughnessy & Spokane, 2013) and self-reported LGB counseling competencies (Bidell, 2013, 2014; O'Shaughnessy & Spokane, 2013). In addition, Burkard, Pruitt, Medler, and Stark-Booth (2009) found that trainees with lower levels of homophobia also had greater self-efficacy for establishing rapport or emotional connections with their LGB clients, but overall trainees were less confident in their own ability to establish appropriate goals and tasks for therapy. Similarly, Graham, Carney, and Kluck (2012) reported that trainees rated themselves as more competent in terms of knowledge and attitudes for working with LGB clients but less so in terms of skills, which is a finding that was true even for those with more experience working with LGB clients and additional training. Bidell (2014) also found that political conservatism was associated with significantly lower levels of self-reported competencies to work with LGB clients. These findings are consistent with earlier research, indicating that it is important for heterosexual counselors-in-training to confront their own heterosexist biases and to reflect on and evaluate their own attitudes, assumptions, and biases before working with LGB clients, including the development of an awareness of heterosexual privilege and an active commitment for continued self-exploration (Dillon et al., 2004).

Notably, identity as LGBTQ is one of the strongest predictors of LGB-affirmative counseling self-efficacy (Dillon et al., 2008). Two pieces of qualitative research (Dillon et al., 2004; Grove, 2009) and one quantitative study (Dillon et al., 2008) suggested that sexual identity exploration and assessment of working models of sexual orientation (e.g., Mohr, 2002) are important components of training or professional development for LGB-affirmative counseling competencies and self-efficacy. In addition, O'Shaughnessy and Spokane (2013) found that trainees' case conceptualizations contained infrequent mentions of sexual orientation or LGB-affirmative therapy themes (sometimes none) in response to therapy vignettes—a finding they speculated may have resulted from a lack of training/experience or uncertainty about how to include sexual orientation or sexual identity development in conceptualizations— possibly out of fear of being perceived as linking sexual orientation to mental illness. Similarly, on the basis of their qualitative study of therapists, Israel, Gorcheva, Walther, Sulzner, and Cohen (2008) suggested that clinicians, though helpful in treating primary concerns relating to sexual orientation and gender identity, might not know how to work effectively with LGBT clients when the concerns presented by clients are not directly related to those issues.

In their study, Israel et al. (2008) used semistructured interviews to identify therapists' perspectives of "helpful situations" and "unhelpful situations." Semistructured interviews revealed that helpful situations were characterized by positive relationships with clients, working successfully with clients toward resolution of their concerns, and involved situations in which therapists were knowledgeable, helpful, appropriate, or affirming in dealing with the client's sexual orientation or gender identity (e.g., exploring options related to identity or coming out, exploring internalized homophobia, providing resources or validation). Unhelpful situations included a number of different negative therapy outcomes, challenges in the therapeutic alliance, client mistrust of the therapist, a lack of preparation or competencies to work with LGBT clients, and an agency setting that was not LGBT affirming.

Burckell and Goldfried (2006) surveyed 42 "nonheterosexual" adult pseudo-clients about preferred characteristics of potential therapists for problems in two conditions: one in which sexual orientation was salient and one in which sexual orientation was not salient. LGB participants in this study consistently rated "exclusionary therapist characteristics" (e.g., heteronormative assumptions, lack of awareness of LGB issues, tentativeness or discomfort working with LGB clients, reluctance to ask questions about sexual identity, overemphasis on sexual identity) as undesirable. There were some differences between conditions in which having LGB-specific knowledge or self-identifying as an LGB therapist were more important when sexual orientation was salient than when it was not a salient aspect of the presenting problem. Therapeutic alliance was more important when considered regarding problems in which sexual orientation was not salient.

Only a small handful of studies addressed counselor training and competencies in working specifically with bisexual clients, as opposed to assessing competencies under the broader LGB rubric. For example, Nova, McGeorge, and Stone Carlson (2013) found that more LGB-affirmative training received by students in their sample was associated with lower levels of biphobia, and that identifying as a woman, identifying as LGB, and being educated at a secular institution were related to more positive attitudes regarding bisexuality. In a survey of 108 psychotherapists, Mohr, Weiner, Chopp, and Wong (2009) found that bisexuality of clients did not influence judgment of functioning, interpersonal attractiveness, or the relevance of clinical issues unrelated to bisexual stereotypes, and that client bisexuality had a strong effect on judgments regarding clinical issues that were related to bisexual stereotypes but unrelated to presenting problems. These findings were particularly salient for ratings of clinical relevance to issues about sexual orientation, sexual dysfunction, and identity development, and did not differ by therapist gender, training in LGB issues, LGB clinical experience, or specialty area. These findings were similar to those of Israel and Mohr (2004) that negative stereotypes specific to bisexuality influence the ways clinicians view their bisexual clients. Similarly, Brooks and Inman (2013) found that attitudes toward bisexuality were significant predictors of both self-reported counseling competencies and case conceptualization ratings for working with bisexual clients. Finally, a qualitative study conducted by Brooks, Inman, Klinger, Malouf, and Kaduvettoor (2010) indicated that ethnic minority bisexual women clients expressed preferences for counselors (a) with specific knowledge of ethnic minority bisexual women; (b) who will provide validation and affirmation of their bisexual identity; (c) with an awareness of potential biases regarding heteronormativity or biphobia; and (d) understanding about client preferences regarding gender, ethnicity, and LGB-affirmativeness.

The quality of the therapeutic relationship plays a pivotal role in counselor efficacy and effectiveness when working with LGBTQ clients. Main factors influencing counselor-client rapport include the counselor's interpersonal characteristics, training, and clinical experience. Ideal personal characteristics include openness and an affirmative stance. Training is an important component of experience in which knowledge is acquired about various sexual orientation identity models, how intersecting identities impact sexual orientation, and how discrimination on a societal level impacts clients individually. It is additionally important to determine the saliency of sexual orientation and gender identity to the client's presenting concerns. More studies need to be conducted with bisexual and trans* clients.

Sexual Orientation Change Efforts

The APA Task Force on Appropriate Therapeutic Responses to Sexual Orientation (2009) produced a cutting-edge report that contained the most comprehensive review of the scientific research on SOCEs, concluding that there is no evidence for their efficacy and there is some evidence to suggest that SOCEs are sometimes harmful. Dissonance and incongruence have received frequent attention in the literature on the intersections of religious and spiritual identities with sexual orientations and gender identities— especially with regard to some highly religious individuals who experience distress regarding same-sex attractions (see Chapter 11, this volume). For many years, the intersections of religion and sexual orientation have been addressed in the context of SOCEs (APA Task Force on Appropriate Therapeutic Responses to Sexual Orientation, 2009; Cramer, Golom, LoPresto, and Kirkley, 2008; Fjelstrom, 2013; Flentje, Heck, & Cochran, 2013; Haldeman, 1994; Worthington, 2004), but a more recent focus has emerged in the literature regarding how to affirmatively and effectively respond to the needs of individuals who are distressed by same-sex attractions while simultaneously attending to their commitment to religious identity (APA Task Force on Appropriate Therapeutic Responses to Sexual Orientation, 2009).

Karten and Wade (2010) surveyed 117 men who had pursued SOCEs to assess social and psychological characteristics associated with self-reports of changes in sexual and psychological functioning. In a major omission, sexual orientation identity was not reported in this study, and instead participants were required only to have at least one past or current form of same-sex attraction that was a source of discomfort and prompted a desire for sexual orientation change. As a result, the survey suffered broadly from a lack of empirical rigor (common to many recent publications about SOCEs in the literature). Flaws prevalent in this research base included a very narrow sample of individuals who were likely to have an investment in reporting positive outcomes of SOCEs. This was a self-report, retrospective survey that relied on subjective comparisons of pre- and posttherapy outcomes that provided no protection against participant biases. Also, this study failed to fully describe the wide-ranging types of SOCEs despite a list of "interventions" that included "psychologist," "psychiatrist," "men's retreat," and "intense individual study," among others. In addition to measurement problems and statistical analyses that detract from (or obscure) the stated findings, demand characteristics inherent to the research procedure were likely to prompt responses suggesting positive outcomes of SOCE findings.

Similarly, Jones and Yarhouse (2011) drew a sample from the now defunct ex-gay group Exodus International, which shut down in 2013 and subsequently issued an apology for its 37-year history of condemnation of LGBT individuals and the promotion of SOCEs. Although the authors claimed that some of their participants achieved significant changes in sexual orientation over the course of 6 to 7 years of involvement in an SOCE, one group (i.e., Phase 1 participants) could best be described as falling along the midline of the Kinsey scale (often referred to as *bisexual* or *equally heterosexual and homosexual*) at the start of the study and remained above the midline at the end of the study, showing no change. The other group (i.e., Phase 2 participants) reported attractions, infatuations, and fantasies at the outset of the study well above the midline of the Kinsey scale (e.g., *predominantly homosexual, only incidentally heterosexual*) but reported scores at or somewhat below the midline at the end of the study, indicating that on average these participants reported substantial levels of same-sex attractions after as many as 6 or 7 years of an SOCE. Furthermore, the authors noted that one of their qualitative categories of success, labeled as *chastity*, should not be regarded as sexual orientation change but instead as a shift in sexual identification (e.g., APA Task Force on Appropriate Therapeutic Responses to Sexual Orientation, 2009; Worthington & Reynolds, 2009). With regard to the potential harmfulness of SOCEs, the authors noted although they reported trends of improved psychological functioning among the final group of participants on the Symptom Checklist–90–Revised (SCL-90-R; Derogatis, 1994), they acknowledged that they were unable to conclude that "particular individuals . . . were not harmed by their attempt to change" (Jones & Yarhouse, 2011, p. 424), primarily because of limitations inherent to the study because of attrition.

More recent research produced by Dehlin, Galliher, Bradshaw, Hyde, and Crowell (2015) examined the cases of 1,612 current and former members of the Church of Jesus Christ of Latter Day Saints who reported experiencing same-sex attraction. These participants completed a comprehensive online survey using both quantitative items and open-ended responses. Seventy-three percent of men and 43 percent of women in this study reported attempts with a wide variety of SOCE methods, including increased religious activity, individual effort, church counseling, psychotherapy, support groups, group therapy, group retreats, psychiatry, and family therapy. Virtually every method was rated as ineffective or potentially harmful (with medium to large effect sizes) when it was used as an SOCE. Of the subsample of 1,019 participants in their research who engaged in SOCEs, only one reported both a heterosexual identity label and a Kinsey attraction score indicating "exclusively attracted to opposite sex" (Dehlin et al., 2015, p. 100). Furthermore, mean Kinsey scores for those reporting attempted an SOCE were not significantly different from those who did not indicate an SOCE attempt. In addition, more than 95% of participants who attempted an SOCE self-identified as something other than "heterosexual," and those who identified as heterosexual reported mean Kinsey attraction scores at a level commonly associated with bisexuality (similar to the findings from the much smaller sample from Jones & Yarhouse, 2011). In addition, the findings indicated that the perceived benefits reported by participants in this study were unrelated to changes in sexual orientation but instead referred to self-acceptance, decreased symptoms of anxiety and depression, and improved family relationships. On the other hand, findings from the open-ended written responses included reports of harm such as "decreased self-esteem, increased self-shame, increased depression and anxiety, wasted time and money, increased distance from God and the church, worsened family relationships, and increased suicidality" (Dehlin et al., 2015, p. 102).

Two studies of ex-ex-gays (i.e., people who had attempted an SOCE and ultimately self-identified as LGB) provide additional insights into the experiences of individuals and characteristics of SOCEs (Fjelstrom, 2013; Flentje, Heck, & Cochran, 2013). In particular, Fjelstrom (2013) noted that participants sometimes identified as heterosexual during the course of an SOCE but never changed their underlying same-sex orientation. Similar to other reports, these studies highlighted the significant role of religious leaders, religious organizations, and personal religious orientation in the practice and pursuit of SOCEs.

Ultimately, SOCEs have been broadly discredited across various disciplines and specializations within the fields that make up the mental health professions. Potential harmful side-effects of SOCEs include depression, anxiety, loss of sexual feelings, and suicidality (APA Task Force on Appropriate Therapeutic Responses to Sexual Orientation, 2009). Similarly, the APA Task Force addressed psychotherapy treatments targeting children diagnosed with "gender identity disorder" by stating that "there is no evidence that teaching or reinforcing stereotyped gender-normative behavior in childhood or adolescence can alter sexual orientation" (APA Task Force on Appropriate Therapeutic Responses to Sexual Orientation, 2009, p. 4). The report acknowledged the need to provide helpful, competent services to individuals who experience conflicts or distress related to same-sex attractions, which often result from shame, isolation, rejection, self-stigma, lack of emotional support, inaccurate information, and conflicts between multiple identities and/or between values and attractions. The report emphasized that a common desire of distressed individuals is to live in congruence between religious values and sexual identity, which is potentially problematic or harmful when the desired congruence is based on stigma and shame. Thus, stigma and shame were identified as focal areas of attention for any individual seeking sexual orientation change or experiencing distress about same-sex attractions.

The report also identified sexual orientation identity rather than sexual orientation as the focus of therapy, which includes affirmative support of the client's processes of healthy identity development without predefined therapy goals regarding sexual orientation self-identification or specific outcome expectations about how to reconcile sexual orientation with religious beliefs. There is emerging consensus regarding the important distinctions among sexual orientation, sexual identity, and sexual identity development (e.g., APA Task Force on Appropriate Therapeutic Responses to Sexual Orientation, 2009; Chung & Katayama, 1996; Dillon, Worthington, & Moradi, 2011; Moradi et al., 2009; Worthington & Reynolds, 2009; Worthington, Savoy, Dillon, & Vernaglia, 2002). Although sexual orientation identity may shift over time (Diamond, 2008; Savin-Williams, Joyner, & Rieger, 2012), and variations in sexual behavior have been noted extensively in the literature (e.g., Vrangalova & Savin-Williams, 2010), there is no empirical evidence to suggest that enduring change in sexual orientation is likely, not even as an outcome of active, intentional efforts to promote change (APA Task Force on Appropriate Therapeutic Responses to Sexual Orientation, 2009). Thus, even when sexual orientation change is requested by a client (or potential client), counselors are recommended to (a) help the client identify and explore the source of distress that prompts the desire for sexual orientation change; (b) provide support, acceptance, and recognition for important values and concerns; (c) allow the client to explore sexual identity issues and concerns without predetermined identity outcome goals; and (d) provide counseling interventions consistent with empirical evidence that homosexuality is not a mental disorder (APA Task Force on Appropriate Therapeutic Responses to Sexual Orientation, 2009). Finally, the report concluded that mental health professionals should not offer or guarantee sexual orientation change as part of a therapy contract with clients expressing distress about same-sex attraction.

Special Populations and Focal Clinical Issues

Mental Health and Well-Being

Research indicates clearly and consistently that most sexual minority individuals are healthy, well adjusted, and have rewarding romantic relationships (King et al., 2008; Mohr, Selterman, & Fassinger, 2013; Moradi et al., 2009). King et al. (2008) conducted a systematic review and meta-analysis of the prevalence of mental disorders, substance misuse, suicide, suicidal ideation, and deliberate self-harm on the basis of data from more than 200,000 heterosexual and 11,971 LGB people. The findings revealed substantially increased risk for suicide attempts, depression, and alcohol and substance dependence among LGB individuals. Within-group gender differences showed that lesbian and bisexual women were at higher risk of substance dependence than heterosexual women, whereas gay and bisexual men had considerably higher lifetime risk for suicide attempts than did heterosexual men. Higher rates of suicidality among LGB and questioning individuals (relative to heterosexual individuals) have received substantial attention in recent years (e.g., Woodward, Pantalone, & Bradford, 2013) along with the additional risk found among LGB ethnic minority youth relative to their White counterparts (O'Donnell, Meyer, & Schwartz, 2011). Although few studies have addressed mental health and suicidality among LGB individuals in counseling or clinical treatment, in one large-sample survey of college counseling center clients, McAleavey, Castonguay, and Locke (2011) reported that sexual minority students had higher rates of service utilization and symptomatic distress. Yet a content analysis of a randomly selected stratified national sample of 203 four-year college counseling center websites found that information and reference services for LGBT students were infrequent, with fewer than one third of college counseling center websites providing descriptions of individual counseling services for LGBT students (Wright & McKinley, 2010). In addition, Diamond et al. (2013) provided preliminary findings from an open trial investigation of attachment-based family therapy for suicidal LGB adolescents that indicated high levels of treatment retention, significant decreases in suicidal ideation, fewer depressive symptoms, and improved indices of attachment. Although this set of studies did not reveal the specific mechanisms by which higher prevalence of suicide rates occur, some authors have speculated that societal conditions such as social hostility, stigma, and discrimination were likely causes (King et al., 2008; O'Donnell et al., 2011). In summary, mental health studies generally support early research (e.g., Hooker, 1957) that suggested that most sexual minority individuals are healthy, well adjusted, and have rewarding romantic relationships. Although clinicians should remain vigilant about the potential for self-harm and potentially self-destructive behaviors among their LGBTQ clients, it is imperative to recognize the sources of these behaviors are rooted in marginalization, stigma, and minority stress.

Minority Stress

Meyer (2013) described *minority stress* as the excess stress experienced by individuals from stigmatized groups as a result of their social position (e.g., as LGBT). He defined minority stress processes along a continuum of proximity to the self, describing *objective stressors*, those most distal to the self (i.e., events and conditions that happen regardless of the individual's characteristics or actions), and *proximal stressors* (i.e., conditions involving an individual's internal perception of the environment as threatening). Distal stressors are based on heterosexism and heteronormativity in the environment, such as homophobic stereotypes, microaggressions, prejudice, and discrimination. Proximal stressors include expectations of rejection and concealment of one's sexual orientation in an effort to cope with stigma. Internalized homophobia is considered the most proximal self-stressor. Minority stress is believed to be the cause of physical and mental health disparities, including but not limited to increased rates of psychological disorders, substance abuse, and suicidal ideation (Balsam et al., 2011; Cochran et al., 2007; Feinstein, Goldfried, & Davila, 2012; Flood, McLaughlin, & Prentice, 2013; Kwon, 2013; McCabe et al., 2010; Meyer, 2013; Senreich, 2009), and minority stress based on gender nonconformity is a leading reason individuals pursue SOCEs (Fjelstrom, 2013; Karten & Wade, 2010).

Threats to mental health due to stigma are well documented in the literature (Clyman & Pachankis, 2014; Hatzenbuehler, Pachankis, & Wolfe, 2012; Meyer, 2013). For example, Pachankis (2007) outlined a substantive list of potential risks for individuals with hidden stigma (e.g., LGBTQ people), such as discrimination in employment, education, health care, and housing, as well as social isolation, abandonment, and violence, ultimately resulting in dilemmas and stresses regarding disclosure.

Research has suggested that multiple minority status compounds an individual's experience of stigma, marginalization, rejection, and discrimination (Balsam et al., 2011; Cochran et al., 2007; David & Knight, 2008; Feinstein et al., 2012). Brewster et al. (2012) found evidence that minority stress variables were related positively with psychological distress and negatively to well-being among a sample of bisexual individuals, in addition to Velez, Moradi, and DeBlaere (2015), who found evidence for the effects of additive and interactive oppressions on the mental health and well-being of Latina/o sexual minority individuals. Thus, a principal focus of counseling and psychotherapy with LGBTQ clients should be on the potential impact minority stress has on psychological functioning and distress.

Whereas relationships in the lives of sexual minority clients are affected by a context of minority stress, there are many characteristics of those relationships that appear to function similarly to relationships among heterosexual couples. In some ways, familial relationships appear to function similarly in that issues unique to sexual minority youth can be understood within the context of minority stresses experienced by both individuals and their family members, adding strains to relationships that function within the broad range of cultural differences that exist in the world. However, because of stigma, discrimination, victimization, and minority stress, clients belonging to sexual minority groups have the potential to experience increased risk for psychological problems and mental disorders, including potentially destructive behaviors associated with substance abuse, suicidal ideation, self-harm, intimate partner violence, and SOCEs. Thus, it is critical for counselors and other mental health professionals to be knowledgeable and competent to address both the sources of minority stress and to directly intervene when there is a risk or presence of potentially destructive behaviors. Intervention efforts may include common forms of counseling processes and social advocacy efforts designed to intervene in the contexts in which problems occur.

Resilience

Coping with minority stress requires individuals to develop a strong sense of connectedness to their minority communities. For example, social support that is explicitly directed toward a person's stigmatized status has the potential to act as a buffer against prejudice and discrimination. Further, having social support promotes mental health (Kwon, 2013). In the context of marginalized same-sex partnerships, Frost (2011) found that strategies used by couples to give meaning to the relationship between stigma and intimacy in their relationships can have positive effects on coping with, resisting, and overcoming stigma.

Family connectedness serves as an additional form of social support that has been found to provide buffering effects against negative health outcomes in sexual minority youth (Needham & Austin, 2010). Specifically, Needham and Austin (2010) found that gay men, lesbians, and bisexual women (but not bisexual men) report lower levels of parental support than heterosexual women and men. Whereas the health-related outcomes were similar for young men regardless of sexual orientation (except that suicidal thoughts were more common among bisexual and gay men than among heterosexual men), lesbians and bisexual women were more likely than were their heterosexual peers to report high depressive symptoms, suicidal thoughts, heavy drinking, marijuana use, and hard drug use (Needham & Austin, 2010). To improve the health of LGBTQ youth, clinicians, counselors, and others who work with young people must be aware of the critical role that parents continue to play in shaping the health of their children as they make the transition from adolescence to young adulthood. Positive family relationships encourage teens to engage in positive behaviors. Depressed adolescents show less secure parental attachment. Thus, a key set of interventions when working with LGBTQ clients experiencing symptomatic effects of minority stress should include focusing on ways to help clients build resilience through strong social support systems and improving family relationships (if possible) or helping clients develop "family of choice" relationships that can foster health and coping.

School Climates

Schools also play an important role in fostering the development of a student's sense of agency, yet an increasing body of research illustrates that middle and high schools have climates that are stigmatizing, unsupportive, and unsafe for many LGBT youth (Kosciw, Greytak, & Diaz, 2009). There is general accord in the research literature about the need for schools to create a more inclusive community by instituting antibullying, harassment, and assault policies with specific protections based on sexual orientation and gender identity/expression (Kosciw, Palmer, Kull, & Greytak, 2013). Discrimination, harassment, and assault are frequent, with 83% of LGB students having reported some sort of victimization at school (Espelage, Aragon, Birkett, & Koenig, 2008). The research literature concludes that this type of marginalization is in part responsible for significantly higher rates of substance use, depression, and suicidality among LGBT teens (Burkard et al., 2009). In addition, schools could provide more supportive environments by offering gay/straight alliances, other LGBT clubs, special training for educators on LGBT issues, and same-sex–inclusive sexual health education programs that address intimate partner violence (IPV; Turell,

Herrmann, Hollander, & Galletly, 2012; see also Chapter 9, this volume). Thus, counselors should be aware of the potential impact schools have on the mental health and well-being of their clients.

Romantic Relationships and Intimate Partner Violence

Balsam, Beauchaine, Rothblum, and Solomon (2008) reported that, compared with heterosexual couples, same-sex couples reported higher levels of overall relationship quality and intimacy and lower levels of ineffective arguing, negative problem solving, partner withdrawal, and self-withdrawal. Mohr et al. (2013) found that the pattern of associations between romantic attachment and relationship functioning among same-sex couples differed in some ways from findings with samples of heterosexual couples, suggesting that same-sex couples may have been influenced by "exposure to negative societal beliefs questioning the sustainability of same-sex relationships, fewer social structures designed to encourage stability in same-sex couples, and greater exposure to norms for negotiating nonmonogamy" (p. 79). Highlighting the impact of limited access to marriage or other forms of legal commitment, Balsam et al. (2008) also found that there were more breakups in non–civil union couples than there were in civil union and heterosexual married couples but that same-sex civil union couples did not differ from heterosexual married couples in rates of breakups during the 3-year duration of the study.

The prevalence of experiences of IPV among men and women in same-sex relationships is difficult to assess because they are often based on small or convenience samples and use varying definitions of violence, time frames, and sampling procedures, with estimates ranging widely between 8% and 60% (Glass et al., 2008), with the best estimates hovering around 25% to 30% (Lewis, Mettelich, Kelley, & Woody, 2012). Although women are the most frequent focus of study in the IPV literature overall, gay men account for the largest proportion of victims within the LGBT community, but they are less likely to report or seek help when they experience IPV and fewer services are available for male victims of IPV (Oliffe et al., 2014). Clearly, there is a need for therapists to assess for IPV among their LGBTQ clients. Threats of outing can be used to control and intimidate same-sex partners who cannot be open about their sexual orientation at work or with family members. Clients may also not recognize abusive behavior because of the myth that IPV only happens in male–female relationships. Other fears include bringing stigma to an already stereotyped group.

Disability Issues

In two studies (Hunt, Matthews, Milsom, & Lammel, 2006; Hunt, Milsom, & Matthews, 2009), researchers interviewed 25 lesbian women with physical disabilities about their counseling experiences and partner-related experiences. In the first study, Hunt et al. (2006) identified themes related to perceptions of their counselors; general satisfaction/dissatisfaction; counselors' general effectiveness; counselors' awareness and education regarding sexual orientation and/or disability, discrimination, and bias; counselor identity; and clients' attempts to negotiate the counseling process regarding coming out or self-disclosure, self-advocacy, and accessibility/accommodations. Phenomenological inquiry produced important insights regarding the difference between overt bias and discrimination versus experiences about whether counselors were aware or educated regarding sexual orientation and disability, and in particular the combination of both disability and sexual orientation. In the second study, Hunt et al. (2009) again used phenomenological inquiry to highlight important themes among couples, such as evolving partner roles (e.g., caregiving, advocating), negotiating the influence of disability on the couple (e.g., effects on the relationship, need for support for the partner, sexuality issues), and navigating legal and financial concerns (e.g., insurance, power of attorney, partner access to medical records or visitation, financial status). In addition, the study revealed important dynamics between the clients and treatment professionals related to how counselors reacted or responded to the same-sex couple and the comfort of clients to be open about their relationship.

Work Experiences and Career Issues

There have been a small number of empirical articles published in recent years regarding the career development or work experiences of LGB individuals. In a large sample of LGB employees in Italy, Prati and Pietrantoni (2014) found that workplace heterosexist climates mediated relationships between workplace outness and job satisfaction, in which anticipated discrimination moderated employee disclosure of sexual orientation identity and job satisfaction. Schmidt and Nilsson (2006) found that LGB adolescents who reported higher levels of inner sexual identity conflict and lower levels of social support also tended to report lower scores on career maturity and higher scores career indecision. Russon and Schmidt (2014) found that specific components of authenticity (e.g., awareness) significantly predicted career decision-making self-efficacy among LGB college students. Given the significance of work in the lives of most clients, it is important for counselors to understand the unique and common ways that workplace experiences can impact the psychological well-being and functioning of LGB clients.

Religious and Spiritual Issues

Buser, Goodrich, Luke, and Buser (2011) conducted a qualitative investigation of the positive and negative experiences of LGBT clients when addressing religious and spiritual issues in counseling. The findings of this study point to the need for counselors and therapists to provide an open and welcoming atmosphere for clients to integrate spiritual and religious identities within their lives as LGBT individuals and call for greater attention to potential biases that might result in discriminatory treatment, microaggressions, lack of training of counselors to address religious and spiritual issues with LGBT clients, and failure to address these issues during the course of therapy. Similarly, Borgman (2009) identified ways psychologists integrate identities as both Christian and LGB allies through increased awareness of potential conflicts between values and identities, experiences of dissonance and confusion, the process of questioning and exploration, challenging and redefining oneself, and identifying integration of identities as a goal.

IMPLICATIONS FOR COUNSELING PRACTITIONERS AND RESEARCHERS

Our review of the recent research and scholarship about sexual orientation and gender variance yielded a substantial body of new knowledge that builds on earlier advances in the field across many decades. Over time, the mental health professions have gradually evolved, at a parallel pace to the broader societal advancements, in removing pathological conceptualizations, treatments, and interventions with respect to LGBTQ individuals. Nevertheless, a great deal of work remains to be done, and despite its relatively rapid expansion, research and scholarship in the area continues to contain significant gaps and deficits. Indeed, a substantial amount of the literature on LGBTQ people and issues remains relatively disconnected from a broader conceptual framework, having been pieced together across time based on wide-ranging and disparate theoretical perspectives and contextual biases arising from historical, generational, cultural, environmental, institutional, and individual sources. Much of the research from different disciplines approaches LGBTQ issues from vastly different perspectives, which produces conflicting or inconsistent findings.

Among the most important problems in research with sexual minority populations remains the lack of consistency from one study to the next on fundamental definitional issues related to sexual orientation, sexual identity, gender identity, gender expression, and gender variance (see Moradi et al., 2009). Furthermore, there is a broad consensus that a more complex model of intersectional identity needs to be incorporated into the research literature on LGBTQ populations (Cheshire, 2013; Frost & Meyer, 2012; Hunt et al., 2006; Moradi et al., 2010; Parent et al., 2013; see also Chapter 4, this volume). An integrative approach is necessary to disentangle the numerous constructs that converge in the lives of sexual minority clients, requiring an understanding of socially constructed as well as essential aspects of sexual orientation and gender identity to form an enduring conceptualization of the complexities of sexuality and gender in counseling and mental health practice (Moradi et al., 2009; see also Chapter 2, this volume). For example, Worthington and colleagues (Dillon et al., 2011; Worthington & Mohr, 2002; Worthington & Reynolds, 2009; Worthington, Savoy, Dillon, & Vernaglia, 2002) have suggested that the stability of sexual orientations can be assumed (e.g., Savin-Williams et al., 2012) without compromising an understanding of the potential flexibility or fluidity of sexual identities (e.g., Diamond, 2008, 2012).

There has been some progress in the advancement of lines of research inquiry specifically designed to address the intersections of race, ethnicity, and sexual orientation (Balsam et al., 2011; Huang et al., 2010), but less progress has been made in the areas of gender identity and expression (Blashill & Hughes, 2009; Blashill & Vander Wal, 2009; McDermott & Schwartz, 2013). Also, a substantial proportion of the research regarding sexual minority clients overwhelmingly involves White participants (Huang et al., 2010). It has become common for many investigators to identify the limitations of almost exclusively White samples; yet, outside of research specifically designed to address the needs of LGBTQ clients of color, very little has been done to increase the numbers of people of color in large-sample research on LGBTQ issues more broadly. This set of conditions continues to constrain advances in understanding the intersections of race, ethnicity, and sexual minority statuses (Huang et al., 2010). One potential explanation of this ongoing issue is that LGBTQ people of color may be less likely to be out than their White counterparts (Gallor & Fassinger, 2010).

Some attempts have been made to integrate intersectionality into clinical research related to minority stress, victimization, and marginalization (Balsam et al., 2011; Bowleg, 2013; David & Knight, 2008; Feinstein et al., 2012). The literature examines the risk and resilience experiences of LGBTQ people of color and how social supports and community connectedness aid in well-being (Frost & Meyer, 2009, 2012; Moradi et al., 2010). Racial/ethnic minority LGBTQ individuals are at a higher risk for mental health disorders, substance abuse, and suicidality than their White LGBTQ counterparts (O'Donnell et al., 2011). The research, however, is limited in addressing ability status, people of color outside of the dominant discourse (e.g., Arab, Jewish, South Asian; Huang et al., 2010; Hunt, Matthews, Milsom, & Lammel, 2006), and LGBTQ individuals living in rural areas. Future research might include greater attention to within-group variability.

Some of the most important advances in research and scholarship on the counseling needs of sexual minority group members have been relatively recent (e.g., ALGBTIC Transgender Committee, 2010; APA, 2012; APA Task Force on Appropriate Therapeutic Responses to Sexual Orientation, 2009; APA Task Force on Gender Identity and Gender Variance, 2009). Professional associations have influenced public policies and legal advancements (e.g., Moradi, 2006), yet societal advances propelled by other political and advocacy efforts outside of the counseling and mental health professions have begun to move so quickly that the field appears to be struggling to keep pace. For example, transgender people often come into contact with counseling and mental health systems that are misinformed or uneducated about the need for counseling competencies with transgender clients (Singh & Burnes, 2010). For this reason, counselor training programs need greater focus on intersectionality to address the complexity of multiple minority statuses, and mental health professionals need to incorporate conceptual and ecological frameworks to understand the complexity of individual experience.

On the basis of our review of the literature and the ongoing emergence of paradigms related to intersecting identities and multiple minority stress in the lives of LGBTQ individuals, we have been careful to avoid recommendations based on broad generalizations about specific counseling and mental health practices and interventions. Specifically, our reading of the literature is one that suggests the need for depth and breadth of understanding of the proximal and distal stressors that impinge on the lives of sexual minority clients based on their multiple and intersecting identities, such that counseling practices will inevitably be based on an idiographic approach to individual cases. Broad recommendations for specific counseling and mental health practices and interventions have the potential to perpetuate stereotypes, overgeneralize on the basis of nongeneralizable qualitative research, or apply findings from idiosyncratic samples in quantitative studies to individuals that ignore the complexities and contexts of sexual minority lives. Nevertheless, the research summaries contained in this chapter serve as a basis for understanding broader contextual forces that affect individual clients and promote greater understanding of the variety of issues that have emerged in the research to be associated with the stresses, health, mental health, and resilience of sexual minority individuals.

REFERENCES

Alessi, E. J. (2013). Acknowledging the impact of social forces on sexual minority clients: Introduction to the special issue. *Clinical Social Work Journal, 41*, 223–227. http://dx.doi.org/10.1007/s10615-013-0458-x

ALGBTIC LGBQQIA Competencies Taskforce. (2013). Association for Lesbian, Gay, Bisexual, and Transgender Issues in Counseling Competencies for Counseling with Lesbian, Gay, Bisexual, Queer, Questioning, Intersex, and Ally Individuals. *Journal of LGBT Issues in Counseling, 7,* 2–4. http://dx.doi.org/10.1080/15538605.2013.755444

ALGBTIC Transgender Committee. (2010). American Counseling Association competencies for counseling with transgender clients. *Journal of LGBT Issues in Counseling, 4,* 135–159. http://dx.doi.org/10.1080/15538605.2010.524839

American Psychological Association. (2012). Guidelines for psychological practice with lesbian, gay, and bisexual clients. *American Psychologist, 67,* 10–42. http://dx.doi.org/10.1037/a0024659

APA Task Force on Appropriate Therapeutic Responses to Sexual Orientation. (2009). *Report of the American Psychological Association Task Force on Appropriate Therapeutic Responses to Sexual Orientation.* Washington, DC: American Psychological Association. Retrieved from https://www.apa.org/pi/lgbt/resources/therapeutic-response.pdf

APA Task Force on Gender Identity and Gender Variance. (2009). *Report of the APA Task Force on Gender Identity and Gender Variance.* Washington, DC: American Psychological Association. Retrieved from https://www.apa.org/pi/lgbt/resources/policy/gender-identity-report.pdf

Balsam, K. F., Beauchaine, T. P., Rothblum, E. D., & Solomon, S. E. (2008). Three-year follow-up of same-sex couples who had civil unions in Vermont, same-sex couples not in civil unions, and heterosexual married couples. *Developmental Psychology, 44,* 102–116. http://dx.doi.org/10.1037/0012-1649.44.1.102

Balsam, K. F., Molina, Y., Beadnell, B., Simoni, J., & Walters, K. (2011). Measuring multiple minority stress: The LGBT People of Color Microaggressions Scale. *Cultural Diversity and Ethic Minority Psychology, 12,* 163–174. http://dx.doi.org/10.1037/a0023244

Bess, J. A., & Stabb, S. D. (2009). The experiences of transgender persons in psychotherapy: Voices and recommendations. *Journal of Mental Health Counseling, 31,* 264–282. http://dx.doi.org/10.17744/mehc.31.3.f624154681133w50

Bidell, M. P. (2013). Addressing disparities: The impact of a lesbian, gay, bisexual and transgender graduate counseling course. *Counselling and Psychotherapy Research, 13,* 300–307. http://dx.doi.org/10.1080/14733145.2012.741139

Bidell, M. P. (2014). Are multicultural courses addressing disparities? Exploring multicultural and affirmative lesbian, gay, and bisexual competencies of counseling and psychology students. *Journal of Multicultural Counseling and Development, 42,* 132–146. http://dx.doi.org/10.1002/j.2161-1912.2014.00050.x

Bieschke, K. J., McClanahan, M., Tozer, E., Grzegorek, J. L., & Park, J. (2000). Programmatic research on the treatment of lesbian, gay, and bisexual clients: The past, the present, and the course for the future. In R. M. Perez, K. A. DeBord, & K. J. Bieschke (Eds.), *Handbook of counseling and psychotherapy with lesbian, gay, and bisexual clients* (pp. 309–336). Washington, DC: American Psychological Association. http://dx.doi.org/10.1037/10339-013

Bieschke, K. J., Paul, P. L., & Blasko, K. A. (2007). Review of empirical research focused on the experience of lesbian, gay, and bisexual clients in counseling and psychotherapy. In K. J. Bieschke, R. M. Perez, & K. A. DeBord, *Handbook of counseling and psychotherapy with lesbian, gay, bisexual, and transgender clients* (2nd ed., pp. 293–315). Washington, DC: American Psychological Association. http://dx.doi.org/10.1037/11482-000

Blashill, A. J., & Hughes, H. M. (2009). Gender role and gender role conflict: Preliminary considerations for psychotherapy with gay men. *Journal of Gay & Lesbian Mental Health, 13,* 170–186. http://dx.doi.org/10.1080/19359700902914300

Blashill, A. J., & Vander Wal, J. S. (2009). Mediation of gender role conflict and eating pathology in gay men. *Psychology of Men & Masculinity, 10,* 204–217. http://dx.doi.org/10.1037/a0016000

Borgman, A. L. (2009). LGB allies and Christian identity: A qualitative exploration of resolving conflicts and integrating identities. *Journal of Counseling Psychology, 56,* 508–520. http://dx.doi.org/10.1037/a0016691

Bowleg, L. (2013). "Once you've blended the cake you can't take the parts back to the main ingredients": Black, gay, and bisexual men's descriptions and experiences of intersectionality. *Sex Roles, 68,* 754–767. http://dx.doi.org/10.1007/s11199-012-0152-4

Brewster, M. E., Moradi, B., Deblaere, C., & Velez, B. L. (2012). Navigating the borderlands: The roles of minority stressors, bicultural self-efficacy, and cognitive flexibility in the mental health of bisexual individuals. *Journal of Counseling Psychology, 60,* 543–556. http://dx.doi.org/10.1037/a0033224

Brewster, M. E., Velez, B., DeBlaere, C., & Moradi, B. (2012). Transgender individuals' workplace experiences: The applicability of sexual minority measures and models. *Journal of Counseling Psychology, 59,* 60–70. http://dx.doi.org/10.1037/a0025206

Brewster, M. E., Velez, B. L., Mennicke, A., & Tebbe, E. (2014). Voices from beyond: A thematic content analysis of transgender employees' workplace experiences. *Psychology of Sexual Orientation and Gender Diversity, 1,* 159–169. http://dx.doi.org/10.1037/sgd0000030

Brooks, L. M., & Inman, A. G. (2013). Bisexual counseling competence: Investigating the role of attitudes and empathy. *Journal of LGBT Issues in Counseling, 7,* 65–86. http://dx.doi.org/10.1080/15538605.2013.756366

Brooks, L. M., Inman, A. G., Klinger, R. S., Malouf, M. A., & Kaduvettoor, A. (2010). In her own words: Ethnic-minority bisexual women's self-reported counseling needs. *Journal of Bisexuality, 10,* 253–267. http://dx.doi.org/10.1080/15299716.2010.500959

Budge, S. L., Adelson, J. L., & Howard, K. A. S. (2013). Anxiety and depression in transgender individuals: The roles of transition status, loss, social support, and coping. *Journal of Consulting and Clinical Psychology, 81,* 545–557. http://dx.doi.org/10.1037/a0031774

Budge, S. L., Tebbe, E. N., & Howard, K. A. S. (2010). The work experiences of transgender individuals: Negotiating the transition and career decision-making processes. *Journal of Counseling Psychology, 57*, 377–393. http://dx.doi.org/10.1037/a0020472

Burckell, L. A., & Goldfried, M. R. (2006). Therapist qualities preferred by sexual-minority individuals. *Psychotherapy, 43*, 32–49. http://dx.doi.org/10.1037/0033-3204.43.1.32

Burkard, A. W., Pruitt, N. T., Medler, B. R., & Stark-Booth, A. M. (2009). Validity and reliability of the lesbian, gay, bisexual working alliance self-efficacy scales. *Training and Education in Professional Psychology, 3*, 37–46. http://dx.doi.org/10.1037/1931-3918.3.1.37

Burnes, T. R., Singh, A. A., Harper, A. J., Harper, B., Maxon-Kann, W., Pickering, D. L., . . . Hosea, J. (2010). American Counseling Association: Competencies for counseling with transgender clients. *Journal of LGBT Issues in Counseling, 4*(3-4), 135–159.

Buser, J. K., Goodrich, K. M., Luke, M., & Buser, T. J. (2011). A narratology of lesbian, gay, bisexual, and transgender clients' experiences addressing religious and spiritual issues in counseling. *Journal of LGBT Issues in Counseling, 5*, 282–303. http://dx.doi.org/10.1080/15538605.2011.632395

Cabaj, R. P. (2008). Substance abuse, internalized homophobia, and gay men and lesbians: Psychodynamic issues and clinical implications. *Journal of Gay & Lesbian Psychotherapy, 3*(3/4), 5–24.

Cerezo, A., Morales, A., Quintero, D., & Rothman, S. (2014). Trans migrations: Exploring life at the intersection of transgender identity and immigration. *Psychology of Sexual Orientation and Gender Diversity, 1*, 170–180. http://dx.doi.org/10.1037/sgd0000031

Cheshire, L. C. (2013). Reconsidering sexual identities: Intersectionality theory and the implications for educating counselors. *Canadian Journal of Counselling and Psychotherapy, 7*(1), 4–13.

Chung, Y. B., & Katayama, M. (1996). Assessment of sexual orientation in lesbian/gay/bisexual studies. *Journal of Homosexuality, 30*(4), 49–62. http://dx.doi.org/10.1300/J082v30n04_03

Clyman, J. A., & Pachankis, J. E. (2014). The relationship between objectivity coded explanatory style and mental health in the stigma-related narratives of young gay men. *Psychology of Men & Masculinity, 15*(1), 110–115. http://dx.doi.org/10.1037/a0031500

Cochran, S. D., Mays, V. M., Alegria, M., Ortega, A. N., & Takeuchi, D. (2007). Mental health and substance use disorders among Latino and Asian American lesbian, gay, and bisexual adults. *Journal of Consulting and Clinical Psychology, 75*, 785–794. http://dx.doi.org/10.1037/0022-006X.75.5.785

Cramer, R. J., Golom, F. D., LoPresto, C. T., & Kirkley, S. L. (2008). Weighing the evidence: Empirical assessment and ethical implications of conversion therapy. *Ethics & Behavior, 18*(1), 93–114. http://dx.doi.org/10.1080/10508420701713014

Cruz, T. M. (2014). Assessing access to care for transgender and gender nonconforming people: A consideration of diversity in combating discrimination.

Social Science & Medicine, 110, 65–73. http://dx.doi.org/10.1016/j.socscimed. 2014.03.032

David, S., & Knight, B. G. (2008). Stress and coping among gay men: Age and ethnic differences. *Psychology and Aging, 23,* 62–69. http://dx.doi.org/10.1037/ 0882-7974.23.1.62

Dehlin, J. P., Galliher, R. V., Bradshaw, W. S., Hyde, D. C., & Crowell, K. A. (2015). Sexual orientation change efforts among current or former LDS church members. *Journal of Counseling Psychology, 62,* 95–105. http://dx.doi.org/10.1037/cou0000011

Derogatis, L. R. (1994). *SCL-90-R Symptom Checklist-90-R administration, scoring and procedures manual.* Minneapolis, MN: National Computer Systems.

Diamond, G. M., Diamond, G. S., Levy, S., Closs, C., Ladipo, T., & Siqueland, L. (2013). Attachment-based family therapy for suicidal lesbian, gay, and bisexual adolescents: A treatment development study and open trial with preliminary findings. *Psychology of Sexual Orientation and Gender Diversity, 1,* 91–100. http:// dx.doi.org/10.1037/2329-0382.1.S.91

Diamond, L. M. (2007). A dynamical systems approach to the development and expression of female same-sex sexuality. *Perspectives on Psychological Science, 2,* 142–161. http://dx.doi.org/10.1111/j.1745-6916.2007.00034.x

Diamond, L. M. (2008). *Sexual fluidity: Understanding women's love and desire.* Cambridge, MA: Harvard University Press.

Diamond, L. M. (2012). The desire disorder in research on sexual orientation in women: Contributions of dynamical systems theory. *Archives of Sexual Behavior, 41,* 73–83. http://dx.doi.org/10.1007/s10508-012-9909-7

dickey, l. m., Burnes, T. R., & Singh, A. A. (2012). Sexual identity development of female-to-male transgender individuals: A grounded theory inquiry. *Journal of LGBT Issues in Counseling, 6,* 118–138. http://dx.doi.org/10.1080/ 15538605.2012.678184

Dillon, F., & Worthington, R. L. (2003). The Lesbian, Gay, and Bisexual Affirmative Counseling Self-Efficacy Inventory (LGB-CSI): Development, validation, and training implications. *Journal of Counseling Psychology, 50,* 235–251. http:// dx.doi.org/10.1037/0022-0167.50.2.235

Dillon, F. R., Worthington, R. L., & Moradi, B. (2011). Sexual identity as a universal process. In S. Schwartz, K. Luyckx, & V. Vignoles (Eds.), *Handbook of identity theory and research* (pp. 649–670). New York, NY: Springer. http://dx.doi.org/ 10.1007/978-1-4419-7988-9_27

Dillon, F. R., Worthington, R. L., Savoy, H. B., Rooney, S. C., Becker-Schutte, A., & Guerra, R. M. (2004). On becoming allies: A qualitative study of lesbian-, gay-, and bisexual-affirmative counselor training. *Counselor Education and Supervision, 43,* 162–178. http://dx.doi.org/10.1002/j.1556-6978.2004.tb01840.x

Dillon, F. R., Worthington, R. L., Soth-McNett, A. M., & Schwartz, S. J. (2008). Gender and sexual identity-based predictors of lesbian, gay, and bisexual affirmative counseling self-efficacy. *Professional Psychology: Research and Practice, 39,* 353–360. http://dx.doi.org/10.1037/0735-7028.39.3.353

Espelage, D. L., Aragon, S. R., Birkett, M., & Koenig, B. W. (2008). Homophobic teasing, psychological outcomes, and sexual orientation among high school students: What influence do parents and schools have? *School Psychology Review, 37,* 202–216.

Fassinger, R. E., & Arseneau, J. R. (2008). Diverse women's sexualities. In F. L. Denmark & M. Paludi (Eds.), *Psychology of women: A handbook of issues and theories* (2nd ed., pp. 484–508). Westport, CT: Praeger.

Feinstein, B. A., Goldfried, M. R., & Davila, J. (2012). The relationship between experiences of discrimination and mental health among lesbians and gay men: An examination of internalized homonegativity and rejection sensitivity as potential mechanisms. *Journal of Consulting and Clinical Psychology, 80,* 917–927. http://dx.doi.org/10.1037/a0029425

Fjelstrom, J. (2013). Sexual orientation change efforts and the search for authenticity. *Journal of Homosexuality, 60,* 801–827. http://dx.doi.org/10.1080/00918369.2013.774830

Flentje, A., Heck, N. C., & Cochran, B. N. (2013). Sexual reorientation therapy interventions: Perspectives of ex-gay individuals. *Journal of Gay & Lesbian Mental Health, 17,* 256–277. http://dx.doi.org/10.1080/19359705.2013.773268

Flood, J., McLaughlin, C., & Prentice, G. (2013). Minority stress, homonegativity, and mental health among college gay males. *Journal of Gay & Lesbian Mental Health, 17,* 367–386. http://dx.doi.org/10.1080/19359705.2013.800006

Frost, D. M. (2011). Stigma and intimacy in same-sex relationships: A narrative approach. *Journal of Family Psychology, 25*(1), 1–10. http://dx.doi.org/10.1037/a0022374

Frost, D. M., & Meyer, I. H. (2009). Internalized homophobia and relationship quality among lesbians, gay men, and bisexuals. *Journal of Counseling Psychology, 56,* 97–109. http://dx.doi.org/10.1037/a0012844

Frost, D. M., & Meyer, I. H. (2012). Measuring community connectedness among diverse sexual minority populations. *Journal of Sex Research, 49,* 36–49. http://dx.doi.org/10.1080/00224499.2011.565427

Gallor, S. M., & Fassinger, R. E. (2010). Social support, ethnic identity, and sexual identity of lesbians and gay men. *Journal of Gay & Lesbian Social Services: The Quarterly Journal of Community & Clinical Practice, 22,* 287–315. http://dx.doi.org/10.1080/10538720903426404

Glass, N., Perrin, N., Hanson, G., Bloom, T., Gardner, E., & Campbell, J. C. (2008). Risk for reassault in abusive female same-sex relationships. *American Journal of Public Health, 98,* 1021–1027. http://dx.doi.org/10.2105/AJPH.2007.117770

Graham, S. R., Carney, J. S., & Kluck, A. S. (2012). Perceived competency in working with LGB clients: Where are we now? *Counselor Education and Supervision, 51,* 2–16. http://dx.doi.org/10.1002/j.1556-6978.2012.00001.x

Grove, J. (2009). How competent are trainee and newly qualified counselors to work with lesbian, gay, and bisexual clients and what do they perceive as their most effective learning experience? *Counselling & Psychotherapy Research, 9,* 78–85. http://dx.doi.org/10.1080/14733140802490622

Haldeman, D. C. (1994). The practice and ethics of sexual orientation conversion therapy. *Journal of Consulting and Clinical Psychology, 62,* 221–227. http://dx.doi.org/10.1037/0022-006X.62.2.221

Hatzenbuehler, M. L., Pachankis, J. E., & Wolfe, J. (2012). Religious climate and health risk behaviors in sexual minority youths: A population-based study. *American Journal of Public Health, 102,* 657–663. http://dx.doi.org/10.2105/AJPH.2011.300517

Heck, N. Y., Croot, L. C., & Robohm, J. S. (2015). Piloting a psychotherapy group for transgender clients: Description and clinical considerations for practitioners. *Professional Psychology: Research and Practice, 46,* 1–7.

Hiestand, K., Horne, S. G., & Levitt, H. M. (2008). Effects of gender identity on experiences of healthcare for sexual minority women. *Journal of LGBT Health Research, 3,* 15–27.

Hooker, E. (1957). The adjustment of the male overt homosexual. *Journal of Projective Techniques, 21,* 18–31. http://dx.doi.org/10.1080/08853126.1957.10380742

Huang, Y., Brewster, M. E., Moradi, B., Goodman, M. B., Wiseman, M. C., & Martin, A. (2010). Content analysis of literature about LGB people of color 1998–2007. *The Counseling Psychologist, 38,* 363–396. http://dx.doi.org/10.1177/0011000009335255

Hunt, B., Matthews, C., Milsom, A., & Lammel, J. A. (2006). Lesbians with physical disabilities: A qualitative study of their experiences with counseling. *Journal of Counseling & Development, 84,* 163–173. http://dx.doi.org/10.1002/j.1556-6678.2006.tb00392.x

Hunt, B., Milsom, A., & Matthews, C. (2009). Partner-related rehabilitation experiences of lesbians with physical disabilities: A qualitative study. *Rehabilitation Counseling Bulletin, 52,* 167–178. http://dx.doi.org/10.1177/0034355208320933

Israel, T. (2005). . . . and sometimes T: Transgender issues in LGBT psychology. *Newsletter of the Society for the Psychological Study of Lesbian, Gay, and Bisexual Issues, 21*(3), 16–18.

Israel, T., Gorcheva, R., Walther, W. A., Sulzner, J. M., & Cohen, J. (2008). Therapists' helpful and unhelpful situations with LGBT clients: An exploratory study. *Professional Psychology: Research and Practice, 39,* 361–368. http://dx.doi.org/10.1037/0735-7028.39.3.361

Israel, T., & Mohr, J. J. (2004). Attitudes toward bisexual women and men. *Journal of Bisexuality, 4*(1-2), 117–134. http://dx.doi.org/10.1300/J159v04n01_09

Jones, S. L., & Yarhouse, M. A. (2011). A longitudinal study of attempted religiously mediated sexual orientation change. *Journal of Sex & Marital Therapy, 37,* 404–427. http://dx.doi.org/10.1080/0092623X.2011.607052

Karten, E. Y., & Wade, J. C. (2010). Sexual orientation change efforts in men: A client perspective. *Journal of Men's Studies, 18*, 84–102. http://dx.doi.org/10.3149/jms.1801.84

King, M., Semlyen, J., Tai, S. S., Killaspy, H., Osborn, D., Popelyuk, D., & Nazareth, I. (2008). A systematic review of mental disorder, suicide, and deliberate self-harm in lesbian, gay and bisexual people. *BMC Psychiatry, 8*, 70–87. http://dx.doi.org/10.1186/1471-244X-8-70

Kosciw, J. G., Greytak, E. A., & Diaz, E. M. (2009). Who, what, where, when, and why: Demographic and ecological factors contributing to hostile school climate for lesbian, gay, bisexual, and transgender youth. *Journal of Youth and Adolescence, 38*, 976–988. http://dx.doi.org/10.1007/s10964-009-9412-1

Kosciw, J. G., Palmer, N. A., Kull, R. M., & Greytak, E. A. (2013). The effect of negative school climate on academic outcomes for LGBT youth and the role of in-school supports. *Journal of School Violence, 12*, 45–63. http://dx.doi.org/10.1080/15388220.2012.732546

Kwon, P. (2013). Resilience in lesbian, gay, and bisexual individuals. *Personality and Social Psychology Review, 17*, 371–383. http://dx.doi.org/10.1177/1088868313490248

Levitt, H. M., & Ippolito, M. R. (2014a). Being transgender: The experience of transgender identity development. *Journal of Homosexuality, 61*, 1727–1758. http://dx.doi.org/10.1080/00918369.2014.951262

Levitt, H. M., & Ippolito, M. R. (2014b). Being transgender: Navigating minority stressors and developing authentic self-presentation. *Psychology of Women Quarterly, 38*, 46–64. http://dx.doi.org/10.1177/0361684313501644

Lewis, R. J., Milletich, R. J., Kelley, M. L., & Woody, A. (2012). Minority stress, substance use, and intimate partner violence among sexual minority women. *Aggression and Violent Behavior, 17*, 247–256. http://dx.doi.org/10.1016/j.avb.2012.02.004

McAleavey, A., Castonguay, L. G., & Locke, B. D. (2011). Sexual orientation minorities in college counseling: Prevalence, distress, and symptom profiles. *Journal of College Counseling, 14*, 127–142. http://dx.doi.org/10.1002/j.2161-1882.2011.tb00268.x

McCabe, S. E., Bostwick, W. B., Hughes, T. L., West, B. T., & Boyd, C. J. (2010). The relationship between discrimination and substance use disorders among lesbian, gay, and bisexual adults in the United States. *American Journal of Public Health, 100*, 1946–1952. http://dx.doi.org/10.2105/AJPH.2009.163147

McDermott, R. C., & Schwartz, J. P. (2013). Toward a better understanding of emerging adult men's gender role journeys: Differences in age, education, race, relationship status, and sexual orientation. *Psychology of Men & Masculinity, 14*, 202–210. http://dx.doi.org/10.1037/a0028538

Meyer, I. H. (2013). Prejudice, social stress, and mental health in lesbian, gay, and bisexual populations: Conceptual issues and research evidence. *Psychology of Sexual Orientation and Gender Diversity, 1*, 3–26. http://dx.doi.org/10.1037/2329-0382.1.S.3

Mohr, J. J. (2002). Heterosexual identity and the heterosexual therapist: Using identity as a framework for understanding sexual orientation issues in psychotherapy. *The Counseling Psychologist, 30,* 532–566.

Mohr, J. J., Selterman, D., & Fassinger, R. E. (2013). Romantic attachment and relationship functioning in same-sex couples. *Journal of Counseling Psychology, 60,* 72–82. http://dx.doi.org/10.1037/a0030994

Mohr, J. J., Weiner, J. L., Chopp, R. M., & Wong, S. J. (2009). Effects of client bisexuality on clinical judgment: When is bias most likely to occur? *Journal of Counseling Psychology, 56,* 164–175. http://dx.doi.org/10.1037/a0012816

Moradi, B. (2006). Perceived sexual-orientation-based harassment in military and civilian contexts. *Military Psychology, 18,* 39–60. http://dx.doi.org/10.1207/s15327876mp1801_3

Moradi, B., DeBlaere, C., & Huang, Y. (2010). Centralizing the experiences of LGB people of color in counseling psychology. *The Counseling Psychologist, 38,* 322–330. http://dx.doi.org/10.1177/0011000008330832

Moradi, B., Mohr, J. J., Worthington, R. L., & Fassinger, R. E. (2009). Counseling psychology research on sexual (orientation) minority issues: Conceptual and methodological challenges and opportunities. *Journal of Counseling Psychology, 56,* 5–22. http://dx.doi.org/10.1037/a0014572

Needham, B. L., & Austin, E. L. (2010). Sexual orientation, parental support, and health during the transition to young adulthood. *Journal of Youth and Adolescence, 39,* 1189–1198. http://dx.doi.org/10.1007/s10964-010-9533-6

Nova, E. A., McGeorge, C. R., & Stone Carlson, T. S. (2013). Bisexuality and lesbian, gay, bisexual affirmative training: An exploration of family therapy students' beliefs and clinical experiences. *Journal of Feminist Family Therapy: An International Forum, 25,* 212–232. http://dx.doi.org/10.1080/08952833.2013.777886

O'Donnell, S., Meyer, I. H., & Schwartz, S. (2011). Increased risk of suicide attempts among Black and Latino lesbians, gay men, and bisexuals. *American Journal of Public Health, 101,* 1055–1059. http://dx.doi.org/10.2105/AJPH.2010.300032

Oliffe, J. L., Han, C., Maria, E. S., Lohan, M., Howard, T., Stewart, D. E., & MacMillan, H. (2014). Gay men and intimate partner violence: A gender analysis. *Sociology of Health & Illness, 36,* 564–579. http://dx.doi.org/10.1111/1467-9566.12099

O'Shaughnessy, T., & Spokane, A. R. (2013). Lesbian and gay affirmative therapy competency, self-efficacy, and personality in psychology trainees. *The Counseling Psychologist, 41,* 825–856. http://dx.doi.org/10.1177/0011000012459364

Pachankis, J. E. (2007). The psychological implications of concealing a stigma: A cognitive-affective behavioral model. *Psychological Bulletin, 133,* 328–345.

Parent, M. C., DeBlaere, C., & Moradi, B. (2013). Approaches to research on inter-sectionality: Perspectives on gender, LGBT, and racial/ethnic identities. *Sex Roles*, 68, 639–645. http://dx.doi.org/10.1007/s11199-013-0283-2

Patterson, C. J. (1995). Sexual orientation and human development: An overview. *Developmental Psychology*, 31, 3–11. http://dx.doi.org/10.1037/0012-1649.31.1.3

Prati, G., & Pietrantoni, L. (2014). Coming out and job satisfaction: A moder-ated mediation model. *The Career Development Quarterly*, 62, 358–371. http://dx.doi.org/10.1002/j.2161-0045.2014.00088.x

Russon, J. M., & Schmidt, C. K. (2014). Authenticity and career decision-making self-efficacy in lesbian, gay, and bisexual college students. *Journal of Gay & Lesbian Social Services*, 26, 207–221. http://dx.doi.org/10.1080/10538720.2014.891090

Savin-Williams, R. C., Joyner, K., & Rieger, G. (2012). Prevalence and stability of self-reported sexual orientation identity during young adulthood. *Archives of Sexual Behavior*, 41, 103–110. http://dx.doi.org/10.1007/s10508-012-9913-y

Schmidt, C. K., & Nilsson, J. E. (2006). The effects of simultaneous developmental processes: Factors related to the career development of lesbian, gay, and bisexual youth. *The Career Development Quarterly*, 55, 22–37. http://dx.doi.org/10.1002/j.2161-0045.2006.tb00002.x

Senreich, E. (2009). A comparison of perceptions, reported abstinence, and comple-tion rates of gay, lesbian, bisexual, and heterosexual clients in substance abuse treatment. *Journal of Gay & Lesbian Mental Health*, 13, 145–169. http://dx.doi.org/10.1080/19359700902870072

Singh, A. A., & Burnes, T. R. (2010). Introduction to the special issue: Translating the competencies for counseling with transgender clients into counseling practice, research, and advocacy. *Journal of LGBT Issues in Counseling*, 4, 126–134. http://dx.doi.org/10.1080/15538605.2010.524837

Szymanski, D. M., & Sung, M. R. (2010). Minority stress and psychological distress among Asian American sexual minority persons. *The Counseling Psychologist*, 38, 848–872. http://dx.doi.org/10.1177/0011000010366167

Turell, S., Herrmann, M., Hollander, G., & Galletly, C. (2012). Lesbian, gay, bisexual, and transgender communities' readiness for intimate partner vio-lence prevention. *Journal of Gay & Lesbian Social Services: The Quarterly Journal of Community & Clinical Practice*, 24, 289–310. http://dx.doi.org/10.1080/10538720.2012.697797

Velez, B. L., Moradi, B., & DeBlaere, C. (2015). Multiple oppressions and the mental health of sexual minority Latina/o individuals. *The Counseling Psychologist*, 43, 7–38.

Vrangalova, Z., & Savin-Williams, R. C. (2010). Correlates of same-sex sexuality in heterosexually identified young adults. *Journal of Sex Research*, 47, 92–102. http://dx.doi.org/10.1080/00224490902954307

Woodward, E. N., Pantalone, D. W., & Bradford, J. (2013). Differential reports of suicidal ideation and attempts of questioning adults compared to heterosexual, lesbian, gay, and bisexual individuals. *Journal of Gay & Lesbian Mental Health, 17*, 278–293. http://dx.doi.org/10.1080/19359705.2012.763081

Worthington, R. L. (2004). Sexual identity, sexual orientation, religious identity, and change: Is it possible to depolarize the debate? *The Counseling Psychologist, 32*, 741–749. http://dx.doi.org/10.1177/0011000004267566

Worthington, R. L., Dillon, F. R., & Becker-Schutte, A. (2005). Development, reliability and validity of the Lesbian, Gay, and Bisexual Knowledge and Attitudes Scale for Heterosexuals (LGB-KASH). *Journal of Counseling Psychology, 52*, 104–118. http://dx.doi.org/10.1037/0022-0167.52.1.104

Worthington, R. L., & Mohr, J. J. (2002). Theorizing heterosexual identity development. *The Counseling Psychologist, 30*, 491–495. http://dx.doi.org/10.1177/00100002030004001

Worthington, R. L., & Navarro, R. L. (2003). Pathways to the future: Analyzing the contents of a content analysis. *The Counseling Psychologist, 31*, 85–92. http://dx.doi.org/10.1177/0011000002239402

Worthington, R. L., & Reynolds, A. L. (2009). Within-group differences in sexual orientation identity. *Journal of Counseling Psychology, 56*, 44–55. http://dx.doi.org/10.1037/a0013498

Worthington, R. L., Savoy, H. B., Dillon, F. R., & Vernaglia, E. R. (2002). Heterosexual identity development: A multidimensional model of individual and social identity. *The Counseling Psychologist, 30*(4), 496–531. http://dx.doi.org/10.1177/00100002030004002

Wright, P. J., & McKinley, C. J. (2010). Mental health resources for LGBT collegians: A content analysis of college counseling center Web sites. *Journal of Homosexuality, 58*, 138–147. http://dx.doi.org/10.1080/00918369.2011.533632

14

BEYOND COMPETENCIES AND GUIDELINES: TRAINING CONSIDERATIONS REGARDING SEXUAL MINORITY AND TRANSGENDER AND GENDER NONCONFORMING PEOPLE

JULIA C. PHILLIPS AND BRIAN R. FITTS

Over the past 40 years, authors have increasingly focused on training mental health practitioners to provide competent psychological and counseling services to sexual minorities and transgender and gender nonconforming (TGNC) people from an affirmative perspective (Miles & Fassinger, 2014). Foundational to this perspective are guidelines and competencies documents produced by major professional organizations, including the World Professional Association for Transgender Health's (WPATH) *Standards of Care (SOC) for the Health of Transsexual, Transgender, and Gender Nonconforming People* (Coleman et al., 2012); the American Psychological Association's (APA) *Guidelines for Psychotherapy With Lesbian, Gay, and Bisexual Clients* (APA, 2012); the American Counseling Association's (ACA) *Competencies for Counseling Lesbian, Gay, Bisexual, Queer, Questioning, Intersex, and Ally Individuals* (Harper et al., 2013); and ACA's *Competencies for Counseling With Transgender Clients* (Burnes et al., 2010). Notably, an APA Task Force

http://dx.doi.org/10.1037/15959-015
Handbook of Sexual Orientation and Gender Diversity in Counseling and Psychotherapy, K. A. DeBord, A. R. Fischer, K. J. Bieschke, and R. M. Perez (Editors)

finalized the *Guidelines for Psychological Practice With Transgender and Gender Nonconforming People* (APA, 2015). These documents are important resources for educators providing training on sexual minority and TGNC issues in counseling.

The purpose of this chapter is to discuss training, with a focus on literature published since the last comprehensive chapter on training in this handbook series (Phillips, 2000). Since that time, scholarship on sexual orientation and gender has blossomed into a broader, more complex and nuanced discussion of intersectional identities in the context of a constricting heteronormative and gender binary, more firmly grounded in empirical knowledge. This complexity is evidenced in the various guidelines and competencies documents (APA, 2012; Burnes et al., 2010; Coleman et al., 2012; Harper et al., 2013), which provide excellent road maps for guiding educators in training graduate students. Still, a reading of these documents should not be mistaken as all that is needed for quality training.

To provide context for the reader, we first introduce ourselves. Next, we review recent indicators of training related to sexual minority and TGNC issues in mental health practitioner programs as documented in the literature, including an examination of what we know about training and its effects on students. We also discuss best practices, including a focus on creative ideas for training. Throughout our chapter, we focus on intersectional identities to highlight that sexual minority and TGNC people have many salient identities. In training, it is especially important to remember that individuals also live with varying ethnicities, races, nationalities, class backgrounds and current economic means, religious and spiritual beliefs or nonbeliefs, abilities or disabilities, and other characteristics. We share information on the coauthors' intersecting social locations for transparency and to model the openness that is critical for students and educators as they engage in training.

BACKGROUND INFORMATION: SOCIAL LOCATIONS OF COAUTHORS

The first author is a White, bisexual, cisgender (i.e., gender corresponds to assigned sex), female, middle to upper class American married to a cisgender man. For 21 years, she was a psychologist in university counseling centers, where she provided training for doctoral students in psychology. Her scholarly interests turned to sexual minority issues (e.g., Phillips & Fischer, 1998) after graduate school, and she moved to academia in 2013. The second author is a 27-year-old doctoral student in a counseling psychology program. He identifies as a White, heterosexual, cisgender man. His life-long education in Catholic schools taught him the principles of social justice, and his access to education raised his awareness of issues of privilege and oppression. His contribution to this chapter continues the work related to sexual minority issues he began with a professor in his master's program.

RECENT INDICATORS OF TRAINING

Early research in the late 1970s through the 1990s raised questions about the quantity and types of training that students in graduate training programs received (for a review, see Phillips, 2000). Studies clearly indicated that graduate training related to sexual minority issues was lacking (e.g., Buhrke, 1989; Phillips & Fischer, 1998). Professional organizations developed the aforementioned guidelines and competencies to improve training and inform practitioners of the skills needed to work with sexual minority and TGNC clients. In this section, we discuss how these documents address training and highlight strengths found within. We explore trainee characteristics that affect counseling competence with sexual minority and TGNC clients. Finally, we examine studies that have updated our knowledge base on training related to sexual minority and TGNC issues since 2000.

GUIDELINES AND COMPETENCIES DOCUMENTS: STRENGTHS FOR EDUCATORS

Although not all professional organizations have developed guidelines or competencies documents specific to sexual minority and TGNC clients, the ones from APA (2012), ACA (Burnes et al., 2010; Harper et al., 2013), and WPATH (Coleman et al., 2012) offer educators road maps for training and gems of wisdom. It is important to note that these documents emphasize viewing sexual minority and TGNC clients in holistic ways such that all of their identities, social locations, and unique issues across the lifespan are considered. The APA Guidelines (2012) explicitly address training, providing educators with a road map to integrate affirmative training. APA Guideline 19 recommends programs integrate LGB issues throughout graduate training, facilitate student exploration of attitudes and biases with honesty and accuracy, and utilize psychologists who have expertise in LGB psychology. While the WPATH SOC do not explicitly address training, they provide a useful framework for competent practice with TGNC clients. Invaluable within the SOC is specific and extensive information about biological and medical issues affecting TGNC individuals across the lifespan. It is likely that cisgender students especially will need this information given that privilege often allows people to remain unaware of the concerns of oppressed people. Still, a majority of psychologists and students report insufficient familiarity to work with TGNC clients (APA Task Force, 2009). Given the differences within the TGNC population (American Psychological Association, 2012; APA Task Force, 2009; Burnes et al., 2010; Coleman et al., 2012), this information may also be useful for TGNC students who may be more familiar with their own experiences and those of similarly identified TGNC individuals, but perhaps less so with those TGNC individuals who are different and/or who make different choices. The inclusion of this information in the curriculum is consistent with recommendations of TGNC students and adds to a positive training environment (APA Task Force, 2009).

The ACA Competencies (Burnes et al., 2010; Harper et al., 2013) implicitly address training in their structural alignment with the eight CACREP education standards for accredited programs. This alignment is designed to facilitate trainee self-exploration and awareness and lead to appropriate intervention strategies. CACREP educators will find this structure particularly useful as they can easily identify where in their course syllabi they should integrate particular competencies related to sexual minority and TGNC issues. Finally, Harper et al. (2013) specifically address competencies of heterosexual counselors-in-training in the allies section of the document, a unique gem of wisdom for all types of educators given that the majority of trainees are heterosexual. Taken together, all of these documents provide invaluable guidance for educators in developing inclusive curricular experiences, and they are comprehensive resources for students to utilize in the course of graduate training in mental health programs.

INVESTIGATIONS INTO THE QUALITY AND QUANTITY OF TRAINING SINCE 2000

Most studies suggest that graduate training continues to be inconsistent at best and that, overall, training programs do not fully integrate sexual minority or TGNC issues into curriculum or supervision (Anhalt, Morris, Scotti, & Cohen, 2003; Burkard, Knox, Hess, & Schultz, 2009; Luke, Goodrich, & Scarborough, 2011; O'Hara, Dispenza, Brack, & Blood, 2013; Rock, Carlson, & McGeorge, 2010). Within psychology, a study of 200 graduate students in 10 clinical psychology doctoral programs with strong faculty interests in behavioral or cognitive–behavioral perspectives suggested that training in these programs lacked even cursory coverage of sexual minority issues in coursework, and few sexual minorities were seen as clients in practica (Anhalt et al., 2003). In a qualitative study, sexual minority doctoral students in psychology indicated mixed experiences with respect to the integration of sexual minority issues in didactic portions of practicum (Burkard et al., 2009). Similarly, participants reported both affirmative and negative experiences during supervision related to their sexual orientation or that of a client, correspondingly resulting in either positive or negative supervisory and client outcomes. Further, a study of 190 couple and family therapy students (Rock et al., 2010) indicated that over 60% reported that affirmative therapy practices and identity development models for sexual minorities were not covered in their classes.

Although the aforementioned studies focused on sexual minority issues, few studies have focused on TGNC issues in training programs (APA Task Force, 2009; Luke et al., 2011; O'Hara et al., 2013). Counselor trainees in one program described a lack of training for TGNC issues in coursework and practical training and confusion about proper terminology (O'Hara et al., 2013). They used both informal sources (e.g., media, personally knowing TGNC individuals) and formal sources (e.g., scholarly texts, didactic training) to gain knowledge. The American Psychological Association Task Force on Gender Identity and Gender Variance (2009) also concluded that few psychologists or students have advanced competencies to work with TGNC clients. Finally, Luke et al. (2011) reported that although 92% of school counselor educators integrated sexual minority and TGNC issues in part of the curriculum, less attention was paid to transgender, bisexual, and intersex individuals, and those who were questioning their gender and sexual identities.

Taken together, these results show a troubling trend of a lack of complexity in training on sexual minority and TGNC issues in mental health programs. Sexual orientation may be continuing to be defined in dualistic ways, excluding bisexuality and queer identities. TGNC individuals are virtually being ignored. Little to no research to date has explored the inclusion of sexual minority or TGNC issues in mental health training programs abroad. Furthermore, it is unclear whether or not programs in the United States are addressing intersectionality since diverse identities beyond gender and sexual orientation (e.g., racial and ethnic identities, nationality, disability, age) have not been evaluated by researchers who are cataloging the state of training. We suggest a comprehensive study in each mental health field on the quantity and quality of training in sexual minority and TGNC issues, with explicit attention to intersectional identities. Such studies would give educators better information with which to evaluate their training programs. Additionally, such studies raise awareness that the mere inclusion of information on gay men and lesbian women while ignoring the complexity and diversity of sexual minority and TGNC individuals is insufficient to meeting the needs of these individuals, both in the United States and internationally.

TRAINEE CHARACTERISTICS

Prior to discussing the body of research on training outcomes, we briefly highlight studies that alert us to trainee characteristics that are associated with competence, self-reported competence, or self-efficacy to counsel sexual minority and TGNC clients. It should be noted that the majority of studies we discuss use measures that assess trainees' self-reported counseling competence rather than actual competence with sexual minority and TGNC clients. For example, Bidell's (2005) Sexual Orientation Counselor Competency Scale (SOCCS), with its three subscales pertaining to Knowledge, Skills, and Attitudes, is often used in research to assess counseling competence with LGB clients (e.g., Bidell, 2014; Graham, Carney, & Kluck, 2012; O'Shaughnessy & Spokane, 2013; Rock et al., 2010).

Regarding personal characteristics, we believe that exploration and cultivation of personal characteristics may be helpful in developing trainees' competence in their work with counseling sexual minority clients. For example, students with higher scores on the Big Five personality variable of Openness to Experience (being intellectually curious and interested in new experiences) as measured by the NEO Personality Inventory—Revised (NEO-PI-R; Costa & McRae, 1992) had higher levels of self-reported counseling competency and self-efficacy for counseling sexual minorities in a sample of trainees who were predominately from doctoral programs in psychology, White, and female (O'Shaughnessy & Spokane, 2013). Bidell (2014) reported that lower levels of religious fundamentalism (not specific to any particular religious faith) uniquely predicted self-reported counseling competency with sexual minorities while holding constant the effects of other variables in a sample of predominately master's level counseling students, the majority of whom were heterosexual, female, and White, but with a sizable representation of ethnic minority participants (37%). We suggest that, taken together, these findings provide preliminary support for the idea that exploration and cultivation of personal characteristics such as openness to experience may be helpful in developing trainees' competence, or at least self-perceived competence, and self-efficacy for counseling sexual minorities.

In other research, being a sexual minority was associated with increased self-efficacy for counseling sexual minorities amongst a mixed group of doctoral and master's level practitioners and students, the majority of whom were heterosexual and female (Dillon, Worthington, Soth-McNett, & Schwartz, 2008). Sources of self-efficacy experienced while living daily life as a sexual minority (e.g., exposure to other sexual minorities, exposure to knowledge about sexual minority concerns, role modeling of how to interact respectfully with sexual minorities, practice with doing so, and coping for managing any anxiety about the learning process) are likely responsible for this relationship (Dillon et al., 2008). The same reasoning may apply to other studies showing the importance of interpersonal contact with sexual minority and TGNC individuals. For example, contact with sexual minority individuals was positively related to competence in an analogue study requiring participants to write case conceptualizations for lesbian and gay male clients (O'Shaughnessy & Spokane, 2013) and to self-reported counseling competence with sexual minorities (Bidell, 2014). Exposure to TGNC individuals was positively related to self-reported competence with TGNC individuals (O'Hara et al., 2013). These findings suggest that training programs may be able to increase trainee competence by providing experiences that increase contact with sexual minority and TGNC individuals. Finally, Dillon et al. (2008) also reported that gender self-definition (i.e., "how strongly one's self-defined femininity or masculinity reflects one's overall identity" [p. 355]) and sexual identity commitment (i.e., how certain one is about various aspects of one's sexual identity) predicted LGB counseling self-efficacy. These findings suggest that it is important that educators provide opportunities for all trainees to explore their own sexual and gender identities in the ways that sexual minority and TGNC students do in daily life as a result of their minority status.

OUTCOMES OF TRAINING

This section addresses outcomes of training in sexual minority and TGNC issues in various mental health fields. Specifically, trainees' levels of competence in various fields are addressed, as is the question of whether self-perceived competence equates to actual competence. In addition, the outcomes of training with respect to its effects on skills, knowledge, and attitudes are discussed.

Levels of Competence

Research on students' self-reported and actual competence for working with sexual minority and TGNC clients is varied in a number of ways and leads to interesting questions about the relationship between actual competence and self-perceptions of competence. Although we can conclude that most students perceive themselves to be at least somewhat competent to work with sexual minority clients (e.g., Anhalt et al., 2003; Graham et al., 2012; O'Shaughnessy & Spokane, 2013), we can only tentatively suggest that they feel incompetent with TGNC clients (O'Hara et al., 2013). There is some evidence that levels of confidence vary by field: Students in clinical psychology report high levels of comfort providing therapy to sexual minorities (Anhalt et al., 2003); students in counseling and counseling psychology view themselves as highly competent with respect to attitudes and at least moderately competent with respect to knowledge and skills with sexual minority clients (Graham et al., 2012; O'Shaughnessy & Spokane, 2013); and couple and family therapy students perceive themselves to be somewhat competent to work with sexual minority clients (Rock et al., 2010). It is unknown whether trainees can work with intersectionality or are confident in their ability to do so because no studies have examined hypotheses about intersectionality. Thus, questions remain regarding trainees' perceptions of their competence when faced with the complexity of intersecting identities for sexual minority and TGNC clients. For example, how competent do trainees feel when faced with an older Latina lesbian female with a physical disability, a biracial genderqueer student athlete, or an immigrant who is also a Christian gay male in the U.S. Armed Forces? It is encouraging that although quantitative analyses indicated that counselor trainees felt incompetent with TGNC clients, qualitative analysis of participants' discussion in focus groups indicated that they were empathetic, took the perspective of transgender individuals, and displayed both an interest and desire to learn more (O'Hara et al., 2013).

Questions about how much actual competence overlaps with self-reported competence remain. The results of O'Shaughnessy and Spokane's (2013) analog study of 212 therapists-in-training indicated that the average score on a clinical case conceptualization task for vignettes of gay male and lesbian clients was less than 4 out of a possible 25. Participants were scored on their responses to five questions, receiving one point each time they mentioned an LGB affirmative factor and more points if the factors were meaningfully integrated in the conceptualization. Even in exemplars for which participants received high scores, some participants still used outmoded language that the APA Guidelines and ACA Competencies recommend against. In this study, the SOCCS Knowledge subscale was the only measure that predicted actual case conceptualization ability, bringing into question the use of self-report measures as indicators of actual counseling competence. That is, the lack of relationships between case conceptualization ability and other subscales of the SOCCS may suggest that this measure is an inadequate indicator of actual competence. Furthermore, it is puzzling why students in the Anhalt et al. (2003) study were so confident of their counseling competence with sexual minority clients when they had virtually no formal training with this population. Analog research has shown clinical bias in judgments by psychotherapists toward bisexual clients related to stereotype-relevant clinical issues (i.e., those involving the client as confused and conflicted; Mohr, Weiner, Chopp, & Wong, 2009) and in male therapists' ratings of LGB clients' potential to harm others (Bowers & Bieschke,

2005). It is important to note that for training, the effect in the Mohr et al. study (2009) was significant even when therapists believed that they were not susceptible to bias. Given these findings, it seems important to teach trainees how to recognize susceptibility to clinical bias, particularly when stereotypes are activated with clients (Mohr et al., 2009). They should learn about this phenomenon in early coursework and later self-reflect on the possibility of clinical bias with clients during clinical supervision. We suggest that educators should be attuned to the likely overestimation of self-reported trainee competence with sexual minority and TGNC clients. Practically speaking, supervisors should use session recordings for evaluation and assessment, and researchers should include some measure of actual competence to accurately and consistently assess trainee competence.

Knowledge, Skills, and Attitudes

Knowledge and Skills

Studies suggest that training in sexual minority and TGNC issues has a positive impact on trainees in a number of ways, including building relevant knowledge and skills. Overall, longevity in graduate programs is associated with increases in the Knowledge and the Skills subscales of the SOCCS (Grove, 2009; O'Shaughnessy & Spokane, 2013; Rock et al., 2010). Even short trainings appear to be effective in increasing trainee knowledge. For example, master's level counseling trainees in a 2.5-hour experimental seminar on sexual minority issues significantly increased their knowledge base as compared with trainees in both a placebo control group who did not receive training and those in a seminar focused on attitude exploration only (Israel & Hackett, 2004). Furthermore, more course content with affirmative perspectives toward sexual minorities was associated with higher self-reported student-counseling competence with sexual minority clients (Rock et al., 2010) among couples and family therapy students. Finally, O'Shaughnessy and Spokane (2013) reported that a positive correlation between trainee case conceptualization skill and number of LGBT clients seen by trainees provided evidence that experiences in clinical training had a positive effect on trainee counseling competencies.

Attitudes

Another focus of research on training in sexual minority and TGNC issues in mental health is on the effects of such training on providers' attitudes. It appears that attitudes are complex and that training programs should take this complexity into consideration. For example, a program evaluation of a 1-day training to educate social workers in an urban area of Great Britain on lesbian and gay issues in foster care and adoption, identified mixed results (Dugmore & Cocker, 2008). These researchers concluded that longer term attitude change required more extensive intervention and contextual supports from participants' home agencies. They suggested that while participants exhibited positive attitude change in the short term, the effect decreased over time when they returned to home agencies that continued to exhibit institutional heterosexism.

Results from a more rigorous study of short-term training (Israel & Hackett, 2004) suggested that participants in the attitude exploration conditions showed a small but significant decrease in positive attitudes toward sexual minority individuals at posttest. These results are similar to results reported by Grove (2009). In both studies, participants reported very positive attitudes at pretest, and thus it may be that the decrease in attitudes is a result of increased self-awareness or honesty in responding at posttest. It may also be that the intensity of this type of training is not well suited to a one-time workshop but instead needs a longer time frame for positive attitude change to occur. Or it may be that small decreases in positive attitudes accurately reflect trainees' increased honesty about or awareness of their own heterosexism. These investigations suggest that continued education and growth is necessary for positive, sustained attitude change beyond one-time workshops or classroom presentations. Thus, for such presentations, a final debriefing is recommended and should be supplemented with written materials on ways for participants to continue to grow. Furthermore, an emphasis on the importance of lifelong learning and self-reflectiveness as a competence for one's professional career well beyond graduate training is critical, especially when considering multiple identities in which increased depth and complexity of thought and understanding are necessary.

Investigations of longer term counselor training suggest that positive attitude change is possible. Participants in a qualitative study of heterosexual counselors-in-training, who volunteered to participate in a two-semester research team that examined their own sexual identity development and attitudes toward sexual minorities, became more aware of societal heterosexism and the experiences of sexual minorities and how their backgrounds shaped their understanding of their own sexual identity development and biases. Participants also became more affirming of sexual minority individuals and more committed to engaging in advocacy as heterosexual allies (Dillon et al., 2004). The importance of a safe environment to engage in self-reflection was noted in this training experience. This study did not describe themes related to intersectionality or gender identity issues despite its longer term nature. Still, evidence of students' attitude change over time was notable as students increased their self-understanding and awareness of societal heterosexism.

In conclusion, studies in a variety of mental health fields, including psychology (Anhalt et al., 2003; Burkard et al., 2009), counselor education

(Graham et al., 2012; Luke et al., 2011), and couple and family therapy (Rock et al., 2010), suggest that the quantity and quality of training in working with sexual minorities and TGNC individuals is inconsistent, at best. There is some evidence of integration in training of issues related to sexual minority individuals (e.g., Burkard et al., 2009; Luke et al., 2011), but without a comprehensive, updated survey of practices, it is difficult to draw firm conclusions. In addition, we know very little about the quality of training being provided to students relative to TGNC issues (APA Task Force, 2009; Rock et al., 2010) and virtually nothing about the training being provided regarding the complexity of multiple identities that sexual minority and TGNC individuals hold. However, we do have evidence that affirmative training environments are related to students' self-perceived competence to work with sexual minorities and that trainee self-exploration, personal interaction with sexual minority and TGNC individuals, and a training environment that is affirmative positively impact students' self-perceived competence. Specifically, we can tentatively conclude that affirmative practices are associated with higher levels of self-perceived counseling competencies (Grove, 2009; Israel & Hackett, 2004; Rock et al., 2010) with sexual minority individuals and that contact with sexual minority and TGNC people is associated with higher levels of self-perceived counseling competency and self-efficacy, and perhaps, actual skills (e.g., Bidell, 2014; O'Hara et al., 2013; O'Shaughnessy & Spokane, 2013). In addition, studies suggest that training affects attitudes and that self-reflectiveness is necessary over longer periods of time in what is often a complex and challenging area for many trainees (Dillon et al., 2004; Dugmore & Cocker, 2008; Grove, 2009; Israel & Hackett, 2004). It is clear from a review of updated research that there is still much to learn about training in various mental health fields, specific outcomes of training, the relationship between self-perceived competency and actual competency, training related to intersectionality, and training related to TGNC individuals.

ADDITIONAL SCHOLARSHIP INFORMING BEST PRACTICES IN TRAINING

Since Phillips (2000), several authors have written articles or chapters with common themes in their suggestions for integrating issues related to sexual minorities and, in some cases, TGNC people in graduate training (e.g., Biaggio, Orchard, Larson, Petrino, & Mihara, 2003; Kashubeck-West, Szymanski, & Meyer, 2008; Long & Serovich, 2003; Miles & Fassinger, 2014). Use of the guidelines, competencies, and standards of care documents is highly recommended as a starting point for increasing knowledge for working with sexual minorities and TGNC clients. All of these documents offer a wealth of resources to educators and their students for increasing knowledge. Given the state of training, we strongly recommend that programs carefully attend to these documents and integrate information from them in the appropriate courses and training experiences. Still, the APA Guidelines and SOC might overwhelm both educators and students with their wealth of information and resources, and the ACA Competencies might leave educators wondering where to go for resources—as the ACA made an intentional choice not to cite references in the text of the Competencies. Thus, our next aim is to highlight recommended curricular content for training in sexual minority and TGNC issues, methods for teaching this content, and materials to focus on and use. New and exemplary supervision models that address intersectionality in practical training are also discussed. Finally, programmatic policy concerns related to recent developments arising from students who have objected to working with sexual minority clients are addressed.

CURRICULUM/MATERIALS

Curriculum: Self-Reflectiveness and Systemic Thinking

A Delphi study of experts in sexual minority issues (Godfrey, Haddock, Fisher, & Lund, 2006) identified two themes as critical for the education of therapists who work with sexual minority clients: (a) a focus on self-reflectiveness with respect to one's own identity and societal heterosexism and (b) a focus on systemic influences on people's lives. Recognizing that self-reflectiveness may not result in immediate positive attitude change in shorter trainings (e.g., Grove, 2009), these Delphi study results are consistent with qualitative research on counselor trainees' perceptions of the benefits of self-reflection when engaged in over the period of a semester (e.g., Dillon et al., 2004). In addition, self-reflective writing is often recommended to develop competence with sexual minority and TGNC people (e.g., Dillon et al., 2004; Godfrey et al., 2006).

Consistent with the Delphi study results (Godfrey et al., 2006), helping students first understand the epistemological differences in essentialist (see Chapter 2, this volume) versus social constructionist perspectives (see Chapter 1, this volume) on sexual orientation and gender identity is important (Miles & Fassinger, 2014). At the same time, students must develop awareness of societal heterosexism and the existence of the gender binary as oppressive ideologies that perpetuate problems for sexual minorities and TGNC clients (Miles & Fassinger, 2014). Further, the need for mental health practitioners to take into account the minority stress model (Meyer, 2003) is noted throughout both the APA Guidelines and the ACA Competencies.

This model is an example of systemic thinking and posits that poor mental health outcomes result from the stress associated with living as a minority in an oppressive environment rather than deficits associated with being a member of a minority (Meyer, 2003; see also Chapter 3, this volume).

To further stimulate self-reflection and systemic thinking, we recommend that educators use Smith, Shin, and Officer's (2012) article for class discussion in which they describe a case of a trainee who communicates in ways that she inaccurately believes to be affirmative. In this case, a cisgender bisexual female client meets with a cisgender heterosexual female counselor trainee who uses language such as "LGBT affirmative." Smith et al. (2012) illustrated how this language inadvertently reinforces a heteronormative framework. Further, they highlight how the trainee both ignores the realities associated with the transgender identity of the client's partner by lumping together the T with the LGB and reinforces the socially constructed gender binary that oppresses persons who are not cisgender. With this article, readers are challenged to reflect on biases, exposed to the use of language acknowledging genderqueer realities (e.g., use of nongendered pronouns *ze*, *zir/zem*, *zirs/zes*, and *zirself*), and introduced to antiheteronormative approaches to counseling as an alternative to LGBT-affirmative approaches (Smith et al., 2012).

Furthermore, consistent with the APA Guidelines and ACA Competencies, the diverse and intersecting identities that sexual minority and TGNC clients hold (e.g., age, religion, socioeconomic class, ethnicity/race, nationality and disability; see Chapter 4, this volume) are critical to teach with emphases on self-reflection and systemic thinking. Experts suggest having guest panels of sexual minority and TGNC individuals speak to classes, taking special care to invite people representing diverse intersectional identities (e.g., Godfrey et al., 2006; Israel & Hackett, 2004; Miles & Fassinger, 2014; O'Hara et al., 2013). Doing so is important because it increases interpersonal contact with sexual minority and TGNC individuals and challenges stereotypes that sexual minority and TGNC individuals only belong to dominant groups (i.e., young, White, physically able, American). Trainees must also understand developmental issues associated with sexual minority and TGNC people, including cohort effects that will make lifespan development different for today's youth as they age compared with adults who were young in the mid-20th century (e.g., Dentato, Orwat, Spira, & Walker, 2014; Yerke & Mitchell, 2011).

The effects of stigma and marginalization on psychological health and the possibility for strength and resilience to buffer stigma are additionally important to teach (Meyer, 2003). In focusing on multiple identities for sexual minority and/or TGNC clients of color in the United States, a discussion of both the challenge of managing multiple stigmatized identities and of the value of transgenerational transmission of resilience strategies related to racism or ethnocentrism might help students understand the complexities of experience.

Furthermore, the experiences of transgender people who choose to transition from one gender to another can serve as a powerful illustration of the effects of stigma and the intersections of identity. For example, class issues related to the cost of transitioning and insurance coverage are highly relevant, as are experiences of transitioning from male to female. These issues may result in loss of power while experiences of transitioning from female to male result in gain of power, especially in the workplace (e.g., Budge, Tebbe, & Howard, 2010).

Godfrey et al.'s (2006) Delphi study results are consistent with suggestions for programs to attend to macrolevel and institutional factors related to sexual minority and TGNC individuals (e.g., Biaggio et al., 2003; Kashubeck-West et al., 2008; Long & Serovich, 2003). Kashubeck-West et al. (2008) discussed ideas for addressing internalized heterosexism with clients, including particularly useful mezzo- and macrolevel suggestions that focus on clients and counselors addressing systemic heterosexism to empower sexual minority clients. Faculty can model advocacy in those institutions not yet having policies inclusive of sexual orientation and gender identity/gender expression. Furthermore, these authors suggested that faculty encourage students to evaluate their own programs' training environments and make recommendations. This activity would be an excellent project in a consultation course, particularly with an emphasis on intersectional identities for sexual minority and TGNC individuals.

Journals

Finally, we highlight essential curricular materials by looking at prominent journals. Although journals specific to sexual minority and TGNC are too numerous to list compared with 15 years ago, notable new additions are the Association for Lesbian, Gay, Bisexual and Transgender Issues in Counseling's *Journal of LGBT Issues in Counseling* and APA Division 44's *Psychology of Sexual Orientation and Gender Diversity*. In addition, *The Counseling Psychologist* published a special issue on sexual minority people of color (Moradi, DeBlaere, & Huang, 2010) that is especially useful for systemic understandings of intersectional identities, and the *Journal of Counseling Psychology* published a special issue on sexual minority issues (Mallinckrodt, 2009) that is an invaluable resource for doing research with sexual minority participants, expanding notions of sexual minority concerns to intersex individuals, and understanding the effects of stigma.

Supervision Literature

The theoretical literature on supervision related to sexual minority and TGNC issues offers educators much material to use, especially with helping trainees develop supervision competencies of their own (Bieschke, Blasko, & Woodhouse, 2014; Halpert, Reinhardt, & Toohey, 2007; Hernández & Rankin, 2008; Singh & Chun, 2010). Bieschke et al. (2014) recommended using a combination of Halpert et al.'s (2007) integrative affirmative supervision model, a model specific to sexual orientation, and Fassinger and Arseneau's (2007) model that focuses more broadly on individuals' gender identities, sexual orientations, and cultural identities. This emphasis moves the focus of affirmative supervision beyond simply considering sexual orientation.

Singh and Chun (2010) further developed the queer people of color resilience-based model of supervision to address issues of intersectionality for supervisors who identify as both ethnic minority and sexual minority and/or TGNC individuals. Their model identifies salient issues and questions that can help queer supervisors of color to focus on their resilience and development in the supervisory relationship. The model asks supervisors to focus on three areas: awareness of privilege and oppression, affirmation of diversity, and supervisor empowerment. With thought-provoking personal disclosure and case examples, the authors provide educators focused on developing supervisory competencies a must read article. Although it was developed for queer people of color, the content of the questions can be relevant to trainees of other, multiple identities.

Further contributing to the supervision literature, Hernández and Rankin (2008) described a case example of group supervision in marriage and family therapy leading to the development of trainee and supervisor competencies with sexual minorities that takes into account multiple social locations and identities for the supervisory triad. Set up in a relationally safe space for persons with oppressed identities to find their voices and persons with privileged identities to understand the impact of their privilege on their relationships with others, they present an international couple from different cultures living in the United States in a same sex relationship. They focus on the interactions of the women's cultures, immigration histories, and socioeconomic status as they affect the clinical situation, and on how their own identities with respect to social class, sexual orientation, immigration status, ethnicity, and culture interact with how they view the case. This case provides a rich example of optimal interactions in the supervisory triad.

PROGRAMMATIC POLICY AND STUDENT CONFLICTS

Conflicts that trainees experience between their own deeply held religious beliefs and the educational requirement to gain competency in working with sexual minority individuals have become a focus of professional discourse in mental health training as a result of recent lawsuits by master's level counseling students in two states who asserted a right on the basis of their religious beliefs to avoid working with sexual minority clients (for reviews, see Behnke, 2012; Herlihy, Hermann, & Greden, 2014). The courts noted that training programs can use professional organizations' ethical codes and competency documents in identifying expectations for students. Although one case was settled out of court and the court ruled in favor of the other educational program, the introduction of "conscience clause" legislation followed these lawsuits in Michigan and Arizona, with passage in Arizona in 2011. These legislative initiatives vary slightly, but in essence, propose to make it illegal for educational institutions to discipline students for refusing to provide services to clients on the basis of the religious beliefs of counselors-in-training.

The American Psychological Association Board of Educational Affairs (APA/BEA) Working Group on Restrictions Affecting Diversity Training in Graduate Education (2013a) later produced a statement to help training programs manage students who have deeply held religious beliefs that conflict with their ability to competently provide services. This statement is thoughtful, weighing the experiences of students who are truly struggling with their own beliefs with the necessity to train all psychologists to competently work with all people. The implication is that outright referral of all sexual minority and TGNC people is not an option for students, particularly because the responsibility for clients and any reassignment of their cases belongs with the supervisor and not with the student (Bieschke, 2014). Because referral may be seen as an ethical action by the courts, the term *reassignment* is encouraged to highlight that students are not engaging in independent practice but in training to gain competence. Although client reassignment may be the most ethical action when a trainee is not ready to provide competent services and before a program works with that trainee to develop competence to work with such clients, students cannot opt out of the process of gaining competence to work with clients on the basis of values conflict. Although the statement is clear that students may hold personal beliefs of their own choosing, they must be able to provide services to the many communities they will encounter when serving the public. The APA/BEA statement notes the importance of faculty and supervisors using a developmental perspective with respect for students at the same time as modeling their own on-going commitment to multicultural competence and growth. The APA/BEA statement is also clear that protection of the public is paramount for the profession of psychology.

The Working Group also developed a flowchart of suggested actions for programs to use (APA/BEA, 2013b). To summarize, programs should have a thoughtful policy that addresses situations in which students might try to "opt out" of providing services to a group of people. This policy should be developed in conjunction with legal counsel and be consistent with other policies in the program and at the institution. In addition, the policy should be well communicated to the public and prospective students in multiple ways to ensure informed consent on admission. Furthermore, the policy should be reinforced throughout students' training (e.g., during orientation, in ethics class, during practicum). Finally, the importance of maintaining a respectful, developmental stance toward students for whom the policy comes into play is emphasized. If with time and remediation, a trainee is not able or willing to demonstrate competence, programs should document steps taken to facilitate the trainee's attainment of competence, lack of progress made, consultation with institutional leaders and legal counsel, and fair application of the policy, especially when dismissal is the end result.

CONCLUSIONS AND RECOMMENDATIONS

In conclusion, results of research suggest that graduate training in sexual minority and TGNC issues remains inconsistent at best despite a strong articulation of competencies needed to work with TGNC clients in the APA Guidelines, ACA Competencies documents, and WPATH SOC. The scholarship has advanced in that we have more research on best practices and validated measures to assist us. With these measures, it appears that training does increase trainees' self-perceived levels of competence and self-efficacy in working with sexual minorities. However, the actual level of competency that trainees exhibit is less clear given methodological weaknesses of the research. Researchers and educators should more frequently use assessments of actual and observed competence rather than self-reported competence or self-efficacy. We especially need more information on the state of training with respect to TGNC individuals and the intersectional identities that all sexual minority and TGNC people hold. Similarly, graduate training programs across the mental health specializations must make efforts to provide instruction on intersectional diversity within sexual minority and TGNC communities.

It is recognized that we cannot expect to teach everything in graduate school. Thus, an emphasis on developing attitudes of self-reflectiveness and lifelong learning in these areas is recommended. Finally, the recent developments related to training issues for students struggling with deeply held religious beliefs and developing competence with sexual minority and TGNC clients will need to be monitored and examined in research. Specifically, questions exist regarding how often programs in various mental health fields encounter these concerns and how successful they are in implementing the best practices as suggested by the APA/BEA Working Group (2013a, 2013b).

Additionally, the political environment related to conscience clause legislation will need to be monitored with political advocacy by mental health practitioners to inform state legislators of best practices for mental health training. In sum, there remains much to learn and much to teach.

REFERENCES

American Psychological Association. (2012). Guidelines for psychological practice with lesbian, gay, and bisexual clients. *American Psychologist, 67,* 10–42. http://dx.doi.org/10.1037/a0024659

American Psychological Association. (2015). Guidelines for psychological practice with transgender and gender nonconforming people. *American Psychologist, 70,* 832–864. http://dx.doi.org/10.1037/a0039906

American Psychological Association Board of Educational Affairs Working Group on Restrictions Affecting Diversity Training in Graduate Education. (2013a). *Preparing professional psychologists to serve a diverse public.* Retrieved from http://www.apa.org/pi/lgbt/resources/policy/diversity-preparation.aspx

American Psychological Association Board of Educational Affairs Working Group on Restrictions Affecting Diversity Training in Graduate Education. (2013b). *Preparing professional psychologists to serve a diverse public: Addressing conflicts between professional competence and trainee beliefs.* Retrieved from http://www.apa.org/pi/lgbt/resources/policy/diversity-preparation.pdf

American Psychological Association Task Force on Gender Identity and Gender Variance. (2009). *Report of the Task Force on Gender Identity and Gender Variance.* Washington, DC: American Psychological Association.

Anhalt, K., Morris, T. L., Scotti, J. R., & Cohen, S. H. (2003). Student perspectives on training in gay, lesbian, and bisexual issues: A survey of behavioral clinical psychology programs. *Cognitive and Behavioral Practice, 10,* 255–263. http://dx.doi.org/10.1016/S1077-7229(03)80038-X

Behnke, S. H. (2012). Constitutional claims in the context of mental health training: Religion, sexual orientations, and tensions between the first amendment and professional ethics. *Training and Education in Professional Psychology, 6,* 189–195. http://dx.doi.org/10.1037/a0030809

Biaggio, M., Orchard, S., Larson, J., Petrino, K., & Mihara, R. (2003). Guidelines for gay/lesbian/bisexual-affirmative educational practices in graduate psychology programs. *Professional Psychology: Research and Practice, 34,* 548–554. http://dx.doi.org/10.1037/0735-7028.34.5.548

Bidell, M. P. (2005). The Sexual Orientation Counselor Competency Scale: Assessing attitudes, skills, and knowledge of counselors working with lesbian, gay, and bisexual clients. *Counselor Education and Supervision, 44,* 267–279. http://dx.doi.org/10.1002/j.1556-6978.2005.tb01755.x

Bidell, M. P. (2014). Personal and professional discord: Examining religious conservatism and lesbian-, gay-, and bisexual-affirmative counselor competence. *Journal of Counseling & Development*, 92, 170–179. http://dx.doi.org/10.1002/j.1556-6676.2014.00145.x

Bieschke, K. J. (2014). Training psychologists to work with diverse clients. *Psychology of Sexual Orientation and Gender Diversity*, 1, 102–105. http://dx.doi.org/10.1037/sgd0000037

Bieschke, K. J., Blasko, K. A., & Woodhouse, S. S. (2014). A comprehensive approach to competently addressing sexual minority issues in clinical supervision. In C. A. Falender, E. P. Shafranske, & C. J. Falicov (Eds.), *Multiculturalism and diversity in clinical supervision: A competency-based approach* (pp. 209–230). Washington, DC: American Psychological Association. http://dx.doi.org/10.1037/14370-009

Bowers, A. M. V., & Bieschke, K. J. (2005). Psychologists' clinical evaluations and attitudes: An examination of the influence of gender and sexual orientation. *Professional Psychology: Research and Practice*, 36, 97–103. http://dx.doi.org/10.1037/0735-7028.36.1.97

Budge, S. L., Tebbe, E. N., & Howard, K. A. S. (2010). The work experiences of transgender individuals: Negotiating the transition and career decision-making process. *Journal of Counseling Psychology*, 59, 60–70.

Buhrke, R. A. (1989). Female student perspectives on training in lesbian and gay issues. *The Counseling Psychologist*, 17, 629–636. http://dx.doi.org/10.1177/0011000089174006

Burkard, A. W., Knox, S., Hess, S. A., & Schultz, J. (2009). Lesbian, gay, and bisexual supervisees' experiences of LGB-affirmative and nonaffirmative supervision. *Journal of Counseling Psychology*, 56, 176–188. http://dx.doi.org/10.1037/0022-0167.56.1.176

Burnes, T. R., Singh, A. A., Harper, A. J., Harper, B., Maxon-Kann, W., Pickering, D. L., . . . Hosea, J. (2010). American Counseling Association: Competencies for counseling with transgender clients. *Journal of LGBT Issues in Counseling*, 4, 135–159.

Coleman, E., Bockting, W., Botzer, M., Cohen-Kettenis, P., DuCuypere, G., Feldman, J., . . . & Zucker, K. (2012). Standards of care for the health of transsexual, transgender, and gender-nonconforming people. *International Journal of Transgenderism*, 13, 165–232. doi:10.1080/155327359.2011.700873

Costa, P. T., & McCrae, R. R. (1992). *Revised NEO Personality Inventory (NEO-PI-R) and NEO Five-Factor Inventory (NEO-FFI) professional manual*. Odessa, FL: Psychological Assessment Resources.

Dentato, M. P., Orwat, J., Spira, M., & Walker, B. (2014). Examining cohort differences and resilience among the aging LGBT community: Implications for education and practice among an expansively diverse population. *Journal of Human Behavior in the Social Environment*, 24, 316–328. http://dx.doi.org/10.1080/10911359.2013.831009

Dillon, F. R., Worthington, R. L., Savoy, H. B., Rooney, S. C., Becker-Schutte, A., & Guerra, R. M. (2004). On becoming allies: A qualitative study of lesbian-, gay-, and bisexual-affirmative counselor training. *Counselor Education and Supervision, 43*, 162–178. http://dx.doi.org/10.1002/j.1556-6978.2004.tb01840.x

Dillon, F. R., Worthington, R. L., Soth-McNett, A. M., & Schwartz, S. J. (2008). Gender and sexual identity-based predictors of lesbian, gay, and bisexual affirmative counseling self-efficacy. *Professional Psychology: Research and Practice, 39*, 353–360. http://dx.doi.org/10.1037/0735-7028.39.3.353

Dugmore, P., & Cocker, C. (2008). Legal, social, and attitudinal changes: An exploration of lesbian and gay issues in a training programme for social workers in fostering and adoption. *Social Work Education, 27*, 159–168. http://dx.doi.org/10.1080/02615470701709600

Fassinger, R. E., & Arseneau, J. R. (2007). "I'd rather get wet than stand under that umbrella": Differentiating the experiences and identities of lesbian, gay, bisexual, and transgender people. In K. J. Bieschke, R. M. Perez, & K. A. DeBord (Eds.), *Handbook of counseling and psychotherapy with lesbian, gay, bisexual, and transgender clients* (2nd ed., pp. 19–49). Washington, DC: American Psychological Association. http://dx.doi.org/10.1037/11482-001

Godfrey, K., Haddock, S. A., Fisher, A., & Lund, L. (2006). Essential components of curricula for preparing therapists to work effectively with lesbian, gay, and bisexual clients: A Delphi study. *Journal of Marital and Family Therapy, 32*, 491–504. http://dx.doi.org/10.1111/j.1752-0606.2006.tb01623.x

Graham, S. R., Carney, J. S., & Kluck, A. S. (2012). Perceived competency in working with LGB clients: Where are we now? *Counselor Education and Supervision, 51*, 2–16. http://dx.doi.org/10.1002/j.1556-6978.2012.00001.x

Grove, J. (2009). How competent are trainee and newly qualified counsellors to work with lesbian, gay, and bisexual clients and what do they perceive as their most effective learning experiences? *Counselling & Psychotherapy Research, 9*, 78–85. http://dx.doi.org/10.1080/14733140802490622

Halpert, S. C., Reinhardt, B., & Toohey, M. J. (2007). Affirmative clinical supervision. In K. J. Bieschke, R. M. Perez, & K. A. DeBord (Eds.), *Handbook of counseling and psychotherapy with lesbian, gay, bisexual, and transgender clients* (2nd ed., pp. 341–358). Washington, DC: American Psychological Association. http://dx.doi.org/10.1037/11482-014

Harper, A., Finnerty, P., Martinez, M., Brace, A., Crethar, H. C., Loos, B., . . . Hammer, T. R. (2013). Association for Lesbian, Gay, Bisexual, and Transgender Counseling competencies for counseling with lesbian, gay, bisexual, queer, questioning, intersex, and ally individuals. *Journal of LGBT Issues in Counseling, 7*, 2–43.

Herlihy, B. J., Hermann, M. A., & Greden, L. R. (2014). Legal and ethical implications of using religious beliefs as the basis for refusing to counsel certain clients. *Journal of Counseling & Development, 92*, 148–153. http://dx.doi.org/10.1002/j.1556-6676.2014.00142.x

Hernández, P., & Rankin, P., IV. (2008). Relational safety and liberating training spaces: An application with a focus on sexual orientation issues. *Journal of Marital and Family Therapy, 34,* 251–264. http://dx.doi.org/10.1111/j.1752-0606.2008.00067.x

Israel, T., & Hackett, G. (2004). Counselor education on lesbian, gay, and bisexual issues: Comparing information and attitude exploration. *Counselor Education and Supervision, 43,* 179–191. http://dx.doi.org/10.1002/j.1556-6978.2004.tb01841.x

Kashubeck-West, S., Szymanski, D., & Meyer, J. (2008). Internalized heterosexism: Clinical implications and training considerations. *The Counseling Psychologist, 36,* 615–630. http://dx.doi.org/10.1177/0011000007309634

Long, J. K., & Serovich, J. M. (2003). Incorporating sexual orientation into MFT training programs: Infusion and inclusion. *Journal of Marital and Family Therapy, 29,* 59–67. http://dx.doi.org/10.1111/j.1752-0606.2003.tb00383.x

Luke, M., Goodrich, K. M., & Scarborough, J. L. (2011). Integration of K-12 LGBTQI student population into school counselor curricula: The current state of affairs. *Journal of LGBT Issues in Counseling, 5,* 80–101. http://dx.doi.org/10.1080/15538605.2011.574530

Mallinckrodt, B. (2009). Advances in research with sexual minority people: Introduction to the special issue. *Journal of Counseling Psychology, 56,* 1–4. http://dx.doi.org/10.1037/a0014652

Meyer, I. H. (2003). Prejudice, social stress, and mental health in lesbian, gay, and bisexual populations: Conceptual issues and research evidence. *Psychological Bulletin, 129,* 674–697.

Miles, J. R., & Fassinger, R. E. (2014). Sexual identity issues in education and training for psychologists. In W. B. Johnson & N. J. Kaslow (Eds.), *The Oxford handbook of education and training in professional psychology* (pp. 452–471). New York, NY: Oxford University Press.

Mohr, J. J., Weiner, J. L., Chopp, R. M., & Wong, S. J. (2009). Effects of client bisexuality on clinical judgment: When is bias most likely to occur? *Journal of Counseling Psychology, 56,* 164–175. http://dx.doi.org/10.1037/a0012816

Moradi, B., DeBlaere, C., & Huang, Y. (2010). Centralizing the experiences of LGB people of color in counseling psychology. *The Counseling Psychologist, 38,* 322–330. http://dx.doi.org/10.1177/0011000008330832

O'Hara, C., Dispenza, F., Brack, G., & Blood, R. A. C. (2013). The preparedness of counselors in training to work with transgender clients: A mixed methods investigation. *Journal of LGBT Issues in Counseling, 7,* 236–256. http://dx.doi.org/10.1080/15538605.2013.812929

O'Shaughnessy, T., & Spokane, A. R. (2013). Lesbian and gay affirmative therapy competency, self-efficacy, and personality in psychology trainees. *The Counseling Psychologist, 41,* 825–856. http://dx.doi.org/10.1177/0011000012459364

Phillips, J. C. (2000). Training issues and considerations. In R. M. Perez, K. A. DeBord, & K. J. Bieschke (Eds.), *Handbook of counseling and psychotherapy with lesbian, gay, and bisexual clients* (pp. 337–358). Washington, DC: American Psychological Association. http://dx.doi.org/10.1037/10339-014

Phillips, J. C., & Fischer, A. R. (1998). Graduate students' training experiences with gay, lesbian, and bisexual issues. *The Counseling Psychologist, 26,* 712–734. http://dx.doi.org/10.1177/0011000098265002

Rock, M., Carlson, T. S., & McGeorge, C. R. (2010). Does affirmative training matter? Assessing CFT students' beliefs about sexual orientation and their level of affirmative training. *Journal of Marital and Family Therapy, 36,* 171–184. http://dx.doi.org/10.1111/j.1752-0606.2009.00172.x

Singh, A. L., & Chun, K. Y. S. (2010). "From the margins to the center:" Moving towards a resilience-based model of supervision for queer people of color supervisors. *Training and Education in Professional Psychology, 4,* 36–46. http://dx.doi.org/10.1037/a0017373

Smith, L. C., Shin, R. Q., & Officer, L. M. (2012). Moving counseling forward on LGB and transgender issues: Speaking queerly on discourses and microaggressions. *The Counseling Psychologist, 40,* 385–408. http://dx.doi.org/10.1177/0011000011403165

Yerke, A. F., & Mitchell, V. (2011). Am I man enough yet? A comparison of the body transitioning, self-labeling, and sexual orientation of two cohorts of female-to-male transsexuals. *International Journal of Transgenderism, 13,* 64–76. http://dx.doi.org/10.1080/15532739.2011.622125

15

LESBIAN, GAY, AND BISEXUAL HEALTH ISSUES: POLICY AND PRACTICE

DOUGLAS C. HALDEMAN AND KRISTIN A. HANCOCK

Throughout the lifespan, no issue is as central to one's existence as is health. Health and ability status affect our lives in major ways. For instance, health and ability status may have a great deal to do with where we can work, what we can do, how we can function socially and recreationally, and how independent we can be. Lesbian, gay, and bisexual (LGB) individuals, like everyone else, place a significant importance on health and, like everyone else, health-related concerns tend to increase as we age.[1] LGB people contend with a wide range of issues associated with health (e.g., aging, mobility, financial security, isolation), access to care, and attitudes on the part of care providers. For the LGB person, who may be more likely than a heterosexual individual to be single and without financial resources (Conron, Mimiaga, & Landers, 2010; Wight, LeBlanc, & Lee Badgett, 2013), these concerns can

---

[1] For information pertaining to transgender issues, please see Chapter 16 of this volume.

http://dx.doi.org/10.1037/15959-016
Handbook of Sexual Orientation and Gender Diversity in Counseling and Psychotherapy, K. A. DeBord, A. R. Fischer, K. J. Bieschke, and R. M. Perez (Editors)

be especially significant. The intent of this chapter is to examine health differences and disparities among LGB individuals and to provide recommendations for policy development and practitioners.

Historically, the literature on sexual orientation attended primarily to issues of mental health and adjustment in a society still based on sexual prejudice and the residual effects of pathologizing same-sex attractions and behavior. Early work on the health-related concerns of LGB individuals for the health care professions and the general public alike focused on disease syndromes (HIV/AIDS, sexually transmitted diseases [STDs]) most common among gay men and to lesser extent, the resultant effects on their caregivers. A specific focus on lesbian health was missing from the literature until the mid-1980s (cf. Bradford, Ryan, & Rothblum, 1994), save for discussions of psychosocial adjustment of lesbians to identity, work, and relationship contexts at midlife and beyond (Kimmel & Sang, 1995). LGB youth were identified as to the degree they might be at risk for suicide or substance abuse (Anhalt & Morris, 1998). It was not until 2000 that a mention of the concept of "wellness" specifically targeted at LGB individuals appeared (Kauth, Hartwig, & Kalichman, 2000).

The subsequent decade, however, ushered in an evolution of attitudes and practice among health care providers and social policymakers alike with respect to LGB health. Organizations were developed, with federal funding (e.g., The Fenway Institute), whose primary focus was improving health care for LGB individuals across the lifespan. Best practices for health care with LGB individuals have been offered to providers in mainstream behavioral health science texts (Meyer & Northridge, 2007; Pantalone, Haldeman, & Martell, 2012), and these have also offered recommendations for health care professionals working with transgender individuals (see Chapter 16, this volume). In 2011, the Institute of Medicine (IOM) issued a groundbreaking report that identified both risk and protective factors for LGB individuals, assessed the epidemiology of various health problems across generational LGB cohorts, and outlined strategies for improving access to health care for LGB individuals. Indeed, much has changed in the 40+ years of the LGB rights movement.

One unfortunate statistic seems to be the same, however. Lesbians, gay men, and bisexuals still rate their overall health as significantly poorer than that of their heterosexual counterparts, and experience higher rates of a variety of diseases and syndromes (Boehmer, Miao, Linkletter, & Clark, 2014). Significant health disparities exist for LGB individuals in all age cohorts (Harcourt, 2006; IOM, 2011).

LGB individuals have unique concerns regarding health and health care (de Vries, 2014; Fredriksen-Goldsen, Kim, Barkan, Balsam, & Mincer, 2010; Harcourt, 2006). There is also evidence that points to the role societal stigma plays "as a pre-disposing and perpetuating factor in many aspects of ill-health" (Williamson, 2000, p. 105). It is essential, therefore, to acknowledge the interplay between psychosocial context and the health and well-being of LGB people. In this light, we intend to examine the institutional, systemic, political, and unique sociocultural factors that can affect the health of LGB individuals and their access to care. In addition, we address personal factors that enhance or detract from general well-being and longevity for LGB individuals. After many years of marginalization, many American LGB individuals now live in a society where their families are protected by policy, their relationships are sanctioned by laws, and major social institutions recognize them as legitimate. This, in turn, has an effect on access to health care which has a beneficial effect on mental and physical well-being (Makadon, Mayer, Potter, & Goldhammer, 2008; Meyer & Northridge, 2007).

It is beyond the scope of this chapter to address the issue of self-identification nomenclature among LGB individuals (note that issues related to gender identity and transgender [T] individuals are addressed elsewhere in this volume). As LGB psychology and research have expanded since the last publication of this handbook, identification nomenclature has also evolved. It is a challenge to find terms that are all-inclusive and accepted by all persons and groups. We have used terms in our chapter related to sexual minority groups that best encompasses the scholarship and research reflected in this chapter. Suffice it to say that terms such as *queer* or *men who have sex with men*, which have a variety of meanings across and within generational cohorts, are embraced by some and scorned by others. This variance in self-identification can add a primary challenge to research. Although the data sets from recent population-based studies (e.g., Wight et al., 2013) are more robust, they may, as de Vries (2014) pointed out, disaggregate groups and incorrectly generalize data that do not capture distinctions such as differences between racial/ethnic groups and age groups. Moreover, such population-based studies rarely include the unique issues among older LGB individuals.

Given this, the purpose of our chapter is to examine the general trends of health concerns and disparities among LGB individuals, starting with the sociocultural factors that may raise stress levels and thus create greater health risks for LGB individuals. We examine generational factors and sexual orientations, socioeconomic status (SES), and the health care environment itself. We then turn our attention to the specific health concerns of lesbians, gay men, and bisexual men and women. Our examination continues with social and institutional policies affecting the health of LGB individuals and ends with policy recommendations and suggestions for psychologists working with LGB clients in the domain of health.

Given the generally sex-negative political climate and policies with which the current generations of LGB elders grew up, it has been difficult until very recently to accurately assess the statistical presence of, or conduct substantial health-related research on, LGB individuals in our society. Although much has changed in recent years, it is still difficult to estimate the number of individuals in the United States who fall into the categories of "LGB" (IOM, 2011). Population-based surveys conducted in the United States indicate that 1.7% to 5.6% identify as lesbian, gay, or bisexual (Gates, 2011). These estimates neither capture individuals who are afraid to identify themselves in surveys, nor do they include individuals, particularly in younger generational cohorts, who may eschew any sort of identifying term when it comes to sexual orientation or gender.

Several large, population-based surveys (Conron et al., 2010; Met Life Mature Market Institute, 2006; Wight et al., 2013) show that LGB individuals are more likely to rate their health status more poorly than are heterosexual individuals, to be single, to be without health insurance, and to fear disclosure to health care providers. These data are partly explained by the fact that lesbians manifest increased rates for certain physical illnesses/ diseases, such as cardiovascular disease, high blood pressure, and diabetes than are their heterosexual counterparts; gay men report higher rates of HIV and STDs (Harcourt, 2006; Hatzenbuehler, McLaughlin, Keyes, & Hasin, 2010). These illnesses or diseases are at least in part the result of accrued stress (Hatzenbuehler et al., 2010). Even more sobering are the results of a study conducted by Hatzenbuehler et al. (2012), which found that the life expectancy rates of LGB individuals living in communities with high levels of antigay prejudice are, on the average, 12 years less than those among LGB individuals who live in the least prejudiced communities.

CULTURAL FACTORS AND LGB HEALTH RISKS

Minority Stress

There are factors that have been shown to have a negative impact upon the health of LGB people, otherwise known as *compromising factors*. The primary compromising health factor for LGB individuals is minority stress (Elliott et al., 2015; Lick, Durso, & Johnson, 2013). Minority stress theory posits that the stigma associated with social devaluation, and attendant concerns about discrimination, hostility and violence, are internalized (Meyer, 2003). Evidence suggests that this internalization is associated with increased levels of depression and anxiety, substance abuse, and lack of adherence to health-promoting behaviors among LGB individuals (de Vries, 2014; Hatzenbuehler et al., 2010).

It is not surprising that LGB individuals living in more affirmative, progressive places tend to fare better in terms of overall mental health and physical well-being than do those living in more conservative areas. Hatzenbuehler et al. (2012) found that LGB individuals living in states banning same-sex marriage endorsed significantly greater levels of depression and anxiety, as well as alcohol abuse, than did their counterparts living in less repressive states. Although this may derive from a general sociocultural level of inclusivity, and not from same-sex marriage per se, it is worth noting that mental health among LGB individuals was found to be significantly better in California and Massachusetts (both jurisdictions with same-sex marriage) than elsewhere (Hatzenbuehler et al., 2012).

The data showing the effect of low social tolerance on LGB people raise concerns about the adverse impact of stress on physical and mental health. One study found that lesbians and gay men begin engaging in risky health behaviors (e.g., substance use, unsafe sex) at much earlier ages than do heterosexual individuals (Boehmer et al., 2014; see Chapter 9, this volume, for more on adolescence). Also, historically, LGB teens have been found to be at significantly greater risk for both attempted and completed suicide than have heterosexual teenagers, based on social rejection related to sexual orientation (C. Bagley & Tremblay, 2000). The concerns for health across the lifespan with this finding are two-fold. Risky health behavior in adolescence or early adulthood tends to be the best predictor of lifelong poor health habits (Ryan, Huebner, Diaz, & Sanchez, 2009). These individuals are more likely to experience chronic struggles with substance abuse, contract HIV or STDs, or develop eating disorders (Mayer, Garofalo, & Makadon, 2014).

Adolescence and Gender

In addition to sexual orientation, gender is seen as a potentially complicating factor in the development of health disparities among adolescents (Saewyc, 2011). This review of the literature shows that health disparities among LGB teens are greatest for lesbians. These health concerns may continue into adulthood. For instance, in her study of heterosexist discrimination and obesity in lesbians, Mereish (2014) found that general chronic stressors were related to higher levels of cortisol. She contends that chronic exposure to minority stress in lesbians may serve to increase cortisol levels which, in turn, puts them at greater risk for obesity. In addition, Mereish noted that lesbians may be more reluctant to seek health care because of potential or perceived heterosexist discrimination on the part of health care providers.

Bisexuality

Bisexual individuals experience health concerns in greater frequency than either heterosexual or lesbian or gay counterparts. Conron et al. (2010), in a population-based study, reported that bisexual women are more likely than lesbians or heterosexual persons to have diabetes, cardiovascular disease, and other stress and behaviorally based concerns. Bisexual men are more likely than gay or heterosexual men to have sexually transmitted diseases. Both bisexual men and women are less likely than heterosexual persons or lesbians and gay men to have access to health care, likely because of "double discrimination" with the most negative attitudes toward bisexual persons endorsed by heterosexual individuals but also held by lesbians and gay men (Conron et al., 2010; Friedman, 2014). Bisexual individuals have been often been viewed with derision by heterosexual persons and with mistrust and resentment by lesbian and gay individuals. In addition, both lesbian and gay individuals, as well as heterosexual persons, have inaccurately viewed bisexuality as a transitional state between heterosexuality and homosexuality (Israel & Mohr, 2004). A randomized study of 339 health records of bisexually identified males and females revealed a significantly higher suicide rate among bisexual individuals than either heterosexual or lesbian/gay individuals (Pompili et al., 2014). Additionally, significantly higher rates of depression and alcohol and drug use were found among bisexual individuals than among either heterosexual or homosexual individuals. Pompili et al. (2014) speculated that these findings may derive from bisexuals feeling rejected by both groups. Other authors, observing socially prevailing "bi-phobic" attitudes, have suggested that bisexual individuals need to create their own sense of community (Israel & Mohr, 2004).

Socioeconomic Status

LGB individuals who are of low SES have historically had greater difficulty than have low-SES heterosexual individuals in accessing health care (Adler et al., 1994), although the Affordable Care Act (ACA) has improved the situation for LGB individuals somewhat. Low SES disproportionately affects people of color (Badgett, 2001). LGB individuals are shown in many studies to be more likely than their heterosexual counterparts to be of low SES, less likely to have health insurance or a partner who can provide it, and thus less likely to access routine or even acute treatment for health conditions (McWilliams, Fournier, Booth, Burke, & Kauffman, 2007). Lack of health insurance is a significant factor in neglecting routine medical care. In fact, Blosnich, Farmer, Lee, Silenzio, and Bowen (2014) found that, when compared with heterosexual women, lesbians were 30% less likely to have had an annual physical examination. The IOM (2011) noted that foregoing routine care is a particularly significant factor in the development of more serious diseases, especially in later life.

The Health Care Environment

Minority stress derives from LGB individuals' fears of unequal treatment in the health care system itself. Health care workers are a significant part of the mainstream cultural environment, and a recent study shows that physicians, mid-level practitioners (nurse practitioners, physicians' assistants) and nurses who hold strong conservative religious beliefs are more likely to evidence greater personal bias and lower levels of acceptance of LGB patients (Wilson et al., 2014). It is of little wonder, then, that LGB individuals in less progressive geographic areas with fewer choices of health care providers might choose to avoid disclosure of their identity or avoid medical care altogether (Hatzenbuehler et al., 2012). This particular issue may lead to serious—even critical—situations in LGB health care (e.g., an aging LGB person becomes dependent upon care in a facility that offers a hostile environment due to a lack of understanding or reluctance to treat the person on the part of care providers). For consideration of the health-related issues specific to older LGB individuals, see Chapter 10, this volume. Similarly, health-related concerns specific to LGB youth are addressed in Chapter 9.

MORBIDITIES

We now turn to the specific health-related problems that disproportionately affect LGB individuals, according to group.

Lesbians and Bisexual Women

Fish (2009) observed that, compared with heterosexual women's health, lesbian health has been largely overlooked in the area of health psychology. In addition, she noted that studies of lesbian and bisexual women's health in this field may only represent 1% of published work in health psychology. Recently, however, though efforts have been made to focus upon the health issues of LGB people, finding studies that focus more upon the health concerns of lesbians—and particularly those of bisexual women—remains challenging in some areas. Nevertheless, this section briefly describes some of the major health concerns of lesbians and bisexual women.

Obesity and Weight Concerns

A number of large, population-based studies (e.g., Case et al., 2004; Cochran et al., 2001) have documented significant obesity among lesbians. Although obesity is quickly becoming a significant risk factor for health problems among women in general (Bowen, Balsam, & Ender, 2008), studies show that lesbians have higher rates of obesity than do heterosexual women (Boehmer et al., 2014; O'Hanlan & Isler, 2007; Struble, Lindley, Montgomery, Hardin, & Burcin, 2010; U.S. Substance Abuse and Mental Health Services Administration [SAMHSA], 2011). Lesbians have been found to be up to twice as likely to be overweight or obese as their heterosexual counterparts (Boehmer, Bowen, & Bauer, 2007; Cochran et al., 2001; Struble et al., 2010).

In their qualitative exploration of lesbians' attitudes and beliefs regarding weight and weight reduction, Roberts, Stuart-Shor, and Oppenheimer (2010) found that the contributing factors to this situation paint a complex picture. Comments from participants in their focus groups suggest that minority stress, depression, and anxiety present barriers to changing unhealthy behaviors. Participants reported believing that "minority stress had the greatest reported impact on the health behavior of participants . . . [they believed] that smoking, drinking and overeating were all methods of soothing themselves and relieving stress, anger and shame" (Roberts et al., 2010, p. 1992). Other findings point to differences in the self-estimates of body weight with heterosexual women overestimating theirs and lesbians underestimating their body weight (Bergeron & Senn, 1998; Cohen & Tannenbaum, 2001).

There may be generational differences among lesbians regarding attitudes toward weight and eating-related problems. In their study of eating disorders, Feldman and Meyer (2007) found that younger lesbians were more likely to have "borderline bulimia" and to be more sensitive to societal standards about weight than were older lesbians. In the Roberts et al. (2010) study, younger lesbians reported not feeling any differently about weight than their heterosexual counterparts while older lesbians tended to reject societal norms regarding women's weight.

It is interesting to note that in a study of lesbians, bisexual women, and body image, Ludwig and Brownell (1999) found that women who rated themselves as "feminine" in appearance and who had more heterosexual friends reported less satisfaction with their bodies than the women who rated themselves as more "masculine" and who had more lesbian friends. This study appears to suggest that gender roles may impact lesbian and bisexual women's attitudes regarding weight and appearance. Moreover, the sex of a woman's partner has been found to be associated with differences in weight expectations. A qualitative study by Taub (1999) found that the weight expectations of the bisexual women with male sexual partners differed from those with female partners. Participants in this study discussed adherence to heterosexual beauty norms when with men and experiencing some pressure to do so. When with women, participants reported experiencing fewer appearance pressures.

Although the Taub (1999) study did not specifically target weight per se, it reflects an important area of concern with regard to sexual orientation differences and obesity. For example, women wishing to attract men continue to deal with different standards and values relative to appearance (including weight) than those wishing to attract women. Is the sex of a woman's partner a major factor in weight differences between lesbians and heterosexual women? In addition, the interesting findings with regard to younger lesbians described above need further investigation and should target whether or not younger lesbians have, in fact, developed standards more reflective of heterosexual women with regard to weight. Further, additional research might examine the extent to which health concerns have motivated such a shift, if found.

The Role of Stress

Another contributing factor to obesity and general health concerns of lesbian and bisexual women is stress. As mentioned earlier, minority stress appears to have a major impact. Recent findings (i.e., Mereish, 2014; Mason & Lewis, 2015) suggest that heterosexist discrimination and minority stress are related to a higher risk of being overweight or obese in lesbians.

Meyer's (2003) work on minority stress describes *distal* (e.g., discrimination, harassment) and *proximal* stressors (e.g., the internalization of negative attitudes). These stressors have been shown to have effects upon the mental health and well-being of gay men and lesbians (Meyer, 2003). Mereish (2014) found that lesbians who experienced discrimination (a distal stressor) were significantly more likely to be overweight or obese than normal weight lesbians. Mason and Lewis (2015) reported that proximal stress (e.g., internalized homophobia, expectation of rejection) appears to be related to binge eating behaviors in lesbians and bisexual women. This occurs via the social isolation, negative affect, and maladaptive emotion-focused coping (i.e., rumination, self-blame, catastrophizing) associated with minority stress. Although minority stress does not necessarily impact all lesbians and bisexual women, when it does, a close social network and adaptive coping skills may serve to reduce the negative impact of stigmatization. The lives of lesbians and bisexual women may be greatly challenged by complex interactions between sexism and heterosexism that can test a woman's capacity for self-care.

One significant area of minority stress for lesbians is the workplace. Ragins, Singh, and Cornwell (2007) found that the fear of negative consequences from being "out" in the workplace resulted in more psychological strain than actually being out in this setting. Lesbians tended to invest considerably more time and energy in preparing for careers than did their heterosexual counterparts (Black, Makar, Sanders, & Taylor, 2003). Being female and negotiating the challenges of being lesbian can involve significant strain which can tax a woman's stress management capabilities. Kuyper (2015) found higher levels of bullying and unequal opportunities among bisexual women in the workplace as compared with heterosexual women and lesbians. Kuyper suggested that, at this point in time, bisexual women may experience more trouble because they are less visible and may have more difficulty finding support than their lesbian counterparts.

Stress and obesity have been shown to be associated with poor general health (Fredriksen-Goldsen et al., 2010). Again, the literature suggests additional challenges for bisexual women. In their investigation of health-related quality-of-life issues in lesbians and bisexual women, Fredriksen-Goldsen et al. (2010) found that "bisexual women showed a higher likelihood of frequent mental distress and poor general health than did lesbians" (p. 2255)—particularly for those bisexual women living in urban areas. The study also revealed stressors such as lower income, more children in the home, less access to health care, and high-risk behaviors (e.g., smoking and acute drinking) were more of a concern for bisexual women when compared with lesbians. It is interesting to note that lesbians in midlife exhibited an elevated risk of poor general health and mental distress (Fredriksen-Goldsen et al., 2010).

It is clear that obesity and weight concerns are among the top health issues for lesbians. The literature reveals connections between being overweight and differing standards of appearance, cohort differences, and the sex of one's partner. It highlights the ways in which minority stress contributes to weight issues in lesbians. The lives of lesbians and bisexual women may be greatly challenged by complex interactions between sexism and heterosexism that can test a woman's capacity for self-care.

Cancer and Cardiovascular Disease

Though there does not appear to be much information available about cancer in lesbian and bisexual women, breast cancer has been shown to manifest in lesbians at a higher rate than in heterosexual women (e.g., Cochran et al., 2001; Dibble, Roberts, & Nussey, 2004). Hutchinson, Thompson, and Cederbaum (2006) noted that "lesbian women have been found to have higher rates of . . . health behaviors that increase their risk for cervical and breast cancers" (p. 395). For example, lesbians and bisexual women appear less often for routine screening procedures, such as mammograms and gynecological examinations. Lesbian and bisexual women also have drinking patterns that put them at risk for cancer and cardiovascular disease (Cochran et al., 2001). Other risk factors for breast cancer in lesbians include higher body mass indices and less frequent exercise per week than their heterosexual counterparts (Zaritsky & Dibble, 2010). It is important to mention that lesbians have been shown to have fewer pregnancies, fewer total months pregnant, and fewer total months breast-feeding than do heterosexual women (Zaritsky & Dibble, 2010); therefore, because estrogen levels drop during pregnancy, women who do not have children (or who have them later in life) are exposed to greater amounts of estrogen. Breast cancer is associated with higher levels of estrogen (Nandi, Guzman, Thordarson, & Rajkumar, 2003). In addition, Cochran et al. (2001) reported that studies show lesbians as having higher rates of abnormal Pap results than do their heterosexual counterparts and lower rates of Pap testing, which is a recipe for risk.

It is not surprising that the issue of some lesbians' reluctance to visit physicians or to disclose their sexual orientation to doctors when they do make appointments is raised in the literature. Discussing this reluctance, Hutchinson et al. (2006) noted that the assumption of heterosexuality on the part of the provider and in the field makes each visit to a physician an occasion for dealing with coming out to that provider. The alternative would be to receive care "passing" as heterosexual. At times, lesbians report having felt disrespected and stigmatized by their providers (Hutchinson et al., 2006). On the other hand, comfort, openness, and disclosure have been found to be significantly related to increased health care use (Bergeron & Senn, 2003).

Research also points to increased risk for cardiovascular disease in lesbians (e.g., Case et al., 2004; Diamant & Wold, 2003). Risk factors such as obesity, smoking, alcohol use, and diet (i.e., eating fewer fruits and vegetables) contribute to the increased vulnerability to cardiovascular problems. Roberts, Deleger, Strawbridge, and Kaplan (2003) found a significant difference between lesbians and heterosexual women in what the authors referred to as *weight cycling* (i.e., losing 10+ pounds and then regaining that weight). Weight cycling has been shown to be related to increased risk for cardiovascular problems (Brownell & Rodin, 1994). Certainly, the issues with minority stress and obesity may be viewed as contributing factors to cardiovascular disease. In addition to this, however, it is important to address smoking and substance use.

Smoking and Substance Use

Hughes, Johnson, and Matthews (2008) found the rates of smoking among lesbians and bisexual women to be substantially higher than those for women in the general population. Lesbians and bisexual women are also more likely to be current smokers than are their heterosexual counterparts (Drabble & Trocki, 2005; Gruskin, Hart, Gordon, & Ackerson, 2001). A study of lesbian and bisexual women smokers by age cohort would be of interest to determine whether these statistics continue to accurately reflect these groups' tobacco use.

Research also points to higher rates of alcohol use among lesbians. Drabble and Trocki (2005) found higher rates of alcohol consumption, smoking, and drug misuse among lesbian and bisexual women than in their heterosexual counterparts. There is also some indication that the higher level of alcohol use may be connected to childhood sexual abuse in lesbians (Roberts, Grindel, Patsdaughter, DeMarco, & Tarmina, 2004). Others (e.g., Hughes, 2005) have suggested that it stems from minority stress. Another issue that has been raised in the literature regarding increased use of alcohol among lesbians is the role of the gay or lesbian bar in the LGB community (Balsam, Beadnell, & Riggs, 2012). "The fact that lesbian life has historically been organized around lesbian bars, where lesbians can find each other as well as enjoy a safe haven . . . has been a major factor explaining the risk of alcohol use and abuse, and alcoholism" (Gedro, 2014, p. 52).

Any review of the health problems among lesbians and bisexual women reveals the complex impact stigma and minority stress have on the health and well-being of lesbians and bisexual women. Researchers have characterized many risk factors and maladaptive health behaviors as responses to discrimination and internalized stigma and abuse. Balsam, Lehavot, and Beadnell (2011) found that multiple victimizations were associated with increased alcohol use and other self-harm behaviors. It therefore appears likely that the discrimination and abuse in the lives of nonheterosexual women would be connected to higher rates of smoking, alcoholism, or other maladaptive health behaviors. It is also important to continue to study the health disparities among lesbians and bisexual women and not to generalize findings to both groups without studying them as separate groups.

Gay and Bisexual Men

HIV/AIDS

The primary health concern for gay men addressed in the health literature, as well as in gay society, for the last 3 decades has been HIV/AIDS (Halkitis, 2013), both in terms of pathways of HIV transmission and treatment options. The AIDS epidemic started in the gay community and decimated the current generation of gay male baby boomers. Estimates suggest that 30% to 40% of gay men born between 1946 and 1965 died in the early years of the epidemic (before the advent of protease inhibitors, which, in conjunction with antiretroviral drugs, are able to keep the virus at or near undetectable levels in most people; Pebody, 2012) and that another 20% are living with HIV (Halkitis, 2013). For gay men, unprotected sex continues to be the most frequent method of *seroconversion* (i.e., contracting the virus; Centers for Disease Control & Prevention [CDC], 2012). The highest-risk groups tend to be young men of color, ages 18 to 34, which represents almost half of all new HIV infections annually for the past several years (CDC, 2012). These findings reveal that young White men are also at risk, although to a lesser extent. These data replicate several years' findings from the CDC (2012), which reports that new HIV infections have been plateauing at about 50,000 per year. It is unclear why, year after year, young men of color account for so many seroconversions (CDC, 2012). It has been speculated that a number of factors may contribute, including low SES, socially oppressive forces of homophobia and racism, and less connection to home community (Halkitis, 2012). In any case, it would be helpful to inquire about the nature and duration of trauma the person may have experienced.

Also unclear is why older gay men, survivors of the initial wave of HIV infections, account for 10,000 new infections every year (CDC, 2012). Ubiquitous public education campaigns about safe sex seem to have slowed, but not stopped, the spread of HIV. One study of gay and bisexual men attributed their seroconversion to a variety of factors: lack of knowledge about HIV transmission, low self-esteem, trusting the "wrong person," and alcohol/drug use (Aguinaldo, Myers, Ryder, Haubrich, & Calzavara, 2009). The CDC (2012) also reported that only 49% of gay and bisexual men know their HIV status, adding to the potential for disseminating the virus in the gay community.

Another recent development in the HIV/AIDS arena, and its effect on MSM (men who have sex with men), is the availability of a prophylaxis in pill form to protect against HIV transmission during unprotected sex called PrEP (preexposure prophylaxis). Helfand (2014) reported on a French study of over 400 participants showing a 92% decrease in HIV infection among sexually active gay men when using the PrEP medication (Truvada) regularly. Opinion in the gay community is divided on the use of this medication. Some see it as a boon to worry-free sex, whereas others fear that it stands to create a culture of indifference to safe sexual practices (Helfand, 2014). In any case, the availability of PrEP is generally limited to those with health insurance—another possible disparity in access to care between gay men of higher SES and those of lower SES, who show the highest new rates of HIV infection (CDC, 2012).

Sexually Transmitted Infections and Cancers

STDs, such as syphilis, gonorrhea, hepatitis B and C, chlamydia and HPV (human papilloma virus, often a precursor to anal warts and cancer), have historically been a significant concern in the gay male community. The rates of STDs and anal cancer are disproportionately higher for gay men than for heterosexual men (Appelbaum, 2008). Further, Asencio et al. (2009) found that gay men are at higher risk than heterosexual men for prostate cancer, especially as they age. This study suggested that many gay men lack adequate information about transmission of sexual infections, particularly with respect to anal health. As a result, Asencio et al. recommended expanded efforts at educating the gay community, particularly its younger element, in preventing the spread of STDs.

Lack of education is not the only factor exacerbating STDs among gay men. Asencio and her colleagues (2009) found that avoidance of medical care plays a role in the incidence of prostate cancer among gay men and their partners, by virtue of the fact that the cancer has often spread significantly by the time medical attention is sought. Hatzenbuehler and colleagues (2012) suggested that a variety of internalized factors related to stigma—including shame about sexuality, fear of disclosure and mistrust of the medical establishment—are significant factors in gay men's avoidance of medical care. Correlated with this are the CDC (2012) estimates that gay men are 17 times more likely than are heterosexual men to develop anal cancer.

The CDC (2012) recommended vaccination for hepatitis B and C, as well as HPV (for men up to age 26). Furthermore, the CDC recommended that all sexually active gay men be tested annually for STDs. In addition, the guidelines include adherence to safer sex practices, including use of condoms, having fewer sexual partners, getting to know the ones one does have, and avoiding excessive use of alcohol or recreational drugs during sexual episodes. It is sometimes the mental health provider, not the physician, who is the first to know an individual's concerns about sexual behavior. In this instance, the mental health provider's role in providing accurate information and support for sexual behavior counseling and STD testing is invaluable.

Substance Abuse

According to the CDC (2012), substance abuse among gay men is significantly higher than that among heterosexual men. Of greatest concern is the epidemic of methamphetamine abuse among gay men, which is well documented (Halkitis, 2013). Methamphetamine is associated with a propensity for unprotected receptive anal sex on the part of the user, the highest risk behavior for HIV transmission. Diaz (2007) found that methamphetamine abuse was significantly correlated with HIV seroconversion among young gay Latino males and posits that young men of color may be at particular risk for new infection via this route.

The statistics on other drugs are noteworthy: Gay and bisexual men are 3.5 times more likely to be dependent on marijuana than are heterosexual men, 5 times more likely to abuse alcohol, and 9.5 times more likely to be addicted to heroin (Ostrow & Stall, 2008). In addition, a variety of "club drugs," such as ecstasy, GHB, and ketamine, and "poppers" (nitrate inhalants used to intensify sexual arousal), are popular with gay and bisexual men and are often used in combination with each other and/or alcohol and other drugs. Ostrow et al. (2009) found that the use of these drugs, either singly or in combination, has led to the majority of recent seroconversions among MSM (Ostrow et al., 2009).

As psychologists, we turn to the question of why gay and bisexual men are more likely to abuse drugs than are their heterosexual counterparts. The literature identifies several possible reasons: a lack of cultural competence of drug and alcohol treatment for gay and bisexual men, disinhibition for drug use at bars or large dances where other drugs are being used, and the factors associated with minority stress. Many gay and bisexual men report having had negative experiences in alcohol/drug treatment programs that are designed for heterosexual people or that are blatantly homophobic (Ostrow & Stall, 2008). In addition, many gay and bisexual men may not openly acknowledge their sexual habits and avoid treatment altogether. Although LGB-specific drug and alcohol treatment centers are now more common than they once were, competent services for MSM in this area are still few and far between.

The rituals associated with gay and bisexual men in bars and at large dances are legendary; bars and clubs were, once upon a time in gay history, the only safe place for gay and bisexual men to gather socially. These venues have also historically been associated with alcohol and drugs, and a recent study of party-goers at large gay dances revealed that up to half of participants decided ahead of time to use some combination of party drugs along with alcohol and agents used to treat erectile dysfunction (to negate the vasoconstrictive effects of many of the party substances; Ramchand, Fisher, Griffin, Becker, & Iguchi, 2013). As we have seen, the disinhibitory effects of these substances can compromise an individual's decisions about sexual partners and behavior, to the detriment of the individual (Ostrow et al., 2009).

As mentioned previously with lesbians and bisexual women, minority stress among gay and bisexual men is noted as a predisposing factor in a variety of health concerns (Meyer, 2012). In this light, we see the systemic effects of cultural homophobia as having a negative impact on a wide range of health issues for gay and bisexual men. A recent population-based survey of almost 10,000 gay and bisexual men indicated that they were significantly more likely to have experienced "severe psychological distress" in the last 3 months than were heterosexual men (Ward, Dahlhamer, Galinsky, & Joestl, 2014). It is reasonable to hypothesize that minority stress plays a role, given the findings previously cited.

The effects of drug and alcohol abuse, which are widespread in the gay community, can be deadly. The psychologist should inquire carefully about the drug/alcohol behaviors and sexual practices of all MSM clients and provide support for behavior modification or recovery if necessary. Such inquiry involves an in-depth exploration of behavioral underpinnings, such as internalized homophobia and mistrust of the health care establishment.

SOCIAL AND INSTITUTIONAL POLICIES

Our discussion now turns to social and institutional policies that serve to protect the health of LGB persons and promote their collective wellness. These domains are not discrete; rather, institutional factors help to define social policy, which, in turn, affect cultural attitudes and, ultimately, the individual. In short, all of the following shifts in sociopolitical and cultural awareness provide reason to be optimistic about the future of LGB health.

The change in the U.S. presidential political administration in 2008 ushered in a slowly evolving shift in positive changes for LGB health care policy. This began with the *President's Memorandum on Hospital Visitation* (The White House, 2010), which mandated that same-sex partners in all federally funded hospitals be granted visitation rights. The end of the military's infamous "Don't Ask, Don't Tell" policy (U.S. Department of Defense, 2010) in the same year added a significant boost to all areas of LGB life in that it represented the fall of a significant institutionalized bastion of prejudice and discrimination against LGB individuals. At the same time, research funding for LGB health initiatives began to increase from the National Institutes of Health (Coulter, Kenst, Bowen, & Scout, 2014). The U.S. Department of Health and Human Services developed LGBT health priorities; funding was generated for the National LGBT Health Education Center for a variety of initiatives, including the establishment of an LGBT-friendly health care workforce; the IOM issued a 2011 report citing health care disparities among LGBT people, and calling for an end to them. Recently, guidelines were promulgated by the American Association of Medical Colleges (2014) for the training of medical students in competent treatment of LGB patients.

This list is further augmented with actions taken by The Joint Commission (TJC), the accrediting body of hospitals. TJC now requires accredited hospitals to include sexual orientation and gender identity in their non-discrimination policies. In the TJC's "field guide" a welcoming environment for LGBT patients and their family members is recommended (The Joint Commission, 2011). Both TJC and Medicare require hospital visitation privileges without respect to sexual orientation or gender identity, significantly broadening the president's order. Access to care for millions of LGB individuals has been improved by federal and private employer mandates, including domestic partners on health insurance policies, regardless of marital status. Starting in 2015, federal law mandates that any private insurer in jurisdictions with same-sex marriage offering medical benefits to married heterosexual couples must do the same for lesbian and gay married couples (Healthcare.gov, 2014).

The foregoing policies stand as one pillar supporting LGB health, but there has been no policy shift as dramatic or as potent as that of same-sex marriage. The U.S. Supreme Court decision of 2015 (*Obergefell v. Hodge*,

2015) that found that same-sex marriage is a constitutional right for lesbians and gay men is the most recent in a series of rulings affirming equality for LGB individuals. This ruling came after a relatively rapid shift in public opinion, as well as lower court rulings following earlier U.S. Supreme Court decisions about the unconstitutionality of the Defense of Marriage Act and California's Proposition 8. This is an area that should be followed with research as marriage equality and its accompanying protections and benefits are recognized across the country. Hatzenbuehler et al. (2010), replicating earlier studies, found that the mental health of LGB individuals in states with same-sex marriage laws is significantly better with respect to depression and anxiety, in contrast with states prohibiting the same. More research is needed to evaluate the overall mental health of LGB citizens in response to these legal and policy changes.

The implications for improving LGB health with same-sex marriage laws are two-fold. Marriage has long been found a protective factor in physical health (Mays & Cochran, 2001; Robles, Slatcher, Trombello, & McGinn, 2014). Additionally, it has been asserted that same-sex marriage improves access to care and diminishes the chances that many LGB individuals will avoid care (Gonzales, 2014). The health and well-being of the estimated 200,000 children being raised in same-sex households also stands to improve (Gonzales, 2014). To be sure, the health care policy landscape is not made perfect for same-sex families; employers may still find ways to circumvent health care mandates in the Affordable Care Act ("The Affordable Care Act Helps LGBT Americans," n.d.) on the basis of recent and sometimes conflicting judicial rulings (N. Bagley, Jones, & Jost, 2015). Still, the health care policy picture for LGBT individuals is vastly different from it was 10 years ago. Implications for practicing psychologists will be addressed in the next section.

Social policies do not develop independently of the cultures they inform. LGB health care policies are connected to the social and cultural evolution relative to understanding and acceptance of homosexuality. Public opinion in this area has shifted dramatically in the past 40 years, in large part owing to the increased visibility of LGB persons (Herek & McLemore, 2013). A majority of Americans now report (Herek & McLemore, 2013) that they know someone who is lesbian or gay, and even those who do not have regular exposure to lesbian or gay characters on television or in films. This familiarity, according to Herek and McLemore (2013), plays a role in mainstream America's endorsement of equality for LGB individuals. Herek has studied and tracked attitudes about LGB individuals for over 3 decades and has found that sexual prejudice is still harbored by many Americans, particularly those who believe that homosexuality is a choice (Herek & McLemore, 2013).

Nevertheless, it has also been observed that members of the LGB communities are resilient. For example, the pre-Stonewall generation survived an age of secrecy and witch hunts. The Stonewall generation survived the AIDS crisis. Kimmel (1978) noted that as diverse communities, we have developed "crisis competence" and a resilience built upon internal strength forged from higher levels of preparedness and education in the face of external socio-political stressors. This resilience is one quality that will hopefully be encouraged with a more open society and be further developed in the evolution of LGB health in coming years.

RECOMMENDATIONS

The world for LGB individuals has seen significant change in social attitudes and policy since the Stonewall era. It has only been a few decades since public opinion throughout almost all of the United States was generally antigay, and LGB people were fearful of being visible. The social climate in America has changed dramatically since then. This change has been reflected in public opinion, social policy, health care policy and laws protecting LGB individuals and their family members. Millions of LGB individuals now live with the knowledge that they may live and work where they choose and love whom they will.

Some LGB individuals still live in fear and danger, without adequate resources, or are trapped in dysfunctional ways of coping with prior stressors that they cannot relinquish. We have seen some of the ways in which there is a synergistic effect between higher rates of health concerns and high-risk behaviors among LGB individuals and health disparities. Psychologists and mental health professionals have a central role to play in the resolution of LGB health disparities. Through a thoughtful and compassionate response to LGB clients, psychologists can serve a vital role in turning the balance from compromising factors to protective ones.

Integration of health care depends upon the ability of mental health professionals to coordinate treatment planning and interventions for LGB clients with other health care professionals. The advent of integrative health care means that psychologists will have increased contact with physicians, nurses, and other primary health care providers. Psychologists with LGB patients who are dealing with medical issues and physicians with LGB patients who are facing behaviorally based or mental health issues will have expanded avenues for interdisciplinary collaboration. This may be of benefit to the LGB client in the health care setting. From the outset, it is clear that psychologists' developing a sense of how to navigate the integrative health care system is a primary opportunity and responsibility. As we have seen, prejudicial treatment in society or the health care environment itself may cause some LGB individuals to be reluctant or unwilling to disclose certain health issues, or even their sexual orientation or gender identity. In such cases, it may be the psychologist or other mental health professional who serves as the first line of defense for providing a safe environment and for eliciting relevant information about the individual's identity and health status (Mayer et al., 2008).

The synergistic effect of ethnoracial identity, SES, and sexual orientation brings added stress and concern about health disparities for LGB persons of color. LGB ethnic minority individuals are disproportionately affected by new HIV seroconversions, obesity, smoking-related health concerns, and diminished access to health care. A recent study suggests that low SES LGB clients, which include a disproportionately large number of persons of color, experience significantly greater discrimination, substandard care, and barriers to care than heterosexual persons (Lambda Legal, 2009). It is incumbent upon psychologists to advocate for equity in health care policy, as well as to work toward ending health disparities in our roles as health care providers.

Creating a "safe space" and being a compassionate listener are primary competencies, but they are not in and of themselves sufficient to support optimal health for the LGB(T) client. Competence on the part of the psychologist is further evidenced in several ways:

- It has been recommended that psychologists develop skills in consulting with other health care professionals; this means learning medical language (e.g., medical conditions, medications) and offering some perspective about psychological strategies and interventions (e.g., behavioral techniques, mindfulness) that are useful in prevention and in the treatment of behaviorally based conditions (IOM, 2011). Additionally, it may be useful for the psychologist to have access to a list of providers competent in the care of LGB individuals. This list may be available from a local LGB counseling organization, LGB Chamber of Commerce, or a local medical society. For those living in rural or more conservative areas without readily accessible providers with LGB competence, a number of internet-based resources are available that provide options for information and even counseling.
- American Psychological Association guidelines encourage a thoughtful inquiry about sexual orientation and behavior, even among those individuals who identify as heterosexual (e.g., in order to assess the potential health risks involved with heterosexually identified men engaging in same-sex behavior on the "down low"). The *Guidelines for Psychological Practice With Lesbian, Gay and Bisexual Clients* (American Psychological Association, 2012) is an excellent resource in general, but in particular for those seeking guidance in terms of asking clients about sexual orientation and behavior.

- Familiarity with health risk factors for LGB individuals, and being willing to inquire about them, is useful for psychologists working with LGB individuals. Cochran (2001) recommended that mental health workers inquire into what particular health risk factors may be present for the patient and how they will be addressed in therapy. Does the person smoke or abuse drugs or alcohol? What are the individual's sexual behavior patterns? Obviously, mental health issues must be taken into consideration; even if depression and anxiety are not part of the initial presentation, they should be reviewed, as a history of such can often be hidden. Aggregate stress level and coping mechanisms should be examined, and understanding the prevailing social attitudes of the world the LGB person inhabits is crucial. As noted, internalized homophobia may have a particularly deleterious effect on physical well-being (Williamson, 2000).
- Recent guidelines recommend that the therapist should discuss the relationship the LGB person has with their primary care provider, or the provider(s) through whom they access health care (American Association of Medical Colleges, 2014; Steele et al., 2006). This relationship is key to preventive medicine as well as effective intervention, but is sometimes impaired by the patient's reluctance to discuss critical information, and/or the primary care provider's lack of knowledge about or sensitivity to health care issues of LGB individuals. For example, LGB individuals are less likely than heterosexuals to seek routine screening for cancer (Buchmueller & Carpenter, 2010). This suggests that the therapist should be attentive to physical as well as mental health concerns. Does the individual feel free to openly share health-related concerns with the primary care provider? Are there barriers to discussing any significant aspect of the health profile? If so, does the individual need assistance in working toward greater honesty with their primary care provider, or do they simply need to find another provider? And if they are unable to do so based upon restrictions of their own coverage, this highlights the need for more advocacy relative to patient choice.
- In addition to the specific health issues identified here, the psychologist should consider what family planning means for LGB individuals in same-sex couples. It is much more common, especially for LGB individuals in younger cohorts, to plan to have children, through a variety of means—adoption, surrogacy, artificial insemination, et cetera. Understanding how to facilitate

such a conversation with an LGB individual, and knowing how to provide appropriate fertility/adoption referrals, is help-ful. From the outset, it is important that the therapist not make unwarranted assumptions about the LGB individual's family situation; "Are you married/partnered?" is less intimidating to many than "Do you have a husband/wife?". "Family" for LGB individuals often consists of individuals to whom the person is not legally or biologically related (American Psychological Association, 2012), and it is affirming for the therapist to ask open-ended questions. "Do you have/would you like to have children?" is an appropriate question for any LGB individual. The therapist may wish to become familiar with resources for individuals planning a family with a same-sex partner. A num-ber of areas of the country now offer resources for lesbians and gay men wishing to adopt or have their own children. These may be found on the internet, or through organizations such as the Fenway Health Center in Boston, which maintains a list of such resources nationwide.

- With heightened stress levels and substance abuse potential for LGB individuals as the results of stigma, therapists should be familiar with the use of behavioral techniques for stress reduc-tion (Carrico et al., 2006). Relief from acute stress, as well as strategies to substitute healthy behaviors for unhealthy ones, all imply utilization of behavioral techniques. Meditation, exercise and of course cognitive behavioral strategies may all be useful tools for the practitioner working with LGB individuals.

CONCLUSION

Psychologists and mental health professionals have a significant role to play in improving health for LGB individuals—on individual, systemic, and institutional levels. We have considered some of the ways and some of the interventions that psychologists may use to be helpful to individual LGB cli-ents in addressing health-related issues. Systemically, the psychologist can be a vital part of an individual's health care team, as well as an advocate for the client. Health of the whole person is, in part, a reflection of the individual's environment. The focus on wellness for the whole person (mind and body), and its relation to the individual's world, involves attention to the poten-tial obstacles for LGB individuals at every stage of life. Is the young person being bullied at school, and therefore at risk for poor academic performance, alcohol and drug use, homelessness, or even suicide (Conron et al., 2010)?

Does the elder LGB person have access to appropriate care? Can the gay man recover from drug addiction, or the lesbian quit smoking, with a treatment program that is appropriate for their needs? Psychologists and mental health professionals can be the facilitator for a number of the LGB individual's mental health needs, in a stigma-free care environment.

REFERENCES

Adler, N. E., Boyce, T., Chesney, M. A., Cohen, S., Folkman, S., Kahn, R. L., & Syme, S. L. (1994). Socioeconomic status and health: The challenge of the gradient. *American Psychologist, 49*, 15–24. http://dx.doi.org/10.1037/0003-066X.49.1.15

The Affordable Care Act helps LGBT Americans. (n.d.). Retrieved from http:// www.whitehouse.gov/sites/default/files/docs/the_aca_helps_lgbt_americans.pdf

Aguinaldo, J. P., Myers, T., Ryder, K., Haubrich, D. J., & Calzavara, L. (2009). Accounts of HIV seroconversion among substance-using gay and bisexual men. *Qualitative Health Research, 19*, 1395–1406.

American Association of Medical Colleges. (2014). *AAMC releases guidelines to improve medical care for patients who are LGBT.* Retrieved from https://www.aamc.org/ newsroom/newsreleases/414490/11182014.html

American Psychological Association. (2012). Guidelines for psychological practice with lesbian, gay, and bisexual clients. *American Psychologist, 67*, 10–42. http:// dx.doi.org/10.1037/a0024659

Anhalt, K., & Morris, T. L. (1998). Developmental and adjustment issues of gay, lesbian, and bisexual adolescents: A review of the empirical literature. *Clinical Child and Family Psychology Review, 1*, 215–230. http://dx.doi.org/10.1023/A:1022660101392

Appelbaum, J. (2008). Late adulthood and aging: Clinical approaches. In H. Makadon, K. H. Mayer, J. Potter, & H. Goldhammer (Eds.), *Fenway guide to lesbian, gay, bisexual and transgender health* (pp. 135–158). Philadelphia, PA: American College of Physicians.

Asencio, M., Blank, T., Descartes, L., & Crawford, A. (2009). The prospect of prostate cancer: A challenge for gay men's sexualities as they age. *Sexuality Research & Social Policy: A Journal of the NSRC, 6*, 38–51. http://dx.doi.org/10.1525/ srsp.2009.6.4.38

Badgett, L. (2001). *Money, myths and change: The economic lives of lesbians and gay men.* Chicago, IL: University of Chicago Press.

Bagley, C., & Tremblay, P. (2000). Elevated rates of suicidal behavior in gay, lesbian, and bisexual youth. *Crisis: The Journal of Intervention and Suicide Prevention, 21*, 111–117. http://dx.doi.org/10.1027//0227-5910.21.3.111

Bagley, N., Jones, D. K., & Jost, T. S. (2015). Predicting the fallout from King v. Burwell—Exchanges and the ACA. *The New England Journal of Medicine, 372*, 101–104. http://dx.doi.org/10.1056/NEJMp1414191

Balsam, K. F., Beadnell, B., & Riggs, K. R. (2012). Understanding sexual orientation health disparities in smoking: A population-based analysis. *American Journal of Orthopsychiatry*, 82, 482–493. http://dx.doi.org/10.1111/j.1939-0025.2012.01186.x

Balsam, K. F., Lehavot, K., & Beadnell, B. (2011). Sexual revictimization and mental health: A comparison of lesbians, gay men, and heterosexual women. *Journal of Interpersonal Violence*, 26, 1796–1814.

Bergeron, S., & Senn, C. (1998). Body image and sociocultural norms: A comparison of heterosexual and lesbian women. *Psychology of Women Quarterly*, 22, 385–401. http://dx.doi.org/10.1111/j.1471-6402.1998.tb00164.x

Bergeron, S., & Senn, C. Y. (2003). Health care utilization in a sample of Canadian lesbian women: Predictors of risk and resilience. *Women's Health*, 37, 19–35. http://dx.doi.org/10.1300/J013v37n03_02

Black, D., Makar, H., Sanders, S., & Taylor, L. (2003). The earnings effects of sexual orientation. *Industrial & Labor Relations Review*, 56, 449–469. http://dx.doi.org/10.1177/001979390305600305

Blosnich, J. R., Farmer, G. W., Lee, J. G. L., Silenzio, V. M. B., & Bowen, D. J. (2014). Health inequalities among sexual minority adults: Evidence from ten U.S. states, 2010. *American Journal of Preventive Medicine*, 46, 337–349. http://dx.doi.org/10.1016/j.amepre.2013.11.010

Boehmer, U., Bowen, D. J., & Bauer, G. R. (2007). Overweight and obesity in sexual-minority women: Evidence from population-based data. *American Journal of Public Health*, 97, 1134–1140. http://dx.doi.org/10.2105/AJPH.2006.088419

Boehmer, U., Miao, X., Linkletter, C., & Clark, M. A. (2014). Health conditions in younger, middle, and older ages: Are there differences by sexual orientation? *LGBT Health*, 1, 168–176. http://dx.doi.org/10.1089/lgbt.2013.0033

Bowen, D. J., Balsam, K. F., & Ender, S. R. (2008). A review of obesity issues in sexual minority women. *Obesity*, 16, 221–228. http://dx.doi.org/10.1038/oby.2007.34

Bradford, J., Ryan, C., & Rothblum, E. D. (1994). National Lesbian Health Care Survey: Implications for mental health care. *Journal of Consulting and Clinical Psychology*, 62, 228–242. http://dx.doi.org/10.1037/0022-006X.62.2.228

Brownell, K. D., & Rodin, J. (1994). Medical, metabolic, and psychological effects of weight cycling. *Archives of Internal Medicine*, 154, 1325–1330. http://dx.doi.org/10.1001/archinte.1994.00420120035004

Buchmueller, T., & Carpenter, C. S. (2010). Disparities in health insurance coverage, access, and outcomes for individuals in same-sex versus different-sex relationships, 2000–2007. *American Journal of Public Health*, 100, 489–495. http://dx.doi.org/10.2105/AJPH.2009.160804

Carrico, A. W., Antoni, M. H., Duran, R. E., Ironson, G., Penedo, F., Fletcher, M. A., . . . Schneiderman, N. (2006). Reductions in depressed mood and denial coping during cognitive behavioral stress management with HIV-positive gay men treated with HAART. *Annals of Behavioral Medicine*, 31, 155–164. http://dx.doi.org/10.1207/s15324796abm3102_7

Case, P., Austin, S. B., Hunter, D. J., Manson, J. E., Malspeis, S., Willett, W. C., & Spiegelman, D. (2004). Sexual orientation, health risk factors, and physical functioning in the Nurses' Health Study II. *Journal of Women's Health*, *13*, 1033–1047. http://dx.doi.org/10.1089/jwh.2004.13.1033

Centers for Disease Control and Prevention. (2012). Diagnoses of HIV infection in the United States and dependent areas, 2012. *HIV Surveillance Report*, *24*, 1–84.

Cochran, S. D. (2001). Emerging issues in research on lesbians' and gay men's mental health: Does sexual orientation really matter? *American Psychologist*, *56*, 931–947. http://dx.doi.org/10.1037/0003-066X.56.11.931

Cochran, S. D., Mays, V. M., Bowen, D., Gage, S., Bybee, D., Roberts, S. J., . . . White, J. (2001). Cancer-related risk indicators and preventive screening behaviors among lesbians and bisexual women. *American Journal of Public Health*, *91*, 591–597. http://dx.doi.org/10.2105/AJPH.91.4.591

Cohen, A., & Tannenbaum, I. (2001). Lesbian and bisexual women's judgments of attractiveness of different body types. *Journal of Sex Research*, *38*, 226–232. http://dx.doi.org/10.1080/00224490109552091

Conron, K. J., Mimiaga, M. J., & Landers, S. J. (2010). A population-based study of sexual orientation identity and gender differences in adult health. *American Journal of Public Health*, *100*, 1953–1960. http://dx.doi.org/10.2105/AJPH.2009.174169

Coulter, R. W., Kenst, K. S., Bowen, D. J., & Scout. (2014). Research funded by the National Institutes of Health on the health of lesbian, gay, bisexual, and transgender populations. *American Journal of Public Health*, *104*, 105–112. http://dx.doi.org/10.2105/AJPH.2013.301501

de Vries, B. (2014). LG(BT) persons in the second half of life: The intersectional influences of stigma and cohort. *LGBT Health*, *1*, 18–23. http://dx.doi.org/10.1089/lgbt.2013.0005

Diamant, A. L., & Wold, C. (2003). Sexual orientation and variation in physical and mental health status among women. *Journal of Women's Health*, *12*, 41–49. http://dx.doi.org/10.1089/154099903321154130

Diaz, R. (2007). Methamphetamine use and its relation to HIV risk: Data from Latino gay men in San Francisco. In I. Meyer & M. Northridge (Eds.), *The health of sexual minorities: Public health perspectives on lesbian, gay, bisexual and transgender populations* (pp. 584–606). New York, NY: Springer.

Dibble, S. L., Roberts, S. A., & Nussey, B. (2004). Comparing breast cancer risk between lesbians and their heterosexual sisters. *Women's Health Issues*, *14*, 60–68. http://dx.doi.org/10.1016/j.whi.2004.03.004

Drabble, L., & Trocki, K. (2005). Alcohol consumption, alcohol-related problems, and other substance use among lesbian and bisexual women. *Journal of Lesbian Studies*, *9*(3), 19–30. http://dx.doi.org/10.1300/J155v09n03_03

Elliott, M. N., Kanouse, D. E., Burkhart, Q., Abel, G. A., Lyratzopoulos, G., Beckett, M. K., . . . Roland, M. (2015). Sexual minorities in England have poorer health and worse health care experiences: A national survey. *Journal of General Internal Medicine*, *30*, 9–16. http://dx.doi.org/10.1007/s11606-014-2905-y

Feldman, M. B., & Meyer, I. H. (2007). Eating disorders in diverse lesbian, gay, and bisexual populations. *International Journal of Eating Disorders, 40,* 218–226. http://dx.doi.org/10.1002/eat.20360

Fish, J. (2009). Our health, our say: Towards a feminist perspective of lesbian health psychology. *Feminism & Psychology, 19,* 437–453. http://dx.doi.org/10.1177/0959353509342692

Fredriksen-Goldsen, K. I., Kim, H. J., Barkan, S. E., Balsam, K. F., & Mincer, S. L. (2010). Disparities in health-related quality of life: A comparison of lesbians and bisexual women. *American Journal of Public Health, 100,* 2255–2261. http://dx.doi.org/10.2105/AJPH.2009.177329

Friedman, M. (2014, May). *Attitudes toward bisexual men and women.* Paper presented at the Annual Meeting of the American Public Health Association, Boston, MA.

Gates, G. (2011). How many people are lesbian, gay, bisexual, and transgender? Retrieved from the Williams Institute website: http://williamsinstitute.law.ucla.edu/wp-content/uploads/Gates-How-Many-People-LGBT-Apr-2011.pdf

Gedro, J. (2014). Alcoholism and lesbians. *New Directions for Adult and Continuing Education, 142,* 49–62. http://dx.doi.org/10.1002/ace.20094

Gonzales, G. (2014). Same-sex marriage—A prescription for better health. *The New England Journal of Medicine, 370,* 1373–1376. http://dx.doi.org/10.1056/NEJMp1400254

Gruskin, E. P., Hart, S., Gordon, N., & Ackerson, L. (2001). Patterns of cigarette smoking and alcohol use among lesbians and bisexual women enrolled in a large health maintenance organization. *American Journal of Public Health, 91,* 976–979. http://dx.doi.org/10.2105/AJPH.91.6.976

Halkitis, P. (2012). Discrimination and homophobia fuel the HIV epidemic in gay and bisexual men. *Psychology and AIDS Exchange Newsletter.* Retrieved from http://www.apa.org/pi/aids/resources/exchange/2012/04/discrimination-homophobia.aspx

Halkitis, P. (2013). *The AIDS generation: Stories of resilience and survival.* New York, NY: Oxford University Press. http://dx.doi.org/10.1093/acprof:oso/9780199944972.001.0001

Harcourt, J. (2006). Current issues in lesbian, gay, bisexual, and transgender (LGBT) health: Introduction. *Journal of Homosexuality, 51,* 1–11. http://dx.doi.org/10.1300/J082v51n01_01

Hatzenbuehler, M. L., McLaughlin, K. A., Keyes, K. M., & Hasin, D. S. (2010). The impact of institutional discrimination on psychiatric disorders in lesbian, gay, and bisexual populations: A prospective study. *American Journal of Public Health, 100,* 452–459. http://dx.doi.org/10.2105/AJPH.2009.168815

Hatzenbuehler, M. L., O'Cleirigh, C., Grasso, C., Mayer, K., Safren, S., & Bradford, J. (2012). Effect of same-sex marriage laws on health care use and expenditures in sexual minority men: A quasi-natural experiment. *American Journal of Public Health, 102,* 285–291. http://dx.doi.org/10.2105/AJPH.2011.300382

Healthcare.gov. (2014). *Health care coverage options for same sex couples.* Retrieved from https://www.healthcare.gov/married-same-sex-couples-and-the-marketplace/

Helfand, M. (2014, October 29). "On demand" PReP may significantly reduce HIV risk. *HIV JournalView*. Retrieved from The Body Pro website: http://www.thebodypro.com/content/75162/on-demand-prep-may-significantly-reduce-hiv-risk-i.html

Herek, G. M., & McLemore, K. A. (2013). Sexual prejudice. *Annual Review of Psychology, 64*, 309–333. http://dx.doi.org/10.1146/annurev-psych-113011-143826

Hughes, T. L. (2005). Alcohol use and alcohol-related problems among lesbians and gay men. *Annual Review of Nursing Research, 23*, 283–325.

Hughes, T. L., Johnson, T. P., & Matthews, A. K. (2008). Sexual orientation and smoking: Results from a multisite women's health study. *Substance Use & Misuse, 43*, 1218–1239. http://dx.doi.org/10.1080/10826080801914170

Hutchinson, M. K., Thompson, A. C., & Cederbaum, J. A. (2006). Multisystem factors contributing to disparities in preventive health care among lesbian women. *Journal of Obstetric, Genecologic, and Neonatal Nursing, 35*, 393–402.

Institute of Medicine. (2011). *The health of lesbian, gay, bisexual and transgender people: Building a foundation for better understanding*. Washington, DC: The National Academies Press.

Israel, T., & Mohr, J. (2004). Attitudes toward bisexual women and men: Current research, future directions. *Journal of Bisexuality, 4*, 117–134. http://dx.doi.org/10.1300/J159v04n01_09

The Joint Commission. (2011). *Advancing effective communication, cultural competence, and patient and family-centered care for the lesbian, gay, bisexual and transgender (LGBT) community*. Retrieved from http://www.jointcommission.org/lgbt/

Kauth, M., Hartwig, M., & Kalichman, S. (2000). Health behavior relevant to psychotherapy with lesbian, gay, and bisexual clients. In R. M. Perez, K. A. DeBord, & K. J. Bieschke (Eds.), *Handbook of counseling and psychotherapy with lesbian, gay, and bisexual clients* (pp. 435–456). Washington, DC: American Psychological Association. http://dx.doi.org/10.1037/10339-018

Kimmel, D. C. (1978). Adult development and aging: A gay perspective. *Journal of Social Issues, 34*, 113–130.

Kimmel, D. C., & Sang, B. E. (1995). Lesbians and gay men in midlife. In A. R. D'Augelli & C. J. Patterson (Eds.), *Lesbian, gay and bisexual identities over the lifespan* (pp. 190–214). New York, NY: Oxford University Press. http://dx.doi.org/10.1093/acprof:oso/9780195082319.003.0008

Kuyper, L. (2015). Differences in workplace experiences between lesbian, gay, bisexual, and heterosexual employees in a representative population study. *Psychology of Sexual Orientation and Gender Diversity, 2*, 1–11.

Lambda Legal. (2009). *When health care isn't caring: Low-income or uninsured LGBT people and persons living with HIV*. Retrieved from https://www.lambdalegal.org/health-care-report

Lick, D. J., Durso, L. E., & Johnson, K. L. (2013). Minority stress and physical health among sexual minorities. *Perspectives on Psychological Science, 8*, 521–548. http://dx.doi.org/10.1177/1745691613497965

Ludwig, M. R., & Brownell, K. D. (1999). Lesbians, bisexual women, and body image: An investigation of gender roles and social group affiliation. *Eating Disorders: The Journal of Treatment & Prevention, 25,* 89–97. http://dx.doi.org/10.1002/(SICI)1098-108X(199901)25:1<89::AID-EAT11>3.0.CO;2-T

Makadon, H., Mayer, K., Potter, J., & Goldhammer, H. (2008). *The Fenway guide to lesbian, gay, bisexual and transgender health.* Philadelphia, PA: American College of Physicians.

Mason, T. B., & Lewis, R. J. (2015). Minority stress and binge eating among lesbian and bisexual women. *Journal of Homosexuality, 62,* 971–992.

Mayer, K. H., Bradford, J. B., Makadon, H. J., Stall, R., Goldhammer, H., & Landers, S. (2008). Sexual and gender minority health: What we know and what needs to be done. *American Journal of Public Health, 98,* 989–995. http://dx.doi.org/10.2105/AJPH.2007.127811

Mayer, K. H., Garofalo, R., & Makadon, H. J. (2014). Promoting the successful development of sexual and gender minority youths. *American Journal of Public Health, 104,* 976–981. http://dx.doi.org/10.2105/AJPH.2014.301876

Mays, V. M., & Cochran, S. D. (2001). Mental health correlates of perceived discrimination among lesbian, gay, and bisexual adults in the United States. *American Journal of Public Health, 91,* 1869–1876. http://dx.doi.org/10.2105/AJPH.91.11.1869

McWilliams, D., Fournier, D., Booth, B., Burke, P., & Kauffman, J. (2007). Legal issues of importance to clinicians. In H. Makadon, K. Mayer, J. Potter, & H. Goldhammer (Eds.), *The Fenway guide to lesbian, gay, bisexual and transgender health* (pp. 443–461). Philadelphia, PA: American College of Physicians.

Mereish, E. H. (2014). The weight of discrimination: The relationship between heterosexist discrimination and obesity among lesbian women. *Psychology of Sexual Orientation and Gender Diversity, 1,* 356–360. http://dx.doi.org/10.1037/sgd0000056

Met Life Mature Market Institute. (2006). *Out and aging.* Westport, CT: Metropolitan Life Insurance.

Meyer, I. H. (2003). Prejudice, social stress, and mental health in lesbian, gay, and bisexual populations: Conceptual issues and research evidence. *Psychological Bulletin, 129,* 674–697. http://dx.doi.org/10.1037/0033-2909.129.5.674

Meyer, I. H. (2012, February). *Minority stress and the health of sexual minorities.* Lecture given at Williams Institute, University of California, Los Angeles. http://dx.doi.org/10.1093/acprof:oso/9780199765218.003.0018

Meyer, I. H., & Northridge, M. E. (2007). *The health of sexual minorities: Public health perspectives on lesbian, gay, bisexual and transgender populations.* New York, NY: Springer. http://dx.doi.org/10.1007/978-0-387-31334-4

Nandi, S., Guzman, R. C., Thordarson, G., & Rajkumar, L. (2003). Pregnancy levels of estrogen prevents breast cancer. *Breast Cancer Research, 5* (Suppl. 1). Retrieved from http://breast-cancer-research.com/supplements/5/S1

Obergefell v. Hodges. (2015). *Syllabus*. Retrieved from http://www.supremecourt. gov/opinions/14pdf/14-556_3204.pdf

O'Hanlan, K., & Isler, C. (2007). Health care of lesbian and bisexual women. In I. Meyer & M. Northridge (Eds.), *The health of sexual minorities: Public health perspectives on lesbian, gay, bisexual and transgender populations* (pp. 506–522). New York, NY: Springer.

Ostrow, D. G., Plankey, M. W., Cox, C., Li, X., Shoptaw, S., Jacobson, L. P., & Stall, R. C. (2009). Specific sex drug combinations contribute to the majority of recent HIV seroconversions among MSM in the MACS. *Journal of Acquired Immune Deficiency Syndromes, 51*, 349–355. http://dx.doi.org/10.1097/ QAI.0b013e3181a24b20

Ostrow, D. G., & Stall, R. (2008). Alcohol, tobacco and drug use among gay and bisexual men. In R. Wolitski, R. Stall, & R. Valdiserri (Eds.), *Unequal opportunity: Health disparities affecting gay and bisexual men in the United States* (pp. 121–158). New York, NY: Oxford University Press.

Pantalone, D., Haldeman, D., & Martell, C. (2012). Health care issues facing lesbian, gay, bisexual and transgender individuals. In O. Sahler & J. Carr (Eds.), *The behavioral sciences and health care* (3rd ed., pp. 173–180). Cambridge, MA: Hogrefe.

Pebody, R. (2012). *Undetectable viral load*. Retrieved from http://www.aidsmap.com

Pompili, M., Lester, D., Forte, A., Seretti, M. E., Erbuto, D., Lamis, D. A., . . . Girardi, P. (2014). Bisexuality and suicide: A systematic review of the current literature. *Journal of Sexual Medicine, 8*, 1903–1913.

Ragins, B. R., Singh, R., & Cornwell, J. M. (2007). Making the invisible visible: Fear and disclosure of sexual orientation at work. *Journal of Applied Psychology, 92*, 1103–1118. http://dx.doi.org/10.1037/0021-9010.92.4.1103

Ramchand, R., Fisher, M., Griffin, B., Becker, K., & Iguchi, M. (2013). Drug use among gay and bisexual men at weekend dance parties. *AIDS and Behavior, 17*, 1540–1549. http://dx.doi.org/10.1007/s10461-012-0382-z

Roberts, R. E., Deleger, S., Strawbridge, W. J., & Kaplan, G. A. (2003). Prospective association between obesity and depression: Evidence from the Alameda County Study. *International Journal of Obesity and Related Disorders, 24*, 514–521.

Roberts, S. J., Grindel, C. G., Patsdaughter, C. A., DeMarco, R., & Tarmina, M. S. (2004). Lesbian use and abuse of alcohol: Results of The Boston Lesbian Health Project II. *Substance Abuse, 25*, 1–9. http://dx.doi.org/10.1300/ J465v25n04_01

Roberts, S. J., Stuart-Shor, E. M., & Oppenheimer, R. A. (2010). Lesbians' attitudes and beliefs regarding overweight and weight reduction. *Journal of Clinical Nursing, 19*, 1986–1994. http://dx.doi.org/10.1111/j.1365-2702.2009.03182.x

Robles, T. F., Slatcher, R. B., Trombello, J. M., & McGinn, M. M. (2014). Marital quality and health: A meta-analytic review. *Psychological Bulletin, 140*, 140–187. http://dx.doi.org/10.1037/a0031859

Ryan, C., Huebner, D., Diaz, R. M., & Sanchez, J. (2009). Family rejection as a predictor of negative health outcomes in white and Latino lesbian, gay, and bisexual young adults. *Pediatrics, 123*, 346–352. http://dx.doi.org/10.1542/peds.2007-3524

Saewyc, E. (2011). Research on adolescent sexual orientation: Development, health disparities, stigma and resilience. *Journal of Research on Adolescence, 21*, 256–272. http://dx.doi.org/10.1111/j.1532-7795.2010.00727.x

Steele, L. S., Tinmouth, J. M., & Lu, A. (2006). Regular health care use by lesbians: A path analysis of predictive factors. *Family Practice, 23*, 631–636. http://dx.doi.org/10.1093/fampra/cml030

Struble, C. B., Lindley, L. L., Montgomery, K., Hardin, J., & Burcin, M. (2010). Overweight and obesity in lesbian and bisexual college women. *Journal of American College Health, 59*, 51–56. http://dx.doi.org/10.1080/07448481.2010.483703

Taub, J. (1999). Bisexual women and beauty norms. *Journal of Lesbian Studies, 3*(4), 27–36. http://dx.doi.org/10.1300/J155v03n04_04

U.S. Department of Defense. (2010). End of the "don't ask, don't tell" policy. Retrieved from http://archive.defense.gov/home/features/2010/0610_dadt/

U.S. Substance Abuse and Mental Health Services Administration. (2011). *Leading change: A plan for SAMHSA's roles and actions 2011–2014* (HHS Publication No. SMA 11-4629). Rockville, MD: Author.

Ward, B., Dahlhamer, J., Galinsky, A., & Joestl, S. (2014, July). Sexual orientation and health among U.S. adults: National Health Interview Survey, 2013. *National Health Statistics Reports*. Retrieved from http://www.cdc.gov/nchs/data/nhsr/nhsr077.pdf

The White House. (2010). *President's memorandum on hospital visitation.* Retrieved from http://www.whitehouse.gov/the-press-office/presidential-memorandum-hospital-visitation

Williamson, I. R. (2000). Internalized homophobia and health issues affecting lesbians and gay men. *Health Education Research, 15*, 97–107. http://dx.doi.org/10.1093/her/15.1.97

Wilson, C., West, L., Stepelman, L., Villarosa, M., Ange, B., Decker, M., & Waller, J. (2014). *Attitudes toward LGBT patients among students in health professions: Influences of demography and discipline.* Retrieved from http://www.jointcommission.org/assets/1/18/LGBTFieldGuide.pdf

Wight, R. G., LeBlanc, A. J., & Lee Badgett, M. V. (2013). Same-sex legal marriage and psychological well-being: Findings from the California Health Interview Survey. *American Journal of Public Health, 103*, 339–346. http://dx.doi.org/10.2105/AJPH.2012.301113

Zaritsky, E., & Dibble, S. L. (2010). Risk factors for reproductive and breast cancers among older lesbians. *Journal of Women's Health, 19*, 125–131. http://dx.doi.org/10.1089/jwh.2008.1094

16

PHYSICAL HEALTH CONCERNS RELATED TO MEDICAL TRANSITIONS FOR TRANSGENDER AND GENDER NONCONFORMING CLIENTS

LORE M. DICKEY AND ANNELIESE A. SINGH

Transgender and gender nonconforming (TGNC) clients have unique health care needs. Although most health care concerns over the course of a TGNC person's lifetime is no different from those of any other person, for TGNC people, there are a number of health concerns that need to be addressed in a culturally competent manner. For the purposes of this chapter, we focus primarily on clients who make a medical transition.

The authors of this chapter have been actively involved in affirmative practice with TGNC people for many years. The first author identifies as a gay-identified, White trans man with a lesbian history. The second author identifies as a multiracial, South Asian, Sikh American who is gender fluid with cisgender (i.e., someone whose gender corresponds to their assigned sex) privilege.

http://dx.doi.org/10.1037/15959-017
Handbook of Sexual Orientation and Gender Diversity in Counseling and Psychotherapy, K. A. DeBord, A. R. Fischer, K. J. Bieschke, and R. M. Perez (Editors)

DEFINITIONS

There are several definitions that warrant attention. *Medical transition* includes any of the variety of health care interventions a TGNC person might access as a means of achieving a gender that is consistent with their internal sense of self. There are two basic elements to a medical transition. The first relates to hormones (Feldman & Safer, 2009). For adolescents, this might include accessing hormone suppression treatments. For adults, this may include some level of hormone treatment. The second type of intervention involves surgery (Ettner, Monstrey, & Eyler, 2007). There are a variety of gender-affirmation surgeries that a person might access. Readers are encouraged to refer to the Introduction to this book for other definitions regarding TGNC identities.

This chapter explores diagnostic concerns, assessment of readiness for transition, medical interventions, the cost of transition, reproductive health, and body image concerns. Where possible, examples are provided to help readers understand the context in which these health care concerns exist.

Prior to exploring these health care concerns, we address two important issues. As stated previously, most of the health care a TGNC individual will access over the course of their life is no different from a cisgender individual's needs. The important difference between the two is the need to have access to providers who will treat the organ systems that are present. For example, a male-to-female (MTF) individual will need screening for prostate cancer, whereas a female-to-male (FTM) will not. Likewise, an FTM may need a pelvic examination. The challenge for the TGNC client is finding a provider who understands these clinical concerns and has the skill to address them in a manner that is supportive of the TGNC person's needs.

Over the past 5 to 10 years providers have increasingly begun to use informed consent or harm reduction models for TGNC people who are accessing hormone treatment (Deutsch, 2012). In the informed consent model, a TGNC person accesses care directly from their medical provider without needing a letter of referral from a mental health practitioner. An endocrinologist, for example, provides TGNC people with the information on the effects that hormones will and will not have and the ways that a medical transition may affect their life (e.g., family relationship, work environment; Deutsch, 2012). Readers are encouraged to explore the models that are used by the various health clinics that are listed in the supplementary materials for this book. Clinics that are marked with an asterisk have established informed consent policies.

Harm reduction models are designed to ensure continued access to medical treatments (e.g., hormones) while ensuring that this access is from safe and reliable sources (Lenton & Single, 1998). In some cases, the TGNC person is already accessing hormone treatment but may be doing so without the benefit of care from a medical provider (e.g., underground market hormones). Providers who use a harm reduction model are likely to provide their TGNC client with care that ensures no interruption in access to hormone treatment. This model prevents the client from experiencing drastic fluctuations in hormone levels, even if the initial source of hormones was the underground market. Practitioners should keep in mind that it is not always possible for TGNC clients to access providers who engage in informed consent practice. In these cases, mental health providers are encouraged to develop a plan for working with clients that is least restrictive in service of meeting their needs.

DIAGNOSTIC CONCERNS

TGNC people have needed to access care from mental health providers for many years (Lev, 2004; Vanderburgh, 2007). This is because medical providers are reluctant to provide care for a medical transition without first having some assurance that a TGNC person is of sound mind (Coleman et al., 2012). Historically, TGNC people were required to access mental health care as part of a process to obtain legitimate permission to proceed with a medical transition. In 2013, the American Psychiatric Association published the fifth edition of the *Diagnostic and Statistical Manual of Mental Disorders* (*DSM–5*). In the previous edition, TGNC people received a diagnosis of gender identity disorder (GID; American Psychiatric Association, 2000). In the *DSM–5*, this diagnosis has been changed to gender dysphoria. In this section, we discuss the ways this diagnosis has changed, how it differs from GID, the implications of the changes, and the ongoing controversy regarding the usefulness of the diagnosis.

Diagnostic Changes

A major change to the diagnosis is the label itself. Previously, the diagnosis of GID signaled that a person's gender identity was disordered. With the new diagnosis of gender dysphoria, the clinical concern is not about a person's identity but about the ways in which their gender may be causing them distress (Carmel, Hopwood, & dickey, 2014). This is an important distinction. Instead of focusing on a person's identity, the diagnostic criteria focus on the ways a person desires to be treated and is perceived as being of a gender that is different from their assigned sex at birth. One of the problems with this approach to diagnosis is that it privileges the gender binary (see the Introduction to this book for definitions) and assumes that there are only two choices to which a person aspires.

The next major change to the diagnosis is that it was moved out of the section titled Sexual and Gender Identity Disorders. Gender dysphoria is now in a category by itself. This is important because many of the disorders that were previously included alongside GID were either inconsistent with understanding gender identity (e.g., sexual dysfunction) or were disorders that involved illegal behaviors (e.g., pedophilia, frotteurism; American Psychiatric Association, 2000).

Another major change to the diagnosis is that there are now diagnostic criteria for children. In addition to the criteria being more "age appropriate," there is a different threshold for achieving diagnostic significance (American Psychiatric Association, 2013). Children need to endorse at least six of the eight criteria, whereas adolescents and adults need only endorse two of six. One advantage to this approach is that it increases the odds that children are not incorrectly diagnosed with gender dysphoria (i.e., false positive; dickey, Fedewa, & Hirsch, 2014). A disadvantage is that it might make addressing the needs of some TGNC children difficult since they do not endorse enough of the criteria to be clinically significant. For example, the parents of a child may seek support from their local school to allow their child access to gender-appropriate facilities. However, if the child only meets three criteria, the school district may be reluctant to provide access to facilities (see Chapter 7 in this volume for additional information about the role of advocacy).

The last two changes to the diagnostic criteria relate to specifiers that might be included with the diagnosis. The previous GID diagnosis had specifiers about the TGNC client's sexual attraction. Specifically, a practitioner was to indicate if the TGNC person was attracted to men, women, both, or neither. This specifier no longer exists, and it may be useful in helping to address previous concerns about the conflation of gender identity with sexual orientation (Bockting, Benner, & Coleman, 2009; Iantaffi & Bockting, 2011; Nagoshi, Brzuzy, & Terrell, 2012).

Controversy

There has been significant controversy within the TGNC community and among trans-affirmative providers as to the usefulness of the diagnosis (Bockting & Ehrbar, 2005; Drescher, 2010, 2013; Lev, 2005, 2013; Winters, 2005, 2008). Some people believe that a diagnosis is necessary to assure access to care (Bockting & Ehrbar, 2005; Knudson, De Cuypere, & Bockting, 2010). However, most TGNC people and trans-affirmative providers agree that the diagnosis should be a medical disorder rather than a mental health disorder (Drescher, Cohen-Kettenis, & Winter, 2012; Gorton, 2013; Ophelian, 2009). Maintaining the disorder as a mental health concern adds to the stigma that TGNC people often face (Drescher et al., 2012; Gorton, 2013; Ophelian,

2009). Efforts are underway to address this concern, and it is possible that gender dysphoria will be considered a medical disorder when the *International Classification of Diseases (ICD)* announces its new classification system (*ICD–11* is scheduled to be released in 2018; Drescher et al., 2012).

Maintaining access to care by way of a diagnosis is important for those individuals who rely on some form of public assistance for care (Gorton, 2007; Spade, Arkles, Duran, Gehi, & Nguyen, 2010). For example, people who are incarcerated rely on the diagnosis to continue medical treatments while serving their prison term. Without the diagnosis, it is likely that requests for hormone treatment will be denied (Brown & McDuffie, 2009). This is also true for some people who rely on Medicaid for treatment (Gorton, 2007). This will be discussed more fully in the section that addresses the cost of medical treatment and insurance coverage.

The concern for many TGNC people about diagnosis is the assumption that there is something inherently wrong with their identity (Winters, 2005, 2008). While it may be true that a TGNC person's identity is not consistent with a cisgender person's identity, this does not, and should not, signal a provider to assume that pathology is present. The World Professional Association for Transgender Health (WPATH; 2010) released a statement calling for the depathologization of gender identity (Coleman et al., 2012). WPATH acknowledges that psychosocial stressors have a strong impact on the well-being of TGNC people. Pathologizing a person as a result of their identity compounds the challenges a person faces and may lead to additional clinical concerns. WPATH recommends that governmental organizations reduce or eliminate barriers that exist for TGNC people. This might include the passage of laws and regulations that are TGNC inclusive. Examples include policies that are supportive of the need for government-sponsored insurance coverage of medical transition. Historically, Medicare and Medicaid in most locations have denied coverage on the basis that these treatments are experimental (Gehi & Arkles, 2007). This began to change in 2014 when the U.S. Department of Health and Human Services revised the ruling. Decisions about care are now handled on a case-by-case basis (National Center for Transgender Equality [NCTE], 2014). However, Medicaid decisions about care are still handled at the state level, with most states denying coverage (Gehi & Arkles, 2007).

At the time of the writing of this chapter, it was too soon to tell whether the TGNC community and trans-affirmative providers would accept the new gender dysphoria diagnosis. Many of the changes, on the surface, seem to favor the needs of TGNC people (dickey et al., 2014). However, many TGNC advocates will likely continue to advocate for the removal of any type of gender identity diagnosis from the *DSM*, as they believe this is not a mental health diagnosis (Drescher, 2010, 2013; Winters, 2008).

ASSESSMENT OF READINESS FOR MEDICAL TRANSITION

The need for psychological assessment relates directly to the requirement many health providers follow regarding the need for a letter of support for medical interventions (Coleman et al., 2012). This assessment might be as simple as a typical clinical intake followed by a brief course of therapy (e.g., 2 to 6 weeks of counseling, depending on the nature of the clinical concerns). This time frame is considered to be sufficient to allow the clinician the time to determine the clinical needs and readiness for a medical transition. It also allows the clinician to determine the client's understanding of the transition process, including addressing questions and concerns as it relates to the client's social circumstances (Lev, 2009). For example, an Asian American trans woman (MTF) may have questions about disclosing her gender identity in the workplace. This same client may also need referrals to medical providers who are trans affirmative. Ultimately, the client's autonomy to determine the need for clinical support should be at the forefront of treatment planning. If a client is expressing the need for additional support it should be provided. If, however, they are not in need of support there is no reason to require a minimum term of treatment.

Counselors and psychologists should explore the coping resources and resilience strategies TGNC clients have, especially due to the trauma experiences that TGNC clients often have had (Singh & McKleroy, 2011). Trauma experiences may include emotional and/or physical violence and harassment and/or experiences of intimate partner violence and sexual abuse (Richmond, Burnes, & Carroll, 2012). Scholars have asserted that the societal barriers TGNC people face, such as barriers to necessary health care and to employment, may result in traumatic experiences (Richmond et al., 2012). Research has suggested that these traumatic experiences may be higher for TGNC people of color (Grant et al., 2010). Counselors and psychologists should, therefore, assess the multiple identities and marginalization experiences that TGNC people may have (e.g., TGNC person of color or a TGNC person living in poverty; Burnes & Chen, 2012).

The need for psychological assessment as a part of understanding a client's readiness for transition might relate to the presence of co-occurring mental health concerns. It should be noted that there is no reliable or valid assessment that can be administered to determine if a client is transgender or ready for transition. The use of various personality assessments, such as the Minnesota Multiphasic Personality Inventory—2 (MMPI–2; Butcher et al., 2001), may be useful in understanding co-occurring mental health concerns (Graham, 2006), but the MMPI–2 (and other personality measures) was not designed to assess gender identity or readiness for transition.

WPATH STANDARDS OF CARE RECOMMENDATIONS

The 2011 WPATH Standards of Care (WPATH SOC) outline specific recommendations for clinical assessment (Coleman et al., 2012). With regard to children and adolescents, these standards make three recommendations. First, a provider is reminded to suspend any judgment they may have about their TGNC client. The provider must be prepared to explore the client's gender identity and to provide resources for the client and their family (see the Appendix for a complete listing of resources). Second, the WPATH SOC recommends assessing the child's psychosocial resources, emotional and intellectual functioning, the status of relationships with friends and family, and their cognitive or intellectual functioning. Finally, when working with adolescents, it is important to assess their understanding of what transition can and cannot accomplish. In some ways, the adolescent's understanding will signal the provider to address misconceptions about being TGNC that may exist. As a result, the needs of the client may change. For instance, a TGNC youth may feel pressure that to be TGNC, they must proceed through a social and/or medical transition. Counselors and psychologists can collaboratively explore these misconceptions as a way to identify the desires and needs of the TGNC youth. As previously stated, there is no assessment for youth that will determine if they have gender dysphoria (Coleman et al., 2012). The diagnostic criteria as set forth in the *DSM–5* cannot be measured through the use of a personality assessment scale, as none currently exist (readers are referred to Chapter 7 for more information about the WPATH SOC).

Issues Affecting Readiness

A variety of issues might affect a client's readiness to transition. These issues may be of a medical nature, related to the client's support system, related to financial concerns, or to emotional readiness.

Medical Contraindications to Transition

For the TGNC client who has co-occurring medical concerns, this can be a very frustrating position in which to be. Hormone therapy has some common health risks (Moore, Wisnewski, & Dobs, 2003). For example, an MTF client with a history of hormone-sensitive cancer may not be able to access hormone treatment. There are other conditions that may cause a person to be at risk for complicating medical concerns, though most of these should not be considered "absolute contraindications" (see Center of Excellence for Transgender Health [COE], 2013, Assessing Readiness for Hormones, para. 2). Historically, other medical conditions have been considered to be of clinical concern for a person who wants to access hormone therapy (e.g., coronary disease). However, in recent years, these conditions have not been a significant concern given the development of new methods for hormone treatment (COE, 2013).

Gorton, Buth, and Spade (2005) published an excellent resource that explores all facets of understanding the medical needs of FTM individuals. The authors addressed absolute contraindications (e.g., pregnancy, androgen sensitive breast cancer, uncontrolled coronary disease, endometrial cancer) as well as "relative medical contraindications" (p. 8). Gorton et al. listed over 15 relative medical concerns that range in severity from severe acne (not life threatening) to bleeding disorders and heart disease. This booklet is a free resource and is written for medical professionals.

Similar concerns may be present for TGNC people who wish to access surgical interventions. The kinds of medical concerns raised by TGNC clients are typically no different from those for any other surgical candidate. For instance, a history of heart disease, uncontrolled diabetes, advanced HIV, bleeding disorders, and hypertension may all be clinical concerns that prevent people from being strong candidates for surgery, regardless of their gender identity.

Supporting the Autonomy of the TGNC Client

Autonomy is one of the core guiding principles of ethical psychological practice (American Psychological Association, 2010). TGNC clients, however, are often forced to access care that feels, at worst, manipulative. At best, a TGNC client may feel as though they have little control over their decision-making process. The need to access mental health care relates directly to the requirement that a TGNC person is often required to provide one letter of support for the initiation of hormone treatment and two letters of support for surgical interventions (Coleman et al., 2012). The continued need to secure letters of referral from mental health providers for transition-related medical care can be, for some, an insurmountable obstacle on their path to realizing their gender. Some providers assume that there are minimum requirements for therapy (e.g., 3 or more months of counseling; Alderson, 2014). With the exception of bariatric surgical procedures (Sarwer et al., 2004), no other medical procedures require a person to secure a letter of support as a requirement to access care. This requirement likely began in the late 1970s after the publication of the first version of the SOC (Berger et al., 1979).

Counselors and psychologists are encouraged to engage their TGNC clients in a collaborative process that enhances the client's control over the treatment process to the extent that is possible. Historically, mental health providers have been seen as gatekeepers (Lev, 2004, 2009). The difficulty this has caused for TGNC people is that they often feel as though they need to relate a very specific story about their gender history. This might include telling a provider that they are disgusted by their genitals or have felt as though they were not a male or female since a very young age. Fortunately, this has begun to change in the last decade as more providers are embracing a trans-affirmative approach to work with TGNC clients (Carroll, 2010).

GENDER-RELATED MEDICAL INTERVENTIONS FOR TGNC PEOPLE

Psychologists and counselors who work with TGNC people who want medical interventions in order to feel comfortable in their gender identity are to be knowledgeable about the medical interventions available to TGNC people and prepared to provide information and resources about these procedures. These medical interventions center around two areas: hormone therapy and gender-affirmation surgeries.

Hormone Therapy

Hormone therapy includes medical interventions designed to change the hormonal make-up of a person by using masculinizing or feminizing hormones (Feldman & Safer, 2009). Endocrinologists typically prescribe hormone therapy, although it may be prescribed by a primary physician (Oriel, 2000). Some major cities (e.g., Chicago, New York City, San Francisco) have informed consent models where TGNC people can access hormone therapy without needing one letter of referral from a mental health practitioner (licensed minimally at the master's level). However, most TGNC adults and all TGNC youth will need this letter of referral as recommended by the WPATH SOC (Coleman et al., 2012). As for surgical treatment, most medical providers will require two letters of referral.

TGNC people may have specific goals for hormone therapy, so it is important for psychologists and counselors to be prepared to explore and discuss these goals with TGNC clients so that the client is prepared to share these goals with their prescribing physician. TGNC people, like everyone, may also have a lack of information or misinformation about the effects of hormones. Therefore, practitioners should be prepared to discuss the myths and stereotypes while also referring clients to trusted sources of information and resources about hormone therapy. In these discussions, psychologists and counselors should explicitly refrain from providing a medical opinion on hormone therapy effects unless they hold a degree as a medical doctor, nurse practitioner, or physician's assistant. Instead, the goal is to support TGNC clients in being able to advocate for themselves with their physicians and to have any questions about hormone therapy answered by a medical provider. For instance, practitioners may refer TGNC clients to websites such as the WPATH SOC and the Center for Transgender Excellence, both of which have helpful charts describing the timelines and potential changes one might expect as a result of initiating hormone therapy. Examples of changes include the amount and texture of body hair, changes in musculature, and voice changes for those initiating the use of testosterone.

When working with TGNC youth, psychologists should be aware of both the WPATH SOC and the Endocrine Society guidelines (Hembree et al., 2009). For TGNC adolescents who would like medical interventions such as hormone therapy or puberty suppression therapy, these guidelines recommend that they see a mental health practitioner and be involved in multidisciplinary care. Practitioners should have a list of endocrinologists who work with TGNC youth in an affirming manner. This list should include endocrinologists who accept insurance, as well as endocrinologists who provide TGNC youth-affirming care at a sliding scale and/or at low cost. Often psychologists will find that even if endocrinologists have worked with TGNC adults, they may not have worked with TGNC youth—or that pediatric endocrinologists do not have experience working with TGNC youth. In these instances, practitioners should initiate collaboration and consultation with endocrinologists in order to facilitate care for TGNC clients who are youth.

The WPATH SOC (Coleman et al., 2012) specified that there are two types of hormone interventions that TGNC youth typically access. Fully reversible interventions are those that delay pubertal changes through the use of hormone therapy are often called puberty suppression. Suppressive hormone treatment delays puberty by pausing physical changes that typically happen to a TGNC youth's body based on their assigned sex at birth. Partially reversible interventions include those that may have some reversible changes and those that cannot be reversed, such as the effect testosterone has on deepening the voice. With either of the two types of hormone treatment, it can be challenging to predict the rate of physical changes from hormone therapy (see WPATH SOC for more information). For instance, two TGNC girls on the same dosage of puberty suppression may experience different rates of changes. Therefore, practitioners should ensure that TGNC youth and their family members are aware of the wide range of potential effects. Psychologists should also encourage TGNC youth and their family members to speak at length with their medical provider about these potential effects. Practitioners should also be aware that the WPATH SOC clearly state that withholding these types of hormone therapy from TGNC youth is "not a neutral option for adolescents" (Coleman et al., 2012, p. 178). This is important to note because often TGNC youth may have significant mental health concerns due to not being able to access hormone suppression therapy or subsequent hormone therapy because they are experiencing what the WPATH SOC term "gender-related abuse" (Coleman et al., 2012, p. 21) from their parents, guardians, or endocrinologists (e.g., hormone therapy is intentionally withheld).

Gender-Affirmation Surgeries

Practitioners should be aware that gender-affirmation surgeries include several different types of surgeries, and should refrain from using the more dated term of *sex reassignment surgery*. Psychologists and counselors should also be aware that many TGNC clients use the terms *bottom surgery* or *lower surgery* to denote genital surgery and *top surgery* or *chest surgery* to refer to breast removal or augmentation. These terms can be more empowering to TGNC clients, as they do not focus on the secondary sex characteristics associated with their birth assignment.

The WPATH SOC (Coleman et al., 2012) suggest that counselors and psychologists assess several components, including a client's persistent gender dysphoria, ability to consent to treatment and make an informed decision, and being the age of majority in a country (in the United States, the age of majority is, most commonly, 18 years old). One letter of referral from a mental health practitioner is needed for top surgeries. The WPATH SOC require two letters of support for bottom surgeries. These letters are provided only after a counselor or psychologist has been assured of the client's ability to consent to treatment and make an informed decision, that the client is the age of majority, and that the client been living consistently for 12 months in one's gender identity. An additional criterion is that there are no serious, extant mental health or medical concerns, and if there are co-occurring conditions, that they are well-controlled. The WPATH SOC do not explicitly require a length of mental health treatment for surgery, although "regular visits with a mental health or other medical professional" are recommended (Coleman et al., 2012, p. 202).

Typical bottom surgeries for TGNC men include metoidioplasty (release of the clitoral tissue), phalloplasty (creation of a penis), scrotoplasty (creation of the scrotum), and/or hysterectomy (removal of uterus, fallopian tubes, and ovaries). Typical bottom surgery procedures for TGNC women include vaginoplasty (creation of a vagina) and orchiectomy (removal of the testes). Other types of surgeries that are gender-affirming for TGNC women but do not require letters of referral include voice modification surgeries, lipoplasty contouring, rhinoplasty (nose surgery), reduction thyroid chondroplasty (reduction of the Adam's apple), and face-lift, among others (Coleman et al., 2012). For TGNC men, gender-affirming surgeries not requiring letters may include pectoral implants, liposuction, lipofilling, and voice chord surgery (Coleman et al., 2012).

Because psychologists and counselors still hold a gatekeeping role with regard to the power to write letters of referral for medical interventions for TGNC people, they should be mindful of how this power differential influences the counseling relationship (see Chapter 7 of this volume for more information). With regard to medical interventions, counselors and psychologists can explore this power differential by thoroughly explaining the content of letters and directly addressing any notions a TGNC client may have about these letters. For instance, TGNC people may have read online or heard through peers that they have to "say the right things" about the length of time of their gender dysphoria in order to get a letter of referral. In another example, many TGNC people have a distrust of mental health practitioners, as might be expected given the history of gatekeeping, and would prefer to access hormone therapy directly from their physician and not have to access a counselor first. Considering the distrust and myths about letter writing that exist, in addition to the inaccurate information that practitioners who are not well-trained may dispense to TGNC clients, it becomes critical to directly explore these issues and any other concerns of TGNC clients (Lev, 2009). A helpful way to address these issues is to remind the client that they have the right to TGNC-affirmative and responsive health care from all their providers, including the counselor or psychologist.

COST OF MEDICAL TRANSITION

The costs associated with a medical transition can be prohibitive. This is especially true for TGNC people who are under- or uninsured or unemployed (Grant et al., 2010). In this section, we address concerns related to insurance coverage, fund-raising ideas, and foundation support for surgical costs.

Insurance Coverage

It is not uncommon for health insurance plans to exclude coverage for transition-related care. This was the case for Medicare for at least 40 years, until the policy was updated in 2014 (NCTE, 2014). Many private insurers have followed a similar approach to exclusionary practices. For example, it is not uncommon for a health insurance policy to exclude transition-related care even if that care has been deemed medically necessary (Blue Cross Blue Shield of Louisiana, 2014). Medicaid rules are set by states, and these rules differ from one state to the next. At the time this chapter was written, it was too soon to tell whether Medicaid changes would be universal. In addition to these changes, the American Medical Association (2008) has called for a removal of the financial barriers that TGNC people face in accessing health care.

Some employers have decided to remove these exclusions. The City of San Francisco was one of the early adopters of providing access to transition-related medical care (Colvin, 2007). This program was so successful that the city ultimately stopped collecting the additional premium when they realized they were collecting more than was needed to meet the demands of care (Colvin, 2007). This additional premium had been deemed to be necessary to ensure sufficient funds in the insurance pool to pay for medical care of TGNC employees (Colvin, 2007). Other large employers have begun covering care (e.g., Apple, Chevron, Orbitz, Raytheon, TIAA-CREF, Xerox). Even the U.S. federal government has joined this group of trans-affirmative employers (Keisling, 2014). The landscape of insurance coverage and exclusions is changing rapidly, such that it is difficult to provide exact information as to where coverage is afforded.

The biggest challenge for TGNC clients is the level of care that is afforded by these employers. It may be the case that an employer will cover hormone treatments but not surgical care. They may cover medical care but not provide mental health care coverage. They may provide coverage for medical interventions but not offer a short-term disability policy that allows the TGNC person to recoup lost wages while accessing care. The Human Rights Campaign (HRC) keeps the most comprehensive compilation of coverage (see http://www.hrc.org/campaigns/corporate-equality-index). As a part of HRC's Corporate Equality Index, employers can indicate the levels of coverage offered to TGNC employees (HRC, 2013). Recent changes in the criteria for achieving a perfect score on the Index include the need to provide coverage for all transition-related care, including mental health services and short-term disability protection.

The Affordable Care Act has the potential to increase access to care (readers are referred to http://www.hhs.gov/healthcare/about-the-law/read-the-law/index.html for more information about the law). There are several areas that are addressed in the law (NCTE, 2016). First, it makes discrimination on the basis of sex illegal. This means that you cannot be denied care on the basis of your sex by a facility that is funded by the federal government. Second, as of January 1, 2014, health care can no longer be denied for preexisting conditions (NCTE, 2016). This is important, as often TGNC people will be denied care because their TGNC health care needs are seen as a preexisting condition. Third, the Affordable Care Act also addresses concerns that some TGNC people have with regard to rescission of policies and denial of care. Insurance companies are no longer allowed to cancel a policy "because of accidental mistakes or omissions in your application, . . . gender transition, or . . . changes in your health" (NCTE, 2016, p. 3).

Fund-Raising for Medical Interventions

Some TGNC people are not fortunate enough to be employed, or if they are, their employer does not provide any coverage for care. These individuals are responsible for covering the costs of care on an out-of-pocket basis. In some cases, this makes access to care impossible. In other cases, a person may be able to save or raise enough money to cover the costs. Fund-raising may be an individual activity or a community event. The first author made a concerted effort to raise the funds necessary for his chest surgery. At the time he was a full-time graduate student with part-time employment. In the end, the first author raised over 70% of the cost of the surgery. Community events may consist of garage sales, drag shows, or other fund-raising events. These events may be used to raise a pool of funds for TGNC people, or they may also be for a specific person. The limits of how to raise these funds or how to use them are restricted only by the creativity of the community.

Foundation Support for Medical Interventions

In 2011, the Jim Collins Foundation (2013) began providing financial support for TGNC people who are unable to afford the costs associated with care. Through 2013, the organization has been able to fund a total of seven people's requests for care. Typically, the people who receive this support are among the poorest applicants. For example, according to the foundation's website, a 2013 recipient was unemployed and homeless at the time of application. To the best of our knowledge, this is the only such foundation providing financial assistance for TGNC people in the United States. The application process is competitive. Unfortunately, there are not enough resources to meet the needs of those asking for assistance (e.g., in 2014 they received over 300 applications for assistance).

SUPPORTING TGNC CLIENT HEALTH THROUGHOUT THE LIFESPAN

Much has been written about the challenges that TGNC people face with regard to accessing health care related to gender concerns and general health (Bradford, Reisner, Honnold, & Xavier, 2013; Nadal, Skolnik, & Wong, 2012). Less research-based information, however, is available about how psychologists and counselors may support TGNC people in terms of staying healthy by minimizing risks and leveraging protective factors. TGNC people have everyday health needs and concerns that may or may not be associated with their gender identity. Practitioners, therefore, can help foster an emphasis on TGNC health by conducting thorough assessments and ongoing explorations of how their TGNC clients feel about their bodies, as well as any risks or protective factors they may have with regard to their health.

Healthy Sexuality

Sex and sexuality can be major physical, psychological, and emotional concerns related to TGNC health. For TGNC people who undergo a social and medical transition, there are physical changes they may experience that can affect sexual desire and sexual function. Sexual attraction may shift as TGNC clients experience transition (dickey, Burnes, & Singh, 2012). For this reason practitioners may want to provide information about potential sexual orientation changes. As in working with any client, it can also be important for counselors and psychologists to assess a client's sexual history. For TGNC clients, this information is also important because TGNC people may be at risk for higher rates of HIV/AIDS and may have important questions about sexuality no matter whether they are selecting a medical and/or social transition. These are also important components that mental health providers should keep in mind during assessment intakes. When taking a sexual history, it is helpful to emphasize a sex-positive approach so that clients feel comfortable in discussing a range of sexual practices (Buehler, 2014). Especially as TGNC clients feel more comfortable in their own gender identity and gender expression, they may naturally want to explore their bodies and possible changes to their bodies. For adult TGNC clients, these changes may mirror a "second" puberty. Practitioners should therefore be prepared to address issues of safer sex, such as the use of barriers, contraception, and condoms. This discussion can take place during intake and throughout counseling with TGNC people in an affirmative manner (Bockting, Robinson, Forberg, & Scheltema, 2005; Bockting, Rosser, & Coleman, 1999).

Many TGNC people across the lifespan may feel uncomfortable accessing sexuality-related health care services (e.g., screening for HIV/AIDS and other sexually transmitted infections) and, research has suggested that this distrust can lead to negative health outcomes for TGNC people (Bockting et al., 2005). Thus, counselors and psychologists should assess how frequently TGNC clients access sexual health and prevention screenings. If TGNC clients are hesitant or unaware of general health and prevention screenings, practitioners should explore these fears and be able to provide a list of TGNC-affirmative physicians and health centers.

Body Image and Eating-Related Concerns

Although research on body image and disordered eating in TGNC adults is limited and research with young TGNC people in this area is absent, these concerns may be evident in counseling with TGNC people across the lifespan. In a qualitative study on disordered eating and gender identity with 20 TGNC people, the authors found that the majority of their sample shared past experiences of disordered eating (Ålgars, Alanko, Santtila, & Sandnabba, 2012). For the TGNC women and men in this sample who reported past or current disordered eating, societal stereotypes of masculinity or femininity were a major influence on their feelings about their bodies. Many of the participants shared that their disordered eating and feelings about their body shifted positively after they had completed a medical transition. TGNC male participants in the study described attempts to reduce body areas such as hips and breasts in order to emphasize masculinity. TGNC female participants shared that they were attempting to become more feminine by losing weight to reduce their body frame.

The implications for counselors and psychologists are many from this study, including the importance of not only assessing previous and current histories of disordered eating but also continuing to explore the influence of social and medical transitions on TGNC people's feelings about their bodies. In addition, providers may normalize changing feelings TGNC clients may have about their bodies and share examples of positive TGNC body image with them. Openly exploring the influence of societal stereotypes on disordered eating and body image is also important (Murray, Boon, & Touyz, 2013). In doing so, counselors and psychologists should be prepared to explore issues of grief and loss related to body image (Murray et al., 2013). For instance, a person assigned male at birth, but who identifies as a woman, may not have experienced as much social pressure around body image when she was socialized as male; however, this same TGNC woman may experience significant distress about the multiple sexist messages in the media or societal assumptions about what women's bodies "should look like." A major barrier to clients accessing services for eating-related issues may be related to fears of experiencing trans-prejudice. Therefore, for those TGNC youth or adults who are experiencing disordered eating, psychologists and counselors should have access to a list of referrals to disordered eating support groups and residential treatment centers that are TGNC affirmative. Providers should be prepared to consult and/or advocate for TGNC clients with these service providers at the beginning and throughout treatment.

Reproductive Health and Family Building

A physical health concern of TGNC people may center on reproductive health and family-building concerns. Psychologists and counselors should explore reproductive concerns with TGNC clients prior to accessing hormone therapy, as this medical intervention may impact current and/or future reproductive health (dickey, Ducheny, & Ehrbar, in press). Practitioners should also be prepared to discuss these concerns with all TGNC people across the lifespan. For instance, a practitioner working with a TGNC adolescent should discuss potential reproductive goals and the challenges of having to consider these concerns at a young age (Coleman et al., 2012; dickey et al., in press). Practitioners should be aware of and able to help TGNC people access health care providers who offer egg (oocyte) or sperm (semen) cryopreservation, if clients are interested in doing so. Practitioners should also be aware of the TGNC-affirmative family-building treatment providers in their area, as TGNC people may want to access in vitro fertilization, surrogacy, or other fertility options (James-Abra, 2012).

As TGNC people access family-building services, providers often work with their partner(s) and other family members in counseling. Counselors and psychologists should note that TGNC people may select many types of family-building options, such as adoption, blended families, and families of choice (dickey et al., in press; Polly & Polly, 2014). Exploring the hopes, fears, challenges, and strengths TGNC people and their loved ones have related to family building is an important practitioner role. In addition, practitioners can refer clients and their families to family-building education and support groups that are geared towards LGBTQ families or are TGNC affirmative. The range of success with reproductive technologies varies. TGNC people who do not have challenges in terms of reproductive concerns and fertility may indeed face other challenges related to family building. For instance, TGNC people may have difficulty in accessing adoption services that are TGNC affirming or completing adoption paperwork. It can be common to address issues of grief and loss during the family-building process. Grief and loss may arise out of difficulties associated with fertility and attempts to carry a child to term. Grief and loss can also be experienced as TGNC people navigate foster and adoptive options for building their family.

CONCLUSION

This chapter addressed a variety of health care concerns that affect the lives of TGNC clients. Psychologists and counselors play a key role in educating and advocating for the health care needs of their clients. It should be clear that there is no one right way for a TGNC person to make a medical transition. Providers are encouraged to build collaborative teams to address the holistic needs of their TGNC clients. Providers must understand that a client's needs may change over time, and one client's needs and expectations are likely to be different from those of the next client. As a result, it is important to remain flexible when working to with TGNC clients. In the end, the clients hold the autonomy for the medical choices they make. Providers are partners who have been invited on the journey of their clients.

REFERENCES

Alderson, K. (2014, September 17). Ethical situation that affects my practice with trans clients [E-mail list message]. Retrieved from https://groups.google.com/a/umn.edu/forum/#!topic/wpath-membership/TLRPIFj7xnU

Ålgars, M., Alanko, K., Santtila, P., & Sandnabba, N. K. (2012). Disordered eating and gender identity disorder: A qualitative study. *Eating Disorders: The Journal of Treatment & Prevention, 20*, 300–311. http://dx.doi.org/10.1080/10640266.2012.668482

American Medical Association. (2008). *Removing financial barriers to care for transgender patients*. Retrieved from http://www.ama-assn.org/ama/pub/about-ama/our-people/member-groups-sections/glbt-advisory-committee/ama-policy-regarding-sexual-orientation.page

American Psychiatric Association. (2000). *Diagnostic and statistical manual of mental disorders* (4th ed., text rev.). Washington, DC: Author.

American Psychiatric Association. (2013). *Diagnostic and statistical manual of mental disorders* (5th ed.). Arlington, VA: Author.

American Psychological Association. (2010). *Ethical principles of psychologists and code of conduct (2002, amended June 1, 2010)*. Retrieved from http://www.apa.org/ethics/code/principles.pdf

Berger, J. C., Green, R., Laub, D. R., Reynolds, C. L., Jr., Walker, P. A., & Wollman, L. (1979). *Standards of care: The hormonal and surgical reassignment of gender dysphoric persons*. Galveston, TX: Janus Information Facility.

Blue Cross Blue Shield of Louisiana. (2014). *Blue Cross HMO plan for state of Louisiana employees and retirees*. Baton Rouge, LA: Author.

Bockting, W. O., Benner, A., & Coleman, E. (2009). Gay and bisexual identity development among female-to-male transsexuals in North America: Emergence of a transgender sexuality. *Archives of Sexual Behavior, 38*, 688–701. http://dx.doi.org/10.1007/s10508-009-9489-3

Bockting, W. O., & Ehrbar, R. D. (2005). Commentary: Gender variance, dissonance, or identity disorder? In D. Karasic & J. Drescher (Eds.), *Sexual and gender diagnoses of the Diagnostic and Statistical Manual (DSM): A reevaluation* (pp. 125–134). New York, NY: Haworth.

Bockting, W. O., Robinson, B. E., Forberg, J., & Scheltema, K. (2005). Evaluation of a sexual health approach to reducing HIV/STD risk in the transgender community. *AIDS Care, 17*, 289–303. http://dx.doi.org/10.1080/09540120412331299825

Bockting, W. O., Rosser, B. R. S., & Coleman, E. (1999). Transgender HIV prevention: Community involvement and empowerment. *International Journal of Transgenderism, 3*(1/2).

Bradford, J., Reisner, S. L., Honnold, J. A., & Xavier, J. (2013). Experiences of trans-gender-related discrimination and implications for health: Results from the Virginia Transgender Health Initiative Study. *American Journal of Public Health, 103*, 1820–1829. http://dx.doi.org/10.2105/AJPH.2012.300796

Brown, G. R., & McDuffie, E. (2009). Health care policies addressing transgender inmates in prison systems in the United States. *Journal of Correctional Health Care, 15*, 280–291. http://dx.doi.org/10.1177/1078345809340423

Buehler, S. (2014). *What every mental health professional needs to know about sex.* New York, NY: Springer.

Burnes, T. R., & Chen, M. M. (2012). The multiple identities of transgender indi-viduals: Incorporating a framework of intersectionality to gender crossing. In R. Josselson & M. Harway (Eds.), *Navigating multiple identities: Race, gender, culture, nationality, and roles* (pp. 113–127). New York, NY: Oxford University. http://dx.doi.org/10.1093/acprof:oso/9780199732074.003.0007

Butcher, J. N., Graham, J. R., Ben-Porath, Y. S., Tellegen, A., Dahlstrom, W. G., & Kaemmer, B. (2001). *Minnesota Multiphasic Personality Inventory—2: Manual for administration, scoring, and interpretation* (Rev. ed.). Minneapolis: University of Minnesota.

Carmel, T., Hopwood, R., & dickey, m. (2014). Mental health. In L. Erickson-Schroth (Ed.), *Trans bodies, trans selves: A resource for the transgender community* (pp. 305–332). New York, NY: Oxford University Press.

Carroll, L. (2010). *Counseling sexual and gender minorities.* Upper Saddle River, NJ: Pearson.

Center of Excellence for Transgender Health. (2013). *Assessing readiness for hormones.* Retrieved from http://transhealth.ucsf.edu/trans?page=protocol-hormone-ready

Coleman, E., Bockting, W., Botzer, M., Cohen-Kettenis, P., DeCuypere, G., Feldman, J., ... Zucker, K. (2012). Standards of care for the health of transsexual, trans-gender, and gender-nonconforming people, Version 7. *International Journal of Transgenderism, 13*, 165–232. http://dx.doi.org/10.1080/15532739.2011.700873

Colvin, R. A. (2007). The rise of transgender-inclusive laws: How well are munici-palities implementing supportive nondiscrimination public employment poli-cies? *Review of Public Personnel Administration, 27*, 336–360. http://dx.doi.org/10.1177/1077800407301777

Deutsch, M. B. (2012). Use of the Informed Consent Model in the provision of cross-sex hormone therapy: A survey of the practices of selected clinics. *International Journal of Transgenderism, 13*, 140–146. http://dx.doi.org/10.1080/15532739.2011.675233

dickey, l. m., Burnes, T. R., & Singh, A. A. (2012). Sexual identity develop-ment of female-to-male transgender individuals: A grounded theory inquiry. *Journal of LGBT Issues in Counseling, 6*, 118–138. http://dx.doi.org/10.1080/15538605.2012.678184

dickey, l. m., Ducheny, K., & Ehrbar, R. D. (in press). Family creation options for transgender and gender nonconforming people. *Psychology of Sexual Orientation and Gender Diversity, 3*(2).

dickey, l. m., Fedewa, A., & Hirsch, A. (2014). Diagnostic changes: Gender dysphoria. *Communique, 42*(7), 1–16.

Drescher, J. (2010). Queer diagnoses: Parallels and contrasts in the history of homosexuality, gender variance, and the Diagnostic and Statistical Manual. *Archives of Sexual Behavior, 39*, 427–460. http://dx.doi.org/10.1007/s10508-009-9531-5

Drescher, J. (2013). Controversies in gender diagnoses. *LGBT Health, 1*, 10–14. http://dx.doi.org/10.1089/lgbt.2013.1500

Drescher, J., Cohen-Kettenis, P., & Winter, S. (2012). Minding the body: Situating gender identity diagnosis in the *ICD–11*. *International Review of Psychiatry, 24*, 568–577. http://dx.doi.org/10.3109/09540261.2012.741575

Ettner, R., Monstrey, S., & Eyler, A. E. (Eds.). (2007). *Principles of transgender medicine and surgery*. New York, NY: Haworth Press.

Feldman, J., & Safer, J. (2009). Hormone therapy in adults: Suggested revisions to the sixth version of the standards of care. *International Journal of Transgenderism, 11*, 146–182. http://dx.doi.org/10.1080/15532730903383757

Gehi, P. S., & Arkles, G. (2007). Unraveling injustice: Race and class impact of Medicaid exclusions of transition-related health care for transgender people. *Sexuality Research & Social Policy, 4*(4), 7–35. http://dx.doi.org/10.1525/srsp.2007.4.4.7

Gorton, R. N. (2007). Transgender health benefits: Collateral damage in the resolution of the National Health care financing dilemma. *Sexuality Research & Social Policy, 4*(4), 81–91. http://dx.doi.org/10.1525/srsp.2007.4.4.81

Gorton, R. N. (2013). Transgender as mental illness: Nosology, social justice, and the tarnished mean. In S. Stryker & A. Z. Aizura (Eds.), *The transgender studies reader* (2nd ed., pp. 644–652). New York, NY: Routledge.

Gorton, R. N., Buth, J., & Spade, D. (2005). *Medical therapy & health maintenance for transgender men: A guide for health care providers*. Retrieved from http://www.nickgorton.org/Medical%20Therapy%20and%20HM%20for%20Transgender%20Men_2005.pdf

Graham, J. R. (2006). *MMPI–2: Assessing personality and psychopathology* (4th ed.). New York, NY: Oxford University.

Grant, J. M., Mottet, L. A., Tanis, J., Herman, J. L., Harrison, J., & Keisling, M. (2010). *Injustice at every turn: A report of the National Transgender Discrimination Survey*. Washington, DC: National Center for Transgender Equality and National Gay and Lesbian Task Force.

Hembree, W. C., Cohen-Kettenis, P., Delemarre-van de Waal, H. A., Gooren, L. J., Meyer, W. J., III, Spack, N. P., . . . Montori, V. M. (2009). Endocrine treatment of transsexual persons: An Endocrine Society clinical practice guideline. *The Journal of Clinical Endocrinology and Metabolism, 94*, 3132–3154. http://dx.doi.org/10.1210/jc.2009-0345

Human Rights Campaign. (2013). *Corporate Equality Index 2014*. Retrieved from http://www.hrc.org/resources/corporate-equality-index-2014-statements-from-employers-that-rated-100-perc

Iantaffi, A., & Bockting, W. O. (2011). Views from both sides of the bridge? Gender, sexual legitimacy and transgender people's experiences of relationships. *Culture, Health & Sexuality, 13*, 355–370. http://dx.doi.org/10.1080/13691058.2010.537770

James-Abra, S. (2012). *Access to assisted human reproduction (AHR) services for trans people in Ontario* (Unpublished master's thesis). Retrieved from http://hdl.handle.net/1807/33252

Jim Collins Foundation. (2013). *Jim Collins Foundation awards its first grant for gender confirming surgery.* Retrieved from http://jimcollinsfoundation.org/jim-collins-foundation-awards-its-first-grant-for-gender-confirming-surgery/

Keisling, M. (2014). *Op-ed: Victories for trans health care are closer than we dreamed.* Retrieved from http://www.advocate.com/commentary/2014/06/24/op-ed-victories-trans-health-care-are-closer-we-dreamed

Knudson, G., De Cuypere, G., & Bockting, W. O. (2010). Recommendations for revision of the DSM diagnoses of gender identity disorders: Consensus statement of the World Professional Association for Transgender Health. *International Journal of Transgenderism, 12*, 115–118. http://dx.doi.org/10.1080/15532739.2010.509215

Lenton, S., & Single, E. (1998). The definition of harm reduction. *Drug and Alcohol Review, 17*, 213–219. http://dx.doi.org/10.1080/09595239800187011

Lev, A. I. (2004). *Transgender emergence: Therapeutic guidelines for working with gender-variant people and their families.* New York, NY: Haworth.

Lev, A. I. (2005). Disordering gender identity: Gender identity disorder in the DSM–IV–TR. In D. Karasic & J. Drescher (Eds.), *Sexual and gender diagnoses of the Diagnostic and Statistical Manual (DSM): A reevaluation* (pp. 35–69). New York, NY: Haworth.

Lev, A. I. (2009). The ten tasks of the mental health provider: Recommendations for revision of the World Professional Association for Transgender Health's Standards of Care. *International Journal of Transgenderism, 11*, 74–99. http://dx.doi.org/10.1080/15532730903008032

Lev, A. I. (2013). Gender dysphoria: Two steps forward, one step back. *Clinical Social Work Journal, 41*, 288–296. http://dx.doi.org/10.1007/s10615-013-0447-0

Moore, E., Wisnewski, A., & Dobs, A. (2003). Endocrine treatment of transsexual people: A review of treatment regimens, outcomes, and adverse effects. *The Journal of Clinical Endocrinology and Metabolism, 88*, 3467–3473. http://dx.doi.org/10.1210/jc.2002-021967

Murray, S. B., Boon, E., & Touyz, S. W. (2013). Diverging eating psychopathology in transgendered eating disorder patients: A report of two cases. *Eating Disorders: The Journal of Treatment & Prevention, 21*, 70–74. http://dx.doi.org/10.1080/10640266.2013.741989

Nadal, K. L., Skolnik, A., & Wong, Y. (2012). Interpersonal and systemic microaggressions toward transgender people: Implications for counseling. *Journal of LGBT Issues in Counseling, 6*, 55–82. http://dx.doi.org/10.1080/15538605.2012.648583

Nagoshi, J. L., Brzuzy, S., & Terrell, H. K. (2012). Deconstructing the complex perceptions of gender roles, gender identity, and sexual orientation among transgender individuals. *Feminism & Psychology, 22*, 405–422. http://dx.doi.org/10.1177/0959353512461929

National Center for Transgender Equality. (2016). *Health care rights and transgender people*. Retrieved from http://transequality.org/sites/default/files/docs/kyr/KYR-Healthcare-May-2016.pdf

National Center for Transgender Equality. (2014). *Medicare and transgender people*. Retrieved from http://transequality.org/PDFs/MedicareAndTransPeople.pdf

Ophelian, A. (2009). *Diagnosing difference* [Motion picture]. San Francisco, CA: Floating Ophelia Productions.

Oriel, K. A. (2000). Clinical update: Medical care of transsexual patients. *Journal of the Gay & Lesbian Medical Association, 4*, 185–194. http://dx.doi.org/10.1023/A:1026563806480

Polly, K., & Polly, R. G. (2014). Parenting. In L. Erickson-Schroth (Ed.), *Trans bodies, trans selves: A resource for the transgender community* (pp. 390–405). New York, NY: Oxford University Press.

Richmond, K. A., Burnes, T. R., & Carroll, K. (2012). Lost in translation: Interpreting systems of trauma for transgender clients. *Traumatology, 18*(1), 45–57. http://dx.doi.org/10.1177/1534765610396726

Sarwer, D. B., Cohn, N. I., Gibbons, L. M., Magee, L., Crerand, C. E., Raper, S. E., ... Wadden, T. A. (2004). Psychiatric diagnoses and psychiatric treatment among bariatric surgery candidates. *Obesity Surgery, 14*(9), 1148–1156. http://dx.doi.org/10.1381/0960892042386922

Singh, A. A., & McKleroy, V. S. (2011). "Just getting out of bed is a revolutionary act": The resilience of transgender people of color who have survived traumatic life events. *Traumatology, 17*(2), 34–44. http://dx.doi.org/10.1177/1534765610369261

Spade, D., Arkles, G., Duran, P., Gehi, P., & Nguyen, H. (2010). Medicaid policy and gender-confirming health care for trans people: An interview with advocates. *Seattle Journal for Social Justice, 8*, 497–514.

Vanderburgh, R. (2007). *Transition and beyond: Observation on gender identity*. Portland, OR: Q Press.

Winters, K. (2005). Gender dissonance: Diagnostic reform of Gender Identity Disorder for adults. In D. Karasic & J. Drescher (Eds.), *Sexual and gender diagnoses of the Diagnostic and Statistical Manual (DSM): A reevaluation* (pp. 71–89). New York, NY: Haworth.

Winters, K. (2008). *Gender madness in American psychiatry: Essays from the struggle for dignity* (text rev.). Dillon, CO: GID Reform Advocates.

World Professional Association for Transgender Health. (2010). *WPATH depsychopathologization statement*. Retrieved from http://www.wpath.org/uploaded_files/140/files/de-psychopathologisation%205-26-10%20on%20letterhead.pdf

AFTERWORD

KURT A. DeBORD, ANN R. FISCHER, KATHLEEN J. BIESCHKE,
AND RUPERTO M. PEREZ

This edition of the *Handbook of Sexual Orientation and Gender Diversity in Counseling and Psychotherapy* was written during a time of significant political and social change for sexual minority (SM) and transgender and gender nonconforming (TGNC) people in the United States. For SM people, the U.S. Supreme Court's decision to recognize and legalize same-sex marriage was not even a year old when this book went to press. As the political legitimization of these relationships seeps into the consciousness of the average U.S. citizen, we anticipate further changes. For TGNC individuals, during the last 3 years the exposure that transgender issues have received in the media and in popular culture mirrors the exposure that sexual minority issues received in the 1990s. If there are parallels to be drawn, we anticipate that positive legal and social changes will likely accompany the increased exposure. However, as many collective identity movements have demonstrated, such changes do not come without struggle. In the paragraphs that follow, we

http://dx.doi.org/10.1037/15959-018
Handbook of Sexual Orientation and Gender Diversity in Counseling and Psychotherapy, K. A. DeBord,
A. R. Fischer, K. J. Bieschke, and R. M. Perez (Editors)

identify some of the challenges that will likely face mental health practitioners and SM and TGNC people before the production of our next edition of the *Handbook*. Excuse us as we get a little bit political.

LANGUAGE AND THE CATEGORIES THAT PEOPLE USE TO IDENTIFY SELF AND OTHERS WILL TRANSFORM AS OUR THINKING DOES

As Nelson (2015) highlighted, we are in constant struggle between our need to categorize and our need to allow the process of "becoming." This dynamic tension led Fassinger, in Chapter 1 of the present volume, to reshape what was traditionally known as lesbian, gay, bisexual, transgender, queer (LGBTQ)–affirmative therapy into a more expansive *transgression-affirmative therapy*. We make no predictions about what terms will emerge during the next few years. At the same time, we agree with Nelson's thoughts on the matter:

> How does one get across the fact that the best way to find out how people feel about their gender or their sexuality—or anything else, really—is to listen to what they tell you, and to try to treat them accordingly, without shellacking over their version of reality with yours? (p. 53)

This is not to say that categories and terms do not matter. This is to say that allowing our clients their space to continuously grow is a priority, as is supporting and empowering our clients as they claim their own spaces and ways to grow.

WE ANTICIPATE POLITICAL BACKLASH

Categories matter because of the implications they have for the lived experiences of our clients. The categories of sexual minority, transgender, and gender nonconforming will have new meaning to people who oppose the civil liberties and equal rights newly afforded to these groups in the U.S. People with prejudice against SM and TGNC individuals will be apt to feel threatened by the direction of social change they perceive. Our goals, as editors of this *Handbook*, include recognizing that change, alone, is threatening to some people. Simultaneously, we aspire to challenge everyone, ourselves included, to be aware of whatever privileges we carry as members of the racial, sexual, gendered, age, socioeconomic status, ability status, and religious groups that we are a part of. Only by consistently confronting the unearned advantages that people benefit from (consciously or unconsciously) and use because of their group memberships can the ethical principles of justice and fairness be upheld in our professional and personal lives.

In a related vein, practitioners and researchers should constantly be mindful of intersectionality while endeavoring to understand and serve our populations of interest. We think the field of SM and TGNC psychology will become enriched as we move away from using simplistic prototypes of bisexual people, lesbian women, gay men, or transgendered people. For example, Black, lesbian women are not often thought about when someone mentions Black person, lesbian, or woman. Marginalization of Black, lesbian women typically manifests itself as invisibility. Their stories are often not heard or considered. The same is true for all who claim or are assigned multiple, stigmatized identities. This marginalization as invisibility process must change if our work is to be truly beneficial to everyone in the future.

ADDITIONAL, MAJOR POLITICAL AND SOCIAL CHALLENGES WILL FACE US IN THE YEARS AHEAD

True equality for TGNC people must be recognized and gender-neutral accommodations in public spaces must be made available (Avery, 2015). The Employment Nondiscrimination Act, if passed, would guarantee work security for thousands of SM and TGNC people. Parenting and adoption rights must be extended to SM and TGNC people as they are to heterosexual, cisgendered (i.e., someone whose gender corresponds to their assigned sex) people. We have a responsibility to ensure that proper senior care is available and accessible to SM/TGNC people. We also have a responsibility to ensure that violence towards SM/TGNC youth decreases. Finally, we can only hope that the coming years see an end to AIDS as a condition that compromises and ends the lives of so many people.

We have identified a few of the issues that we anticipate will hold our attention and, hopefully, motivate us to action in the years ahead. As editors of this *Handbook*, we have been tremendously inspired by the changes that have occurred since we started producing the first edition in 1996. We hope that the pages in this edition will serve to nourish continued, positive growth in the years that it is in print.

REFERENCES

Avery, D. (2015, June 30). *What's next: 7 issues facing the LGBT community after marriage equality*. Retrieved from http://www.newnownext.com/whats-next-7-issues-facing-the-lgbt-community-after-marriage-equality/06/2015/

Nelson, M. (2015). *The Argonauts*. Minneapolis, MN: Graywolf Press.

APPENDIX: RESOURCE LIST

WEBSITES

American Counseling Association: http://www.algbtic.org
American Psychological Association: http://www.apa.org/pi/lgbt/programs/ transgender/
APA Division 44: http://www.apadivisions.org/division-44/index.aspx
Center of Excellence for Transgender Health: http://transhealth.ucsf.edu
FORGE: http://www.forge-forward.org
Gay Lesbian Medical Association: http://glma.org/
Gay, Lesbian & Straight Education Network: http://www.glsen.org
GSA Network: http://www.gsanetwork.org
Gender Odyssey: http://www.genderodyssey.org/
Gender Spectrum: http://www.genderspectrum.org/
Jim Collins Foundation: http://jimcollinsfoundation.org/
Lambda Legal: http://www.lambdalegal.org
LGBT Senior Living Resources: http://www.seniorliving.org/lifestyles/ gay-senior-living/
National Center for Transgender Equality: http://www.transequality.org
National LGBTQ Task Force: http://www.thetaskforce.org
National Youth Advocacy Coalition: http://www.nyacyouth.org
PFLAG: http://community.pflag.org/
Servicemembers Legal Defense Network: http://www.sldn.org/
Services & Advocacy for Gay, Lesbian, Bisexual & Transgender Elders: http://www.sageusa.org
Soulforce: http://www.soulforce.org
Sylvia Rivera Law Project: http://www.srlp.org
Trans Youth and Family Allies: http://www.imatyfa.org
Transgender Law Center: http://www.transgenderlawcenter.org
Transgender Legal Defense & Education Fund: http://www.transgenderlegal.org
World Professional Association of Transgender Health: http://www.wpath.org

BOOKS[1]

On the Couch With Dr. Angello: A Guide to Raising and Supporting Transgender Youth by Michele Angello*
The Lives of Transgender People by Genny Beemyn and Susan Rankin

---

[1]All of these books are helpful for psychologists to read, and the books specifically addressing counseling transgender nonconforming people are marked with asterisks.

Speaking Out: LGBTQ Youth Stand Up by Steve Berman

Gender Outlaw by Kate Bornstein

She's Not the Man I Married: My Life With a Transgender Husband
    by Helen Boyd

The Transgender Child: A Handbook for Families and Professionals
    by Stephanie Brill and Rachel Pepper*

Counseling Sexual and Gender Minorities by Lynne Carroll*

Brown Boi Project: Freeing Ourselves edited by B. Cole and Luna Han

Hung Jury: Testimonies of Genital Surgery by Transsexual Men by Trystan
    Theosophus Cotten

From the Inside Out: Radical Gender Transformation, FTM and Beyond
    by Morty Diamond

Gender Born, Gender Made: Raising Healthy Gender-Nonconforming Children
    by Diane Ehrensaft

Head Over Heels: Wives Who Stay With Crossdressers and Transsexuals
    by Virginia Erhardt

Trans Bodies, Trans Selves: A Resource for the Transgender Community edited
    by Laura Erickson-Schroth

Transgender Warriors: Making History From Joan of Arc to Dennis Rodman
    by Leslie Feinberg

Becoming a Visible Man by Jamison Green

*Where's MY Book? A Guide for Transgender and Gender Non-Conforming
    Youth, Their Parents, & Everyone Else* by Linda Gromko

*Transgender Emergence: Therapeutic Guidelines for Working With Gender-
    Variant People and Their Families* by Arlene Lev*

*When the Opposite Sex Isn't: Sexual Orientation in Male-to-Female Transgender
    People* by Sandra L. Samons

*Whipping Girl: A Transsexual Woman on Sexism and the Scapegoating of
    Femininity* by Julia Serano

The Complete Guide to Transgender in the Workplace by Vanessa Sheridan

*The Testosterone Files: My Hormonal and Social Transformation from Female to
    Male* by Max Wolf Valerio

Transition and Beyond: Observations on Gender Identity by Reid Vanderburgh*

FILMS

The Adventures of Priscilla, Queen of the Desert (1994)

Against a Trans Narrative (2008)

The Aggressives (2005)

Albert Nobbs (2011)

Be Like Others (2008)

Beautiful Boxer (2004)

Becoming Chaz (2011)
The Birdcage (1996)
Bob's New Suit (2011)
Boy I Am (2006)
Boys Don't Cry (1999)
The Brandon Teena Story (1998)
Breakfast on Pluto (2005)
By Hook or By Crook (2000)
Cabaret (1972)
The Cockettes (2002)
Cruel & Unusual (2006)
The Crying Game (1992)
The Danish Girl (2012)
Diagnosing Difference (2009)
Different for Girls (1996)
Ed Wood (1994)
Female Trouble (1975)
Forever's Gonna Start Tonight (2009)
Gendernauts (1999)
Gun Hill Road (2011)
Hedwig and the Angry Inch (2001)
I Want What I Want (1972)
Just Call Me Kade (2001)
Kinky Boots (2005)
Kiss of the Spider Woman (1985)
La Cage Aux Folles (1978)
The Last Summer of La Boyita (2009)
Leave It On The Floor (2011)
M. Butterfly (1993)
Ma Vie en Rose (1997)
Madame X (2011)
Miwa: A Japanese Icon (2011)
The Mouth of the Wolf (2011)
Mrs. Doubtfire (1993)
Myra Breckenridge (1970)
No Dumb Questions (2001)
Normal (2003)
Orchids: My Intersex Adventure (2011)
Orlando (1992)
Outrageous (1977)
Pageant (2008)
Paris Is Burning (1990)

Prodigal Sons (2008)
Red Without Blue (2007)
Renee (2011)
The Rocky Horror Picture Show (1975)
Romeos (2011)
Screaming Queens: The Riot at Compton's Cafeteria (2005)
Second Serve (1986)
She's a Boy I Knew (2008)
Shortbus (2006)
Soldier's Girl (2003)
Southern Comfort (2001)
Tales of the Waria (2010)
Tomboy (2011)
To Wong Foo, Thanks for Everything! Julie Newmar (1995)
Torch Song Trilogy (1987)
Trained in the Ways of Men (2007)
Trans: The Movie (2012)
TransAmerica (2005)
TransGenderf*ation (2011)
TransGeneration (2005)
Transparent (2005)
Unveiled (2005)
Vera (1986)
Victor/Victoria (1982)
Yentl (1983)
You Don't Know Dick (1997)

CRISIS HOTLINES AND SUPPORT GROUPS

Camp Aranu'tiq for TGNC Youth: http://www.camparanutiq.org
Laura's Playground Online Support Groups: http://www.lauras-playground.com
Philadelphia Trans Health Conference: http://www.trans-health.org/
The Trevor Project Crisis Line: http://www.thetrevorproject.org

HEALTH CLINICS[2]

Callen-Lorde Community Health Center (New York, NY)*
Chase Brexton Health Care (Baltimore, MD)

---

[2]Clinics marked with asterisks are known to use informed consent treatment for hormones. For a complete listing of LGBTQ Health Centers readers are referred to CenterLink, The Community of LGBT Centers: http://www.lgbtcenters.org/

Feminist Women's Health Center (Atlanta, GA)
Fenway Health (Boston, MA)*
Gay Men's Health Crisis (New York, NY)
Hartford Gay & Lesbian Health Collective (Hartford, CT)
Howard Brown Health Center (Chicago, IL)*
L.A. Gay & Lesbian Center (Los Angeles, CA)*
Legacy Community Health Services (Houston, TX)
Lyon-Martin Health Services (San Francisco, CA)*
Mazzoni Center (Philadelphia, PA)*
Persad Center (Pittsburgh, PA)
Tom Wadell Clinic (San Francisco, CA)*
Whitman-Walker Health Center (Washington, DC)*

INDEX

Association of Welcoming and Affirm-
ing Baptists, 217
Atran, S., 87
Attachment theory, 244

Baiocco, R., 242
Balsam, K. F., 350, 398
Baptist faith, 217–218
Bariatric surgical procedures, 424
Barnes, D. M., 221
Barres, B., 33
Barrett, R., 224
Bartkowski, J. P., 53–54
Bartoli, E., 223, 302
Barzan, R., 224
Bathrooms, 10, 203, 281. *See also*
restrooms
Beadnell, B., 398
Beckstead, (A.) L., 138, 223, 297, 302
Berger, P., 76
Berry, J. W., 146
Bess, J. A., 338
Bidell, M. P., 340, 370
Bieschke, K. J., 131, 138, 146, 148
Bimbi, D. S., 222
Biological research, 51–65
and forbidden knowledge, 55
on the "gay gene," 54–55
on genetics, 58–60, 64
on hormones, 56–58
media portrayal of, 51
on neuroanatomy, 60–63
and public opinion, 53–54
types of, 56–63
Biopsychosocial model, 53
Biphobia
internalized, 91
and minority stress, 136
Birth certificates, 175
Bisexuality, 9, 51, 81, 114, 136, 198,
221, 313, 339, 340, 341, 342, 343,
344, 348, 349, 369, 372, 392, 393,
394, 396. *See also* Health issues of
lesbian, gay, and bisexual clients;
Sexual minority people
Bisson, J. I., 192
Black feminism, 105–109
Body image, 431–432
Bohan, J. S., 23
Bordeyne, P., 216

Borgman, A. L., 352
Bottom surgery, 427
Bowleg, L., 115
Boys Don't Cry (film), 197
Bozard, R. J., 226, 228
Bradshaw, W. S., 344
Brain
autopsies of, 60–62
MRI studies of, 62–63
sexual dimorphism, 61, 63, 64
structure, 61, 63, 64, 65
Breast cancer, 396–397
Brewster, M. E., 136
Brill, S., 171
Brooks, L. M., 342
Brown, L. S., 95, 134
Brownell, K. D., 394
Buddhism, 215
Budge, S. L., 338, 339
Bullying
prevalence of, 243, 396
in school environments, 171, 349
and trauma, 190, 195, 243
Burckell, L. A., 341
Burkard, A. W., 340
Burke, A., 222
Burnes, T. R., 337
Buser, J. K., 225, 351–352
Buser, T. J., 225, 351–352
Buth, J., 424
Butler, Judith, 35
Butterworth, M., 118

California, 166, 169, 298
Campbell, H. A., 215
Canada, 279
Cancer, 396–397
Cardiovascular disease, 392, 396–397
Caregivers, 167–168
Caregiving, 275
Carney, J. S., 340
Career. *See also* Employment
and social constructionism, 37–40, 44
Carter, L., 136
Cass, V. C., 76
Castonguay, L. G., 346
Catholicism, 216–217, 225
CDC (Centers for Disease Control),
245, 400
Cederbaum, J. A., 396–397

Counseling and therapy, 83–92. *See also specific headings*

The Counseling Psychologist (journal), 378

Couples therapy, 254, 294, 375

Crenshaw, Kimberle, 108, 121–122

Crisis competence, 94

Croteau, J. M., 119, 138

Crowell, K. A., 344

Cultural competence, 186, 281

Custody arrangements, 172, 315, 317, 323

D'Augelli, A. R., 94, 241, 243

Davis, Angela, 107

Davison, Gerald C., 292, 298

Death penalty, 150

DeBlaere, C., 348

DeBord, K. A., 131

Defense of Marriage Act (DOMA), 279, 403

Dehlin, J. P., 224, 344

Deleon, J., 244

Delgado-Romero, E. A., 139, 225

Demographic competence, 148

Dency, A. K., 146

Depression, 246, 305, 345, 391

DES (diethylstilbestrol), 57–58

De Vries, B., 389

Diabetes, 390, 392, 424

Diagnostic and Statistical Manual of Mental Disorders (DSM)
  gender identity disorder terminology in, 337, 419, 421, 423
  removal of homosexuality from, 26
  trauma in, 184, 185, 191, 192

Diamond, L. M., 32, 63, 118, 347

Dickinson, Robert, 25

Diethylstilbestrol (DES), 57–58

DignityUSA, 216

Dillon, F. R., 371

Disability
  and affirmative counseling with sexual minority clients, 141, 144
  and hate crimes, 5
  and insurance coverage during medical transition, 429
  and LGB/TGNC aging adults, 275, 277, 278

research on, 350–351

and TGNC-affirmative counseling, 159

Discreditable identity, 88–89

Discredited identity, 88–89

Discrimination. *See also specific forms of discrimination, e.g.:* Sexism
  and affirmative counseling with sexual minority clients, 143, 150
  and beliefs about genetics, 54
  decreases in, 318
  as distal stressor, 160, 186, 188, 347, 395
  high rates of, 3
  institutionalized forms of, 22, 335, 402
  and intersectionality, 108, 113, 115–116. *See also* Intersectionality
  legal protection against, 80, 81, 82, 108, 174
  and LGB/TGNC aging adults, 269–270, 278
  and minority stress, 36, 136, 390
  and obesity, 391, 395
  and psychological distress, 113, 114, 116, 135, 136
  in school environments, 349
  and sexual orientation change interventions, 292
  and social constructionism, 30
  and stigma, 78, 86–87, 143
  and trauma, 190, 195

Distal stressors, 160, 188, 347

Division of labor, 38, 321–322

Doll, M., 244

DOMA (Defense of Marriage Act), 279, 403

Donor insemination, 323–324, 406–407

Don't Ask, Don't Tell law, 315, 402

Double jeopardy, 107, 267

Down-low (subculture), 119, 405

Drabble, L., 398

Driver's licenses, 175

DSM. *See Diagnostic and Statistical Manual of Mental Disorders*

Dual-use research, 55

Durso, L. E., 136

Dynamic inclusivity, 148

Eating disorders, 177, 191, 391, 394, 395, 431–432
Ecstasy, 244, 400
Educational institutions, 175
Effectiveness, therapist, 340–342, 351
Eibach, R. P., 109, 110
Eidhamar, L. G., 220
Electronic records, 163–164
Eliason, M. J., 222
Ellis, Havelock, 25
EMDR (eye-movement desensitization reprocessing), 192, 294
Emerging adulthood, 239–240
Employment
    bans on discrimination in, 174, 315, 316
    legal and social policy contexts for, 315, 316, 318
    and minority stress, 395–396
    research on issues in, 339, 351
Employment Non-Discrimination Act of 2013, 80
Empowerment, 40, 226, 227, 378
Endocrine Society, 426
End-of-life planning and care, 278, 280
Endogenous hormones, 57
Essentialism, 51–65
    biological research as. *See* Biological research
    challenges to, 63–64, 76
    constructionism vs., 23, 29–33, 52–53
    defined, 22, 52–53
    and stigma, 76–78
Ethgender, 108
Ethics
    and sexual orientation change interventions, 299–302
    in TGNC-affirmative counseling, 173–174
    trainings in, 146
Ethnicity. *See* Race and ethnicity
Evans, N. J., 119
Evidence-based treatments, 192–198
"Ex-gay" (sexual orientation change interventions term), 294, 297, 344–345
Ex-Gay Survivor's Survey, 297
Exodus International, 294

Exposure (therapy technique), 90, 192, 198–201
Eye-movement desensitization reprocessing (EMDR), 192, 294
Eyler, A. E., 214

Face-lifts, 427
Families
    of choice, 274–275
    of LGB/TGNC aging adults, 273–276
    rejection by, 242–243
    and resilience, 349
    services for building, 432–433
    of sexual minority/TGNC adolescents, 167–169, 250–252
    as sources of support and stress, 172
    and TGNC-affirming counseling, 142–143, 168–170
    and trauma, 196
Family Research Council, 295
Family therapy, 170, 294, 375
Family Watch International (FWI), 295
Fassinger, R. E., 138, 379
Feldbaum, M., 54
Feldman, M. B., 394
Femininity, 9, 10, 371, 394
Feminism, 23, 27, 28, 29, 30, 31, 33, 34, 106, 337. *See also* Black feminism
Feminist therapy
    egalitarian approach of, 40, 44
    model for empowerment in, 226
Fenway Institute and Center for American Progress, 164
Ferree, M. M., 118
Financial issues, 279–280
Finger-length ratio, 58
Fish, J., 393
Fluidity, 8, 28, 38–39, 41, 63, 167–168, 241, 271, 303, 353, 417. *See also* Gender identity; Sexual identity
fMRI (functional magnetic resonance imaging), 62–63
Foa, E. B., 184
Follins, L. D., 222
Forbidden knowledge, 55
Foucault, Michel, 24, 34–35
Francis, Pope, 216
Frank, J. A., 241
Fredriksen-Goldsen, K. I., 223, 396

Freud, Sigmund, 25
Friend, R. A., 270, 271
Frost, D. M., 78, 83–93, 95, 348–349
Functional magnetic resonance imaging (fMRI), 62–63
FWI (Family Watch International), 295

Gagnon, John, 24–26, 28
Galliher, R. V., 344
Gallup Research, 80
Garofalo, R., 244
Gay, Jan, 25
Gay-affirmative therapy. *See* LGBTQQIA-affirmative therapy; Affirmative counseling with sexual minority clients; Affirmative counseling with transgender and gender nonconforming clients
"Gay gene," 54–55
Gay sexual orientation, 9. *See also* Health issues of lesbian, gay, and bisexual clients; Sexual minority people
Gender-affirmation surgery
    complications from, 272
    and counseling issues with trans* clients, 336–337
    medical contraindications with, 423, 424
    overview, 418
    overview of types of, 427–428
    and religion, 218, 219
    and TGNC-affirmative counseling, 160
Gender binary, 9, 336, 419
Gender blender/bender identity, 159
Gender development, 240–241. *See also* Gender identity
Gender dysphoria, 161, 167, 171, 337, 419–423, 427–428. *See also* Gender identity disorder (GID)
Gendered racism, 108
Gender expansive individuals, 9, 75, 80, 167. *See also* Sexual minority people; Transgender and gender nonconforming (TGNC) people
Gender expression, 10
Gender fluidity, 166–167. *See also* Fluidity

Gender identity
    biological research on. *See* Biological research
    conflation of sexual orientation with, 335
    defined, 9
    legal protections for, 316
    of LGB/TGNC aging adults, 271
    and social constructivism, 22–24
Gender identity disorder (GID), 337, 419–420. *See also* Gender dysphoria
Genderism, internalized, 91–92
Gender nonconforming people. *See* Transgender and gender nonconforming people; Gender expansive individuals
Gender non-normative people, 75n1
Gender play, 167
Genderqueer, 10, 106, 111, 158, 336, 372, 377
Gender roles, 52, 119, 162, 198, 199, 200, 201, 214, 221, 242, 267, 270, 337, 394
Gender-transgressive sexual minorities, 41, 43, 45, 138, 355
Genetic linkage analysis, 59
Genetics, 21, 23, 29, 51, 53, 54, 55, 58–60, 64, 65
Genomic imprinting, 59
Gergen, K. J., 28–29, 76
Gibson, R. C., 266
GID (gender identity disorder), 337, 419–420. *See also* Gender dysphoria
Gillem, A. R., 223, 302
Ginges, J., 87
Godfrey, K., 378
Goff, P., 110
Goffman, E., 78, 88
Goldfried, M. R., 138, 341
Golub, S. A., 222
Gonsiorek, J. C., 138, 300
Goodrich, K. M., 225, 351–352
Gooren, L. J. G., 61
Gorcheva, R., 341
Gorski, R. A., 61
Gorton, R. N., 424
GRACE (goals, renewal, action, connection, empowerment) model, 226–227

Jim Collins Foundation, 430
Johnson, K. L., 136
Jones, S. L., 343
Journal of Counseling Psychology, 378
Journal of LGBT Issues in Counseling, 378
Journals, 378
Judaism, 216, 218–219

Kaduvettoor, A., 342
Karten, E. Y., 343
Kashubeck-West, S., 221
Kertbeny, Karl-Maria, 24
Kidd, J. D., 214
Kimmel, D. C., 94, 404
Kincaid, T., 299
King, M., 346
Kinsey, Alfred, 25–26
Kitzinger, Celia, 23
Kitzinger, E., 28, 32
Klinger, R. S., 342
Kluck, A. S., 340
Kort, J., 138
Krafft-Ebing, Richard von, 24–25

Ladin, Joy, 219
Lambda Legal, 80, 81, 175, 280
Lance, T. S., 119
Landén, M., 54
Language, 158–159, 440
LaSala, M. C., 252
Late adulthood, 172–173
Latino/Latina Americans, 114, 116, 119
Latter-Day Saints (Mormons), 218
Laurentis, Teresa de, 33
Lawrence v. Texas, 315
LDS (Latter-Day Saints), 218
Lease, S. H., 224
Legal and social policy issues, 313–327
    in employment situations, 315, 318
    and health of LGB clients, 402–404
    and intersectionality, 335. See also
        Intersectionality
    of LGB/TGNC aging adults,
        279–280
    overview, 314–318
    parenthood, 316–320, 323–325
    and protections for LGBTQ people,
        295
    and protections for TGNC people, 174

and psychosocial issues for couples,
    320–323
same-sex marriage. See Same-sex
    marriage
Legal documents, 175–176
Legislation, 150
Lehavot, K., 398
Lesbian, gay, bisexual, transgender, and
    queer (LGBTQ) individuals. See
    also Sexual minority people
    distinctions between trans* people
        and, 335–336
    health issues of. See Health issues
        of lesbian, gay, and bisexual
        clients
    violence against, 3, 5
Lesbians. See Sexual minority people
Lev, A. I., 170
LeVay, Simon, 60–61
Levitt, H. M., 338
Levy, D. L., 214
Lewis, R. J., 395
LGBT Movement Advancement
    Project, 80
LGBTQQIA-affirmative therapy, 19–46
    case study, 19–21, 43–46
    and constructionist–constructivist
        approach to therapy, 37–40
    and constructionist vs. constructivist
        stances, 37
    and constructions of homosexuality,
        24–27
    elements of, 3
    and queer theory, 27–29, 33–36
    and social constructionist stance,
        22–36
    and transgression-affirmative
        nested-narrative identity
        construction and enactment
        model, 41–43
Lick, D. J., 136
Liddle, B. J., 214, 221
Lindahl, K. M., 221
Lindström, P., 62
Lipofilling, 428
Lipoplasty contouring, 427
Liposuction, 428
Lo, J. R., 214
Locke, B. D., 346
Locus of control, 136

ABOUT THE EDITORS

Kurt A. DeBord, PhD, is a professor of psychology at Lincoln University, a historically Black university in Jefferson City, Missouri. He conducts and presents research with students on topics that are of primary interest to his students. He has earned the Governor's Award for Outstanding Teaching at Lincoln. In addition, he conducts a private counseling practice in Columbia, Missouri. Dr. DeBord works with a diverse set of clients, including many from the sexual minority, transgender, and gender nonconforming communities. He is a member of the Transgender Health Network in Mid-Missouri.

Ann R. Fischer, PhD, spent two decades as a faculty member in American Psychological Association–accredited graduate programs in counseling psychology, most recently in the Department of Psychology at Southern Illinois University. Over the years, she and her students have published a number of studies involving core questions about how gender, sexuality, and culture are infused with issues of power and identity. A fellow of American Psychological Association Division 35, she has taught a range of undergraduate and graduate courses in both psychology and women, gender, and sexuality studies. As she transitions out of academia, Dr. Fischer enjoys freelance writing and editing, as well as creative work in photography and music.

Kathleen J. Bieschke, PhD, is a professor of education (counseling psychology) at Pennsylvania State University, head of the Department of Educational Psychology, Counseling, and Special Education, and a licensed psychologist. She earned her PhD in counseling psychology from Michigan State University. Dr. Bieschke's research focuses on the provision of services to members of underrepresented populations, particularly those who identify as members of sexual or gender minorities. Dr. Bieschke is also actively involved with the Center for Collegiate Mental Health. She recently served as the associate editor of the journal *Training and Education of Professional Psychology*, and she is currently a commissioner and chair of the American Psychological Association's Commission on Accreditation. Dr. Bieschke was named a fellow for two divisions of the American Psychological Association (Division 17—Counseling Psychology; and Division 44—Society for the Psychological Study of Lesbian, Gay, Bisexual, and Transgender Issues).

Ruperto M. Perez, PhD, is director of the Counseling Center and adjunct assistant professor in the School of Psychology at the Georgia Institute of Technology. He is a licensed psychologist in Georgia and Florida and is credentialed with the National Register Health Service Providers in Psychology. He has authored various publications and programs and provided consultation in the areas of diversity and inclusion and counseling lesbian, gay, bisexual, and transgender clients. Dr. Perez is a fellow of the American Psychological Association (Division 17—Society of Counseling Psychology; and Division 44—Society for the Psychological Study of Lesbian, Gay, Bisexual, and Transgender Issues), a Diamond Honoree Award Recipient of the American College Personnel Association, and a member of the Asian American Psychological Association and the Georgia Psychological Association.